The British School at Athens

THE POTTERY FROM KARPHI

A RE-EXAMINATION

THE POTTERY FROM KARPHI

A RE-EXAMINATION

By
Leslie Preston Day

BRITISH SCHOOL AT ATHENS
STUDIES 19

Published and distributed by
The British School at Athens
10 Carlton House Terrace, London SW1Y 5AH
©The Council, the British School at Athens

Series Editor: Olga Krzyszkowska

First published in Great Britain 2011

ISBN 978-0-904887-63-1

This book is set in Times New Roman 11/12 pt
Designed and computer typeset by Rayna Andrew
Printed in Great Britain by Short Run Press Ltd,
25 Bittern Road, Exeter, Devon EX2 7LW

Contents

List of abbreviations   vi
List of figures   vii
List of plates   x
List of tables   xi
Acknowledgements   xii
Preface   xiii

1   Introduction   1

2   Mikre Koprana (K 147–150), the Eastern Side of the Settlement: The Eastern Quarter (K 135–144),   7
Barracks (K 2–7, K 134), Road House (K 145), and Southeast Block (K 130–131)

3   The Northeast Quadrant: the Temple (K 1) and its dependencies (K 19–20, K 38–41), Great House   43
(K 9–14) and Great House Shrine (K 15–18), Temple Road (K 70, K 72, K 76), and Baker's House
(K 71, K 73–74)

4   The Southeast Quadrant: the Square (K 10, K 32), Magazines (K 21–23, K 29–31, K 33–37),   83
Southern Houses (K 24–28, K 42–51), Broad Road (K 52–54, K 56), and Small Shrine (K 55–57)

5   The Southwest Quadrant: the Priest's House (K 58–61, K 80), Central West Quarter (K 66–69,   137
K 81–88, K 96–97, K 100), Southern Shelters (K 62–65, K 90–95, K 98–99), Broad Road II
(K 101, K 103, K 105, K 117)

6   The Northwest Quadrant: the Commercial Quarter (K 77–79, K 89, K 112, K 116), Eastern Cliff   169
Houses (K 75, K 110, K 118–119), Western Cliff Houses (K 102, K 106, K 113–115, K 120–121,
K 126), Northern Shelters (K 104, K 107–109, K 122–125, K 127), and Summit (K 128–129)

7   The Vitzelovrysis Spring and Tombs at Ta Mnemata (M 1–17) and Atsividhero (A 1–4)   221

8   Pottery from uncertain contexts   243

9   Pottery analysis   253

10   Conclusions   325

11   Appendix. Analysis of Postpalatial pottery from Karphi   337
      Eleni Nodarou and Ioannis Iliopoulos

Bibliography   349

Index   355

Abbreviations

BA	Bronze Age		H	Helladic
C	Cycladic		M	Minoan
CG	Cypro-Geometric		PG	Protogeometric
E / M / L	Early / Middle / Late		SM	Subminoan

D.	diameter		m	metre
est.	estimated		max.	maximum
FS	Furumark Shape		mm	millimetre
g.	grammes		pres.	preserved
H.	height		Th.	thickness
HM	Herakleion Museum		W.	width
int.	interior		Wt.	weight
L.	length			

Bibliographic abbreviations appear on p. 349

List of figures

1.1   Plan of Karphi (with permission of the British School at Athens).   2

2.1   Mikre Koprana, pottery from K 147 (**K147.1–15**).   9
2.2   Mikre Koprana, pottery from K 147 (**K147.16–18**) and K 149 (**K149.1–7**).   10
2.3   Mikre Koprana, pottery from K 149 (**K149.8–25**).   13
2.4   Mikre Koprana, pottery from K 148 (**K148.1–7**).   15
2.5   Mikre Koprana, pottery from K 150 (**K150.1–5**).   17
2.6   Mikre Koprana, pottery (**MK.1–5**).   18
2.7   Mikre Koprana, pottery (**MK.6–12**).   20
2.8   Mikre Koprana, pottery (**MK.13–15**).   22
2.9   Eastern Quarter, pottery from K 137 (**K137.1**), K 140 (**K140.1–3**), K 139 (**K139.1**), and K 138 (**K138.1**).   25
2.10   Eastern Quarter, pottery from K 142 (**K142.1**), K 143 (**K143.1–3**), and K 144 (**K144.1**).   27
2.11   Barracks, pottery from K 2 (**K2.1–4**).   28
2.12   Barracks, pottery from K 2 (**K2.5–10**).   30
2.13   Barracks, pottery from K 2 (**K2.11–14**) and K 3 (**K3.1–6**).   31
2.14   Barracks, pottery from K 3 (**K3.7–14**).   33
2.15   Barracks, pottery from K 7 (**K7.1–5**) and outside K 2-7 (**K2-7.1**).   36
2.16   Barracks, pottery from K 134 (**K134.1–5**).   38
2.17   Southeast House, pottery from K 130 (**K130.1**) and K 131 (**K131.1–3**).   40
2.18   Southeast House, decorated krater from K 131 (**K131.4**).   41
2.19   Southeast House, pottery from K 132 (**K130.1–4**).   42

3.1   Temple, pottery from K 1 (**K1.1–10**).   46
3.2   Temple, pottery from K 1 (**K1.11–15**).   48
3.3   Temple, pottery from K 1 (**K1.16–22**).   49
3.4   Temple dependencies, pottery from K 19 (**K19.1–5**), K 20 (**K20.1**), K 40 (**K40.1–5**), K 41 (**K41.1–2**), and K 40-41 (**K40-41.1–2**).   51
3.5   Temple dependencies, pottery from K 38 (**K38.1–9**) and K 39 (**K39.1–6**).   54
3.6   Great House, pottery from K 8 (**K8.1–2**) and K 9 (**K9.1–7**).   57
3.7   Great House, pottery from K 9 (**K9.8–11**).   59
3.8   Great House, pottery from K 11 (**K11.1–11**).   61
3.9   Great House, pottery from K 12 floor (**K12.1–8**) and lower deposit (**K12.9–16**).   63
3.10   Great House, pottery from K 12 lowest deposit (**K12.17–33**) and K 8-12 (**K8-12.1**).   65
3.11   Great House, pottery from K 14 (**K14.1–2**) and Great House Shrine, pottery from K 16 (**K16.1–2**).   67
3.12   Great House Shrine, pottery from K 17 (**K17.1–2**), K 17 lower deposit (**K17.3–9**), and K 17 lowest deposit (**K17.10–33**).   70
3.13   Great House Shrine, pottery from K 16-17 (**K16-17.1–4**) and K 18 (**K18.1–2**).   72
3.14   Temple Road East, pottery from K 70 (**K70.1–3**) and K 72 (**K72.1–2**).   75
3.15   Temple Road West, pottery from K 76 (**K76.1–38**).   77
3.16   Temple Road West, pottery from K 76 (**K76.39–56**).   79
3.17   Baker's House, pottery from K 71 (**K71.1**), K 73 (**K73.1–4**), and K 74 (**K74.1**).   81

4.1   Magazines, pottery from K 21 (**K21.1–3**).   84
4.2   Magazines, pottery from K 22 (**K22.1–5**).   85
4.3   Magazines, pottery from K 22 (**K22.6–13**).   86
4.4   Magazines, pottery from K 23 (**K23.1–18**).   89
4.5   Magazines, pottery from K 23 (**K23.19–26**).   91
4.6   Magazines, pottery from K 23 (**K23.27–32**).   92
4.7   Magazines, pottery from K 23 lower deposit (**K23.33–47**).   94
4.8   Magazines, pottery from K 23 (**K23.48–71**) and outside K 23 (**K23.72–73**).   96
4.9   Magazines, pottery from K 29 (**K29.1–17**).   98
4.10   Magazines, pottery from K 30 (**K30.1**) and K 31 (**K31.1–16**).   100

4.11	Magazines, pottery from K 33 (**K33.1–5**).	103
4.12	Magazines, pottery from K 36 (**K36.1–2**) and K 37 (**K37.1–3**).	104
4.13	Square and street, pottery from K10 (**K10.1**) and K 32 (**K32.1–21**).	106
4.14	Street, pottery from K 48 (**K48.1–8**).	108
4.15	Southern Houses, pottery from K 24 (**K24.1–2**) and K 25 (**K25.1**).	110
4.16	Southern Houses, pottery from K 26 (**K26.1–6**).	111
4.17	Southern Houses, pottery from K 26 (**K26.7–12**).	113
4.18	Southern Houses, pottery from K 26 (**K26.13–14**).	114
4.19	Southern Houses, pottery from K 27 (**K27.1–3**).	116
4.20	Southern Houses, pottery from K 27 (**K27.4–8**).	117
4.21	Southern Houses, pottery from K 28 (**K28.1–6**).	119
4.22	Southern Houses, pottery from K 43 (**K43.1–13**).	120
4.23	Southern Houses, pottery from K 43 (**K43.14–17**).	122
4.24	Southern Houses, pottery from K 44 (**K44.1–10**).	124
4.25	Southern Houses, pottery from K 46 (**K46.1–7**) and K 47 (**K47.1–2**).	126
4.26	Southern Houses, pottery from K 47 (**K47.3–6**).	128
4.27	Southern Houses, pottery from K 45 (**K45.1–9**), K 50 (**K50.1–2**), and K 51 (**K51.1–2**).	129
4.28	Southern Houses, pottery from K 49 (**K49.1–2**).	131
4.29	Broad Road, pottery from K 52 (**K52.1–6**), K 54 (**K54.1–6**), and K 56 (**K56.1–5**).	133
4.30	Small Shrine, pottery from K 57 (**K57.1–6**) and K 55 (**K55.1–3**).	135
5.1	Priest's House, pottery from K 58 (**K58.1–5**).	139
5.2	Priest's House, pottery from K 61 (**K61.1–15**).	141
5.3	Priest's House, pottery from K 59 (**K59.1**).	142
5.4	Priest's House, pottery from K 80 (**K80.1–10**).	143
5.5	Central West Quarter, Building K 66-67-68-81, pottery from K 66 (**K66.1**), K 67 (**K67.1–3**), K 81 (**K81.1–5**), and K 81-82 (**K81-82.1**).	146
5.6	Central West Quarter, Building K 66-67-68-81, pottery from K 68 (**K68.1–11**).	148
5.7	Central West Quarter, Building K 66-67-68-81, pottery from K 68 (**K68.12–14**).	150
5.8	Central West Quarter, Building K 82-83-84-86-88, pottery from K 82 (**K82.1–5**).	151
5.9	Central West Quarter, Building K 82-83-84-86-88, pottery from K 83 (**K83.1–4**), K 84 (**K84.1**), K 86 (**K86.1**), K 88 (**K88.1–2**).	153
5.10	Central West Quarter, Building K 85-87-69, pottery from K 85 (**K85.1–9**).	156
5.11	Central West Quarter, Building K 85-87-69, pottery from K 85 (**K85.10–14**).	158
5.12	Central West Quarter, Building K 85-87-69, pottery from K 87 (**K87.1–3**) and K 69 (**K69.1–3**).	159
5.13	Central West Quarter, Building K 96-97-100, pottery from K 96 (**K96.1–2**), K 97 (**K97.1–7**), and K 100 (**K100.1–5**).	161
5.14	Southern Shelters, pottery from K 62 (**K62.1–2**), K 90 (**K90.1–3**), K 91 (**K91.1–5**), K 93 (**K93.1**), and K 94 (**K94.1**).	164
5.15	Broad Road II, pottery from K 101 (**K101.1–11**) and K 103 (**K103.1–3**).	167
6.1	Commercial Quarter, pottery from K 79 (**K79.1–8**).	170
6.2	Commercial Quarter, pottery from K 79-89 (**K79-89.1–16**).	173
6.3	Commercial Quarter, pottery from K 79-89 (**K79-89.17–30**).	175
6.4	Commercial Quarter, pottery from K 112 (**K112.1–5**) and K 77 (**K77.1–5**).	177
6.5	Commercial Quarter, pottery from K 116 (**K116.1–8**).	179
6.6	Eastern Cliff Houses, pottery from K 75 (**K75.1–15**).	181
6.7	Eastern Cliff Houses, pottery from K 110 (**K110.1–8**).	184
6.8	Eastern Cliff Houses, pottery from K 110 (**K110.9–15**).	186
6.9	Eastern Cliff Houses, pottery from K 110 (**K110.16**).	187
6.10	Eastern Cliff Houses, pottery from K 110 (**K110.17–21**).	188
6.11	Broad Road, pottery from K 117 (**K117.1–3**) and Western Cliff Houses, Building K 113-114-120, pottery from K 113 (**K113.1–5**).	190
6.12	Western Cliff Houses, Building K 113-114-120, pottery from K 114 (**K114.1–5**).	193
6.13	Western Cliff Houses, Building K 113-114-120, pottery from K 114 (**K114.6–10**).	194
6.14	Western Cliff Houses, Building K 113-114-120, pottery from K 120 (**K120.1–4**) and area outside K 120 (**K120N.1**).	196
6.15	Western Cliff Houses, pottery from K 121 (**K121.1–14**).	198
6.16	Western Cliff Houses, Building K 102-106-115-126, pottery from K 102 (**K102.1–2**) and K 106 (**K106.1–20**).	201
6.17	Western Cliff Houses, Building K 102-106-115-126, pottery from K 106 (**K106.21–26**).	203
6.18	Western Cliff Houses, Building K 102-106-115-126, pottery from K 115 (**K115.1–5**).	205
6.19	Western Cliff Houses, Building K 102-106-115-126, pottery from K 115 (**K115.6–7**).	207

6.20	Western Cliff Houses, Building K 102-106-115-126, pottery from K 115 (**K115.8–12**).	208
6.21	Western Cliff Houses, Building K 102-106-115-126, pottery from K 115 (**K115.13–19**).	209
6.22	Western Cliff Houses, Building K 102-106-115-126, pottery from K 126 (**K126.1–3**).	211
6.23	Northern Shelters, pottery from K 104 (**K104.1–2**) and K 107 (**K107.1–10**).	212
6.24	Northern Shelters, pottery from K 108 (**K108.1–8**), K 109 (**K109.1**), K 122 (**K122.1–4**), and K 123 (**K123.1**).	214
6.25	Northern Shelters, pottery from K 124 (**K124.1–10**) and K 125 (**K125.1–2**).	217
6.26	Northern Shelters, pottery from K 127 (**K127.1–7**).	219
7.1	Vitzelovrysis, pottery from spring (**V.1**) and Ta Mnemata tombs M 1 (**M1.1–3**) and M 2 (**M2.1**).	222
7.2	Ta Mnemata tombs, pottery from M 3 (**M3.1–2**).	224
7.3	Ta Mnemata tombs, pottery from M 4 (**M4.1–7**).	226
7.4	Ta Mnemata tombs, pottery from M 8 (**M8.1–3**).	229
7.5	Ta Mnemata tombs, pottery from M 8 (**M8.4–13**).	231
7.6	Ta Mnemata tombs, pottery from M 9 (**M9.1–2**).	232
7.7	Ta Mnemata tombs, pottery from M 11 (**M11.1–5**).	234
7.8	Ta Mnemata tombs, pottery from M 12 (**M12.1**), M 13 (**M13.1**), and M 14 (**M14.1–8**).	235
7.9	Ta Mnemata tombs, pottery from M 15 (**M15.1**) and M 16 (**M16.1–5**).	237
7.10	Ta Mnemata tombs, pottery from M 17 (**M17.1–6**).	239
7.11	Atsividhero tombs, pottery from A 1 (**A1.1–2**), A 2 (**A2.1–2**), and A 3 (**A3.1–6**).	241
8.1	Pottery from unknown contexts (**K.1–17**).	244
8.2	Pottery from unknown contexts (**K.18–31**).	245
8.3	Pottery from unknown contexts (**K.32–39**).	247
8.4	Pottery from unknown contexts (**K.40–49**).	249
8.5	Pottery from unknown contexts (**K.50–53**).	250
8.6	Pottery from unknown contexts (**K.54–65**).	251
9.1	Cups.	256
9.2	Deep bowls.	258
9.3	Motifs on deep bowls.	261
9.4	Shallow bowls, bowls, skyphos, and krateriskoi.	266
9.5	Kylikes, goblets, and chalice.	268
9.6	Mugs and tankards.	271
9.7	Basket kalathos and other fine kalathoi.	272
9.8	Coarse kalathoi.	273
9.9	Scuttles.	275
9.10	Kraters.	277
9.11	Bowls and basins.	280
9.12	Basins.	281
9.13	Deep basin or bowl.	283
9.14	Lids.	284
9.15	Pyxides.	287
9.16	Hut urns.	289
9.17	Fine stirrup jars.	291
9.18	Large fine and coarse stirrup jars.	292
9.19	Thelastron, juglets, and bottle.	295
9.20	Jugs.	297
9.21	Jugs.	299
9.22	Amphoras.	301
9:23	Jars.	303
9:24	Pithoid jars.	306
9.25	Pithoi.	308
9.26	Pithos decorations.	309
9.27	Rhyta, bird vases, head vase, ring vase.	311
9.28	Stands.	313
9.29	Cooking dishes, trays, and tripod trays.	316
9.30	Cooking jugs.	318
9.31	Tripod cooking pots.	321
11.1	Geological map of the area of Karphi (after IGME 1989).	340
11.2	Diagram CaO/MgO for the SEM samples.	344

List of plates

1   (*a*) Fragments of deep bowls (**K147.3**, **K147.8**, **K121.1**, **K44.1**); (*b*) fragments of deep bowls (**K76.2**, **K32.6**, **K44.3**, **K61.4**, **K147.6**, **K32.4**); (*c*) stirrup jar fragments (**K147.14**, **K149.17**); (*d*) pyxis **K147.16**; (*e*) hut urn **K147.17**; (*f*) basin **K147.18**; (*g*) deep bowl **K149.3**; (*h*) deep bowl fragments (**K85.1**, **K71.1**, **K106.8**, **K149.5**, **K149.6**); (*i*) deep bowl fragments (**K149.10**, **K110.1**, **K75.1**).

2   (*a*) Krater fragments **K75.8**, **K149.14**, **K47.1**; (*b*) amphora **K149.20**; (*c*) kalathos **K149.21**; (*d*) jug **K149.23**; (*e*) jug **K148.6**; (*f*) kalathos **K148.7**; (*g*) deep bowls (**K31.2**, **K120.1**, **K150.1**).

3   (*a*) Pyxis **K150.2**; (*b–d*) stirrup jar **K150.3**; (*e*) basin **K150.4**; (*f*) multiple vessel **K150.5**.

4   (*a*) Pithos **MK.2**; (*b*) cooking jug **MK.4**; (*c*) MK spools; (*d*) deep bowl **MK.6**; (*e*) stirrup jar **MK.7**; (*f*) hut urn **MK.11**.

5   (*a*) Krater **MK.13**; (*b*) jug **MK.15**; (*c*) spools (K 2, K 46); (*d*) kalathos **K2.3**; (*e*) cooking jug **K2.7**; (*f*) pithos **K2.15**; (*g*) kalathos **K3.10**; (*h*) pithos fragments (**K7.5**, **K19.5**).

6   (*a*) Pyxis **K134.1**; (*b*) stirrup jar **K134.4**; (*c–d*) krater **K131.4**; (*e*) K 1 goddess fragment; (*f*) K 1 goddess fragment; (*g*) K 1 goddess fragment.

7   (*a*) K 1 bird attributes; (*b*) K 1 animal figurines; (*c*) K 1 goddess attributes; (*d*) deep bowl **K1.1**; (*e*) deep bowl **K1.2**; (*f*) thelastron **K1.4**; (*g*) thelastron **K1.7**; (*h*) chalice **K1.9**.

8   (*a*) Basin **K1.10**; (*b*) basin **K1.11**; (*c*) stirrup jar **K1.13**; (*d*) cooking dish **K1.16**; (*e*) cooking jug **K1.20**; (*f*) tripod **K1.21**; (*g*) juglet **K39.5**.

9   (*a*) Jug **K11.4**; (*b*) jug **K11.5**; (*c*) thelastron **K11.6**; (*d*) pithos **K13.1**; (*e–f*) pyxis **K14.1**; (*g*) tripod **K14.2**; (*h*) goddess head K 8-18, stand or goddess crown K 76, rectangular stand K 85.

10   (*a*) Hut urn **K16.1**; (*b*) amphora **K70.2**; (*c*) deep bowl **K76.1**; (*d*) deep bowl fragments (**K21.1**, **K38.3**, **K61.6**, **K76.13**, **K100.2**, **K147.2**); (*e*) deep bowl bases (**K57.2**, **K76.19**, **K76.21**); (*f*) stirrup jar fragments (**K45.9**, **K54.6**, **K76.55**, **K77.4**); (*g*) pyxis **K22.2**.

11   (*a*) Pyxis **K22.3**; (*b*) pyxis **K22.6**; (*c*) lid **K22.9**; (*d*) tankard fragments (**K23.8**, **K28.2**, **K.17**); (*e*) tankard fragment **K23.9** and kylix fragment **K80.4**; (*f*) krater **K23.11**; (*g*) amphora **K23.17**; (*h*) thelastron **K23.18**.

12   (*a*) Jug **K23.29**; (*b*) amphora **K23.73**; (*c*) deep bowl fragments (**K29.1**, **K29.3**, **K66.1**); (*d*) larnax **K29.17**; (*e*) jug **K31.11**; (*f*) lid fragments (**K19.1**, **K31.5**, **K38.9**, **K44.9**); (*g*) hut urn **K33.2**.

13   (*a*) Stirrup jar **K33.4**; (*b*) deep bowl **K36.1**; (*c*) pithos **K36.2**; (*d*) pithos **K24.2**; (*e–f*) tankard **K26.4**; (*g*) kalathos **K26.7**; (*h*) stirrup jar **K26.10**.

14   (*a*) Tripod **K26.11**; (*b*) tripod **K26.12**; (*c*) deep bowl **K27.1**; (*d*) rhyton **K27.3**; (*e*) bird vase **K28.4**.

15   (*a*) Kalathos **K28.6**; (*b*) kalathos **K43.14**; (*c*) K 44 spools; (*d–e*) stirrup jar **K47.2**; (*f*) lid **K47.4**; (*g*) cooking jug **K47.5**.

16   (*a*) Deep bowl **K51.1**; (*b*) jug **K57.4**; (*c*) cup **K58.1**; (*d*) kalathos **K58.2**; (*e*) stand **K58.4**; (*f*) stand **K58.5**.

17   (*a*) Pyxis **K61.12**; (*b*) tripod **K61.15**; (*c*) stirrup jar **K59.1**; (*d*) jug **K80.5**; (*e–f*) basket kalathos **K68.11**; (*g*) pyxis **K80.8**; (*h*) pyxis **K68.12**.

18   (*a*) Stirrup jar **K83.2**; (*b*) pithos **K83.4**; (*c*) pyxis **K85.5**; (*d*) jug **K85.7**; (*e*) jug **K87.1**; (*f*) kalathos **K87.3**; (*g*) hut urn **K69.2**; (*h*) juglet **K96.2**; (*i*) kylikes (**K100.3**, **K106.17**, **K.106.16**); (*j*) thelastron **K100.4**.

19   (*a*) Amphora **K90.3**; (*b*) krater **K79-89.18**; (*c*) pyxis **K116.1**; (*d*) stirrup jar **K116.4**; (*e*) deep bowl **K116.5**; (*f*) jug **K116.6**.

20   (*a*) Jar **K116.7**; (*b*) pyxis **K75.9**; (*c*) deep bowl **K110.2**; (*d*) jug **K110.8**; (*e*) stirrup jar **K110.9**; (*f*) stirrup jar **K110.10**; (*g*) kalathos **K110.15**; (*h*) lid **K110.19**.

21   (*a*) Pyxis **K113.1**; (*b*) stirrup jar **K113.2**; (*c*) cooking slab **K113.5**; (*d*) cup **K114.2**; (*e*) pyxis **K114.3**; (*f*) pyxis **K114.4** and lid **K114.5**; (*g*) stirrup jar **K114.6**.

22   (*a*) Jug **K114.9**; (*b*) cooking jug **K114.10**; (*c*) deep bowl **K120N.1**; (*d*) bowl **K121.6**; (*e*) tankards **K.77.1**, **K121.7**; (*f*) stirrup jar **K121.10**; (*g*) tripod **K121.13**; (*h*) deep bowl **K115.2**; (*i*) skyphos **K115.4**.

23   (*a*) Pyxis **K115.7**; (*b*) hut urn **K115.8**; (*c*) stirrup jar **K115.9**; (*d*) scuttle **K115.13**; (*e*) jar **K115.16**; (*f*) plaque **K104.2**; (*g*) jug **K107.5**; (*h*) stand **K107.10**; (*i*) stirrup jar **K109.1**.

24   (*a*) Krater **K122.3**; (*b*) hut urn **K122.4**; (*c*) rhyton **K123.1**; (*d*) deep bowl **K124.1**; (*e*) Byzantine sherd from K 127; (*f*) PG jug **V.1**; (*g*) bottle **M1.2**; (*h*) stirrup jar **M3.1**; (*i*) stirrup jar **M3.2**.

25   (*a*) Stirrup jar **M4.4**; (*b*) stirrup jar **M4.5**; (*c*) mug **M4.7**; (*d*) skyphos **M8.1**; (*e*) krater **M8.2**; (*f*) stirrup jar **M8.3**; (*g*) thelastron **M8.12**; (*h*) fenestrated stand **M8.4**.

26   (*a*) Rhyton **M11.1**; (*b*) bird vase **M11.2**; (*c*) thelastron **M11.3**; (*d*) stirrup jar **M11.4**; (*e*) stirrup jar **M11.6**; (*f*) juglet **M14.3**; (*g*) stirrup jar **M14.5**; (*h*) stirrup jar **M14.6**; (*i*) flask **M16.2**; (*j*) oinochoe **M16.5**.

27   (*a*) Krateriskos **M17.1**; (*b*) thelastron **M17.5**; (*c*) thelastron **M17.6**; (*d*) cup **A3.1**; (*e*) kylix **K.15**; (*f*) pyxis **K.24**; (*g*) fenestrated stand **K.32**; (*h*) snake tube **K.33**; (*i*) stirrup jar **K.36**; (*j*) coarse krater **K.40**.

28   (*a*) Stirrup jar **K.46**; (*b*) pithos **K.53**; (*c*) plaque, no good context.

29 (*a*) Low calcareous group, body fragment, no vitrification (NV); (*b*) moderately calcareous group, sample KAR 06/ 32, advanced vitrification (V); (*c*) moderately calcareous group, sample KAR 06/ 78, no vitrification (NV); (*d*) highly calcareous group, sample KAR 06/ 10, extensive vitrification (Vc+); (*e*) highly calcareous group, sample KAR 06/ 27, initial vitrification (IV); (*f*) highly calcareous group, sample KAR 06/ 31, initial vitrification (IV).

COLOUR PLATES

1 (*a*) Fabric 1, subgroup (a) (×25); (*b*) Fabric 1, subgroup (a) (×25); (*c*) Fabric 1, subgroup (b) (×25); (*d*) Fabric 2 (×25); (*e*) sample KAR 06/ 38 (×50); (*f*) sample KAR 06/ 18 (×25); (*g*) sample KAR 06/ 21 (×25); (*h*) sample KAR 06/ 2 (×25).

2 (*a*) Fabric 3 (×25); (*b*) Fabric 4 (×25); (*c*) Fabric 5 (×50); (*d*) sample from the Pediada Survey (×50); (*e*) sample KAR 06/ 15 (×50); (*f*) sample KAR 06/ 23 (×50); (*g*) sample KAR 06/ 37 (×50); (*h*) sample KAR 06/ 40 (×50); (*i*) sample KAR 06/ 41 (×50).

List of tables

9.1   Concordance of spools.   323

11.1   Concordance of vessels sampled for analysis.   338
11.2   Compositional data from SEM analysis.   343
11.3   Concordance of petrography and SEM data.   343

Acknowledgements

The restudy of the Karphi pottery was a large undertaking, and many people and institutions have helped me accomplish it. First of all, I am grateful to the Managing Committee (now Council) of the British School at Athens for granting the permission to undertake the study and to use the notebooks and photographs from the 1937–39 excavations stored in the archives in Athens. During this study Directors of the British School at Athens provided much help, and I owe thanks to all of them: Elizabeth French, David Blackman, James Whitley, and Catherine Morgan. The librarian of the British School, Penny Wilson, and the archivist, Amalia Kikissis, were of great help in providing me with photos and especially with access to the Karphi notebooks.

I could not have done the work without the support of the then Knossos Curator, Colin Macdonald, who helped in every conceivable way, from the logistics of transporting the boxes from the Museum to discussions of LM IIIC pottery. The staff of the British School at Knossos and numerous visiting scholars were also of great assistance, in particular Steffi Chlouveraki, Eleni Hatzaki, Carl Knappett, Conn Murphy, and Joanne Murphy. My thanks also go to Gail Hoffman, with whom I worked in the museum in 1994 and who shared with me her knowledge of Phoenician and Cypriote pottery.

I am particularly grateful to the former Directors of the Herakleion Museum, Charalambos Kritsas and Alexandra Karetsou, to the epimeletria in charge of my work, Ioanna Serpetenaki, and to all the guards who watched over the work so diligently. Tassos and Irini Karoussas, then conservators at the Herakleion Museum, helped to find and make available the large krater from K 131 so that we could draw it despite its deteriorating condition.

Permits were obtained for this study from the American School of Classical Studies at Athens, and I am grateful to the staff of the School for its support and help. In particular, I wish to thank Maria Pilali for taking care of all of the details and to the Directors of the School, William Coulson, James Muhly, and Steven Tracy for their support. Much of the study and writing of this analysis was carried out in the Blegen Library of the American School of Classical Studies, and I owe thanks to all the staff who keep it running so well. Finally, I am grateful to Natalia Vogeikoff-Brogan for providing storage of and access to the drawings in the archives of the American School during the study.

Most of the drawings of the pottery were done by the author and Roxana Docsan, who also inked all of the figures; I am grateful to her for her meticulous care with a difficult body of material. In 1991 Margaret Mook drew some of the vessels. In 1997 Lyla Pinch Brock and Christopher White also joined me in drawing and conservation of the pottery. Thanks also go to Ann Brysbaert, who helped in 1997 with temporary conservation on the pottery so that it could be recorded. Photographs were taken by the author and printed by Katherine May at the INSTAP Study Center for East Crete with the help of a publication grant from the Institute for Aegean Prehistory. I am also grateful to Eleanor Huffman, who digitised all of the drawings.

Funding for this study came from a variety of sources. In 1991 I was aided by the Harriet Pomerance Fellowship from the Archaeological Institute of America and a Fellowship from the American Council of Learned Societies. The work in 1994 was made possible by the McLean-McTurnan-Arnold Faculty Research Fellowship from Wabash College. In 1996 and 1997 support was provided by the Institute for Aegean Prehistory. Research on the Karphi material was made possible by Faculty Development Grants and Sabbatical leave grants from Wabash College. I am grateful for all of this financial assistance.

Over the years, many productive discussions with other scholars have helped in the analysis of the Karphi material. In particular, I would like to thank the following: Gerald Cadogan, Kostis Christakis, the late William Coulson, Anna Lucia D'Agata, Theodoros Eliopoulos, Geraldine Gesell, Kevin Glowacki, Birgitta Hallager, Barbara Hayden, Athanasia Kanta, Nancy Klein, Colin Macdonald, Joseph Maran, Jennifer Moody, Margaret Mook, Penelope Mountjoy, Krzysztof Nowicki, Jeremy Rutter, Metaxia Tsipopoulou, Lee Ann Turner, Saro Wallace, Peter Warren, Vance Watrous, James Whitley, and Assaf Yasur-Landau. Saro Wallace's excellent book, *Ancient Crete*, unfortunately came out too late to take into account in my presentation, but it is listed in the bibliography (Wallace 2010). Finally I thank the British School at Athens for including this volume in the Studies Series, and specifically Alan Johnston (Chairman of the BSA Publication Committee), Olga Krzyszkowska (Series Editor) and Rayna Andrew (Production Editor).

Finally, I wish to thank my husband, Joseph Day, without whose financial, intellectual, and moral support over the long years, this study could never have been completed.

Leslie Preston Day
March 2011

Preface

This volume presents a re-examination of the pottery from the excavations at Karphi conducted by the British School at Athens under the direction of John Pendlebury from 1937–39. Although Pendlebury published a final report of those excavations before his untimely death in 1941, the pottery study had not been completed at that time, and it was not until 1960 that Mercy Seiradaki published her analysis of this material. The publication spurred renewed interest in the transitional period that spanned the period after the collapse of the great palatial centres on Crete and before the rise of the *polis*, but almost immediately questions arose about the dating of the Karphi settlement and the nature of the buildings, questions which could only be answered by a restudy of the pottery and by renewed excavation.

This report represents the result of fieldwork undertaken on Crete between 1991 and 1998. What began as an interest in LM IIIC pottery assemblages that might help in the interpretation of the material from the excavations at Kavousi–*Vronda* (of which I was co-director) became a long-term project to study and publish more fully the material from Karphi that was still extant in the Herakleion Museum. In May of 1991 a brief initial study of the material in boxes then in the east storerooms of the Herakleion Museum showed how much was preserved. Ironically, the work had to be cut short because of activities commemorating the 50th anniversary of the German invasion of Crete, the military engagement in which John Pendlebury lost his life. Even this brief exposure to the Karphi pottery showed two things that demanded further consideration. First, there was far more preserved pottery than was drawn and photographed in the publication. Second, nearly every vessel, including fragments, had its find spot marked in ink, making it possible to consider and illustrate the pottery in context.

A more thorough study began in the winter of 1994, when I was able to draw, photograph, and describe the nearly complete vases in the west storerooms of the Herakleion Museum, a task that was completed in May of that year. Study seasons continued in May of 1995 and 1996, when the sherd material in the boxes

was moved to the Stratigraphical Museum at Knossos for analysis. A final season took place in September through November of 1997 at Knossos. The period from 1997 to the present has been spent in the analysis of the pottery, taking into account the large number of sites of the period that have been excavated in the last 50 years.

During the study seasons at Knossos I was able to strew much of the material from the boxes stored in the museum. The larger storage jars that were still preserved could not be restored, and many of the vessels were only pieced together long enough to draw and photograph. It was not possible to examine the nearly complete pottery along with the fragments in the boxes at the same time, and some joins that might have been possible were never made. Nevertheless, the vessels presented here represent a more complete view of the Karphi assemblages than is available in the 1960 report.

Although every attempt was made to find a ceramic petrographer willing to undertake the analysis of the Karphi coarse wares, it was not until 2006 that such an analysis became possible. Eleni Nodarou helped to choose the samples from the Karphi material and carried out the petrographic analysis at the INSTAP Study Center for East Crete. We chose to concentrate on the boxes of material recovered from the Temple in 1937, since all sherd material from that season was kept and was still in the original boxes. Although the pottery represents a highly specialised group of vessels for a specific and unusual function, the fragments come from a more complete range of coarse fabrics than the individual pieces selected by the excavators to keep because of some special feature. This group was supplemented by fragments of other types of vessels from the buildings.

The material is still in the Herakleion Museum. The fragments were re-boxed and have been moved to a remote storage space, and at the time of the writing the rest is still in the Museum, which remains closed for renovations. While I might have liked to check a few details, it has not been possible to do so. The original pencil drawings and the inked drawings now reside in the archives of the British School at Athens.

1

Introduction

The site of Karphi, high on a mountain peak overlooking the Lasithi Plain in eastern Crete, has elicited interest since its excavation by members of the British School at Athens from 1937–1939 under the direction of John Pendlebury (FIG. 1.1). Belonging to the transitional period between the fall of the Minoan palaces and the rise of the Greek city-state, it was one of the first sites thoroughly investigated on Crete from that little-known period often referred to as the dark ages. Pendlebury published his findings with admirable speed, spurred on by the imminent war.[1] The final report on the architecture, objects, and history of the site was brief but thorough, with one exception; no analysis of the pottery was included. The pottery was plentiful and particularly difficult to clean, and vessels could not be mended, drawn, and photographed in time for the publication. Although a manuscript on the pottery was completed by Mercy Money-Coutts (Seiradaki) before the war and approved by Pendlebury at that time, the publication did not actually appear until 1960.[2] For this article Seiradaki added some photographs and drawings to her earlier manuscript, but she did not go back and make a new study in light of subsequent archaeological discoveries on Crete. Nevertheless, this publication was most welcome, as Karphi was and still is the most extensively excavated site of the LM IIIC–PG period on Crete, and it enters into every discussion of the period.

The published material immediately gave rise to questions about the dating of the settlement and its place in the history of Crete. The excavators observed little or no meaningful stratigraphy, leading to the conclusion that Karphi was a one-period site in use for a rather short period of time, roughly two hundred years from c. 1100–900 BC.[3] Any phasing of the parts of the city had to be done on the basis of architectural remains.[4] Pendlebury dated the site to the 'Intermediate Period', a label which he saw as more accurate than either SM or PG.[5] The term SM implies that the people producing the pottery were Minoans even if mainland elements had come into Crete during LM II–III, while PG suggests that the people had strong mainland connections and stood at the beginning of the Hellenic culture that ultimately dominated the island. 'Intermediate Period' was considered a more neutral term without implications about the ethnicity of the people who inhabited Crete during that period. Nonetheless, the term has been abandoned for more specific chronological or stylistic terminology.

Pendlebury called the majority of the pottery SM, with a small amount of PG;[6] only after Seiradaki's publication of the pottery in 1960 was it clear that most of the material was LM IIIC. Vincent Desborough was the first to attribute the material to LM IIIC, maintaining that the settlement, while it was founded in the middle or latter part of IIIC, lasted only a hundred years rather than the two hundred assigned it by Pendlebury.[7] Mervyn Popham refined the phasing, suggesting that Karphi belonged to the second half of the LM IIIC period, although he admitted that it may have been founded earlier.[8] Other scholars have agreed that there was earlier material, including Athanasia Kanta,[9] who concluded that the site was first inhabited during an early stage of LM IIIC and that inhabitation continued into the SM Period. Birgitta Hallager pointed to the LM IIIB character of some of the published Karphi pottery and believed that the settlement was inhabited at the very beginning of the LM IIIC period.[10]

As to when the settlement was abandoned there is even greater confusion. Several scholars have pointed to the report of PG sherds at Karphi,[11] and Watrous reiterated this late date on the basis of conversations he had with Mercy Money-Coutts Seiradaki before her death.[12] Certainly some of the published pottery can be assigned to the SM or even to the EPG periods, but it was unclear how much later material was found on the site and whether the entire settlement was inhabited into the 10th century.

As more material of the LM IIIC–PG periods has come to light on Crete, the question of dating the Karphi material has become more pressing. The sites of Khania,[13] Khamalevri,[14] Sybrita/Thronos,[15] Knossos,[16]

1   *Karphi*.
2   Seiradaki, 1.
3   *Karphi*, 140–1.
4   *Karphi*, 134–5; this analysis was heavily influenced by Pendlebury's experiences at Tell el-ʿAmarna in Egypt.
5   *Karphi*, 134.
6   *Karphi*, 134.
7   Desborough 1964, 172–6.
8   *Kastri*, 281–2.
9   Kanta 1980, 121.
10 *Khania II*, 174, n. 343.
11 *Karphi*, 134.
12 Watrous 1992, 40.
13 *Khania II*.
14 Andreadaki-Vlasaki and Papadopoulou 2005, 2007.
15 Prokopiou 1997; D'Agata 1999, 2003, 2007.
16 Warren 1983, 2007.

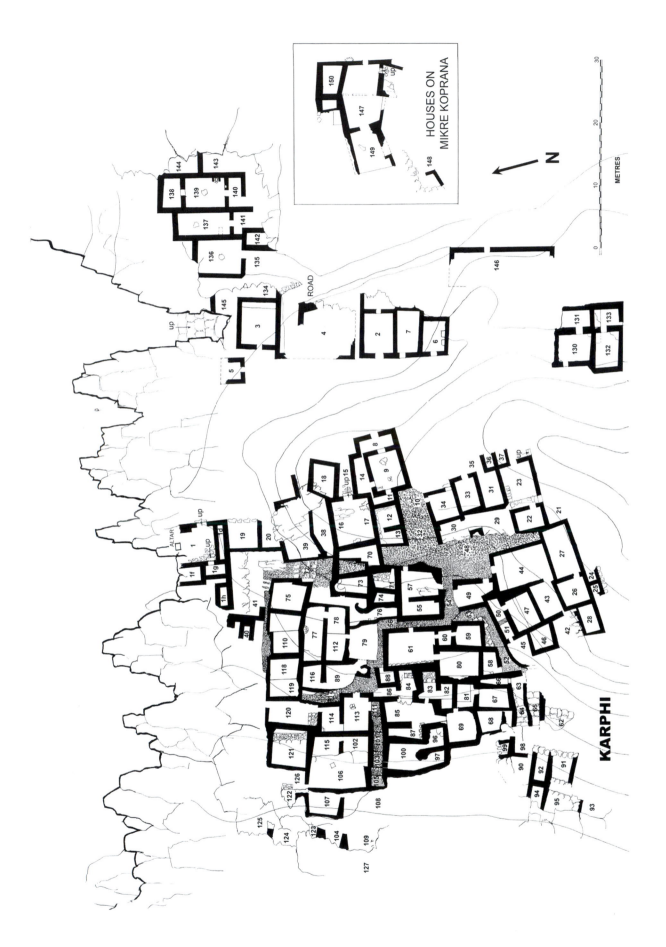

Fig. 1.1. Plan of Karphi (with permission of the British School at Athens).

Kastelli Pediada,[17] Kavousi,[18] Khalasmenos,[19] and Kastri[20] have provided stratified sequences or closed deposits that allow us to distinguish at least three phases of LM IIIC,[21] although there is still no consensus on what these should be called or how they are correlated with the phases of LH IIIC on the mainland.[22] The very earliest phase of LM IIIC, in which LM IIIB styles were still prevalent, has been distinguished at Kavousi–*Kastro* and Khania.[23] Many sites, including Khania, Khamalevri, Sybrita/Thronos, Kastrokephala, Knossos, Kastelli Pediada, Kavousi–*Vronda*, Kavousi–*Kastro*, and Kastri have produced material that has been identified as early LM IIIC, and at Sybrita/Thronos, Knossos, and Khamalevri two phases of early LM IIIC have been distinguished. It is, however, still difficult at this time to define a middle phase of LM IIIC. As for late LM IIIC, we now know more from other sites in eastern Crete: Kavousi–*Vronda*, Kavousi–*Kastro*, and Khalasmenos; some pits at Sybrita/Thronos also date to this late phase of LM IIIC stylistically, if not stratigraphically.

The SM phase has been more difficult to distinguish, and much of the material attributed to this period comes from cemeteries, rather than stratified habitation sites. Knossos has produced several non-funerary deposits of the SM period, including the Spring chamber,[24] the Stratigraphical Museum excavations,[25] and the Unexplored Mansion.[26] At Sybrita/Thronos several pits can be attributed to SM, and two separate phases of this period have been distinguished by the excavator.[27] The cemeteries at Knossos have further helped to understand the PG period.[28] This new information has created more questions about the place of Karphi in the history of this period. A re-examination of the pottery, then, is much needed.

Recent work on Karphi has also concentrated on reconstructing the social, religious, and political organisation of the settlement,[29] and the re-examination of the pottery in its context can provide some evidence for the social organisation of Karphi. Since every piece of pottery and every vessel that was kept from the site had the number of the room in which it was found written on it in ink, and most of these numbers survive and are still legible, it is possible to recontextualise the extant pottery to see whole assemblages that might give clues about the lives and social organisation of the people. Thus, in this publication, the pottery is catalogued by room and building or by grave, rather than by type, as Seiradaki organised her publication; the pottery is analysed by type in a separate chapter (Chapter 9). A consideration of the contexts that produced the vessels can also show where the earliest and latest materials were found. In particular, it is important to distinguish whether a vessel or group of vessels comes from within a house, from a street or court, or from one of the tombs, since the depositional histories of these different areas were not necessarily the same.

The assemblages presented here are not in any way complete; much pottery was thrown away during excavation. It is fortunate that the excavation notebooks still survive in the archives of the British School at Athens, and one of these notebooks records lists of pottery from every room on the site. Whenever possible, the lists of pottery recorded in the notebook are given in the discussion of the room, as these accounts in general are more detailed than the brief mention in Pendlebury's final report.

The buildings at Karphi were uncovered over a three-year period, and the pottery was handled in a different way in each season. In 1937 work concentrated on the Temple, although local workers also removed material from Mikre Koprana, a small peak to the east. All the fragments of pottery from this season were saved. In 1938 Rooms 2–57 were uncovered. The pottery was taken down to Tzermiado for washing and study, and much of it was discarded there.[30] 1939 saw the excavation of Rooms 58–150. In this season, the pottery was sorted on site, and although all of the fine ware was kept, the majority of the coarse vessels were thrown away without washing. In the last two seasons, some information about the discarded pottery was recorded in the excavation notebook, and in 1939 the recognisable types of the various shapes were recorded (e.g. three dishes of Type 2). It is not possible, however, to know what percentage of the pottery found was described or kept. Thus, what is available for study is the result not only of the site formation process, but also of the decisions made by the excavators about the worth of the artefacts. All of the fine wares remain, in addition to whole or nearly complete coarse vessels, or any pieces that were deemed of interest. The preserved pottery, then, is not necessarily a representative sample of the shapes, decoration, or fabrics of the

17 Rethemiotakis 1997.
18 Mook and Coulson 1997; Mook 2004; Day 1997; *Kavousi IIA*.
19 Coulson and Tsipopoulou 1994; Tsipopoulou 2004.
20 *Kastri*.
21 See D'Agata 2007 for a good summary, especially 101, table 3.
22 Hallager 2007, Mountjoy 2007.
23 Mook and Coulson 1997, 342–4 (Kavousi–*Kastro*, Phase I); Mook 2004, 164–9; Hallager 2000, 173.
24 Evans 1928, 123–39.
25 Warren 1983, 76–83.
26 Popham 1992, 59–66.
27 D'Agata 1999, 201–06; 2007, 95, 99–101. I do not, however, agree with her terminology, particularly in her distinction of two phases of SM, which I take here as a single chronological phase; much of what she calls SM I would fit better into the category of very late LM IIIC in my opinion.
28 Brock 1957; Catling and Coldstream 1996.
29 Nowicki 1999; Wallace 2005; Day and Snyder 2004.
30 Seiradaki, 1.

Karphi assemblages; nevertheless, a large amount of material does remain and can be used with the publications to make conclusions about the history and society of the settlement.

The Karphi material is now stored in the Herakleion Museum and its satellite storerooms. Over the years, with the vicissitudes of history, some of the pottery was inevitably lost. Some vessels had disappeared already at the time of Seiradaki's work, while others seem to have been lost or misplaced in subsequent years. Nearly 140 restored vessels and 65 boxes of fragments were present in the Herakleion Museum when the project began in 1991.

During the course of this study, an attempt was made to draw all of the extant pottery for which some shape or decoration was discernable. Many tiny fragments were too small to draw or too worn to determine their precise shape or decoration, and only a brief verbal description was made of them. Frequently sherds from different layers in a room or area were kept in separate compartments in the boxes, each with its own label, and although fragmentary these pieces do provide some information about the depositional histories of the rooms in which they were found. None of the small finds was studied, with the exception of several terracotta objects found with the pottery, such as spools, loomweights, and a potter's wheel. The metal and stone objects that had been inventoried were kept separate from the pottery, and no attempt was made to re-examine them; similarly, a large box of stone tools was left unstudied. The figurines from the Middle Minoan peak sanctuary on the summit of Karphi are part of an on-going study by Alan Peatfield, and the terracotta figurines from the settlement are also part of a separate study by Geraldine Gesell, who has also looked at the cult equipment from the Temple. A few pieces of the ritual equipment from the site are catalogued; snake tubes and stands are considered part of the ceramic assemblages of Karphi, with the exception of the 'altar' from K 57, which forms part of Gesell's study. The goddess statues have been well studied by Rethemiotakis[31] and Gesell,[32] and the large chariot rhyton by Robert Koehl,[33] so they are not included in the catalogues.

The pottery is discussed and catalogued according to its building, room, or area, beginning with Mikre Koprana and the eastern side of the settlement. The centre of the settlement has been divided into four quadrants: the northeast (the Temple, Temple dependencies, Great House, Baker's House and surrounding streets), the southeast (the Magazines, Southern Houses, Small Shrine, and surrounding streets and squares), the southwest (the Priest's House, Central West Quarter, and Southern Shelters, with their associated streets), and the northwest (the Commercial Quarter, Eastern and Western Cliff Houses, Northern Shelters, and Summit). The tombs follow in a separate chapter, and finally the ceramics of uncertain context are discussed.

No attempt has been made to modify Pendlebury's original building and room designations, although more recent studies by Rutkowski of the Temple and Wallace of several of the buildings have been taken into account.[34] The discussion for each room includes a brief description of its features. If there was any indication of stratigraphy in the room, every attempt has been made to distinguish the pottery from the different layers. Also included is a list of pottery recorded in the excavation notebook for each room, often more detailed than the published account. To help in understanding room function, a list of inventoried objects is also included, with their numbers and references to illustrations in the original publication. Any other objects that were not inventoried but mentioned in the notebook or publication are also noted.

Each vessel or fragment has been catalogued according to its context, and for most of these pieces of pottery, the context was assumed to be the number written on it in ink or occasionally pencil (e.g. K 57, M 1). Sometimes the number was not clear, because the ink had flaked off or the number had been written on sediment that had been washed or worn off. If a number could be reasonably guessed at, the object has been catalogued in that context, although note is made that the number was unclear and alternative possibilities are also given. If the number was totally illegible or lacking, the object is catalogued as from an uncertain context. At times, the number on a published vessel did not agree with that in the publication. Whenever discrepancies occurred, it was assumed that the number written on the surface was more likely to be correct, especially since the publication came out 20 years after the excavation and Seiradaki did not go back and look at all the pottery again. Occasionally Seiradaki gave the same vessel a different context number in the figures and plates; if one of these agreed with the number written on the vessel, that was accepted as more accurate, but if not, then references in the publication or notebook were used to make a reasonable guess at the correct context.

Catalogue numbers have been assigned according to context (e.g. **K1.1**). Vessels of uncertain context are simply labelled **K.1–K.65**. Pottery is catalogued according to fabric in the following order: fine wares, medium-coarse wares, coarse wares, and cooking wares; cooking wares are, of course, always coarse wares, but show evidence of having been used directly in the fire for food preparation. Within each of these four categories, the open vessels are given first, then

31 Rethemiotakis 1998, 2001.
32 Gesell, Glowacki and Klein forthcoming.
33 Koehl 2006, 83.
34 Rutkowski 1987; Wallace 2005.

the closed shapes, beginning with the smallest shapes (e.g. cup) and proceeding to the largest (e.g. pithos). Whole or nearly complete vessels of each shape are given first, then rim, base, and handle fragments, and finally body sherds.

Catalogue entries include the following:

Catalogue number (PLATE and FIG. references). Identification of object. Preservation. Measurements. Description of material and details of manufacture (including fabric, colour, wear, and surface appearance). Details of shape or decoration. Type if applicable. Previous publications if applicable. Comparanda. Date.

Measurements are in centimetres. Colours are given according to the Munsell Soil Chart. Whenever possible, the colours were taken in direct sunlight, with the sun behind the viewer. The nearly complete vessels in the Museum, however, were often done without direct sunlight. Such colours are, of course, arbitrary, but the Munsells give some consistency to the recording of colour.

An attempt was made to describe the inclusions in the coarse and cooking pottery based on macroscopic analysis; since the investigator is not a geologist, these may be incorrect, but they are based on previous experience with coarse fabrics at Kavousi. During the actual study seasons, it was not possible to do a systematic sampling of fabrics for petrographic analysis, but in 2006 petrographic analysis of the Karphi pottery was carried out by Eleni Nodarou on some 85 fragments, primarily from the Temple. The material from the Temple seems to have included most of the coarse fabric types found on the cooking and storage vessels in the houses, even if the pottery does represent a collection of highly specialised shapes. Since all of the pottery from the Temple was kept, it represents a more complete sample of the range of coarse fabrics. The results of the petrographic analysis can be found in the Appendix.

The pottery is analysed in Chapter 9 according to shape. A basic description of the fine wares, medium-coarse wares, coarse wares, and cooking wares is followed by an analysis of the pottery by shapes; decoration is generally discussed within each shape. No attempt has been made to change or supplement Seiradaki's typology. In general the distinguishing features of each of her types were not explained; when she has made an error in identification (as in mistaking a tripod cooking pot for a jar), she has created types that do not exist. It seemed best to discuss the shapes in general, rather than adding to an already problematic typology.

The final chapter considers the new evidence for the chronology of the Karphi settlement, as well as making suggestions about the functions of rooms and buildings based on the pottery and objects found within. This section is necessarily brief, based as it is on incomplete evidence. It is hoped that the reopening of excavations at Karphi will provide more evidence to reconstruct the society of this important settlement.

2

The eastern side of the settlement

Mikre Koprana (K 147–K 150), Eastern Quarter (K 135–K 144), Barracks
(K 2–K 7, K 134) and Road House (K 145), Southeast Block (K 130–K 132)

MIKRE KOPRANA (ROOMS K 147–K 150)

Lying on a peak to the northeast of the main settlement are the rooms excavated as Mikre Koprana (FIG. 1.1).[1] Although the major excavation of the area took place late in the 1939 season, there had also been some archaeological activity in 1937. The notebook for 1937 simply notes that 'sherds were dug up by peasants' while the excavators were working at the Temple, and there were no traces of walls in the excavated area. The notebook records pithoi or large jars, eleven large and four small spools, and stone pounders (three of Type 3 and one of Type 6). Much pottery preserved in the storerooms bears the following designations: MK 1, MK 1E, MK 1NE, MK 1N, or MK 1W. This material came from the 1937 investigation or was excavated before the rooms were defined. When published by Seiradaki, some of these vessels were given a room designation, and sometimes there are conflicting room numbers in different places in the report; if there is any doubt, such pieces are here catalogued according to the designation written on the vessel.

The excavators believed that there was a single building on a plateau on top of the summit.[2] There was little soil deposition, and the bedrock often appeared 20 cm below the surface; few traces of roofing appeared in the rooms. The main entrance into the building was from the east into K 147. Outside this entrance lay a semicircular vat or bin paved with flat slabs and containing a pithos base and a whetstone. Although he compared this object to what may be a dyeing vat at Archaic Kolonna, Pendlebury thought it was more likely to be a watering trough.[3]

Room K 147

The building on Mikre Koprana was entered by a doorway into K 147 from the east. This was a large room that may have been divided into two. The excavators suggested that it was built against a pre-existing room, but they did not indicate whether this room was K 149 or K 150. Steps led down to the south from the southeast corner to a denuded room. A door on the west led into K 149.

The notebook gives much information about the pottery to add to the limited discussion in the publication. Coarse ware included at least five pithoi, one very large one of Type 15, with rope decoration

and chevrons and chevrons on the handles, two of Types 6 and 23, and one each of Types 7 and 14; eight pithoid jars, six of Type 3, two of Type 7; several jars of Types 2 and 3; tripod legs and a rim of Type 1; a tripod pithos; eleven dishes, eight of Type 6, three of Type 1; a tripod 'lebes;' a kalathos of Type 1; small basin of Type 7; and a trefoil 'lamp'(i.e. a scuttle). Fine wares included a hut urn (**K147.17**), a small spouted jar, a jug with ridged neck, a cup in blue ware of Type 1, two pyxides of Type 2 (**K147.16**), two stirrup jars of Type 2, and several bowls of Types 1 and 2. The krater base pictured in Seiradaki was not located.[4] Other published pottery was not found, including the large basin[5] and a pithos with incised chevrons on bands and incised serpentine rope bands, probably the one mentioned in the notebook.[6] In addition to the catalogued pottery, the boxes produced the following: three handle fragments from deep bowls bearing multiple pendent loops, a spiral, and a multiple curvilinear design, and a body fragment of a deep bowl with vertical strokes or fringe, and another from a deep bowl or krater with strokes, a decorated feeding bottle spout, a cooking pot with ridged decoration, and a pithos handle, flattened, with raised vertical bands and impressed circles.

Objects from K 147 included a bronze knife with twisted handle (687),[7] two bronze angle pieces (688, 689), a bronze fibula (690),[8] a fragment of a knobbed stone lid (683), two conical stone beads or whorls (684, 685), a double-pierced stone disc (686), four terracotta spindle whorls (two conical, one cylindrical, one biconical in shape) (691, 692, 693, 694), three terracotta spools (695), and animal bones.

The pottery from K 147 gives clues to the function of the building. The large number of pithoi (5) and

---

1   The plan published by Nowicki 1987, figs. 2 and 3 gives a good picture of where these rooms lie in relation to the main part of the excavated settlement and other features of the site of Karphi.
2   *Karphi*, 69–70.
3   *Karphi*, 69.
4   Seiradaki, fig. 16.9.
5   Seiradaki, pl. 3c, left.
6   Seiradaki, pl. 1b.
7   *Karphi*, pl. 28.2.
8   *Karphi*, pl. 29.2.

pithoid jars (7), along with the tripod pithos and the large stirrup jar (**K147.15**) confirm that the room was used primarily for storage. The large basins may have been used for food preparation, and the cooking dishes and tripod 'lebes' (probably a round-bottomed cooking pot) were also used in cooking. The material points to storage and ordinary domestic use, although the pithoid jars and basins may also have served for washing or for some industrial function, such as dyeing of wool.

Most of the whole vessels found on the floor were coarse and utilitarian and cannot provide a date for the final occupation. The basin (**K147.18**) is, however, a good LM IIIC shape, similar to examples from Kastri, Knossos, and Khamalevri of early LM IIIC date,[9] and Kavousi–*Vronda* of late LM IIIC.[10] Another exception is the fine stirrup jar (**K147.15**), which finds a close parallel at Khania of early LM IIIC date, where it is thought to be an import from Knossos.[11] The other fine wares, however, particularly the deep bowls and kraters, are quite fragmentary, and they could have lain broken on or in the floor for some time. There is nothing that appears particularly late. On deep bowl fragments, the running spirals, hatched lozenges or lozenge chain, Minoan flower, and tricurved streamer all are motifs that appear in early deposits of LM IIIC.[12] The upright multiple loops on **K147.1** find parallels at Kastri, but also in Phase III at Kavousi–*Kastro* of Late LM IIIC date.[13] Certainly the delicate octopus stirrup jar (**K147.14**), another fragment of which was found in K 149, is not late, although it is without any good parallels.

Pottery Catalogue: K 147

Fine Wares

K147.1 Cup or deep bowl (FIG. 2.1). D. rim est. 13–14. Two joining and one non-joining fragments from rim. Fine, rather hard reddish yellow fabric (7.5YR 7/6). Very pale brown slip 10YR 8/2. Paint brown to reddish yellow (5YR 6/6) (interior). Well-preserved surfaces, especially on interior. Upright multiple loops. No label, but published as being from K 147. Publication: Seiradaki, fig. 21c. LM IIIC early.

K147.2 Deep bowl or cup (FIG. 2.1). D. rim. est. 15. Single fragment from rim. Fine, soft, porous reddish yellow fabric (7.5YR 7/6). Very pale brown slip (10YR 8/2). Shadow of red to brown paint. Very worn surfaces. Running spirals. Reserved band on interior. Publication: Seiradaki, fig. 21a. For decoration, cf. **K147.3**; *Khania II*, pl. 52.77-P 0079; Popham 1965, 326, fig. 6.31 (Knossos). LM IIIC early.

K147.3 Deep bowl or cup (PLATE 1 *a*, FIG. 2.1). D. rim est. 15. Single fragment from rim. Fine, very soft reddish yellow (5YR 7/6) fabric. Pinkish white slip (7.5YR 8/2). Worn black paint, streaky on interior. Some patches of burning. Running spirals. For decoration, cf. **K147.2**. LM IIIC early.

K147.4 Deep bowl or cup (FIG. 2.1). D. rim est. 15. Single fragment from rim. Fine, soft, very pale brown fabric (10YR 8/3). Very pale brown slip (10YR 8/3). Black paint worn to reddish brown (5YR 4/4). Rather well-preserved surfaces. Tricurved streamer? For shape and decoration, cf. Andreadaki-Vlasaki and Papadopoulou 2007, 47, fig. 4.4 (Khamalevri, Phase Ib). LM IIIC early.

K147.5 Deep bowl or cup (FIG. 2.1). D. rim est. 15. Single fragment from rim. Fine, soft, porous, very pale brown (10YR

8/4) fabric. Very pale brown slip (10YR 8/3). Black paint. Well-preserved surfaces, especially on interior. Hatched lozenges. May be same vessel as **K147.6**. For decoration, cf. Andreadaki-Vlasaki and Papadopoulou 2007, 51, fig. 8.4 (Khamalevri, Phase Ib). LM IIIC early.

K147.6 Deep bowl or cup (PLATE 1 *b*, FIG. 2.1). Max. pres. H. 4.5. Single fragment from rim. Fine, soft, porous, reddish yellow (7.5YR 7/6) fabric, with voids where inclusions have burned out. Very pale brown slip (10YR 8/2). Paint red (2.5YR 4/8) to black (interior). Worn surfaces. Hatched lozenges. May be same vessel as **K147.5**. For decoration, cf. Popham 1965, 326, fig. 6.36 (Knossos); Borgna 1997a, 280, fig. 15. LM IIIC early.

K147.7 Deep bowl or cup (FIG. 2.1). D. rim est. 16. Single fragment from rim. Fine, soft, reddish yellow (7.5YR 7/6) fabric. Glossy very pale brown slip (10YR 8/3). Worn red paint (2.5YR 4/8). Well-preserved interior surfaces, worn exterior. Running spiral. Label unclear, looks like K 147. LM IIIC early.

K147.8 Deep bowl or cup (PLATE 1 *a*, FIG. 2.1). D. rim est. 16. Single fragment from rim. Fine, soft fabric, completely burned. Wheel ridging on interior. Spiral. LM IIIC early.

K147.9 Deep bowl or cup (FIG. 2.1). Max. pres. H. 7.3. Single large body fragment. Fine, soft, very pale brown (10YR 8/4) fabric. Very pale brown slip (10YR 8/4). Worn black paint. Minoan flower. For decoration, cf. Popham 1965, 328, fig. 7.42 (stirrup jar, Knossos, LM IIIC); Popham 1970b, pl. 47c (Knossos, LM IIIB). LM IIIC early.

K147.10 Deep bowl or cup (FIG. 2.1). Max. pres. H. 5.7. Single worn fragment from rim. Fine, soft, reddish yellow (5YR 7/6) fabric. Very pale brown slip (10YR 8/3). Black paint. Worn surfaces. Curvilinear motif with filler. LM IIIC.

K147.11 Deep bowl or cup (FIG. 2.1). Max. pres. H. 3.8. Single fragment from body. Fine, medium-hard, reddish yellow (5YR 7/6) fabric. Very pale brown slip (10YR 8/3). Red paint (2.5YR 5/8). Rather well-preserved surfaces on exterior, worn on interior. Multiple stacked arcs between multiple stems. LM IIIC.

K147.12 Krater (FIG. 2.1). D. rim est. 22. Single fragment from rim. Fine, soft, reddish yellow (5YR 7/6) fabric. Very pale brown slip 10YR 8/3. Red (2.5YR 4/8) paint. Very worn surfaces. Spiral. LM IIIC.

K147.13 Krater (FIG. 2.1). D. rim est. 21. Single fragment from rim. Fine, medium-hard, reddish yellow (7.5YR 7/6) fabric. Very pale brown slip (10YR 8/3). Black paint worn to brown shadow. Well-preserved surfaces. Wavy band on top of rim. Curvilinear motif below rim. LM IIIC.

K147.14 Stirrup jar (PLATE 1 *c*, FIG. 2.1). Max. pres. H. 3.3. Single fragment from body. Fine, soft, pink (7.5YR 7/4) fabric. Very pale brown slip 10YR 8/3. Red (2.5YR 5/6) paint. Well-preserved surfaces. Octopus with dotted multiple tentacles; eye preserved. Publication: Seiradaki, fig. 22g. Cf. **K149.17**, which certainly comes from the same vessel. LM IIIC early.

---

9 *Kastri*, 296, fig. 16 P11; Warren 1982–83, 84, fig. 56; Andreadaki-Vlasaki and Papadopoulou 2007, 51, fig. 8.33 (Phase II).

10 Gesell, Day and Coulson 1995, pl. 18d; *Kavousi IIA*, fig. 74.D4 P4.

11 *Khania II*, pl. 50.71-P 0736/0763/0779/77-P 0719.

12 All these motifs except the lozenge chain appear in the earliest deposits at Kavousi–*Kastro*, for example: Mook and Coulson 1997, 344–51. The lozenge chain appears at Kastri and Knossos; see *Kastri*, 296, 294–5 (lozenge and loop) and Popham 1965, 324–6.

13 *Kastri*, 296, 288, fig. 9m; Mook and Coulson 1997, 362, fig. 37.150 (Kavousi–*Kastro*).

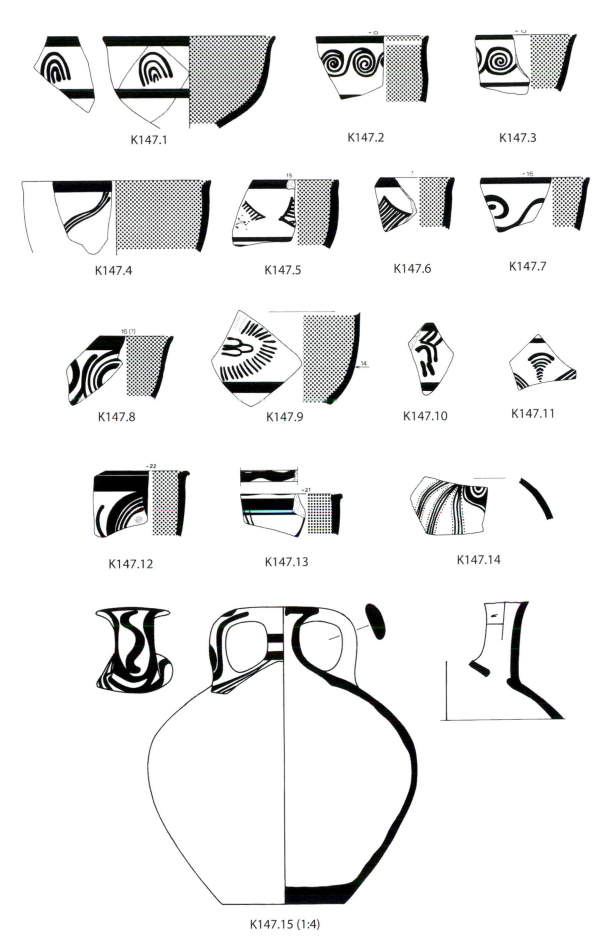

K147.1

K147.2

K147.3

K147.4

K147.5

K147.6

K147.7

K147.8

K147.9

K147.10

K147.11

K147.12

K147.13

K147.14

K147.15 (1:4)

*Fig. 2.1. Mikre Koprana, pottery from K 147 (**K147.1–15**). Scale 1:3 unless otherwise indicated.*

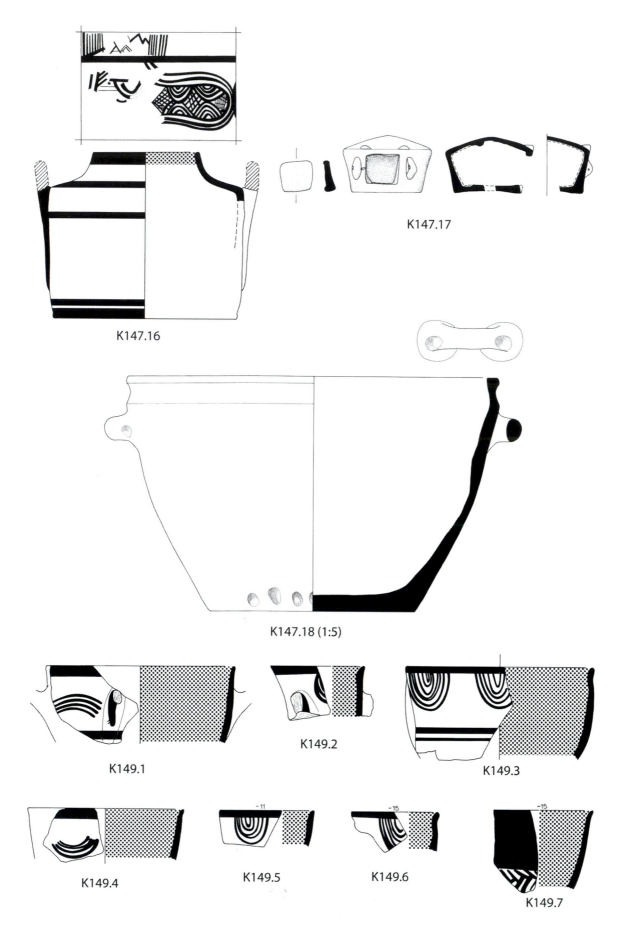

*Fig. 2.2. Mikre Koprana, pottery from K 147 (**K147.16–18**) and K 149 (**K149.1–7**).*
Scale 1:3 unless otherwise indicated.

K147.15   Stirrup jar (FIG. 2.1). H. 32; D. base 12.8. Partially mended from 157 fragments. *c.* 60% preserved, including full profile, entire base, 75% of lower body, 35% of upper body, base of spout, false spout, both handles; missing rim of spout. Fine, medium-soft, light grey (5Y 7/1) to greenish grey (5GY 5/1) fabric with a few grey phyllite inclusions. Totally burned except for false spout, which is only burned on interior. Very pale brown slip (10YR 8/4) where not burned. Black paint. Worn surfaces. False spout pierced in centre. Bands on neck of false spout; wavy band down handle. LM IIIC early.

K147.16   Pyxis (PLATE 1 *d*, FIG. 2.2). H. 13.9; D. base 14.7; D. rim 8.7. Restored from 23 fragments. 85% preserved; missing tops of handles and body sherds. Fine, soft, very pale brown (10YR 7/3) fabric with frequent tiny black inclusions and occasional mica. Paint worn to shadow. Very worn surfaces. Type 2 pyxis. Zigzag between vertical lines below shoulder; on body, large loops containing multiple pendent loops alternating with multiple upright loops on a background of crosshatching. Publication: Seiradaki, fig. 24b, pl. 7c, right (labelled K 147). For shape and decoration, cf. D'Agata 2007, 113, fig. 13 (Mouliana, Tomb A). LM IIIC late.

K147.17   Hut urn (HM 11054) (PLATE 1 *e*, FIG. 2.2). H. 4.7; D. base 5.6. Mended from seven fragments. 90% preserved, only missing small pieces of top and base. Door preserved. Fine, soft, very pale brown (10YR 8/2) fabric. No trace of paint. Worn and flaky surfaces; much of surface still coated with sediment. Small projections at join of roof and walls, possibly horns of consecration. Publication: Seiradaki, pl. 10a, bottom left; Gesell 1985, 52, pl. 176; Hägg 1990, 105, fig. 5.5; Mersereau 1993, 34–5, fig. 24.16. LM IIIC.

Coarse Wares

K147.18   Basin (PLATE 1 *f*, FIG. 2.2). H. 31; D. base 27; D. rim 49. Restored from numerous fragments. 75% preserved, including full profile; missing part of base, body fragments, and one handle. Coarse red (2.5YR 5/6) fabric, with frequent red and grey phyllite inclusions (3–4 mm). Surface blackened on one side and much coated with sediment. Interior blackened. Interior shows construction in sections. Dints at both attachments of handles. Finger impressions around base. Publication: Seiradaki, pl. 3b (where labelled from K 147); fig. 5.4 (where labelled from K 150; the vessel itself is labelled MK). LM IIIC.

Rooms K 148 and K 149

The material from these two rooms was lumped together in the publication, but kept separate in the notebook. The objects listed in the publication as coming from the two rooms are said to be from MK in the notebook, and they will be listed there.

Room K 149

Room K 149 was connected to K 147 through a doorway, and it also had an additional exit on the south. There was in the room a tank in floor that the excavators thought may have been used for fermenting milk.[14]

The notebook lists much pottery from the room. There were at least 17 pithoi, four of Type 6, two each of Types 2 and 25, one each of Types 1, 3, 8, 12, 14, 15, 21, and 22, and one for which no rim found, and the feet of four tripod pithoi; the pithoi were decorated with the usual designs, including impressed circles, squares, alternating hatched triangles, zigzag with dots, X-pattern, vertical slashes, oblique slashes, and alternating oblique slashes (**K149.24**). There were also seven pithoid jars, three of Type 3, two of Type 7, two of Type 9; several jars of Types 1, 2, 5, and 7; a very large number of tripod rims and legs of all types; at least 16 dishes, three of Type 1, one of Type 5, twelve of Type 6, with the usual holes, spouts, and handles; three basins, one of Type 5, two of Type 6; three kalathoi, one of Type 1 with a rim of Type 2, 1 of Type 4 with rim of Type 3, one with goddess inside (**K149.21**); three one-handled jugs of Types 1, 7, and 8; two cups of Type 2; several small bowls; an 'egg-cup;' and a coarse kylix stem. Finer and painted pottery included a very fine krater of Type 1 with scale pattern in blue and red paint (**K148.5**), krater bases of Types 1 and 3, two pyxides of Type 2, a large jar with octopus pattern, a jar of Type 3, a one-handled jug of Type 7, two stirrup jars of Type 2, two spouted jars, two kylikes of Type 1, two dishes of Type 1, a pyxis rim of Type 4, small pots with straight sides, and several small bowls of Types 1 and 2 with usual patterns including dotted curvilinear motifs and a hatched lozenge with tricurved streamer (**K149.10**). There were several fragments from K 149 in the boxes that were not catalogued, including deep bowl fragments with spirals, curvilinear ornaments, floral designs, a rayed panel, and one burned example. Also found were a stirrup jar fragment with fringed decoration and a cup or kylix handle. The tray pictured in Seiradaki was not located.[15]

That this room was used primarily for storage is indicated by the unusually large number of pithoi (17) and pithoid jars (7) recovered from it. This was the largest number of storage vessels recorded for a single room on the site. It is hard to imagine that there was room for any other activities, yet the number of cooking dishes and tripods suggests that the room was used for cooking, or at least storage of cooking vessels. The kalathos with a goddess figurine (**K149.21**) inside may have served a ritual function, perhaps for daily religious observance.

As is usual, nearly all of the fine pottery was in fragments, and thus it may represent broken earlier material on or in the floor of the room, not what was in use at the time of abandonment. As with the fragments from K 147, the deep bowls, kraters, and stirrup jars are of early LM IIIC style. The deep bowls or cups with multiple pendent loops (**K149.3, K149.5**) find parallels in LM IIIC deposits at Knossos,[16] although on the earlier example the loops do not hang from

---

14   *Karphi*, 69.

15   Seiradaki, fig. 6.1, pl. 2f.

16   Popham 1965, 325, fig. 5.27 (early LM IIIC); Cadogan 1967, 260, fig. 2.8 (Knossos, Kephala tholos, early LM IIIC). The date of individual vessels from the Kephala tomb is uncertain. Preston 2005, 101, places this deep bowl (P 67) within the tomb above 2.3 m, not as high in the debris as the latest LM IIIC material. D'Agata (2007, 101, table 3, 104, fig. 1) places this material in LM IIIC early.

the rim band; multiple loops hanging from the rim band may be a later feature. **K149.10** with its tricurved streamer has parallels at Khania, where it is a LM IIIC pattern on a LM IIIB2 shape.[17] **K149.8** finds parallels at Knossos and Phaistos.[18] The bird motif with dotted breast on krater **K149.14** is similar to krater **K62.1** and to an example from Phase II at Khamalevri,[19] while the palm motif finds a parallel at Khania;[20] it is possible that the fragment **K149.15** may belong to the same vessel.

Pottery Catalogue: K 149

Fine Wares

K149.1   Deep bowl (FIG. 2.2). D. rim est. 16. Single fragment from rim, preserving one handle attachment. Fine, soft, reddish yellow (7.5YR 7/6) fabric. Very pale brown slip (10YR 8/3). Paint black to red (2.5YR 4/6). Well-preserved surfaces. Multiple stems. LM IIIC early?

K149.2   Deep bowl (FIG. 2.2). Max. pres. H. 4. Single fragment from rim, preserving one handle attachment. Fine, medium-soft, reddish yellow (7.5YR 7/6) fabric. Very pale brown slip (10YR 8/4). Dark brown paint (7.5YR 3/2). Well-preserved surfaces. Spiral? LM IIIC.

K149.3   Deep bowl or cup (PLATE 1 g, FIG. 2.2). D. rim est. 15. Two joining fragments from rim. Fine, rather soft, reddish yellow (7.5YR 7/6) fabric. Very pale brown slip (10YR 8/4). Black paint, worn on exterior. Multiple pendent loops hanging from rim band. LM IIIC.

K149.4   Deep bowl or cup (FIG. 2.2). D. rim est. 12.6. Single fragment from rim. Fine, soft, reddish yellow (7.5YR 7/6) fabric. Very pale brown slip (10YR 8/3). Red paint (2.5YR 4/8). Worn surfaces. Multiple pendent loops. LM IIIC.

K149.5   Deep bowl or cup (PLATE 1 h, FIG. 2.2). D. rim est. 11. Single fragment from rim. Fine, soft, reddish yellow (7.5YR 7/6) fabric. Very pale brown slip (10YR 8/3). Worn black to brown paint. Worn and flaky surfaces. Multiple pendent loops. Label hard to read, possibly K 99. LM IIIC.

K149.6   Deep bowl or cup (PLATE 1 h, FIG. 2.2). D. rim est. 15. Single fragment from rim. Rather hard reddish yellow (7.5YR 7/6) fabric. Very pale brown slip (10YR 8/3). Black paint. Well-preserved surfaces, especially on interior. Multiple pendent loops. For decoration, cf. **K148.3**, **K149.3**. LM IIIC.

K149.7   Deep bowl or cup (FIG. 2.2). D. rim est. 15. Single fragment from rim. Fine, soft, reddish yellow (7.5YR 7/6) fabric. Very pale brown slip (10YR 8/3). Crackled black paint worn to streaky red-brown. Flaky interior surfaces, well-preserved exterior. Chevrons or crosshatching. LM IIIC.

K149.8   Deep bowl or cup (FIG. 2.3). D. rim est. 15. Single fragment from rim. Fine, soft, rather porous, reddish yellow (7.5YR 7/6) fabric, with tiny black and white inclusions. Very pale brown slip (10YR 8/3). Black paint worn to red-brown shadow. Flaky interior surfaces, well-preserved exterior surfaces. Multiple stems with arc fillers and scallops. LM IIIC early.

K149.9   Deep bowl or cup (FIG. 2.3). D. rim est. 16. Single fragment from rim. Fine, soft, rather porous, very pale brown (10YR 7/4) fabric. Worn, very pale brown (10YR 8/4) slip. Red (2.5YR 4/8) paint. Well-preserved exterior surfaces; interior worn. Multiple stem with arc fillers. LM IIIC.

K149.10   Deep bowl or cup (PLATE 1 i, FIG. 2.3). D. rim est. 11. Single fragment from rim. Fine, soft, porous, very pale brown (10YR 7/4–8/4) fabric. Worn, very pale brown (10YR 8/4) slip. Black paint. Tricurved streamer with crosshatched lozenge with spirals on either side. Probably monochrome interior, but worn. Cf. **K149.11**; this may be the same vessel. LM IIIC early.

K149.11   Deep bowl or cup (FIG. 2.3). D. rim est. 12–13. Single fragment from rim. Fine, rather soft, very pale brown (10YR 7/3) fabric. Light grey slip (2.5Y 7/2). Black paint worn to shadow. Worn surfaces. Possibly burned. Multiple stem and spiral. Cf. **K149.10**; this may be the same vessel. LM IIIC early.

K149.12   Deep bowl or cup (FIG. 2.3). Max. pres. H. 3.9. Single fragment from body. Fine, medium-soft, very pale brown (10YR 7/3) fabric. Very pale brown slip (10YR 8/3). Dark reddish brown (5YR 3/3) to yellowish red (5YR 4/6) paint. Well-preserved surfaces. Careless upright multiple loops and multiple stems. LM IIIC.

K149.13   Deep bowl or kylix (FIG. 2.3). Max. pres. H. 3.4. Single fragment from body. Fine, hard, reddish yellow (7.5YR 7/6) fabric. Very pale brown slip (10YR 8/3). Worn black paint. Well-preserved surfaces. Crosshatched outlined lozenge. LM IIIC.

K149.14   Krater (PLATE 2 a, FIG. 2.3). D. rim est. 26. Single large fragment from rim. Fine reddish yellow (7.5YR 7/6) fabric. Glossy, very pale brown slip (10YR 8/3). Worn black paint. Well-preserved surfaces. Wheel-ridging on interior. Palm motif with dotted outline, bird to right with beak and dotted breast. LM IIIC early.

K149.15   Krater (FIG. 2.3). D. rim est. 22. Single fragment from rim. Fine, soft, reddish yellow (7.5YR 7/6) fabric. Very pale brown slip (10YR 8/4). Crackled black paint. Well-preserved surfaces. Bird with head outlined in dots. Cf. **K149.14**, to which it may belong. LM IIIC early.

K149.16   Krater (FIG. 2.3). Max. pres. H. 6; Th. 1.0. Single fragment from body. Fine, medium-soft, very pale brown (10YR 8/4) fabric. Very pale brown slip (10YR 8/4). Red (2.5YR 5/8) paint, brown inside. Well-preserved surfaces. Panelled pattern, with curvilinear motif. LM IIIC.

K149.17   Stirrup jar (PLATE 1 c, FIG. 2.3). Max. pres. H. 6. Two joining fragments from shoulder of body. Fine, soft, pink (7.5YR 7/4) fabric. Very pale brown slip (10YR 8/3). Red paint (2.5YR 5/6). Dotted multiple tentacles of octopus, including edge of one eye. Cf. **K147.14**, which certainly comes from the same vessel. LM IIIC early.

K149.18   Stirrup jar (FIG. 2.3). Max. pres. H. 4.2. Single fragment from body. Fine, soft, reddish yellow (7.5YR 7/6) fabric. Very pale brown slip (10YR 8/2). Red paint (2.5YR 4/8). Worn surfaces. Burned in patches inside and out. Closed vessel, possibly a stirrup jar, or a jug. Vertical strokes and arcs between horizontal bands. LM IIIC.

K149.19   Stirrup jar (FIG. 2.3). Max. pres. H. 2.8. Single body fragment. Fine, medium-soft, reddish yellow (7.5YR 7/6) fabric, with small, sharp, elongated black inclusions. Very pale brown slip (10YR 8/3). Black paint worn to shadow. Worn surfaces. Closed vessel, possibly stirrup jar. Minoan flower. LM IIIC early.

K149.20   Amphora (PLATE 2 b, FIG. 2.3). Max. pres. H. 12.8; H. est. 17; D. base 5.2. Restored from 14 fragments. 60% preserved, including entire base, most of body, and lower handle attachments; missing neck, rim, and handles. Very sandy, fine, light grey (2.5Y 7/2) fabric, with small black inclusions. Light grey slip (2.5Y 7/2). Dull black paint. Ridge at base of neck. Irregular base. Dent in one side, as if misfired. Panelled pattern: crosshatched panel with

---

17   *Khania II*, 138, pl. 48.77-P 0522, dated to LM IIIC because of the fringes, but on a cup of LM IIIB2 shape. See also Rethemiotakis 1997, 322, fig. 33b for a similar decoration from Kastelli Pediada. The shape of this vessel finds a parallel at Phaistos (Borgna 1997a, 278, fig. 6.7).

18   Popham 1965, pl. 82a, bottom left (Knossos); Borgna 1997a, 289, fig. 24.

19   Andreadaki-Vlasaki and Papadopoulou 2005, 380, fig. 45.

20   *Khania II*, pl. 53.77-P 0147 and pl. 52.70-P 0234.

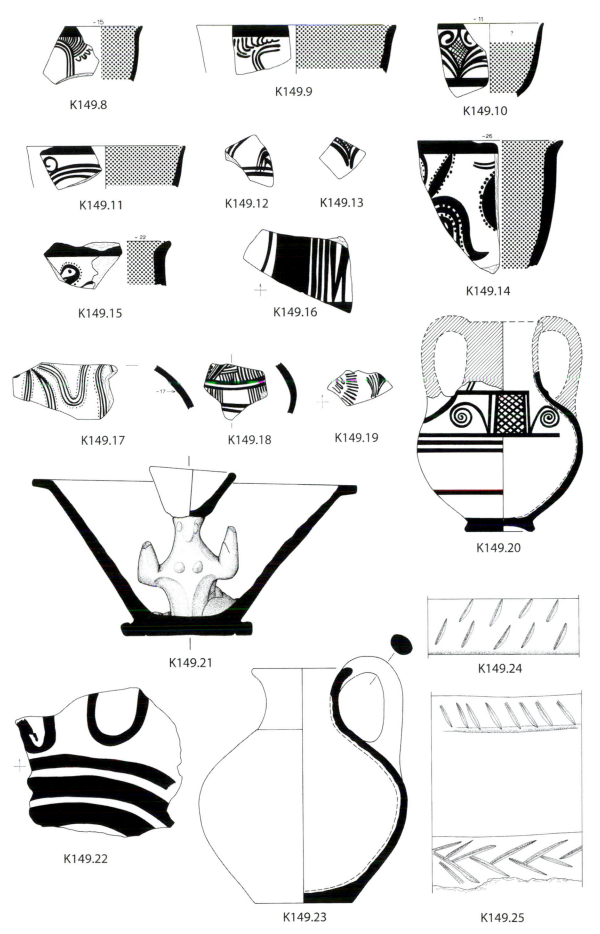

K149.8

K149.9

K149.10

K149.11

K149.12

K149.13

K149.14

K149.15

K149.16

K149.17

K149.18

K149.19

K149.20

K149.21

K149.22

K149.23

K149.24

K149.25

*Fig. 2.3. Mikre Koprana, pottery from K 149 (**K149.8–25**). Scale 1:3.*

stemmed spirals on either side. Publication: Seiradaki, pl. 5d, top, 2nd from right (labelled K 149), possibly fig. 8.1 (labelled K 148). For decoration, cf. Coldstream and Catling 1996, 88, fig. 84.16 (SM). LM IIIC late.

Coarse Wares

K149.21   Kalathos (HM 11047) (PLATE 2 *c*, FIG. 2.3).[21] H. 12 (with inner cup 12.9); D. base 10.5; D. rim 26.2–26.6; D. rim cup 6.7. Restored from several fragments. 35% preserved, including 25% of rim, 66% of base, 50% of body; entire goddess preserved except for hands. Coarse, hard, light red (2.5YR 6/6) fabric, with phyllite and hard white angular inclusions (0–2 mm). Smooth surface. Publication: *Karphi*, pl. 35.6; Seiradaki, pl. 4c; Gesell 2004, 142, fig. 7.10. LM IIIC late.

K149.22   Stirrup jar (FIG. 2.3). Max. pres. H. 12; Th. 0.8–1.1. Single large body fragment. Very coarse, light grey (5Y 7/2) fabric, with frequent hard white and black inclusions (1–2 mm). Light grey slip (5Y 7/2). Worn black paint. Wavy band or debased octopus. LM IIIC.

K149.23   Jug (PLATE 2 *d*, FIG. 2.3). H. 19; D. base 7.8; D. rim 8.2. Restored from five fragments. 80% preserved, including entire base, 30% of rim and handle; missing 66% of rim and one body fragment. Hard, coarse, red (2.5YR 5/6) fabric, with frequent small black and white inclusions and phyllites. May be decorated, but surfaces still coated with sediment. Publication: Seiradaki, pl. 5d, top, second from left (labelled K 149). LM IIIC.

K149.24   Pithos (FIG. 2.3). Two fragments from body. Coarse, light red (10R 6/8) fabric, with very frequent red phyllite (1–5 mm) and hard white angular inclusions. Raised band with two rows of incised alternating oblique strokes. LM IIIC.

K149.25   Pithos (FIG. 2.3). Single decorated body fragment. Coarse, reddish yellow (5YR 7/6) fabric, with very frequent red phyllites, some schist, and hard white angular inclusions. Two raised bands, one with incised oblique strokes, the other with incised chevrons. LM IIIC.

Room K 148

Room K 148 is a small out-building to the southwest of K 149. According to the notebook, the following coarse pottery was found in this room: three pithos rims of Types 2, 8, and 23; three pithoid jars, two of Type 3, one of Type 9; a jar of Type 2; the usual tripod legs; a dish of Type 6; a kalathos of Type 1 (**K148.7**); and two basins of Type 7. Neither the amphora shown in Seiradaki,[22] nor the cooking jug[23] was certainly located, although the amphora may be the one from MK 1 (**K149.20**) and the cooking jug is possibly **K.48**. Animal bones are also recorded from this room.

The pottery suggests an ordinary domestic function for the room. The material is not closely datable, but it looks early in LM IIIC; **K148.2** finds parallels for shape in LM IIIA1 at Knossos, as well as at LM IIIC Phaistos,[24] and the decoration on krater **K148.4** finds a parallel in Phase II at Khamalevri.[25]

Pottery Catalogue: K 148

Fine Wares

K148.1   Cup (FIG. 2.4). H. 7.7 (with handle 8.2); D. base 3.1; D. rim 8. Mended from four fragments. 75% preserved, including handle. Fine, soft, light brown (7.5YR 6/4) fabric. Almost totally burned, apparently after breaking. Very worn surfaces. Plain, monochrome, or blob decoration. LM IIIC.

K148.2   Deep bowl or cup (FIG. 2.4). Max. pres. H. 5.7. Single fragment from rim. Medium-fine, soft, reddish yellow (5YR 6/6) fabric, with infrequent inclusions (<1mm). Thick, creamy, yellow (10YR 8/6) slip. Black to brown paint. Well-preserved exterior surfaces, worn on interior. Arc filler on curvilinear design. LM IIIC early.

K148.3   Deep bowl or cup (FIG. 2.4). D. rim est. 15–16. Single fragment from rim. Fine, rather soft, very pale brown (10YR 7/4) fabric. Very pale brown slip (10YR 8/2). Worn black paint. Multiple pendent loops. LM IIIC.

K148.4   Krater (FIG. 2.4). D. rim est. <40. Single fragment from rim. Fine, soft, very pale brown (10YR 7/4) fabric, possibly burned. Very pale brown (10YR 8/3) slip. Yellowish red (5YR 4/6) paint. Spiral or other curvilinear motif with filler arcs. Strokes on top of rim. LM IIIC.

K148.5   Krater (FIG. 2.4). Max. pres. H. 16.4. Large body fragment (8 sherds) and three non-joining fragments; missing rim, base, handles. Fine, rather soft, reddish yellow (5YR 7/6) fabric. Very pale brown (10YR 8/3) slip. Red (2.5YR 4/6) paint. One patch of burning. Panelled decoration: scale pattern, vertical bands with hatching and U-pattern, scale, chequerboard, vertical bands, and S-pattern. The fragment is labelled K 148, although it is described in the notebook as from K 149; possibly fragments were found in both places. For chequerboard pattern, cf. *Kastri*, 288, fig. 9x; Andreadaki-Vlasaki and Papadopoulou 2007, 47, fig. 4.14 (Khamalevri, Phase Ib). LM IIIC early.

Medium-Coarse Wares

K148.6   Jug (PLATE 2 *e*, FIG. 2.4). H. 22 (with handle 23.4); D. base 7.8; D. rim 8.4. Restored from numerous fragments. 60% preserved, including base, handle, full profile; missing 50% of body and rim. Medium-coarse, soft, porous, light grey (10YR 7/2) fabric, with small black inclusions. Possibly grey from burning. Elliptical handle with added roll of clay in centre. Monochrome. Publication: Seiradaki, fig. 9.2 (labelled K 148), pl. 5d, bottom left (labelled K 148). LM IIIC.

Coarse Wares

K148.7   Kalathos (PLATE 2 *f*, FIG. 2.4). H. 7.9–8.3; D. base 5.7; D. rim 17.7. Three joining fragments preserving full profile. 66% preserved, including entire base; missing 75% of rim. Coarse red (2.5YR 5/6) to reddish yellow (7.5YR 6/6) fabric, with frequent phyllite and dark grey inclusions (1–2 mm), rather finer than usual. Burned all over interior bottom and in patches on exterior. Publication: Seiradaki, fig. 7.1 (labelled K 148). LM IIIC.

Room 150

The last room excavated at Karphi, K 150 was a small room north of K 147. Next to it on the west was a tiny room, identified by the excavators as a closet. The pottery listed in the notebook included at least

---

21 The label says this is from MK. The notebook puts it into K 149. Seiradaki gives two different find spots for it: on p. 11 she says it is from K 149, while on pl. 4c she identifies it as from K 148. Since it is clearly listed with the material from K 149 in the notebook, it has been catalogued here.

22 Seiradaki, fig. 8.1.

23 Seiradaki, fig. 9.8.

24 Warren 1997, 166, fig. 16, bottom left (Knossos); Borgna 1997a, 278, fig. 6.10 (Phaistos).

25 Andreadaki-Vlasaki and Papadopoulou 2007, 53, fig. 10.21.

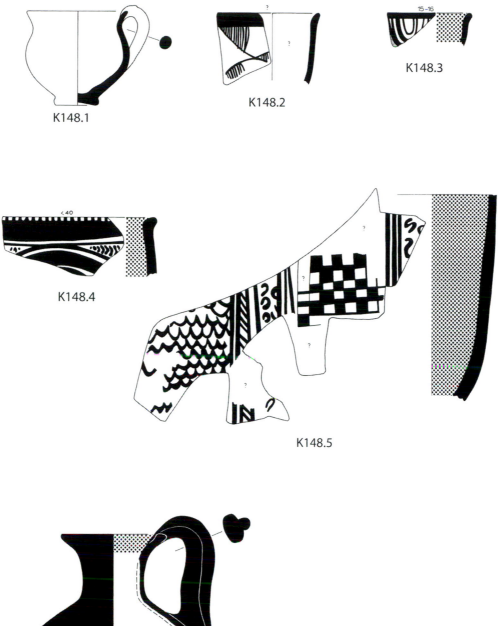

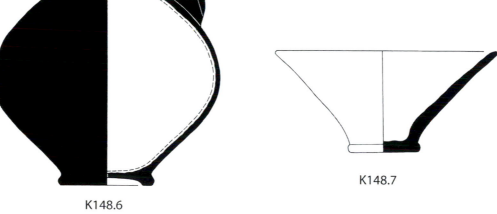

*Fig. 2.4. Mikre Koprana, pottery from K 148 (**K148.1–7**). Scale 1:3.*

three pithoi of Types 2, 4, and 14; several pithoid jars, including one of Type 1; at least five tripods; a large red stirrup jar; a dish of Type 3 with horizontal handles; a one-handled jug of Type 8; the top of a jar, like Type 6, but with a grooved rim, and a firebox (**K150.5**). Recorded objects included a stone bead or whorl (696), a whetstone (694),[26] and many clay spools: two large square, two large round, thirteen medium, and one small. There were also the remains of a pierced boar's tusk.

The octopus stirrup jar (**K150.3**) is close to **K134.3**, and probably dates to early LM IIIC.[27] Of similar date is the pyxis (**K150.2**), which find parallels at Kastri,[28] and the basin (**K150.4**), which is similar to examples from Khania and Kastri.[29] The small multiple tripod (**K150.5**) is unique and may have been used for aromatics.

Pottery Catalogue: K 150

Fine Wares

K150.1   Deep bowl (PLATE 2 g, FIG. 2.5). D. rim est. 13. Single fragment from rim with handle attachment. Fine, rather hard, reddish yellow (5YR 7/6) fabric. Very pale brown (10YR 8/2) slip. Dark red (10R 3/6) to red (10R 5/8) paint, black on interior. Multiple stems with arc filler and dot. For shape, cf. Borgna 1997, 278, fig. 6.7 (Phaistos); for decoration, cf. Warren 2007, 337, fig. 2 P252 (Knossos, Phase II). LM IIIC.

K150.2   Pyxis (PLATE 3 a, FIG. 2.5). H. 9 (with handles 9.3); D. base 12; D. rim 9. Partially mended from 14 fragments, seven non-joining fragments. 75% preserved, including full profile; missing centre of base, 25% of body, 50% of rim, and tops of handles. Fine, soft, reddish yellow (7.5YR 6/6) fabric, slightly discoloured from fire. Very pale brown (10YR 7/3) slip. Red (2.5YR 4/8) paint. Worn surfaces. Panelled pattern with oblique strokes and scalloped edges. LM IIIC early.

K150.3   Stirrup jar (PLATE 3 b–d, FIG. 2.5). H. 18; D. base 6.2; max. D. 18. Restored from numerous fragments. 75% preserved; missing spout, fragments of body; base not mended, but found in one of boxes in two fragments. Fine, medium-soft, rather porous, very pale brown (10YR 7/3) fabric. Creamy, very pale brown (10YR 7/4) slip. Black paint worn to dark yellowish brown shadow (10YR 4/4). Almost entirely burned after breaking; in some areas so badly burned that the decoration has become a negative image (slip is black, paint white). Lower part of body badly burned, while parts of upper body not burned at all. Well-preserved surfaces, except on back side. Sampled KAR 06/55. Bands on base and lower body. Octopus with body and eyes under spout and tentacles curving around top and possibly part of body with filler arcs and triangles. On back, tentacles end in medallions with filled lozenges and leaf pattern. Metopal panels on sides with two dotted scalloped borders and multiple horizontal zigzags. Fringes and strokes and arcs as filler. Top of false spout has arcs with scalloped edges in centre. Publication: Seiradaki, pl. 6.6 (mislabelled K 134). Cf. **K134.3–4**. LM IIIC early.

Medium-Coarse Wares

K150.4   Basin (PLATE 3 e, FIG. 2.5). H. 10.5; D. base 16; D. rim 20. Mended from 29 fragments and broken. 80% preserved, including full profile. Another unlabelled rim fragment may belong. Medium-coarse, soft, reddish yellow (5YR 7/6) fabric, with frequent phyllite (1–2 mm) and hard white angular inclusions. Very pale brown (10YR 8/4) slip. Yellowish red (5YR 4/6) paint. Worn

surfaces. Burned after broken. Bands on interior and exterior. Spiral on bottom. Labelled K 150, but one fragment says K 116. Publication: Seiradaki, fig. 5.11, pl. 3a. LM IIIC early.

Coarse Wares

K150.5   Multiple tripod (PLATE 3 f, FIG. 2.5). H. 5.3–5.6; D. rim (outer) 12.5; D. rim (inner) 6; D. base 12.2. Restored from five fragments. 75% preserved; missing pieces of rim and base and one leg. Coarse, hard, red (2.5YR 5/6–5/8) fabric, with some phyllites, hard white and hard black inclusions. Surfaces smoothed and mottled black and red. Interior burned and exterior on one side. Three small legs, elliptical in section. Outside vessel is simple tray, and inside is a second vessel with inwardly curved sides and ridge around middle. Publication: Seiradaki, fig. 4.7, pl. 4d middle. LM IIIC.

Mikre Koprana

There is much material labelled simply MK (for Mikre Koprana), sometimes with the designation of MK 1, often with further identifications as to whether the piece came from N, S, E, or W. This is probably the material excavated in 1937 by the local villagers, and it is not clear precisely where the objects came from. Some of this material was published as coming from K 148– 149, and occasionally Seiradaki gave a room number, although the same object can be labelled with more than one room number. A large unlabelled box in the storerooms may contain the remainder of the material excavated that year. The fragments seem to represent an assemblage of pottery before discards were made. In 1937 all the material from the Temple and Mikre Koprana would have been kept.

Pottery Catalogue: MK

Fine Wares

MK.1   Kylix (FIG. 2.6). D. rim est. 17. Single fragment from rim. Fine, soft, rather porous, very pale brown (10YR 8/3) fabric. Very pale brown (10YR 8/3) slip. Red (10R 4/8) paint. Worn surfaces. Vertical strokes on rim, octopus or flower below. LM IIIC.

Coarse Wares

MK.2   Pithos (PLATE 4 a, FIG. 2.6). Max. pres. H. 32.2; D. rim est. 38. Once partially restored from many fragments. 45% preserved, including entire rim and upper body, three handles; missing base and lower body. Coarse reddish yellow (5YR 6/6) fabric, with frequent grey phyllites and hard angular white inclusions (up to 2 mm). Surfaces still coated with sediment. Ridge below rim. Raised band at lower handle attachment with impressed circles. Rope-slashed serpentine band below. Raised band with vertical incised strokes. Labelled MK 1937. LM IIIC.

---

26   *Karphi*, pl. 30.2.
27   Mountjoy, personal communication. For the medallion *RMDP*, 1045–6, pl. 8a, b (Ialysos, Rhodes, imported from Crete). For the strokes *RMDP*, 1051, pl. 8e, f (Ialysos, Rhodes, imported from Crete, LM IIIC).
28   *Kastri*, 296, 289, fig. 10j.
29   *Khania II*, pl. 54.77-P 1622; *Kastri*, 296, 290, fig. 11e.

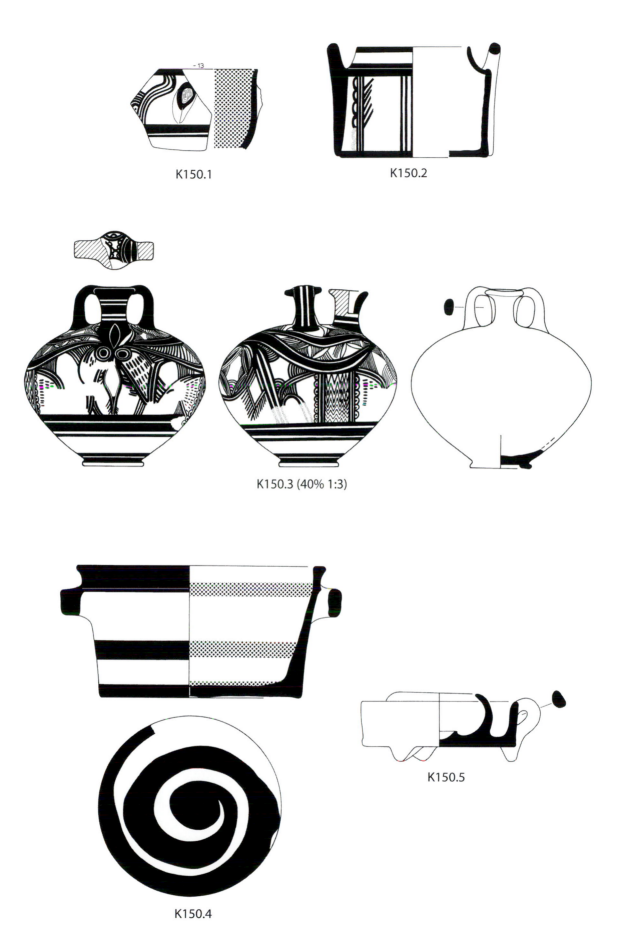

K150.1

K150.2

K150.3 (40% 1:3)

K150.5

K150.4

Fig. 2.5. Mikre Koprana, pottery from K 150 (**K150.1–5**). Scale 1:3 unless otherwise indicated.

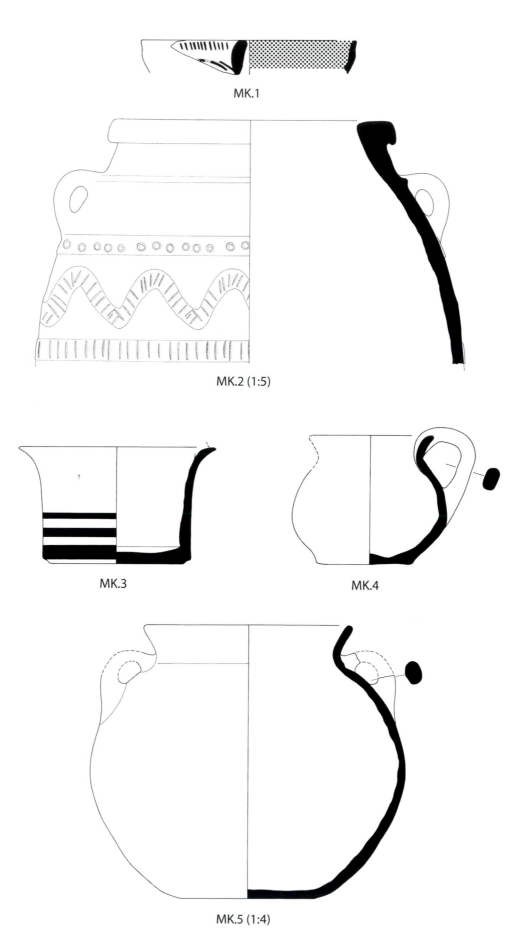

*Fig. 2.6. Mikre Koprana, pottery (**MK.1**–**5**). Scale 1:3 unless otherwise indicated.*

MK 1

In addition to the catalogued pottery, there was also a jug handle with a knob from the surface of MK 1. Objects recorded from this area in the notebook were as follows: a grey steatite bowl (185),[30] two conical stone beads or whorls (198, 199), and the head of a terracotta ox figurine (187).[31]

Pottery Catalogue: MK 1

Fine Wares
MK.3   Basket kalathos (FIG. 2.6). Max. pres. H. 9.3; D. base 10.6; D. rim est. 15.8. Once mended from 12 fragments. 35% preserved, including nearly complete profile; missing handles and handle attachments. Rim fragment does not join. Fine, soft, reddish yellow (7.5YR 7/6) fabric, with some phyllites, gold mica, and hard white angular inclusions. Reddish yellow (7.5YR 7/6) slip. Traces of red paint (2.5YR 4/6). Worn surfaces. Slight burning on one side. Handle on top of rim? Bands below. Possibly an import. LM IIIC.

Coarse Wares
MK.4   Cooking jug (PLATE 4 *b*, FIG. 2.6). H. 11; D. base 7.2; D. rim est. 10. Mended from two fragments. 70% preserved, including full profile and handle; missing most of rim. Coarse reddish yellow (5YR 6/6) fabric with frequent phyllite and schist inclusions. Surface still coated with sediment. Interior blackened, probably burned. LM IIIC.

MK.5   Pitharaki (FIG. 2.6). H. est. 28.8; D. base 14; D. rim 19–22. Mended from 35 fragments. 25% preserved, including entire base, parts of one handle, 75% of rim; profile can be restored. Very coarse, hard, red (2.5YR 5/8) fabric with frequent phyllites, gold mica, hard angular and soft smooth white inclusions (1–4 mm). Almost entirely burned to dark greenish grey (5G 4/1); irregular and warped as if misfired. LM IIIC.

MK 1E

In addition to the catalogued pottery, one of the boxes also contained a fragment of a small spouted jug from MK 1E and two coarse stirrup jar tops of similar fabric (sampled KAR 06/25, KAR 06/28). A clay 'palette', possibly the doorway of a hut urn,[32] was also found in this vicinity (186). Also preserved are three large and twenty small spools (PLATE 4 *c*). All were intact, crudely made of coarse fabrics (5YR 6/4), and burned on one side. The three large spools were 5.6 high with a maximum diameter of 4.3; they weighed 60–100 g. The small spools were all of approximately the same size, with a height of 4.2 and a maximum diameter of 3.3; these varied in weight from 25–50 g.

Pottery Catalogue: MK 1E

Fine Wares
MK.6   Deep bowl (PLATE 4 *d*, FIG. 2.7). H. 12.5; D. base 6.2; D. rim 16.6. Restored from 15 fragments. 50% preserved, including full profile; missing most of base, one handle, 80% of rim. Fine, soft, very pale brown (10YR 8/4) fabric. Black to brown paint. Very worn surfaces. Partly burned. Monochrome. LM IIIC.

MK.7   Stirrup jar (PLATE 4 *e*, FIG. 2.7). Max. pres. H. 12.3. Partially restored from five fragments. 30% preserved; missing lower body and base, rim of spout. Fine, soft, very pale brown (10YR 7/3) fabric with some tiny black inclusions. Shadow paint. Worn surfaces, pocked, and pitted. Traces of burning. False spout pierced in centre. Top thrown with rest of pot, not an added disc. Bands and two loops or scroll pattern. Publication: Seiradaki, pl. 6c left (?) (mislabelled K 47, perhaps an error for K 147). LM IIIC.

Medium-Coarse Wares
MK.8   Pyxis (FIG. 2.7). H. 9; D. base 12.8; D. rim 14 (D. ledge 11.2). Four joining and two non-joining fragments preserving full profile; missing handles. Rather hard medium-coarse, reddish yellow (5YR 6/6) fabric with frequent small (<1 mm) hard black and white inclusions. Very burned. Publication: Seiradaki, fig. 12.5 (without handles; labelled K 147). LM IIIC.

Coarse Wares
MK.9   Krater (FIG. 2.7). D. base 13.2. Mended from three fragments. 90% of base preserved. Coarse reddish yellow (5YR 6/8) fabric, with frequent schist inclusions (2–3 mm). Burned on underside and on bottom. Low pedestal base. LM IIIC.

MK.10   Kalathos (FIG. 2.7). H. 8; D. base 5; D. rim 18.4. Large fragment (four sherds) preserving full profile, and two non-joining fragments. 60% preserved. Coarse reddish yellow (5YR 7/8–6/6) fabric, with frequent large (1–3 mm) grey phyllites and small hard white angular inclusions. Burned inside and out, including interior of base. Sampled KAR 06/08. Incisions on interior of rim. LM IIIC.

MK.11   Hut urn (PLATE 4 *f*, FIG. 2.7). Max. pres. H. 4.3; D. base 8.2. Single fragment from base. Lower 30% preserved, including bottom of handles and doorway. Missing upper part, including roof and added door. Coarse reddish yellow (7.5YR 6/6) fabric, with schist (mostly 1–2 mm, up to 5 mm) and hard white angular inclusions. Worn surfaces. Burning on one edge of base and interior coloured green, possibly from a bronze pin. LM IIIC.

MK 1NE

From MK 1 NE came a conical stone bead (189), according to the notebook.

Pottery Catalogue: MK 1 NE

Fine Wares
MK.12   Lid (FIG. 2.7). H. 1.3; D. rim 4.6. Mended from two fragments. Complete except for chip in rim. Fine, rather soft, grey (N5/) blue ware fabric. Flat base, flaring sides, irregular shallow knob at top. LM IIIC.

MK 1N

The notebook reports the following objects as coming from this vicinity: three conical (191, 192, 193) and one cylindrical (190) stone beads or whorls, and four cylindrical terracotta spindle whorls (190).

---

30   *Karphi*, pl. 30.1.
31   *Karphi*, pl. 32.4.
32   Hägg 1990, 107.

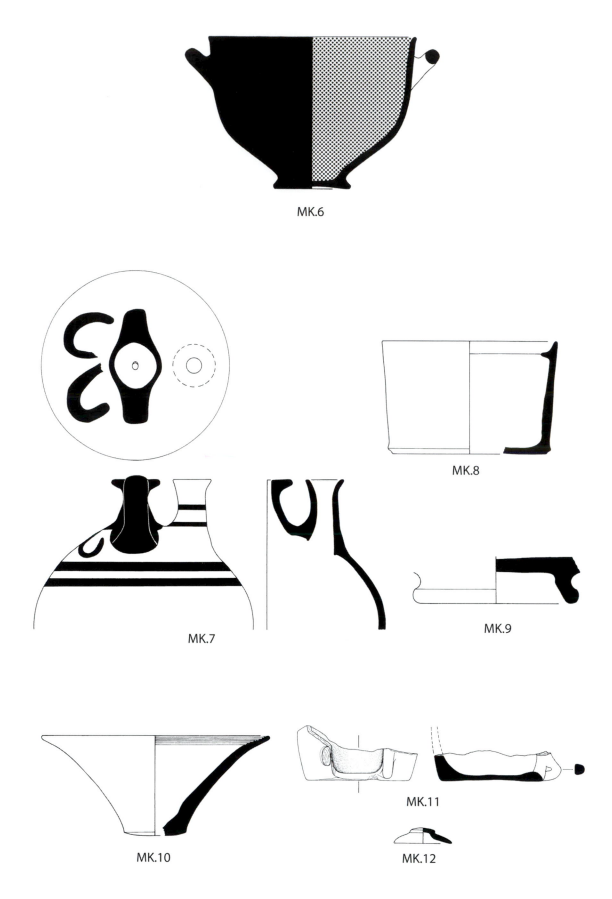

Fig. 2.7. *Mikre Koprana, pottery (**MK.6–12**). Scale 1:3.*

Pottery Catalogue: MK I N

Coarse Wares

MK.13 Krater (PLATE 5 *a*, FIG. 2.8). H. 29–30.5; D. base 13.6; D. rim 45. Restored from 45 fragments. 90% preserved; missing only parts of body. Coarse, very pale brown (10YR 8/2) fabric, with frequent grey phyllite and some hard white angular inclusions (1–3 mm). Dull black paint worn to shadow. Very worn surfaces. Traces of burning on outside of lower body and foot. Panelled design with central motif rounded at top with alternating hatched triangles; spiral to left and vertical bands with horizontal strokes, some curvilinear design; to right, fringed curvilinear design. Strokes on rim. Publication: Seiradaki, pl. 9a (labelled K 148–9). For shape and decoration, cf. *Kavousi IIA*, fig. 68.D1 P10. LM IIIC.

MK.14 Stirrup jar (FIG. 2.8). Max. pres. H. 23.5; D. base 13. Once mended from 37 fragments, and others are missing. 30% preserved, including nearly complete profile, both handles, bottom of spout; missing false spout. Coarse, light red (2.5YR 6/6) to reddish yellow (5YR 7/6) fabric with infrequent grey phyllites. Grey (N 6/) on interior. Traces of pale slip. Black paint. Very worn surfaces. Baggy ovoid body with large flat base. No sign of added disk for false spout. LM IIIC.

MK 1W

Only one object was listed as coming from this area of Mikre Koprana: a knobbed stone lid (377?). The jug (**MK.15**) is highly unusual, both in shape and decoration. Its high ring base with a ridge at the attachment, impressed decoration on neck ridge, and elaborate painted design make it unique. There are no parallels, but similar double tangent spirals in a secondary zone can be found on a vessel from Naxos.[33]

Pottery Catalogue: MK 1 W

Fine Wares

MK.15 Jug (PLATE 5 b, FIG. 2.8). H. 21.5 (with handle 22.2). Restored from *c.* 37 fragments. 60% preserved, including lower body to near base, neck to near rim, lower handle attachment; missing base, half of body, most of neck, all of rim, and much of handle. Fine, soft, pink (7.5YR 7/4) fabric, with tiny black and white inclusions. Pink slip (7.5YR 7/4). Brown to red paint (2.5YR 4/8) paint. Very worn surfaces, still coated with sediment. Fragments of shoulder burned, so decoration is negative image. Ridge at attachment of neck with incised or impressed decoration. Ridge at attachment of foot. Shoulder has pendent crosshatched triangles alternating with upright loops. Body has running spirals with double tails. Publication: Seiradaki, fig. 9.6 (labelled K 147), pl. 5c left and 5d right (labelled K 149). LM IIIC.

MK 1S

No pottery was found from this area, but the notebook records several objects, including a bronze knife fragment (197), a grey limestone amulet (188), a slate amulet or whetstone (195),[34] a double-pierced steatite amulet (196),[35] and a conical stone bead or whorl (194).

EASTERN QUARTER (ROOMS K 135–K 144)

Three separate houses were identified in this area, all of megaron type, laid out in a very regular way, each with a large rectangular room, occasionally with a back room (House K 138-139-140), sometimes with an ante-room or 'prodromos' (Houses K 137-141 and K 138-139-140).[36] Pendlebury was the first to call attention to the unusual plans of these houses and how they differed from the other houses in the settlement. He also was the first to suggest that these belonged to a Greek-speaking population,[37] an idea reiterated by others,[38] which has led to the theory that the whole complex forms a single unit that functioned as a ruler's dwelling for the Greek-speaking leaders of the Karphi settlement.[39] More recently, Nowicki suggested that the houses were not inhabited by mainlanders, but by an outside group of inhabitants who were under Mycenaean influence,[40] although he later suggested that topographic constraints may have played a more important role in the arrangement of these houses.[41] The regularity and layout of these houses may have more to do with utilising the available space and with the topography than with the ethnicity of the inhabitants. The rooms in the so-called Barracks, for example, are also very regular. Wallace has pointed out the differences among these houses in terms of size and configuration, based on her new observations and plans.[42] These houses in the Eastern Quarter may also be of later date than those in the rest of the settlement, although it is difficult to tell, since so little was found in them. All three houses had hearths in the large rooms, and while such fixed hearths may indicate foreign influence,[43] they do occur widely in LM IIIC sites throughout the island.[44] None of the rooms produced a large amount of pottery or other material.

House K 135-136

This area was approached from a road on the south, leading up from the Barracks.

Room K 135

Only two walls were preserved on the east and north, but the excavators thought that the roof on the west side might have been supported on poles.[45] The roofing material found within suggests that it could not have been a courtyard. The excavators reported finding little fine ware in the room. The notebook adds the following

---

33 *RMDP*, 954, fig. 389.47 (Naxos, LH IIIC middle).
34 *Karphi*, pl. 30.3.
35 *Karphi*, pl. 30.4.
36 *Karphi*, 70–2.
37 *Karphi*, 137–8.
38 Desborough 1964, 172–3.
39 Mazarakis Ainian 1997, 219–20.
40 Nowicki 1999, 148.
41 Nowicki 2002, 163–4.
42 Wallace 2005, 238.
43 Nowicki 1999, 150.
44 At Kavousi–*Vronda*, for example see Day, Glowacki and Klein 1996. Also at Khania; *Khania II*, 128–9.
45 *Karphi*, 71.

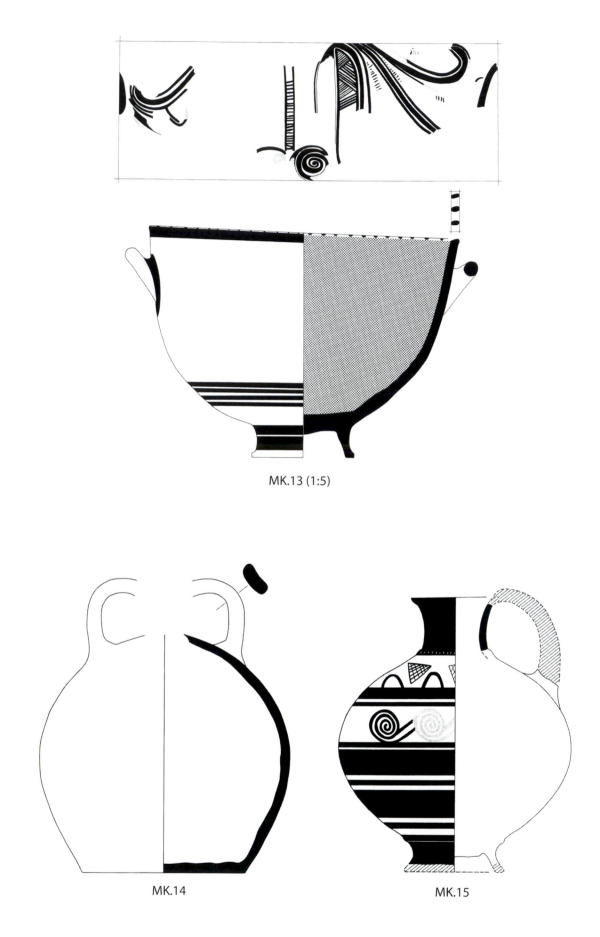

MK.13 (1:5)

MK.14   MK.15

Fig. 2.8. Mikre Koprana, pottery (**MK.13–15**). Scale 1:3 unless otherwise indicated.

list of pottery: a pithoid jar of Type 3, a dish of Type 6, a basin of Type 7, and tripod legs. Only one fragment labelled K 135 was found in the boxes, a deep bowl rim with a fringed loop, but this was not catalogued. There are no objects recorded from this room.

Room K 136

This large room had a patch of burned earth and much charcoal in the centre of room, no doubt a hearth. There was also a possible square bench in northwest corner, but it was not indicated on the plan. Although too large for the roof to have been unsupported, the room showed no trace of interior supports. The notebook records the following coarse pottery: two pithoi of Types 1 and 14; a pithoid jar of Type 3; four two-handled jars, one of Type 2, three of Type 3; the usual tripod legs; three dishes, one of Type 1, two of Type 6; three basins, one of Type 5, two of Type 7; a kalathos of Type 4; and two stirrup jars of Type 2. Fine wares included a small cup, a jug, bowls of Types 1 and 2, and a tankard spout. No pottery has been preserved from the room. Objects from K 136 included a decorated bronze plate from a fibula (636),[46] a stone bowl base (634), a cylindrical stone bead or whorl (635), a faience fragment (637), and 21 terracotta spools. The notebook adds that pumice and animal bones were found in the room. The pottery suggests ordinary domestic use, although the finds, especially the fibula, are unusual; the rarity of such objects found in settlement contexts might indicate a higher level of wealth than appears from the other objects.[47] The large number of spools may indicate that weaving went on in the room.

House K 137-141

This is a two-room structure, with a 'prodromos' (K 141) and a main room (K 137). Nowicki emended the plan of the building, making it appear more regular, and suggested that it could only have housed a family of five.[48] K 142 may have belonged with this building rather than with House K 135-136, as the west wall is slightly thicker, but the excavators were unwilling to commit themselves to this idea. There is so little material from the building that it is impossible to date, and most of the finds suggest ordinary domestic use.

Room K 141

Little roofing material was found in this room, suggesting to the excavators that it might have been open. Little was found in it, but the proportion of fine sherds was larger than usual, and they were very broken; perhaps they represent vessels that were broken and discarded during the use of the building. The pottery represented the usual types, and none has been kept. Objects from K 141 included a pierced schist lid (656) and a conical terracotta spindle whorl (657). The description of the pottery suggests refuse or material in or below floors.

Room K 137

The large room of the 'megaron' may have been subdivided; a possible foundation of another wall projected from the west wall, and another linear accumulation may also have been a wall.[49] There was a hearth in centre of the northern half of room, a patch of burned earth with charcoal still on it. The pottery included sherds from a jar in coarse ware with medallions and other mouldings (called a goat's head in the notebook), and the notebook adds at least three pithoi with rims of Types 7 and 10, several pithoid jars, a basin of Type 3, a jar of Type 1, a stirrup jar of Type 5, a lid of Type 1 with rope design, and three fine stirrup jars. A tripod pithos published in Seiradaki was not located.[50] Objects from this room included a bronze octagonal leg of a tripod (638),[51] a bronze blade fragment (654), a conical stone bead or whorl (639), and a tetragonal whetstone (655). The notebook adds that there was some bone. The single preserved nearly complete vessel, a pyxis, does not help to determine the date or the function of this room. The bronze octagonal tripod leg may be the remains of a large, high status object used in the room, and has been used to support the identification of this entire complex as the ruler's house.[52]

Pottery Catalogue: K 137

Coarse Wares

K137.1 Pyxis (FIG. 2.9). Max. pres. H. 18; D. base 20.5. Partially mended from 17 fragments, 19 non-joining fragments. 50% preserved, including entire base, 75% of lower body, handle attachments; missing entire rim and tops of handles. Coarse, hard, red (10R 5/6–2.5YR 5/6) fabric, like Kavousi Type IV, with phyllites and hard white angular inclusions. Creamy yellow slip (10YR 8/6). Possible traces of red paint. Worn surfaces. Burned inside and out, mostly on one side, not on underside of base. Possibly decorated. LM IIIC.

House K 138-139-140

The largest of the megaron-type houses is composed of three rooms: a 'prodromos' (K 140), a large room

---

46 *Karphi*, pl. 29.2.

47 Mazarakis Ainian 1997, 304 points out how rarely fibulas are found in settlement contexts and uses this fact to support his idea that the Eastern Quarter belonged to a very wealthy 'ruler'. Bronze jewellery, implements, and weapons have been found all over the site, however, and in several places in greater numbers and with more variety than the few bronzes in the Eastern Quarter (e.g. in Room 12 of the Great House, Room 26 of the Southern Houses, and in Room 106 of the western Cliff Houses.

48 Nowicki 1999, 150.

49 Wallace 2005, 238–9.

50 Seiradaki, pl. 2a.

51 *Karphi*, pl. 29.2.

52 Mazarakis Ainian 1997, 220, 274. He uses Homer to show the importance of bronze tripods in the gift economy of the epic world, a world that may, however, have little to do with 12th century Karphi.

with a hearth (K 139), and a smaller back room (K 138). The door into K 140 was not on axis, but the doors leading to K 139 and to K 138 were. Rooms K 143 and K 144 to the east may have served as storage chambers for the building, which could have housed a family of eight.[53]

Room K 140

This room served as the entranceway to the building. It contained the usual sort of pottery, except that there were no pithos fragments. The notebook adds that there were two pithoid jars, three fine stirrup jars (one of Type 6), a kylix stem of Type 1 (**K140.1**), and a fine pyxis of Type 4. The publication mentions a fragment of a head of a figurine (644), although the notebook says that this inventoried fragment is actually from K 139. The fragments from cult objects mentioned as coming from K 140 were not described; it is possible that the reference is to the piece identified here as a fenestrated stand (**K140.2**). There was clearly some small-scale storage in the room, seen in the pithoid jars, and perhaps the very large kylix is the sort that could have been used in elite drinking rituals;[54] it is similar in shape and decoration to kylix **K120.5**, and to an example from Kavousi–*Vronda* of late LM IIIC;[55] the decoration finds another parallel on a cup from Sybrita/Thronos.[56]

Pottery Catalogue: K 140

Fine Wares

K140.1   Kylix (FIG. 2.9). Max. pres. H. 21.2; max. pres. D. 23.2. Partially mended from seven fragments, five non-joining fragments, including handle attachment; no rim, no base. Fine, soft, light red (2.5YR 6/8) to reddish yellow (5YR 6/6) fabric. Very pale brown slip (10YR 8/4). Dark reddish brown paint (2.5YR 3/4). Worn surfaces. Tall pierced stem. Stem made separately and added; base of bowl and top of stem scored in rays to make attachment. Octopus decoration (?): hourglass-shaped solid body with outlines, curved streamers or tentacles with arc fillers. Publication: stem published in Seiradaki, pl. 12b, bottom, second from left (2 fragments). LM IIIC late.

K140.2   Fenestrated stand (?) (FIG. 2.9). Max. pres. H. 9. Single fragment. Fine, soft, porous, pink (5YR 7/4) fabric at core, very pale brown (10YR 8/4) on surfaces. Very worn surfaces. Flat, rectangular object, with some curve to body; possibly part of fenestrated stand, between fenestrations. LM IIIC.

Coarse Wares

K140.3   Tripod (FIG. 2.9). Max. pres. H. 17.8. Single fragment preserving one leg. Coarse red (10R 5/8) fabric, with frequent large (2–5 mm) schist inclusions and mica. Burning on interior of upper leg. Three vertical slashes at top of round leg. Label unclear; probably K 140. LM IIIC.

Room K 139

The main room of the building had a central hearth and a cupboard in the wall to the right of the door. Against the east wall were two upright slabs with a paving between that probably served as a jar stand or

an oven. The notebook lists the following coarse pottery from this room: at least three pithoi of Types 8, 13, and 14; three pithoid jars of Types 3 and 11; a two-handled jar of Type 2; the usual tripods; six dishes, two of Type 1, four of Type 6; two kalathoi of Type 4; a basin of Type 7; two stirrup jars of Type 2; a pyxis of Type 2; and three small bowls. Fine ware included a spouted jug, a stirrup jar of Type 2 (**K139.1**) and a pyxis of Type 1. Objects found in the room were scanty: two conical stone beads or whorls (642, 643), five terracotta spools, and some animal bones; the notebook indicates that the fragment of a terracotta figurine (644) listed in the publication as from K 140 actually comes from K 139. From the drawing of this object, it is difficult to determine from what sort of figurine the fragment comes, but apparently it represents the top of the crown and one eyebrow, possibly of a human figure, possibly an animal. The only nearly complete vessel was a medium-coarse storage stirrup jar. The whole assemblage is quite meagre and certainly not in keeping with ideas that this was a ruler's dwelling. Similarly, there is nothing in the assemblage to suggest that a different ethnic group inhabited the house.

Pottery Catalogue: K 139

Medium-Coarse Wares

K139.1   Stirrup jar (FIG. 2.9). Max. pres. H. 16.2; D. base est. 7. Partially mended into two large fragments, one from base (seven sherds), one from top (eight sherds), and 14 non-joining fragments. 75% preserved, including 35% of base spout, one handle and part of another; missing false spout. Medium-coarse light red (2.5YR 6/6) fabric, with tiny soft white inclusions. Totally burned grey (5Y/61) to black. Very worn surfaces. May have once been decorated, but too worn to tell. LM IIIC.

Room K 138

This back room was a steep step up from the main room. It had traces of a stone-paved floor, but otherwise showed no unusual features. The notebook lists the coarse ware that came from the room: at least five pithoi with rims of Types 4, 5, 13, 15, and 22; two pithoid jars of Type 3; tripods with rims of Types 1 and 2 and tripod legs; three dishes of Type 6, one with a spout; two kalathoi of Types 1 and 2; a basin of Type 7; and three small bowls of Type 1. Fine ware included two stirrup jars of Types 1 and 2, five bowls of Type 1, a basin of Type 7, and a pyxis of Type 2. Pumice and animal bones were also mentioned in the notebook.

The early LM IIIC deep bowl fragment with multiple loops pictured in Seiradaki was not located.[57] The only

---

53   Nowicki 1999, 150.
54   Day and Snyder 2004.
55   Day 1997, 399, fig. 5.2; *Kavousi IIA*, 37, fig. 22.B3 P3.
56   Prokopiou 1997, 384, fig. 30d.
57   Seiradaki, fig. 21d.

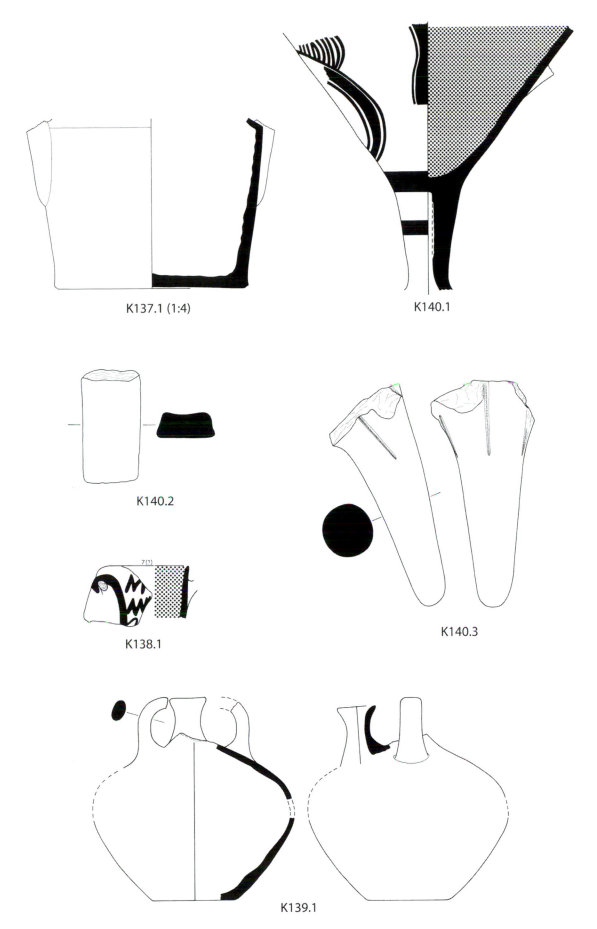

K137.1 (1:4)

K140.1

K140.2

K138.1

K140.3

K139.1

*Fig. 2.9. Eastern Quarter, pottery from K 137 (**K137.1**), K 140 (**K140.1–3**), K 139 (**K139.1**), and K 138 (**K138.1**). Scale 1:3 unless otherwise indicated.*

preserved pottery fragment from the room, a small deep bowl with zigzags, is not closely datable, since the motif was popular throughout LM IIIC; a similar example with several rows of zigzags can be found in Kastelli Pediada.[58]

As Nowicki has noted, this back room seems to have been used primarily for storage, although it may also have served for food preparation and cooking.[59]

Pottery Catalogue: K 138

Fine Wares

K138.1   Deep bowl (FIG. 2.9). D. rim est. 7. Single fragment from rim, preserving handle attachment. Fine, soft, reddish yellow (7.5YR 7/6) fabric. Very pale brown slip (10YR 8/3). Black to red paint. Well-preserved surfaces. Double row of zigzags, possibly more rows. No band on exterior of rim. LM IIIC.

Other Rooms in the Area

Room K 142

This small out-building may have served either House K 135-136 or House K 137-141. Little was found within it. The publication says that the pottery is much broken, and the notebook says none of the coarse sherds was in good enough condition to determine a type. Fine ware included several bowls and about three stirrup jars. Aside from the catalogued small krater there was also the base of a plain jug in one of the boxes. The small krater has a deep, almost carinated shape with a fairly high foot. It has a reserved band on the interior and is decorated with buttonhook spirals. The spirals are common on deep bowls in early LM IIIC deposits at Kavousi–*Vronda*, Kastri, Knossos, and Khania,[60] and often are accompanied by reserved bands on the interior.

Pottery Catalogue: K 142

Fine Wares

K142.1   Krater (FIG. 2.10). Max. pres. H. 8 (H. est. 15). D. base 5.8. D. rim 22. Partially mended into several fragments, one from rim to lower body (11 sherds), one from rim (five sherds), one from base (eight fragments), and 36 non-joining fragments. 40% preserved, including entire base, 50% of lower body, and 25% of rim and upper body; missing both handles. Fine, soft, reddish yellow (7.5YR 7/6) fabric. Very pale brown slip (10YR 8/3). Worn red (2.5YR 5/8) paint. Buttonhook spirals. Reserved band on interior of rim. LM IIIC.

Room K 143

K 143 and K 144 may have been storage chambers, possibly belonging to House K 138-139-140. The east wall of K 143 was cut out of bedrock, and no south wall was preserved so it may have been an open courtyard.[61] The north wall was incorrectly placed on the original plan, and Wallace corrected it on her plans and suggested that the room may have been used for temporary storage.[62] The notebook records the

following pottery: at least five pithoi of Types 3, 5, 8 and 2 of Type 25; seven pithoid jars, four of Type 3, two of Type 7, and one of Type 10; the usual tripod legs; a tripod dish; nine dishes, five of Type 1, four of Type 6; a strainer; two kalathoi of Types 1 and 4; a small lid of Type 1 (**K143.3**); and small jugs or jars. Fine ware included two small bowls of Types 1 and 2 and a double handle. Objects included fragments of five bone pins (660–664),[63] two conical stone beads or whorls (658, 681), a pierced stone disc (680), a conical (682) and a cylindrical (659) terracotta spindle whorl. The notebook also records animal bones and pumice. The pottery would indicate ordinary domestic functions of storage and cooking, but the preserved pottery is not closely datable. The carinated bowl (**K143.2**) is an unusual shape, but the decoration of a crosshatched lozenge chain is found in LM IIIC.[64]

Pottery Catalogue: K 143

Fine Wares

K143.1   Deep bowl or cup (FIG. 2.10). Max. pres. H. 4.2. Single fragment from rim. Fine, soft, reddish yellow (5YR 7/6) fabric. Very pale brown slip (10YR 8/4). Red (2.5YR 4/8) paint. Worn surfaces. Running spiral (?). LM IIIC.

K143.2   Carinated bowl (FIG. 2.10). D. rim est. 25.5. Single fragment from rim. Fine, soft, porous, reddish yellow (5YR 7/6) fabric. Very pale brown slip 10YR 8/4. Black paint worn to dark reddish brown (5YR 3/4). Worn surfaces. Crosshatched lozenge chain, with an X-pattern below. Interior has oblique grooves near rim, painted band on inside of carination. Publication: Seiradaki, fig. 24d (called a pyxis). LM IIIC.

Coarse Wares

K143.3   Lid (FIG. 2.10). Max. pres. H. 2.7; D. base 2.5. Intact. 65% preserved, including knob in centre; missing rim and much of upper body. Coarse reddish yellow (5YR 7/8) fabric, with frequent small (1 mm) red phyllites and hard white angular inclusions. Flat base, body like conical cup; central domed knob in centre of interior. Incisions on middle of body, outside. LM IIIC.

Room K 144

Room K 144 may have been another storage chamber, and the excavators thought it was entered from K 138, although no door was found connecting the two

58   Rethemiotakis 1997, 319, fig. 28j.
59   Nowicki 1999, 150–1.
60   Day and Snyder 2004, 68, fig. 5.6:6 (Kavousi–*Vronda*); *Kastri*, 296, 288, fig. 9d, e; Warren 2007, 337, fig. 2.P251, P253 (Knossos); *Khania II*, pl. 35.77-P 0189, 77-P 0674/71-P 1425/0938 b, c.
61   Nowicki 1999, 151, fig. 3.
62   Wallace 2005, 239, 240–1, figs. 13–14.
63   *Karphi*, pl. 28.4.
64   See, for example, a deep bowl from Kavousi–*Kastro*: Mook and Coulson 1997, 358, fig. 30.103 (Phase I–II dump). See also a krater from Khania: *Khania II*, pl. 41.83-P 0351. The crosshatched lozenge combined with other motifs is more common than the crosshatched lozenge chain, however.

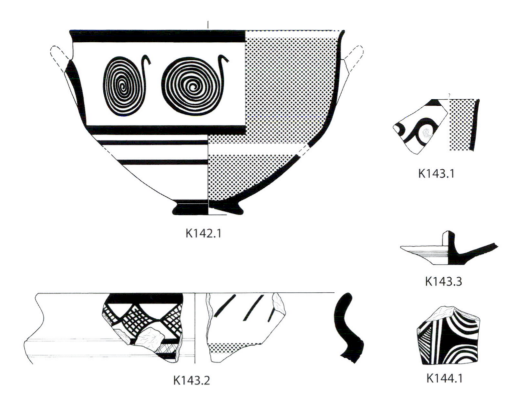

K142.1

K143.1

K143.3

K143.2

K144.1

*Fig. 2.10. Eastern Quarter, pottery from K 142 (**K142.1**), K 143 (**K143.1–3**), and K 144 (**K144.1**). Scale 1:3.*

rooms.[65] The notebook gives the following list of coarse pottery: a jar of Type 6, a tripod rim and legs of Type 2, a basin of Type 3, and a bowl of Type 1. Fine wares included three bowls of Type 1, and a sherd from a kylix. The preserved deep bowl fragment has a good LM IIIC panelled pattern with a double axe or butterfly motif with multiple outlines.[66]

Pottery Catalogue: K 144

Fine Wares

K144.1   Deep bowl (FIG. 2.10). Max. pres. H. 4.6. Single fragment from body. Fine, porous, reddish yellow (7.5YR 7/6) fabric, with tiny black and white inclusions. Very pale brown slip 10YR 8/2. Red (2.5YR 4/8) paint. Panelled pattern: hatched vertical triangle, double axe or butterfly with multiple outlines. LM IIIC.

THE BARRACKS (K 2–7, K 134, K 145)

This area was excavated in 1938 (Rooms 2–7) and 1939 (Rooms 134, 145). The position at the entrance to the settlement and the bare rooms suggested at first the function implied in the name, but the simplicity of the rooms was later attributed to their being among the earliest buildings on the settlement.[67] It is not clear whether each room constituted a single house or the rooms belonged to a single complex or multiple houses. The large amount of coarse pottery preserved from the rooms suggests that for the most part these were ordinary dwellings. The proportion of coarse ware, however, may be misleading; at the beginning of the

1938 season, when most of the rooms were excavated, more coarse ware was kept than in later seasons.

Room K 2

K 2 was a simple room entered from the west with a hatchway or window at the east end, opening onto a space to the east. Traces of roofing material show that this room was roofed. Of the pottery mentioned in Seiradaki as being from this room, only a single basin could not be located.[68] The notebook also mentioned several pithoi decorated with bands bearing a variety of incised decorations: straight or chevron cuts (horizontal, diagonal, or looped), impressed circles, or finger dints. Also mentioned were a tripod bowl, a pithoid jar, a pyxis with handles continuing down the sides, stirrup vases, rough dishes with flaring sides, rounded jars with horizontal uptilted handles, small bowls in fine buff (one with a side spout), a flat lid with loop handle, and a high pedestal base. The handles and tripod legs were said to have dints where attached to the bodies, and the tripod legs also had vertical cuts.

---

65   Wallace 2005, 242.

66   For parallels, see Prokopiou 1997, 377, fig. 18e (on a krater from Sybrita/Thronos).

67   *Karphi*, 72–3.

68   Seiradaki, fig. 5.1; it may be the same as one pictured on pl. 3d, bottom, left (K 39); this is also missing.

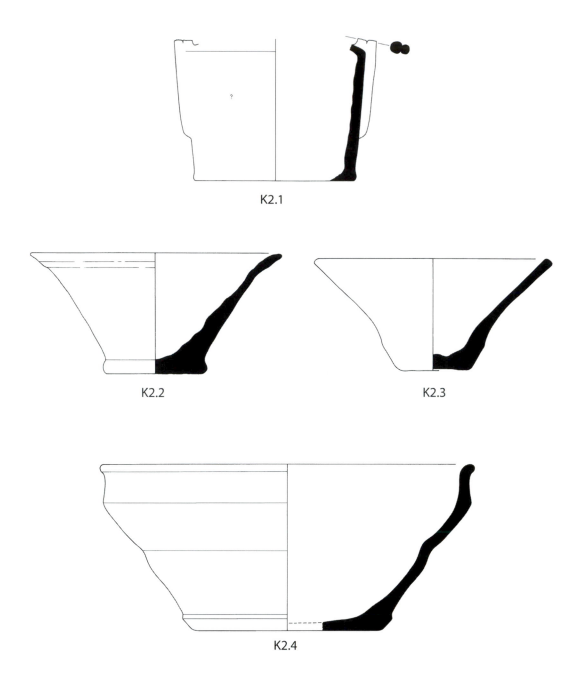

*Fig. 2.11. Barracks, pottery from K 2 (**K2.1–4**). Scale 1:3.*

The pottery included a great deal of coarse and very little fine ware. Not catalogued was the top of a large, coarse stirrup jar (sampled as KAR 06/30). Three spools were found (PLATE 5 *c*).[69] These are intact except for a chip on one, and were made of very coarse fabrics; their weights are 21, 75, and 60 g.

Clearly the room was used for storage (the pithos, jar, stirrup jar, and amphora, possibly the askos), as well as cooking (the cooking dish and cooking jug), and other domestic activities (basins, pyxis, jugs, and lid). The function of the kalathoi is uncertain; elsewhere they were apparently multifunctional, used for offerings

in shrines, and perhaps as lamps or braziers. There is no trace of burning on either of the two kalathoi from this room, nor is there anything else found here to suggest a religious function, unless the lid or plaque is the sort used in shrines. The three spools may have been used for weaving, but there were not enough to suggest the presence of a loom.

---

69   Mentioned in *Karphi*, 73.

Pottery Catalogue: K 2[70]

Fine Wares

K2.1 Pyxis (FIG. 2.11). Max. pres. H. 11.6; D. base 13. Once mended from 13 fragments. 45% preserved, including nearly full profile; rim, tops of handles, much of base, and half of body missing. Fine, soft, chalky fabric, reddish yellow (5YR 7/6) at core with some small (<1 mm) phyllite inclusions. Reddish yellow surface (7.5YR 8/6). Surface very worn, probably once painted. Twisted handles rise above shoulder. LM IIIC.

Coarse Wares

K2.2 Kalathos (PLATE 5 *d*, FIG. 2.11). H. 9.7; D. base 8; D. rim 21. Restored from 15 fragments. 75% preserved, including full profile and entire base, half of rim. Coarse red (2.5YR 5/8) fabric with frequent black and white hard angular inclusions, red phyllites (*c*. 1 mm). Pronounced wheel ridging on interior. Publication: Seiradaki, pl. 3d, top right. LM IIIC.

K2.3 Kalathos (FIG. 2.11). H. 8.9, D. base 5.8, D. rim 19. Restored from seven fragments. 75% preserved; missing 33% of upper body (fresh breaks). Coarse red (2.5YR 5/8) fabric with grey core; frequent red and grey phyllites and hard white angular inclusions (up to 4 mm). No traces of burning, but much of surface still coated with sediment. Publication: Seiradaki, pl. 3d, bottom right. LM IIIC.

K2.4 Basin (FIG. 2.11). H. 13.3; D. base est. 15; D. rim est. 30. Ten joining and six non-joining fragments preserving 50% of vessel, including full profile; handles missing. Coarse reddish yellow (5YR 6/6) fabric with frequent schist and hard white angular inclusions (1–3 mm). Surface barely cleaned, but traces of burning inside and out. Publication: Seiradaki, fig. 5.2 (labelled as from K 88). LM IIIC.

K2.5 Basin (FIG. 2.12). Max. pres. H. 12.2; D. rim est. 36–38. Partially mended from more than 80 fragments. 20% preserved. One large fragment from rim with handle; three other large fragments of rim, another from handle. No base or lower body. Coarse light red (2.5YR 6/8) to black fabric with frequent phyllites (mostly 1–3 mm) and hard white angular inclusions. Surface mottled black on exterior, burned on one side; possibly a cooking pot. LM IIIC.

K2.6 Cooking dish (FIG. 2.12). Max. pres. H 5.2; D. rim est. 50–52. At least 16 fragments from rim and body, one additional fragment from rim.[71] Coarse red (2.5YR 5/6) fabric with frequent large (2–3 mm) schist, phyllites, mica, and hard white angular inclusions. Burned on outside, bottom rough. One side pinched to form spout, two holes pierced through rim. Probably had rounded bottom. Publication: Seiradaki, pl. 12a, third row, second from right. For shape, cf. *Kastri*, 290, fig. 11s; Mook 1999, pl. 110.32 (Kavousi–*Kastro*). LM IIIC.

K2.7 Cooking jug (PLATE 5 *e*, FIG. 2.12). H. 12.7; D. base 11; D. rim est. 14.8. Mended from 22 joining and four non-joining fragments. 75% preserved, including full profile and handle; missing one-third of rim and upper body. Coarse yellowish red (5YR 5/6) fabric, with frequent phyllites and hard white angular inclusions (1–5 mm). Base burned on interior; forms a band at bottom with a definite line. Exterior burned on one side around handle. Surface smoothed and very cracked. LM IIIC.

K2.8 Lid (FIG. 2.12). Max. pres. H. 4; D. est. 9. Single fragment preserving half of lid, including handle. Coarse red (10R 5/6) fabric with black core; frequent schist, mica, and hard white angular inclusions (1–3 mm). Burned. Flat base with round horizontal handle at top. Edges worn; possibly rest of lid broken off. Publication: Seiradaki, fig. 19.2. LM IIIC.

K2.9 Amphora (FIG. 2.12). H. est. 37 (with handles 38.6); D. base 16.4; D. rim 11.8. Partially mended into two large fragments (100 sherds). One fragment preserves 75% of rim, neck, handles, and shoulder; the other preserves 50% of base and lower body. Approximately 60% of total vessel preserved. Coarse reddish yellow (5YR 7/6) fabric, with frequent grey phyllites and hard angular grey and white inclusions (2–3 mm). Very pale brown (10YR 8/3) slip. Some of surface slip burned black. Black paint. Bands at base and on lower body; three bands at lower handle attachment; bands on neck and at rim. Snaky bands down handle. For shape, cf. *Kastri*, 296, fig. 16.P31, P25; Watrous 1992, 82, fig. 54.1415, 1412 (Kommos, LM IIIB). LM IIIC.

K2.10 Jug or amphora (FIG. 2.12). Max. pres. H. 11.3; D. base 8.8. Mended from nine fragments. 40% preserved, including most of base and lower body; missing upper body, neck, rim, handles. Coarse, once reddish yellow (5YR 6/6) fabric, but burned grey throughout; tiny (sand-sized) white and some larger hard white angular inclusions. Surfaces still heavily coated with sediment, but preserved surfaces worn. LM IIIC.

K2.11 Askos (FIG. 2.13). Max. pres. H. 11.7; D. rim 4.2. Two joining fragments from neck and two other large fragments (5 sherds) from neck and shoulder; neck and both handle attachments preserved. Lower body and base missing. Coarse light red (2.5YR 6/6–6/8) fabric with frequent phyllites and hard angular black and white inclusions, gold mica, and schist. Thick, chalky, yellow (10YR 8/6) slip, possibly originally decorated. Surface very hard and cracked. Some burned patches on interior. Sampled KAR 06/36. Shape uncertain, but asymmetrical. Has neck like stirrup jar, and top has been inserted as a disc, as on stirrup jars. Decorated with knobs. LM IIIC.

K2.12 Jar (FIG. 2.13). Max. pres. H. 9; D. rim est. 14. Single fragment from rim, neck, and handle. Lower body and base missing. Coarse reddish yellow (5YR 6/6) fabric with frequent white and grey phyllite inclusions (2–4 mm). Fugitive very pale brown slip (10YR 8/3). Reddish brown (5YR 4/4) paint. Worn surfaces. Sampled KAR 06/58. Decorated with curvilinear design going under handles and a rectilinear design on shoulder. Publication: Seiradaki, fig. 3.5. LM IIIC.

K2.13 Lid or plaque (FIG. 2.13). D. est. 54–55, Th. 1.5. Single fragment from rim. Coarse reddish brown (5YR 5/4) fabric, with frequent schist (2–3 mm) and some hard white angular inclusions. Flat plaque or round cooking lid; not enough preserved to be certain. LM IIIC.

K2.14 Pithoid jar (FIG. 2.13). Max. pres. H. 14; D. est. 48. Single fragment from rim, preserving one handle. Soft, chalky, coarse, light red (2.5YR 6/8) fabric with frequent large (2–4 mm) phyllite, schist, and hard white angular inclusions. Surface heavily coated with sediment. Sampled KAR 06/71. Publication: Seiradaki, fig. 2.10. LM IIIC.

K2.15 Pithos (PLATE 5 *f*). Many fragments found in single box; one fragment labelled K2. Very hard red (2.5YR 5/8) fabric with schist inclusions. Decorated with bands bearing incised triple chevrons and a serpentine rope pattern with an incised chevron pattern. LM IIIC.

---

70 There was a problem in identifying correctly the material from this room because of the numbering system, which clearly changed early in the 1938 season. Many of the fragments are labelled 'K 2', using Arabic numbers. Others are numbered 'K II', using Roman numerals. Most often the Roman numeral II has bars across the top and bottom, but occasionally the bars are lacking. It may be that those vessels without the bar came from K 11, rather than K 2. Where Seiradaki's publication provides a check, the questionable pieces are listed as being from K 11.

71 Found with it were fragments of at least two other cooking dishes of different fabrics, one with more schist, the other with only phyllites.

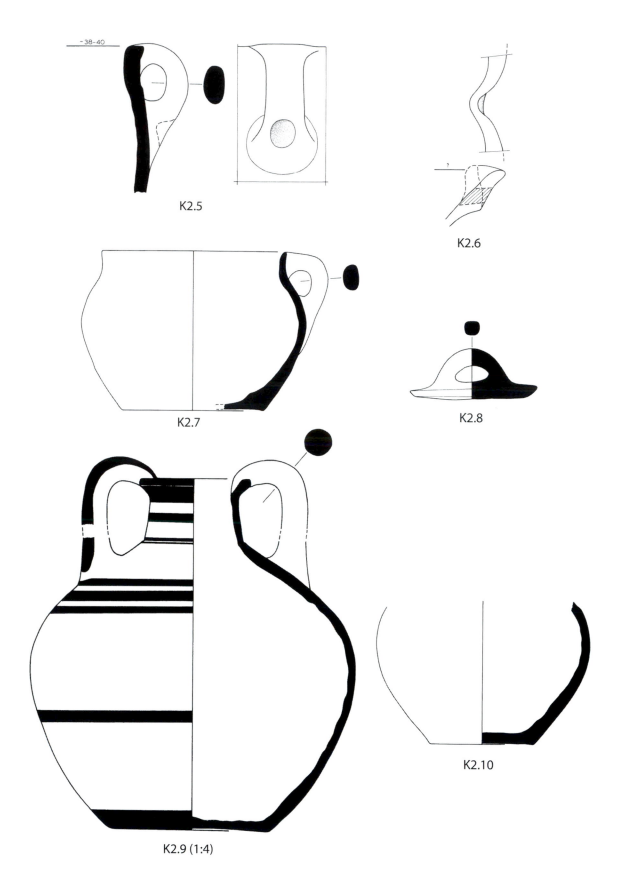

Fig. 2.12. Barracks, pottery from K 2 (**K2.5–10**). Scale 1:3 unless otherwise indicated.

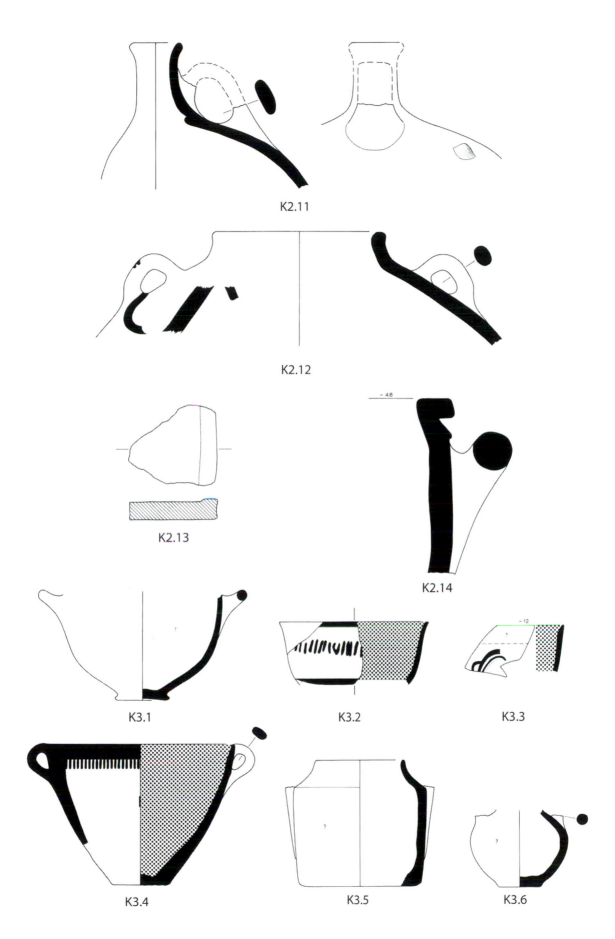

*Fig. 2.13. Barracks, pottery from K 2 (**K2.11–14**) and K 3 (**K3.1–6**). Scale 1:3.*

Room K 3

This large room was plain and denuded, but had some roofing material. A bench lay at the east end against the bedrock.

Of the published pottery said to come from this room, two pieces were not located: a jug[72] and a lid.[73] The notebook records pithoi (as from K 2), typical rounded pithos rims, ten kalathoi, jugs or jars with wide necks, and very large coarse-ware stirrup jars; the false spout of one of these stirrup jars is preserved, but was not catalogued (Sampled KAR 06/29). Another false spout of a smaller stirrup jar was also found, along with a pithos or pithoid jar with strokes and circles on a raised ridge at the bottom of the neck.

The objects recorded from the room included a bronze needle (207), a circular stone bead (616), and a cylindrical terracotta spindle whorl (206).

There was a good deal of fine ware, including many deep bowls or cups (**K3.1–3**), a kylix (**K3.4**), a pyxis (**K3.5**), two jugs (**K3.7–8**), and a small amphora (**K3.6**). All the pottery was ordinary domestic serving and dining equipment. The coarse wares suggest that the inhabitants used the room for storage (the pithoi, jar, and coarse stirrup jars), cooking (cooking dish), and other domestic uses. The ten kalathoi, however, are highly unusual and constitute the largest number found in a single room. Other rooms on the site that produced large numbers were K 58 (8), K 26 (8), K 28 (7), K 80 (7), K 114 (6), most identified as either cult rooms themselves (K 58) or adjacent to cult areas (K 26, K 28, K 80). As with K 114, however, here is no ritual association in K 3. Both of the preserved kalathoi (**K3.10–11**) show burning on the interior, so at least these two held burning material, perhaps used as lamps or braziers; if they were offering bowls, they held burning material.

It is presumed that the nearly complete vessels represent what was in use in the room at the time the site was abandoned. The fragments of deep bowls or cups (**K3.2–3**) are possibly earlier, and indeed the decoration of strokes on **K3.2** looks early.[74] The kylix (**K3.4**) is similar to large examples from the later part of LM IIIC at Kavousi–*Vronda*.[75] The narrow-necked jug (**K3.8**) is a most unusual shape; it was manufactured like the stirrup jars by throwing the neck separately and adding it to the body with a ridge of clay to strengthen the join. It may be an adaptation of FS 120, which was popular on the mainland through LH IIIB1,[76] but has not been recognised on Crete.

Pottery Catalogue: K 3

Fine Wares

K3.1   Deep bowl (FIG. 2.13). Max. pres. H. 8.9; D. base 4.2. Partially mended from four fragments. 20% preserved, including entire base, 25% of body and one handle. Rim and second handle missing. Very soft, fine, reddish yellow (5YR 7/6) fabric. Very pale brown (10YR 7/4) surface. Worn surfaces. Burned badly inside

and out on one side. Blob decoration or monochrome, but too burned to be certain. LM IIIC.

K3.2   Deep bowl or cup (FIG. 2.13). D. rim est. 12. Three joining fragments from rim. Soft, fine, porous, pink (7.5YR 8/4) fabric with dark sand-sized inclusions. Very pale brown (10YR 8/4) slip. Worn red (2.5YR 5/8) paint. Vertical strokes with V in centre. LM IIIC early.

K3.3   Deep bowl or cup (FIG. 2.13). D. rim est. 12. Single fragment from rim. Fine, soft, reddish yellow (5YR 6/6) fabric. Very pale brown (10YR 8/3) slip. Black (?) paint. Very worn surfaces. Multiple curvilinear decoration, possibly a spiral. LM IIIC.

K3.4   Kylix (FIG. 2.13). Max. pres. H. 11.4; D. rim 10. Once restored, now made up of 17 sherds preserving 60% of rim and body and one handle; missing stem and second handle. Severe secondary burning. Stem originally preserved and is in publication, but now missing. Fine, soft, pale brown (10YR 6/3) fabric. Black paint (originally red?). Very worn surfaces. Heavy ridging on interior. Vertical strokes below rim band, other decoration worn. Publication: Seiradaki, fig. 18.2; pl. 10b, right. LM IIIC late.

K3.5   Pyxis (FIG. 2.13). H. 12; D. base 10; D. rim 7.3. Once mended from 14 fragments. 50% preserved, including full profile, 75% of base; missing tops of handles, Fine, soft reddish yellow fabric, 5YR 7/8. Surface still coated with sediment, but where removed, surfaces worn. No burning. Sampled KAR 06/35. Decorated, but too worn and coated to determine motifs. LM IIIC.

K3.6   Miniature amphora (FIG. 2.13). Max. pres. H. 6.3; D. base 3.5. Mended from five fragments. 75% preserved, including entire base and lower body, half of shoulder, and both lower handle attachments; missing neck, rim, and most of handles. Rather fine, soft, reddish yellow (5YR 6/6) fabric, with tiny white carbonates (less than sand-sized). Black paint. Burned all over. Interior surface flaking. Possibly monochrome, but it is difficult to tell if this is a thin layer of carbon between surface and sediment, or paint. LM IIIC.

K3.7   Jug (FIG. 2.14). Max. pres. H. 18.3; D. base 10.5. Once mended from 19 joining fragments, with seven non-joining sherds; glue marks suggest there were other fragments. 75% preserved, including entire base, half of upper body; missing most of neck, entire rim, and handle. Fine, soft, porous, reddish yellow (5YR 7/6) fabric with some grey phyllite inclusions (1–3 mm). Very pale brown (10YR 8/3) slip. Traces of black paint, very worn. Surface heavily coated with sediment, and surfaces come off with washing or scraping. Decorated with bands and possibly other motifs. LM IIIC.

K3.8   Jug (FIG. 2.14). H. 21.4; D. base 6.8; D. rim 4.5. Once mended from 19 joining and 16 non-joining sherds; other fragments once joined. 75% preserved, including most of rim and neck, half of body and base. Fine, soft, light red (2.5YR 6/6) fabric, very flaky inside and covered with sediment outside, with some phyllite inclusions (1–2 mm). Very pale brown (10YR 8/4) surface. Dark reddish brown (2.5YR 3/4) to red (2.5YR 4/8) paint. Neck added on like disc of stirrup jar; ridge on interior where joined. Decorated, but too worn to make out motifs. LM IIIC.

K3.9   Jar (FIG. 2.14). Max. pres. H. 9.5; D. rim 12. Eight joining and eight non-joining fragments from rim and upper body, both handles. 10% preserved including both handles; missing base

72   Seiradaki, fig. 9.1.
73   Seiradaki, fig. 19.4.
74   This example is very close to one from Phaistos; Borgna 1997a, 280, fig. 16, top right, but it cannot be closely dated.
75   Day 1997, 399, fig. 5.3; *Kavousi IIA*, fig. 22.
76   Mountjoy 1986, 101–2, fig. 122.

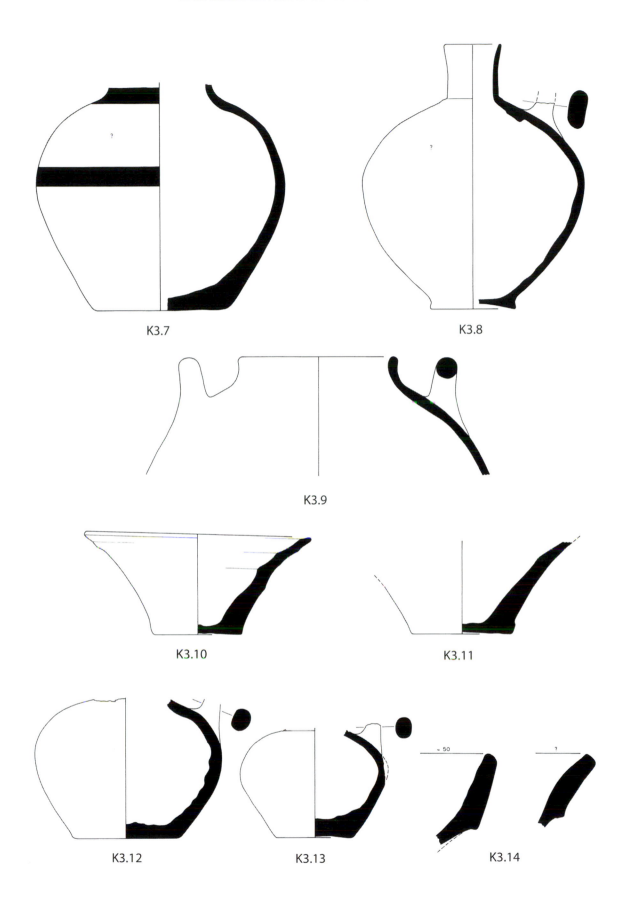

*Fig. 2.14. Barracks, pottery from K 3 (**K3.7–14**). Scale 1:3.*

and lower body. Fine, soft, reddish yellow (5YR 6/6) fabric with tiny white sand-sized inclusions and a few red and grey phyllites. Surface coated with sediment, which takes away surface when removed. LM IIIC.

Coarse Wares

K3.10   Kalathos (PLATE 5 *g*, FIG. 2.14). H. 7.8–8.3; D. base 7; D. rim 18. Mended from eight fragments. 90% preserved, including most of base and lower body, full profile; missing 75% of rim. Coarse fabric with large and frequent chunky red and white inclusions and the consistency of coarse cement. Light red (2.5YR 6/8) fabric, grey at core. Burned in patches on interior, no burning on exterior. Heavy ridging on interior. LM IIIC.

K3.11   Kalathos (FIG. 2.14). Max. pres. H. 7.4; D. base 8. Three joining fragments preserving 50% of vessel, including entire base and much of lower body; rim missing. Coarse light red (2.5YR 6/8) fabric, with frequent mudstone inclusions (1–3 mm) and hard white and black ones. Burned on interior bottom and on one side of exterior. Sampled KAR 06/5. LM IIIC.

K3.12   Jug (FIG. 2.14). Max. pres. H. 11.2; D. base 8.6. Mended from 18 fragments. 75% preserved, including entire base and lower body, lower handle attachment; missing neck, rim, and handle. Very coarse and friable red (2.5YR 5/6) fabric, with frequent grey phyllite inclusions (1–2 mm) like cooking pottery. Black at core. Blackened inside as if it held burning material, but mostly on inside of shoulder. Exterior blackened around handle attachment. Heavy ridging on interior. LM IIIC.

K3.13   Jug (FIG. 2.14). Max. pres. H. 9.2; D. base 6.2. Single fragment preserving 70% of vessel, including entire base and most of body; missing entire neck and rim, and most of handle. Coarse reddish yellow (5YR 6/8) fabric with frequent small hard white inclusions (<1 mm) and a few larger white and black inclusions, some mica. Reddish yellow (7.5YR 7/6) surface, heavily encrusted with sediment. Cf. **K3.12.** Labelled Karphi 3, outside. LM IIIC.

K3.14   Cooking dish (FIG. 2.14). Max. pres. H. 7.3; D. rim est. 50. Large fragment of rim (four sherds) and small fragment of rim with different profile (two sherds), perhaps from same vessel (profiles are different, but fabric is the same, and dishes are often pinched out at rim). 10% preserved, including rim and part of base; missing centre of base, much of rim. Very crumbly, coarse, red (2.5YR 5/8) fabric with frequent large schist and hard white angular inclusions (2–4 mm); almost more inclusions than fabric. Surface wiped and mottled. Burned thoroughly in patches. Part of rim pinched out. Rough on bottom. For shape, cf. Mook 1999, pl. 110.29 (Kavousi–*Kastro*, Phase III); *Kastri*, 290, fig. 11p. LM IIIC.

Room K 4

This room was thought to be an open courtyard because of its large size and lack of roofing material. It may have had a long bench at the north end. The notebook mentions the following coarse ware: pithos fragments, tripod bowls, a pyxis, a jug handle, and flat dishes. The recorded fine ware (as in K 2 and K 3) included a spouted saucer, a stirrup jar, and pedestal bases. Only one fragment was found from K 4, a deep bowl with a spiral, and it was too fragmentary to be catalogued. Objects included a human figurine fragment (208) and two terracotta spools.

Room K 5

This was a separate small square building, which the excavators interpreted as a watchtower. They reported few traces of roofing and had difficulty determining the entrances.[77]

The notebook records pithoi, pithoid jars, tripod bowls, flat dishes, pedestal bases, a tripod bowl with an angular profile, and small pieces of fine pottery. No pottery was saved from the room. Objects included a conical stone bead or whorl (263).

Room K 6

This was another simple room. The excavators suggest that two large flat slabs found against the south wall may have formed a bench.[78] As in other rooms, there were good traces of roofing. The notebook added that the earth was very carbonised.

The pottery is reported to have contained a larger proportion of fine ware than usual. The notebook mentions pithos fragments, flat dishes with flared sides and wavy edges, fine bowls with all sorts of bases (flat, low, ring, pedestal), a jug or large bottle, a krater, and tumbler bases. Pottery preserved in the boxes included a large, coarse, elliptical handle with two ridges and a leg or handle decorated with five round finger impressions.

Objects from the room included fragments of a stone cup (209),[79] a conical stone bead or whorl (264), a cylindrical terracotta spindle whorl (652), and a terracotta spool.

Room K 7

This was another simple room with no distinguishing features and no visible entrance, although one is visible in the east wall on the plan. There was little pottery. In addition to the catalogued vessels, the following pottery was found in the Karphi boxes: the rim of a possible kylix, a stirrup jar or jug fragment, fragments from a deep bowl in blue ware, and a round vertical handle also in blue ware. A pierced schist palette (615)[80] was also found.

The extant pottery suggests simple functions of storage (pithos, jar), cooking (tripod bowl), and drinking. The kylix is of the large variety with small foot that might have been used in drinking rituals.[81] The tripod bowl is probably a round-bottomed tripod cooking pot, similar to others on the site; this shape may originally have been imported into Crete from the mainland.[82]

---

77   *Karphi*, 73.
78   *Karphi*, 73.
79   *Karphi*, pl. 30.1.
80   *Karphi*, pl. 30.3.
81   Day and Snyder 2004, 73.
82   Borgna 1997*b*, 200–1, fig. 11.

Pottery Catalogue: K 7

Fine Wares

K7.1   Kylix (FIG. 2.15). Max. pres. H. 25.8; D. base 7; max. pres. D. 24. Partially mended from seven fragments. 70% preserved, including whole stem, parts of base, entire lower body; missing rim and both handles. Uncatalogued rim fragment may belong. Fine, very soft, pink (7.5YR 7/4) fabric. Very pale brown (10YR 8/3) surface, possibly a slip. Traces of black paint, but surfaces almost entirely gone and decoration indistinguishable. Small base, tall stem with swelling in middle, hollow at bottom; ridge at attachment of conical body. Publication: Seiradaki, fig. 18.3. LM IIIC late.

Medium-Coarse Wares

K7.2   Juglet (FIG. 2.15). Max. pres. H. 4.8; D. base 2.6. Partially mended from four joining fragments, two more non-joining fragments, preserving most of base and lower body. Hard, medium-coarse, blue ware fabric, reddish yellow (5YR 7/6) to greenish grey (5BG 5/1) on exterior; greenish grey (5BG 5/1) on interior. LM IIIC.

Coarse Wares

K7.3   Tripod bowl (FIG. 2.15). Max. pres. H. 15.5; D. rim est. 40. Two joining and five non-joining fragments preserving 10% of vessel, including nearly complete profile and one leg attachment; missing centre of base, handles, and legs. Coarse reddish yellow (5YR 7/8) fabric with grey (5Y 6/1) core. Frequent schist, phyllite, and hard white angular inclusions (2–4 mm). Burned on base and body (exterior), mottled burning on interior. Shallow bowl, possibly with rounded bottom. LM IIIC.

K7.4   Jar (FIG. 2.15). Max. pres. H. 16.3; D. rim est. 18. Partially mended from seven joining fragments from rim and handle, three more joining fragments from second handle, 13 body fragments. Base and lower body missing. Coarse, soft, yellowish red (5YR 5/8) fabric with infrequent medium white inclusions (1–2 mm). Very worn surfaces. Shape similar to cooking pots. LM IIIC.

K7.5   Pithos (PLATE 5 *h*, FIG. 2.15). Two non-joining body fragments. Coarse reddish yellow (5YR 7/6) fabric, with small (1–2 mm) but frequent soft black phyllite inclusions. Very pale brown (10YR 8/4) on surface. Decoration of raised band with incised X-pattern. Publication: Seiradaki, pl. 12a, second row, middle. For decoration, cf. Day and Glowacki forthcoming (Vronda Building E: E1 P145). LM IIIC.

Street outside K 2–7

The notebook records pottery from an area outside K 2–7, perhaps the road shown to the east of the building complex. Included were pithos sherds with rope patterns, tripod legs, dishes with flared sides, tripod bowls, a scuttle with a grooved and wavy rim and stick handle (**K2–7.1**), a fragment of bowl in thin blue ware with orange red slip, a large bowl in fine buff clay, and small buff and cream-colored bowls. A huge jug or amphora handle in one of the boxes is labelled as coming from here.

The pottery shows little similarity to assemblages found in other areas identified as streets, which generally consist of large quantities of small fragments of fine ware, mostly from deep bowls or cups and kraters (see below).

Pottery Catalogue: K 2–7 (Street)

Coarse Wares

K2–7.1   Scuttle (FIG. 2.15). Max. pres. H. 7.1. Single fragment from rim, preserving handle attachment and beginning of handle. Coarse reddish yellow (7.5YR 6/6) fabric with frequent grey phyllites (up to 6 mm), some red phyllites (2–3 mm), and hard black and white inclusions (1 mm and less). No traces of burning inside or out. Incisions on interior of rim. LM IIIC.

Room K 134

This area, a kind of rock chamber, was considered an outside space, in which the publication records that nothing was found 'of any importance'.[83] It was thought to belong more with the Barracks than the Eastern Block. The statement about the lack of finds is surprising, given the amount of interesting fine decorated wares marked as coming from the space.

The pottery mentioned in the notebook included many sherds from a pithos with a chevron pattern, a large coarse stirrup jar of Type 5, a base with incised lines, at least two fine stirrup jars (**K134.3–4**), two fine one-handled jugs (**K134.5**), some fine cups, and pyxides (**K134.1**). Uncatalogued pottery from the room included a burned base or stopper, a krater with a dotted curvilinear design, a jug or stirrup jar base with bands, and a small coarse jug base. Objects from the room included a terracotta spindle whorl cut from a kylix stem and a fragment of a bone handle (678).

While there was not a great deal of pottery here, the same function of storage (pithos, large stirrup jar) appears as in most of the buildings. There was no pottery clearly related to cooking. Perhaps the space was used for storage, both for goods and for pottery. The two octopus stirrup jars are unusual, and they are both badly burned. Possibly they were damaged and discarded in this space. The stirrup jars find their closest parallels with the octopus stirrup jar **K150.3**. The pyxis (**K134.1**) has decoration similar to a LM IIIC krater from Sybrita/Thronos, while the splatters on the interior can be compared to a pyxis from Kastri;[84] at Karphi there is a good deal of similarity between the decorative schemes on these two large shapes. The stirrup jars and the pyxis look earlier than some of the material found on the floors, perhaps early LM IIIC.

Pottery Catalogue: K 134

Fine Wares

K134.1   Pyxis (PLATE 6 *a*, FIG. 2.16). H. 12.2–12.4; D. base 13; D. rim 9.5. Restored from 40 fragments. 75% preserved; missing part of base and some body fragments. Fine, soft, pinkish white (7.5YR 8/2) fabric, grey at core, with tiny dark sand-sized

---

83   *Karphi*, 72.

84   D'Agata 1999, 199, fig.10.36.19 (Sybrita/Thronos, LM IIIC late); *Kastri*, 296, 289, fig. 10j (early LM IIIC).

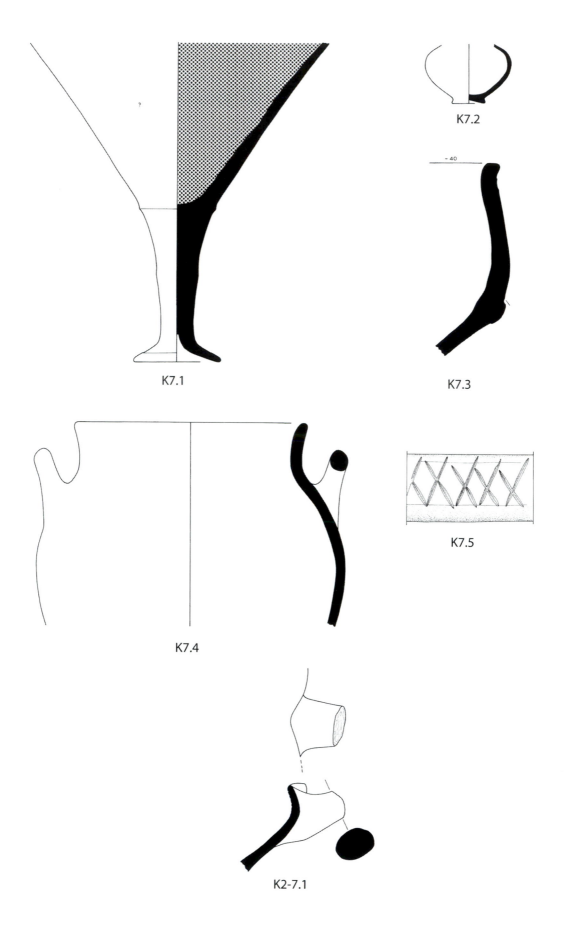

*Fig. 2.15. Barracks, pottery from K 7 (**K7.1–5**) and outside K 2–7 (**K2–7.1**). Scale 1:3.*

inclusions. Black paint worn to brown shadow. Very worn surfaces. Elaborate panelled decoration, similar on both sides: in centre, two vertical rows of U-patterns, multiple curved streamers, with filler arcs, spirals, and filled half medallions on either side. Interior has splatters. Publication: Seiradaki, fig. 24f; pl. 7b, lower left. LM IIIC late.

K134.2 Amphora (FIG. 2.16). Max. pres. H. 11.7; D. base 4.4. Mended from 15 fragments. 85% preserved, including entire base, most of body, both lower handle attachments; missing both handles, much of neck, whole rim. Fine, soft, pink (7.5YR 7/3) fabric. Traces of black paint, but surfaces almost entirely gone. Burned. Probably painted. Incised rings at base of neck. LM IIIC.

K134.3 Stirrup jar (FIG. 2.16). Max. pres. H. 20.5; max. D. 22.3. Partially mended. Large fragment of 30 sherds preserving 75% of top, including false spout and lower handle attachments; four fragments from base, 12 more from lower body, 15 additional sherds. 60% of vessel preserved; nearly full profile can be restored. Missing spout and top of handles. Fine, soft, pink (5YR 7/4) fabric, laminating especially on bottom. Very pale brown (10YR 8/3) slip. Black paint. Top is burned totally black, and burned sherds join onto unburned or partially burned pieces. Sampled KAR 06/57. Top manufactured separately as disc and added on with additional clay inside. Bands on lower body. Octopus decoration, with eyes and body under spout. Tentacles curve around top and end in two medallions with lozenges filled with arcs in centre, arc filler around. Much hatching, fringes, and arcs as filler. Sides have metopal panels of horizontal multiple zigzags outlined with vertical lines and dotted scalloped edge. On disc of false spout, arcade pattern with arc fillers. Decoration almost identical to stirrup jar **K150.3**. For medallions, cf. Prokopiou 1997, 378, fig. 19k (Sybrita/Thronos, LM IIIC Pit 44). LM IIIC early.

K134.4 Stirrup jar (PLATE 6 *b*, FIG. 2.16). H. est. 17.4; D. base 5; max. D. 16.8. Partially mended from 15 fragments, preserving nearly complete profile. Much of top preserved, including handle and false spout, parts of body and base. Many fragments associated with **K134.3** may go with this vessel. Fine, soft fabric, grey to black through and through. Black paint. Burned, especially around false spout on top; less burned on lower body. Sampled KAR 06/56. Top added on as disc, as with **K134.3**. Decorated with fringed multiple chevrons, medallions with crosshatched lozenges, filler — possibly another octopus, with eyes and body under spout. On disc of false spout: arcade pattern. LM IIIC early.

K134.5 Jug (FIG. 2.16). H. 12 (with handle 12.6); D. base 4.7; D. rim 5.1. Partially mended from 15 fragments. 80% preserved, including full profile, entire base, most of upper body, handle and small fragment of neck. Fine, soft, pale red (2.5YR 7/2) fabric, flaking and laminating; mainly grey as if burned or misfired, with some very black patches. No traces of paint. Irregular base has string marks and possibly mat impressions. Decorated with small knobs on shoulder. LM IIIC.

Room K 145

This space was not really a room, but only a short passage leading to Room K 134. Again, the excavators reported nothing of importance found here. The notebook confirms that the pottery was scanty. Nothing is preserved that can be attributed to this area.

THE ROAD HOUSE

Room K 146

This large building lay to the southeast of the Barracks and northeast of the Southeast Quarter. It was badly destroyed; only the eastern long side and small sections of the north and south walls were preserved. It was entered from one of the long sides. There are no recorded finds in the publication or notebook. The notebook suggests that this area was called MK 2. If so, then a burned stopper or lid preserved in one of the boxes came from here.

THE SOUTHEAST BLOCK (ROOMS K 130–K 133)

In the notebook this group of four rooms was originally called the Southern Barracks.[85] It consisted of at least two separate buildings: House K 130–131 and House K 132–133. The excavators originally thought that some stratigraphy was preserved, but the stones in regular order above a black layer turned out to be a chance fall of stones above roofing. Although neither the publication nor the notebook says so, it would seem that these rooms were all roofed.

House K 130–131

House K 130–131 was a simple two-room structure entered from the west into K 130. A doorway led from K 130 into a back room K 131; the doorways were not on axis, and the door into K 131 was not aligned with the entrance into the building, providing privacy for this back room.

Room K 130

This nearly square room had a platform in the corner. It was entered in the northwest. The pottery was unusual only because there were few pithos sherds. The notebook lists only one pithoid jar, but says that there were at least three examples of each coarse shape. There were one or more buff stirrup jars of 'porridge' ware. Fine pottery came mostly from bowls of Types 1–3, but there were some krater sherds, two kylix bases and the spout of a duck vase. Found in the boxes were also a fragment of a possible bird vase and a pithos base decorated with oblique slashes. Only a spindle whorl cut from a kylix stem was found in the room. There is nothing found in the room to indicate any special functions, nor can the single catalogued krater give a close date.

Pottery Catalogue: K 130

Medium-Coarse Wares

K130.1 Krater (FIG. 2.17). D. rim est. 31–32. Single fragment from rim. Medium-coarse very pale brown (10YR 8/4) fabric with red phyllites and sharp angular black and white inclusions

---

[85] *Karphi*, 74–5.

*Fig. 2.16. Barracks, pottery from K 134 (**K134.1–5**). Scale 1:3 unless otherwise indicated.*

(1–2 mm) and mica. Very pale brown (10YR 8/2) slip. Dark brown (7.5YR 3/2) paint. Worn surfaces. Outlined curvilinear motif, with arc fillers. LM IIIC.

Room K 131

This small room was entered through a doorway on the southwest from K 130. Its north side was bedrock. According to the publication, the pottery included more fine wares than usual, most probably from a large decorated krater (**K131.4**). A strainer top is also mentioned. The notebook lists the following pottery: sherds from at least two pithoi of Types 8 and 11, kalathoi of Types 1 and 2, and a large stirrup jar of Type 6; the rest was too fragmentary to distinguish types. The only object from the room was a conical stone bead or whorl (618).

The catalogued pottery from this room represents vessels used for drinking and serving of food and drink: a large and elaborately decorated krater (**K131.4**) and two or three kylikes (**K131.1–3**), two of them very large. One of the kylikes catalogued here was labelled K 131/138 and may come from either this complex (a mistake for K 131/133) or from the Eastern Quarter (a mistake for K 137/138); no mention is made of kylikes in either group of rooms, although two kylikes were mentioned from K 130. Since neither combination seems more likely than the other, the vessel has been catalogued here. It is possible that this equipment was used for elite drinking rituals such as may have gone on in some of the larger houses at Karphi and at the Big House at Kavousi–*Vronda*.[86] The vessels all look late LM IIIC; there is nothing particularly early. The elaborate fringed and scalloped motifs of one kylix and the exotic animals on the krater look late, but these vessels are not among the latest pottery at Karphi. The krater, in particular, is highly unusual, and surely of local inspiration. It is unfortunate that its surfaces are so poorly preserved that one cannot make out the motifs with certainty. It looks as if there are two animals, possibly mythological animals, on either side of a central motif that may be horns of consecration. The figures have the clawed feet of lions, but their bodies look more like those of horses. One is clearly male. Either they have elaborate headdresses, or their mouths/beaks are open with trees or plants growing out of them. It is possible that these are griffins, but they may also be fanciful representations of real animals. The other side is also panelled, but the motifs could not be determined. There are good parallels for the subsidiary decoration of this piece; the running spiral occurs on a terracotta window frame from Kavousi–*Vronda*.[87] The deep rounded shape is common in LM IIIC.[88]

Pottery Catalogue: K 131

Fine Wares

K131.1   Kylix (FIG. 2.17). Max. pres. H. 10.5; D. rim est. 27. Once restored from 30 fragments, preserving profile from rim to lower body, including both handle attachments; missing stem and most of rim. Fine, very soft, reddish yellow (5YR 6/6) fabric. Very pale brown (10YR 8/4) slip. Red (2.5YR 4/6) paint, worn to shadow. Very worn surfaces. Exterior burned. Elaborate decoration, poorly preserved: loops or scallops from rim, with fringed motif below. Perhaps octopus decoration, with solid body and multiple outlines, tentacles with hatching between. For decoration, cf. Andreadaki-Vlasaki and Papadopoulou 2007, 53, fig. 10.27 (Khamalevri, Phase II). LM IIIC late.

K131.2   Kylix (FIG. 2.17). D. rim 22. Three non-joining fragments two from rim, one from body. Fine, soft, very pale brown (10YR 8/2) fabric and slip. Crackled black paint. Well-preserved surfaces, but still much coated with sediment. Hatched lozenges with spirals on either side. LM IIIC early.

K131.3   Kylix (FIG. 2.17). Max. pres. H. 13; max. D. 10.6. Four joining fragments preserving entire stem and part of lower body; missing base and upper body. Fine, very soft, very pale brown (10YR 8/4) fabric, with tiny white inclusions. Black paint. Very worn surfaces. Stem not pierced. Label says K 131/138, probably either K 137/8 or K 131/3. LM IIIC.

K131.4   Krater (PLATE 6 *c–d*, FIG. 2.18). Max. pres. H. 42; D. rim 55.8. Once restored from numerous fragments; now falling apart. 80% preserved, including both handles; missing base, fragments of body and rim. Fine, very soft, light red (2.5YR 6/6) to red (2.5YR 5/6) fabric, with infrequent grey phyllite inclusions (1–2.5 mm). Very pale brown (10YR 8/3) slip. Paint black to yellowish red (5YR 4/6). Very worn surfaces, especially on side B. Patches of burning on exterior rim and body. Pedestal base is restored. Deep rounded body. Round horizontal handles set high on body. Elaborately decorated. Side A: large central panel with horns of consecration and filler, possibly a tree with hatched leaves; on either side are vertical panels of running spirals with wave pattern on either side of the spiral tails; then large animals, quadrupeds, with claw-like feet. One clearly male. Small beak-like head or open mouth with 'fish tree' or fringed multiple curvilinear motif growing out of it; perhaps this is an elaborate headdress. Side B: panel with scalloped edges, curvilinear motifs, but too poorly preserved to make out. Publication: Seiradaki, fig. 17.10, pl. 9e–f. For decoration, cf. *RMDP*, 288, fig. 98.219 (Laconia, LH IIIC middle); Mountjoy 2007, 234, fig. 6 (Lefkandi pyxis with griffins, LH IIIC middle, advanced). LM IIIC late.

House K 132–133

This two-room house is entered from the south into K 133. There are traces of a kalderimi, or paved road, to the south of the building. The contents of the rooms suggest ordinary domestic functions. There was a rather large amount of misfired pottery (blue ware).

Room K 133

This small room was thought of as an entrance hall to K 132. It had a bench along its north wall. No pottery is extant. The notebook lists the following coarse pottery: two pithoi of Types 21 and 23, a pithoid jar of

---

86   Day and Snyder 2004.

87   Day 1999, pl. 38b; *Kavousi IIA*, fig. 43.

88   *Kastri*, 296, 292, fig. 13; Warren 1982–83, 79, fig. 43 (Knossos); *Kavousi IIA*, fig. 43 (Kavousi–*Vronda*, LM IIIC late).

K 130.1

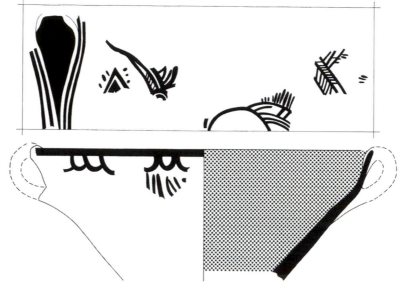

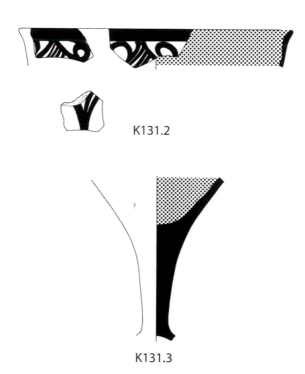

K131.1

K131.2

K131.3

Fig. 2.17. Southeast House, pottery from K 130 (**K130.1**) and K 131 (**K131.1–3**). Scale 1:3.

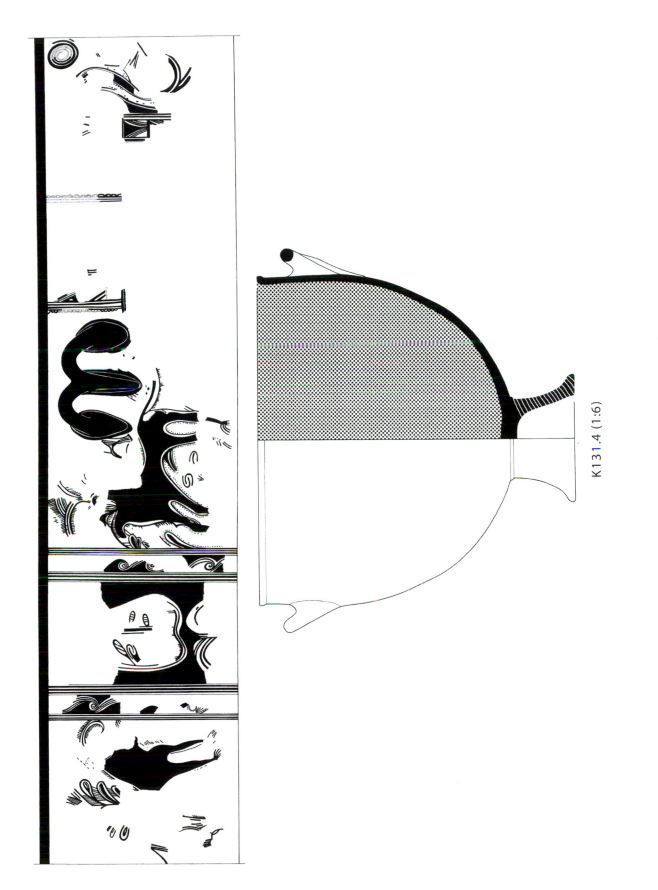

K131.4 (1:6)

*Fig. 2.18. Southeast House, decorated krater from K 131 (**K131.4**). Scale 1:6.*

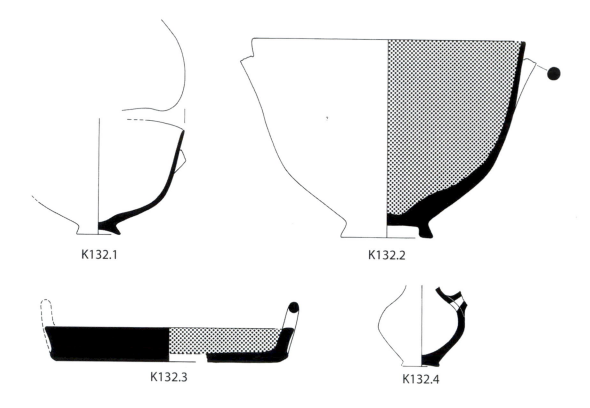

*Fig. 2.19. Southeast House, pottery from K 132 (**K130.1–4**). Scale 1:3.*

Type 3, a tripod rim and leg of Type 2, a kalathos of Type 1, a scuttle handle, a bowl of Type 1, and a small bowl or cup. There was little fine pottery listed, only a stirrup jar of Type 2, a blue ware bowl of Type 1, and a few small bowl fragments. Objects included a conical stone bead or whorl (619) and a lentoid sealstone of red jasper with a lion (620),[89] no doubt an heirloom. Pumice was also found.

Room K 132

The larger room of the house was entered down two steps from K 133. There was a bench along the north side of the room. The notebook lists the following coarse vessels: at least four pithoi, two of Type 1, one each of Types 3 and 11; a pithoid jar of Type 8; a tripod of Type 2; three dishes of Type 6, with holes; and a large blue stirrup jar of Type 2. In addition to the catalogued fine pottery, there were also two stirrup jars of Type 2, one with a hole in the false spout. Objects from the room included a stone lid (621),[90] a conical stone bead or whorl (622), and a whetstone (623).

There is little from this room to suggest date, and the pottery indicates an ordinary domestic function. The deep bowl of blue ware has the rather high raised and concave foot that is found on late LM IIIC vessels. The ring base of the small krater also may be a late feature.

Pottery Catalogue: K 132

Fine Wares

K132.1   Deep bowl (FIG. 2.19). H. 8.5–9.3; D. base 3.6. Partially mended from ten fragments. 40% preserved, including entire base, full profile, one handle attachment. Very hard, fine, grey (N5/) blue ware fabric, with tiny white inclusions. Traces of black paint. Totally burned and warped from misfiring. LM IIIC.

K132.2   Krater (FIG. 2.19). H. 16.1; D. base 7.3; D. rim 22. Mended from 11 fragments. 40% preserved, including full profile, handle attachment; missing top of handle. Fine, very soft, yellow (10YR 7/4) fabric. Very pale yellow (2.5YR 8/4) surface. Black paint. Very worn surfaces. Ring base. Handles set high on body. Decoration too worn to determine; vertical parallel bands suggests panelled pattern. LM IIIC late.

K131.3   Tray (FIG. 2.19). H. 2.7 (with handles 4.8); D. rim 20. Single large fragment. 20–25% preserved, including full profile, one handle. Fine reddish yellow (5YR 7/6) fabric with pink (7.5YR 8/4) surface. Black paint. Burned. Uneven bevelled base. Basket handle. Monochrome. Publication: Seiradaki, fig. 6.8; pl. 4d, right. Cf. **K43.12**; Borgna 2007, 72, fig. 3.10 (Phaistos, LM IIIC late). LM IIIC.

K131.4   Thelastron (FIG. 2.19). Max. pres. H. 6.4; D. base 3. Intact. 80% preserved; missing rim, upper neck, basket handle, end of spout. Fine, soft, light red (2.5YR 6/8) fabric with tiny black and white inclusions (<1 mm). Surface still coated with sediment. LM IIIC.

---

89   *Karphi*, 132, fig. 3; *CMS* II.3 no. 227.
90   *Karphi*, pl. 30.4.

3

The Northeast Quadrant

The Temple (K 1) and its dependencies (K 19–20, K 38–41), the Great House
(K 9–14) and Great House Shrine (K 15–18), the Temple Road (K 70, K 72, K 76),
and the Baker's House (K 71, K 73–74)

THE TEMPLE (K 1)

The first building excavated at Karphi in 1937 was the
Temple. Since many large stones were left *in situ* at the
end of that season, the building was also cleaned in
subsequent seasons (especially 1938).[1] Although several
rooms comprise the temple complex, the entire area was
labelled K 1. In his 1987 study of the Temple,[2]
Rutkowski provided designations for the various rooms
in the complex which will be used here (FIG. 1.1): K 1
for the large room, K 1d for the bench along the south
wall, K 1g for the small room entered from K 1 by a
staircase, K 1f for the room to the northwest with
Goddess 1, and K 1h for the small compartment to the
southwest which had a burned red clay floor and
produced many vessels of 'blue ware'. To the east,
beyond the entrance to K 1 was a large open area that
Rutkowski identified as a public open courtyard (K 1m).
Aside from a few other objects whose precise locations
were recorded on the plan in the notebook, the find spots
of the pottery are uncertain. Some of the material may
have accompanied the ritual objects in K 1 and K 1f,
but other pieces may have been found in other
compartments or rooms and may have only a tenuous
connection to the ritual activities that went on in K 1.

Room K 1

Room K 1 was a large, rectangular room at the very
northernmost edge of the settlement. The excavators
believed that it was an open courtyard, since they found
no roofing debris within. In his later study of the
Temple, Rutkowski suggested more plausibly, if
without any definite evidence, that the room had been
roofed.[3] K 1 had an uneven floor of bedrock that was
levelled with red clay, and a rectangular stone pier
towards the north end, one course high, was interpreted
as an altar. The northern edge of the room and its north
wall had fallen off the cliff before excavation began.
The room was entered over a heavy threshold on the
east. Another door, at the top of a staircase, led up from
K 1 to compartment K 1g and a second room, K 1f.
Statues of goddesses with upraised arms were clearly
recorded in the notebook as standing on the broad ledge
on the south side of K 1 (K 1d); the ledge had rubble
fill underneath. Along the west wall was a shelf of

stones approximately 0.80 m high, next to the steps
that went up to K 1g. Goddess 1, the largest of the
terracotta figures, is recorded as having been found
standing on a bench that ran along the east side of
K 1f. The compartment in the southwest corner (K 1h)
contained the blue ware vessels and most of the other
whole pots, according to the notebook; its floor was
described as of red mud, but the 1937 drawing in the
notebook calls it burnt earth.

From the description in the publication and
notebook, it would appear that much of the ritual
equipment was left standing when the settlement was
abandoned. The other whole vessels from K 1h,
including the blue ware vases, may have been in
storage, and at any rate had little or nothing to do with
the display and deployment of the ritual equipment in
the cult centre itself. In addition to the ritual equipment,
much of which is on display in the Herakleion Museum,
there were a number of boxes in the storerooms
containing material from the Temple; nothing was
discarded in 1937. One box was labelled 'K 1
Cleaning', while two others simply said 'Karphi I'. One
further box had a label that read 'Karphi: Dump and
Outside Shrine', but neither the notebook nor the
publication gives any specific information about where
this material comes from; there may have been a dump
uncovered in proximity to the Temple,[4] or this box
held material that came from the excavation dump
from 1937 and was recovered in subsequent seasons.
Other Karphi boxes contained ritual equipment
(plaques in one box, snake tube fragments in another,
goddess fragments and other religious material in yet
another box), but none of it is certainly from the

---

1   *Karphi*, 75–6.
2   Rutkowski 1987, 268, fig. 3.
3   Rutkowski 1987, 261.
4   The inventory book does list 'Karphi 1 dump' as a find spot,
    and the entries seem to belong to the 1938 season, based on
    the handwriting and the fact that these objects are recorded
    after objects from Ta Mnemata 8, which was dug in 1938; they
    may have been excavated in 1937, however, and not inventoried
    until 1938. The material is most likely to have come from the
    Temple, possibly from the dump of the 1937 season.

Temple, and much of it can be assigned to other religious buildings on the site.

The publication described the pottery from K 1 as usual, both fine and coarse.[5] The notebook gives little more information, adding only that there were many cult objects and statues, flat anthropomorphic plaques, some coarse wares, including large stirrup jars, pithoi with rope designs, and blue wares. The date given for all this material in the notebook is Protogeometric. The small dish published by Seiradaki with other material from the Temple could not be located.[6]

Five goddess statues from the Temple were reconstructed and have been published: Goddess 1 (HM 11042),[7] Goddess 2 (HM 11043),[8] and three more unnumbered Goddesses (HM 11041,[9] HM 11045,[10] and HM 11044).[11] A terracotta plaque with a face in relief was also found (HM 10872).[12] Other objects from the Temple include the following: a MM II button-shaped seal with rosette motif (409),[13] a disc shaped limestone spindle whorl (110),[14] three conical stone beads or whorls (201, 274, 657), four to six limestone pounders (111–114), an obsidian fragment (205, from outside to the east), a globular terracotta bead (115), a cylindrical terracotta spindle whorl (202, from the dump), two cowrie shells (203, 204, from the dump), and a triton shell (369, from Karphi 1 cleaning).

In addition to the vessels catalogued below, the four boxes labelled as coming from the Temple, or K 1 produced a great deal of material, and although not catalogued, some of it is listed below.[15]

Four goddess faces came from the box labelled 'K1 cleaning'. The first fragment (PLATE 6 e), preserving the top part of face and the eyes, was made of a very pale brown (10YR 8/4) fabric, with small dark grey inclusions.[16] The eyes are unusual because they are deeply incised, rather than moulded. The second fragment from the lower face (PLATE 6 f top) preserved a rather pointed chin and smiling small mouth; it was made of a coarse red (2.5YR 5/6) fabric with large red and grey schist inclusions (2–3 mm).[17] The third fragment (PLATE 6 f bottom) preserved the nose, mouth, chin, and one cheek; it was made of a soft reddish yellow (5YR 6/8) fabric with schist inclusions.[18] The fourth fragment came from a large face (PLATE 6 g), and only the mouth, cheek, and chin were preserved. It was made of a coarse red (2.5YR 5/8) fabric with schist inclusions (1–2 mm). The head was made unusually in two layers; a clay cylinder formed the basis, and on top of that was a second layer with the moulded face. Attributes from the crowns or headdresses of the statues were also found: a small bird with outstretched wings, another small bird on a pedestal with folded wings, and a dove offering (PLATE 7 a). Fragments of other ritual objects included arms, a flat plaque with no raised edge, the breast of a goddess, and a goddess in very pale brown clay with knobs (breasts?) and possibly snakes.[19] Pottery included an amphora neck, fragments of blue ware, and a few decorated fragments.

From the box labelled 'Karphi 1' came fragments of a fine snake tube in very pale brown fabric (sampled KAR 06/45), the heads of two animal figurines (one bovine, one possibly equine) (PLATE 7 b),[20] a fragment of a fine ware goddess in buff fabric, 41 arm or hand fragments, a fragment of a thin (Th. 1.8) plaque with a wide flat edge of fine pale fabric with very pale brown (10YR 8/4) slip, and a fragment of another plaque with a narrow flat edge of coarse red (10R 5/6) fabric with frequent large schist inclusions. Pottery included several painted fine body sherds, a cooking tray, a kalathos with a horn on the rim, a coarse rhyton base (?), and a scuttle handle ending in a bird's head.

The second box labelled 'Karphi I' produced the following: a scuttle handle, a possible hut urn doorway (or a coarse fenestrated stand), a fine flat tripod leg or section of fenestrated stand, the skirt of an incense burner with burning only on one side of the interior ridge, fragments possibly from two small chalices, and a great number of coarse body fragments

The box labelled 'Karphi: dump and outside shrine' produced fragments of the following ritual objects: the skirt and base of a goddess (sampled KAR 06/10); snake tubes; goddess arms, including one elbow; the heads of several goddesses with different hair treatments, including plain applied bands, bands with finger impressions, and several types of chevron bands; a goddess face preserving nose and chin; several ears, noses, breasts from goddesses; and attributes from crowns or headdresses of goddesses, including a poppy, three incised cones, one of which looks like snail shell, two palettes, and the top of a crown with discs (PLATE 7 c). Pottery included twisted handles from a jug or amphora.

If all this material does come from the Temple, then it provides more information about the ritual equipment used in this building than has been published. There

5   *Karphi*, 76.
6   Seiradaki, pl. 4b, top, third from right.
7   *Karphi*, pl. 31 left; Rethemiotakis 1998, 22.18, pl. 59–63.18, fig. 57.
8   *Karphi*, pl. 31 right; Rethemiotakis 1998, 22.18.
9   Seiradaki, pl. 14a–c left; Rethemiotakis 1998, 22.17, pl. 52–3.
10   Seiradaki, pl. 14a–c right; Rethemiotakis 1998, 22.20, pl. 50–51.
11   Seiradaki, pl. 14a–c middle; Rethemiotakis 1998, 22.19, pl. 48–9, fig. 56.
12   *Karphi*, pl. 35.1; Gesell 2004, 142, fig. 7.13.
13   *Karphi*, 131, fig. 2; *CMS* II.2 no. 199.
14   *Karphi*, pl. 30.4.
15   This material is now being studied by Geraldine Gesell.
16   Day 2009, 142, fig. 12.4.
17   Day 2009, 141, fig. 12.3.
18   Day 2009, 141, fig. 12.3.
19   Possibly the one mentioned by Gesell 2010, 137–8.
20   Day 2009, 142, fig. 12.5.

were five nearly complete goddess statues, and fragments of at least four other heads of statues (both faces and hair);[21] the 41 arm fragments could indicate as many as 20 statues, although some pieces may come from different parts of the same arm. An estimate of 10–15 statues would not seem unreasonable, and there are parallels for such a large number at Kavousi–*Vronda*, where as many as 30 statues may be represented.[22] Two cylindrical stands were catalogued and there were also fragments in the boxes of at least ten others (sampled KAR 06/11–12, KAR 06/31–32, KAR 06/46–52); one had a snake crawling through the handle.[23] Fragments of at least three plaques appeared, in addition to the published one with the head. It is surprising that there were few kalathoi, as large numbers of kalathoi were found in the Vronda and Khalasmenos shrines. Several chalices, scuttles, an incense burner, and some animal figurines make up the remainder of the assemblage, and all are known from other shrines of goddesses with upraised arms. Chalices are unusual in LM IIIC shrines, but found at Kavousi–*Vronda* and possibly Gazi.[24]

The pottery presents an unusual assemblage for a shrine. The blue ware deep bowls look late in terms of shape and whatever decoration is preserved. The feet of all the vessels are particularly suggestive of a late date, as they are all high raised concave bases that approach the later conical feet of SM and PG date. The coarse cup (**K1.8**), lid (**K1.12**), basins (**K1.10–11**), and stirrup jar (**K1.13**) all resemble examples from elsewhere on the site, as do the cooking wares. Basin **K1.11** is similar to one from Kastri, though not as shallow.[25] Basin **K1.10** is closer to a basin than a kalathos, as Seiradaki characterised it; it is a unique shape for this period. The lid (**K1.12**) finds parallels at Kastri.[26] The tripod **K1.21** with triple handles, originally published as a jar, is a shape otherwise unattested at Karphi and finds no good parallels. The cooking dish (**K1.16**) is of a type common on other LM IIIC sites and is one of the best examples preserved of this very common shape.[27]

Although the vessels may have been in storage and not displayed or used, the pottery suggests activities that occurred in the temple.[28] It would be interesting to know if the cooking vessels were actually in the cult rooms themselves and were used in a ritual setting, or whether they were found in K 1h or outside and were not necessarily part of the ritual equipment. They may have been used for ritual meals for the community or for preparation of meals for a smaller group of religious or political figures.

Likewise, it would be useful to know if the blue ware vessels were employed in the ritual setting, or if their deposition in K 1h was chance. Blue ware vessels are found widely scattered over the site, and although they do appear in other ritual contexts (for example in K 106 and K 116) they are not exclusively associated with religious areas. This particular group may have been the result of a misfiring in a kiln, perhaps intended for religious purposes, and deliberately buried in K 1h. On the other hand, a kiln may have stood in the vicinity, and this material may represent wasters from it; certainly the contemporary kiln at Kavousi–*Vronda* was quite close to the Shrine.[29] These vessels may also have been used despite the warping, either for aesthetic reasons or because they had been specially fired for the Temple.

Pottery Catalogue: K 1

Fine Wares

K1.1   Deep bowl (PLATE 7 *d*, FIG. 3.1). H. 10.5; D. base 4.2; D. rim 13.6–15. Restored from 14 fragments. 67% preserved, including full profile and entire base; missing half or rim, one handle, and part of body. Fine, very porous 'blue ware' fabric, bluish grey (5B 5/1) to red (10R 5/6) or weak red (10R 4/3) in colour, with some small white inclusions and many voids where burned out. Very pale brown (10YR 7/3) slip. Black paint. Surfaces very worn. Curvilinear decoration. Publication: *Karphi*, pl. 24.5, middle; Seiradaki, fig. 14.1, pl. 4b, top left; Day 2009, fig. 12.2. Cf. Andreadaki-Vlasaki and Papadopoulou 2007, 47, fig. 4.28 (Khamalevri, Phase I). LM IIIC late.

K1.2   Deep bowl (PLATE 7 *e*, FIG. 3.1). H. 8.1–8.4; D. base 3.4; D. rim 6.1–13.5. Restored from 16 fragments. Missing one handle, but glue marks indicate that originally preserved. Badly misfired; rim is particularly misshapen. Rather fine, soft, porous 'blue ware' fabric, grey (5Y 5/1) in colour with hard white angular inclusions. Publication: *Karphi*, pl. 24.5 left; Seiradaki, pl. 4b, top, third from left; Day 2009, fig. 12.2. LM IIIC.

K1.3   Deep bowl or cup (FIG. 3.1). H. 7–8; D. base 4; D. rim 9.2–12.8. Restored from nine fragments. 66% preserved, including full profile; missing handles. Hard 'blue ware' fabric, dark grey (5Y 4/1) in colour, with small white inclusions. Very irregular; misfired. Publication: Seiradaki, pl. 4b, top, second from left; Day 2009, fig. 12.2. LM IIIC.

K1.4   Thelastron (PLATE 7 *f*, FIG. 3.1). H. 11.9; D. base 3.4, D. rim 2.5–3.2. Mended from 27 fragments. 80% preserved; missing parts of upper body and spout. Fine, hard, 'blue ware' fabric with voids and hard white inclusions, red (2.5YR 5/6) to dark red (2.5YR 3/6) where not burned, grey (10YR 4/0) on surface. Badly burned or misfired. Traces of black paint where not completely burned. Very uneven in shape; neck has partly collapsed. Horizontal multiple loops on shoulder. Publication: *Karphi*, pl. 24.5, right; Seiradaki, pl. 4b, top, second from right; Day 2009, fig. 12.2. For decoration, cf. **K79-89.9**; Mook and Coulson 1997, 358, fig. 30.117 (Kavousi–*Kastro*, Phase I–II); Popham 1965, 325, fig. 5.26 (Knossos). LM IIIC early?

---

21   This number accords with Pendlebury's initial count of nine goddesses in a preliminary publication (Young 1937, 142).

22   Gesell, Glowacki and Klein forthcoming.

23   Gesell 2010, 137–8.

24   Kanta 1980, fig. 9.2 (Gazi); Gesell, Glowacki and Klein forthcoming (Kavousi–*Vronda*).

25   *Kastri*, 295, fig. 15.P 34.

26   *Kastri*, 295, fig. 15.P 33.

27   *Kastri*, 290, fig. 11p, q; Mook 1999, pl. 110.23 (Kavousi–*Kastro*, Phase III); *Khania II*, pl. 46.71-P0831; Borgna 1997*b*, 197, fig. 6.4 (Phaistos).

28   Day 2009, 139–40.

29   Day, Coulson and Gesell 1989.

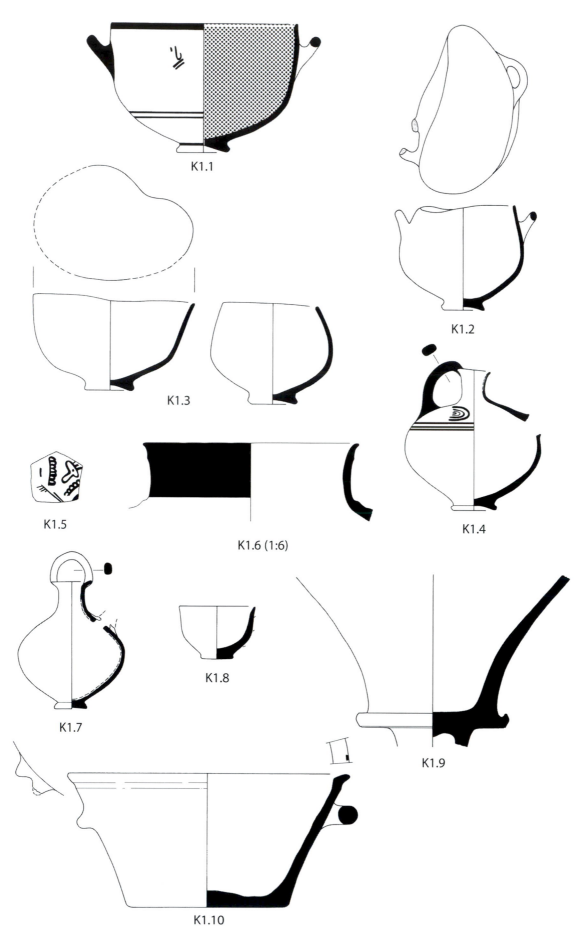

*Fig. 3.1. Temple, pottery from K 1 (**K1.1–10**). Scale 1:3 unless otherwise indicated.*

K1.5   Closed vessel (FIG. 3.1). Th. 0.4. Single decorated body fragment, possibly from stirrup jar. Fine reddish yellow (5YR 6/6) fabric. Very pale brown (10YR 8/2) slip. Black paint. Decorated with filler ornaments, including chain of loops. From 'Shrine Dump'. LM IIIC.

K1.6   Jar (FIG. 3.1). D. rim 34.5. Large fragment (four sherds) from rim of large jar. Fine, soft, light red (2.5YR 6/6) fabric, pink (7.5YR 8/4–7/4) on surface, with some grey phyllite inclusions. Streaky black paint worn to dark reddish brown (5YR 3/4), inside and out. Ridge below rim, larger on one side as if something was attached, possibly a handle. Ridge at base of neck. LM IIIC.

Medium-Coarse Wares

K1.7   Thelastron (PLATE 7 *g*, FIG. 3.1). H. 12.5; D. rim 3.2; D. base 2.6. Nearly complete; missing spout and chips of base; two additional fragments of handle. Medium-coarse yellowish red (5YR 5/6–5/8) fabric with grey core and frequent sand-sized black and white inclusions (<1 mm). Some larger sharp black and white rectangular inclusions (up to 6.5 mm long). Publication: Seiradaki, pl. 4a, top right; Day 2009, fig. 12.2. LM IIIC.

Coarse Wares

K1.8   Miniature cup (FIG. 3.1). H. 4.2, D. rim 6. Intact. 65% preserved, including handle scars; missing one quarter of upper body and handle. Coarse reddish yellow (5YR 6/6) fabric, with frequent schist and mica, some hard white inclusions, all <1 mm. Almost completely burned inside and out. Publication: Day 2009, fig. 12.2. LM IIIC.

K1.9   Chalice (PLATE 7 *h*, FIG. 3.1). Max. pres. H. 13.7. Mended from seven fragments. 40% preserved; missing rim, stem, and 25% of body. Coarse red (10R 5/6) fabric with infrequent schist inclusions (2–3 mm); mottled surface. Interior discoloured, slightly burned? Publication: Day 2009, fig. 12.2. LM IIIC.

K1.10   Basin (PLATE 8 *a*, FIG. 3.1). H. 10.8; D. base 13; D. rim 22.4. Restored from 12 fragments. 75% preserved; missing fragments of base and rim. Coarse red (2.5YR 5/6) fabric with frequent phyllite, black basalt, and hard, white, angular inclusions (1–2 mm); grey core near base. Possible traces of paint on rim. Surface still largely coated with sediment. Interior of bottom burned. Two-pronged or horned lug. Publication: Seiradaki, pl. 4b, middle, second from left; fig. 7.4 (kalathos); Day 2009, fig. 12.2. LM IIIC.

K1.11   Basin (PLATE 8 *b*, FIG. 3.2). H. 13; D. base est. 17; D. rim 33.5–36. Restored from 16 fragments. 60% preserved, including full profile and part of handle. Coarse red (2.5YR 5/6) cooking pot fabric with red and grey phyllite inclusions. Traces of burning on one side. Very worn surfaces. Exterior of rim may have black paint in some sort of crosshatched pattern, but too worn to be certain. Publication: Seiradaki, fig. 5.3, pl. 4b, bottom, left; Day 2009, fig. 12.2. LM IIIC.

K1.12   Lid (FIG. 3.2). H. 6.2; D. 12. Partially restored from four fragments. 75–80% preserved; missing 33% of rim. Coarse, light red (2.5YR 6/6) fabric with large quartz, red and grey phyllites, and some calcareous inclusions. Pink (7.5YR 8/4) slip. Many voids where inclusions have burned out. Surfaces very worn. Publication: Seiradaki, fig. 19.3; pl. 4b, bottom middle; Day 2009, fig. 12.2. LM IIIC.

K1.13   Stirrup jar (PLATE 8 *c*, FIG. 3.2). H. 28; D. base 14; max. D. 25.3. Restored from 30 fragments. 75–80% preserved; missing 33% of base, 67% of one handle, and body fragments, including most of one side. Coarse greyish brown (10YR 5/2) fabric, with frequent large white and grey inclusions, mostly 1–3 mm, but some up to 4 mm. Fabric burned. Surfaces totally scrubbed off or still covered with sediment. Spout almost touches false spout. False spout slightly concave, with hole pierced on top (not going all the way through). May have been decorated. Publication: Seiradaki, pl. 4b, bottom right; Day 2009, fig. 12.2. LM IIIC.

K1.14   Cylindrical stand or basin (FIG. 3.2). Max. pres. H. 10.1; D. 28. Single fragment from rim or base; once mended and restored. Coarse, soft, light red fabric (2.5YR 6/6–6/8) with a few grey phyllite inclusions, 1–2 mm. Publication: Day 2009, fig. 12.2. LM IIIC.

K1.15   Snake tube or cylindrical stand (FIG. 3.2). Max. pres. H. 17; D. base est. 20. Five joining fragments, once mended and restored. 30% of bottom part of stand preserved; fragment from close to top may belong; missing handles. Coarse, soft, light red fabric (2.5YR 6/6–6/8) with a few grey phyllite inclusions (1–2 mm). Base has ledge on exterior, is flattened on bottom, and has ledge on interior. Sides curve in then begin to flare outward. Publication: Day 2009, fig. 12.2. LM IIIC.

Cooking Wares

K1.16   Cooking dish (PLATE 8 *d*, FIG. 3.3). D. rim est. 50; max. pres. H. 8.2. Partially mended into three large fragments from rim (6, 13, and 3 sherds respectively), once restored in plaster. Missing base, but fabric thins out and rounds off toward bottom. Coarse red (2.5YR 5/8) fabric with large and frequent schist and hard white angular inclusions (2–3 mm). Exterior burned except on one side. Almost rounded rough bottom; rim pulled out on one side and irregular. Publication: Day 2009, fig. 12.2. For shape, cf. Andreadaki-Vlasaki and Papadopoulou 2007, 50, fig. 7.4 (Khamalevri, Phase I). LM IIIC.

K1.17   Cooking tray (FIG. 3.3). D. rim 16.5. Single fragment from rim and base, preserving complete profile. Coarse light red (2.5YR 6/6) fabric with phyllites and hard white inclusions. Burning on exterior and interior; surface mottled. Oblique incised slashes on rim. LM IIIC.

K1.18   Cooking tray (FIG. 3.3). D. rim est. 19. Single fragment from rim and base, preserving complete profile. Very coarse and friable red fabric (10R 4/8) with phyllites. Some blackening on exterior of rim. LM IIIC.

K1.19   Tripod cooking tray (FIG. 3.3). D. rim est. 18. Single fragment from rim and base, preserving complete profile of body and one lug handle; missing legs. Coarse red (2.5YR 5/6) fabric with schist and hard angular inclusions. Mottled surface. Scar from attachment of foot preserved. LM IIIC.

K1.20   Cooking jug (PLATE 8 *e*, FIG. 3.3). H. 12.3; D. rim 12.4–13.2; D. base 8.5. Restored from 32 fragments. 75% preserved. Missing fragments of body. Coarse red (2.5YR 5/6) fabric, grey at core, with frequent phyllite and hard white angular and black inclusions. Much burning inside and out, particularly on base. Rim pulled out on one side to form spout. Publication: Seiradaki, pl. 4b, middle row, right; Day 2009, fig. 12.2. LM IIIC.

K1.21   Tripod cooking pot (PLATE 8 *f*, FIG. 3.3). Max. pres. H. 12.6; D. rim est. 9. Single large fragment preserving 40% of vessel from rim to base, two handles and third handle attachment; missing legs (attachments preserved) and one handle. Coarse fabric burned dark grey through to core; coated with sediment. Fragments of another similar handle and body fragments found with it are red (2.5YR 5/6–5/8) with schist and mica, some hard black and white inclusions. Scar at bottom where leg attached. Globular body, short, slightly everted rim; three vertical elliptical handles on shoulder, alternating in position with legs. Publication: Seiradaki, fig. 3.2 (called a jar); pl. 4b, lower, second from right; Day 2009, fig. 12.2. LM IIIC.

K1.22   Tripod cooking pot (FIG. 3.3). H. 18.3 (with handle 18.6); D. rim 10.5. Mended from five fragments (one large body sherd, two leg fragments, two rim fragments, one with handle) 90–95% preserved; missing one leg, part of another, and bit of rim. Very coarse red (2.5YR 5/8) fabric, grey at core, with schist, hard white angular inclusions (generally 2–3 mm up to 6 mm long), and small mica. Burned on one side, legs, and interior. Ridging on interior. Dint at top of leg. Publication: probably Seiradaki, pl. 4b, middle left; Day 2009, fig. 12.2. LM IIIC.

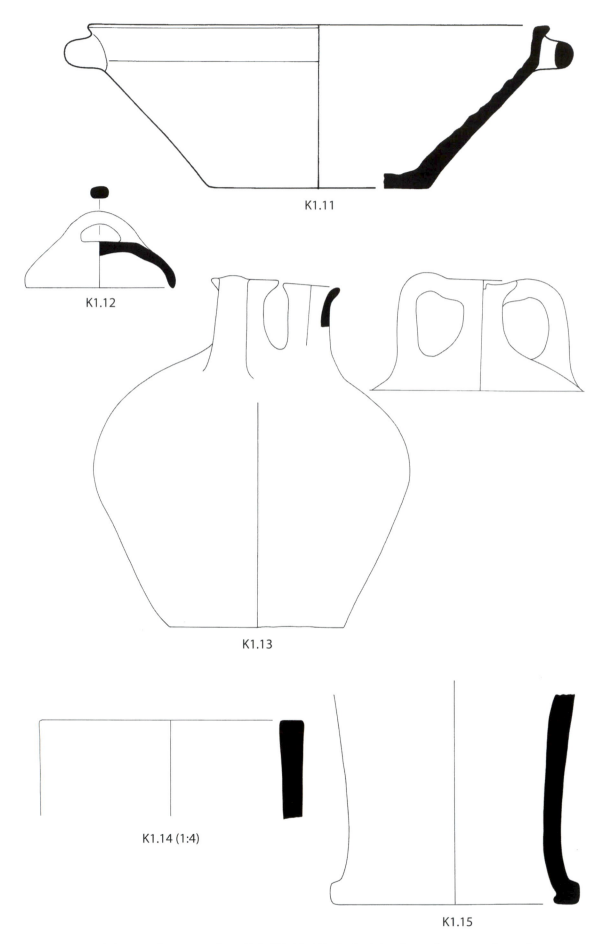

*Fig. 3.2. Temple, pottery from K 1 (**K1.11–15**). Scale 1:3 unless otherwise indicated.*

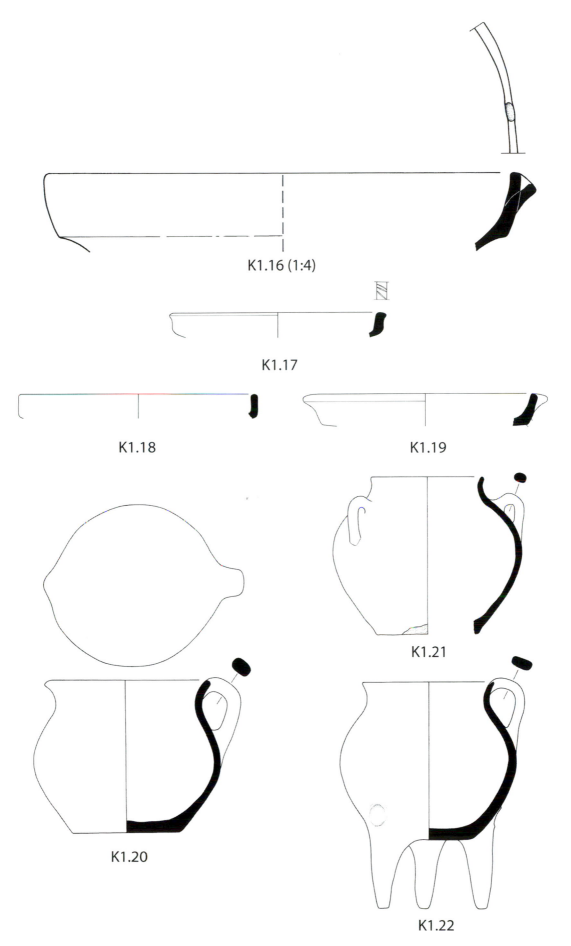

Fig. 3.3. Temple, pottery from K 1 (**K1.16–22**). Scale 1:3 unless otherwise indicated.

DEPENDENCIES OF THE TEMPLE (ROOMS K 19, K 20, K 38–K 41)

The rooms that lie to the south of the Temple were interpreted as dependencies of the Temple,[30] although none of them has any clear connection with that building. Rutkowski reconstructed the area south of K 1 as an open space (K 41) reached from street K 72 (including the portion under K 70), with storage sheds on either side (K 40 and K 19–20).[31] K 38 and K 39 were apparently open spaces; they are also in close proximity to K 15–18 and at a level lower than the Temple, and they may just as easily have belonged with that complex as the Temple.

Room K 19

This large room just south of the Temple was said to be open to sky, suggesting that no roofing material was found in it. K 19 and K 20 are on nearly the same level as the Temple. The notebook lists the following pottery from this area: a few plain pithos sherds; sherds from a pithoid jar in light clay with traces of dark paint; part of a large jug or jar in similar ware; rims of at least three tripods and tripod legs; sherds from a large number of open dishes; trays, one with a horizontal handle at rim; a scuttle handle; and many sherds from rounded vessels with remains of a whitish slip on red clay. The fine ware was described as usual, but included 'rather more fineish pink ware than usual'. In addition to the catalogued pottery a fine stirrup jar fragment, a cooking dish with chevrons on a flat rim, and a tray with spit depressions on the rim were found in the boxes. There were no recorded objects from this room.

The pottery is too scanty to suggest a function for this room, and there is nothing to indicate a date. A large proportion of fragments come from trays and dishes, as well as a cooking lid. The rosette pattern on the pithos (**K19.5**) is unusual, and there are no other examples preserved from the site.

Pottery Catalogue: K 19

Fine Wares
K19.1   Deep bowl (FIG. 3.4). D. base 4. Single fragment preserving entire base. Fine, hard, porous, greenish grey (5GY 5/1) 'blue ware' fabric. LM IIIC.

Coarse Wares
K19.2   Tray (FIG. 3.4). H. 4.4; D. est. 50. Single fragment of rim and base. Soft, coarse, red (2.5YR 5/8) cooking pot fabric with numerous schist inclusions (2–3 mm). Rim decorated with round finger impressions. Publication: Seiradaki, pl. 12a, third row, right (?). For shape, cf. Andreadaki-Vlasaki and Papadopoulou 2007, 46, fig. 3.12 (Khamalevri, Phase I). LM IIIC.
K19.3   Tray (FIG. 3.4). H. 3.8; D. rim est. 30–32. Single fragment from base to rim. Coarse red (10R 5/8) fabric with schist and phyllite inclusions, some mica. Smoothed, mottled surface. For shape, cf. Borgna 1997b, 196, fig. 5.1 (Phaistos). LM IIIC.
K19.4   Lid (PLATE 12 f, FIG. 3.4). D. est. 24. Single fragment from rim. Coarse red (10R 5/6) fabric with schist inclusions, 1–2

mm. Bottom totally burned. Flat disc. At edge top has two raised ridges with rope slashes, incised concentric circles toward centre. LM IIIC.
K19.5   Pithos (PLATE 5 h, FIG. 3.4). Single body fragment with decoration. Coarse reddish yellow (7.5YR 8/6) fabric with frequent red phyllites and some black and hard white angular inclusions. Decoration of raised band with impressed rosettes. Publication: Seiradaki, pl. 12a, top, right. LM IIIC.

Room K 20

This room lying south of K 19, was also said to be open to the sky. The pottery was similar to that from K 19, and no pottery was represented in sufficient quantity to be mendable. The deep bowl published by Seiradaki as being from this room actually came from K 120, according to the number in ink on the fragment.[32] The cooking dish finds a close parallel at Sybrita/Thronos.[33]

Pottery Catalogue: K 20

Coarse Wares
K20.1   Cooking dish (FIG. 3.4). H. 6.6. Single fragment preserving profile, part of base. Coarse red (2.5YR 6/8) fabric with schist (2–4 mm), tiny gold mica, and hard white angular inclusions. Sampled KAR 06/59. Rim pulled inward to form spout. Thinner base, probably rounding out like wok. LM IIIC.

Room K 40

This tiny compartment was one of several small 'closets' to the south and west of the Temple. The west end had collapsed over the cliff. The room is one of the few associated with the temple for which evidence of roofing existed.

The notebook records the usual coarse pottery, including tripods, open dishes, pithoid jars, kalathoi, and stirrup jars. The fine ware was all in small, worn sherds. There is mention of a few fragments that may be from cult objects. The dish published by Seiradaki was not located.[34] The boxes produced many fragments of deep bowls, including two rims (one with vertical strokes, one with a loop), three handles, and body fragments with a Minoan flower, spirals, curvilinear motifs, short strokes, and bands. A plain cooking tray was also found. Other objects from the room included a bronze shoemaker's awl (258),[35] a haematite weight (256),[36] two conical terracotta spindle whorls (257, 259), and a pierced plaque of mother-of-pearl (260).[37]

---

30   *Karphi*, 76.
31   Rutkowski 1987, 261–2 and fig. 7.
32   Seiradaki, pl. 10a top, second from right.
33   Prokopiou 1997, 376, fig. 17b.
34   Seiradaki, fig. 6.5.
35   *Karphi*, pl. 29.1.
36   *Karphi*, pl. 30.1.
37   *Karphi*, pl. 30.4.

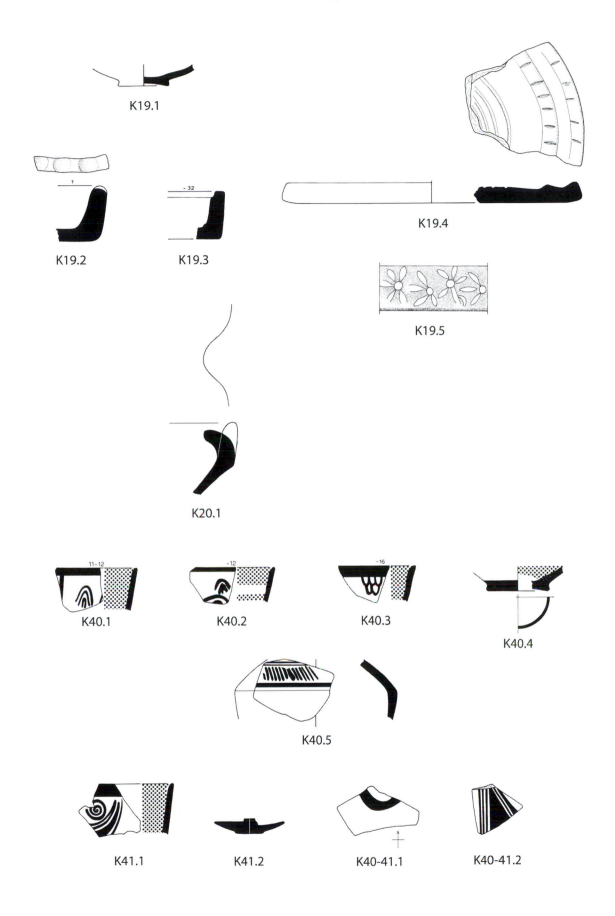

Fig. 3.4. Temple dependencies, pottery from K 19 (**K19.1–5**), K 20 (**K20.1**), K 40 (**K40.1–5**), K 41 (**K41.1–2**), and K 40-41 (**K40-41.1–2**). Scale 1:3.

The preserved pottery from this tiny room is in very small fragments, and none of it is closely dateable. The pieces may not represent what was in use in the room at the time the settlement was abandoned, but rather refuse in the floors or material fallen from farther upslope. The deep bowl base (**K40.4**), with its slightly concave raised shape, painted edge, and reserved disc does not look particularly late. **K40.1**, however, with its upright multiple loops, could be either early or late in LM IIIC; the motif is found on other deep bowls, like **K147.1** and **K79-89.2**, and appears in early LM IIIC contexts at Khania, Kastri, and Knossos and late IIIC at Kavousi–*Kastro*.[38] The motif of pendent triangle made up of scales, like that on **K40.3**, appears on LM IIIB deep bowl from Knossos.[39] The non-catalogued deep bowls have motifs that would fit into any phase of LM IIIC, but the whole deposit looks early rather than late.

Pottery Catalogue: K 40

Fine Wares

K40.1   Deep bowl or cup (FIG. 3.4). D. 11–12. Single fragment from rim. Fine, soft, porous, very pale brown (10YR 7/4) fabric. Very pale brown (10YR 8/3) slip. Worn streaky black paint. Multiple upright loops in panel. LM IIIC early.

K40.2   Deep bowl or cup (FIG. 3.4). D. rim est. 12. Fragment (two sherds) from rim. Fine, soft, porous, very pale brown (10YR 7/4) fabric. Worn very pale brown (10YR 8/4) slip. Dull, worn black paint. Decoration of multiple loops and spiral? Reserved band below rim on interior. LM IIIC.

K40.3   Deep bowl or cup (FIG. 3.4). D. rim est. 16. Single fragment from rim. Fine, soft, reddish yellow (7.5YR 7/6) fabric. Very pale brown (10YR 8/4) slip. Dark brown (7.5YR 3/2) paint. Well-preserved surfaces. Triangle of pendent loops from rim. LM IIIC early.

K40.4   Deep bowl or cup (FIG. 3.4). D. base 5. Single fragment from base. Fine, medium soft, reddish yellow (7.5YR 7/6) fabric. Very pale brown (10YR 8/2) slip. Red (2.5YR 5/8) paint on exterior, dusky red (2.5YR 3/2) on interior. Well-preserved surfaces. Band on exterior; band around edge on bottom. Reserved disc on interior. LM IIIC.

K40.5   Closed vessel (FIG. 3.4). Max. pres. H. 4.8; max. D. est. 13. Single fragment from shoulder. Very soft, flaky, yellowish red (5YR 5/6) fabric. Very pale brown (10YR 8/4) slip. Red (2.5YR 4/8) paint. Very poorly preserved surfaces. Closed vessel with carinated shoulder, possibly a hut urn, stirrup jar, or jug. Oblique strokes between bands on shoulder. LM IIIC.

Room K 41

The area labelled K 41 was probably an open court, as both Pendlebury and Rutkowski suggested.[40] It was divided in two by a line of stones, and the north half was 0.40 higher than the south. That it was a significant area is indicated by the fact that the Temple Road led directly to it.

The pottery was said to be similar to that from K 40. In addition to the catalogued pottery, a number of small fragments were found in the boxes from K 41. Deep bowls were the most plentiful and included two rims (one burned, one with a multiple curvilinear motif),

three handles, and three body sherds (one with a possible whorl shell, one with a curvilinear motif, one with bands). A spout from a medium-coarse thelastron, the rim of a jug with a handle, a coarse jug of greenish fabric with a black band at the rim, and some blue ware body sherds were also found.

Other objects from the area included a pear-shaped bone bead (262), a shell (321), and a fragment of a limestone weight (261). The pottery is too scanty to tell anything about the date or function of this area. A few fragments came from K 40-41 or outside K 40-41. From the latter context is a fragment of a snake tube (sampled KAR 06/19). A fragment of a stirrup jar of coarse greenish fabric with a curvilinear motif and bands is labelled K 40-49, but it was not catalogued.

Pottery Catalogue: K 41

Fine Wares

K41.1   Deep bowl or cup (FIG. 3.4). Max. pres. H. 4.2. Fragment (3 sherds) from rim. Fine, soft, rather porous, reddish yellow (7.5YR 7/6) fabric. Very pale brown (10YR 8/2) slip. Black paint. Worn surfaces. Spiral. LM IIIC.

K41.2   Lid (FIG. 3.4). Max. pres. H. 1.2; D. base 2.3; D. rim 5.6. Single fragment preserving 65% of base and sides; missing knob at top. Fine, soft, reddish yellow (5YR 7/8) fabric. Black paint. Slightly raised base, conical sides; knob in centre on interior. Monochrome. Label worn, probably from K 41. LM IIIC.

Pottery Catalogue: K 40-41

Fine Wares

K40-41.1   Stirrup jar or jar (FIG. 3.4). Max. pres. H. 3.6, Th. 0.4. Single fragment from body. Fine, soft, very pale brown (10YR 8/4) fabric. Very pale brown (10YR 8/4) slip. Worn black paint. Wavy line or octopus. LM IIIC.

Pottery Catalogue: K 40-41 Outside

Fine Wares

K40-41.2   Deep bowl or cup (FIG. 3.4). Max. pres. H. 3.5. Single body fragment. Fine soft, reddish yellow (7.5YR 7/6) fabric. Very pale brown (10YR 8/2) slip. Red (2.5YR 4/8) paint, worn inside. Double axe with multiple outlines? LM IIIC.

Room K 38

Pendlebury originally recorded in the notebook that only K 38 was roofed, but in the publication he emended this idea and included K 39 among the roofed areas.[41] Rutkowski suggested that both rooms were unroofed sheds.[42] The excavators believed that the rooms were

---

38   *Khania II*, pl. 35.70-P 0755; Mook and Coulson 1997, 362, fig. 37.150 (Kavousi–*Kastro*, Phase III); *Kastri*, 287, fig. 8:o; 288, fig. 9m; Warren 2007, 342, fig. 7.P183 (Knossos).

39   Popham 1970*b*, pl. 47e.

40   *Karphi*, 76; Rutkowski 1987, 261–2.

41   *Karphi*, 76.

42   Rutkowski 1987, 262.

entered by ladder from K 20, but it is also possible that they were part of the Great House Shrine or represent another complex entirely. The floors are closer in level to those in K 16-17 than those of the Temple, to judge from the site section.

The pottery was as usual, but without any pithos fragments, and the notebook adds that a miniature tumbler fragment was found. Fragments from this room that were not catalogued include deep bowl sherds (one burned rim with a spiral, one rim with a tailed spiral, and three body fragments with vertical lines, a curvilinear motif, and a rayed design), a krater fragment with banded decoration, a coarse jug or jar with a yellow slip and black paint, a flat piece with plastic decoration (part of a plaque?), and part of the face of a goddess statue. Two vessels published by Seiradaki as from this room were not located: a kalathos[43] and a deep bowl fragment with a zigzag decoration;[44] the kalathos in Seiradaki's drawing resembles one identified on the label as from K 28, and the number may have been misread at the time of the publication. Other objects from the room included a bronze hook (306),[45] two bronze rings (307, 308),[46] a chip of obsidian (309), a cylindrical terracotta spindle whorl (310), and a shell (311).

The pottery is mostly fragmentary; the single exception is **K38.1**, which is an unusual piece. It is shallower than usual and has a slightly more flaring rim. The reserved disc on the interior and the rather low and wide foot would seem to place this example early in LM IIIC; deep bowls of similar shape can be found at Knossos in LM IIIB.[47] The decoration, however, finds a close match at Phaistos of LM IIIB–C date, as well as at Knossos and Kommos.[48] Of the sherds, the decoration of **K38.2** has parallels at Kastri, Phaistos, Knossos, and Khamalevri, suggesting a date in early LM IIIC;[49] **K38.4** is similar to a deep bowl from Khamalevri of Phase I.[50] The stirrup jar (**K38.6**) has parallels at Mouliana and Kritsa and may be slightly later in LM IIIC.[51] The sherd material, then would appear to belong to the early part of the LM IIIC period. It is possible that the rubbish dump that underlay K 16-17 also went under part of K 38 and K 39. The fragment of a goddess may belong in the room, or it may have come from the dump underneath.

Pottery Catalogue: K 38

Fine Wares

K38.1 Deep bowl (FIG. 3.5). H. 8.5; D. base 4.7; D. rim. 14.2. Mended from seven fragments, four more not joining. 75% preserved, including entire base and most of one handle; other handle and body fragments missing. Fine, hard, very pale brown (10YR 7/4) fabric. Pinkish white (2.5YR 8/2) slip. Black paint. Well-preserved surfaces. Sampled KAR 06/15. Multiple stem or tongue pattern (derived from sacral ivy?) between bands. Interior coated except for reserved disc. LM IIIC early.

K38.2 Deep bowl or cup (FIG. 3.5). D. rim. est. 11. Single fragment from rim. Fine, soft, reddish yellow (7.5YR 7/6) fabric.

Very pale brown (10YR 8/3) slip. Only shadow of paint. Very worn surfaces. Multiple horizontal chevrons filled with loops. Reserved band on interior. LM IIIC early.

K38.3 Deep bowl or cup (PLATE 10 d, FIG. 3.5). Max. pres. H. 6.7. Single fragment from rim. Fine, fairly hard, reddish yellow (7.5YR 7/6) fabric. Very pale brown (10YR 8/2) slip. Crackled black paint, worn to brown on exterior. Interlocking spirals, with filling arcs and hanging multiple loops from rim. Publication: Seiradaki, fig. 21i. LM IIIC early.

K38.4 Deep bowl or cup (FIG. 3.5). D. rim est. 13.2. Single fragment from rim. Fine, porous, very pale brown (10YR 8/2) fabric and slip. Red (2.5YR 4/8) paint. Well-preserved surfaces. Minoan flower. LM IIIC early.

K38.5 Deep bowl or cup (FIG. 3.5). Max. pres. H. 4.6. Single fragment from near rim. Fine, porous, soft, reddish yellow (7.5YR 7/6) fabric. Very pale brown (10YR 8/2) slip. Black paint. Exterior surfaces worn, well-preserved interior paint. Multiple stem pattern. LM IIIC.

K38.6 Stirrup jar (FIG. 3.5). Max. pres. H. 5.3. Fragment from top of stirrup jar (four sherds). False spout, both handles, lower part of spout preserved. Missing most of body and base. Fine, rather hard, reddish yellow (7.5YR 7/6) fabric. Very pale brown (10YR 8/3) slip. Dark reddish brown (2.5YR 3/4) to red (2.5YR 5/8) paint. Well-preserved surfaces. Small stirrup jar. False spout made separately and added on as disc; ridge of clay where joins. Medallions with hatched and dotted arcs. Top has arcs, handles have horizontal stripes. LM IIIC early.

K38.7 Stirrup jar (FIG. 3.5). Max. pres. H. 5. Two non-joining body fragments probably from stirrup jar. Fine, soft, reddish yellow (7.5YR 8/6) fabric. Very pale brown (10YR 8/3) slip. Dusky red (2.5YR 3/2) paint. Worn surfaces; paint only preserved as shadow. Multiple spiral filled with arcs and dots; dotted lozenge. LM IIIC early.

Coarse Wares

K38.8 Lid (FIG. 3.5). H. 3.4; D. top 5.2. Single fragment preserving top and part of body. Coarse, soft, light red (2.5YR 6/8) to reddish-yellow (5YR 6/8) fabric with numerous quartz and phyllite inclusions (1–3 mm). Knob handle, hollowed. No decoration. LM IIIC.

K38.9 Lid (PLATE 12 g, FIG. 3.5). D. est. 22–23. Two joining fragments from rim and body. Coarse red (10R 5/6) fabric, with red and grey phyllites (1–2 mm), some schist and hard white angular inclusions (1–2 mm). Top surface mottled red and black; bottom is

43 Seiradaki, fig. 7.3.

44 Seiradaki, fig. 21e.

45 *Karphi*, pl. 29.2.

46 *Karphi*, pl. 29.2.

47 Popham 1970*b*, pl. 52b.

48 Borgna 2003, 439, pl. 13.121; see also Popham 1965, pl. 85c, d (Knossos, LM IIIB); Warren 2007, 338, fig. 3.P2143 (Stage II); Watrous 1992, 72, fig. 45 and pl. 28.1201 (Kommos, LM IIIB:1 cup).

49 Borgna 1997*a*, 279, fig. 7, top left (Phaistos, LM IIIC); *Kastri*, 288, fig. 9h; Popham 1965, 329, fig. 8.50 (Knossos), Andreadaki-Vlasaki and Papadopoulou 2007, 47, fig. 4.3 (Khamalevri, Phase Ib).

50 Andreadaki-Vlasaki and Papadopoulou 2007, 47, fig. 4.27.

51 Kanta 1980, 175, fig. 82.4 and 7 (Mouliana); 138, fig. 121.7 (Kritsa); 71, fig. 121.4 (Kera). The dotted almonds or arcs have been suggested as Naxian in inspiration (P. Mountjoy, personal communication).

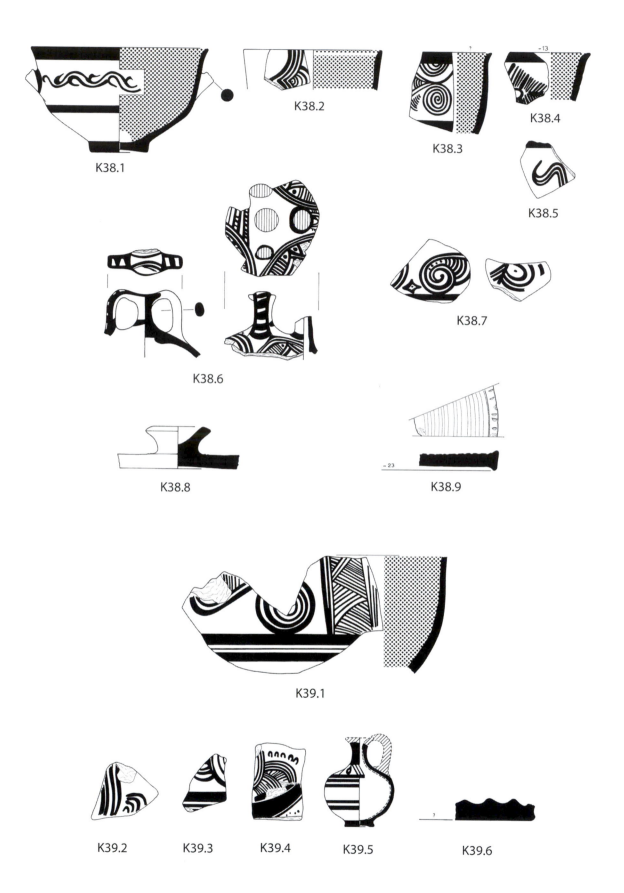

*Fig. 3.5. Temple dependencies, pottery from K 38 (**K38.1–9**) and K 39 (**K39.1–6**). Scale 1:3.*

blackened around the outside about 3 cm. Flat disc lid with knob. Decorated with slashes on rim, incised concentric circles. Publication: Seiradaki, pl. 12a, bottom row, third from left. LM IIIC.

Room K 39

The excavators thought that this was another roofed room, possibly entered by ladder, but it may have been open.[52] The proportion of fine ware was recorded as larger in this room, and it was much broken. The notebook also mentions that fragments of rough red fabric with a yellow white slip were common. The basin fragment published by Seiradaki was not catalogued.[53] Also found in the boxes were handle and body fragments with bands from deep bowls and a jug or stirrup jar handle. Other objects from the room included two pierced schist discs (272, 273),[54] a bone handle for a knife (312), and a conical terracotta spindle whorl (271).

The pottery is fragmentary and thus probably does not represent what was in use at the end of the room's history. The single exception is the small juglet, which is highly unusual and which looks later than the rest of the deposit. Taken out of context, the juglet might appear to be Late Geometric to Early Orientalising in date, but the shape appears earlier on Crete, long before it enjoys popularity in the later periods.[55] On the mainland, the small juglet begins in LH IIIC.[56]

Pottery Catalogue: K 39

Fine Wares

K39.1   Deep bowl (FIG. 3.5). Max. pres. H. 9.3; max. pres. D. 21. Large body fragment (three sherds). No rim, no base, no handles. Fine, rather hard, pink (5YR 7/4) fabric. Glossy, very pale brown (10YR 8/4) slip, Worn black paint, red (2.5YR 5/6) on interior. Panels. Vertical band of alternating hatched triangles between vertical bands. Spirals with filling arcs. For decoration, cf. Rethemiotakis, 1997, 319, fig. 28k (Kastelli Pediada). LM IIIC.

K39.2   Deep bowl or cup (FIG. 3.5). Max. pres. H. 4.4. Single body fragment. Fine, soft, porous, micaceous, reddish yellow (7.5YR 7/4) fabric. Very pale brown (10YR 8/3) slip. Black paint, worn to brown shadow. Worn surfaces. Decoration of vertical lines, multiple arcs. LM IIIC.

K39.3   Krater (FIG. 3.5). Max. pres. H. 4. Single body fragment. Fine, soft, very pale brown (10YR 7/4) fabric. Very pale brown (10YR 8/3) slip. Black paint. Well-preserved surfaces. Spiral (?) with filler arcs. LM IIIC.

K39.4   Krater (FIG. 3.4). Max. pres. H. 6; Th. 0.5–0.7. Single body fragment (two sherds). Fine, soft, reddish yellow (7.5YR 7/6) fabric. Very pale brown (10YR 8/3) slip. Black paint. Worn surfaces. Large curvilinear motif with multiple filling arcs and U-pattern. For decoration, cf. Warren 2007, 341, fig. 6.P2469 (Phase III). LM IIIC early.

K39.5   Juglet (PLATE 8 g, FIG. 3.5). H. 7.1 (with handle 7.4); D. base 23. Restored from five fragments. 75% preserved, including entire base (chipped), all but one piece of body, lower handle attachment, and neck; handle and rim missing. Fine, soft, reddish yellow (5YR 7/6) fabric, with tiny black inclusions. Reddish yellow (7.5YR 7/6) slip. Yellowish red (5YR 5/8) paint, very worn. On shoulder, teardrop between oblique lines; bands below. Publication: possibly in Young 1938, 235, fig. 12, right, bottom right; possibly

Seiradaki, fig. 9.5, which is listed from K 89, perhaps an error for K 39. LM IIIC late.

Coarse Wares

K39.6   Lid (FIG. 3.5). H. 13–18. Single fragment from rim. Coarse red (2.5YR 5/8) fabric with frequent schist (1–2 mm) and silver mica inclusions. Bottom burned around edge in a 3-cm wide band. Concentric raised ridges on top. LM IIIC.

THE GREAT HOUSE (ROOMS K 8, K 9, K 11–K 18)

The excavators thought that one building (Rooms 8–9, 11–18) stood out as superior to the others, and for this reason they labelled it the 'Great House', and suggested it as the ruler's dwelling.[57] Although Rooms 15–18 were assigned to this complex, their connection with the other rooms of the Great House has been called into question, and they have been considered a separate unit.[58] Wallace's restudy of the architecture shows that, although there is no clear connection between the two groups of rooms (8–14 and 15–18), a good deal of care was taken to build the rooms on the same alignment.[59] The large threshold block between Rooms 15 and 16-17 was encroached upon by the north wall of Room 14, so it would seem that there was some collaboration in or acceptance of its construction.[60] The two groups of rooms are here treated as separate structures; Rooms K 8–9 and K 11–14 are taken as an elite dwelling, the Great House, while Rooms K 15–18 are treated independently, as the Great House Shrine.

Much care was taken in the construction of the walls of the Great House. In addition, the finds from the building suggest its elite function; it produced unusual luxury objects, not as many as found in some other houses, but showing a greater variety. Subsequent scholars, however, have questioned the identification of the building as a ruler's dwelling. Both Nowicki[61] and Mazarakis Ainian[62] suggested that the Great House is only one of several elite dwellings, and that the megarons of the Eastern Quarter and the Priest's House have an equal claim to the title of ruler's dwelling. The combination of the size of the building, its unusual architectural refinements, and the variety of objects

---

52   *Karphi*, 76.
53   Seiradaki, fig. 5.5.
54   *Karphi*, pl. 30.4.
55   Coldstream and Catling 1996, 356 say the shape begins well back in Protogeometric, although this example looks more elegant in shape.
56   Mountjoy 1986, 143, fig. 177 from Perati, LH IIIC early.
57   *Karphi*, 77–8.
58   Hayden 1981, 151; Gesell 1985, 79–81.
59   Wallace 2005, 233.
60   Wallace 2005, 237.
61   Nowicki 1999, 148–9.
62   Mazarakis Ainian 1997, 219–20, 304.

found within it seems to indicate that the building was the dwelling of an elite individual or group, and the many kylikes suggests that drinking rituals may have gone on in the building.[63]

The Great House Shrine (Rooms K 15–18) contained ritual equipment, including fragments of goddess statues and snake tubes, and may have served a religious function, although some of this ritual material may have come from a rubbish dump underneath the area.[64] If Rooms 15–18 were part of a religious building, the proximity of the elite Great House suggests that the inhabitants may have been prominent in the religious life of the community, or even have been asserting control over religious matters. The location may, however, be a matter of chance.

The Great House Shrine is not without problems of interpretation, and its role as a religious building in the later stages of the settlement's history is not clear. Some of the material found in these rooms may in fact have come from a rubbish dump under K 16 and K 17, one that also extended under K 12 and K 13. A fragment of a plaque was definitely found below the floor in K 17, and additional ritual equipment came from other areas which may have been built over the dump. From K 70, which may have been a cellar storeroom for K 15–17, came the arm, hand, and skirt of a goddess, along with a plaque and snake tube, but it is unclear if these came from the dump below or were being stored in the room at the time the building went out of use. Other fragments of cult equipment were found nearby: part of a goddess face, a plaque and a kalathos from K 38 (a space contiguous with K 16), and the corner of a plaque and a goddess fragment from K 72 (to the north and west of the Great House Shrine). In addition, the pottery from K 16-17 showed later disturbance, possibly in the Hellenistic Period.

The Great House: K 8–9, K 11–14

The Great House was so called because of its size and certain refinements noticed by the excavators: the building is in the most sheltered position on the site, is the largest building of the period, and is most elaborate in terms of arrangement. In addition, the walls employed fine cut blocks of limestone, with especially elaborate doorjambs.[65] At least three phases of construction were defined: Room K 9 was built first, then K 11 and K 14 were added on, and finally, Rooms K 8 (an anteroom) and K 12–13 (basement storerooms); Wallace's investigations confirmed this sequence.[66]

Room K 8

This small room was an entranceway with fine doorjambs. The entrance from outside is on axis, as is the door into K 9. The notebook mentions a ledge or bench to the right of the door leading into K 9.

The notebook lists the following coarse wares: pithoi, flat dishes, a large red jug, tripod legs, the mouth of a stirrup jar, and a kylix stem. The fine ware included some small buff carinated bowls and a handle of fine blue ware. In addition to the two catalogued vessels, the boxes yielded a large tripod leg with a slash and two dints, probably one of the tripod legs mentioned in the notebook.

The pottery found in the room suggests some storage and possibly cooking. The pyxis is difficult to date, and we do not know what vessels of this shape were used for, except the obvious one of storage for small items. The decoration suggests that it was made in early LM IIIC, and the interior splatters, which find parallels at Kastri, also point to that date.[67]

Pottery Catalogue: K 8

Medium-Coarse Wares

K8.1 Pyxis (FIG. 3.6). H. 11; D. base 11.7; D. rim est. 8. Mended from seven fragments. 75% preserved, including full profile, both handles; missing parts of base and lower body, most of rim. Medium-coarse yellow (10YR 7/6) fabric with frequent large (1 mm), sharp, black and white inclusions. Surfaces worn in places, and black crackled paint only occasionally preserved; otherwise fugitive. Panelled decoration: crosshatched panel in centre, with hatched triangles on one side, and curvilinear motifs on the other, including bivalve shell and two 'fishes'. Vertical wavy lines under handles. Loops hanging from rim band. Splatters on interior. Publication: Seiradaki, fig. 12.1; pl. 7c, far left; Mountjoy 2007, 232, fig. 4.3. LM IIIC early.

K8.2 Basin or pithoid jar (FIG. 3.6). Max. pres. H. 8.8; D. rim est. 44–46. Single fragment from rim. Coarse reddish yellow (7.5YR 7/6) fabric with grey (5YR 6/4) core and large (1–2 mm) phyllite, schist, and hard white angular inclusions. No traces of burning. May be a pithoid jar or a basin. Pinched rope decoration and ridge just below rim. Listed as from K 8 in notebook, labelled K8–18. Publication: Seiradaki, fig. 2.6 (where said to be from K 8), and pl. 12a, top, second from left. LM IIIC.

Room K 9

Originally the only room in the building, this large rectangular room was interpreted as another megaron.[68] It had a good door with a raised stone threshold. At the west end was a square column base, and a depression marked the place of a matching column on the east. Carbonised cross-beams were preserved from the ceiling, and the beams were approximately 15 cm square and 1.25 cm apart. There was a jar stand in the northwest corner. The west wall cut through the room and was not bonded with the other walls. The notebook

---

63 Day and Snyder 2004, 73–8.
64 *Karphi*, 135.
65 *Karphi*, pl. 18.1–4.
66 Wallace 2005, 233.
67 Mountjoy (personal communication) also suggests that the 'fish' motif (or dotted oval) is Naxian, where it dates from mid LH IIIC to late IIIC. For splatters on interior: *Kastri*, 289, fig. 10j.
68 *Karphi*, 77.

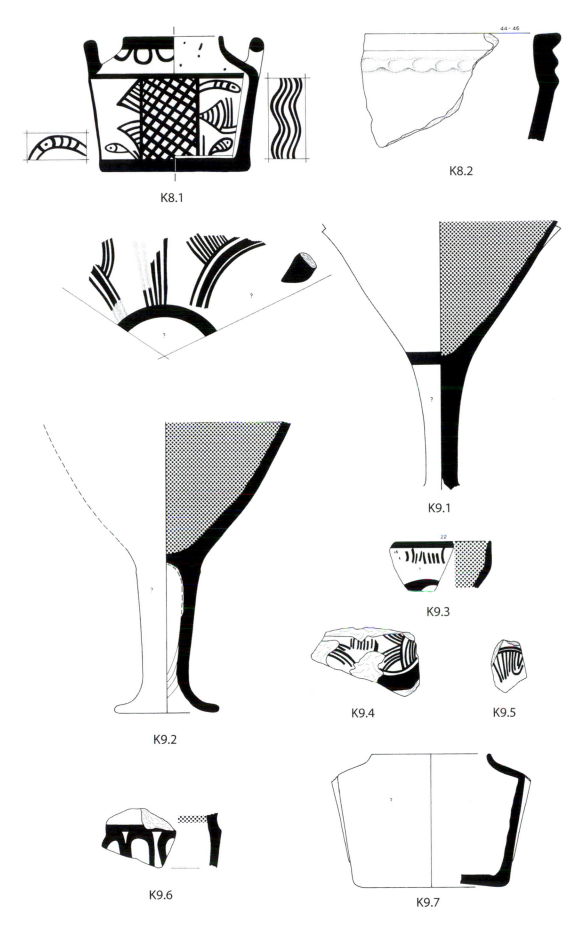

K8.1

K8.2

K9.1

K9.2

K9.3

K9.4

K9.5

K9.6

K9.7

*Fig. 3.6. Great House, pottery from K 8 (**K8.1**–**2**) and K 9 (**K9.1**–**7**). Scale 1:3.*

provides an idealised section of the stratigraphy in the room. At the bottom was a floor of yellow clay (*dhomatokhoma*), varying in depth from 6–10 cm, with the beams resting on it. Over this was a layer of red clayey earth, with another 6 cm layer of yellow roofing material above.

According to the notebook the pottery included many pithoi with projecting bases, one with an angular rim; a black-glazed pithoid jar with grooves around the body and an unusual squared rim; large buff kylikes, one with a hollow stem that shows spiral ridges of pulled clay inside (**K9.2**), and one scored to help attachment of bowl; tripod bowls; flat dishes with low straight sides (i.e. trays) or higher flared sides (i.e. dishes); handles and shoulder fragments of jugs; and pedestal bases. Fine ware included a carinated kylix rim with diagonal lines of paint (**K9.3**) and a tubular side spout. In addition to the catalogued pottery, the boxes produced the following fragments: two deep bowls with spiral or vertical strokes and bands, another kylix fragment with vertical strokes on the rim, a stirrup jar fragment with bands, a vertical handle with punctuated decoration in a vertical chevron pattern (this may come from K 7, but the writing is not clear), a horizontal basket handle, a small cylindrical vessel, a square flat vessel, and a fine tile fragment.

Objects from K 9 included fragments of a bronze ring (367), a terracotta figurine (275),[69] a cylindrical terracotta spindle whorl (276), and oyster shells (365, 366).

The pottery is not unusual, but it includes a larger number of kylikes than usual, and these are of the large variety that may have been used in elite competitive drinking rituals.[70] The rest of the material seems like an ordinary domestic assemblage. If this building was the house of an elite group or individual, and Room 9 is the largest in the building, the amount of available space given over to storage seems unusual. The notebook, while not providing actual numbers of pithoi, indicates that there were many, and one large example is preserved (**K9.11**). Nowicki suggested that when K 8 was added on, it replaced K 9 as the hearth room, allowing for more temporary storage in K 9.[71] As in other LM IIIC sites, however, storage at Karphi was not limited to the storerooms, and the rooms of the buildings were multi-functional.[72] The black-glazed pithoid jar mentioned in the notebooks suggests a later disturbance or occupation of the area of the Great House in later periods, perhaps the Hellenistic Period, as with K 16-17.

Pottery Catalogue: K 9

Fine Wares

K9.1   Kylix (FIG. 3.6). Max. pres. H. 21; max. D. 18.7. Partially mended from three fragments of stem and body. 25% preserved, including much of profile, most of stem, and two lower handle attachments; missing most of base, all of upper body and rim, both handles. Fine, soft, reddish yellow (5YR 7/6) fabric. Very

pale brown (10YR 8/3) slip. Red (2.5YR 4/8) paint. Tall unpierced stem without bulb. Ridging on interior of bowl. Decorated with vertical lines, with curvilinear motifs on either side (broad outlined streamer) and filler. Cf. **K140.1**. LM IIIC late.

K9.2   Kylix (FIG. 3.6). Max. pres. H. 23.2; D. base 8.2; max. pres. D. 19.5. Partially mended from 11 fragments. 35% preserved, including most of base, all of stem and lower body; missing entire rim and handles. Fine, soft, chalky, reddish yellow (5YR 7/6) fabric. Very pale brown (10YR 8/3) slip. Traces of black to brown paint around top of stem, but surfaces almost entirely gone. Tall, thick stem pierced all the way up, with oblique striations inside near base. Decorated, but too worn to make out motifs. LM IIIC.

K9.3   Kylix (FIG. 3.6). D. rim est. 22. Single fragment from rim. Fine, soft, reddish yellow (7.5YR 7/6) fabric. Very pale brown (10YR 8/3) slip; black paint worn to shadow. Very worn surfaces. Vertical strokes below rim band, curvilinear motif below carination. May belong to **K9.2** or **K9.3**. LM IIIC.

K9.4   Krater (FIG. 3.6). Max. pres. H. 5.1; Th. 1.2. Single fragment from body. Fine, soft, very pale brown (10YR 8/4) fabric. Very pale brown (10YR 8/2) slip. Black paint. Worn and pocked surfaces. Decorated with alternating multiple arcs and filler arcs. LM IIIC.

K9.5   Krater (FIG. 3.6). Max. pres. H. 4.1; Th. 6.5. Single fragment from body. Fine, soft, rather porous, very pale brown (10YR 8/2) fabric and slip. Black paint. Surfaces rather worn. Decoration of fringed arcs. LM IIIC.

K9.6   Basin (FIG. 3.6). Max. pres. H. 4.5. Single fragment from near rim, preserving ridge below rim. Fine, rather sandy, reddish yellow (7.5YR 7/6) fabric with some small (1–2 mm) inclusions and voids. Very pale brown (10YR 8/4) slip. Red (10R 5/8) paint, rather well-preserved. Decorated with wavy line or debased octopus motif; interior band at rim. LM IIIC.

K9.7   Pyxis (FIG. 3.6). H. 10.8; D. base 12.5; D. rim 9.6. Once mended; six joining fragments preserving full profile, 30 other fragments. 30% preserved; missing tops of both handles. Fine, soft, chalky, reddish yellow (5YR 6/8) fabric with tiny white carbonate inclusions. Flaky and worn surfaces. Traces of paint suggest that once decorated, but too worn to make out. LM IIIC.

Medium-Coarse Wares

K9.8   Closed vessel (FIG. 3.7). Max. pres. H. 4.7; D. base 3.8. Three joining and two non-joining fragments preserving most of base. Medium-coarse, greenish grey (5GY 5/1), 'blue ware' fabric, with angular white inclusions up to 2 mm. Mottled surface, grey to reddish yellow (5YR 6/6). Raised concave base with knob on interior. Deep rounded body. LM IIIC.

Coarse Wares

K9.9   Kalathos (FIG. 3.7). H. 12–12.4; D. base 9; D. rim 2.4. Mended from 13 fragments; three non-joining fragments. 50% preserved, including most of base and half of rim. Coarse red (10R 5/8) fabric with frequent grey and some hard white angular inclusions. Burned on one side, inside and out and on the interior of the base. Grooves on top of rim. Publication: Seiradaki, fig. 7.2. LM IIIC.

69   *Karphi*, pl. 32.4.
70   Day and Snyder 2004.
71   Nowicki 1999, 149.
72   An important exception was Building A–B at Kavousi–Vronda, which contained specialised storage rooms. *Kavousi IIA*, 61.

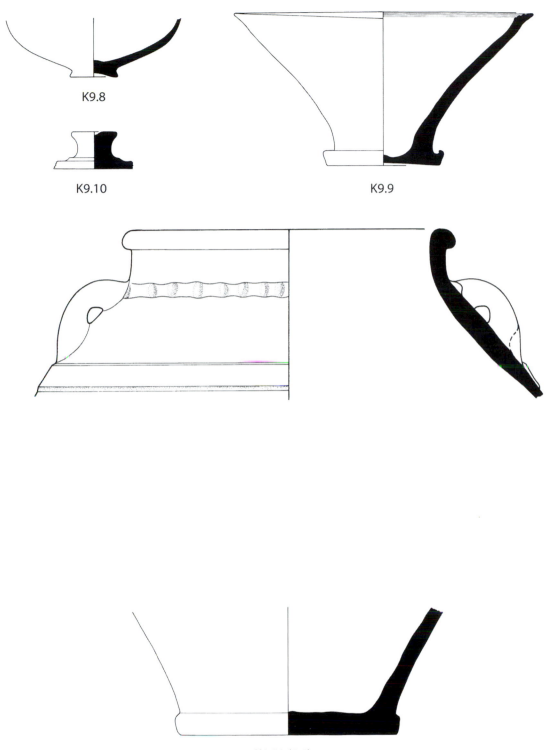

K9.8

K9.10

K9.9

K9.11 (1:4)

*Fig. 3.7. Great House, pottery from K 9 (**K9.8–11**). Scale 1:3 unless otherwise indicated.*

K9.10   Lid (FIG. 3.7). Max. pres. H. 3; D. knob 3.6. Single fragment from the knob of a coarse lid; missing most of body and all of rim. Coarse reddish yellow (5YR 6/6–6/8) fabric, grey at core, with frequent schist and hard white inclusions. Flat disc with knob handle, slightly hollowed on top. Decorated with concentric ridges. LM IIIC.

K9.11   Pithos (FIG. 3.5). Max. pres. H. 17.2; D. rim est. 30; D. base 23. Large fragment (eight sherds) from rim and upper body, entire base in single fragment, and eight other fragments. 90% of rim and upper body preserved, with both handles, and entire base; missing centre of body. Coarse red (2.5YR 5/8) fabric with infrequent large (2 mm) and sand-sized inclusions of red phyllites, some spongy grey, some hard red, hard black, and frequent hard white angular inclusions. Burned patches. Sampled KAR 06/77. Flat base with ledge. Ridge at upper handle attachment. Plain band at lower handle attachment, finger impressions on ridge; dint at base of handles. LM IIIC.

Room K 11

This small room was added on to Room K 9, possibly at the same time as K 14. The notebook records the following pottery: pithoi and pithoid jars, dishes, jugs, and tripods, a fragment of a shoulder with a double groove, and a fine miniature tumbler, perhaps the tiny base preserved in one of the boxes. Two small krater fragments, one with loops and an S-pattern, were found in one of the boxes, but were not catalogued. The lid pictured in Seiradaki was missing.[73] Objects were few: a fragment of yellow sandstone with a carved ridge (211), one cylindrical (277) and one biconical (212) terracotta spindle whorl, and a lead ferrule (372) were all that was found.

Of the pottery, most of the fine deep bowls or cups and kylikes are in small fragments and may represent earlier material discarded in the floor. The quirk pattern on **K11.1** certainly appears early at the site. The hatched circle of **K11.2** finds parallels in Khania.[74] The decoration on the kylix also resembles that on a similar vessel from Khania.[75] The fragment of a jar or stirrup jar with wavy line (**K11.11**) is also probably an earlier piece; similar fragments abound on the site, often in dumps of earlier material.[76] The two jugs (**K11.4–5**) are nearly complete and were probably part of the floor deposit. They are rather similar in shape, although **K11.5** is less globular and has a wider mouth; it may have a moustache or scroll design on the shoulder. Parallels for **K11.4** can be found in LH IIIC on the mainland.[77] The jar and two cooking jugs also were probably on the floor. The jar has the knobbed decoration that was so popular at Karphi. The cooking jugs tell us little except that cooking may have been a function of the room.

Pottery Catalogue: K 11

Fine Wares

K11.1   Deep bowl or cup (FIG. 3.8). D. rim est. 8. Single fragment from rim. Fine, hard, reddish yellow (7.5YR 7/6) fabric. Thick, creamy, very pale brown (10YR 8/2) slip. Black paint. Imported? Running quirk. LM IIIC early.

K11.2   Deep bowl or cup (FIG. 3.8). Max. pres. H. 3.7. Single fragment from rim. Fine, soft, reddish yellow (7.5YR 7/6) fabric. Very pale brown (10YR 8/3) slip. Red (10R 4/8) paint. Worn surfaces. Hatched circular pattern and multiple stems. LM IIIC early.

K11.3   Kylix (FIG. 3.8). Max. pres. H. (rim fragment) 3, (body fragment) 6.5. Two fragments, one from rim, the other from body. Fine, soft, very pale brown (10YR 8/3) fabric and slip. Worn black paint. Vertical strokes below rim, filled curvilinear pattern below carination. LM IIIC.

K11.4   Jug (PLATE 9 a, FIG. 3.8). H. 17.7 (with handle 18.6); D. base 6; D. rim 5.7. Restored from 16 fragments. 60% preserved,

including full profile; missing 40% of rim, lower part of handle, half of body. Very soft, fine, very pale brown (10YR 7/3) fabric with tiny black inclusions. Very worn surfaces. Some decoration, but too worn to determine. Interior band on rim. Publication: Seiradaki, fig. 9.7; pl. 5d, bottom, second from left (in caption, identified as from K 57, but next jug to the right is from K 57, but mislabelled K 11). LM IIIC.

K11.5   Jug (PLATE 9 b, FIG. 3.8). H. 19; D. base 7.6. Mended from 16 fragments. 90% preserved, including full profile; missing part of neck and rim. Medium-coarse brown (10YR 5/3) fabric, with many sharp angular black and white inclusions. Worn black paint. Surfaces worn and pocked. Burned on one side below handle. Bands on lower body; curvilinear pattern on shoulder. Curved loop on handle. Label may read K II or K 11. LM IIIC.

Coarse Wares

K11.6   Thelastron (PLATE 9 c, FIG. 3.8). Max. pres. H. 14.8; D. base 7; D. rim 8. Restored. Single fragment, preserving 90% of vessel; spout, handle, and part of rim missing. Coarse red (2.5YR 5/6) fabric, with frequent grey and hard white angular inclusions. Greenish blue (5BG 4/1) and warped as if misfired. Very irregular in shape. Publication: Seiradaki, fig. 10.2 (mislabelled as from K 23) pl. 5d, top right. LM IIIC.

K11.7   Jug or amphora (FIG. 3.8). Max. pres. H. 7. Single fragment from handle. Coarse, soft, yellow (10YR 8/6) to brownish yellow (10YR 6/6) fabric with infrequent hard black and white inclusions. Black paint. Round vertical handle, twisted. LM IIIC.

K11.8   Jar (FIG. 3.8). H. est. 16; D. base 9; D. rim est. 10.2. Once mended from numerous fragments; 13 sherds from base, six from rim, and 14 non-joining. 30% preserved, including entire base and 35% of rim and upper body. Coarse red (2.5YR 5/8) fabric with phyllites and some angular white inclusions. Traces of creamy very pale brown (10YR 8/4) slip. Decorated with small knobs on shoulder. LM IIIC.

K11.9   Cooking jug (FIG. 3.8). H. est. 13; D. base 9; D. rim 9–10. Two large fragments from base (four sherds) and rim and upper body (11 sherds); ten additional fragments. 50% preserved, including handle attachment; missing full profile, handle. Coarse reddish yellow (5YR 6/8) fabric with grey (5Y5/1) core and frequent schist inclusions, 1–3 mm. Burned. LM IIIC.

K11.10   Cooking jug (FIG. 3.8). Max. pres. H. 8.6. Three joining fragments from body, including handle. Coarse reddish yellow (5YR 6/6) fabric with frequent schist and mica inclusions, 1–2 mm. Exterior burned all over. Not labelled but found with material from K 11. LM IIIC.

K11.11   Stirrup jar (FIG. 3.8). Th. 1.0. Single body fragment. Coarse reddish yellow (7.5YR 8/6) fabric with frequent hard black and white inclusions (1–2 mm). Very pale brown (10YR 8/3) slip. Worn red (10R 4/8) paint. Very worn surfaces. Decorated with wavy line or debased octopus pattern. LM IIIC.

---

73   Seiradaki, fig. 19.5; also shown in Young 1938, 235, fig. 12, right, bottom, second from left.

74   *Khania II*, 104, pl. 36.84-P 0689 (LM IIIB2/C), although this example has cross hatching.

75   *Khania II*, pl. 54.77-P 0179.

76   Day 2005, 434.

77   Mountjoy 1986, 165, fig. 209 (FS 106) (Perati, LH IIIC Middle); *RMDP*, 948, fig. 386.28 (Naxos, LH IIIC Middle).

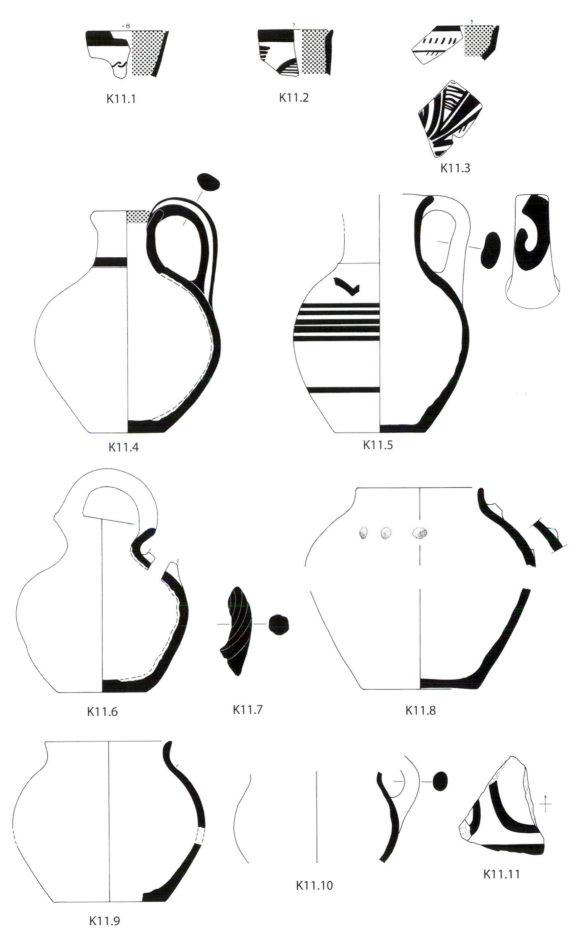

K11.1

K11.2

K11.3

K11.4

K11.5

K11.6

K11.7

K11.8

K11.9

K11.10

K11.11

*Fig. 3.8. Great House, pottery from K 11 (**K11.1–11**). Scale 1:3.*

Room K 12

This room was thought to be a cellar, only reached from the roof above by a trap door, as there were no doors into the room. Benches lay on the north and east. The room was constructed over the rubbish dump, which continued also under K 13 and K 17; the same rubbish dump may have run under K 70 and K 72. Although the material from the dump was not stratigraphically distinguished from that on or above the floors, the excavators did keep the sherds separate, and this material was found in different compartments of one of the boxes. There were two groups, one labelled 'above the floor', the other 'below the level of the walls to 0.70'. These probably correspond to the levels mentioned in the notebook as 'above 1.70' and 'below 1.70', and an accompanying sketch of the stratigraphy in the notebook supports this idea. From the level of the bottom of the outer walls, a deposit of finer sherds and bones was shown above bedrock; this no doubt represented the pottery dump, while above this level coarse sherds were reported.

Some pottery was simply labelled K 12, and it is assumed that this material came from the deposit on or above the floor of the room. In addition to the catalogued vessels, there were a few others, including a deep bowl with spiral or multiple loops, a krater with curved strokes and outlined curvilinear motif, a basin rim, a stirrup jar with a spiral, the false spout of a stirrup jar (sampled KAR 06/27), and a tripod leg decorated with a dint. The material is scrappy, and did not include many whole vessels. Most of the pottery is not closely diagnostic, although it is nearly all LM IIIC. The cup or deep bowl (**K12.2**) may be a fragment of a wavy band cup of SM date, like those at Knossos and Sybrita/Thronos.[78] It may also be an import, because of the banded rather than the usual monochrome interior; similar interior bands in pairs near rim and lower occur on mainland examples.[79] An unusual piece is the jar (**K12.8**) of micaceous fabric with ridges on the neck. Although not much of this vessel is preserved, it looks very different from the rest of the Karphi material, both in fabric and in its incised decoration. Such jars do exist in the PG period on Crete, but they also occur in the Geometric and Archaic Periods.[80] This example may be later; there is some evidence of late disturbance, possibly in the Hellenistic Period in this area (see also below under K 16).

Objects listed as coming from this room, but without any additional information about which stratum, were the following bronze objects: a sickle (213),[81] a dagger (214),[82] a saw (215), a chisel (216),[83] a nail (217), a needle (218), a fragment of decorated bronze (219), a fragment of a ring (222), and two other fragments (220). Also found were two fragments of lead (221), a globular glass bead (245), a biconical bead of faience (246), and a cylindrical terracotta spindle whorl (244). These objects may have come from the deposit above the floor, rather than the rubbish dump below.

Pottery Catalogue: K 12

Fine Wares

K12.1   Cup (FIG. 3.9). Max. pres. H. 6; D. rim 7. Three joining fragments, preserving most of profile. 75% preserved; missing base, three-quarters of rim and handle. Rather fine, sandy, very pale brown (10YR 8/4) fabric with grey (5Y 5/1) core. Dull black paint. Monochrome. LM IIIC.

K12.2   Cup or deep bowl (FIG. 3.9). Max. pres. H. 6. Single fragment from rim. Fine, soft, reddish yellow (7.5YR 8/6) fabric. Thick, creamy, very pale brown (10YR 8/3) slip. Red (10R 5/8) paint. Well-preserved surfaces. Wavy line; bands on interior. SM.

K12.3   Deep bowl or cup (FIG. 3.9). Max. pres. H. 4.4. Single fragment from body. Fine, soft, reddish yellow (7.5YR 7/6) fabric. Very pale brown (10YR 8/3) slip. Worn black paint. Worn surfaces. Decorated with rosette and upright multiple loops. LM IIIC.

K12.4   Closed vessel (FIG. 3.9). Max. pres. H. 3.6. Single fragment from body. Fine, soft, reddish yellow (7.5YR 7/6) fabric. Very pale brown (10YR 8/3) slip. Black paint worn to brown shadow. Worn surfaces. Panel motif with wavy vertical lines and scalloped vertical lines separating spirals. LM IIIC.

Coarse Wares

K12.5   Kalathos (FIG. 3.9). Max. pres. H. 9.2; D. base 7.6. Base mended from six fragments. 60% preserved, including entire base and lower body; missing upper body and rim. Coarse red (2.5YR 5/8) fabric with frequent red and grey phyllites (2–3 mm), smaller (<1 mm) black and white inclusions. Possible traces of burning inside. Groove around outside of bottom. LM IIIC.

K12.6   Kalathos (FIG. 3.9). H. 9.6–9.9; D. base 8.7; D. rim 21.6. Eight joining and two non-joining fragments preserving 75% of vessel, including full profile, entire base, much of lower body, and 25% of rim. Coarse red (2.5YR 6/8) fabric with frequent small schist and red phyllite inclusions. Sampled KAR 06/69. Groove around outside on underside of base. Ridging on interior. Two grooves on top of rim. LM IIIC.

K12.7   Kalathos (FIG. 3.9). D. rim est. 18–22. Single fragment from rim. Coarse red (10R 5/6) fabric with schist inclusions, up to 4 mm. Heavy wheel ridging on interior. LM IIIC.

K12.8   Jar (FIG. 3.9). Max. pres. H. 3.5; D. rim est. 11. Two joining fragments from rim. Coarse red (2.5YR 5/8) cooking fabric with grey (2.5YR 4/0) core; frequent phyllite and hard white inclusions, very micaceous. Exterior surface burned. Incised grooves on neck. PG–G or Hellenistic.

K12, Deposit Above Floor

This deposit, separated in the boxes and labelled 'above floor' in the notebook, is probably that simply listed as K 12 in the publication. The notebook mentions in the deposit above 1.70 m the following: a yellow pithos

---

78   Warren 1982–83, 85, fig. 60 (Knossos); D'Agata 1999, 201, fig. 14.41.5 (Sybrita/Thronos).

79   *RMDP* 185, fig. 56.427 (Asine, LH IIIC late); 956, fig. 390.56 (Naxos, LH IIIC middle).

80   Mook 1993, fig. 98. P2 99 and P2 100 (Kavousi–*Kastro*, LM IIIC–PG). See also Coldstream 1960, 162, fig. 5.31 (Geometric) and Sackett (ed.) 1992, pl. 75.H3.8, pl. 79.3 (Archaic).

81   *Karphi*, pl. 28.2.

82   *Karphi*, pl. 28.2.

83   *Karphi*, pl. 28.2.

*Fig. 3.9. Great House, pottery from K 12 floor (**K12.1–8**) and lower deposit (**K12.9–16**). Scale 1:3.*

base, an angular red pithos rim, a pithoid jar with X-pattern on a band, a fragment of a bowl in rough 'porridgy' ware, a large dish with flaring sides and pulled out lip, fragments of kylix and krater, fragments of a large buff krater with panelled decoration, and a large bottle shape in coarse ware with a small base and a round lug. Found in the box with other fragments from this deposit were a pithos fragment with raised band and an X-pattern, a fine body fragment with bands, and what looks like a modern body fragment. Unfortunately, this deposit does not offer much information about either the use of K 12 or its date.

The goblet (probably a champagne cup) (**K12.11**) is generally found early in LM IIIC.[84] The deep bowl **K12.9** has a flat raised base like examples from Kastrokephala of early LM IIIC date,[85] while the other (**K12.10**) has a genuine ring base.

Pottery Catalogue: K 12, Above Floor

Fine Wares

K12.9   Deep bowl or cup (FIG. 3.9). D. base est. 5.5. Single fragment preserving half of base. Fine, soft, reddish yellow (5YR 7/6) fabric. Very pale brown (10YR 8/4) slip. Brown to black paint. Band on base; painted on interior. LM IIIC early.

K12.10   Deep bowl or cup (FIG. 3.9). D. base est. 4.7. Single fragment from base. Fine, soft, reddish yellow (5YR 7/6) fabric. Very pale brown (10YR 8/4) slip. Traces of red (2.5YR 4/6) paint. Band at base; interior painted. LM IIIC.

K12.11   Goblet (FIG. 3.9). Max. pres. H. 3. Single fragment preserving entire stem; missing foot and body. Fine, soft, red (2.5YR 5/8) fabric; traces of worn black paint. Very worn surfaces. Short stem with circular depression on underside. Cf. **K76.39**, **K61.8**. LM IIIC early.

K12.12   Kylix (FIG. 3.9). Max. pres. H. 2.9. Single fragment preserving top of stem and bottom of bowl. Fine, soft, reddish yellow (5YR 7/6) fabric. Very pale brown (10YR 8/4) slip. Paint black on exterior, red (2.5YR 4/6) on interior. Ridge at attachment of stem and bowl. Decorated with bands. LM IIIC.

K12.13   Closed vessel (FIG. 3.9). D. base est. 7. Single fragment preserving half of base. Fine, soft, porous, very pale brown (10YR 8/4) fabric. Traces of worn black paint. String marks on bottom. Patch of burning on interior. Band at base. LM IIIC.

K12.14   Closed vessel (FIG. 3.9). D. base est. 13. Single fragment preserving 15% of base. Fine, soft reddish yellow (5YR 7/6) fabric. Red (2.5YR 4/8) paint on exterior. LM IIIC.

K12.15   Closed vessel (FIG. 3.9). D. base est. 4. Single fragment from base. Fine, soft, light red (2.5YR 6/6) fabric, with some red phyllite and small white angular inclusions. Worn surfaces. LM IIIC.

Medium-Coarse Wares

K12.16   Closed vessel (FIG. 3.9). D. base 3.6. Single fragment preserving entire base (or knob) of lid. Medium-coarse light red (2.5YR 6/6) fabric, with infrequent hard white angular inclusions and silver mica. Entire surface eroded. Small flat base with deep depression in centre. LM IIIC.

K 12, Lower Deposit

The notebook calls this deposit 'below 1.70', and the tag with the pottery reads 'below level of walls to 0.70'. The deposit included more fine ware than in the upper deposit, and the fragments were less burned. The notebook records pithoi of rounded type with projecting bases and plain bases, the usual type of jar, a tripod leg, two pedestal bases of small bowls and much pale buff pottery, including a large jar, and rims of small bowls. Uncatalogued fragments from this lower deposit included the following: a round cooking pot handle, body fragments of a greenish colour in a phyllite fabric, three medium-coarse body sherds with red bands, three rim fragments from deep bowls with rim bands, two deep bowl handles and one fragment with a handle attachment, five body fragments from

deep bowls, two rims from kraters, one handle attachment from a krater, five krater body sherds with bands and one plain body sherd, a false spout of a stirrup jar, a flat base with bands, seven body fragments with bands, and two plain body fragments. Unfortunately, there is nothing particularly diagnostic for dating in the fragments from this lower deposit. The one base of **K12.28**, raised and slightly hollowed, looks early. The Minoan flower motif, which may appear on several fragments, seems to be popular in the early LM IIIC material, or at least it is found in other deposits, like this one, which have much fine early pottery, but small and broken pieces. The pendent loops that do not hang from the rim on **K12.24** are reminiscent of those on deep bowls **K32.3**, **K71.1**, and **K106.7–8**.

Pottery Catalogue: K 12, Deposit below level of walls to 0.70

Fine Wares

K12.17   Cup (FIG. 3.10). Max. pres. H. 1.5. Single fragment from rim and handle. Fine, soft, reddish yellow (7.5YR 7/6) fabric. No traces of paint. LM IIIC.

K12.18   Deep bowl or cup (FIG. 3.10). D. rim est. 15. Single fragment from rim. Fine, soft, reddish yellow (5YR 7/6) fabric. Very pale brown (10YR 8/4) slip. Red (2.5YR 4/6) paint. Well-preserved surfaces. Flower motif and comb pattern; reserved band on interior of lip. LM IIIC early.

K12.19   Deep bowl or cup (FIG. 3.10). D. rim est. 16. Single fragment from rim. Fine very pale brown (10YR 8/4) and slip (slightly grey). Black paint. Fringed decoration or Minoan flower. LM IIIC early (?).

K12.20   Deep bowl or cup (FIG. 3.10). Max. pres. H. 2.6. Single fragment from rim. Fine, soft, reddish yellow (5YR 7/6) fabric. Very pale brown (10YR 8/4) slip. Worn dark brown (7.5YR 3/2) paint. Concentric arcs? LM IIIC.

K12.21   Deep bowl or cup (FIG. 3.10). D. rim est. 17. Single fragment from rim. Fine, soft reddish yellow (5YR 7/6) fabric. Very pale brown (10YR 8/4) slip. Yellowish red (5YR 4/6) paint. Outlined oblique leaf pattern. LM IIIC.

K12.22   Deep bowl or cup (FIG. 3.10). D. rim est. 17. Single fragment from rim. Fine, soft, reddish yellow (5YR 7/6) fabric. Very pale brown (10YR 8/4) slip. Worn dark reddish brown (5YR 3/4) paint. Decoration too worn to make out. LM IIIC.

K12.23   Deep bowl or cup (FIG. 3.10). Max. pres. H. 3.2. Single fragment from rim. Fine, soft, reddish yellow (5YR 7/6) fabric. Very pale brown (10YR 8/4) slip. Red (2.5YR 4/8) paint. Very worn surfaces. Multiple vertical strokes, Minoan flower, or fringe. LM IIIC.

K12.24   Deep bowl or cup (FIG. 3.10). D. rim est. 14. Single fragment from rim. Fine, soft, very pale brown (10YR 8/4) fabric and slip. Dark red (2.5YR 3/6) paint. Multiple pendent loops. LM IIIC.

---

84   See Day and Snyder 2004, 68, fig.5.6.2–3. An example can also be found at Kastri; see *Kastri*, 289, fig. 10b, c; 295, fig. 15.P 22.

85   Kanta and Karetsou 2003, 153, fig. 3a, c.

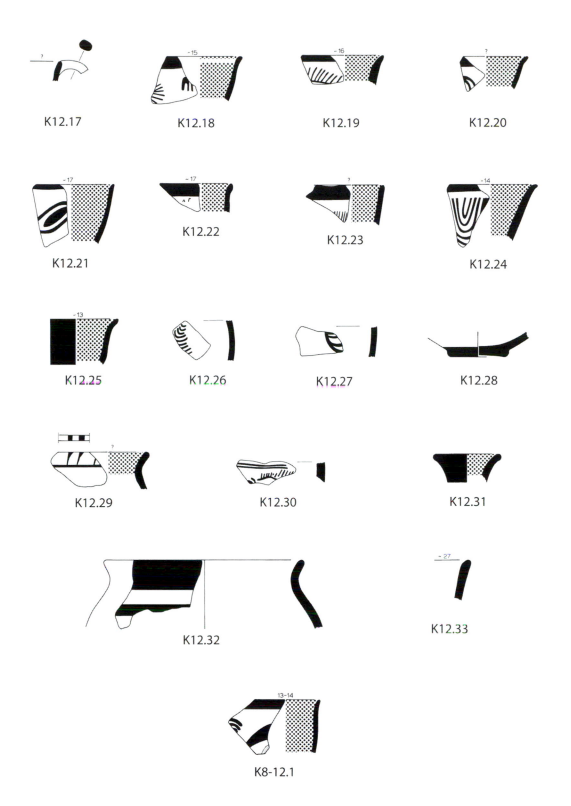

*Fig. 3.10. Great House, pottery from K 12 lowest deposit (**K12.17–33**) and K 8-12 (**K8-12.1**). Scale 1:3.*

K12.25 Deep bowl or cup (FIG. 3.10). D. rim est. 13. Single fragment from rim. Fine, soft, very pale brown (10YR 8/4) fabric. Dark brown (7.5YR 3/2) paint. Blob or monochrome. LM IIIC.

K12.26 Deep bowl or cup (FIG. 3.10). Max. pres. H. 3.2. Single body fragment. Fine, soft, reddish yellow (7.5YR 7/6) fabric. Very pale brown (10YR 8/4) slip. Black paint. Worn surfaces. Multiple concentric arcs. Interior coated. LM IIIC.

K12.27 Deep bowl or cup (FIG. 3.10). Max. pres. H. 2.5. Single fragment from body. Fine, soft, reddish yellow (5YR 7/6) fabric. Very pale brown (10YR 8/4) slip. Worn red (2.5YR 4/6) paint. Hatched oval or 'tennis racquet'. LM IIIC.

K12.28 Deep bowl or cup (FIG. 3.10). D. base 5. Single fragment from base. Fine, soft, reddish yellow (5YR 7/6) fabric. Very pale brown (10YR 8/4) slip. Red (2.5YR 4/8) paint. Band at base. LM IIIC.

K12.29   Jar (FIG. 3.10). Max. pres. H. 3. Single fragment from rim. Fine, soft, reddish yellow (5YR 7/6) fabric, with some inclusions. Very pale brown (10YR 8/4) slip. Dark reddish brown (2.5YR 3/4) paint. Strokes on top of rim. LM IIIC.

K12.30   Closed vessel (FIG. 3.10). Max. pres. H. 1.5. Single worn body fragment. Fine, soft, reddish yellow (7.5YR 7/6) fabric. Very pale brown (10YR 8/4) slip. Dark reddish brown (5YR 3/4) paint. Fringed decoration. LM IIIC.

Medium-Coarse Wares

K12.31   Jug (FIG. 3.10). D. rim est. 5.5. Single fragment from rim. Medium-coarse reddish yellow (5YR 7/6) fabric. Very dark grey (5YR 3/1) paint. LM IIIC.

K12.32   Jar (FIG. 3.10). D. rim est. 16. Two joining fragments from rim. Medium-coarse reddish yellow (5YR 7/6) fabric. Very pale brown (10YR 8/4) slip. Black to dark reddish brown (5YR 3/2) paint. Bands on neck and shoulder. LM IIIC.

Coarse Wares

K12.33   Krater (FIG. 3.10). D. rim est. 27. Single fragment from rim. Coarse reddish yellow (5YR 7/6) fabric with red phyllites. LM IIIC.

K 8 and K 12 (Cleaning)

No information was given on this cleaning of the rooms of the Great House, which produced the following fragment.

K8–12.1   Deep bowl or cup (FIG. 3.10). D. rim est. 13–14. Single fragment from rim. Fine, rather hard, reddish yellow (7.5YR 7/6) fabric. Very pale brown (10YR 8/3) slip. Black paint worn to brown; interior paint streaky, but well-preserved; exterior fugitive. Curvilinear motif with concentric multiple arcs. LM IIIC.

Room K 13

K 13 was interpreted as another cellar, like K 12, reached by a ladder from above; it was connected to K 12 but lacked doorways from other rooms.[86] Like K 12, this room also had a bench on the north side, as well as an outcrop of rock in the northwest corner. Also like K 12 and K 17, it was built over a rubbish dump. The notebook records the following pottery from this room: fragments from a few pithoi of the usual types, fragments of speckled green ware with red wash, kalathoi of common type, fragments of buff kraters, small bowls, and tripod legs. Little pottery was preserved well enough to be catalogued, but the boxes produced a pithoid jar rim and a possible neck of a flask. One jar of Type 9 published by Seiradaki as from this room could not be located.[87] The identification of the find spot may be an error, as the profile looks like the larnax rim from K 81–82.

Pottery Catalogue: K 13

Coarse Wares

K13.1   Pithos (PLATE 9 *d*). Single fragment from body. Coarse, medium-hard, red (2.5YR 5/8) fabric with hard angular white and black inclusions, many voids. Decorated with serpentine rope pattern and band with wide oblique slashes in alternating directions. LM IIIC.

Room 14

K 14 was also thought to be a storeroom. The excavators suggested that it was constructed in the second phase of the building's use, along with K 11.[88] It may have been entered from K 9 by ladder, as there were no doorways, only a window or hatch on the south wall that may have led up to K 14.

The notebook lists the following pottery of coarse ware, mostly reddish in colour: pithos sherds with chevrons and vertically slashed rope patterns; pithoid jars; five tripods; open dishes, one with vertical sides and a horizontal handle at rim. There was a good deal of gritty buff ware mostly from jars with handle(s) starting from the rim, but also including a pyxis (**K14.1**) and a sherd from a circular lid with slashed rope design. A point of a steatite implement (223) and fragments of wood (224) also came from the room.

The two nearly complete vessels from the room are a decorated pyxis (**K14.1**) with pleonastic decoration of the fringed style that includes horns of consecration, and a standard LM IIIC tripod (**K14.2**), with numerous parallels on Crete of LM IIIC date.[89]

Pottery Catalogue: K 14

Fine Wares

K14.1   Pyxis (PLATE 9 *e–f*, FIG. 3.11). H. 10.2; D. base 11; D. rim 7. Restored from 17 fragments. 90% preserved; missing pieces of rim and upper body. Fine, soft, reddish yellow (5YR 7/6) fabric with occasional small red and brown inclusions. Pink (7.5YR 8/4) slip. Red (2.5YR 3/6) paint. Some surface pitting may indicate inclusions that dropped or burned out. Well-preserved surfaces. No traces of burning. Panelled decoration. Side A: horns of consecration with central outlined rib and panels of vertical chevrons; filler arcs. Side B: two panels of vertical chevrons outlined with bands and scalloped edge; vertical bulbous motif, outlined and fringed. Publication: *Karphi,* pl. 24.6, right; Seiradaki, pl. 7c, second from left; figs 12.2, 23b and c. For shape and pleonastic decoration, cf. Andreadaki-Vlasaki and Papadopoulou 2007, 51, fig. 8.34 (Khamalevri, Phase II). LM IIIC early.

Coarse Wares

K14.2   Tripod cooking pot (PLATE 9 *g*, FIG. 3.11). H. 25; D. rim 16.8. Restored from about 42 fragments; some pieces have fallen off. 75% preserved, including full profile, all three legs, one handle; missing one handle, fragments of rim and body. Coarse reddish brown (2.5YR 4/4) fabric with frequent grey phyllites, white sand-sized, and hard white angular inclusions (1–3 mm); many voids where inclusions dropped or burned out. Surface mottled; burned patches all over, interior and exterior. Legs round in section; dint at top of each leg. Publication: Seiradaki, pl. 2d, fig. 4.1. LM IIIC.

---

86   *Karphi,* 77.
87   Seiradaki, fig. 3.9.
88   *Karphi,* 77.
89   *Kastri,* 297, fig. 17.P20; Warren 1982–83, 84, fig. 53 (Knossos); Prokopiou 1997, 376, fig. 17a (Sybrita/Thronos); *Khania II,* pl. 45.77-P 1178; Andreadaki-Vlasaki and Papadopoulou 2007, 45, fig. 2.15 (Khamalevri, Phase I); Tsipopoulou 2004, 113, fig. 8.7.95-397 (Khalasmenos).

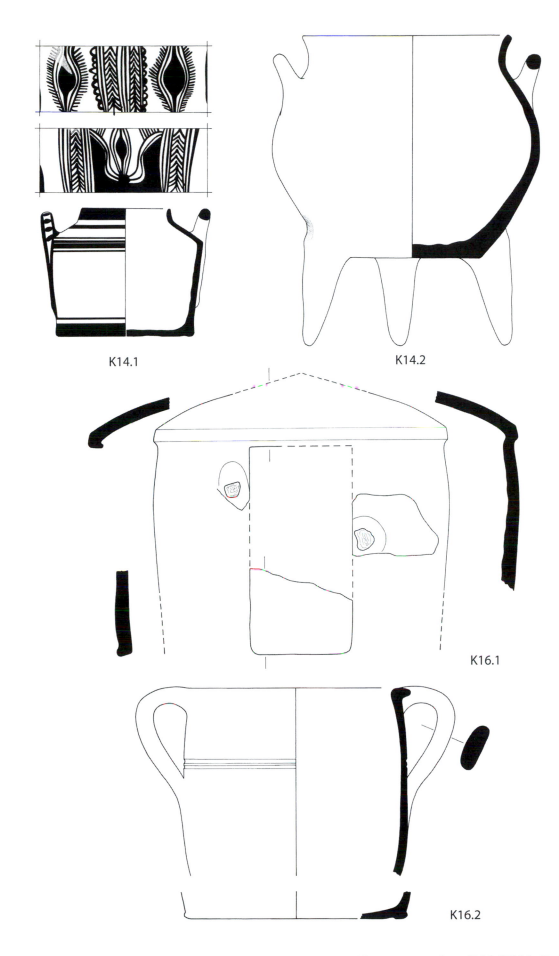

K14.1

K14.2

K16.1

K16.2

*Fig. 3.11. Great House, pottery from K 14 (**K14.1–2**) and Great House Shrine, pottery from K 16 (**K16.1–2**). Scale 1:3.*

The Great House Shrine (K 15–18)

There was no obvious connection between these rooms and those comprising the Great House, although they are oriented along the same lines. This was a building of a single large room (K 16-17) entered through a narrow corridor (K 15) with a trapezoidal room (K 18) to the north and east that has no connection with either K 16-17 or K 38–39. K 70 may have belonged with the building at some point. K 17 was built over the same rubbish tip that ran under K 12 and K 13, as well as under K 70 and K 72. A good deal of religious material was found in this vicinity, both inside K 16 and outside in K 70, K 72, and K 8–14–15. It would appear, then, that K 15–18 was a shrine, but it is not clear whether the religious material belonged to the later stages of the settlement or whether it represents a dump of material from an earlier shrine either on the site or brought from elsewhere. There seem to be three possibilities about this shrine in K 15–18. The first is that all the ritual material found throughout this area may have come from the dump underneath or tumbled down the slope from the Temple and have nothing to do with Rooms K 15–18. The second explanation is that this material came from a shrine in K 15–18. The third possibility is that a shrine in K 15–18 was built on top of an earlier ritual deposit. The last explanation would account for the apparent presence of ritual equipment both below and above the floors of rooms. There is also evidence for later activity, long after the abandonment of the settlement, probably in the Hellenistic period.

Room K 15

K 15 was an open, paved and stepped passage leading up into K 16-17. Pottery listed in the notebook from this area included pithoi decorated with incised cross hatching, chevron, multiple bands of finger impressions, and serpentine rope slashed patterns. Also recorded are tripods, dishes mostly with flat bases, some buff gritty wares including handles as from K 14, and fine kylix stems and part of a stirrup jar. No pottery was catalogued, but a huge handle was found in one of the boxes from K 15. Objects from the room included a terracotta loomweight (225), two boar's tusks (226), and the horn of a bull (247).

Outside Rooms K 8–14–15

Somewhere in this area was found a fragment from the face of a terracotta goddess figure (PLATE 9 h).[90]

Room K 16

Room K 16-17 was labelled a large open court. The division between the two rooms was not distinct, and it may have been a buttress, or as Wallace suggests, the remains of an earlier wall.[91] The notebook mentions that K 17 was built on top of a rubbish tip, but in the publication, the rubbish tip is said to have run under only K 12 and K 13. The notebook lists the following pottery from K 16: at least four pithoi decorated with finger impressions, rope, double row of dinted rope, and chevron patterns; five pithoid jars, two in gritty buff, the others in red ware; tripods; dishes, one pulled in at rim with holes on either side near base; kalathoi; part of a large coarse stirrup vase; sherds of a vase in red clay apparently with slits cut out near base (**K16.1**); jugs or jars in sandy orange clay, and a sherd from a heavy tripod lamp. The goblet stem illustrated in Seiradaki was found in one of the boxes but was not catalogued; it is probably Hellenistic in date.[92] Objects included fragments of figures of goddesses and other ritual objects, a terracotta figurine (228),[93] a terracotta spool, and fragments of a conch shell (227).

Not much pottery is preserved from this part of the room. The hut urn (**K16.1**) is unusual because of its size, and is the largest known from the site. The two-handled jar (**K16.2**) and the goblet stem (identified as a krater base by Seiradaki) are probably Hellenistic in date and show later activity in the area in that period. The jar may in fact represent two vessels of identical fabric, as the base does not seem to fit the profile of the rim and handles. Although no precise parallel could be found, the general shape seems similar to pottery of the Hellenistic period.[94]

Pottery Catalogue: K 16

Coarse Wares

K16.1   Hut urn (PLATE 10 *a*, FIG. 3.11). Max. pres. H. 16. Three large fragments (22 sherds). 10% (?) preserved, including top of doorway, fragments of two sides, part of roof, one handle attachment on each side, and assorted body fragments; also preserved are parts of inserted cut-out doorway. Missing base, most of body, much of roof, and top of door cutout. Coarse red (2.5YR 5/6) fabric with frequent large (1–2 mm) schist and some hard white inclusions. Surface mottled black and red, but not burned. Handles, probably vertical round or lugs, on either side of doorway. LM IIIC.

K16.2   Two-handled jar (FIG. 3.11). Max. pres. H. 15; D. rim 18–19; D. base 18–20. Numerous sherds making up into large rim fragment, large base fragment, and several large body fragments. Nearly complete profile can be restored. 10–20% preserved, including some of rim, one handle, and parts of a second. Base of same fabric doesn't seem to fit and may represent another vessel. Coarse reddish yellow (5YR 6/8) fabric with greenish grey (5GY 6/1–5/1) core and soft red siltstones (*c.* 2 mm), hard white inclusions, and gold mica; some schist, some hard black inclusions. Horizontal grooves just above lower handle attachment. Hellenistic?

---

90   Day 2009, 141, fig. 12.7.
91   Wallace 2005, 238.
92   Seiradaki, fig. 16.6. For similar goblet stems and bases, see Callaghan and Johnston 2001, 257, pl. 4.21.456 (mid 4th century), 262, pl. 4.22.504 (400–375 BC).
93   *Karphi*, pl. 32.4.
94   For shape, see. Sackett (ed.) 1992, pl. 100.37 (fine kantharos, Hellenistic); pl. 104.12 (50-28 A.C.) It looks late — Hellenistic or Roman — but there are no precise parallels.

Room K 17

This room was north of K 16 and separated from it by a buttress. There was, however, a lower deposit in the room (none was recorded from K 16), identified in the notebook as the same rubbish tip underlying K 12 and K 13. Fragments from two strata below the walls were kept separate in one of the boxes; both come from below the walls, the upper from 0–0.50 below the walls, the lower from 0.50–1.0 below the walls. The following pottery was listed in the notebooks from the main deposit in K 17: two pithoi, about three pithoid jars, five tripods, dishes, the neck of jar in gritty buff ware, and a tubular vessel like a pipe in gritty buff ware. Uncatalogued sherds included a krater fragment with a curvilinear motif. Many objects of bronze were found in the room, including a fragment of a blade (230), a sickle (232),[95] an awl (236),[96] a fragment of a saw (237), and a nail (238). Other objects included a stone bead (231), a worked piece of steatite (268), a terracotta horn from a figurine (233), a tubular cult object, two cylindrical terracotta spindle whorls (234, 235), and a pierced boar's tusk (231).

There was also some material found in the boxes labelled K 16-17 or K 16–18. Some of these fragments are catalogued below, but also included was a krater fragment with a floral motif, a possible snake tube fragment, and a coarse handle.

The miniature tankard (**K17.1**) can be paralleled by larger LM IIIC examples.[97] The krater (**K17.2**), with its good LM IIIC decorative scheme of filling angles and between bands is similar to a krater from Knossos of early LM IIIC date.[98]

Pottery Catalogue: K 17

Fine Wares

K17.1   Miniature tankard (FIG. 3.12). H. 5.6; D. base 5.2; D. rim 7.4. Nearly complete; missing most of handle and end of spout. Fine, soft, yellow (10YR 7/6) fabric with fine black inclusions and small voids. Very pale brown (10YR 8/4) slip. Black paint. Surfaces very worn. Vertical band with scallops on either side between vertical bands. Publication: Seiradaki, fig. 13.3. LM IIIC.

K17.2   Krater (FIG. 3.12). D. rim est. 20. Single fragment from rim. Fine, soft, light red (2.5YR 6/8) fabric with grey core. Very pale brown (10YR 8/4) slip. Dark red (2.5YR 3/6) paint. Worn surfaces. Multiple curvilinear motifs with multiple arc fillers. LM IIIC early.

K 17, Below Walls 0–0.50

The notebook reports more fine ware than usual in this layer, but the sherds were very small and broken. The coarse ware included tripod dishes and jars. In addition to the catalogued pottery, the boxes also contained a handle and a plain body fragment from deep bowls, a double handle, a handle attachment on a coarse jar, a possible thelastron spout, a burned coarse body sherd of 'oatmeal' ware, and a body sherd of phyllite fabric.

The pottery is scrappy and not very diagnostic. **K17.4** has a crosshatched pattern within multiple loops,

a motif which can be found on a number of LM IIIC pots. The low foot of **K17.3** may indicate an early date. The hatched oval on the stirrup jar is also a common LM IIIC motif. The pithoid jar or basin and tripod leg are good LM IIIC shapes.

Pottery Catalogue: K 17, Deposit Below Walls, 0–0.50

Fine Wares

K17.3   Deep bowl or cup (FIG. 3.12). D. base est. 5.5. Single fragment preserving 25% of base. Fine, soft, red (2.5YR 5/8) fabric. LM IIIC.

K17.4   Deep bowl or cup (FIG. 3.12). Max. pres. H. 6. Single fragment from body. Fine reddish yellow (5YR 7/6) fabric. Very pale brown (10YR 8/4) slip. Reddish brown (5YR 4/4) to yellowish red (5YR 4/6) paint. Crosshatched lozenge and multiple arcs. LM IIIC.

K17.5   Stirrup jar or jug (FIG. 3.12). Max. pres. H. 3.6. Single body fragment. Fine reddish yellow (5YR 7/6) fabric. Very pale brown (10YR 8/4) slip. Shadow of paint. Hatched loop or tennis racquet above hatched motif. LM IIIC.

Medium-Coarse Wares

K17.6   Jar (FIG. 3.12). D. rim est. 21. Single fragment from rim. Medium-coarse, light red (2.5YR 6/6) fabric with small phyllites, some hard black and white inclusions, and gold mica. Band on rim on exterior and interior. LM IIIC.

K17.7   Jug (FIG. 3.12). D. rim est. 9. Single fragment from rim and handle. Medium-coarse reddish yellow (5YR 7/6) fabric with the consistency of oatmeal, with grey phyllites, some hard black and white inclusions, and gold mica. Very pale brown (10YR 8/3) slip. Black paint. LM IIIC.

Coarse Wares

K17.8   Pithoid jar (FIG. 3.12). D. rim est. 34. Single fragment from rim. Coarse grey (7.5YR 5/0) fabric with frequent hard white inclusions; totally burned. LM IIIC.

K17.9   Tripod cooking pot (FIG. 3.12). Max. pres. H. 5. Single fragment from top of leg. Coarse yellowish red (5YR 5/6) fabric with phyllites and some silver mica. Burned. Dint at top of leg where joins body. LM IIIC.

K 17, Lower Deposit, 0.50–1.00 Below Walls

According to the notebook, this stratum was identical to that above, except there were no obvious pithos sherds. Part of a red painted 'skyphos' joined a sherd from the floor level. Mention was also made in the notebook of a lower level in K 16 and K 17, which was the same as the other two strata; the base of a ribbed cylindrical cup of MM date (**K17.10**) came from this lowest deposit. A rather large amount of material was kept separate from this lower deposit in K 17 and was found in a compartment in one of the boxes. Many pieces were not catalogued. Of these, fine wares

---

95   *Karphi*, pl. 28.2.
96   *Karphi*, pl. 29.1.
97   Kanta 1980, 172, fig. 67.4 (Myrsini); Catling 1968, 127, fig. 8.36.
98   Warren 2007, 340, fig. 5. P1917 (Stage II).

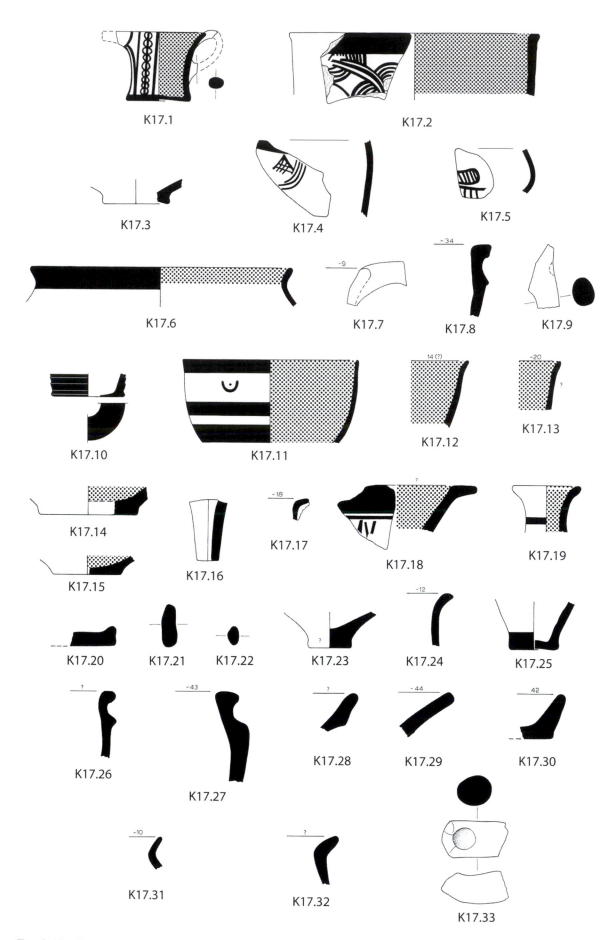

Fig. 3.12. Great House Shrine, pottery from K 17 (**K17.1–2**), K 17 lower deposit (**K17.3–9**), and K 17 lowest deposit (**K17.10–33**). Scale 1:3.

included a fragment of a monochrome deep bowl, two deep bowl rims with bands, two deep bowl handles and three body sherds with handle attachments, three body fragments from deep bowls with bands, two krater fragments, one with a curvilinear motif, and a spout attachment from a thelastron. Coarse wares included a spout fragment from a stirrup jar, the handle of a cooking jug, and a fragment of a jug or amphora in phyllite fabric.

Unfortunately, the catalogued pottery from this deposit is not closely diagnostic. The ribbed cylindrical cup (**K17.10**) is clearly MM II in date, belonging to the period when the peak sanctuary was in use. The rest of the material is LM IIIC, and none of it has to be particularly late. The deep bowls lack the raised and hollowed bases found on later examples; the flat bases can be paralleled by some from Kastrokephala.[99] Of great interest is the fragment of a plaque, which suggests that ritual material was being dumped in the area. This information accords well with the cult equipment in K 70, K 72, and K 32, all of which may have been from the same rubbish pit; the cult equipment from K 38 might also have come from the same dump. This material could have been brought from anywhere, but it is interesting that K 16-17 may also have been in use as a shrine of the goddess with upraised arms later on. It is possible that this building was used for ritual from its construction, and that the cult equipment found in the rubbish pit came from a cleaning up of an earlier phase of the shrine. It might also have come from another location, however.

Pottery Catalogue: K 17, Lower Deposit Below Walls, 0.50–1.0

Fine Wares

K17.10   Cup or tumbler (FIG. 3.12). D. base est. 6. Single fragment from base. Fine, soft, very pale brown (10YR 8/4) fabric. Thick black paint. Thin, flat base, nearly cylindrical sides. Ribbed. MM II.

K17.11   Deep bowl or cup (FIG. 3.12). D. rim est. 14. Three joining fragments from rim. Fine, soft, reddish yellow (5YR 7/6) fabric. Very pale brown (10YR 8/4) slip. Black crackled paint worn to shadow on exterior. Dotted loop between bands. LM IIIC.

K17.12   Deep bowl or cup (FIG. 3.12). D. rim est. 14. Single fragment from rim. Fine, soft, reddish yellow (7.5YR 7/6) fabric. Very pale brown (10YR 8/4) slip. Very worn black paint. Decoration too worn to determine. LM IIIC.

K17.13   Deep bowl or cup (FIG. 3.12). D. rim est. 20. Single fragment from rim. Fine, soft, very pale brown (10YR 8/4) fabric. Crackled black paint. Worn surfaces. Decoration on exterior, but worn. LM IIIC.

K17.14   Deep bowl or cup (FIG. 3.12). D. base est. 8. Single fragment from base. Fine, soft, reddish yellow (7.5YR 7/6) fabric. Dusky red (2.5YR 3/2) paint. Worn surfaces. LM IIIC.

K17.15   Deep bowl or cup (FIG. 3.12). D. base est. 5.5. Single fragment from base. Fine, soft, reddish yellow (7.5YR 7/6) fabric. Very pale brown (10YR 8/4) slip. Worn black paint. LM IIIC.

K17.16   Kylix or rhyton (FIG. 3.12). Max. pres. H. 4.6. Single fragment from stem. Fine, soft, reddish yellow (5YR 7/6) fabric, grey at core. Surfaces almost entirely gone. Pierced stem. LM IIIC.

K17.17   Shallow bowl (FIG. 3.12). D. rim est. 18. Single fragment from rim. Fine, soft, reddish yellow (5YR 7/6) fabric. Very pale brown (10YR 8/4) slip. Black paint. Traces of horizontal handle at rim. LM IIIC.

K17.18   Kalathos (FIG. 3.12). Max. pres. H. 3.8. Single fragment from rim. Fine, soft, reddish yellow (7.5YR 7/6) fabric. Very pale brown (10YR 8/4) slip. Dark reddish brown (5YR 3/3) paint, very worn. Decorated with zigzags. LM IIIC.

K17.19   Juglet or stirrup jar (FIG. 3.12). D. rim est. 5.5. Single fragment preserving full profile of rim and neck. Fine, soft, reddish yellow (7.5YR 7/6) fabric. Very pale brown (10YR 8/4) slip. Worn black paint. Possibly from a jug or the spout of a stirrup jar. Band on neck, reserved band on interior. LM IIIC.

K17.20   Plaque (FIG. 3.12). W. 1.5; Th 1.2. Single fragment from edge. Fine, soft, reddish yellow (7.5YR 7/6) fabric, very chalky and worn. Flat, with slightly raised edge. LM IIIC.

K17.21   Jug (FIG. 3.12). W. 3.4; Th. 1.2. Single fragment of a handle. Fine, soft, reddish yellow (5YR 7/6) fabric. Very pale brown (10YR 8/4) slip. Flat handle. LM IIIC.

K17.22   Jug (FIG. 3.12). W. 1.5; Th. 1.0. Single fragment from handle of jug. Fine, soft, reddish yellow (7.5YR 7/6) fabric. Elliptical handle. LM IIIC.

Medium-Coarse Wares

K17.23   Closed vessel (FIG. 3.12). D. base 3.5. Single fragment preserving entire base. Medium-coarse reddish yellow (5YR 7/6) fabric with infrequent small (1–2 mm) red phyllites. Small raised base from a jug? Possibly once decorated, but too worn to tell. LM IIIC.

Coarse Wares

K17.24   Jar (FIG. 3.12). D. rim est. 12. Single fragment from rim. Coarse reddish yellow (5YR 6/8) fabric with frequent red phyllites, some hard black and white inclusions, and gold mica. Very pale brown (10YR 8/4) slip. No trace of decoration, but slip suggests it was decorated. LM IIIC.

K17.25   Closed vessel (FIG. 3.12). D. base 4. Single fragment preserving entire base. Coarse, fairly soft, red (2.5YR 6/8) fabric with phyllites and hard white inclusions. Dull black paint. Small, flat base, probably from a jug. Band at base. LM IIIC.

K17.26   Pithoid jar (FIG. 3.12). Max. pres. H. 5.3. Single fragment from rim. Coarse red (2.5YR 5/6) fabric with frequent phyllites, hard dark grey and hard white inclusions, and some white carbonates. Black paint? Burned dark grey on rim. Possibly painted. LM IIIC.

K17.27   Pithoid jar (FIG. 3.12). D. rim 43.6. Single fragment from rim. Coarse light red (2.5YR 6/8) fabric with frequent red phyllites, some hard white inclusions, and gold mica. Could be either a deep jar or a shallower basin or lekane. LM IIIC.

K17.28   Cooking dish (FIG. 3.12). Max. pres. H. 3. Single fragment from rim. Coarse yellowish red (5YR 4/6) fabric with frequent phyllite inclusions. Burned on exterior. LM IIIC.

K17.29   Cooking dish (FIG. 3.12). D. rim est. 44. Single fragment from rim. Coarse red (2.5YR 4/8) fabric with frequent phyllite inclusions. Friable. Mottled black and red surface. Slight ridge at beginning of base. LM IIIC.

K17.30   Cooking tray (FIG. 3.12). H. 3.5; D. rim est. 42. Single fragment from rim and base, preserving full profile. Coarse, soft, red (2.5YR 5/8) fabric with phyllite inclusions. Burned on exterior, but not burned on bottom. Base roughened as on cooking dishes. For shape, cf. *Kastri*, 296, fig. 16.P13. LM IIIC.

---

99   Kanta and Karetsou 2003, 153, fig. 3A, C, F, G.

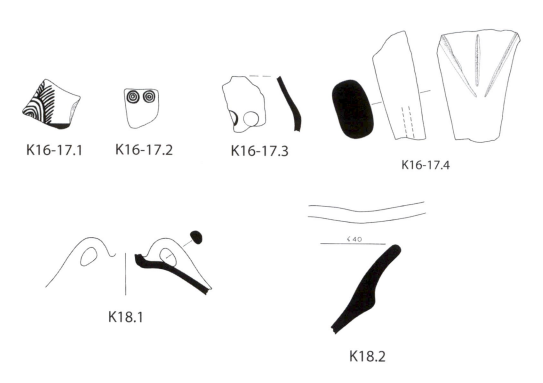

*Fig. 3.13. Great House Shrine, pottery from K 16-17 (**K16-17.1–4**) and K 18 (**K18.1–2**). Scale 1:3.*

K17.31   Cooking pot (FIG. 3.12). D. rim est. 10. Single fragment from rim. Coarse, friable, reddish yellow (5YR 6/6) fabric with hard grey and white inclusions, gold mica. Burned inside and out. LM IIIC.

K17.32   Cooking pot (FIG. 3.12). Max. pres. H. 4. Single fragment from rim. Coarse red (2.5YR 5/6) fabric with phyllite inclusions, like Kavousi Type IV. LM IIIC.

K17.33   Scuttle (FIG. 3.12). D. handle 2.2–2.7. Single fragment preserving end of handle. Coarse red (2.5YR 5/6) fabric with frequent hard black and white inclusions and gold mica. Almost round handle with dint near end. LM IIIC.

K 16-17

A number of vessels were simply labelled K 16-17, as if the excavators could not determine precisely where they came from. The stirrup jar (**K16-17.1**) is in fringed style. The other fragments are small and coarse; the closed vessel (**K16-17.2**) may be a Hellenistic intrusion, as its fabric is unlike the usual LM IIIC types for Karphi.

Pottery Catalogue: K 16-17

Fine Wares

K16-17.1   Stirrup jar (?) (FIG. 3.13). Max. pres. H. 3.8. Single body fragment. Fine, soft reddish yellow (7.5YR 7/6) fabric. Very pale brown (10YR 8/3) slip. Red (2.5YR 4/8) paint. Worn surfaces. Fringed multiple upright loops. LM IIIC.

Medium-Coarse Wares

K16-17.2   Closed vessel (FIG. 3.13). Max. pres. H. 3.1. Single body fragment. Medium-coarse light red (2.5YR 6/8) fabric with tiny white sand-sized inclusions and mica. Decorated with stamped concentric circles. Hellenistic?

K16-17.3   Small jug or closed vessel (FIG. 3.13). Max. pres. H 4.5. Single body fragment from shoulder. Medium-coarse brown (7.5YR 5/4) fabric with tiny white inclusions and mica. Decorated with impressed circles, deeper on one side than the other. LM IIIC?

Coarse Wares

K16-17.4   Tripod cooking pot (FIG. 3.13). Max. pres. H. 9. Single fragment from near top of leg. Coarse red (10R 5/6) fabric with frequent schist (2–4 mm) and some hard white inclusions. No traces of burning. Three deep slashes at top of leg. Publication: possibly pictured in Seiradaki, pl. 12b, middle, third from left. LM IIIC.

Room K 18

Room K 18 was another small unroofed 'yard' with no visible door. The excavators suggested that animals could step over the low walls.[100] If the walls were so low, however, it would not have served well as an animal enclosure, and it seems more likely that it was entered from above, like so many of the other rooms on the site. The function is not clear, nor is it certain whether the room belonged with K 15–17 or K 38–39, since it is contiguous to both. The notebook reports the following pottery from the room: at least four pithoi decorated with pinched rope, chevron and wavy rope motifs; pithoid jars; three tripods; four dishes; and the top of a large red stirrup jar. The fragment of a small tripod found in one of the boxes may be one of the tripods mentioned in the notebook. The only object found in the room was a bronze ring (679).[101]

---

100   *Karphi*, 77–8.
101   *Karphi*, 29.2.

The catalogued pottery includes the top of what appears to be a lentoid flask of an unusual shape, with both handles on the shoulder, not from the neck to the shoulder (**K18.1**); similar flasks come from Pseira and Alalakh in Syria.[102] The cooking dish (**K18.2**) is of the standard Type 6, perhaps the most common on the site; there are many parallels for it in LM IIIC contexts.[103]

Pottery Catalogue: K 18

K18.1   Lentoid flask (FIG. 3.13). Max. pres. H. 4.5. Four joining fragments preserving both handles and lower neck. Fine, soft, very pale brown (10YR 7/3) fabric. Very pale brown surface (10YR 8/2), apparently without slip. Burned? Sampled KAR 06/23. Wide, irregular shoulder, narrow neck; two round vertical handles from lower neck to shoulder. LM IIIC.

K18.2   Cooking dish (FIG. 3.13). D. rim est. <40. Five joining and one non-joining fragments from rim. 20% preserved, including much of profile; missing most of base. Coarse red (2.5YR 4/6) fabric with frequent large (4 mm) phyllite inclusions. Burned on exterior, not on interior. Rim pulled out to form rough spout; rounded base. LM IIIC.

TEMPLE ROAD EAST (ROOMS K 70, K 72)

The road labelled the Temple Road had retained much of its paving.[104] The excavators thought that it originally branched to the right from the top of K 32 and ran between the Great House and Temple Dependencies on the east and the Commercial Quarter on the west up to the Temple, bending to the left to avoid the rubbish dump that ran under K 16-17. The construction of the Baker's House, however, changed the route. At that time K 70 was built on top of the dump, continuing the lines of the walls of K 16-17. Although K 70 was never identified as part of the Great House, it may have belonged in its last phases with K 16-17. A retaining wall for the dump was visible below K 70, and there was also a heavy banking of masonry below K 71 that went with the earlier arrangement of the area.

Room K 70

Room K 70 was a cellar built over the same rubbish dump found under K 16-17. The pottery was recorded as usual, but with little fine ware. The notebook mentions coarse sherds in red and gritty buff clay from tripods or pithoid jars, fragments of dishes, perhaps all from a single vessel of Type 6. There were only a few fine sherds, probably from bowls, and no certain pithos fragments. Objects found in the space included a black stone bowl (600)[105] and a cylindrical stone pestle (426).[106] A good deal of terracotta ritual equipment was also found in this area, but whether it came from the dump beneath or belonged with the use of the later room as a back room for K 16-17 is uncertain. The notebook mentions the arms, hand, and part of the skirt of a terracotta goddess, a fragment from a flat plaque, and part of a ridged tubular vessel, possibly a snake tube. Fragments of a possible snake tube were found in one of the boxes, and another one

from uncertain context (**K.33**) may also come from here. The plaque fragment was found, but was not catalogued. Only the rounded corner was preserved, with a wide flat edge around it. It was of a coarse reddish yellow (5YR 6/8) fabric with hard black and white inclusions and gold mica.

The catalogued material seems to come from the second use of the area as a cellar room, rather than belonging to the earlier rubbish dump or the street. There was no fragmentary fine ware such as was found in other areas of the dump, only large fragments of a coarse stirrup jar (**K70.1**), an amphora (**K70.2**), and a lid (**K70.3**). The stirrup jar has the customary hole pierced through the top, and the top seems to have been made as a separate disc and added on, a trait that is customary in LM IIIC. The large amphora has rope-twisted handles, which although not usual, are found in later LM IIIC contexts, particularly at Kavousi–*Vronda*.[107] They are popular in the middle phase of LH IIIC on the mainland.[108] The disc lid is also common on the site and its popularity may be a LM IIIC trait.[109]

Pottery Catalogue: K 70

Coarse Wares

K70.1   Stirrup jar (FIG. 3.14). Max. pres. H. 20. Nine joining and 12 non-joining fragments from top. 25–30% preserved, including one handle, half of false spout, most of spout, 90% of shoulder; missing base and lower body, other handle. Coarse red (2.5YR 5/8) fabric with frequent phyllites (1–2 mm) and small (<1 mm), hard, white, angular inclusions. False spout is concave on top and pierced through centre. Spout tilted back to touch false spout. Ridge on interior where top added on as separate disc.

K70.2   Amphora (PLATE 10 *b*, FIG. 3.14). Max. pres. H. 26.1; D. rim est. 22.4. Partially restored; entire tray of fragments. 50% of neck and both handles preserved, many body fragments, part of base. Very coarse red (2.5YR 5/8) fabric, grey at core, with frequent large (2–6 mm) inclusions of red, black, grey, and hard white angular stone; more inclusions in base than neck. Very pale brown (10YR 8/3) slip. Black or red paint. Mottled red and black surfaces. Burning on interior. Surfaces very worn. Ridge at base of neck. Two rope-twisted handles from below rim to shoulder. Decorated with bands on some of body fragments; paint totally gone, but pattern visible. Publication: Seiradaki, fig. 8.4, pl. 5c, top. LM IIIC late.

K70.3   Lid (FIG. 3.14). H. 3; D. knob 3.1. Single fragment from centre of lid, preserving knob handle. Coarse, light red (10R 6/8) fabric, with frequent small (1–3 mm) phyllites and hard white angular inclusions. Underside burned. Flat disc with concave knob in centre. Oblique incised strokes around knob. LM IIIC.

102   Betancourt 1998, 49, fig. 1; Woolley 1955, 324, pl. 112.44c.
103   *Kastri*, 290, fig. 11q; Borgna 1997*b*, 197, fig. 6.3 (Phaistos); Mook 1999, pl. 110.31 (Kavousi–*Kastro*).
104   *Karphi*, 86.
105   *Karphi*, pl. 30.1.
106   *Karphi*, pl. 30.1.
107   Day, Coulson and Gesell 1986, pl. 84a.
108   Mountjoy 1986, 163, fig. 206 (Mycenae, LH IIIC middle).
109   Hallager 2000, 163.

Area K 72

Originally a rubbish dump, K 72 became a stepped street leading up to K 41, a courtyard outside the Temple. The road was a series of widely spaced steps rising to the north. The notebook records the following coarse pottery: a pithos rim of Type 9, two pithoid jars of Types 8 and 10, rims and legs of at least two large tripods of Type 3, several dishes of Types 4 and 6. There was a little fine ware, mainly from bowls, and a kylix stem. Other objects from this area included a curved bronze blade (450),[110] an oblong stone object that was not inventoried, and a fragment of a terracotta goddess, as well as animal bones. One of the boxes included the corner of a terracotta plaque of very coarse reddish yellow (5YR 6/6) fabric with large and frequent schist inclusions (2–4 mm); this thick plaque had a flat ridge running around the edge of it. The two preserved vessels were fragmentary and may have come either from the dump beneath the street or from the street itself. The stirrup jar (**K72.2**), with its disc top, hole pierced near the false spout, and linear decoration is surely late in LM IIIC. Late features include the way in which the spout touches the false spout, and the air hole also is thought to be a sign of the late LM IIIC and SM styles.[111] This example lacks the cone on the false spout that is a hallmark of the late LM IIIC stirrup jars elsewhere, but such cones are not common at Karphi, even in the later tomb material. A burned body fragment of a stirrup jar with a crosshatched triangle or lozenge found in one of the boxes and labelled K 72 floor may belong to the same vessel.

Pottery Catalogue: K 72

Fine Wares

K72.1　　Kylix (?) (FIG. 3.14). Max. pres. H. 3.4. Single fragment from body. Fine, soft, porous, reddish yellow fabric (7.5YR 7/6). Very pale brown slip (10YR 8/3). Black paint. Worn surfaces. Multiple stems, dotted curvilinear pattern. LM IIIC.

K72.2　　Stirrup jar (FIG. 3.14). Max. pres. H. 6. Large fragment (three sherds) preserving nearly complete top; missing lower body and base. Fine, soft, pink fabric (7.5YR 7/4–8/4) with tiny angular black inclusions. Pale yellow (2.5Y 8/2) slip. Black paint. Very worn surfaces. Unusual fabric; may be imported. Top made separately and added as disc with ridge of clay on interior. Slightly concave top on false spout. Spout nearly vertical, almost touches false spout. Hole pierced through body at base of false spout. Top decorated with crosshatching. Oblique strokes on handles. LM IIIC late.

TEMPLE ROAD WEST (AREA K 76)

Area K 76

This area was very confused; essentially it wound its way from street K 56 on the south to K 72 on the north. Although roofing material was found in it, the excavators believed that the roofing came from buildings to either side of it and that it was always open to the sky. It may, however, have been covered over in its last phase of use. There were two orthostats up against the south end of the west wall of this 'room'; these were the best on the site. Originally thought to be jambs of a doorway from K 56 into K 76, they were later interpreted as table legs or a framed small shrine.[112] The extreme south end of the area was paved with a good plaque floor, perhaps from the time when it was part of the street, as the pavers are level with K 56. Pendlebury thought the curved wall on the north resembled Egyptian manure tips.[113] There was much burning at the extreme north end, but this seems to be from the oven heating, not from a fire.

According to the notebook, the pottery was very fragmentary. All the usual types were represented, but there were few pithoi and many vertical handles from large jars of Types 3 and 4. Fine wares were identified as from bowls or stirrup jars, but all other types were represented except pyxides and tankards. There were two small cups in soft clay of Types 1 and 2, and part of a flat cult plaque. Sherds of a krater with a red-painted bird,[114] as well as the krater illustrated in Seiradaki,[115] were not found. A large amount of fine ware appeared in the boxes from this location. In addition to that catalogued below, there were many deep bowl fragments: seven rims with spirals, one with pendent multiple loops, one with fringe, two with fringe or flower motif, one with a panelled pattern, one with a fringe, three with arcs, and four too worn to tell. Also from deep bowls were seven handles (one with fringed motif next to it) and 25 body sherds: three decorated with spirals, five with curvilinear motifs, three with multiple loops, one with fringe, two with vertical strokes, two with multiple-outlined rays, one with drip pattern, one with a vertical element, one with dots and lines, and six with bands. There was also a fragment from the handle of a cup, a kylix with multiple-outlined rays, six kraters with lozenge chain or hatched ovals (possibly 'kissing fishes'), curvilinear motifs, filler arcs, and elaborately fringed motifs. Eleven stirrup jar fragments were found, decorated with bands, curvilinear motifs, a possible debased octopus, a U-pattern, a flower, and fringed motifs. Also found were a small fine spout, a thelastron spout attachment, a jug fragment with wavy bands, a large jug with crude spiral, a coarse jar or jug with a curvilinear motif, the vertical handle of a jug, and a cylindrical piece with ridges and pallette or horns, possibly the top of a goddess, snake tube, or altar (PLATE 9 *h*). Other objects recorded as from this space included a decorated bronze axe head

---

110　*Karphi*, pl. 28.2.
111　Hallager 2000, 146 provides the most recent discussion of the air holes in LM IIIC stirrup jars.
112　*Karphi*, 87.
113　*Karphi*, 87.
114　Seiradaki, fig. 25a.
115　Seiradaki, fig. 25d.

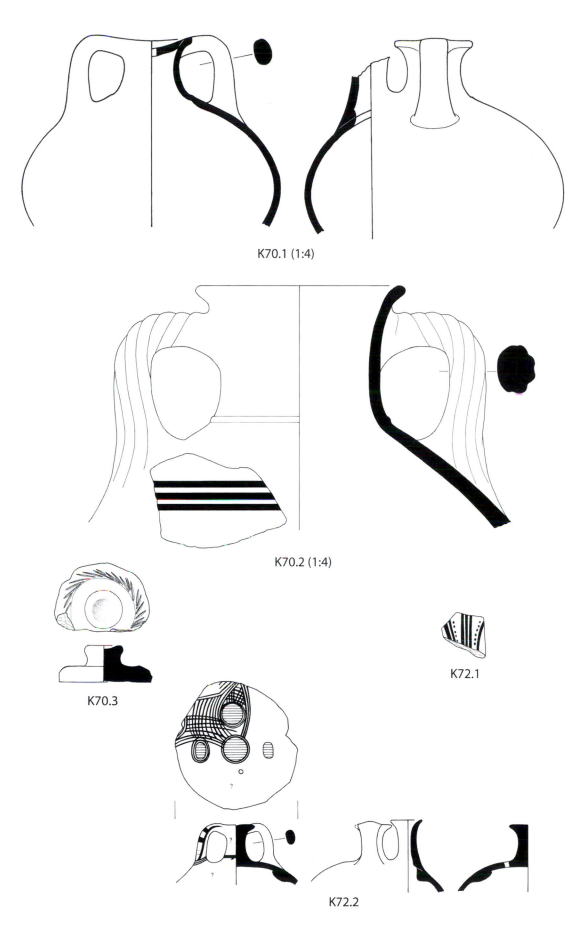

K70.1 (1:4)

K70.2 (1:4)

K70.3

K72.1

K72.2

*Fig. 3.14. Temple Road East, pottery from K 70 (**K70.1–3**) and K 72 (**K72.1–2**).*
Scale 1:3 unless otherwise indicated.

(455),[116] bronze tweezers (456),[117] two fragments of bronze (491, 492), the end of a bone pin (490),[118] and a cylindrical terracotta spindle whorl (493). The plaque fragment was found in one of the boxes; it is of a very soft reddish yellow (7.5YR 7/6) fabric, and the corner is preserved with a flat ridge around the top edge.

It is difficult to interpret this area. Part of it may have been included in the rubbish pit found farther east. It was probably a street first, perhaps becoming part of the Baker's House or Commercial Quarter in its last phase of use. The pottery suggests that it was not a living space, as it consists of very small pieces, mostly early in date. The material is very similar to that found also in K 79–89, and there may have been a large court in this area that was later carved into smaller units. Like the material from K 79–89, this probably represents refuse from earlier habitation of the site.

The fine pottery is consistent in style and very useful as an assemblage of material from the earliest part of LM IIIC. First of all, there seem to be more possible cups in this deposit than is the case elsewhere. It is always difficult to distinguish cups from deep bowls when only a small fragment of the rim or body is preserved, but several examples in this group look more like cups than deep bowls, including **K76.7**, **K76.12**, **K76.15** and **K76.17**; the cup handle found in one of the boxes may be from one of these or similar cups. **K76.37** and **K76.38** are from shallow cups or bowls, like those found at Khania.[119] The best preserved of the deep bowls (**K76.1**) may be somewhat later, but still within early LM IIIC; the foot is a bit higher than most, and it finds its closest parallel in a deep bowl from the Kephala tholos at Knossos, probably of early LM IIIC date, despite the late date of the tomb.[120] Like many of the other deep bowls in this deposit, the interior has a reserved disc. This piece may belong to the later use of the area, as its preservation also suggests. The bases of the other deep bowls are raised and slightly concave, except for **K76.24**, which has a true ring base, and **K76.25** with its flat base. Many of the bases have reserved discs (**K76.18**, **K76.19**, **K76.23**, **K76.24**). Two of the bases have paint on the edges of their undersides (**K76.19**, **K76.21**) or are monochrome underneath (**K76.20**) or have a spiral or circle (**K76.22**). The most popular motifs on cups or deep bowls are blob (four examples), multiple pendent loops (four examples), quirk (two examples), zigzag (two examples), and Minoan flower (two examples). These motifs are also common in early LM IIIC deposits at Kastri and Knossos,[121] as well as in Phase I of Kavousi–*Kastro*, although the pendent multiple loops do not appear there until Phase II.[122] The early deposits from Building B at Kavousi–*Vronda* are also similar.[123] Several of the sherds are of LM IIIB style, as with **K76.26** and **K76.29**. The goblet stem **K76.39** is probably from a champagne cup, a shape which seems to die out in popularity after the early phases of LM IIIC.[124] The other pottery is more fragmentary and difficult to date.

Pottery Catalogue: K 76

Fine Wares

K76.1   Deep bowl (PLATE 10 *c*, FIG. 3.15). H. 9.8; D. base 4.2; D. rim 14. Restored, but broken; only eight fragments remain. Now 40% preserved, including full profile and one handle. Fine, rather hard, pink (7.5YR 7/4) fabric. Very pale brown (10YR 8/4) slip. Dull black paint. Well-preserved surfaces. Multiple pendent loops. Strokes on handle. Reserved disc on interior base. For shape, cf. Andreadaki-Vlasaki and Papadopoulou 2007, fig. 4.28 (Khamalevri, Phase I); decoration: Prokopiou 1997, 372, fig. 6 (Sybrita/Thronos, early IIIC). LM IIIC early.

K76.2   Deep bowl or cup (PLATE 1 *b*, FIG. 3.15). D. rim est. 13–14. Single fragment from rim. Fine, medium-soft, very pale brown (10YR 7/4) fabric. Very pale brown (10YR 8/3) slip. Black paint, somewhat worn. Well-preserved surfaces, especially on interior. Multiple stems meeting in arc, with uncertain central motif. For decoration, cf. Mook and Coulson 1997, 358, fig. 30.107 (Kavousi–*Kastro*). LM IIIC early.

K76.3   Deep bowl or cup (FIG. 3.15). D. rim est. 13. Single fragment from rim. Fine, medium soft, reddish yellow (7.5YR 7/6) fabric. Very pale brown (10YR 8/3) slip. Worn black paint. Worn surfaces. Curvilinear pattern with arc fillers. LM IIIC.

K76.4   Deep bowl or cup (FIG. 3.15). D. rim est. 14–15. Single fragment from rim. Fine, soft, porous, yellowish red (5YR 5/6) fabric. Very pale brown (10YR 8/2) slip. Worn black paint. Spiral, possibly buttonhook. LM IIIC early.

K76.5   Deep bowl or cup (FIG. 3.15). Max. pres. H. 3.6. Single fragment from rim. Fine, porous, very pale brown (10YR 7/4) fabric. Very pale brown (10YR 8/2) slip. Black to dark brown paint. Well-preserved surfaces. Multiple pendent loops (?). LM IIIC.

K76.6   Deep bowl or cup (FIG. 3.15). D. rim est. 11. Single fragment from rim. Fine, medium-hard, reddish yellow (7.5YR 7/6) fabric. Very pale brown (10YR 8/2) slip. Worn crackled black paint. Multiple pendent loops. LM IIIC early.

K76.7   Deep bowl or cup (FIG. 3.15). D. rim est. 8–9. Single fragment from rim. Fine, medium-hard, reddish yellow (7.5YR 7/6) fabric. Very pale brown (10YR 8/3) slip. Red (10R 4/8) paint. Worn surfaces, especially on interior. Shallower body than usual and small diameter suggest it may be a cup. Multiple pendent loops above two narrow bands. For shape and decoration, cf. Andreadaki-Vlasaki and Papadopoulou 2007, 52, fig. 9.3 (Khamalevri, Phase I). LM IIIC early.

K76.8   Deep bowl or cup (FIG. 3.15). D. rim est. 18. Single fragment from rim. Fine, soft, very pale brown (10YR 7/4) fabric. Very pale brown (10YR 8/3) slip. Red (10R 4/8) paint. Worn surfaces. Possible spiral. LM IIIC early.

K76.9   Deep bowl or cup (FIG. 3.15). D. rim est. 14. Single fragment from rim. Fine, soft, porous, reddish yellow (7.5YR 7/6) fabric. Very pale brown (10YR 8/2) slip. Black to red (2.5YR 5/8) paint. Worn surfaces. Leaf and flower? LM IIIC.

---

116   *Karphi*, pl. 29.2.
117   *Karphi*, pl. 29.1.
118   *Karphi*, pl. 28.4.
119   *Khania II*, pl. 34.87-P 0011
120   Cadogan 1967, 260, fig. 2.8; D'Agata 2007, 104, fig. 1.
121   *Kastri*, 286–91; Popham 1965, 324–7 (Knossos).
122   Mook and Coulson 1997, 354.
123   *Kavousi IIA*, figs. 25–31, 37–8.
124   Hallager 1997, 39–40. At Kavousi–*Vronda* they occur in the earlier deposits in Building B, but not in the latest phases of that settlement. See Day *et al.* forthcoming.

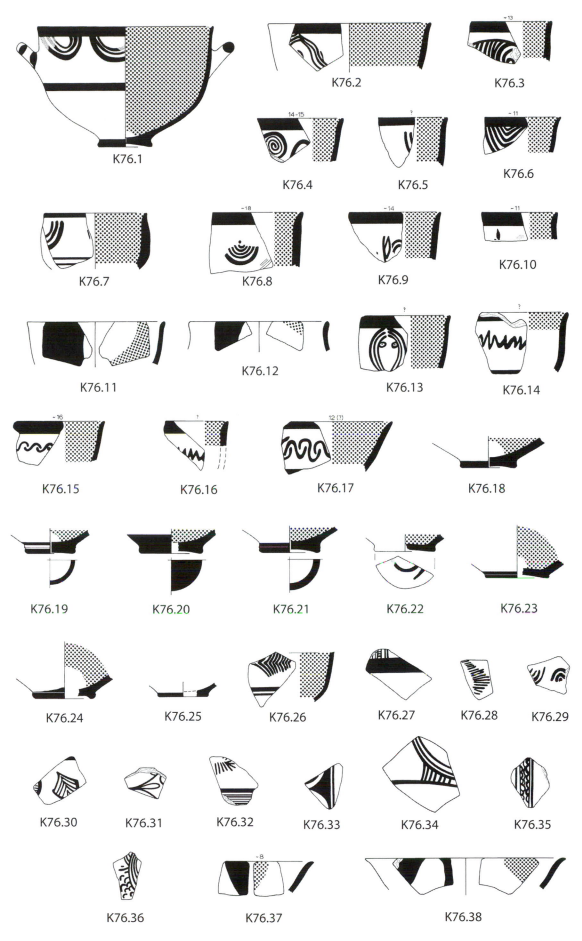

*Fig. 3.15. Temple Road West, pottery from K 76 (**K76.1–38**). Scale 1:3.*

K76.10 Deep bowl or cup (FIG. 3.15). D. rim est. 11. Single fragment from rim. Fine, soft, reddish yellow (7.5YR 7/6) fabric. Very pale brown (10YR 8/4) slip. Worn red (2.5YR 5/8) paint. Tip of floral or quatrefoil motif. LM IIIC.

K76.11 Deep bowl or cup (FIG. 3.15). D. rim est. 11. Single fragment from rim. Fine, medium-hard, reddish yellow (7.5YR 8/6) fabric. Very pale brown (10YR 8/3) slip. Red (2.5YR 4/8) paint. Blob decoration. For shape and decoration, cf. Andreadaki-Vlasaki and Papadopoulou 2007 46, fig. 3.19 (Khamalevri, Phase Ib). LM IIIC early.

K76.12 Deep bowl or cup (FIG. 3.15). D. rim est. 11. Single fragment from rim. Fine, soft, very pale brown (10YR 8/2) fabric and slip. Black paint. Blob decoration. LM IIIC early.

K76.13 Deep bowl or cup (PLATE 10 d, FIG. 3.15). Max. pres. H. 4.2. Single fragment from rim. Fine, soft, porous, reddish yellow (7.5YR 7/6) fabric. Very pale brown (10YR 8/2) slip. Red (10R 5/6) paint. Well-preserved surfaces. Decorated with 'face' (multiple arcs with eyes). Publication: Seiradaki, fig. 21h. Cf. Rethemiotakis 1997, 317, fig. 26g (Kastelli Pediada); *Kastri*, 288, fig. 9q. LM IIIC early.

K76.14 Deep bowl or cup (FIG. 3.15). Max. pres. H. 4.8. Single fragment from rim; rim chipped. Fine, very soft, reddish yellow (7.5YR 7/6) fabric. Very pale brown (10YR 8/3) slip. Worn red (10R 4/8) paint. Worn surfaces. Zigzag. Band on interior of rim, remainder has slip. LM IIIC early.

K76.15 Deep bowl or cup (FIG. 3.15). D. rim est. 16. Single fragment from rim. Fine, hard, reddish yellow (7.5YR 7/6) fabric. Thick, creamy, very pale brown (10YR 8/2) slip. Black paint. Running quirk. Imported? LM IIIC early.

K76.16 Deep bowl or cup (FIG. 3.15). Max. pres. H. 2. Single fragment from rim. Fine, medium-hard, very pale brown (10YR 7/4) fabric. Very pale brown (10YR 8/4) slip. Dark reddish brown (5YR 3/3) paint. Well-preserved surfaces. Zigzag. For motif, cf. *Kastri*, 287, fig. 8a–d (LM IIIC early). LM IIIC early.

K76.17 Deep bowl or cup (FIG. 3.15). D. rim est. 12. Single fragment from rim. Fine, very soft, porous, pinkish white (2.5YR 8/2) fabric. Dark reddish brown (5YR 3/3) paint. Very worn surfaces. Quirk. LM IIIC early.

K76.18 Deep bowl or cup (FIG. 3.15). D. base 4.6. Single fragment from base. Fine, very soft, reddish yellow (7.5YR 6/6) fabric. White (10YR 8/1) slip. Black to red (10R 4/8) paint. Well-preserved surfaces. Band at base, reserved disc on interior of bottom. LM IIIC early.

K76.19 Deep bowl or cup (PLATE 10 e, FIG. 3.15). D. base 4. Single fragment from base. Fine, soft, reddish yellow (5YR 7/6) fabric. Very pale brown (10YR 8/3) slip. Black to red (10R 4/8) paint. Worn surfaces. Raised, slightly concave base, with small ridge around outside. Two bands on exterior. Reserved disc on bottom of interior. Band around outer edge of underside. LM IIIC early.

K76.20 Deep bowl or cup (FIG. 3.15). D. base 5. Three joining fragments from base. Fine, soft, reddish yellow (7.5YR 7/6) fabric. Streaky dark brown (7.5YR 3/2) paint. Monochrome inside and out and on underside. LM IIIC early.

K76.21 Deep bowl or cup (PLATE 10 e, FIG. 3.15). D. base 5. Single fragment from base. Fine, soft, reddish yellow (5YR 7/6) fabric. Very pale brown (10YR 8/3) slip. Red (10R 4/8) paint. Well-preserved surfaces. Band on exterior. Band around outer edge of underside. LM IIIC early.

K76.22 Deep bowl or cup (FIG. 3.15). D. base 5. Single fragment from base. Fine, soft, reddish yellow (7.5YR 7/6) fabric. Very pale brown (10YR 8/2) slip. Crackled black paint. Well-preserved surfaces. Circle or spiral on underside. LM IIIC early.

K76.23 Deep bowl or cup (FIG. 3.15). D. base 5. Single fragment from base. Fine, medium-hard, reddish yellow (5YR 7/6) fabric. Very pale brown (10YR 8/3) slip. Red (10R 4/8) to light red (2.5YR 6/8) paint. Well-preserved surfaces. Band on exterior, reserved disc on interior. LM IIIC early.

K76.24 Deep bowl or cup (FIG. 3.15). D. base 5. Single fragment from base. Fine, soft, porous, reddish yellow (7.5YR 7/6) fabric with red phyllites. Very pale brown (10YR 8/2) slip. Red (2.5YR 4/8) to dark red (2.5YR 3/6) paint. Band on exterior, reserved disc on interior. Ring base. LM IIIC early.

K76.25 Deep bowl or cup (FIG. 3.15). D. base est. 4. Single fragment from base. Fine, medium-hard, very pale brown (10YR 7/3) fabric. Very pale brown (10YR 8/3) slip. Black paint. Well-preserved surfaces. Band on exterior. Flat base. LM IIIC early.

K76.26 Deep bowl or cup (FIG. 3.15). Max. pres. H. 4. Single fragment from lower body. Fine, rather hard, reddish yellow (7.5YR 7/6) fabric. Very pale brown (10YR 8/2) slip. Red (2.5YR 5/8) paint. Worn surfaces. Carinated body. Chevron spray. For decoration, cf. Andreadaki-Vlasaki and Papadopoulou 2007, 50, fig. 7.14 (Khamalevri, Phase Ib); Borgna 1997a, 279, fig. 7, top middle (Phaistos); Watrous 1992, 109, fig. 68.1921 (Kommos LM IIIB–C). LM IIIB/C.

K76.27 Deep bowl or cup (FIG. 3.15). Max. pres. H. 3.5. Single fragment from body. Fine, soft, yellow (10YR 7/6) fabric. Very pale brown (10YR 8/3) slip. Black paint. Worn surfaces. Panelled pattern, with hatching between vertical bands. LM IIIC.

K76.28 Deep bowl or cup (FIG. 3.15). Max. pres. H. 3.3. Single fragment from body. Fine, soft, reddish yellow (5YR 6/6) fabric. Very pale brown (10YR 8/3) slip. Worn black paint, streaky on interior. Minoan flower, placed horizontally. LM IIIC early.

K76.29 Deep bowl or cup (FIG. 3.15). Max. pres. H. 3. Single fragment from body. Fine, medium-soft, porous, very pale brown (10YR 7/4) fabric. Very pale brown (10YR 8/2) slip. Red (2.5YR 5/8) paint. Worn surfaces. Pendent multiple loops alternating with upright multiple loops. For decoration, cf. Warren 2007, 342, fig. 7 P183; Rethemiotakis 1997, 309, fig. 10c (Kastelli Pediada); Popham 1965, pl. 86b (Knossos, Little Palace, LM IIIA and B). LM IIIB/C.

K76.30 Deep bowl or cup (FIG. 3.15). Max. pres. H. 3.1. Single fragment from body, near rim. Fine, medium-hard, reddish yellow (7.5YR 7/6) fabric. Very pale brown (10YR 8/3) slip. Black paint worn to brown. Worn surfaces. Hatched loop and chevrons in loop. LM IIIC early.

K76.31 Deep bowl or cup (FIG. 3.15). Max. pres. H. 2.4. Single fragment from body. Fine, medium-soft, reddish yellow (7.5YR 8/6) fabric. Very pale brown (10YR 8/3) slip. Worn red (2.5YR 4/8) paint. Lozenge with loops as filler. For decoration, cf. **K127.3**; *Kastri*, 287, fig. 8j. LM IIIC early.

K76.32 Deep bowl or cup (FIG. 3.15). Max. pres. H. 3.3. Single fragment from body. Fine, soft, reddish yellow (7.5YR 7/6) fabric. Very pale brown (10YR 8/3) slip. Red (10R 5/8) paint. Worn exterior surfaces, well-preserved on interior. Minoan flower, set horizontally. LM IIIC early.

K76.33 Deep bowl or cup (FIG. 3.15). Max. pres. H. 3.2. Single fragment from body. Fine, medium-soft, reddish yellow (7.5YR 7/6) fabric. Very pale brown (10YR 8/2) slip. Streaky black paint, worn to shadow. Double axe (?). For decoration, cf. *Kastri*, 287, fig. 8r. LM IIIC early.

K76.34 Deep bowl or cup (FIG. 3.15). Max. pres. H. 5.5. Single fragment from body. Fine, very soft, reddish yellow (5YR 7/6) fabric with tiny white inclusions. Creamy, very pale brown (10YR 8/2) slip. Worn, dark reddish brown (5YR 3/3) paint. Worn surfaces. Curvilinear design with arc fillers. Interior paint over slip. LM IIIC early.

K76.35 Deep bowl or cup (FIG. 3.15). Max. pres. H. 4. Single fragment from body. Fine, soft, reddish yellow (7.5YR 7/6) fabric. Very pale brown (10YR 8/3) slip. Dark brown (7.5YR 3/2) paint. Panelled decoration with scalloped edges. For decoration, cf. Andreadaki-Vlasaki and Papadopoulou 2007, 46, fig. 3.5 (Khamalevri, Phase I). LM IIIC early.

K76.36 Deep bowl or cup (FIG. 3.15). Max. pres. H. 4. Single fragment from body. Fine, soft, reddish yellow (5YR 7/6) fabric.

K76.39

K76.40

K76.41

K76.43

K76.42

K76.44

K76.45

K76.46

K76.47

K76.48

K76.49

K76.50

K76.51

K76.52

K76.53

K76.54

K76.55

K76.56

*Fig. 3.16. Temple Road West, pottery from K 76 (**K76.39–56**). Scale 1:3.*

Very pale brown (10YR 8/2) slip. Red (10R 4/6) paint. Worn surfaces. Curvilinear pattern with arc fillers, U-pattern or scale pattern. LM IIIC.

K76.37   Shallow cup or bowl (FIG. 3.15). D. rim est. 8. Single fragment from rim. Fine, very soft, reddish yellow (7.5YR 7/6) fabric. Very pale brown (10YR 8/2) slip. Red (2.5YR 4/8) paint. Worn surfaces. Blob decoration. For shape and decoration, cf. *Khania II*, pl. 34.87-P 0011, 77-P 0268. LM IIIC early.

K76.38   Shallow bowl or cup (FIG. 3.15). D. rim est. 16. Single fragment from rim. Fine, soft, very pale brown (10YR 8/2) fabric and slip. Worn black paint. Blob decoration. For shape and decoration, cf. *Khania II*, pl. 34.87-P 0011, 77-P 0268. LM IIIC early.

K76.39   Champagne cup (FIG. 3.16). D. base 7. Single fragment from base and stem. Fine, soft, reddish yellow (5YR 6/6) fabric with dark grey phyllites (<1mm). Black paint. Short stem, with deep circular depression in centre. Monochrome, including underside. LM IIIC early.

K76.40   Kylix (FIG. 3.16). Max. pres. H. 2.3. Single fragment from rim. Fine, soft, reddish yellow (7.5YR 7/6) fabric. Very pale brown (10YR 8/3) slip. Black paint. Worn surfaces. Curvilinear motif, possibly fringed. LM IIIC.

K76.41   Krater (FIG. 3.16). Max. pres. H. 5.5. Single fragment from rim, non-joining fragment from body. Fine, very soft, reddish yellow (7.5YR 7/6) fabric. Very pale brown (10YR 8/2). Red paint, but only shadow preserved. Very worn surfaces. Multiple curvilinear motif with arc fillers and scalloped edges. LM IIIC early.

K76.42   Krater (FIG. 3.16). Max. pres. H. 4.8. Single fragment from rim, non-joining body fragment. Fine, medium-soft, pink (5YR 7/4) fabric. Very pale brown (10YR 8/3) slip. Red (10R 4/6) paint. Worn surfaces. Outlined curvilinear motif, fringes or flower. LM IIIC early.

K76.43   Krater (FIG. 3.16). D. rim est. 22. Single fragment from rim. Fine, medium-hard, reddish yellow (5YR 7/6) fabric. Very pale brown (10YR 8/4) slip. Black paint worn to yellowish red (5YR 5/6). Well-preserved surfaces. Stacked triangles between curvilinear motifs. Strokes on rim. For decoration, cf. Rethemiotakis 1997, 322, fig. 33b (Kastelli Pediada). LM IIIC early.

K76.44   Krater (FIG. 3.16). D. rim est. 30. Single fragment from rim. Fine, medium-soft, porous, very pale brown (10YR 8/2) fabric and slip. Black paint. Worn surfaces. Fringed motif. Strokes on rim. LM IIIC.

K76.45   Krater (FIG. 3.16). D. base 11.5. Single fragment preserving 50% of base. Fine, soft, very pale brown (10YR 8/4) fabric. Black paint. Short pedestal base. Decorated with bands. LM IIIC.

K76.46   Krater (FIG. 3.16). Max. pres. H. 5.8; Th. 0.5–0.7. Single fragment from body. Fine, medium-soft, reddish yellow (5YR 7/6) fabric. Very pale brown (10YR 8/3) slip. Red (10R 5/8) paint. Worn surfaces. Curvilinear pattern with fringes and circle. LM IIIC.

K76.47   Krater (FIG. 3.16). Max. pres. H. 4; Th. 0.6. Single fragment from body. Fine, soft, reddish yellow (7.5YR 7/6) fabric. Very pale brown (10YR 8/3) slip. Red (2.5YR 4/8) paint. Worn surfaces. Curvilinear pattern with arc fillers. LM IIIC.

K76.48   Krater (FIG. 3.16). Max. pres. H. 2.8; Th. 0.5. Single fragment from body. Fine, soft, porous, reddish yellow (5YR 7/6) fabric. Very pale brown (10YR 8/2) paint. Worn brown paint. Worn surfaces. Foliate band or floral motif. LM IIIC.

K76.49   Pyxis (?) (FIG. 3.16). Max. pres. H. 2.2. Single fragment from base. Fine, soft, reddish yellow (7.5YR 7/6) fabric. Very pale brown (10YR 8/4) slip. Black paint worn to red. Worn surfaces. Bands. Possibly painted on interior. LM IIIC.

K76.50   Stirrup jar (FIG. 3.16). Max. pres. H. 4.4. Single fragment (two sherds) from body. Fine, soft, reddish yellow (5YR 7/6) fabric. Very pale brown (10YR 8/3) slip. Black paint worn to

brown shadow. Rather well-preserved surfaces. Hatched multiple triangles alternating with curvilinear motif. LM IIIC.

K76.51   Stirrup jar (FIG. 3.16). Max. pres. H. 3. Single fragment from body. Fine, soft, porous, reddish yellow (7.5YR 7/6) fabric. Very pale brown (10YR 8/3) slip. Worn black paint. Worn surfaces. Closed vessel, probably stirrup jar. Crosshatched lozenge with fringes in arc. LM IIIC.

K76.52   Stirrup jar (FIG. 3.16). D. base 4.5–5. Single fragment from base. Fine, soft, reddish yellow (7.5YR 7/6) fabric. Very pale brown (10YR 8/3) slip. Black to red (2.5YR 4/6). Closed vessel, probably stirrup jar. Ring base. Bands. LM IIIC.

K76.53   Lid (FIG. 3.16). H. 2.5; D. rim est. 19. Single fragment from rim and base, preserving entire profile; missing handle. Fine, soft, reddish yellow (7.5YR 7/6) fabric. Very pale brown (10YR 8/2) slip. Black paint. Well-preserved surfaces. Monochrome. For shape, cf. *Khania II*, pl. 44.80-P 0087. LM IIIC early.

Coarse Wares

K76.54   Stirrup jar (FIG. 3.16). Max. pres. H. 5.5; Th. 0.6. Single fragment from body. Coarse reddish yellow (5YR 7/6) fabric, with frequent large (1–2 mm) grey phyllites. Very pale brown (10YR 8/3) slip. Worn reddish yellow (7.5YR 6/6) paint. Wavy band above bands, possibly debased octopus. Publication: Day 2005, 435, fig. 1.2. LM IIIC early.

K76.55   Stirrup jar (PLATE 10 *f*, FIG. 3.16). Max. pres. H. 5; Th. 0.6. Single fragment from body. Coarse, rather hard, pale red (2.5Y 7/2) fabric with very frequent hard black and white inclusions. Pale yellow (2.5Y 8/2) slip. Very dark grey (10YR 3/1) paint. Well-preserved surfaces. Burned? Wavy band above bands, possibly debased octopus. Publication: Day 2005, 435, fig. 1.3. LM IIIC early.

K76.56   Stopper or lid (FIG. 3.16). D. 5.5. Intact. Coarse reddish yellow (5YR 6/8) fabric with infrequent schist inclusions (1–2 mm). Coarse body fragment from another vessel chipped into round disc to be used as stopper. LM IIIC.

THE BAKER'S HOUSE (ROOMS K 71, K 73, K 74)

This entire building was considered a later addition to the settlement, and it underwent modifications during the course of its history.[125] The building was constructed over a street and possibly part of the rubbish dump that was in the area to the west of the Great House. There is an earlier wall under room 71 shown on the plan that may have served as a boundary for the rubbish pit to the east. Rooms 70 and 71 were probably originally single room, entered on the south; the partition wall between them was built later on top of collapsed rubble and may have served as buttress. A so-called bread oven stands in the north end. Little was found in the building, and little survives today.

Room K 71

There were comparatively few tripod legs and little fine ware found in this room. In addition to what is listed in the publication, the notebook records at least three pithoi, one with a rope moulding on the rim, several pithoid jars, jars of Types 1–4, a coarse krater; fine

---

125   *Karphi*, 86–7.

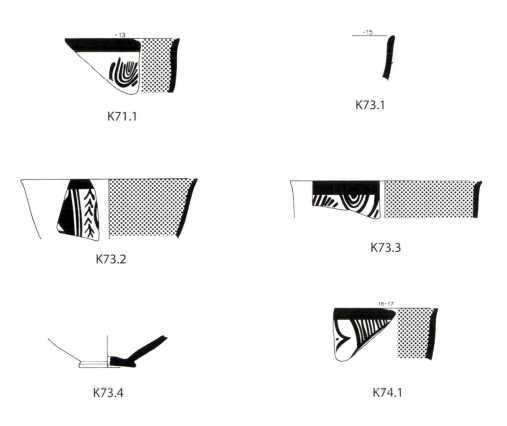

*Fig. 3.17. Baker's House, pottery from K 71 (**K71.1**), K 73 (**K73.1**–4), and K 74 (**K74.1**). Scale 1:3.*

wares included a kylix stem and a small pyxis. Many animal bones and goat horns are recorded. In addition to the catalogued pottery, there was another deep bowl with vertical chevrons and two fragments from stirrup jars, one with crosshatching, and the other with loops. There is not enough material to date this room securely; the deep bowl with pendent multiple loops appears in the very earliest LM IIIC, and there are parallels for it in LM IIIB.[126]

Pottery Catalogue: K 71

Fine Wares

K71.1   Deep bowl or cup (PLATE 1 *h*, FIG. 3.17). D. rim est. 13. Single fragment from rim. Fine, soft, reddish yellow (7.5YR 7/6) fabric. Very pale brown (10YR 8/3) slip. Worn red (2.5YR 4/8) paint. Multiple pendent loops. For decoration, cf. *Kastri*, 295, fig. 15 P27. LM IIIC early.

Room K 73

Room K 73 contained a small, partly vaulted, bread oven lined with burned clay; two cooking dishes of Type 6 were actually found within it. The room was unusual in that it had no discernable floor.

In addition to the many dishes mentioned in the publication, the notebook records pithos rims of Types 2 and 9, a pithoid jar of Type 10 that joined with a vessel in K 76, many jars and tripods, and much broken fine ware. In addition to the catalogued pottery, there

is also a fragment of a deep bowl with multiple loops and three fragments from stirrup jars, one decorated with a spiral, one with a scalloped edge, another with an intricate pattern that included a hatched oval. Other objects included a hollow bone tube (451).[127]

The fine pottery is fragmentary and probably represents earlier material from underneath, rather than vessels in use at the time the settlement ended. The fact that there were joins with K 76 suggests that all this material might belong to an earlier dump. The preserved sherds do not look late; the schematic double axe pattern of **K73.2** is found in earlier contexts and at any rate is an earlier LM IIIB2 motif that continues into LM IIIC.[128]

Pottery Catalogue: K 73

Fine Wares

K73.1   Deep bowl (FIG. 3.17). D. rim est. 15. Single fragment from rim, preserving part of handle scar. Fine, medium-hard, very pale brown (10YR 7/4) fabric. Crackled black paint. Monochrome (or blob) decoration. LM IIIC early.

---

126   Popham 1970*b*, pl. 47e (Knossos, Little Palace) one of which is quite close to this example.

127   *Karphi*, pl. 28.4.

128   Hallager 2000, 174 n. 343.

K73.2   Deep bowl or cup (FIG. 3.17). D. rim est. 12. Single fragment from rim. Fine, medium-hard, reddish yellow (7.5YR 8/6) fabric. Creamy pink (7.5YR 8/4) slip. Black to red (2.5YR 5/8) paint. Well-preserved surfaces. Panelled pattern with vertical stacked chevrons and double axe (?). LM IIIC early.

K73.3   Deep bowl or cup (FIG. 3.17). D. rim est. 15–16. Single fragment from rim. Fine, soft, reddish yellow (5YR 7/6) fabric. Very pale brown (10YR 8/3) slip. Black paint worn to brown (7.5YR 4/4) on interior. Worn surfaces. Multiple pendent loops next to fringed or floral design. LM IIIC early.

K73.4   Closed vessel (FIG. 3.17). D. base 4.6. Single fragment preserving half of base and part of lower body. Fine, soft, greenish grey (5BG 5/1), blue ware fabric. Possibly a stirrup jar or jug. LM IIIC.

Room K 74

This room was said to have produced little fine ware, and Seiradaki illustrated one fragment from the room, a jar of Type 8, which was not found.[129] The notebook lists also pithos rims of Types 2 and 5, a jar of Type 7, tripod legs, a kalathos of Type 1, a one-handled jug of Type 3, a spout (perhaps from dish of Type 6), and a few fragments of fine ware from bowls. Animal bones are also recorded. Two additional deep bowl fragments were found, one decorated with a fringed streamer, the other with vertical strokes; these were not catalogued. The single catalogued sherd, with its arc filler and dotted lozenge, is surely LM IIIC, but whether it is early in that pottery phase or later is not certain.

Pottery Catalogue: K 74

Fine Wares

K74.1   Deep bowl or cup (FIG. 3.17). D. rim est. 16–17. Single fragment (2 sherds) from rim. Fine, soft, very pale brown (10YR 7/4) fabric. Very pale brown (10YR 8/4) slip. Red (10R 4/6) paint. Worn surfaces. Lozenge with dot, curvilinear decoration with filler arcs. LM IIIC.

---

129   Seiradaki, fig. 3.8. It may have been mislabelled; it is similar to the fragment catalogued as pyxis **K46.6**.

4

The Southeast Quadrant

The Magazines (Rooms K 21–K 23, K 29–K 31, K 33–K 37), the Squares (Areas K 10, K 32, K 48), the Southern Houses (K 24–28, K 42–51), the Broad Road (Rooms K 52–K 54, K 56), and the Small Shrine (Rooms K 55, K 57)

THE MAGAZINES (ROOMS K 21–K 23, K 29–K 31, K 33–K 37)

This group of rooms, excavated in 1938, was built up against a steep wall of rock on the west.[1] The rooms were dubbed the 'Magazines', presumably because of the large number of storage vessels and ordinary domestic wares found in them, or perhaps because the line of rooms facing east resembled storerooms. There was no indication of different phases of construction; rather, the excavators thought that all the rooms were part of the same building programme.[2] Rooms K 22, K 23, K 29, and K 30 were all connected by doorways and belonged to the same building. Rooms K 31, K 33, and K 34, however, were separate units, with entrances on a possible street outside to the east.

Room K 21

Only part of this room was excavated; the rest is said to have disappeared into a field.[3] There is no further information on the area, and it is not clear if it was a room or an exterior space. The notebook reports that the pottery was mostly coarse and much worn, including a few pithos fragments; tripods, at least three with flaring rims; at least two dishes; pithoid jar bases; a gritty buff rim, perhaps of a jar, with a vertical handle; and a pyxis in red ware. Fine wares included flat and ring bases, two decorated rims, arched horizontal bowl handles, and a kylix base. The pithoid jar pictured in Seiradaki was not located in the museum boxes.[4] Few other objects were found in the room, but two terracotta spools were still preserved, one weighing 50, the other 70 g.

The deep bowl with Minoan flower (**K21.1**) may be an import, as it had a distinctively different fabric and paint; the flower motif seems to be more popular in the early LM IIIC period than later, so this piece may belong to the period of construction of the building. The other pottery gives little indication as to date or function of the area.

Pottery Catalogue: K 21

Fine Wares

K21.1 Deep bowl or cup (PLATE 10 *d*, FIG. 4.1). Max. pres. H. 5.7. Single fragment from rim. Fine, fairly hard, very pale brown (10YR 7/4) fabric. Very pale brown (10YR 8/4) slip. Red (2.5YR 5/8) paint. Very well-preserved surfaces. Minoan flower. Imported? Publication: Seiradaki, fig. 21h. For shape, cf. Borgna 1997*a*, 278, fig. 6.2 (Phaistos). LM IIIC early.

K21.2 Cup or deep bowl (FIG. 4.1). D. rim est. 10. Single fragment from rim. Fine, soft, yellow (10YR 7/6) fabric, possibly burned. Very pale brown (10YR 8/4) slip. Black paint worn to shadow. Panel decoration with multiple vertical lines separating horizontal wavy lines and wavy lines and chain motif. LM IIIC.

Coarse Wares

K21.3 Tripod tray (FIG. 4.1). Max. pres. H. 9.7. Single fragment preserving nearly complete profile; missing tip of leg and most of base. Coarse red (2.5YR 5/8) fabric, with large (1–5 mm) and frequent phyllites, some schist, and hard white angular inclusions. No traces of burning. Finger impressions on top of flattened rim, dint at top of leg, and two sets of oblique slashes on either side of leg forming a V-pattern. Publication: Seiradaki, pl. 12b, middle, second from left. LM IIIC.

Room K 22

Room K 22 was identified as a magazine west of K 23.[5] The room showed many traces of burning, including a patch of baked roofing clay with marks of a rafter 5 cm in section; it is thus possible that a hearth had existed in the room. There was a much larger quantity of pottery than usual for the size of the room. The publication reports that there were eight pithoi, all other common coarse types except open dishes, and little fine ware. The notebook adds the following information. Of the eight pithoi, one was of red clay with a fine chevron pattern, a rope-slashed ridge, and a plain ridge below the rim, and a base that had flaked away; a second was of yellow gritty clay, with chevron and diagonally slashed bands, heavy rim, and a plain base; a third was also of yellow gritty clay with vertically slashed bands, no attached rim or base; a fourth of the same fabric had a pinched rope below the

---

1   *Karphi*, 79–81.
2   *Karphi*, 135.
3   *Karphi*, 80.
4   Seiradaki, fig. 2.7.
5   *Karphi*, 80.

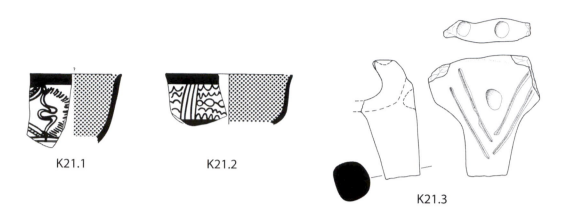

*Fig. 4.1. Magazines, pottery from K 21 (**K21.1–3**). Scale 1:3.*

rim and probably a plain base; a fifth was of reddish clay with pinched rope at the rim and plain bands below; a sixth also of reddish clay had a ridge with finger impressions below and a triple line of finger-impressed rope further down; the seventh was also of reddish clay and had plain ridges; and the eighth was apparently plain. There were also fragments from large jars that were not pithoi, an amphora with two large twisted handles (**K22.11**), as well as three very large tripod legs, one with three impressed holes at the top, a flaring rim, a rim that was angular in section, small bases with straight sides, an offset base, one or two jars (**K22.12**), a sherd from a lid with rope pattern with finger impressions, a white painted sherd in thick red ware, two notched sherds, a large stirrup jar, perhaps with octopus design, and two pyxides (**K22.2, K22.3**). Among the fragments still preserved in the boxes but not catalogued was a huge handle from a pithos with three holes at the base,[6] a tripod leg (sampled KAR 06/24), and a body sherd with a large flat knob as decoration. There were also fragments of a second pyxis similar to **K22.6** in fabric.

Objects included two cylindrical terracotta spindle whorls (239, 240) and five spools, of which two have been preserved. These are of different fabric and shape, but both spools weigh 60 g.

The pottery has some unusual features. Although many pithoi were found in other rooms, the notebook gives enough information about rims, bases, and decoration to suggest that these vessels were well preserved, not just the discrete fragments found in many of the rooms. The number of elaborately decorated pyxides is high as well; they come in many different types and with decoration ranging from the early LM IIIC date of **K22.2**[7] and slightly later **K22.6**,[8] to the late LM IIIC dates for pyxides **K22.3** and **K22.4**. The deposit is also unusual for the paucity of deep bowls or other vessels for eating and drinking. The only deep bowl (**K22.1**) has blob decoration.

Pottery Catalogue: K 22

Fine Wares

K22.1   Deep bowl (FIG. 4.2). D. rim est. 10. Two joining fragments from rim, preserving one handle; missing base. Fine, soft, very pale brown (10YR 8/3) fabric, with small black sand-sized inclusions. Worn black paint. Blob decoration inside and out. Cf. Borgna 1997a, 278, fig. 6.9 (Phaistos); Andreadaki-Vlasaki and Papadopoulou 2007, 48, fig. 5.11 (Khamalevri, Phase Ib). LM IIIC early?

K22.2   Pyxis (HM 11056) (PLATE 10 *g*, FIG. 4.2). H. 9.5; D. base 10.4; D. rim 7.3–7.5. Mended from ten fragments. Complete except for one handle and a small piece of rim and second handle. Fine, soft, reddish yellow (7.5YR 7/6) fabric with black sand-sized and gold mica inclusions (almost medium-coarse). Reddish yellow (7.5YR 7/6) slip. Very dark greyish brown (10YR 3/2) to brown (7.5YR 4/4) paint. Panelled decoration. Side A has reserved quatrefoil on a black background, with filled triangles that have dotted spiral ends. Side B has panel with dotted and outlined vertical wavy bands, with triangles filled with arcs on either side. Publication: Seiradaki, fig. 24c; pl. 7c second from right, pl. 8b; Mountjoy 2007, 232, fig. 4.2. LM IIIC early.

K22.3   Pyxis (HM 11061) (PLATE 11 *a*, FIG. 4.2). H. 16.7 (with handles 19.8); D. base 22.6; D. rim 18.6. Restored from 28 fragments. 85% preserved, including entire base, two-thirds of rim, both handles; missing pieces of body, tops of both handles, one-third of rim. Fine, soft, reddish yellow (5YR 6/6) fabric, rather harder than usual, with some grey and black tiny inclusions (possibly phyllites). White (10YR 8/2) slip. Black paint, worn to shadow in some places. Surfaces quite well-preserved. Burning on one side and bottom; not uniform and occurred before breaking. Elaborately decorated with panels that include horns of consecration, 'windmills', vertical chevrons, crosshatched lozenges, all with fringes, fillers, dots, and scallops. Publication: Seiradaki, pl. 7a, right; figs. 12.3, 23a, 1–2; Young 1938, 235, fig. 12, right, upper right; Desborough 1964, pl. 11. LM IIIC late.

---

6   Possibly the tripod leg mentioned in the notebook and pictured in Seiradaki, pl. 12b, top left.

7   P. Mountjoy, personal communication.

8   P. Mountjoy, personal communication; for the quatrefoil leaf with loop decoration see Rethemiotakis 1997, 319, fig. 28ag.

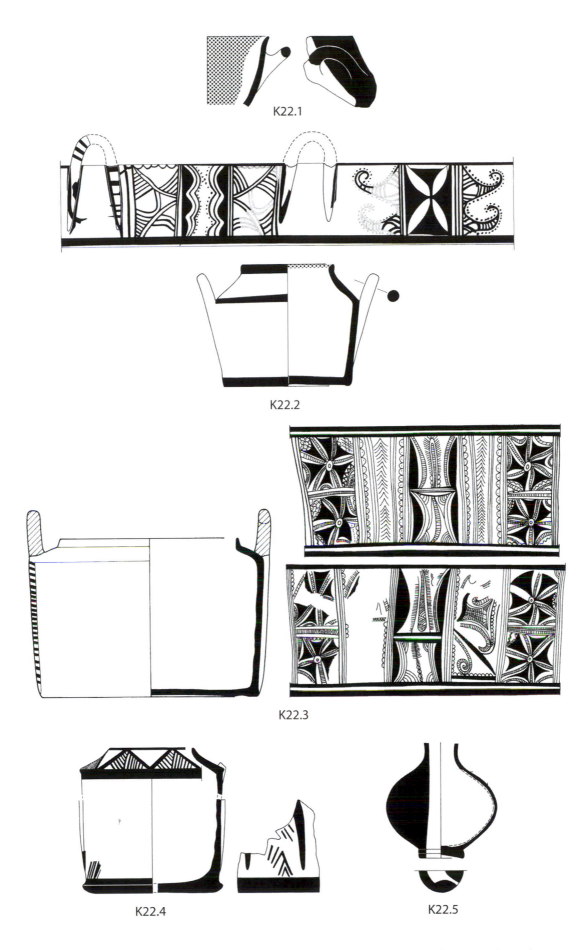

*Fig. 4.2. Magazines, pottery from K 22 (**K22.1–5**). Scale 1:3 unless otherwise indicated.*

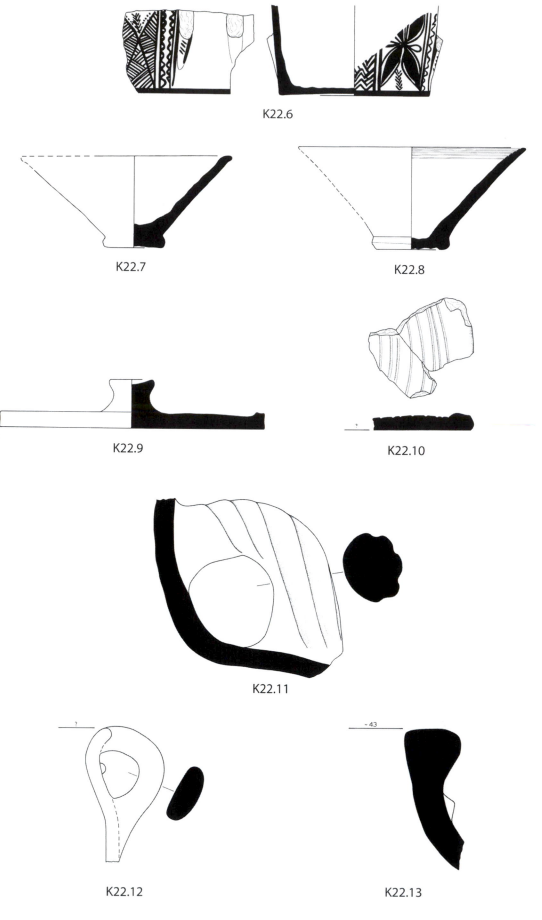

K22.6

K22.7

K22.8

K22.9

K22.10

K22.11

K22.12

K22.13

*Fig. 4.3. Magazines, pottery from K 22 (**K22.6–13**). Scale 1:3.*

K22.4   Pyxis (FIG. 4.2). H. est. 11.8; max. pres. H. 7.6; D. base 11.1; D. rim 6–7. Partially mended from 17 fragments. 50% preserved, including 65% of base, 60% of rim; missing full profile, both handles. Fine, very soft, very pale brown (10YR 8/3) fabric. Decoration in dull, thin, black paint, but worn. Sampled KAR 06/37. Filled triangles on shoulder, worn linear pattern on body; chevrons within handle attachments. For a similar decoration, cf. Tsipopoulou 2004, 112, fig. 8.6.97-4 (Khalasmenos). LM IIIC late.

K22.5   Juglet (FIG. 4.2). Max. pres. H. 9.3; D. base 3.6. Partially restored from 18 fragments. 90% of body and lower neck preserved, including lower handle attachment; missing handle, top of neck, and rim (fresh breaks suggest that it may have been there originally). Fine, soft, reddish yellow (5YR 6/6) fabric. Pink (7.5YR 7/4) slip. Red (2.5YR 4/6) paint. Worn surfaces. Blob decoration. LM IIIC.

Medium-Coarse Wares

K22.6   Pyxis (PLATE 11 *b*, FIG. 4.3). Max. pres. H. 8.3; D. base est. 12. Partially mended from six fragments from base and lower body. 75% preserved; missing upper body, rim and handles. Rather coarse, red (2.5YR 5/8) fabric, with fine (less than 1 mm) hard white inclusions and mica. Thick, very pale brown (10YR 8/4) slip. Black paint. Some surfaces very worn. Burned. Panelled decoration: Side A has panel of outlined quatrefoil leaves with loops, with multiple horizontal zigzags on one side and vertical wavy line on other by handle. Side B has triangles with alternating strokes as filler, and vertical lines with scalloped edges by handle. For the decoration, cf. Andreadaki-Vlasaki and Papadopoulou 2007, 51, fig. 8.34 (Khamalevri, Phase II). LM IIIC early.

Coarse Wares

K22.7   Kalathos (FIG. 4.3). H. 7.2–7.5; D. base 5; D. rim 15.6–18.4. Nearly intact; two sherds from rim mended on, fresh breaks; rim chipped. 80% preserved. Coarse, red (2.5YR 5/8) cookpot fabric, with frequent large (3 mm) phyllite inclusions. Some surface mottling on interior and exterior. Irregular rim, almost oval in shape. LM IIIC.

K22.8   Kalathos (FIG. 4.3). H. 8.3; D. base 6.2; D. rim est. 18.2. Partially mended from four fragments, with nine more non-joining. 40% preserved, including full profile. Coarse light red (2.5YR 6/6) fabric with very frequent red phyllites and hard white angular inclusions (2–3 mm). Sampled KAR 06/68. Uneven base. Incisions on interior of rim. For incisions, cf. Gesell 1999, pl. 61e (Kavousi–*Vronda*). LM IIIC.

K22.9   Lid (PLATE 11 *c*, FIG. 4.3). H. 3.9; D. 21.2. Restored from three fragments. 75% preserved; missing three fragments of body and edge of knob handle. Coarse reddish yellow (5YR 6/6) fabric with frequent grey phyllite inclusions (1–2 mm, up to 6 mm on bottom). No traces of burning. Bottom very rough. Flat disc with knob handle, hollowed on top; slightly raised edge. Publication: Seiradaki, fig. 19.6; pl. 10c, left. LM IIIC.

K22.10   Lid (FIG. 4.3). Max. pres. H. 1–1.4. Two joining fragments from rim. Coarse, friable, red (2.5YR 5/8) fabric with very frequent grey and red phyllites and hard white angular inclusions (1–3 mm). No traces of burning. Sampled KAR 06/03. Flat disc, with roughened underside. Incised concentric circles on top. Cf. **K83.3**, **K113.4**. LM IIIC.

K22.11   Amphora (FIG. 4.3). Max. pres. H. 13.2; D. neck 15. Single fragment from neck, shoulder, and handle; rim missing. Coarse, soft, reddish yellow (5YR 6/8) fabric with frequent schist and hard white angular inclusions (1–3 mm). Reddish brown (5YR 4/3) paint. Rope twisted handle. Monochrome? For rope-twisted handles, cf. **K70.2**; Day and Glowacki forthcoming (Kavousi–*Vronda*, Building E1: E1 P119). LM IIIC.

K22.12   Jar (FIG. 4.3). Max. pres. H. 10.9. Single fragment from rim and handle. Coarse reddish yellow (5YR 6/8) fabric with frequent grey and hard white angular inclusions (1–3 mm). Black paint. Ridge below rim. Monochrome? Publication: Seiradaki, fig. 3.4. LM IIIC.

K22.13   Pithos (FIG. 4.3). D. rim est. 43. Single fragment from rim. Coarse red (2.5YR 5/6) fabric with very frequent phyllite and hard white angular inclusions. Ridge below rim. LM IIIC.

Room K 23

K 23 was identified as the most important room of block, and indeed is the largest single room in the building. The room was entered through a doorway on the east, and there may have been an additional stepped entrance from K 21 on the south. On the west end was a steep step up through a doorway into K 22; an additional doorway may have led through stairs into K 29 on the northwest, where there was also a possible small pot stand. Perhaps a window led into K 31 on the north.[9]

This room had more complex stratigraphy than any other at Karphi. The excavators recognised two separate layers, interpreting them at first as evidence for a second story, but because the lower layer was burned and the upper was not, they were seen as two phases.[10] According to the published account, the walls were blackened to a height of 1.24 m, and there was burned destruction debris in the lower layer. The upper layer, however, was not burned, so the excavators suggested that the builders used the clay of the earlier burned roofing as the foundation for a paved floor. It looks as though the building suffered fire damage during its history and was rebuilt.

Much of the pottery from this room was labelled K 23 or K 23 floor. There was, however, a large box which was divided into two compartments with material from below the floor. The tag in the one of the compartments read 'K 23: below floor, upper', while the other was labelled 'K 23: below floor, lower'. Only one level below the floor was mentioned in the publication and notebook, and it is uncertain what distinction exists between the two separate groups. The labels suggest that both of these deposits are below the final floor in the building. It is possible that the material from the upper of these two deposits represents what was between the two floors, and that from the lower deposit came from below the earlier floor. The two may also have been kept separate arbitrarily and the distinction has no meaning in terms of date. Since the deposits were kept distinct by the excavators, they are here presented separately. What is certain is that the lower deposits represent material earlier than that from the latest floor.

Much of the pottery preserved from the room is labelled K 23, floor. It is assumed that this represents the material on the final floor in use at the time the

---

9   *Karphi*, 80.
10   *Karphi*, 80.

building was abandoned. Vessels labelled simply K 23 may have come from either layer.

The floor deposit (i.e. what was on and above the later floor) was published as being usual but with little fine ware. The notebook adds the following list of pottery: pithoi, pithoid jars, a large jar with twisted handles similar to the amphora from K 22, sherds from large red stirrup vases, at least two with white-painted decoration, a jug with white paint on harsh grey clay, and smaller coarse vases. The fine ware was said to be scanty and mostly blackened by fire. A good deal of pottery in the boxes labelled 'K 23 floor' was not catalogued. Included in this group were deep bowl fragments: a vertical burned rim fragment with curvilinear motif, a flaring rim fragment with a band at the rim, a burned body fragment with a curvilinear pattern and two more unburned body sherds with curvilinear patterns, one with filler motifs, and a monochrome cup or deep bowl. Also from this deposit were fragments of a spouted jug, a flat vertical handle, a closed vessel with creamy slip and three red bands, the neck and handle of a jug in coarse very pale brown fabric, and a scuttle handle with spiral fluting. From the boxes came a coarse base with an added disc near the base and the rim fragment of a pithos, both labelled K 23.

Several vessels published by Seiradaki as coming from K 23 present problems. The carinated bowl of Type 5[11] and a coarse stirrup jar[12] were not located in the boxes or on the shelves. The small tripod looks like one of the tripods from K 121, and the number given in the publication may be an error.[13]

Objects found in the room included a fragment of a bronze bowl (278), three Neolithic stone axes (284, 285, 286),[14] three conical (279, 280, 283) and four cylindrical (281, 282, 287, 291) terracotta spindle whorls, nine terracotta spools (two large and seven medium), a pierced bone sword pommel (289), and shell (290). One spool is still preserved. It was made of very coarse fabric and was burned. It weighs 100 g.

Much of the pottery from the floor deposit that was whole or nearly complete was burned, including the krater (**K23.11**), miniature amphora (**K23.17**), thelastron (**K23.18**), stirrup jars (**K23.19** and **K23.23**), jugs (**K23.20**, **K23.28**, **K23.29**), and jar (**K23.31**). The fragments found in the room, however, including most of the deep bowls and kraters, were not burned. The fact that the vessels on the floor were burned but not the sherds that may have come from the earlier floor contradicts what was said in the excavation report and notebook.

Dating of the two deposits is difficult. Of the nearly complete pots from the floor, the earliest may be the stirrup jar **K23.19**, with its fringed and dotted crosshatched triangles; the decoration places it toward the end of early LM IIIC.[15] Perhaps somewhat later in date is jug **K23.20**, which finds parallels both at

Kavousi–*Kastro* of early LM IIIC and at Sybrita/Thronos of late LM IIIC.[16] The latest vessel is certainly the large carinated krater **K23.11**, with its most unusual shape and decoration. The rows of crosshatched triangles, with their linear character and regularity, along with the absence of any of the lively LM IIIC filler ornaments, suggest that it could be termed Subminoan in style, although exact parallels are lacking. The piece is similar to a kantharos from Kephallonia of the late LH IIIC period,[17] and the decoration may be paralleled on an amphoroid krater of LM III date from Tourtouloi.[18] Other whole or nearly complete pots are less closely datable.

As far as the fragments go, the deep bowls bear typical LM IIIC patterns of wavy line, spiral, panels, loops, and a possible double axe that find parallels in early LM IIIC sites. The tankards are clearly LM IIIC; one with a beaded rim (**K23.8**) is similar to an example from **K28.2**; the decoration of filled pendent triangles finds parallels on the mainland in middle LH IIIC.[19] Another (**K23.9**) has decoration similar to that on a vessel in LM IIIC Khania,[20] while the third (**K23.10**) bears a decoration of alternating arcs that look back to the LM IIIA period.[21] The other pottery is not closely datable.

Pottery Catalogue: K 23, Floor Deposit

Fine Wares

K23.1   Deep bowl or cup (FIG. 4.4). D. rim est. 13–14. Single fragment from rim. Fine, soft, yellow (10YR 7/6) fabric. Worn black paint. Spiral. LM IIIC early.

K23.2   Deep bowl or cup (FIG. 4.4). Max. pres. H. 4.7. Single fragment from rim. Fine, medium-soft, very pale brown (10YR 8/4) fabric and slip. Black paint worn to yellowish red (5YR 4/6). Worn surfaces. Loops with hatched oval. LM IIIC early.

K23.3   Deep bowl or cup (FIG. 4.4). Max. pres. H. 3.5. Single fragment from rim. Fine, soft, porous, very pale brown (10YR 8/4) fabric. White (10YR 8/2) slip. Dull streaky black paint, very worn.

11   Seiradaki, fig. 14.5.
12   Seiradaki, pl. 6e.
13   Seiradaki, pl. 4d, second from right.
14   *Karphi*, pl. 30.2.
15   Mountjoy, personal communication; see also Catling 1968, 116, fig. 6.24 of LM IIIC date; Paschalides 2009, 11, fig 14 (but with net pattern instead of crosshatching) of early LM IIIC.
16   Mook and Coulson 1997, 356, fig. 25.85 (Kavousi–*Kastro*, Phase II); D'Agata 1999, 197, fig. 9, 31.4; 2007, 101 (Sybrita/Thronos).
17   *RMDP*, 462–3, fig. 167.73 (Kephallonia, LH IIIC late).
18   Kanta 1980, 178–9, fig. 65.7.
19   Mountjoy 1986, 174, fig. 224.3.
20   *Khania II*, 112, pl. 54.71-P 1378.
21   Warren 1997, 163, fig. 13 (Knossos, LM IIIA early); Popham 1970b, 198, fig. 2.7 (Knossos, LM IIIB).

*Fig. 4.4. Magazines, pottery from K 23 (**K23.1–8**). Scale 1:3.*

Low wavy band. For decoration, cf. *Khania II*, 119, pl. 78.f.4 (Khania, early LM IIIC). LM IIIC early.

K23.4 Deep bowl or cup (FIG. 4.4). Max. pres. H. 3. Single fragment from rim. Fine, rather porous, soft, reddish yellow (7.5YR 7/6) fabric. Very pale brown (10YR 8/3) slip. Worn black paint. Spiral ? LM IIIC.

K23.5 Deep bowl or cup (FIG. 4.4). Max. pres. H. 2. Single body fragment. Fine, soft, reddish yellow (7.5YR 7/6) fabric. Very pale brown (10YR 8/3) slip. Very worn brown to red (2.5YR 4/8) paint. Panelled decoration with outlined double axe (?) with fringes, scalloped panel, spiral. LM IIIC early.

K23.6 Deep bowl or cup (FIG. 4.4). Max. pres. H. 3. Single body fragment. Fine, soft, reddish yellow (7.5YR 7/6) fabric. Very pale brown (10YR 8/3) slip. Red (2.5YR 5/8) paint. Very worn surfaces. Panelled decoration, with crosshatched vertical panel. LM IIIC.

K23.7 Deep bowl or cup (FIG. 4.4). Max. pres. H. 3.3. Single body fragment. Fine, soft, reddish yellow (7.5YR 7/6) fabric. White (10YR 8/2) slip. Dark reddish brown (5YR 3/3) paint. Well-preserved surfaces. Chevron? LM IIIC.

K23.8 Mug or tankard (PLATE 11 *d*, FIG. 4.4). D. rim est. <20. Two joining fragments from rim, including handle attachment. Fine, soft, reddish yellow (5YR 7/6) fabric. Very pale brown (10YR 8/3) slip. Worn red (10R 4/8) paint. Worn surfaces. Beaded decoration on rim; below rim, painted decoration of dotted pendent triangles. Cf. **K28.2**. LM IIIC.

K23.9 Mug or tankard (PLATE 11 *e*, FIG. 4.4). Max. pres. H. 8.3. Single body fragment. Fine, medium-soft, very pale brown (10YR 8/4) fabric and slip. Crackled paint, black to dark reddish brown (2.5YR 2.5/4). Well-preserved surfaces. Filled, outlined triangles. LM IIIC.

K23.10 Mug or tankard (FIG. 4.4). D. base est. 12. Single fragment from base. Fine, soft, very pale brown (10YR 8/4) fabric. Black paint. Very worn surfaces. Alternating arcs with fringe filler; monochrome interior. For shape, cf. *RMDP*, 576–7, fig. 213.368–70 (Perati, LH IIIC early). LM IIIB/C.

K23.11 Krater (PLATE 11 *f*, FIG. 4.4). H. est. 23 (with handles 24.3); D. rim 28.5. Restored from 65 fragments. 55% preserved, including both handles; missing entire base, half of body, fragments of rim. Fine, soft, dark brown (7.5YR 4/4) to light grey (5Y 7/1) fabric with tiny black inclusions, badly burned. Black paint. Handles have plastic band down centre. Crosshatched triangles below rim, and another band of triangles on rim; pendent crosshatched triangles on other side. Publication: Seiradaki, pl. 9b, fig. 16.4. LM IIIC late–SM.

K23.12 Krater (FIG. 4.4). Max. pres. H. 8.5. Two joining body fragments. Fine, soft, reddish yellow (7.5YR 7/6) fabric. Very pale brown (10YR 8/4) slip. Red (2.5YR 4/8) paint. Very worn surfaces. Running spirals with filler arcs. LM IIIC.

K23.13 Krater (FIG. 4.4). Max. pres. H. 4.6; Th. 0.65. Single fragment from body. Fine, rather hard, reddish yellow (5YR 6/8) fabric. Very pale brown (10YR 8/4) slip. Black crackled paint worn to red (10R 4/8). Well-preserved surfaces. Panel of dotted multiple horizontal zigzags. For zigzag in panel (without dots), cf. *Kastri*, 292, fig. 13.KP 31 (LM IIIC early). LM IIIC.

K23.14 Krater (FIG. 4.4). Max. pres. H. 7; Th 1.0. Single body fragment. Fine, soft, very pale brown (10YR 7/4) fabric. Very pale brown (10YR 8/4) slip. Black paint. Worn surfaces. Fringed vertical V-pattern. LM IIIC.

K23.15 Krater (FIG. 4.4). Max. pres. H. 3.7; Th 0.53. Single body fragment. Fine, soft, reddish yellow (7.5YR 7/6) fabric. Very pale brown (10YR 8/4) slip. Black paint. Worn exterior surfaces. Spiral (?) with fillers. LM IIIC.

K23.16 Jar or rhyton (FIG. 4.4). D. rim est. 18. Single fragment from rim, preserving handle attachment. Fine, soft, reddish yellow (5YR 7/6) fabric. Very pale brown (10YR 8/3) slip. Worn red (10R 4/8) paint. Rim rolled over so flat on top; handle attachment on top

of rim. Sides of rim have chevrons; top decorated with triangles within arcs, with filler arcs; interior painted. For folded-over rim, though rounded, not squared, cf. Watrous 1992, 76, fig. 48.1303 (Kommos, LM IIIA:2–B:1). LM IIIC.

K23.17 Miniature amphora (HM 11064) (PLATE 11 *g*, FIG. 4.4). H. 6.75; D. base 2.8–3; D. rim 2.85. Nearly complete. 90% preserved; missing a chip from body, half of rim, both handles. Fine, soft, light grey (10YR 7/2) to grey (5Y 6/1) fabric, almost totally burned. Horned projections on rim. Publication: Seiradaki, fig. 8.2; pl. 5b, right. For shape, cf. Cadogan 1967, 261–2, fig. 3.3 (Knossos, late LM IIIC). LM IIIC late.

K23.18 Thelastron (HM 11063) (PLATE 11 *h*, FIG. 4.4). Max. pres. H. 8.2; H. est. (with handle) 11; D. base 3.4; D. rim 4. Nearly intact, including handle attachment and base of spout; missing handle and spout. Fine, rather soft, grey (5Y 6/1) fabric with some tiny black inclusions. Black paint. Surface pocked and marked. Entirely burned. Monochrome. Publication: Seiradaki, fig. 10.1 (mislabelled K 11); pl. 5b, middle; Young 1938, 235, fig. 12 right, bottom, second from right. LM IIIC.

K23.19 Stirrup jar (FIG. 4.5). Max. pres. H. 9.6; max. D. 10. Three joining fragments from body and top of stirrup jar. 35% preserved, including half of body and one handle; missing half of body, second handle, spout, false spout, and base. Fine, soft, very pale brown (10YR 8/3) fabric and slip. Black paint. Completely burned except for one patch of body. Top added on as disc, with added clay ridge where joins body. Multiple narrow bands on lower body; on shoulder crosshatched, dotted, and fringed triangle, wavy lines, and fringed horizontal bands. Publication: Seiradaki, fig. 22j. LM IIIC early.

K23.20 Jug (FIG. 4.5). Max. pres. H. 16.8. Partially mended into two large fragments, one from near base (eight sherds), one from neck and shoulder (eight sherds); eight non-joining sherds. 25% preserved; missing base, rim, handle. Fine, soft, light grey (5Y 7/1) fabric. Surface entirely burned, with some darker patches of burning. Black paint. Bands on lower body, foliate band or necklace on shoulder. LM IIIC.

Medium-Coarse Wares

K23.21 Cup (FIG. 4.5). H. est. 10; D. base 3.6; D. rim est. 10.4. One large fragment from base, three joining sherds from rim, five non-joining sherds. 20% preserved, including nearly complete profile, handle. Medium-coarse, light brown (7.5YR 6/4) to grey (5Y 5/1) blue ware fabric with frequent large (1–3 mm) phyllite inclusions. Very worn surfaces and smoothed edges. LM IIIC.

K23.22 Jug (FIG. 4.5). H. est. 10; D. base 6.5. Single fragment preserving entire base, two joining fragments from neck and shoulder, including handle, and one body fragment; missing neck and rim. Medium-coarse, soft, reddish yellow (5YR 6/6) blue ware fabric with greenish grey (5G 5/1) core and hard white inclusions. Incised circles below lower handle attachment. LM IIIC.

K23.23 Stirrup jar (FIG. 4.5). Max. pres. H. 12.4. Single large fragment from top, preserving spout. Medium-coarse grey (5Y 6/1) fabric with gold mica and hard white angular inclusions (0.5 mm). Black paint. Burned inside and out. Top with spout not an added disc. Curved lines around spout and filler arcs between spout and bands. LM IIIC.

K23.24 Stirrup jar (FIG. 4.5). Max. pres. H. 5.2; Th. 0.5. Two non-joining body fragments. Medium-coarse, rather hard, light grey (10YR 7/2) fabric, possibly burned, with some hard dark grey inclusions. White (10YR 8/2) slip. Worn black paint. Stirrup jar or jar. Wavy line or debased octopus. LM IIIC.

Coarse Wares

K23.25 Cooking dish (FIG. 4.5). D. est. 40. Single small fragment from rim. Coarse red (10R 5/6) fabric with frequent

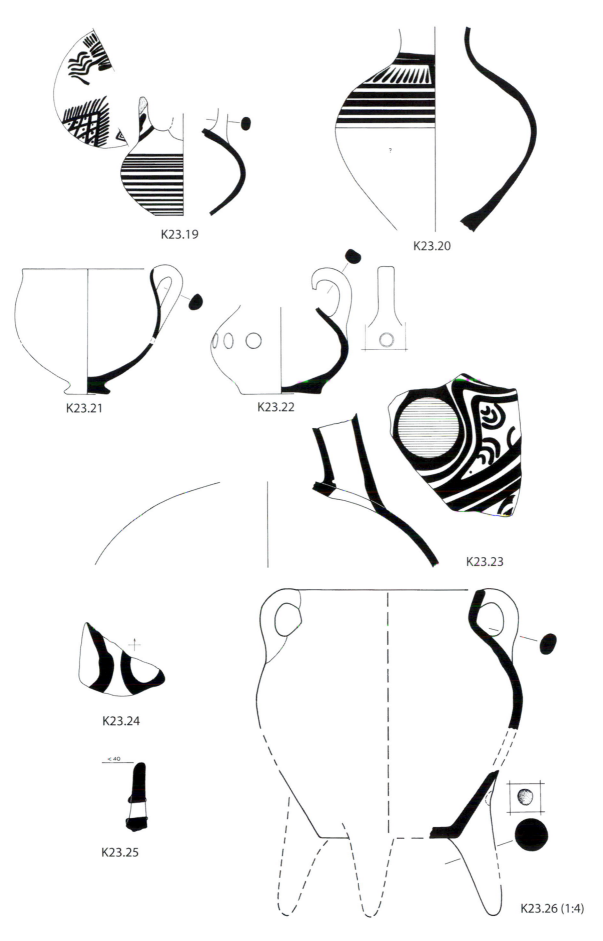

K23.19

K23.20

K23.21

K23.22

K23.23

K23.24

< 40

K23.25

K23.26 (1:4)

Fig. 4.5. Magazines, pottery from K 23 (**K23.19–26**). Scale 1:3 unless otherwise indicated.

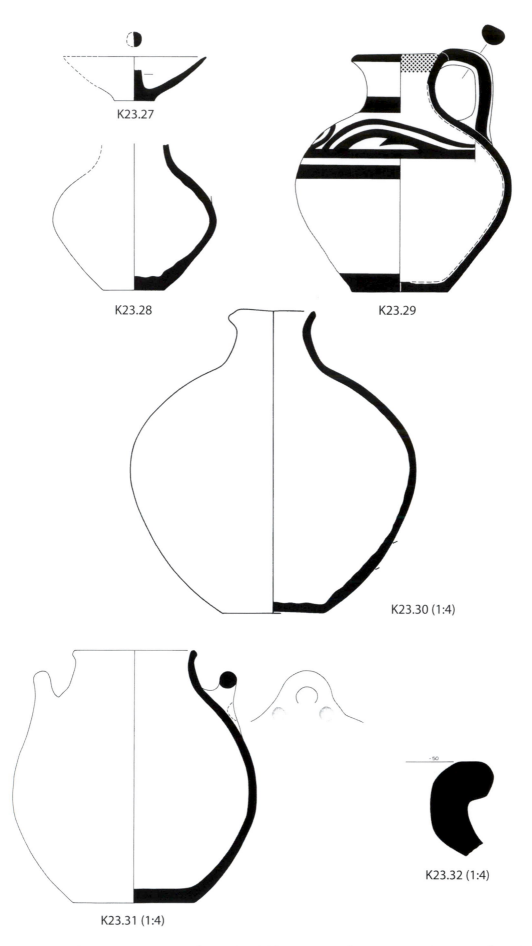

*Fig. 4.6. Magazines, pottery from K 23 (**K23.27–31**). Scale 1:3 unless otherwise indicated.*

phyllites, schist, and hard white angular inclusions (1–4 mm). Burned on exterior. Hole pierced through vertical rim. Label simply reads K 23. LM IIIC.

K23.26 Tripod cooking pot (FIG. 4.5). H. est. 34.5; D. rim est. 20. Once partially mended from 26 sherds. Half of rim, one handle and another handle attachment preserved, three legs (one may not belong). Coarse red (10R 5/8) fabric with frequent hard sharp white inclusions, grey and red phyllites, and much fine mica schist. Surface burned black in patches on exterior. Sampled KAR 06/38. Three fragments of badly burned base, including one leg, probably do not belong, since other fragments of the base are totally unburned, and there may be at least two tripod cooking pots. Dint at top of leg, where attached to body. For shape, cf. *Kastri*, 290, fig. 11.1; Borgna 1997*b*, 194, fig. 3.1b (Phaistos). LM IIIC.

K23.27 Lid (FIG. 4.6). Max. pres. H. 3.6; D. base 3.25; D. rim est. 11.4. Partially mended from six joining fragments. 30% preserved, including nearly complete profile, entire base; missing top of knob, most of one side. Coarse red (2.5YR 4/8) cookpot fabric with frequent large phyllite inclusions (2–3 mm); dark grey core. Surface smoothed and mottled. Shape like conical cup with knob in centre. Publication: Seiradaki, pl. 3d, top middle (mislabelled K 3). LM IIIC.

K23.28 Jug (FIG. 4.6). Max. pres. H. 11.8; D. base 5. Mended from 13 fragments, another large fragment (5 sherds) from near neck, and 9 non-joining sherds. 65% preserved, including all of base and lower handle attachment; missing most of neck, all of rim, handle. Very coarse yellowish red (5YR 5/6) fabric with frequent phyllite (?) inclusions (1–2 mm). Burned on bottom and one side. Ridging on interior. LM IIIC.

K23.29 Jug (PLATE 12 *a*, FIG. 4.6). H. 19.2 (with handle 19.6); D. base 7.8; D. rim 7.7. Restored from *c*. 40 fragments. 90% preserved; missing fragments of neck and body. Coarse, dark greenish grey (5GY 4/1) fabric with frequent large (1–2 mm) hard white and grey inclusions. Totally burned. Very pale brown (10YR 7/3) slip. Black paint. Spiral or concentric loops on shoulder, with double streamer. Publication: Seiradaki, pl. 5d, top left; fig. 9.3, labelled K 23. For shape, cf. Warren 2007, 343, fig. 8.P197 (Knossos, LM IIIC early). LM IIIC.

K23.30 Jug (FIG. 4.6). H. 32; D. base 11; D. rim 8.5–9.2. Once mended from 53 fragments. 60% preserved, including entire base and 75% of lower body and large fragment of upper body and rim; missing handle. Coarse red (10R 5/8) fabric with frequent red and grey phyllites, chunky black, and hard white angular inclusions. Handle attachment on lower body, so low that shape resembles a hydria rather than an oinochoe. Wheel ridging on interior. For shape, cf. *Kastri*, 296, fig. 16.P16. LM IIIC.

K23.31 Jar (FIG. 4.6). H. 26.7; D. base 13; D. rim 13. Restored from 19 fragments. 95% preserved; missing pieces of rim and body. Coarse very pale brown (10YR 7/3) to yellowish brown (10YR 5/4) fabric with very frequent red and grey phyllites and large sharp white inclusions from sand-sized to 4 mm. Burned on one side around handle and on other side entirely. Base very burned on bottom. Dints on base of handle where attaches to body. Labelled K 23. Publication: Seiradaki, fig. 3.1; pl. 1d. LM IIIC.

K23.32 Pithos (FIG. 4.6). D. rim est. 50. Single fragment from rim. Coarse reddish yellow (7.5YR 8/6) fabric with red phyllite inclusions. Red (10R 4/6) paint. LM IIIC.

K 23, Lower Floor Level

The notebook calls this level 'below the floor'. The publication says that the pottery consists of sherds of the usual types, but much broken and blackened by fire.[22] The notebook, however, attributes the burned fragments to the floor deposit and mentions a large proportion of fine sherds. The material from the museum

box was divided into two separate compartments, and these have been kept separate, although they may belong together. The preserved pottery was not noteworthy for its burning, and in fact, more of the fragments from the floor deposit of K 23 are burned than from this deposit. One cylindrical terracotta spindle whorl (293) was found in the lower deposit.

The upper deposit from below the floor contained, in addition to the catalogued sherds, the following pottery. From deep bowls there were three rim fragments (one with a rim band, one with a curvilinear pattern, one worn or plain), a flat raised base, and four body sherds (two with handle attachments, two with bands). Other open shapes included a krater with bands and three other body fragments with blob decoration, filler, and an indeterminate motif, as well as the handle from a cup or kylix. Closed vessels included a fragment of a stirrup jar or jug with filler design, three body fragments with bands, and a possible pyxis fragment with bands.

The material is not closely datable, in part because it is so small and scrappy. The octopus deep bowl (**K23.41**) may be early, as the depiction of tentacles with suckers is not regular on octopods of LM IIIC; a LM IIIC parallel can be found for this treatment, however, on a krater from Phase I at Kavousi–*Kastro*.[23] The decorative motif on the pyxis (**K23.44**) resembles a vessel from early LM IIIC Kastelli Pediada.[24] The deep bowl bases are raised and slightly hollowed, but not so much as on later examples, which almost approach the later conical foot of the PG style.

Pottery Catalogue: K 23, Below Floor, Upper Deposit

Fine Wares

K23.33 Cup (FIG. 4.7). Max. pres. H. 5.2. Single fragment from handle and rim. Fine, soft, reddish yellow (5YR 7/6) fabric. Worn black paint. LM IIIC.

K23.34 Deep bowl (FIG. 4.7). D. rim est. 12. Single fragment from rim and handle. Fine, soft, reddish yellow (5YR 7/6) fabric. Red (2.5YR 4/6) paint. Monochrome or blob decoration. LM IIIC.

K23.35 Deep bowl or cup (FIG. 4.7). D. rim est. 8. Single fragment from rim. Fine, soft, reddish yellow (5YR 7/6) fabric. Very pale brown (10YR 8/4) slip. Red (2.5YR 4/8) paint. Wavy line or loop? LM IIIC.

K23.36 Deep bowl or cup (FIG. 4.7). D. rim est. 12. Single fragment from rim. Fine, soft, reddish yellow (5YR 7/6) fabric. Very pale brown (10YR 8/4) slip. Dark reddish brown (2.5YR 3/4) paint, black inside. Wavy band. LM IIIC.

K23.37 Deep bowl or cup (FIG. 4.7). Max. pres. H. 3.4. Single body fragment. Fine, soft, reddish yellow (5YR 7/6) fabric. Very pale brown (10YR 8/4) slip. Reddish brown (2.5YR 4/4) to black paint. Metopal panel with multiple upright loops. LM IIIC.

K23.38 Deep bowl or cup (FIG. 4.7). Max. pres. H. 4.2. Single body fragment with worn surfaces. Fine, soft, reddish yellow (5YR

22 *Karphi*, 80.
23 Mook and Coulson 1997, 346, fig. 11.32.
24 Rethemiotakis 1997, 319, fig. 28ag.

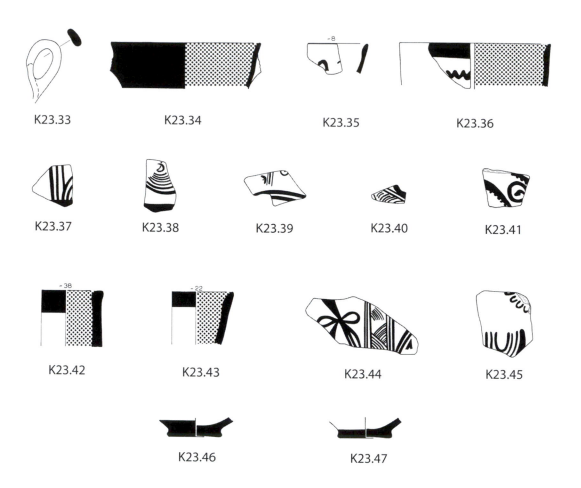

*Fig. 4.7. Magazines, pottery from K 23 lower deposit (**K23.32–46**). Scale 1:3.*

7/6) fabric. Very pale brown (10YR 8/4) slip. Dusky red (2.5YR 3/2) to red (2.5YR 4/8) paint. Spiral. LM IIIC.

K23.39   Deep bowl or cup (FIG. 4.7). Max. pres. H. 2.8. Two joining body fragments. Fine, soft, reddish yellow (5YR 7/6) fabric. Very pale brown (10YR 8/4) slip. Red (2.5YR 4/8) paint. Metopal panel with dotted loop on either side of multiple vertical lines. LM IIIC.

K23.40   Deep bowl or cup (FIG. 4.7). Max. pres. H. 1.4. Single body fragment. Fine, soft, reddish yellow (5YR 7/6) fabric. Very pale brown (10YR 8/4) slip. Dusky red (2.5YR 3/2) paint. Filler arcs. LM IIIC.

K23.41   Deep bowl or cup (FIG. 4.7). Max. pres. H. 3. Single body fragment. Fine, rather hard, light red (2.5YR 6/6) fabric. Very pale brown (10YR 8/4) slip. Black paint. Octopus? LM IIIC?

K23.42   Krater (FIG. 4.7). D. rim est. 38. Single fragment from rim. Fine, soft, reddish yellow (7.5YR 7/6) fabric. Very pale brown (10YR 8/4) slip. Dusky red (2.5YR 3/2) to very dark grey (2.5YR 3/0) paint. Very worn surfaces. Curvilinear motif. LM IIIC.

K23.43   Krater (FIG. 4.7). D. rim est. 22. Single fragment from rim. Fine, soft, reddish yellow (7.5YR 7/6) fabric. Very pale brown (10YR 8/4) slip. Black crackled paint. Curvilinear motif (spiral?). LM IIIC.

K23.44   Pyxis (FIG. 4.7). Max. pres. H. 4. Two joining body fragments. Fine, rather hard, reddish yellow (5YR 7/6) fabric. Very pale brown (10YR 8/4) slip. Red (2.5YR 4/8) paint, fairly well-preserved. Panelled decoration: alternating arcs between vertical bands, leaf pattern with loops or bow, curvilinear pattern.

K23.45   Closed vessel (FIG. 4.7). Max. pres. H. 5.2; Th. 0.7. Single body fragment. Fine, soft, reddish yellow (5YR 7/6) fabric. Very pale brown (10YR 8/3) slip. Red (2.5YR 5/8) paint. Multiple pendent loops, curvilinear motif outlined with U-pattern. LM IIIC.

K23.46   Closed vessel (FIG. 4.7). D. base 4.4. Single fragment preserving entire base. Fine, soft, reddish yellow (7.5YR 7/6) fabric. Very pale brown (10YR 8/4) slip. Worn paint. Worn surfaces. Raised, slightly hollowed base. LM IIIC.

K23.47   Closed vessel (FIG. 4.7). D. base 4.4. Single fragment preserving entire base. Fine, soft, reddish yellow (5YR 7/6) fabric. Very pale brown (10YR 8/4) slip. Red (2.5YR 4/6) paint. LM IIIC.

K 23, Below Floor, Lower Deposit

The lower deposit from below the floor contained much pottery that was too small to be catalogued. Deep bowls included a rim with pendent multiple loops and a body fragment with a handle attachment. Fragments of cups or deep bowls were decorated with blobs, vertical lines, leaf and bands, or bands, or they were monochrome or plain. Other fine ware included a krater body fragment with multiple streamers, a stirrup jar shoulder, a spout from a tankard, and three body fragments from closed vessels, one with spiral and filler, another with oblique strokes, and the third with bands. As with the material from the upper deposit below the floor, there were fewer burned fragments than expected from the report in the publication.

Like the material from the upper deposit below the floor, this pottery is difficult to date. There seems to be a great number of monochrome deep bowls or cups, although many of these may instead be parts of blob decoration. Cups and deep bowls with blob decoration are typical of the earlier LM IIIC deposits in Building B at Kavousi–*Vronda*,[25] and blob or monochrome cups also appear in Phase II at Kavousi–*Kastro*.[26] The decorative motifs on several of the deep bowls also find parallels with material from early LM IIIC, including **K23.50**,[27] **K23.51**,[28] and **K23.59**.[29] The kylix (**K23.62**) is similar to one found at Kavousi–*Vronda*, in the early LM IIIC deposits.[30]

The bases on the deep bowls are raised and either flat or concave, but again, there are no examples of the very high feet of the latest phases. The material in this deposit, then, is probably not the earliest LM IIIC, but early in LM IIIC.

Pottery Catalogue: Below Floor, Lower Deposit

Fine Wares

K23.48   Deep bowl (FIG. 4.8). D. rim est. 14. Single fragment from rim and handle. Fine, soft, reddish yellow (5YR 7/6) fabric. Very pale brown (10YR 8/4) slip. Worn reddish brown (2.5YR 4/4) paint. Band at rim. Decoration unclear because of worn surfaces. LM IIIC.

K23.49   Deep bowl (FIG. 4.8). Max. pres. H. 3.8. Single fragment preserving one handle. Fine, soft, light red (2.5YR 6/8) fabric. Black paint, only preserved on top of handle. Round horizontal handle. LM IIIC.

K23.50   Deep bowl or cup (FIG. 4.8). D. rim est. 20. Single fragment from rim. Fine, soft, reddish yellow (5YR 7/6) fabric. Very pale brown (10YR 8/4) slip. Reddish brown (2.5YR 4/4) paint. Worn surfaces. Multiple pendent loops, with hatching between two innermost; circle in centre. LM IIIC early.

K23.51   Deep bowl or cup (FIG. 4.8). D. rim est. 14. Single fragment from rim. Fine, soft, reddish yellow (5YR 7/6) fabric. Very pale brown (10YR 8/4) slip. Dark reddish brown (2.5YR 3/4) paint, black on interior. Panelled decoration with leaf or quatrefoil. LM IIIC early.

K23.52   Deep bowl or cup (FIG. 4.8). D. rim est. 12. Single fragment from rim. Fine, soft, reddish yellow (7.5YR 7/6) fabric. Dark brown (7.5YR 3/2) paint. Monochrome or blob decoration. LM IIIC early.

K23.53   Deep bowl or cup (FIG. 4.8). D. rim est. 14. Single fragment from rim. Fine, fairly hard, reddish yellow (5YR 7/6) fabric. Dark brown (7.5YR 3/2) to very dark grey (7.5YR 3/0) paint. Monochrome or blob decoration. LM IIIC early.

K23.54   Deep bowl or cup (FIG. 4.8). Max. pres. H. 3. Single fragment from rim. Fine, soft, reddish yellow (5YR 7/6) fabric. Red (2.5YR 5/8) paint. Monochrome or blob decoration. LM IIIC.

K23.55   Deep bowl or cup (FIG. 4.8). D. rim est. 13 Single large fragment from rim. Fine, soft, reddish yellow (5YR 7/6) fabric. Dark reddish brown (5YR 3/2) paint. Monochrome or blob decoration. LM IIIC.

K23.56   Deep bowl or cup (FIG. 4.8). D. rim est. 8. Two fragments, one from rim, another from base. Fine, hard, grey (N5/) blue ware fabric. LM IIIC.

K23.57   Deep bowl or cup (FIG. 4.8). D. base 4.1. Single fragment, preserving entire base. Fine, soft, reddish yellow (5YR 7/6) fabric. Dark red (2.5YR 3/6) paint. Bands on base and lower body. LM IIIC.

K23.58   Deep bowl or cup (FIG. 4.8). D. base est. 4. Single fragment preserving half of base. Fine, soft, reddish yellow (5YR 7/6) fabric. Red (2.5YR 5/8) paint. Surfaces entirely painted, probably monochrome. LM IIIC.

K23.59   Deep bowl or cup (FIG. 4.8). Max. pres. H. 2.5. Single body fragment. Fine, soft, reddish yellow (7.5YR 7/6) fabric. Very pale brown (10YR 8/4) slip. Black to brown paint. Bivalve shell. For decoration, cf. **K43.7**. LM IIIC early.

K23.60   Deep bowl or cup (FIG. 4.8). Max. pres. H. 4. Single body fragment. Fine, soft, reddish yellow (5YR 7/6) fabric. Very pale brown (10YR 8/4) slip. Red (2.5YR 4/6) paint. Hatched motifs. LM IIIC.

K23.61   Deep bowl or cup (FIG. 4.8). Max. pres. H. 3. Single body fragment. Fine, soft, reddish yellow (5YR 7/6) fabric. Very pale brown (10YR 8/4) slip. Red (2.5YR 4/8) paint. Hatched leaf ? LM IIIC.

K23.62   Shallow bowl or kylix (FIG. 4.8). D. rim est. 14. Single fragment from rim. Fine, soft, reddish yellow (5YR 7/6) fabric. Pink (7.5YR 8/4) surface. Plain or blob decoration. LM IIIC.

K23.63   Kylix (FIG. 4.8). D. rim est. 12. Single tiny fragment from rim. Fine, soft, reddish yellow (7.5YR 7/6) fabric. Worn black paint. Monochrome? LM IIIC.

K23.64   Krater (FIG. 4.8). Max. pres. H. 3.6. Single body fragment. Fine, soft, reddish yellow (7.5YR 7/6) fabric. Very pale brown (10YR 8/3) slip. Red (2.5YR 5/8) paint. Curvilinear motifs, possibly panelled. LM IIIC.

K23.65   Krater (FIG. 4.8). Max. pres. H. 4.1. Single body fragment. Fine, soft, reddish yellow (5YR 7/6) fabric. Very pale brown (10YR 8/3) slip. Shadow of paint. Spiral. LM IIIC.

K23.66   Pyxis (FIG. 4.8). D. rim est. 16. Single large fragment from rim and upper body, preserving handle attachment. Fine, soft, reddish yellow (5YR 7/6) fabric, rather harder than usual. Very pale brown (10YR 8/4) slip. Red (2.5YR 4/8) paint. Multiple pendent loops (?). LM IIIC.

K23.67   Stirrup jar (FIG. 4.8). Max. pres. H. 3.5. Single body fragment from area of spout. Fine, soft, reddish yellow (5YR 7/6) fabric. Very pale brown (10YR 8/4) slip. Dark reddish brown (2.5YR 3/4) paint. Fringed multiple loops. LM IIIC.

K23.68   Stirrup jar (FIG. 4.8). Max. pres. H. 2.4. Single body fragment from shoulder. Fine, soft, reddish yellow (5YR 7/6) fabric. Very pale brown (10YR 8/4) slip. Crackled black paint, worn. Multiple loops with arc fillers. LM IIIC.

K23.69   Jug (FIG. 4.8). D. rim est. 11. Single fragment from rim. Fine, soft, reddish yellow (7.5YR 7/6) fabric. Very pale brown (10YR 8/3) slip. Red (2.5YR 4/6) paint. Banded decoration, inside and out. LM IIIC?

K23.70   Jar or jug? (FIG. 4.8). D. rim est. 11. Single fragment from rim. Fine, soft, chalky, light red (2.5YR 6/8) fabric. Very pale brown (10YR 8/4) slip. Dusky red (2.5YR 3/2) paint. Worn surfaces. LM IIIC?

---

25   *Kavousi IIA*, fig. 25; Day and Snyder 2004, 68, fig. 5.6.1–3; Day 1997, 400, fig. 6.

26   Mook and Coulson 1997, 352, fig. 1.72-81.

27   Mook and Coulson 1997, 358, fig. 30.109 (Kavousi–*Kastro*, Phase I–II).

28   Mook and Coulson 1997, 352, fig. 18.55 (Kavousi–*Kastro*, Phase II).

29   *Kastri*, 287, fig. 8k; Gesell, Day, and Coulson 1995, 118, fig. 22 (Kavousi–*Kastro*, LM IIIB/C).

30   *Kavousi IIA*, 44, fig. 26.B4 P20.

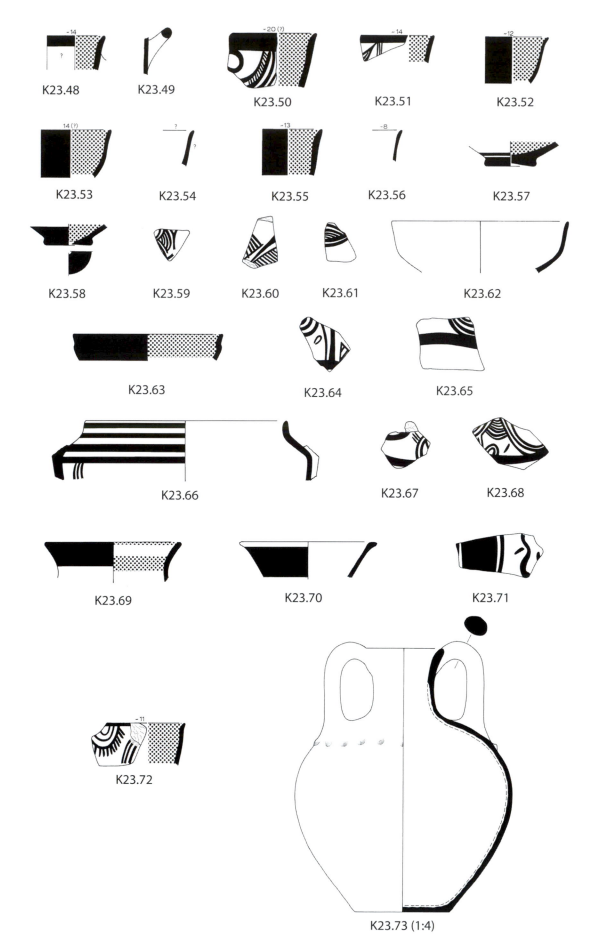

Fig. 4.8. Magazines, pottery from K 23 (**K23.47–70**) and outside K 23 (**K23.71–72**). Scale 1:3 unless otherwise indicated.

K23.71   Closed vessel (FIG. 4.8). Max. pres. H. 3.4; Th 0.55. Single body fragment. Fine, soft, reddish yellow (7.5YR 7/6) fabric. Very pale brown (10YR 8/4) slip. Red (2.5YR 5/8) paint. Uncertain curvilinear motif. LM IIIC.

Just Outside K 23 to E

According to the notebook, in 1939 pottery was found just outside K 23 to the east, including few sherds, very fragmentary, with a large proportion of fine ware. Included in this deposit were the top of a large red stirrup jar, a lid with rope moulding, and two jars of Type 3, one of which had knobs around the shoulder (**K23.73**).

Pottery Catalogue: Outside K 23

Fine Wares

K23.72   Deep bowl or cup (FIG. 4.8). D. rim est. 11. Two joining fragments from rim. Fine, rather soft, very pale brown (10YR 7/4) fabric. Very pale brown (10YR 8/4) slip. Worn black paint, better preserved on interior than exterior. Fringed multiple pendent loops alternating with multiple upright loops or multiple stems. LM IIIC.

Coarse Wares

K23.73   Amphora (PLATE 12 *b*, FIG. 4.8). H. 28 (with handles 28.8); D. base 10; D. rim 8.5. Restored; nearly complete in single fragment. 95% preserved; missing much of one handle and 75% of neck. Coarse, yellowish red (5YR 5/8–5/6) fabric with frequent schist, some black basalt, and hard white angular inclusions (<3 mm). Surface smooth and mottled. Ring of black burning on one side. Knobs just below lower handle attachment. Labelled outside K 23 to E. LM IIIC.

Room K 29

Rooms K 29 and K 30 may have been two separate rooms or a single room separated by a buttress. K 29 was a small compartment approached by stairs from K 23, and it was built up against a wall of bedrock on the east. Pottery was listed as usual, but mention was made of a larnax fragment (**K29.17**). The notebook lists the following additional pottery from this room: a flat open dish with upright side and horizontal handle (i.e. a tray), a large red stirrup vase, a gritty blue bowl (**K29.10**), and a ridged pedestal base. Fragments from this room found in the boxes but not catalogued included two deep bowls with spirals, a fine jug handle, a thelastron spout, two stirrup jars, and a jar or jug with creamy white slip and red paint. A pithoid jar published by Seiradaki is actually the larnax rim mentioned in the publication;[31] the jar pictured in Seiradaki was not located.[32]

Other objects from K 29 included a bronze curved disc or cap (265),[33] a bronze sickle (267), a bronze ring (268),[34] a conical lump of steatite (269), a Neolithic stone axe (292),[35] a cylindrical terracotta spindle whorl (270), and a fragment of a bone implement (266).

The fine pottery from the room comes chiefly from deep bowls or cups. Many of the motifs are those that are popular very early in LM IIIC: the buttonhook spiral, the quirk, and the outlined double axe. The very tight form of the quirk on **K29.4** may be an earlier feature; it appears, for example, at Kastri.[36] The buttonhook spiral seems popular in the early part of LM IIIC at Kastri and Knossos.[37] Deep bowl **K29.6** finds parallels at LM IIIC Phaistos, but cannot be more closely dated.[38] The larnax (**K29.17**) finds its closest parallels in east Cretan burials of LM IIIB or LM IIIB/C; the dark fish with wavy lines in a central panel is most similar to one on a LM IIIB larnax from Pacheia Ammos,[39] but it also resembles the fish on the interiors of a group of sarcophagi from the same workshop dating to LM IIIB/C from Tourtouli, Piskokephalo, and Praisos–*Papoures*.[40] The material, then, looks rather earlier than some of the late LM IIIC deposits found elsewhere at Karphi, although not perhaps as early as the deposits in K 76 or those below the floors of the Great House or K 23. The material provides little information on the function of this room. The larnax (**K29.17**), which is of the bathtub variety, is probably not funerary but practical.

Pottery Catalogue: K 29

Fine Wares

K29.1   Deep bowl or cup (PLATE 12 *c*, FIG. 4.9). D. rim 14. Two joining fragments from rim. Fine, soft, dark yellowish brown (10YR 4/4) fabric. Worn very pale brown (10YR 8/4) slip. Black paint worn to brown, streaky inside. Buttonhook spirals. LM IIIC early.

K29.2   Deep bowl or cup (FIG. 4.9). D. rim est. 16. Single fragment from rim. Fine, rather hard, reddish yellow (7.5YR 7/6) fabric. White (10YR 8/2) slip. Worn black paint. Buttonhook spirals. LM IIIC early.

K29.3   Deep bowl or cup (PLATE 12 *c*, FIG. 4.9). D. rim est. 11. Single fragment from rim, tip broken off. Fine, fairly hard, reddish yellow (7.5YR 7/6) fabric with white sand-sized inclusions. Very pale brown (10YR 8/4) slip. Worn black paint, streaky inside. Carinated. Buttonhook spiral. Publication: Seiradaki, fig. 21b (upside down). LM IIIC early.

K29.4   Deep bowl or cup (FIG. 4.9). D. rim est. 16–18. Single fragment from rim. Fine, soft, very pale brown (10YR 7/4) fabric and slip. Very worn black paint. Quirk. Seiradaki, fig. 21. LM IIIC early.

K29.5   Deep bowl or cup (FIG. 4.9). Max. pres. H. 4.6; max. D. 13. Single fragment from lower body. Fine, hard, reddish yellow

31   Seiradaki, fig. 2.1.

32   Seiradaki, fig. 3.3.

33   *Karphi*, pl. 29.1.

34   *Karphi*, pl. 29.2.

35   *Karphi*, pl. 30.2.

36   *Kastri*, 288, fig. 9 l. Hallager 2000, 174, n. 343, places this fragment in early LM IIIC, since the motif continues from LM IIIB.

37   *Kastri*, 288, fig. 9d, e; Warren 2007, 337, fig. 2.

38   Borgna 1997*a*, 281, fig. 19 and fig. 5.7.

39   Kanta 1980, 144, fig. 56.3–4.

40   Kanta 1980, 177, 292, figs. 65.3–4, 66.1–2, 73.10.

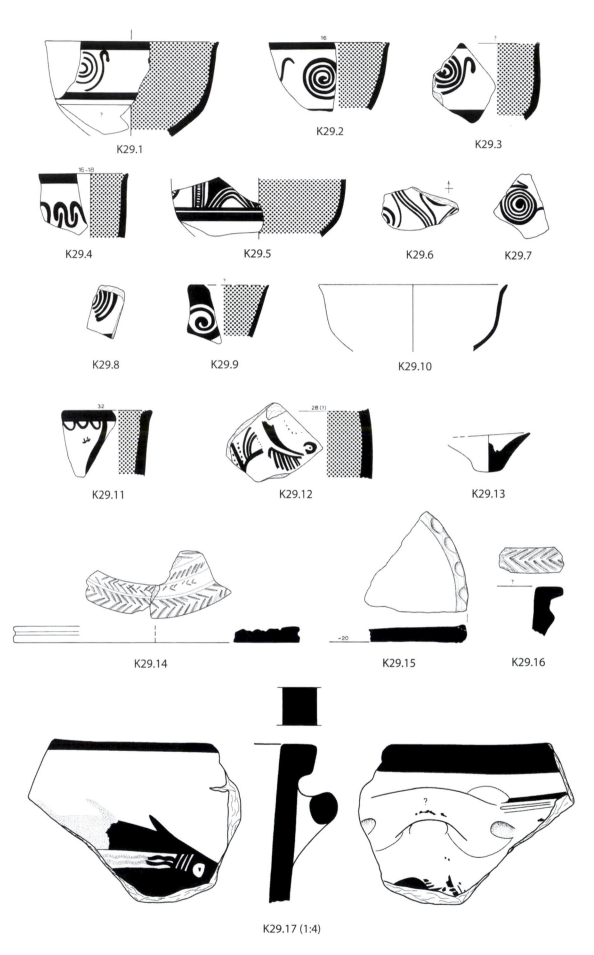

*Fig. 4.9. Magazines, pottery from K 29 (**K29.1–17**). Scale 1:3 unless otherwise indicated.*

(7.5YR 7/6) fabric. Pink (7.5YR 8/4) slip. Dusky red (2.5YR 3/2) to red (2.5YR 4/8) paint. Well-preserved surfaces. Carinated. Fabric looks imported. Metopal panel design: double axe (?) with loops underneath; vertical bands with horizontal hatching, curvilinear design with hatching. LM IIIC early.

K29.6   Deep bowl or cup (FIG. 4.9). Max. pres. H. 3.5. Single body fragment. Fine, rather hard, reddish yellow (7.5YR 7/6) fabric. Very pale brown (10YR 8/4) slip. Black paint. Well-preserved surfaces. Alternating stemmed spirals and multiple curved bands. LM IIIC.

K29.7   Deep bowl or cup (FIG. 4.9). Max. pres. H. 5.2. Two joining body fragments. Fine, soft, reddish yellow (5YR 7/6) fabric. Very pale brown (10YR 8/3) slip. Red (2.5YR 4/8) paint. Worn surfaces. Buttonhook spiral with hook over back. For motif, cf. Borgna 1997*a*, 277, fig. 2 (Phaistos, LM IIIB–C). LM IIIC early.

K29.8   Deep bowl or cup (FIG. 4.9). Max. pres. H. 4.2. Single body fragment. Fine, soft, reddish yellow (5YR 7/6) fabric. Very pale brown (10YR 8/3) slip. Worn black paint. Multiple upright loops. LM IIIC.

K29.9   Deep bowl or kylix (FIG. 4.9). Max. pres. H. 4.2. Single fragment from rim. Fine, soft, reddish yellow (7.5YR 7/6) fabric. Very pale brown (10YR 8/3) slip. Red (10R 4/8) paint. Worn surfaces. Spiral. LM IIIC.

K29.10   Shallow bowl (FIG. 4.9). D. rim est. 15. Single fragment from rim preserving *c*. 20% of rim. Fine, hard, dark greenish grey (5BG 4/1) blue ware fabric with tiny inclusions of mica. Traces of black paint. Once decorated? LM IIIC.

K29.11   Krater (FIG. 4.9). D. rim est. 32. Single fragment from rim. Fine, soft, reddish yellow (7.5YR 7/6) fabric. Very pale brown (10YR 8/3) slip. Worn black paint. Surfaces very worn. Loops hanging from rim, curvilinear motif below. LM IIIC.

K29.12   Krater (FIG. 4.9). Max. pres. H. 5.6; max. D. 28. Single body fragment. Fine, soft, reddish yellow (7.5YR 7/6) fabric. Very pale brown (10YR 8/3) slip. Black cracked paint, worn in places. Fringed and dotted curvilinear motif, possibly a bird. LM IIIC.

K29.13   Lid (FIG. 4.9). Max. pres. H. 3.1. Intact except for chips from rim and broken knob. Fine, soft, light red (2.5YR 6/6) fabric with some tiny white inclusions. Very pale brown (10YR 7/3) surface. Shaped like conical cup, but with rounded bottom. Knob inside centre. Very crude. LM IIIC?

Coarse Wares

K29.14   Lid (FIG. 4.9). D. est. 23–24. Two joining fragments from rim; missing centre and handle. Coarse red (10R 5/6) fabric with frequent phyllites and hard white angular inclusions (1–2 mm); hard, smoothed surfaces. Fire blackened on bottom around edge for about 2.5 cm. Sampled KAR 06/01. Flat circular disc with groove on edge. Ridges with incised chevron patterns. Publication: Seiradaki, pl. 12a, bottom row, left (one fragment). For shape and decoration, cf. Andreadaki-Vlasaki and Papadopoulou 2005, 378, fig 43.94.4.301 (Khamalevri, Phase II). LM IIIC.

K29.15   Lid (FIG. 4.9). D. est. 20. Single fragment from rim. Coarse red (10R 5/6) fabric with frequent large (1–2 mm) schist inclusions; surface smooth and mottled. Bottom fire-blackened around edge for 5.5 cm. Flat disc with raised ridge with finger impressions around edge on top, incisions around edge on bottom. For decoration, cf. *Khania II*, pl. 47.71-P 1312. LM IIIC.

K29.16   Pithoid jar or basin (FIG. 4.9). Max. pres. H. 4. Single small fragment from rim. Coarse red (10R 5/8) fabric with schist inclusions (1–2 mm). Incised chevrons on rim. Number unclear, may be from either K 29 or K 79. LM IIIC.

K29.17   Larnax (PLATE 12 *d*, FIG. 4.9). Max. pres. H. 17. Single fragment from rim, including handle. Coarse fabric, reddish yellow at core (5YR 6/6) and on surface (7.5YR 7/6), with frequent dark grey phyllites and schist. Black paint, badly worn. Bathtub larnax. Exterior has fringed motif, too fragmentary to identify; interior has fish. Publication: Seiradaki, fig. 2.1 (as pithoid jar). LM IIIB/C.

Room K 30

Like K 29, this was a small compartment backed up against the rock and separated from K 29 by a buttress. The published fine krater with rows of double loops in a scale pattern[41] was not located. This vessel finds a close parallel at Kavousi–*Vronda*.[42] The notebook only mentions a tripod bowl (**K30.1**) and a flat dish (possibly a tray) with wavy rim and finger dints. Objects found in the room included a fragment of bronze (295) and a cylindrical terracotta spindle whorl (294). The tripod bowl (**K30.1**) is of an unusual type, open, with a rim like a pithoid jar and apparently a rounded bottom. It may be an example of the round-bottomed tripod cooking pot that is thought to have been introduced into Crete in LM III from the mainland.[43]

Pottery Catalogue: K 30

Coarse Wares

K30.1   Tripod cooking pot (FIG. 4.10). D. rim est. 48. Single large fragment from rim with leg attachment. Coarse red (2.5YR 5/8) fabric with frequent large (1–3 mm) phyllite inclusions. Exterior very burned. Flat rim, outwardly thickened; foot attached on body above base. Probably round-bottomed. Publication: Seiradaki, fig. 2.8 (pithoid jar, Type 8). LM IIIC.

Room K 31

This small room just north of K 23 was perhaps divided into two unequal halves by a partition that is not shown on the plan.[44] It was entered through a doorway on the east, and possibly also by ladder through a hatch from K 23. The pottery was recorded in the publication as usual, but without pyxides. The notebook mentions that there were few pithos sherds, and most of these came from a single pithos with a chevron design. Other pottery listed in the notebook includes the following: coarse stirrup jars, tripods, dishes, kalathoi, jars, some straight-sided bases, a punctuated sherd, and quite a large proportion of fine ware, including parts of two kylikes, one large krater, and a very small sherd that appeared to be a Mycenaean or Knossian import. Pottery from the boxes that was not catalogued includes four deep bowl fragments (decorated with multiple loops, spirals, and panelled pattern), a krater with multiple strokes, a stirrup jar, three pithoid jar rims (one of buff fabric with raised bands and incised circles),[45] and a strainer spout. There were also two cooking trays, one with a horizontal handle and another

---

41   Seiradaki, fig. 16.3 and pl. 9c.

42   Gesell, Day and Coulson 1995, 90, fig. 7.2.

43   Borgna 1997*b*, 200. While the round bottomed variety does not become common until LM III, it does occur in Neopalatial contexts; see Kanta and Karetsou 2003, 150.

44   *Karphi*, 79.

45   Possibly the one pictured in Seiradaki, fig. 2.9.

*Fig. 4.10. Magazines, pottery from K 30 (**K30.1**) and K 31 (**K31.1–16**). Scale 1:3.*

shallow one. Objects found in the room included a fragment of a bronze knife (298), a Neolithic axe (297),[46] a fragment of a steatite bowl (299), a cylindrical terracotta spindle whorl (296), a pierced, sharpened boar's tusk (300), and the antler of a red deer.

The preserved pottery does not look particularly late, although it is clearly LM IIIC. The deep bowl or cup without a rim band (**K31.5**) is unusual, but the feature does not seem to be a chronological indicator. The metopal panel on deep bowl **K31.1** finds many parallels in LM IIIB and it appears in the earliest LM IIIC levels at Kavousi–*Kastro*[47] and in early LM IIIC deposits at Kastelli Pediada, Phaistos, and Kastri.[48] The panelled pattern of deep bowl or cup **K31.4** has parallels in the second phase of the Kavousi–*Kastro* deposit[49] and at Petras and Knossos of advanced LM IIIB date.[50] Thus it looks as though the pottery (much of it fragmentary) belongs to the LM IIIB/C transition or early LM IIIC and does not represent the latest material from the site. The coarse wares, of course, do not provide a date, nor do they suggest a function for Room K 31; it seems unlikely to have been used solely for storage, given the few pithoi found in it. The lids and trays may indicate cooking.

Pottery Catalogue: K 31

Fine Wares

K31.1 Deep bowl (FIG. 4.10). D. rim est. 13. Single fragment from rim, preserving handle attachment. Fine, rather hard, reddish yellow (7.5YR 7/6) fabric. Very pale brown (10YR 8/3) slip. Dark reddish brown (5YR 3/4) to red (10R 5/8) paint. Panelled decoration: vertical lines, with solid band at end, curved, and outlined. For decoration, cf. **K79-89.5**. LM IIIC early.

K31.2 Deep bowl or cup (PLATE 2 *g*, FIG. 4.10). D. rim est. 16. Single fragment from rim. Fine, soft, rather porous, reddish yellow (5YR 7/6) fabric. Very pale brown (10YR 8/4) slip. Red (2.5YR 4/8) paint. Well-preserved surfaces. Multiple arcs with antithetic single loops between. For shape, cf. Borgna 1997a, 278, fig. 6.7 (Phaistos, LM IIIB–C); for motif, cf. Kanta 1980, fig. 15.12 (Amnisos); Hatzaki 2005, 137, fig. 4.11.1; *RMDP*, 780, fig. 306.229–38 (Phocis, LH IIIC early). LM IIIC early.

K31.3 Deep bowl or cup (FIG. 4.10). Max. pres. H. 3.5. Single small fragment from rim. Fine, medium-soft, reddish yellow (7.5YR 7/6) fabric. White (10YR 8/2) slip. Black to dark red (2.5YR 3/6) paint. Exterior surfaces poorly preserved, well-preserved interior. Pendent loops with arc fillers. LM IIIC.

K31.4 Deep bowl or cup (FIG. 4.10). D. rim est. 10–11. Single fragment from rim. Fine, rather soft, reddish yellow (7.5YR 7/6) fabric. Very pale brown (10YR 8/3) slip. Worn black paint. Metopal panel design: quatrefoil leaf pattern, vertical panel of alternating arcs. LM IIIC early.

K31.5 Deep bowl or cup (FIG. 4.10). D. rim 14. Single fragment from rim. Fine, soft porous, reddish yellow (7.5YR 7/6) fabric. Very pale brown (10YR 8/3) slip. Reddish brown (2.5YR 4/4) paint. Worn surfaces. Pendent multiple loops with solid centre, multiple rectilinear pattern. No rim band. LM IIIC.

K31.6 Deep bowl or cup (FIG. 4.10). D. rim est. 12. Single fragment from rim. Fine, soft, reddish yellow (7.5YR 7/6) fabric. White (10YR 8/2) slip. Black paint worn to brown. Worn surfaces. Buttonhook spiral (?) or other tailed spiral. LM IIIC early.

K31.7 Deep bowl or cup (FIG. 4.10). D. rim est. 15. Single fragment from rim. Fine, soft, reddish yellow (7.5YR 7/6) fabric.

Very pale brown (10YR 8/3) slip. Dull black paint. Worn surfaces. Spiral. LM IIIC.

K31.8 Krater (FIG. 4.10). D. rim est. 34. Two large fragments, one from rim (3 sherds), one from body (2 sherds). Fine, soft, reddish yellow (7.5YR 7/6) fabric. White (10YR 8/2) slip. Dark brown (7.5YR 3/4) paint. Very worn surfaces. Entire upper surface of vessel covered with interlocking horizontal multiple loops with arc and stroke fillers. For decoration, cf. Popham 1970b, pl. 50b (Knossos LM IIIB). LM IIIC.

K31.9 Krater (FIG. 4.10). Max. pres. H. 5.8. Single fragment from rim. Fine, soft, reddish yellow (7.5YR 7/6) fabric with mica inclusions. White (10YR 8/2) slip. Dark red (2.5YR 3/6) paint. Worn surfaces. Metopal panel with quatrefoil leaf or double axe; strokes on top of rim. LM IIIC.

K31.10 Basin (FIG. 4.10). D. rim est. 19.3. Single fragment from rim. Fine, soft, reddish yellow (7.5YR 7/6) fabric with voids where inclusions have come out. Very pale brown (10YR 8/3) slip. Red (10R 4/8) paint. Worn surfaces. Wavy line or debased octopus. Label worn; may be from K 21. LM IIIC.

K31.11 Jug (PLATE 12 *e*, FIG. 4.10). Max. pres. H. 9.4; H. est. 12; D. base 4; D. rim est. 4.7. Intact, but not complete; restored. 75% preserved; missing neck, rim, and half of handle. Fine, soft, reddish yellow (5YR 6/6) fabric, pinkish grey (7.5YR 6/2) where burned, with tiny black inclusions; surface pocked as if inclusions fallen or burned out. Red (10R 4/8) to black paint. Surfaces worn and almost entirely burned. Wavy line on shoulder, bands below. For shape and decoration, cf. Nowicki 2008, 101, fig. 52.KP 282 (Katalimata, LM IIIC). LM IIIC.

K31.12 Closed vessel (FIG. 4.10). Max. pres. H. 2.9; Th. 0.7. Single body fragment. Fine, soft, rather porous, very pale brown (10YR 8/4) fabric. Very pale brown (10YR 8/3) slip. Paint black to dark yellowish brown (10YR 3/4). Rather well-preserved surfaces. Spiral with dots. LM IIIC.

Medium-Coarse Wares

K31.13 Stirrup jar (FIG. 4.10). Max. pres. H. 6; Th. 0.5. Single body fragment. Medium-coarse, soft, reddish yellow (7.5YR 8/6) fabric with frequent voids (1–7 mm) where inclusions have come out. Very pale brown (10YR 8/3) slip. Red (10R 4/8) paint. Wavy line or debased octopus. LM IIIC.

Coarse Wares

K31.14 Tray (FIG. 4.10). H. 3.8; D. base est. 38. Two joining fragments from rim and base. Coarse red (10R 5/6) fabric with frequent schist and mica inclusions (1–2 mm); surface mottled, smoothed, and cracked. One fragment burned. Shallow flat tray with band of finger impressions on rim. Publication: Seiradaki, fig. 6.4, where it is called a dish. For shape, cf. *Kastri*, 296, fig. 16.P3. LM IIIC.

K31.15 Lid (PLATE 12 *g*, FIG. 4.10). D. est. 22. Single fragment from rim. Coarse red (10R 5/6) fabric with frequent schist and mica inclusions (1–2 mm). Smoothed and mottled surface. Bottom fire-burned except for 2 cm around outer edge. Flat disc with raised rim, flattened ridges around edge and near edge with incised rope slashing. LM IIIC.

46   *Karphi*, pl. 30.2.

47   Mook and Coulson 1997, 344, fig. 8.23.

48   Rethemiotakis 1997, 323, fig. 34a; Borgna 1997a, 277, fig. 2; *Kastri*, 287, fig. 8q.

49   Mook and Coulson 1997, 352, fig. 18.63.

50   Tsipopoulou 1997, 220, fig. 18d. 91.144.2; Popham 1964, pl. 8a.

K31.16   Pierced lug (FIG. 4.10). Max. pres. L. 4.4. Single fragment from end of handle. Coarse red (2.5YR 5/8) clay with schist inclusions. Elliptical handle, squared off and pierced near end. May be from scuttle or ladle. LM IIIC.

Room K 33

Room K 33 was a simple small room with a doorway out onto K 35 to the east; it may have been an independent building. In the publication, the pottery was said to be as usual, but there was little fine ware.[51] The notebook lists a good deal of pottery from this room. There were sherds from four pithoi, but only one in any quantity, and it has a pinched rope below the rim. Additional coarse ware included tripods with both vertical and horizontal handles (two of each type), four dishes, and two kalathoi. Fine wares were rather fewer than usual; there were parts of two kraters, stirrup jars, a kylix stem, and a hut urn (**K33.2**). Found in the boxes but not catalogued were two fine deep bowls, one burned with a spiral design, the other with vertical strokes. Stirrup jar fragments were decorated with fringed half circles, vertical strokes, filling motifs, fringes, and scale pattern. The krater illustrated in Seiradaki may be the same as the coarse bowl catalogued below (**K33.3**).[52] Objects from the room included two cylindrical terracotta spindle whorls (301, 302) and the antler of a red deer.

Pottery Catalogue: K 33

Fine Wares

K33.1   Deep bowl or cup (FIG. 4.11). D. rim est. 11. Single fragment from rim. Fine, fairly hard, reddish yellow (7.5YR7/6) fabric. Very pale brown (10YR 8/3) slip. Black paint. Well-preserved surfaces. Multiple alternating arcs, curvilinear design. LM IIIC.

K33.2   Hut urn (HM 11055) (PLATE 12 *g*, FIG. 4.11). H. 6.75; D. base 10.3. Restored from 15 fragments. 90% preserved, including full profile and both lugs; missing much of centre of base and a few body fragments, door. Fine, soft, light brown (7.5YR 6/4) to reddish yellow (7.5YR 6/6) fabric with tiny black inclusions. Black paint, well-preserved on one side. Monochrome; incisions at base and on roof. Publication: Seiradaki, pl. 10a, bottom, second from left; Hägg 1990, 99, fig. 6, 105.6; Mersereau 1993, 31.11, figs. 18–9. For shape, cf. *Kastri*, 294, fig. 14.P8. LM IIIC.

Coarse Wares

K33.3   Small bowl (FIG. 4.11). D. base est. 12–13. Single fragment from base. Coarse dark grey (N5/) fabric with mica and hard white angular inclusions (1–2 mm). Surface painted black, with white band. Ring base with ridge around base. Rim rounded (may be a worn break). Monochrome black, with white band around bottom. Publication: Seiradaki, fig. 16.8 (?), krater base from K 33 (upside down). LM IIIC.

K33.4   Stirrup jar (PLATE 13 *a*, FIG. 4.11). H. 20.3; D. base 10.2. Restored from *c.* 40 fragments. 90% preserved. Coarse, porous, reddish yellow (7.5YR 7/6) fabric with frequent grey and red phyllites and hard white angular inclusions (all *c.* 1 mm). Very pale brown (10YR 8/3) slip. Traces of worn brown paint. Some grey patches on bottom, from burning? False spout pierced through centre. Bands on lower body, spirals on shoulder. Publication: Seiradaki, pl. 6d (mislabelled K 23), fig. 11.5. LM IIIC.

Outside K 33 (?)

K33.5   Deep bowl or cup (FIG. 4.11). Max. pres. H. 3. Single body fragment. Fine, soft, reddish yellow (5YR 7/6) fabric. Pink (7.5YR 8/4) slip. Red (5R 4/8) paint. Worn surfaces. Panelled design with scalloped edge, curvilinear motif. LM IIIC.

Room K 34

Room K 34 is another small and simple room that may have been an independent unit. It had two entrances, one from square 10 on the north, and the other from street 35 on the east. It was slightly set back from the other rooms (K 23, K 31, K 33).

The publication mentions that three kraters came from this room, but they have not been preserved.[53] According to the notebook, there were only a few pithos sherds, and also fragments of two pyxides. A fragment of a hollowed square vessel was found in one of the boxes, but it was not catalogued. Objects found in the room included a conical stone bead (303) and a pierced sandstone disc (304).[54]

Area K 35

K 35 was not a room, but a street to the east of the magazines. The pottery consisted chiefly of small and worn sherds, the type of material usually found in the streets and courtyards of the settlement. The krater published in Seiradaki looks rather like a champagne cup or goblet base and could not be located;[55] a stem and foot is similar to the one pictured from K 76 (**K76.39**), and a mistake may have occurred in recording the numbers. The notebook mentions that a fragment was found in K 35 from the same krater as appeared in K 33, but this was not located, as there was nothing in the boxes labelled K 35.

Room K 36

Rooms K 36 and K 37 were narrow little rooms or magazines that ran towards the east just north of the door of K 23 and to the south of the door into K 31. It is uncertain where these rooms belong. They were not fully excavated and continued to run toward the east. The pottery from K 36 included many fragments of a pithos with serpentine rope pattern between bands (**K36.2**), all decorated with incised chevrons, and there were few other sherds, mostly coarse. The basin illustrated in Seiradaki was not located.[56] Objects from the room included a bronze needle (305) and a cylindrical terracotta spindle whorl (320). This room was certainly used for storage, but any other functions are unknown.

---

51   *Karphi*, 81.
52   Seiradaki, fig. 16.8.
53   *Karphi*, 81.
54   *Karphi*, pl. 30.4.
55   Seiradaki, fig. 16.7.
56   Seiradaki, fig. 5.7.

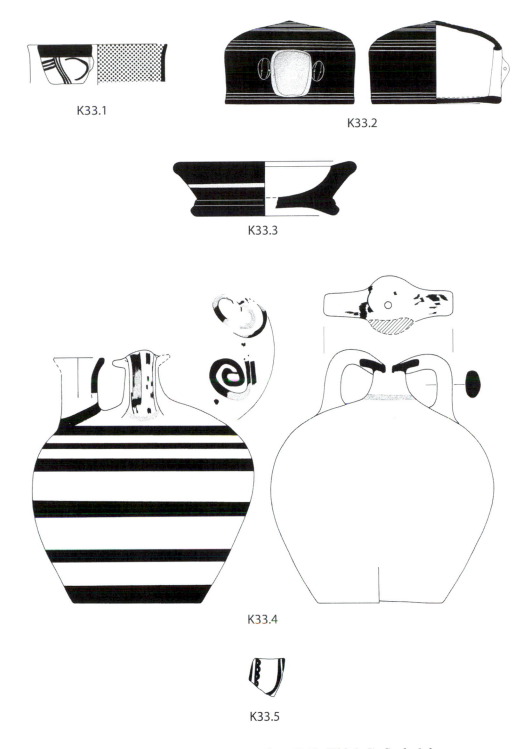

K33.1

K33.2

K33.3

K33.4

K33.5

*Fig. 4.11. Magazines, pottery from K 33 (**K33.1–5**). Scale 1:3.*

The deep bowl with buttonhook decoration and reserved disc on the base looks early, with parallels at Khania, Kastelli Pediada, and Knossos.[57]

Pottery Catalogue: K 36

Fine Wares

K36.1   Deep bowl (PLATE 13 *b*, FIG. 4.12). H. est. 12.5; D. base 4.8; D. rim 16–16.4. Restored from 42 fragments. 75% preserved, including full profile; missing 75% of rim and part of upper bowl, including one handle; second handle once preserved,

to judge from glue marks, but now missing. Fine, soft, pink (7.5YR 8/4) fabric with reddish yellow (7.5YR 7/6) core. Red (2.5YR 4/6–4/8) paint. Worn surfaces. Buttonhook spirals. Interior reserved disc on foot. LM IIIC early.

---

57   *Khania II*, pl. 35.71-P 0728, 71-P 0739, 77-P 0674, 77-P 0189; Rethemiotakis 1997, 321, fig. 31n; Warren 2007, 337, fig. 2 (Knossos, early LM IIIC).

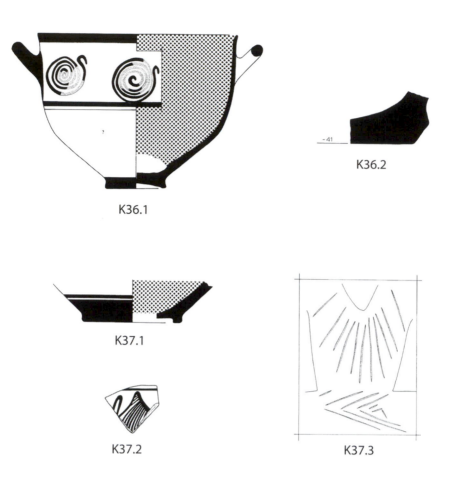

*Fig. 4.12. Magazines, pottery from K 36 (**K36.1–2**) and K 37 (**K37.1–3**). Scale 1:3.*

Coarse Wares

K36.2   Pithos (FIG. 4.12). D. base est. 41. Box full of body sherds; several fragments of base. Coarse, rather soft, reddish yellow (7.5YR 7/6) fabric with frequent large phyllite (2–4 mm), some hard white angular inclusions. Sampled KAR 06/65. Applied bands with chevron, pointing left, serpentine rope pattern with rope slashes. LM IIIC.

Room K 37

As with K 36, it is uncertain to which building this room belonged. Found in it were a few sherds from same pithos as found in Room K 36. The deep bowl base (**K37.1**) is a genuine ring base, and the pyxis fragment (**K37.2**) bears the hatched lozenge and loop decoration found on numerous deep bowls in the early phases of LM IIIC.[58]

Pottery Catalogue: K 37

Fine Wares

K37.1   Deep bowl or cup (FIG. 4.12). D. base est. 8. Single fragment from base. Fine, soft, reddish yellow (7.5YR 7/6) fabric. Very pale brown (10YR 8/3) slip. Paint black to reddish brown (5YR 4/4). Rather worn surfaces. Ring base. Band at base with narrow band above. LM IIIC.

K37.2   Pyxis (FIG. 4.12). Max. pres. H. 3.7. Single body fragment. Fine, soft, reddish yellow (5YR 6/8) fabric. Very pale brown (10YR 8/3) slip. Worn red (2.5YR 4/8) paint. Hatched lozenge chain with loops. LM IIIC.

Coarse Wares

K37.3   Pithos (PLATE 13 *c*, FIG. 4.12). Single body fragment. Coarse reddish yellow (5YR 7/6) fabric with red and grey phyllites, and green inclusions. Raised band with incised chevron, serpentine rope pattern, slashed. Same pithos as **K36.2**? LM IIIC.

THE SQUARES AND BROAD ROAD (AREAS K 10, K 32, K 48)

These three areas comprise two large squares (K 10 and K 48) and a street (K 32) that extended between the Magazines and the Great House on the north and the Magazines and the Small Shrine and Southern Houses on the west. Although this area may once have been paved, and is shown paved on the site plan, no paving stones were actually preserved.

---

58   *Kastri*, pl. 73b.

Area K 10

K 10 was a small square. The publication states that it produced the usual sorts of pottery, but all the sherds were worn and small.[59] The notebook records the following: pithoi and jars, a round-based tripod bowl and other tripods, a tray with waved rim, several flat bases of jugs or jars, a jug handle and fragment of a shoulder with a double groove, and two spouts from fine, large stirrup jars. In addition to the single fragment catalogued below, the boxes produced a handle from a double vessel, a handle with a small horned projection, and two fragments from fine stirrup jars, one with a pendent scale pattern. A conical stone bead (210) was also found. All of the pottery looks early in LM IIIC.

Pottery Catalogue: K 10

Fine Wares

K10.1   Closed vessel (FIG. 4.13). Max. pres. H. 4.6. Single body fragment. Fine, very soft, reddish yellow (5YR 7/6) fabric. Very pale brown (10YR 8/4) slip. Red (2.5YR 4/8) paint. Possibly from a stirrup jar. Crosshatched triangles or lozenges. LM IIIC.

Area K 32

K 32 was a steep road leading from the square K 10 up to the west. The sherds found in this area were small and much worn, and according to the notebook they came mostly from tripods or dishes. The notebook also mentions that there were a few fine pieces, including one krater fragment with a bird, and some flat cult plaque fragments, one with a moulded ear. In addition to the vessels catalogued below, there were five deep bowl or cup rims (three with spirals, one with a spiral and pendent multiple loops, one too worn to determine), a deep bowl handle with arcs as filler, and eight deep bowl or cup body fragments decorated with spirals, multiple loops, arc filler, upright Minoan flower, multiple stems, multiple strokes and bands, and other curvilinear motifs. In addition, there were two krater fragments with alternating broad and narrow curvilinear bands or other curvilinear motifs, a cup fragment, fragments of one large stirrup jar and a smaller one with bands. Only one plaque fragment was found from this area. It had a large hole pierced through it and did not look like the usual sort of plaque found in the shrines. The fragment with the possible ear was not located. Other objects were of bronze and included a knife (508),[60] a blade with a long tang (510),[61] a rod in five pieces (511), and fragments of a bronze bowl (509).

The pottery consists of many small fine fragments, of the sort that often are found in the streets and courtyards at Karphi and which probably represent refuse rather than vessels in use at the time of the abandonment; perhaps they were even beneath the paving stones that subsequently disappeared. Nearly all of the deep bowl or cup fragments have simple decorations, and many of them look early. The bivalve shell on **K32.4** in particular has parallels in material of

LM IIIB style from Kavousi–*Kastro*, Phaistos, and Knossos,[62] and from early LM IIIC at Knossos.[63] The motif is similar to other fragments at Karphi, particularly **K23.59** from the lower deposit in K 23 and from **K43.7**. The quirk and the buttonhook spiral appear together in early LM IIIC deposits at Knossos, Kastri, and Khania;[64] the rather open shape of the bowls would also fit in with an early date. The motif of multiple stems meeting to form a 'face' is also found on **K76.13**, and finds parallels at Kastelli Pediada and Kastri of early LM IIIC date.[65] **K32.10**, with its panelled rather geometric pattern and use of arc fillers looks later, but it is too fragmentary to be certain. The kylikes and kraters all fit into the early phases of LM IIIC; the motifs on **K32.12** find parallels at Kastelli Pediada and Kavousi–*Kastro*.[66] In short, while there is little that is closely diagnostic, most of the material fits into the early phases of LM IIIC. The plaques may have washed down into this area from above to the north and west, perhaps from the same dump found under the Great House, which itself contained a good number of plaque fragments, although it is possible that the plaques came from the Small Shrine.

Pottery Catalogue: K 32

Fine Wares

K32.1   Deep bowl or cup (FIG. 4.13). D. rim est. 10–11. Single fragment from rim. Fine, soft, reddish yellow (7.5YR 7/6) fabric with infrequent red inclusions. White (10YR 8/2) slip. Very worn black paint. Buttonhook spiral. No rim band. LM IIIC early.

K32.2   Deep bowl or cup (FIG. 4.13). D. rim est. 13. Single fragment from rim. Fine, soft, very pale brown (10YR 7/4) fabric. Very pale brown (10YR 8/3) slip. Black paint. Worn surfaces. Tailed spiral. LM IIIC.

K32.3   Deep bowl or cup (FIG. 4.13). Max. pres. H. 4.1. Single fragment from rim. Fine, soft, reddish yellow (5YR 7/6) fabric. Very pale brown (10YR 8/3) slip. Red (10R 4/8) paint. Very worn surfaces. Pendent multiple loops. LM IIIC early.

K32.4   Deep bowl or cup (PLATE 1 *b*, FIG. 4.13). D. rim 13–14. Single fragment from rim. Fine, medium-soft, very pale brown (10YR 7/4) fabric. Very pale brown (10YR 8/3) slip. Dull black paint. Well-preserved surfaces. Bivalve shell. LM IIIB.

59   *Karphi*, 79.
60   *Karphi*, pl. 28.2.
61   *Karphi*, pl. 28.2.
62   Gesell, Day and Coulson 1995, 118, fig. 22.2; Borgna 1997*a*, 277, fig. 4 top left; Popham 1970*b*, 198, fig. 2.12, pl. 47d (Knossos, LM IIIB).
63   Warren 2007, 338, fig. 3.P250 (Knossos, Stage II).
64   Popham 1965, 325, fig. 5; 326, fig. 6; *Kastri*, 287; fig. 8; 288, fig. 9; *Khania II*, pl. 35.
65   Rethemiotakis 1997, 317, fig. 26g (Kastelli Pediada); *Kastri*, 288, fig 9q.
66   Rethemiotakis 1997, 319, fig 28af (Kastelli Pediada); Mook and Coulson 1997, 352, fig. 18.63 (Kavousi–*Kastro*, Phase II).

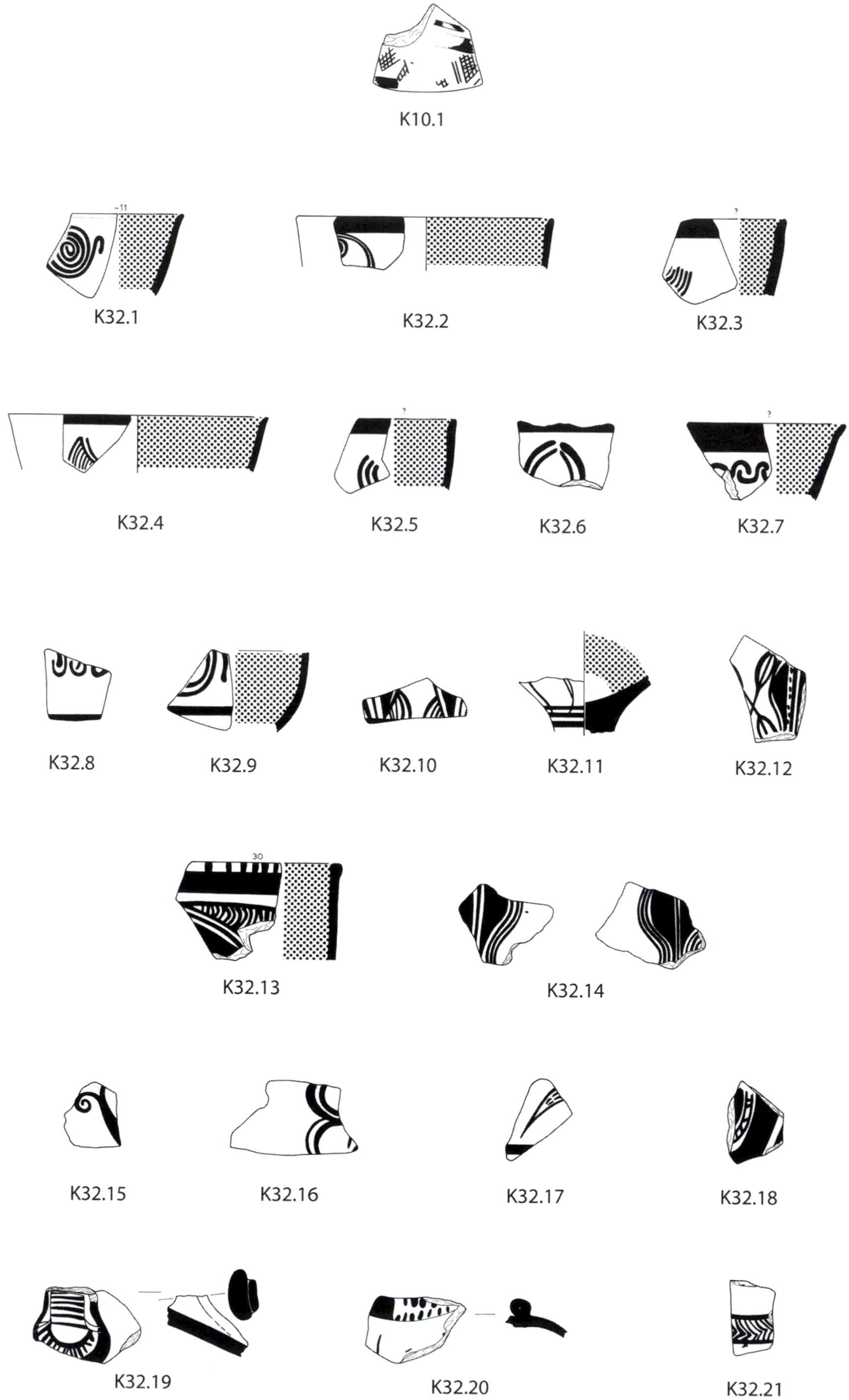

K10.1

K32.1

K32.2

K32.3

K32.4

K32.5

K32.6

K32.7

K32.8

K32.9

K32.10

K32.11

K32.12

K32.13

K32.14

K32.15

K32.16

K32.17

K32.18

K32.19

K32.20

K32.21

*Fig. 4.13. Square and street, pottery from K 10 (**K10.1**) and K 32 (**K32.1–21**). Scale 1:3.*

K32.5 Deep bowl or cup (FIG. 4.1). Max. pres. H. 3.5. Single fragment from rim. Fine, soft, reddish yellow (7.5YR 7/6) fabric. White (10YR 8/2) slip. Yellowish red (5YR 5/6) paint. Worn surfaces. Multiple pendent loops (?). LM IIIC early.

K32.6 Deep bowl or cup (PLATE 1 *b*, FIG. 4.13). Max. pres. H. 3.4. Single fragment from rim; rim chipped and worn. Fine, medium-hard, reddish yellow (7.5YR 7/6) fabric. Very pale brown (10YR 8/3) slip. Worn black paint. Worn surfaces. Multiple stems meeting below rim. LM IIIC early.

K32.7 Deep bowl or cup (FIG. 4.13). Max. pres. H. 4. Single fragment from rim. Fine, very soft, reddish yellow (5YR 7/6) fabric with some tiny white inclusions. Very pale brown (10YR 8/4) slip. Red (10R 5/8) paint. Quirk. LM IIIC early.

K32.8 Deep bowl or cup (FIG. 4.13). Max. pres. H. 3.6. Single fragment from body. Fine, medium-hard, very pale brown (10YR 8/3) fabric and slip. Worn black paint. Worn exterior surfaces, well-preserved on interior. Quirk. LM IIIC early.

K32.9 Deep bowl or cup (FIG. 4.13). Max. pres. H. 4.2. Single fragment from body. Fine, soft, reddish yellow (7.5YR 7/6) fabric. Very pale brown (10YR 8/3) slip. Worn yellowish red (5YR 5/6) paint, well-preserved on interior. Buttonhook spiral (?). LM IIIC.

K32.10 Deep bowl or cup (FIG. 4.13). Max. pres. H. 2. Single fragment from body. Fine, medium-hard, reddish yellow (5YR 7/6) fabric. Very pale brown (10YR 8/2) slip. Black to yellowish red (5YR 5/6) paint. Well-preserved surfaces. Outlined solid motifs with arc fillers. LM IIIC.

K32.11 Kylix (FIG. 4.13). Max. pres. H. 2.8. Single fragment from top of stem and bottom of body. Fine, medium-soft, reddish yellow (5YR 7/6) fabric. Very pale brown (10YR 8/3) slip. Black paint worn to brown shadow. Well-preserved interior surfaces. Stem pierced almost to bowl. Multiple stems on body. Bands on stem. Reserved disc on interior. LM IIIC.

K32.12 Kylix (FIG. 4.13). Max. pres. H. 5. Single fragment from body. Fine, soft, reddish yellow (5YR 7/6) fabric, with one large (4 mm) white inclusion. Very pale brown (10YR 8/3) slip. Black paint worn to brown. Worn surfaces. Quatrefoil leaf pattern with central ribs. Panelled pattern with half round and dots. LM IIIC early.

K32.13 Krater (FIG. 4.13). D. rim est. 30. Single fragment from rim. Fine, soft, reddish yellow (5YR 7/6) fabric. Very pale brown (10YR 8/3) slip. Black to red (2.5YR 5/8) paint. Well-preserved surfaces. Outlined curvilinear decoration with arc fillers. Strokes on rim. LM IIIC.

K32.14 Krater (FIG. 4.13). Max. pres. H. 4; Th. 0.5–0.55. Two non-joining fragments from body. Fine, very soft, reddish yellow (7.5YR 7/6) fabric. Very pale brown (10YR 8/3) slip. Red (10R 4/8) paint. Worn surfaces. Opposite half rounds with multiple outlines. For decoration, cf. Rethemiotakis 1997, 323, fig. 34a (Kastelli Pediada). LM IIIC.

K32.15 Krater (FIG. 4.13). Max. pres. H. 3.4; Th 0.5. Single fragment from body. Fine, soft, yellow (10YR 7/6) fabric. Very pale brown (10YR 8/3) slip. Black to dark red (2.5YR 3/6) paint. Worn surfaces. Stemmed spiral. Interior only partly painted. For motif, cf. Popham 1970*b*, pl. 49b (Knossos, LM IIIB). LM IIIC early.

K32.16 Krater (FIG. 4.13). Max. pres. H. 3.8; Th 0.05–0.7. Single fragment from body. Fine, medium-hard, reddish yellow (5YR 7/6) fabric with some tiny dark grey inclusions. Very pale brown (10YR 8/3) slip. Black paint, worn to shadow. Worn surfaces. Floral spray (?). LM IIIC.

K32.17 Krater (FIG. 4.13). Max. pres. H. 3; Th. 0.5. Single fragment from body. Fine, soft, yellow (10YR 8/6) fabric. Very pale brown (10YR 8/3) slip. Dull black paint. Worn surfaces. Leaf or quatrefoil with rows of short strokes inside. LM IIIC.

K32.18 Krater (FIG. 4.13). Max. pres. H. 4.2; Th. 0.7. Single fragment from body. Fine, soft, pink (7.5YR 7/4) fabric with tiny white inclusions. Very pale brown (10YR 8/3) slip. Black paint worn to shadow. Worn surfaces. Curvilinear motif with hatching between narrow bands. LM IIIC.

K32.19 Jug? (FIG. 4.13). Max. pres. H. 2.3. Single fragment from handle attachment. Fine, soft, reddish yellow (5YR 7/6) fabric. Very pale brown (10YR 8/3) slip. Black paint worn to brown. Worn surfaces. Vertical elliptical handle with added ridge of clay. Decorated with horizontal bands and fringes around attachment. LM IIIC.

K32.20 Closed vessel (FIG. 4.13). Max. pres. H. 2. Single fragment from neck. Fine, soft, very pale brown (10YR 7/3) fabric. Very pale brown (10YR 8/4) slip. Black paint. Worn surfaces. Neck has plastic decoration, possibly a snake. Short painted strokes on plastic decoration. LM IIIC.

K32.21 Closed vessel (FIG. 4.13). Max. pres. H. 3.9. Single fragment from body. Fine, very soft, reddish yellow (5YR 6/6) fabric with schist inclusions. Very pale brown (10YR 8/3) slip. Worn black paint. Worn surfaces. Band of chevrons. LM IIIC.

Area K 48

The area labelled K 48 was not a room but an open square that lay between the Southern Houses and the Magazines. The notebook reported that there were many pithoi, a miniature kalathos with plain base, a large bowl with a flat rim, a jar rim, a very squat vase that may have been a jug, a gritty blue sherd with a white band, and a jug with bosses. Sherds found in the boxes but not catalogued include a deep bowl with multiple stems, two stirrup jars (one handle attachment with a scale pattern, the other a burned base), the base of a stirrup jar or jug, and a coarse jug or jar with yellow slip and black bands. Other objects from the room included a conical stone bead (335), a pierced schist plaque (354),[67] seven cylindrical (329, 330, 331, 332, 333, 334, 338) and one biconical (346) spindle whorls, and two shells (336, 337).

The material from this deposit was unusual in that there were fewer small fine fragments than usual in an open area and there were two basins that were nearly complete; perhaps these basins were used for washing just outside one of the houses. The small deep cup **K48.1** is a shape that is rare at the site, but it does occur in the tombs; a close parallel comes from Atsividhero 3 (**A3.3**). These tombs are not as late as the Ta Mnemata tombs, and they look rather early in LM IIIC. The base on **K48.5**, however, is rather high and looks late. Blob cups and bowls appear in the earliest LM IIIC deposits and continue in use, so **K48.3** is of little help in dating.

Pottery Catalogue: K 48

Fine Wares

K48.1 Cup (FIG. 4.14). H. 6.3; D. base 2.2; D. rim 4.8. Sixteen joining fragments. 85% preserved, including base and full profile, both upper and lower handle attachments; missing handle and 70% of rim. Fine, soft, reddish yellow (5YR 6/6) fabric. Red (2.5YR 5/6) paint. Worn surfaces. Bottom entirely burned inside and out. Decoration unclear. LM IIIC.

---

67   *Karphi*, pl. 30.3.

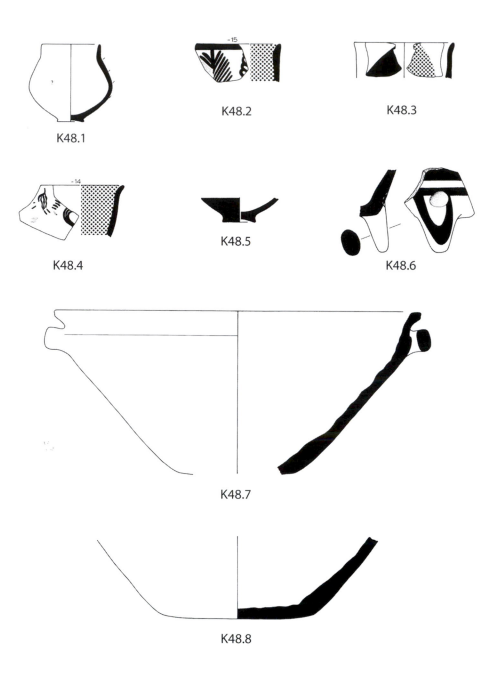

*Fig. 4.14. Street, pottery from K 48 (**K48.1–8**). Scale 1:3.*

K48.2   Deep bowl or cup (FIG. 4.14). D. rim est. 15. Single fragment from rim. Fine, porous, very pale brown (10YR 7/4) fabric. Very pale brown (10YR 8/4) slip. Worn black paint. Tree or floral spray, next to scalloped pattern. LM IIIC.

K48.3   Cup or deep bowl (FIG. 4.14). D. rim est. 8. Single fragment from rim. Fine, soft fabric, burned dark grey. Black paint. Blob decoration. LM IIIC.

K48.4   Deep bowl or cup (FIG. 4.14). D. rim est. 14. Single fragment from rim. Fine, soft, very pale brown (10YR 8/4) fabric and slip. Worn black paint. Curvilinear pattern with strokes and fringes. LM IIIC.

K48.5   Closed vessel (FIG. 4.14). D. base 2.6. Single fragment preserving entire base. Fine, soft, pale brown (10YR 6/3) fabric. Black paint. Worn surfaces. Burned? Monochrome. LM IIIC.

K48.6   Tripod (FIG. 4.14). Max. pres. H. 6.8; D. base est. 26–28. Single fragment preserving one leg and part of base. Fine, soft, reddish yellow (5YR 6/6) fabric. Very pale brown (10YR 8/4) slip.

Black paint now worn to dull brown. Flat base, legs elliptical in section, with dint at attachment. Loop on leg and bands around exterior of base. LM IIIC.

Coarse Wares

K48.7   Basin (FIG. 4.14). H. est. 13; D. base est. 8–10; D. rim est. 26–28. Large fragment from rim (four sherds), one non-joining base fragment. 15% preserved, including half of rim and one handle; missing most of base and other handle, much of body. Coarse reddish yellow (5YR 6/8) fabric with frequent schist and hard white angular inclusions (<1 mm). Reddish yellow (7.5YR 7/6) slip. Burned around handle. Surface still heavily coated with sediment. For shape, but shallower, cf. *Kastri*, 296, fig. 16.P11. LM IIIC.

K48.8   Basin (?) (FIG. 4.14). D. base 10. Mended from four fragments, preserving entire base. Coarse reddish yellow (5YR 6/8) fabric, with small (<2 mm) white, frequent black and white inclusions, some phyllites. Very pale brown (7.5YR 7/6) slip. Surfaces still coated with sediment. Flat base. Cf. **K48.7**. LM IIIC.

THE SOUTHERN HOUSES (K 24–28, K 42–51)

This block is said to show two phases of use,[68] but it was more difficult to divide it up into individual houses, because there were few doorways. The excavators attributed to an earlier phase Rooms K 43, K 46, and K 47, with an open space K 42, and a curving street to the north where later there were three small rooms: K 45-50-51. They believed that Room K 44 was added later, along with the southern rooms K 24–28, the public room K 49, and the square K 48. At that time the street K 45-50-51 was blocked and divided into the three small compartments shown on the plan.

It is likely that the later southern rooms (K 24–28) formed one unit, and the others (K 42–50) formed a second unit, part of which was early (K 43, K 46, K 47) and part later (K 44, K 45, K 50, K 51). K 49 may have been an independent unit.

The Southern Rooms (K 24–28)

Room K 24

Both K 24 and K 25 were tiny compartments, whose precise relation to the other rooms is not clear. Room K 24 had no unusual features and little deposition, although the notebook records that it contained roofing debris. The pottery from the room was much broken, as though it had been dumped here.[69] The notebook lists the following coarse wares: the rim of a pithos in yellow gritty ware, which vitrified from fire (**K24.2**); a sherd of another pithos with serpentine rope pattern; bases of pithoid jars, some plain and two offset; a rim in gritty buff perhaps from large bowl or jar and another with pinched rope below; three tripods; three bowls with horizontal handles; rims of six open dishes, one with bent-in lip and holes in the base on either side; some horizontal handles from jugs, and four small bases in red ware, one fairly fine. Fine ware came mostly from deep bowls, but included at least one stirrup jar. The pithoid jar published by Seiradaki as from this room was not located.[70] Other objects from the room included a Neolithic stone axe (288),[71] two cylindrical terracotta spindle whorls (242, 243), and three terracotta spools.

The preserved pottery from the room was not diagnostic. The deep bowl with hatched lozenge chain (**K24.1**) finds close parallels at Khania, Phaistos, and Kavousi–*Kastro*,[72] and it should probably date to early in LM IIIC.

Pottery Catalogue: K 24

Fine Wares

K24.1   Deep bowl or cup (FIG. 4.15). D. rim est. 18. Single fragment from rim. Fine, medium-hard, reddish yellow (7.5YR 7/6) fabric. Very pale brown (10YR 8/3) slip. Black to red (2.5YR 5/6) paint. Worn surfaces. Hatched lozenge chain. Labelled K 24–28. LM IIIC.

Coarse Wares

K24.2   Pithos (PLATE 13 *d*, FIG. 4.15). Max. pres. H. 28.4; D. rim est. 36. Restored from numerous fragments. 40% preserved, including 80% of upper body, four handles; missing lower body and base. Coarse light grey (2.5Y 7/2) fabric with frequent grey phyllites. Burned extensively, almost vitrified in places. Ridge has pinched rope or piecrust decoration. LM IIIC.

Room K 25

The other small room, K 25, was also denuded, but it had no traces of roofing. There were no unusual features. There was very little pottery, and in fact the notebook records none. The pithoid jar published by Seiradaki was not found.[73]

Pottery Catalogue: K 25

Fine Ware

K25.1   Miniature kylix (FIG. 4.15). H. 4.5; D. base 3; D. rim 4. Intact. 60% preserved, including entire base and stem, full profile, one handle; missing 90% of rim and upper body. Fine, soft, light red (2.5YR 6/8) fabric with reddish yellow (5YR 7/6) surface. Burned grey at handle and on one side of body. No trace of decoration. LM IIIC.

Room K 26

A small room connected to a larger room (K 27), K 26 also lacked deposition; the notebook reports that it contained roofing clay and much evidence of burning. There were no other unusual features.

Much pottery was found in this small room. The publication reports ten pithoi and pithoid jars and many kalathoi.[74] The notebook lists at least four pithoi (one with chevron bands and probably two registers of serpentine rope pattern, one with a plain band, one with double rope with finger impressions and serpentine rope pattern, a fourth with chevron bands); five pithoid jars, one with pinched rope on the ridge below the rim (**K26.13**), one with a white painted design, a third in blue ware; eight kalathoi; five tripods; and some open dishes. Fine wares listed in the notebook included a kylix base, pyxis sherds, some miniature bowls, small stirrup jars, and a tankard (**K26.4**). The stirrup jar published by Seiradaki as from K 26 is from K 121,[75] and the published stirrup jar with fringed decoration

---

68   *Karphi*, 81.
69   *Karphi*, 81.
70   Seiradaki, fig. 2.4.
71   *Karphi*, pl. 30.2.
72   *Khania II*, pl. 36.70-P 0160; Borgna 1997a, 280, fig. 15; Mook and Coulson 1997, 358, fig. 30.103.
73   Seiradaki, fig. 2.5.
74   *Karphi*, 82.
75   Seiradaki, pl. 6a, right.

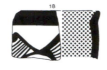

K24.1

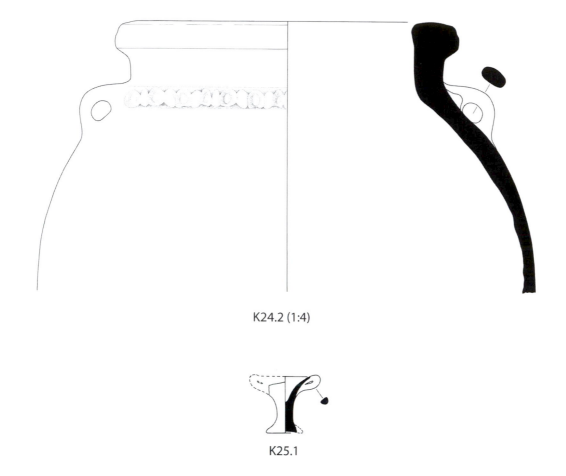

K24.2 (1:4)

K25.1

*Fig. 4.15. Southern Houses, pottery from K 24 (**K24.1**–2) and K 25 (**K25.1**). Scale 1:3 unless otherwise indicated.*

came from K 125.[76] In the boxes were fragments of a burned rope-twisted handle from a pyxis and laminated stirrup jar fragments, some burned, with a dotted U-pattern and arcs. Objects found in the room included a good deal of bronze: a votive double axe (248),[77] a disc (249), a dagger hilt (250),[78] an awl with a bone handle (251),[79] a disc with bosses (252), and thin fragments (253). Other objects included a stone 'inlay' (254),[80] a terracotta burnished flattened cylinder (255),[81] and two terracotta spools.

The krater (**K26.5**), juglet (**K26.6**), and tankard (**K26.4**) were well preserved and were probably in use in the room at the time of abandonment. The tankard is a good example of pleonastic late LM IIIC style, but dating the krater is more problematic. The shape looks late and can be paralleled by an example from a late LM IIIC deposit at Kastelli Pediada,[82] but the decoration, for which there is no good parallel,

looks earlier in LM IIIC. The juglet is not closely dated; such juglets occur as early as LM IIIC early at Khania, but continue later in the period.[83] The cups and deep bowls are only fragments and may belong to an earlier use; the shape of cup **K26.1** finds a good parallel at Knossos in the earliest stages of LM IIIC.[84]

---

76   Seiradaki, fig. 22h.
77   *Karphi*, pl. 29.1.
78   *Karphi*, pl. 29.1.
79   *Karphi*, pl. 29.1.
80   *Karphi*, pl. 30.3.
81   *Karphi*, pl. 30.4.
82   Rethemiotakis 1997, 322, fig. 33c.
83   Hallager 2000, 150–1.
84   Warren 2007, 337, fig. 2.P1919 (LM IIIB/C or earliest LM IIIB).

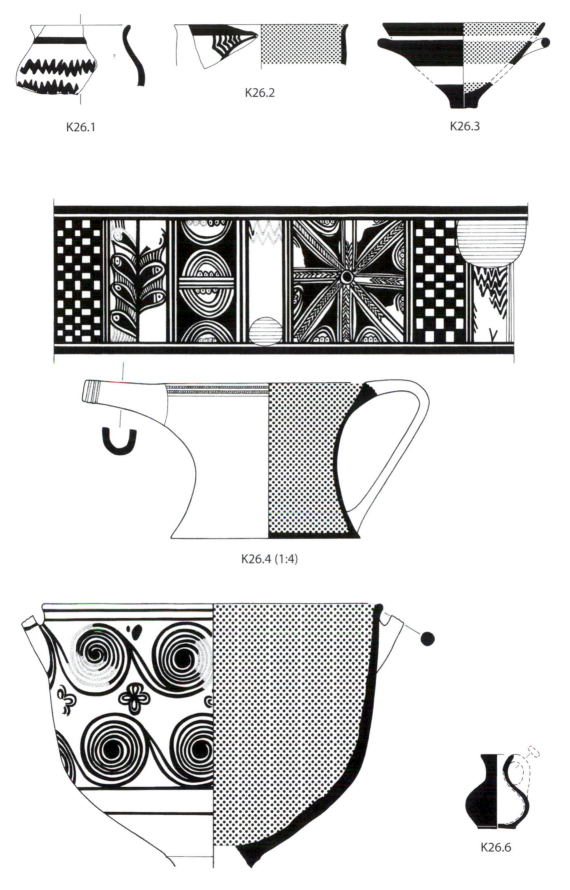

*Fig. 4.16. Southern Houses, pottery from K 26 (**K26.1–6**). Scale 1:3 unless otherwise indicated.*

The presence of so many pithoi and pithoid jars, along with the coarse stirrup jar, indicates that this room was used for storage, and it is possible that the bronzes were also stored here; there were many bronzes also found in the Great House in a storeroom (K 12). The bronze double axe may have served as a votive, as suggested by Gesell,[85] or it may have been stored in this room for use in the libation rituals that may have taken place in K 27. The number of nearly complete tripod cooking pots suggests that the room may have also been used for cooking.

Pottery Catalogue: K 26

Fine Wares

K26.1   Cup (FIG. 4.16). D. rim est. 8. Single fragment from rim. Fine, medium-hard, light grey (2.5Y 7/2) fabric. Black paint. Very burned so decoration becomes negative. Double row of zigzags. LM IIIC early.

K26.2   Deep bowl or cup (FIG. 4.16). D. rim est. 14. Single fragment from rim. Fine, soft, white (10YR 8/2) fabric and slip. Worn paint, once black. Curvilinear motif with chevron filler in angle. LM IIIC.

K26.3   Kalathos or deep bowl (FIG. 4.16). D. base 2.1; D. rim est. 13. Fragment preserving entire base, two small fragments of rim, large body fragment (four sherds) with handle attachment, second handle, five non-joining body fragments. Fine, soft, reddish yellow (7.5YR 7/6) fabric. Black paint. Burned in many areas. Tiny raised base may not belong with the other fragments. Monochrome. SM?

K26.4   Tankard (HM 11052) (PLATE 13 *e, f*, FIG. 4.16). H. 16.5; D. base 20.2; D. rim 20. Restored from numerous fragments. 75–80% preserved; missing handle, 25% of rim, and fragments of body. Fine, medium-hard, very pale brown (10YR 8/4–7/3) fabric and slip. Paint black to dark brown (7.5YR 4/2–4/4). Well-preserved surfaces. Burned all over, but particularly on base, before breaking. Punctuated pattern on rim: thick rim slashed horizontally forming three ridges, which then were slashed vertically to form small 'pillows'. Incisions on end of spout. Elaborate painted decoration in panels: next to handle, X-pattern in cross, with hatching or chevrons, solid triangles between rays, with multiple loops and scale pattern with dots (called 'windmill' pattern); chequerboard; vertical row of multiple zigzags under spout. On other side, next to spout: chequerboard; 'tree' with almond-shaped leaves that are solid except for circle with dot at end, hatching or arcs between leaves; stacked double axes (?) with multiple loops between blades and small loops with dots. Publication: Seiradaki, fig. 13.1, fig. 22a, pl. 8c. For the 'fish tree' motif, cf. **K131.4**; Kanta 1980, fig. 73.5 (Zakros); *RMDP*, 288, fig. 98.219 (Laconia, LH IIIC middle: barred ovals or almond). LM IIIC.

K26.5   Krater (FIG. 4.16). Max. pres. H. 28; D. rim est. 36. Partially mended from numerous sherds into three large fragments: base and lower body (14 sherds), rim and upper body (four sherds), body (18 sherds). 25% preserved; missing base and part of both handles. Fine, soft, porous, reddish yellow (5YR 7/6) fabric with tiny black inclusions. Very pale brown (10YR 8/4) slip. Black paint, worn to shadow. Very worn surfaces, better-preserved on interior. Burned after broken. Two rows of running spirals, with outlined quatrefoils on either side of double tails. LM IIIC.

K26.6   Juglet (HM 11065) (FIG. 4.16). H. 6; D. base 3; D. rim est. 2.6. Restored from four fragments. 80% preserved, including full profile, lower handle attachment; missing most of rim and handle. Fine, soft, light grey (10YR 7/2–5Y 7/1) fabric. Black paint. Burned uniformly. Monochrome. LM IIIC.

Coarse Wares

K26.7   Kalathos (PLATE 13 *g*, FIG. 4.17). H. 8.1–8.8; D. base 6.7; D. rim 17.7. Mended from seven fragments; four non-joining fragments, and glue marks suggest that originally there was more. 70% preserved, including entire base and full profile. Coarse light red (2.5YR 6/8) fabric with infrequent small (<1mm) grey phyllites and hard white angular inclusions. Sampled KAR 06/72. Flat, uneven, bevelled base. Ridging on interior. Two ridges on lower body, above base. For shape, cf. Andreadaki-Vlasaki and Papadopolou 2007, 45, fig. 2.14 (Khamalevri, Phase I). LM IIIC.

K26.8   Kalathos (FIG. 4.17). H. 7.3–8.9; D. base 6.5; D. rim est. 19.6. Large fragment from base (three sherds) and four non-joining rim fragments. 60% preserved, including full profile and entire base; missing half of body and rim. Coarse red (2.5YR 5/8) fabric with phyllites and hard white angular inclusions. Surface smoothed. No burning. Sampled KAR 06/73. Irregular in shape; higher on one side than the other. Shelf rim. Groove on interior below rim. LM IIIC.

K26.9   Basin (FIG. 4.17). D. rim est. 34–36. Single fragment from rim, preserving one handle; missing base. Coarse, light red (2.5YR 6/8) fabric with frequent large (2–4 mm) schist and hard white angular inclusions. Surfaces smoothed and mottled red and black. Possibly burned. Publication: Seiradaki, fig. 5.8. LM IIIC.

K26.10   Stirrup jar (HM 11060) (PLATE 12 *h*, FIG. 4.17). H. 39; D. base 17; max. D. 37. Restored from numerous fragments. 70% preserved, including full profile, both handles, false spout; missing half of rim of spout and sections of body. Coarse red (2.5YR 5/6) fabric with frequent grey phyllites (1–5 mm) and some hard angular white and black inclusions. Red (2.5YR 4/6) to very dusky red (2.5YR 2.5/2) paint. Some patches of burning, but very slight. False spout is concave on top, with hole pierced through it. Spout is tilted back to touch false spout. Monochrome. Publication: Seiradaki, fig. 11.8, pl. 6g. LM IIIC.

K26.11   Tripod cooking pot (PLATE 14 *a*, FIG. 4.17). Max. pres. H. 19.7; D. rim 18.6. Restored from numerous fragments. 75% preserved, including most of body, 66% of rim, both handles, scar for leg attachment; missing base and all legs. Coarse yellowish red (5YR 5/6) fabric with frequent hard black and white inclusions, some mica. Surface smoothed and mottled. No burning on preserved part. Heavy ridging on interior. Publication: Seiradaki, pl. 2e, right. For shape, cf. **K14.2** and parallels listed there; *Kastri*, 297, fig. 17. P17. LM IIIC.

K26.12   Tripod cooking pot (PLATE 14 *b*, FIG. 4.17). Max. pres. H. 24.5; D. base 20; D. rim est. 22.2. Restored from *c.* 40 fragments. 65% preserved, including nearly complete profile, both handles, top of legs; missing half of rim, large fragments of upper and lower body, all three legs. Coarse red (2.5YR 5/8) fabric with frequent small (1 mm) inclusions of phyllites, hard white and black inclusions, and gold mica. A few possible patches of burning. Legs probably round in section. Dint or finger impressions at top of legs. Publication: Seiradaki, pl. 2e, left. LM IIIC.

K26.13   Pithoid jar (FIG. 4.18). D. rim est. 40–42. Single large fragment from rim and handle. Coarse red (2.5YR 5/6) fabric, grey at core, with frequent schist (1–7 mm) and hard white angular inclusions. Deep wide jar with ridge below rim. Ridge decorated with finger impressions. Publication: Seiradaki, fig. 2.3. LM IIIC.

K26.14   Pithos (FIG. 4.18). H. 50.5; D. base 24; D. rim 30. Once restored from many fragments, now broken. 75% preserved, including full profile, entire base, 30% of rim, one handle; missing one handle part of body. Coarse reddish yellow (5YR 6/6) fabric with frequent grey and red phyllites (1–4 mm), hard white angular inclusions. Burned all over and uniformly (during firing?). Body

---

85   Gesell 1985, 81.

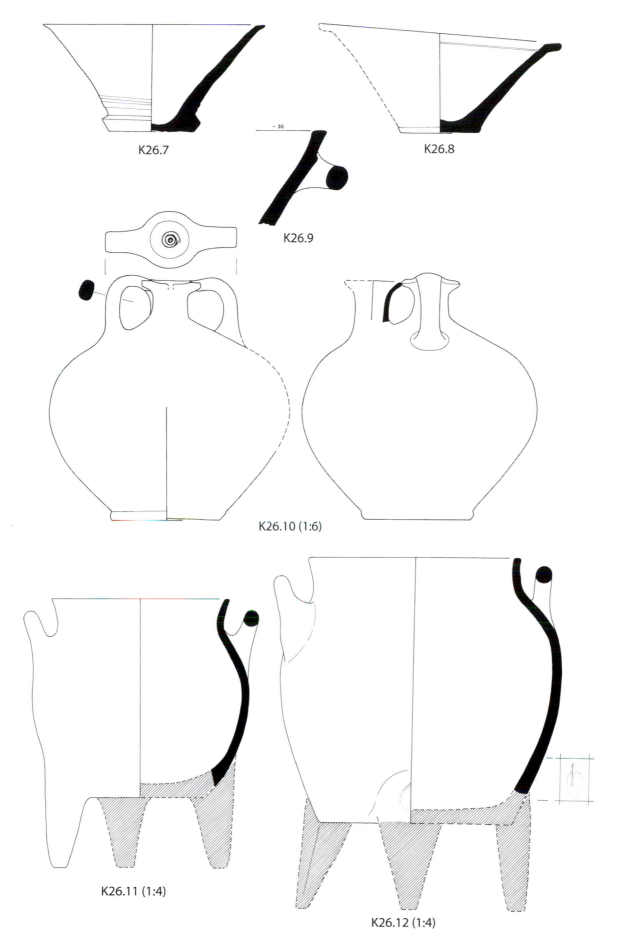

Fig. 4.17. *Southern Houses, pottery from K 26 (**K26.7–12**). Scale 1:3 unless otherwise indicated.*

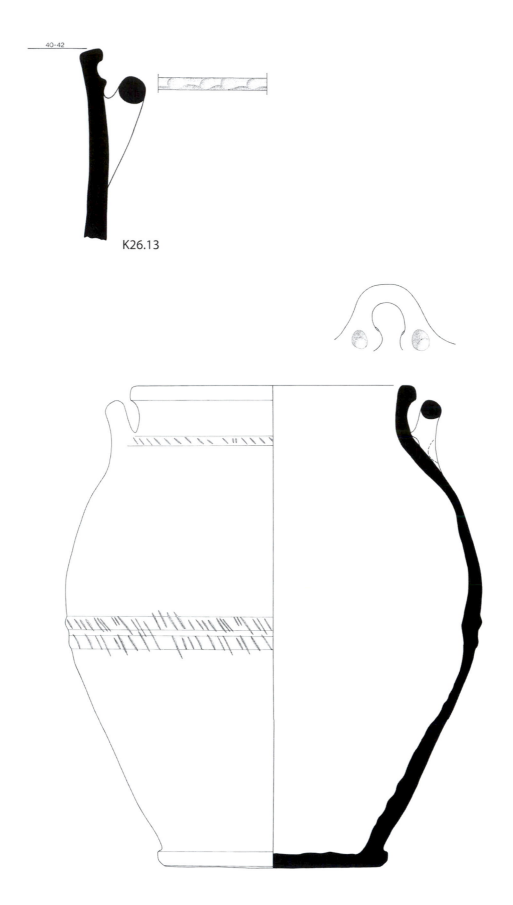

40-42

K26.13

K26.14 (1:4)

*Fig. 4.18. Southern Houses, pottery from K 26 (**K26.13–14**). Scale 1:3 unless otherwise indicated.*

made in two sections and joined at middle with a raised band to reinforce the joint. Two ridges on mid body with crude rope slashing. Rope-slashed ridge at base of neck. Dints at bases of handles. LM IIIC.

Room K 27

The largest room in the southern group was K 27. Little roofing material was found in it, suggesting to the excavators that it may have been an open space; it was also floored with the same sort of red clay found in the Temple, also interpreted as an open space.[86] The recorded presence of some roofing clay, however, suggests that the room may once have been roofed. On the north side was sloping bedrock, with a thin slab of faced marble nearby; the two rhyta were found on this bedrock. These two ritual objects suggested to the excavators that the room may have been a shrine, an idea which found support also from the bronze votive double axe found in the neighbouring room K 26.

The notebook lists the following coarse ware from K 27: three pithoi, two in yellow gritty clay, one with pinched rope below rim, the other with a chevron band, and another in red clay with chevrons; two pithoid jars with white painted designs on red clay; eight large jars; four stirrup jars; three kalathoi; a pyxis; five tripods; dish rims; two scuttle handles of Type 1; and a strainer top in buff ware. Fine wares are described as much blackened by fire, but included the two rhyta, which were originally thought to be three rhyta and two vases with human heads, along with a ring stand.

Other objects from the room included a cylindrical terracotta spindle whorl (256) and 20 terracotta spools. Seven of the spools are still preserved; they are all of approximately the same size and shape and their weights vary from 50–75 g. All are intact, but worn, and all show burning.

The two rhyta have been used to identify the room as a possible cult building. Certainly the large and elaborate rhyton that represents a cart on three wheels with a human figure on top and three ox heads on the front (HM 11046)[87] must have been used for religious observance; it has no other possible use, except as decoration. It may have stood on a bench or platform and served as the focus for ritual activity. It is a unique piece and nothing like it exists.[88] The other rhyton, with the human head, resembles a canonical piriform rhyton in shape, except for the head, and it is not nearly so large nor so elaborate. It finds a possible parallel in one of the tombs at Ta Mnemata (M11.1). Were it not for these two objects, however, K 27 would not be identified as a cult room. The rest of the material from the room is certainly like that found in the other buildings on the site. The spools, if they indeed represent a form of loomweight, suggest that weaving went on in the room, since there are so many and of such even size and shape. Possibly there was a combination of religious observance and weaving here, the products of the room somehow in the service of

religion or under the protection of a deity.[89] Certainly no other room at Karphi is like this, and the usual accoutrements of cult associated with the worship of the goddess with upraised arms (snake tubes, figurines, plaques) are missing. The two preserved kalathoi show traces of interior burning and may have contained coals, aromatics, or burned offerings. The rhyton, used for pouring liquid libations into the ground or into a vessel below, represents a different sort of ritual activity from offering on a stand, where the offering is raised up from the earth; libation from a rhyton may thus indicate that a different deity or aspect of a deity was being honoured (a fertility or underworld divinity) or that the ritual was expected to produce a different result from offering on a stand or setting up figurines.[90]

There is nothing from this room that looks particularly early in date, although the deep bowl **K27.1** finds some parallels with Kastri, which is early LM IIIC. The decoration on the rhyton **K27.3**, with its combination of curvilinear fringed motifs and some linear decoration could be later.

Pottery Catalogue: K 27

Fine Wares

K27.1　Deep bowl (PLATE 14 *c*, FIG. 4.19). H. 11.1; D. base 5; D. rim 14.3–15.6. Restored from 27 fragments. 70% preserved, including entire base, full profile; missing some of rim and body, both handles. Fine, porous, very pale brown (10YR 7/3) fabric with sand-sized black inclusions. Dull black paint. Entire vessel burned, but different fragments burned differently; one fragment burned so badly that decoration has become negative. Carinated. Handles set unevenly. Rim irregular. Buttonhook spirals. Reserved band on interior of rim; reserved disc on interior of base. Publication: Seiradaki, fig. 14.3; pl. 10a. top right; Mountjoy 2007, fig. 4.4. For decoration, cf. Popham 1965, 326, figs. 6.28–29 (Knossos); Andreadaki-Vlasaki and Papadopoulou 2007, 50, fig. 7.22. For shape, cf. Watrous 1992, 109, fig. 68.1921 (Kommos, LM IIIB–C); Andreadaki-Vlasaki and Papadopoulou 2007, 47, fig. 4.30. LM IIIC.

K27.2　Deep bowl or cup (FIG. 4.19). D. base 1.8. Large fragment (five sherds) preserving entire base, two non-joining fragments. Fine, soft, very pale brown (10YR 7/3) fabric, almost totally burned to grey (5Y 5/1). Black paint. Small flat base from a small cup or deep bowl. Monochrome (?) Number unclear, but looks like K 27. LM IIIC.

K27.3　Rhyton (HM 11050) (PLATE 14 *d*, FIG. 4.19). Max. pres. H. 27; max. D. 14. Restored from numerous fragments. 85% preserved, including rim and neck, most of body, handle attachments; missing base, all three handles. Fine, soft, pink (7.5YR 7/4) fabric. Black to brown paint. Very worn surfaces. Uniformly burned or misfired? Ridge at attachment of neck. Human head as

86　*Karphi*, 27.

87　Seiradaki, pl. 13; Rethemiotakis 1998, 22, pl. 64–5.21; Koehl 2006, 83, pl. 7.71.

88　Koehl 2006, 262–3 gives the best description of how this vessel may have worked.

89　Koehl 2006, 334–5 discusses the association of rhyta with weaving implements and finds that it is not uncommon.

90　Day 2009, 147–8.

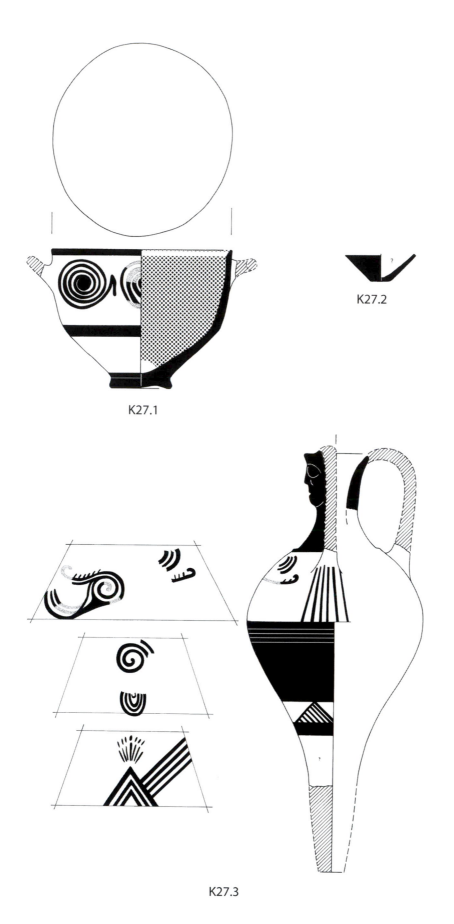

Fig. 4.19. *Southern Houses, pottery from K 27 (**K27.1–3**). Scale 1:3.*

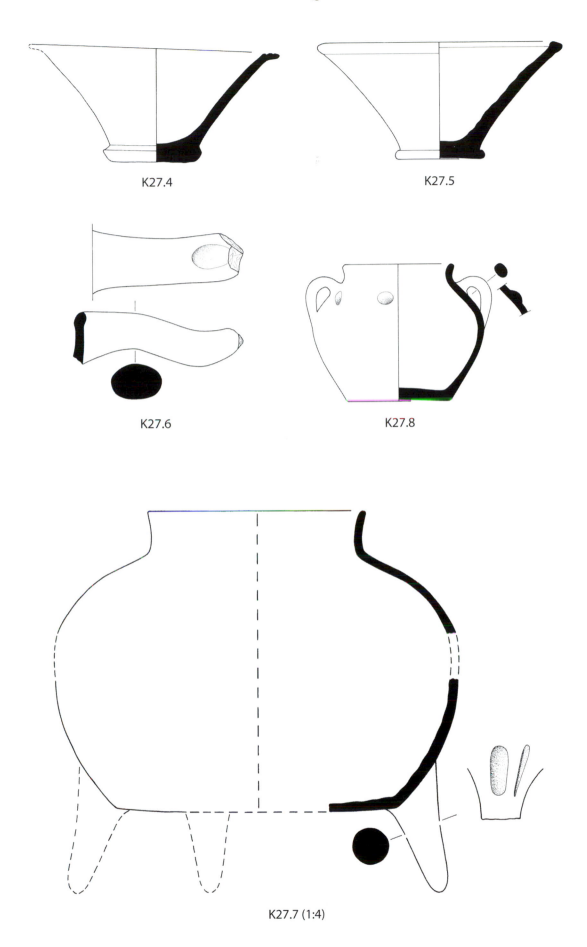

K27.4

K27.5

K27.6

K27.8

K27.7 (1:4)

*Fig. 4.20. Southern Houses, pottery from K 27 (**K27.4–8**). Scale 1:3 unless otherwise indicated.*

neck, with eyes, nose, mouth, and ears indicated. Three handles, two on sides, one on back of head. On shoulder, three panels with different decoration: fringed spirals, spirals and multiple loops, multiple triangles with fringes and oblique strokes. On lower body, hatched triangles. Publication: *Karphi*, pl. 35.2–3; Young 1938, 235, fig. 12 right, bottom left; Rethemiotakis 1998, fig. 50.22; Koehl 2006, 86, fig. 5.88, pl. 10. For shape, cf. **M11.1**; Day and Snyder 2004, 72, fig. 5.11.9 (Kavousi–*Vronda*, late LM IIIC). LM IIIC.

Coarse Wares

K27.4   Kalathos (FIG. 4.20). H. 8.7–9.5; D. base 7.5; D. rim 19.4–20.4. Mended from six fragments. 65% preserved, including base and full profile; missing much of rim. Very coarse red (2.5YR 5/8) fabric, grey at core, with frequent large (2–3 mm) schist inclusions. Burned on exterior at base and on one side; possibly burned on interior. Very irregular. Ledge rim with two grooves on top. LM IIIC.

K27.5   Kalathos (FIG. 4.20). H. 9.5; D. base 7.2; D. rim 19.6. Mended from seven fragments. 70% preserved, including full profile; missing 50% of rim. Coarse yellowish red (5YR 5/6) fabric with grey core toward base; frequent worn, oblong, and round white inclusions (1–2 mm). Burned on one side, inside and out. Groove on interior of rim. Ridging on interior. LM IIIC.

K27.6   Scuttle (FIG. 4.20). Max. pres. L. 13.5. Single fragment preserving small part of rim and handle, chipped at end. Coarse red (2.5YR 5/8) fabric with infrequent phyllites and hard white angular inclusions. Very smooth surface, mottled black and red. No burning. Thumb impression or dint at end. LM IIIC.

K27.7   Tripod cooking pot (FIG. 4.20). Max. pres. H. 22.6; D. rim est. 23. Once mended from 18 fragments, with ten non-joining fragments. 66% of base and tips of two legs, three fragments of rim preserved; missing upper body and handles. Coarse reddish yellow (5YR 7/6) fabric with frequent phyllites, clay pellets (2 mm), hard black and white angular inclusions and some mica. No signs of burning inside or out. Long oval impression with oblique slash to one side where leg attaches to body. For shape cf. Borgna 1997b, 192, fig. 2.3 (Phaistos). LM IIIC.

K27.8   Cooking jar (FIG. 4.20). H. 10.9; D. base 8.2; D. rim 9. Large fragment from base (nine sherds) and rim/handle (five sherds) and 14 body fragments. 30% preserved, including nearly all of base, part of rim, and one handle. Coarse reddish yellow (5YR 6/6) fabric, grey (5Y 5/1) at core, with frequent phyllites (2–3 mm), green striated stone, mica, and hard white angular inclusions. Sampled KAR 06/34. Interior burned grey; some burning on exterior. Knobs on shoulder. For shape, cf. Andreadaki-Vlasaki and Papadopoulou 2007, 53, fig. 10.4 (Khamalevri, Phase 1). LM IIIC.

Room K 28

This small room had no connection with the other rooms. It lacks doorways and was much denuded. The notebook suggests that there may have been a cupboard in the northeast corner. Pottery mentioned in the notebook includes the following: a pithos with chevron bands; a pithoid jar rim with rope-slashed ridge below the rim; tripod bowls, one shallow, one small red; at least seven kalathoi, one with a high pedestal; and a kylix stem. There was a good deal of pottery in the boxes that was not catalogued, including five deep bowl fragments (with multiple arcs, spirals, floral motifs, and bands), a krater fragment with bands, a stirrup jar with a scalloped loop and fringes, and a medium-coarse handle of blue ware (sampled KAR 06/26). The fine decorated krater pictured in Seiradaki was not located.[91]

The only object found in this area was a cylindrical terracotta spindle whorl (351) found in the cleaning of rooms K 24–K 28.

There is little here to indicate the function of this small room, nor is its date clear. The deep bowl with quirk could belong to any phase of LM IIIC. The tankard rim is almost identical to one from K 23. The bird vase may belong to LM IIIB. The kalathos is unusual for its projections on the rim, and finds no parallels. The decoration on the missing krater resembles motifs on early LM IIIC kraters.

Pottery Catalogue: K 28

Fine Wares

K28.1   Deep bowl or cup (FIG. 4.21). Max. pres. H. 3. Single fragment from body. Fine, medium-soft, reddish yellow (7.5YR 7/6) fabric. Very pale brown (10YR 8/3) slip. Red (2.5YR 4/8) paint. Worn surfaces. Quirk. For decoration, cf. Popham 1965, 325, fig. 5.18–9. LM IIIC.

K28.2   Mug or tankard (PLATE 11 *d*, FIG. 4.21). D. rim est. 18–19. Single fragment from rim. Fine, soft, reddish yellow (5YR 7/6) fabric. Very pale brown (10YR 8/3) slip. Worn red (10R 4/8) paint. Very worn surfaces. Beaded or punctuated decoration on rim, inside and out. Painted dotted pendent triangles on exterior. For shape and decoration, cf. **K23.8**. LM IIIC.

K28.3   Lid (FIG. 4.21). D. rim 14. Single fragment from rim. Fine, soft, yellowish red (5YR 5/6) fabric. White (10YR 8/2) slip. Worn red paint. Worn surfaces. Domed or flat top. Bands on exterior. For shape and decoration, cf. Rethemiotakis 1997, 314, fig. 17 (Kastelli Pediada, Phase 2). LM IIIC.

K28.4   Bird vase or rhyton (PLATE 14 *e*, FIG. 4.21). Max. pres. H. 5.7. Four joining fragments from body. Fine, soft, light brown (7.5YR 6/4) fabric. Very pale brown (10YR 8/3) slip. Black paint worn to brown shadow. Surfaces glossy and well-preserved. Irregular in shape; looks like body of bird, possibly a rhyton. Decorated with wings: curvilinear pattern with arc fillers, wavy lines, short strokes. For shape and decoration with wings, cf. Kanta 1980, 44, fig. 11.4 (Nirou Chani, LM IIIB). LM IIIB.

Coarse Wares

K28.5   Goblet (FIG. 4.21). Max. pres. H. 9.5; D. base 8.6. Single fragment preserving entire stem and part of base; missing body. Coarse, red (10R 5/6) fabric, black at core, with frequent schist, hard angular white inclusions (2–4 mm), and gold mica. Burned on bottom of interior and on underside of base in two patches. Ring base, with lip around bottom; thick stem, flaring sides. Publication: Seiradaki, fig. 16.5. LM IIIC.

K28.6   Kalathos (PLATE 14 *a*, FIG. 4.21). H. 9.7–10.2; D. base 8.6; D. rim 19.2. Mended from nine fragments. 65% preserved, including entire base; missing 33% of rim and parts of lower body. Very coarse red (10R 5/8) fabric with frequent large (2–3 mm) schist, phyllite, and hard white angular inclusions. Smoothed and mottled surface. No burning. Sampled KAR 06/07. Slightly concave bevelled base. Flaring sides, with slight ridge below rim. Small projections on rim, projecting outward 0.25 cm; one preserved, and scars of two others show where broken off. Irregularly spaced, originally five or six. LM IIIC.

---

91   Seiradaki, fig. 26a.

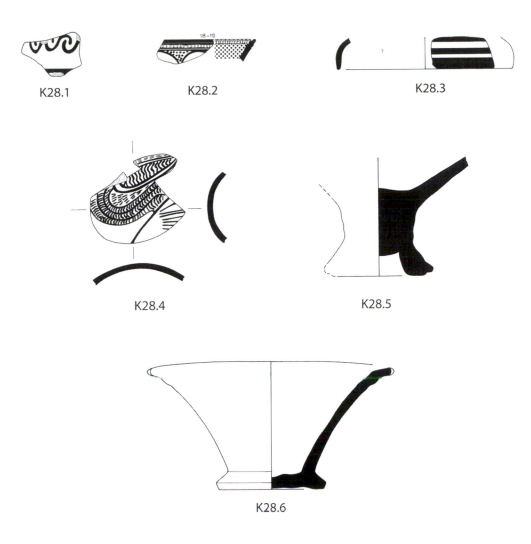

K28.1 K28.2 K28.3

K28.4 K28.5

K28.6

*Fig. 4.21. Southern Houses, pottery from K 28 (**K28.1–6**). Scale 1:3.*

NORTHERN HOUSE (ROOMS K 42, K 43, K 44, K 45, K 46, K 47, K 50, K 51)

Area K 42

This was not a room, but an open space. The pottery was reported to be as usual, but nothing was recorded in the notebook, nor were any sherds found from this location.

Room K 43

This room was thought to belong to the earliest phase of the block. It was entered from K 44, probably by a door in the southeast corner. Only one vessel was mentioned in the publication, a pyxis of Type 4 (**K43.13**).[92] The notebook records the following additional pottery: a jar with in-turned rim (**K43.16**), a rounded cauldron with coil pattern in relief on shoulder (tripod cauldron), fragments of three large stirrup jars (**K43.17**), a burnt jar with out-turned rim, a very fine painted tripod cauldron with short legs,

and an unusual rim. The painted tripod was illustrated by Seiradaki,[93] but was not located in the storerooms of the museum. The boxes produced a number of fragments that were not catalogued: deep bowls (plain or decorated with oblique strokes, spirals, or multiple arcs), two kylikes, two stirrup jars with curvilinear motifs and dotted filler arcs, and a jug or jar of coarse fabric with bands. There were few other objects in the room; only a fragment of a large conch shell (347) was recorded.

The pyxis (**K43.13**), kalathos (**K43.14**), and stirrup jar (**K43.17**) are reasonably complete and may be representative of the material in use at the time the room was abandoned. They are not particularly helpful either in determining date or function for the room. Most of the decorated fine ware is fragmentary, and

---

92 *Karphi*, 82.
93 Seiradaki, pl. 2c.

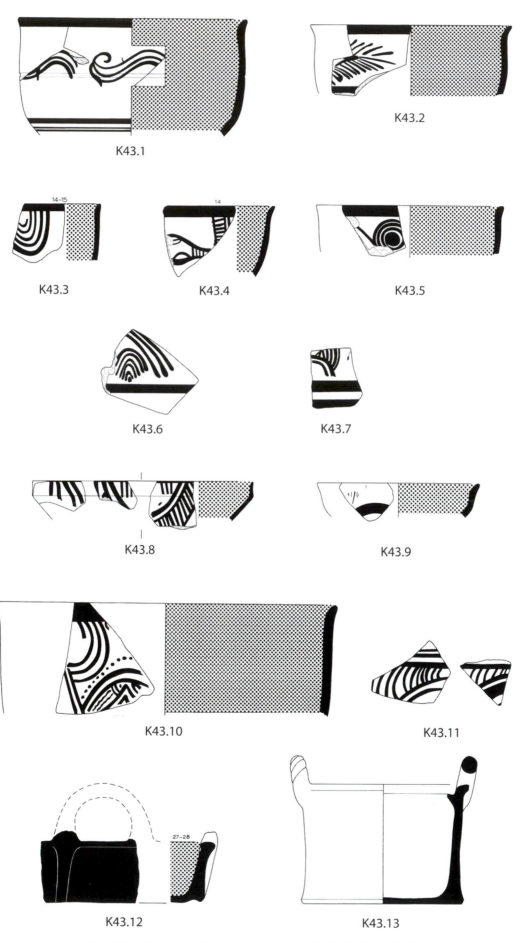

*Fig. 4.22. Southern Houses, pottery from K 43 (**K43.1–13**). Scale 1:3.*

some of it looks quite early. The cup or deep bowl with stemmed spirals (**K43.1**), for example, finds close parallels among LM IIIB pottery at Knossos,[94] but also appears in LM IIIC contexts there and at Phaistos.[95] The Minoan flower on deep bowl or cup **K43.2** resembles examples on LM IIIB pottery from Knossos[96] and LM IIIB–C pottery at Phaistos.[97] The bivalve shell on deep bowl or cup **K43.7** is another motif that is common in LM IIIB and also in early LM IIIC, for example at Kavousi–*Kastro*.[98] Deep bowl or cup **K43.3**, with its multiple pendent loops, finds parallels in early LM IIIC deposits at Kastelli Pediada and Knossos.[99] Kylix **K43.8**, however, looks later. Some of these deep bowls were doubtless around from the earlier phases of the building's use. The pottery confirms the excavators' idea that this room belonged to the earliest use of the area of the Southern Houses, very early in LM IIIC.

Pottery Catalogue: K 43

Fine Wares

K43.1   Deep bowl or cup (FIG. 4.22). D. rim 18–19. Two joining fragments from rim and body; missing base and handle(s). Fine, rather hard, pink (7.5YR 7/4) fabric. Very pale brown (10YR 8/4) slip. Black paint. Curved multiple stems or multiple stemmed spirals. LM IIIB/C.

K43.2   Deep bowl or cup (FIG. 4.22). D. rim 16. Single fragment (two sherds) from rim. Fine, medium-hard, white (10YR 8/2) fabric. Very pale brown (10YR 8/3) slip. Dull black to red (2.5YR 5/8) paint. Worn surfaces. Minoan flower. LM IIIB/C.

K43.3   Deep bowl or cup (FIG. 4.22). D. rim est. 14–15. Single fragment from rim. Fine, soft, reddish yellow (7.5YR 7/6) fabric. White (10YR 8/2) slip. Worn black paint. Multiple pendent loops hanging from rim. For decoration, cf. **K149.3**, **K149.5**. LM IIIC.

K43.4   Deep bowl or cup (FIG. 4.22). D. rim est. 14. Single fragment from rim. Fine, rather hard, reddish yellow (7.5YR 7/6) fabric. Very pale brown (10YR 8/4) slip. Red (10R 5/6) paint. Well-preserved surfaces. Panelled decoration with ladder pattern and vertical lines, loops or ovals with filler. LM IIIC.

K43.5   Deep bowl or cup (FIG. 4.22). D. rim est. 15. Single fragment from rim. Fine, soft, reddish yellow (5YR 7/6) fabric. Very pale brown (10YR 8/3) slip. Red (2.5YR 4/8) paint. Worn surfaces. Running spiral with solid centre. For motif, cf. Borgna 2007, 70, fig. 1.7 (Phaistos, LM IIIC early). LM IIIC.

K43.6   Deep bowl or cup (FIG. 4.22). Max. pres. H. 6. Single fragment from body. Fine, soft, rather porous, very pale brown (10YR 7/4) fabric. White (2.5Y 8/2) slip. Black paint worn to dark reddish brown (2.5YR 3/4). Worn surfaces. Multiple upright loops under streamers. LM IIIC.

K43.7   Deep bowl or cup (FIG. 4.22). Max. pres. H. 4.7. Single fragment from body. Fine, medium-hard, reddish yellow (5YR 7/6) fabric. Very pale brown (10YR 8/3) slip. Red (2.5YR 5/8) paint. Bivalve shell. LM IIIB/C.

K43.8   Kylix (FIG. 4.22). D. rim 17–18. Two joining and two non-joining fragments from rim. Fine, soft, reddish yellow (7.5YR 7/6) fabric. Very pale brown (10YR 8/3) slip. Black paint worn to shadow. Worn surfaces. Carinated just below rim. Hatched curvilinear motif; strokes on rim. For shape, cf. Day 1997, 399, fig. 5.4, 9; *Kavousi IIA*, fig. 22.B3 P6, B3 P7 (Kavousi–*Vronda*, LM IIIC late). LM IIIC.

K43.9   Kylix (FIG. 4.22). D. rim est. 13. Single fragment from rim. Fine, soft, reddish yellow (7.5YR 7/6) fabric. Very pale brown (10YR 8/3) slip. Black paint. Very worn surfaces. Curvilinear motif

with fringes. For shape, cf. Mook and Coulson 1997, 359, fig. 31.135 (Kavousi–*Kastro*, Phase I–II). LM IIIC.

K43.10   Krater (FIG. 4.22). D. rim est. 27. Single fragment (two sherds) from rim. Fine, rather hard, white (10YR 8/2) fabric. Worn black paint. Worn surfaces. Medallion filled with arc and dot, some sort of multiple triangle, dotted outline, arc fillers. For decoration, cf. Prokopiou 1997, 378, 397, fig. 19k (Sybrita/Thronos pit 44, LM IIIC early). LM IIIC early.

K43.11   Krater (FIG. 4.22). Max. pres. H. 5. Two non-joining fragments from body. Fine, medium-hard, light grey (2.5Y 7/2) fabric. Very pale brown (10YR 8/4) slip. Black paint worn to shadow. Worn surfaces. Outlined curvilinear motifs with arc fillers. LM IIIC.

K43.12   Tray (FIG. 4.22). Max. pres. H. 5.8; D. rim 27–28. Three joining fragments preserving 25% of rim and body, including handle attachments; missing most of base and handles. Fine, very soft, light reddish brown (5YR 6/4) fabric. Red (2.5YR 5/6) paint. Surfaces very worn. Flat base with groove around underside. Basket handle on rim. Monochrome (?). Cf. **K132.3**; Borgna 2007, 72, fig. 3.19 (Phaistos, LM IIIC late). LM IIIC.

K43.13   Pyxis (FIG. 4.22). H. 9.7 (with handles 11.9); D. base 13; D. rim 13.6. Large fragment (two sherds) preserving full profile, two fragments from base, two from second handle. 35% preserved. Fine, very soft, chalky, reddish yellow (5YR 7/6) fabric with grey (5Y 6/1) core. Very pale brown (10YR 8/3) slip. Very worn red (2.5YR 4/6) paint. Surfaces almost totally gone. Sampled KAR 06/40. Type 4 pyxis with rope-twisted handles rising above rim. Once decorated, but now so worn that all decoration lost. Publication: Seiradaki, fig. 12.4. LM IIIC.

Coarse Wares

K43.14   Kalathos (PLATE 14 *b*, FIG. 4.23). H. 11; D. base 10.7; D. rim 22. Restored from four fragments. 95% preserved; missing small bits of rim and two projections. Coarse red (2.5YR 4/8) fabric with frequent large (3–4 mm) grey and hard white angular inclusions. Surface encrusted with sediment. No evidence of burning. Flat ledge base. Flattened rim with three incised grooves; projections on outside of rim. Publication: Seiradaki, pl. 3d, top left. LM IIIC.

K43.15   Basin (FIG. 4.23). D. rim est. 35. Single fragment from rim, including handle attachment. Coarse, light red (2.5YR 6/6) fabric with frequent schist (1–3 mm) and hard white angular inclusions. Smoothed surface. Burned inside and out, more intensely on interior. Round horizontal handle. LM IIIC.

K43.16   Jar (FIG. 4.23). D. rim est. 29. Single large fragment from rim. Coarse red (2.5YR 5/8) fabric with frequent large (1–4 mm) schist and red phyllite inclusions. Sampled KAR 06/64. Ledge around top (inset slightly), as if for lid. Hole pierced through body below rim; burning around hole, only on interior. LM IIIC.

K43.17   Stirrup jar (FIG. 4.23). Max. pres. H. 21.6; D. base 12.4; max. D. 21.4. Mended from 21 fragments, five non-joining fragments. 65% preserved, including base, lower handle attachments; missing spout and false spout. Coarse red (2.5YR 5/6) fabric with frequent, very large (3–5 mm) schist and phyllite inclusions. Surfaces still coated with sediment. Top made separately and added onto body as disc. LM IIIC.

94   Popham 1965, pl. 85c, d; Popham 1970*b*, 196, fig. 1.3.

95   Warren 2007, 338, fig. 3.P2143 (early LM IIIC); Borgna 1997*a*, 279, fig. 8, top left.

96   Popham 1970*b*, pl. 50a, fourth row, third from left.

97   Borgna 1997*a*, 278, fig. 6.6.

98   Gesell, Day and Coulson 1995, 117, fig. 22.2.

99   Rethemiotakis 1997, 309, fig. 10h; Cadogan 1967, 260, fig. 2.8.

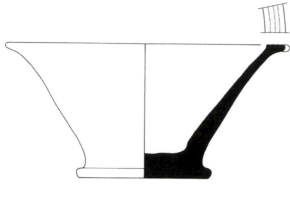

K43.14

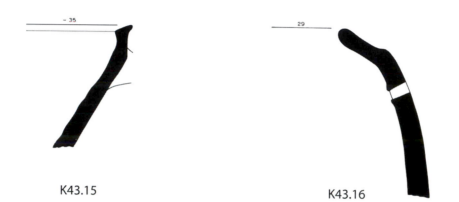

K43.15

K43.16

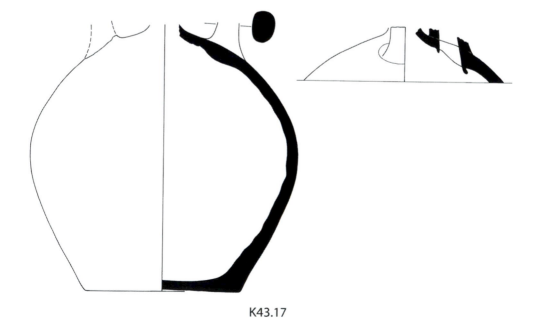

K43.17

*Fig. 4.23. Southern Houses, pottery from K 43 (**K43.14–17**). Scale 1:3.*

Room K 44

The excavators believed that this room was some sort of public structure fronting onto square K 48, and they likened it to a *kapheneion* in a traditional Cretan village.[100] It was added at an angle to the already existing rooms of the building, possibly at the same time as the southern rooms were built (K 24–28). Wallace, however, on the basis of her more recent work on the site concluded that K 44 was not a later addition.[101] It was one of the largest rooms on the site, and it was entered from K 48 through a doorway on the north.

The notebook lists three pithoi, including many sherds from one in gritty yellow clay with chevron decoration; the usual pithoid jars; tripods; dishes; stirrup jars; kalathoi; a lid with pinched rope decoration (**K44.9**); a scuttle handle (**K44.8**); and fine ware. A great deal of pottery was found in the boxes but not catalogued. There were many deep bowl fragments, including rims with multiple pendent loops, spirals, and other multiple curvilinear motifs, a handle attachment with multiple pendent loops, and body fragments with spiral and other curvilinear motifs, one of them burned. A krater handle attachment was also found and burned stirrup jar fragments with filled triangles.

Objects from the room included two conical stone beads (318, 319), a sandstone pounder (339), five cylindrical terracotta spindle whorls (313, 314, 315, 316, 317), and six terracotta spools (one large, five medium). Five of the spools have been preserved (PLATE 15 *c*). They are all intact, with smoothed surfaces, almost burnished, and their colour varies from reddish yellow (5YR 6/8–7.5YR 6/6) to pale red (10R 6/4) where burned. They are approximately the same size and shape, 2.8 high and weighing 25–35 g. They look like a matched set.

The pottery from this room consisted of small and broken pieces, with only one nearly complete vessel that may have been on the floor when the room was abandoned. This coarse jug (**K44.10**) belongs to Seiradaki's Type 3, one of the most common on the site, and it does not help to determine either the date of abandonment or the function of the room. The deep bowl or cup fragments have buttonhook spirals (**K44.1**), pendent multiple loops (**K44.2**), and floral motifs (**K44.3**) that appear both in LM IIIB deposits[102] and in LM IIIC.[103] The perforated lid (**K44.5**) finds a parallel in early LM IIIC Khania.[104] This pottery suggests an early LM IIIC date for Room K 44. Nothing, however, supports the idea of a public function for the room.

Pottery Catalogue: *K 44*

Fine Wares

K44.1   Deep bowl or cup (PLATE 1 *a*, FIG. 4.24). D. rim est. 14–15. Single fragment (two sherds) from rim. Fine, soft, reddish yellow (7.5YR 7/6) fabric. Very pale brown (10YR 8/3) slip. Worn black paint. Buttonhook spiral? LM IIIC early.

K44.2   Deep bowl or cup (FIG. 4.24). Max. pres. H. 3.5. Single fragment from rim. Fine, very soft, very pale brown (10YR 7/4) fabric. Worn very pale brown (10YR 8/4) slip. Worn black paint. Multiple pendent loops (?). LM IIIC.

K44.3   Deep bowl or cup (PLATE 1 *b*, FIG. 4.24). D. rim est. 13. Single fragment from rim. Fine, medium-soft, very pale brown (10YR 7/4) fabric. Very pale brown (10YR 8/3) slip. Worn, streaky black paint. Flower (?). For decoration, cf. Prokopiou 1997, 379, fig. 20:1 (Sybrita/Thronos, LM IIIC); Rethemiotakis 1997, 322, fig. 33e (Kastelli Pediada, Phase 2). LM IIIC.

K44.4   Stirrup jar (?) (FIG. 4.24). Max. pres. H. 6.2. Single fragment from body. Fine, rather hard, very pale brown (10YR 7/4) fabric. White (2.5Y 8/2) slip. Black paint worn to shadow. Worn surfaces. Possibly an import, based on fabric. On side: vertical wavy lines between bands. LM IIIC.

K44.5   Strainer lid (FIG. 4.24). Max. pres. H. 2. Single fragment from top of vessel. Fine, porous, very pale brown (10YR 8/4) fabric. Red (2.5YR 5/8) paint. Domed, with holes pierced through vessel. No indication of rest of shape. Monochrome except for reserved band around edge. LM IIIC.

Medium-Coarse Wares

K44.6   Amphora (FIG. 4.24). D. base 4.7; D. rim 48. Fragment preserving entire base, large fragment (three sherds) from neck and handles, three body fragments. Medium-coarse, gritty, hard, grey (5Y 6/1) blue ware fabric with small (1 mm and smaller) black and hard white angular inclusions. Ring base, with knobs on interior and underside. LM IIIC.

Coarse Wares

K44.7   Basin (FIG. 4.24). D. rim est. 38. Single large fragment preserving 10% of rim and one handle; missing base. Coarse, light red (2.5YR 6/8) fabric with frequent phyllites, schist, and hard angular white inclusions (1–3 mm). Traces of very pale brown (10YR 8/4) slip. Possible traces of burning on interior. Sampled KAR 06/62. Publication: Seiradaki, fig. 5.9. LM IIIC.

K44.8   Scuttle (FIG. 4.24). Max. pres. L. 16.5. Single fragment preserving entire handle. Coarse light red (10R 6/8) fabric with infrequent red and grey phyllites (1–2 mm) and mica. Possible traces of yellow slip. S-curved handle, round in section, with hook at end. Publication: Seiradaki, pl. 12b, middle, right. LM IIIC.

K44.9   Lid (PLATE 12 *c*, FIG. 4.24). Max. pres. H. 1.9; D. base 28. Single fragment from rim, preserving *c*. 5% of lid; missing knob handle. Coarse red (2.5YR 5/6) fabric with infrequent hard white and black inclusions (1–2 mm) and gold mica. Surface mottled black and red on top and bottom. No burning on bottom. Disc lid. Ridge with finger impressions on top of rim, plain ridge, and second ridge with finger impressions. Publication Seiradaki, pl. 12a, bottom, third from right. For shape and decoration, cf. **K80.7**, **K.41**. LM IIIC.

K44.10   Jug (FIG. 4.24). H. 28.4 (with handle 30); D. base 12.2; D. rim est. 11.4. Once mended from 31 fragments, 19 non-joining fragments. 50% preserved, including full profile, entire base, handle, and one rim fragment; missing most of neck and rim. Coarse pink (7.5YR 8/4) fabric with frequent hard red, grey, and white angular inclusions (1–2 mm). Surface light red (2.5YR 6/6) in patches. Burned patches toward bottom and on underside of base. LM IIIC.

---

100   *Karphi*, 81.
101   Wallace 2005, 248.
102   Popham 1970*b*, fig. 2.22, pl. 47e, pl. 49a, 50a (Knossos).
103   Mook and Coulson 1997, 352, fig. 18.45 (Kavousi–*Kastro*, Phase II); *Khania II*, pl. 36.82-P 1650.
104   *Khania II*, pl. 44.83-P 0352.

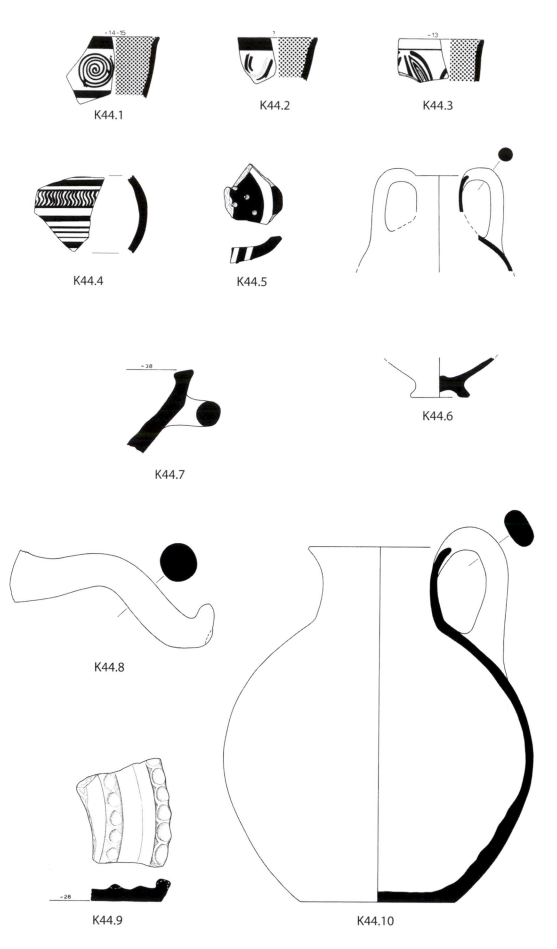

K44.1

K44.2

K44.3

K44.4

K44.5

K44.7

K44.6

K44.8

K44.9

K44.10

*Fig. 4.24. Southern Houses, pottery from K 44 (**K44.1–10**). Scale 1:3.*

Room K 46

This small room without visible doors belonged to the early phase of the building. The pottery found in it was reported as usual, except that there were few pithos sherds.[105] The notebook provides no additional information on the pottery. Uncatalogued sherds in the boxes included two body fragments from deep bowls, one with bands, one with a curvilinear decoration, and two stirrup jar fragments with bands. Other objects from the room included two terracotta spindle whorls, one conical (323), the other cylindrical (322) in shape, and seven spools (two large, five medium). Two of the spools are still preserved (PLATE 5 *c*). They are approximately the same size and weight (75 g), but one is chipped.

All of the pottery from this room is small and fragmentary. It probably represents discarded material on the floor or embedded in it. The deep bowls or cups all look early in LM IIIC. The Minoan flower of **K46.1** looks like examples from Knossos of LM IIIB,[106] with its Y-shaped stamen, but the IIIB examples usually have the strokes for the 'petals' attached to the stamen, not as a separate arc; that is more common in LM IIIC.[107] The rim of this bowl looks like examples found in the Phaistos area in LM IIIB–C.[108] **K46.2** may be a mainland import, as it is not monochrome painted inside and has only a narrow interior rim band. The comb motif has parallels, however, at Kastelli Pediada, and LM IIIB Knossos.[109] The body fragment **K46.4** with its outlined quatrefoil in panelled pattern recalls an example from Phase II at Kavousi–*Kastro*.[110] The fragments, then, look like early LM IIIC and fit well with the excavators' observations that this room belongs to an early phase of the settlement's history.

Pottery Catalogue: K 46

Fine Wares

K46.1 Deep bowl or cup (FIG. 4.25). D. rim est. 14. Single fragment from rim. Fine, soft, porous, very pale brown (10YR 7/4) fabric. Thick, very pale brown (10YR 8/3) slip. Worn black paint, especially on interior. Minoan flower. LM IIIB/C.

K46.2 Deep bowl or cup (FIG. 4.25). D. rim est. 12. Single fragment from rim. Fine, medium-hard, reddish yellow (5YR 7/6) fabric. Very pale brown (10YR 8/3) slip. Black paint worn to brown shadow. Well-preserved surfaces. Fringes or comb. Interior unpainted, except for band at rim. Mainland import? LM IIIC.

K46.3 Deep bowl or cup (FIG. 4.25). D. base 6. Single fragment from base. Fine, soft, very pale brown (10YR 7/4) fabric. Very pale brown (10YR 8/3) slip. Streaky black paint worn to brown. Worn surfaces. Band at base. LM IIIC.

K46.4 Deep bowl or cup (FIG. 4.25). Max. pres. H. 2.8. Single fragment from body. Fine, soft, reddish yellow (7.5YR 7/6) fabric. Very pale brown (10YR 8/3) slip. Red (2.5YR 4/8) paint. Worn surfaces. Panelled decoration with quatrefoil leaf. LM IIIC.

K46.5 Deep bowl or cup (FIG. 4.25). Max. pres. H. 3.8. Single fragment from body. Fine, soft, reddish yellow (7.5YR 7/6) fabric. Very pale brown (10YR 8/3) slip. Black paint. Worn surfaces. Hatched oval with tail. LM IIIC.

Medium-Coarse Wares

K46.6 Pyxis (FIG. 4.25). D. rim est. 25. Single fragment (two sherds) from rim. Medium-coarse reddish yellow (5YR 7/6) fabric with infrequent phyllites and schist (1–2 mm). Very pale brown (10YR 8/4) surface. Traces of red (10R 4/8) paint on exterior. Decorated with four incised grooves just below body. Several fragments of the same vessel came from K 47. LM IIIC.

Coarse Wares

K46.7 Lid (FIG. 4.25). Max. pres. H. 1.4. Two joining fragments from rim; missing centre with knob. Coarse, soft, red (2.5YR 5/8) fabric, dark grey (N4/) at core, with schist (up to 3 mm) and hard black and white inclusions. No burning on underside. Flat disc. Incised strokes on edge, incised concentric grooves farther in. LM IIIC.

Room K 47

This room also was thought to belong to the earlier phase of the building. The notebook says that it had a wall down the middle making two terraces in the room. The pottery listed in the notebook included the following: variations on usual rim types for pithoi and pithoid jars with undercutting, a red pithoid jar with yellow-white slip, a tripod bowl rim, and a red jug with yellow-white slip and globular body.[111] The jar of Type 7 illustrated by Seiradaki was not located;[112] the stirrup jar fragment identified as from K 47 is actually from K 147,[113] and another stirrup jar shown in Seiradaki is probably from Mikre Koprana (MK 1E).[114] A body fragment with handle attachment from a deep bowl with running spiral decoration was found in one of the boxes. Other objects found in this room included four cylindrical terracotta spindle whorls (324, 325, 326, 327) and a fragment of shell (328).

Most of the pottery found in this room is nearly complete and may have been in use when the building was abandoned. The krater fragment (**K47.1**), however, may be an earlier piece. The stirrup jar (**K47.2**) is of an unusual carinated shape, and its best parallels can be found in LM IIIB;[115] it is a shape that was not popular in LM IIIC, but does appear in early LM IIIC deposits

---

105 *Karphi*, 82.

106 Popham 1970*b*, 200, fig. 3.33, pl. 49a.

107 Popham 1965, 328, fig. 7.

108 Watrous 1992, 109, fig. 68.1921; Borgna 1997*a*, 278, fig. 6.6.

109 Rethemiotakis 1997, 318, fig. 27I; Popham 1970*b*, 200, fig. 3.41.

110 Mook and Coulson 1997, 352, fig. 18.55, 59, 63.

111 *Karphi*, 83.

112 Seiradaki, fig. 3.7.

113 Seiradaki, fig. 22g.

114 Seiradaki, pl. 6c, left.

115 Watrous 1992, 81, fig. 52.1397 (Kommos); Marinatos 1920–21, 155, fig. 1 (Milatos); Kanta 1980, fig. 55.5 (Kritsa), fig. 73.3 (Zakros); Catling 1968, 121.29, fig. 5.

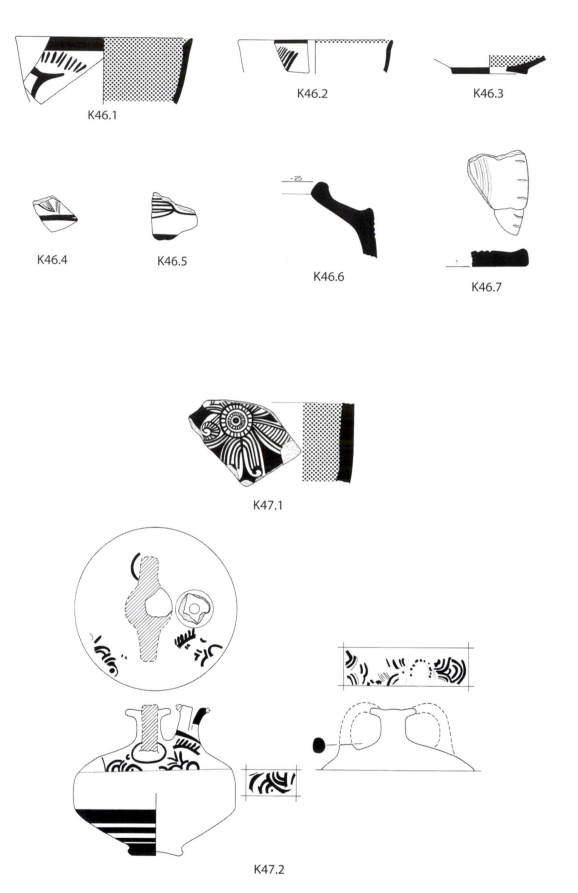

Fig. 4.25. Southern Houses, pottery from K 46 (**K46.1**–7) and K 47 (**K47.1**–2). Scale 1:3.

at Khamalevri.[116] The fringes on this example suggest LM IIIC, although the alternating arcs were more popular in LM IIIB. At any rate, this is an early piece that may have been in use over a long period of time. The basin, cooking jug, cooking lid, and stand all point to cooking and the preparation of food as a major function in the room.

Pottery Catalogue: K 47

Fine Wares

K47.1　Krater (PLATE 2 *a*, FIG. 4.25). Max. pres. H. 6.5. Single fragment from body. Fine, soft, very pale brown (10YR 8/4) fabric. Crackled black paint, worn on exterior, streaky on interior. Elaborate pattern with concentric circles at centre, many with hatching between, solid motifs (triangles?) radiating from centre, with arcs as hatching in the loops between and spiraliform ends. LM IIIC.

K47.2　Stirrup jar (PLATE 15 *d–e*, FIG. 4.25). H. 12; D. base 4.5; max. D. 13. Restored from 12 fragments; several fragments which were once there have fallen out. 50% preserved; missing 75% of lower body, parts of upper body, both handles, edges of spout, and most of rim of false spout. Fine, soft, brown (7.5YR 5/4) fabric. Entire surface burned grey. Traces of black paint. Worn surfaces. Carinated profile. On shoulder, loops and fringes. On body, alternating arcs above bands. Publication: Seiradaki, fig. 11.7, pl. 6c, right. LM IIIB/C.

Coarse Wares

K47.3　Basin (FIG. 4.26). H. 25.3; D. base est. 8.5; D. rim est. 35.2. Partially mended into two large fragments from base (11 sherds) and rim (18 sherds). 65% preserved, including full profile, entire base, half of lower body, 70% of rim, one handle; missing second handle. Coarse light red (2.5YR 6/8) to reddish yellow (5YR 6/8) fabric with frequent phyllites, and hard white and grey angular inclusions (2–3 mm). Creamy, very pale brown (10YR 8/4) slip. Red (10R 4/8) paint. Worn surfaces. Bands inside and out. For shape, cf. *Kastri*, 296, fig. 16.P11. LM IIIC.

K47.4　Lid (HM 11066) (PLATE 15 *f*, FIG. 4. 26). H. 4; D. base 24. Restored from six fragments. 50% preserved, including knob handle. Coarse red (2.5YR 5/6–5/8) fabric with frequent phyllites. Burning on top and side; bottom too coated with sediment to be certain of burning pattern. Flat disc lid, with knob handle in centre, concave on top. Four ridges, beginning at rim with finger impressions. Publication: Seiradaki, fig. 19.1, pl. 10c, right (mislabelled K 22). LM IIIC.

K47.5　Cooking jug (PLATE 15 *g*, FIG. 4.26). H. 9.4–9.8; D. base 6.4; D. rim 9. Mended from three fragments. 65% preserved, including full profile and entire base; missing 75% of rim and handle, much of upper body. Coarse reddish yellow (5YR 6/6–6/8) fabric with frequent red and grey phyllites and hard angular white inclusions. Burned on bottom and one side of exterior; burned on interior. Rim pinched out to form spout opposite handle. LM IIIC.

K47.6　Drain tile (FIG. 4.26). H. 6.8; max. pres. L. 14.1. Single fragment preserving full profile. Coarse, soft, reddish yellow (5YR 6/8) fabric with schist inclusions (1–2 mm). Flat irregular base, straight sides, and vertical rim. Not much curve, but not quite straight. May be a drain channel or a stand. LM IIIC.

Room K 45

Room K 45 is a small compartment built with K 50 and K 51 over a curving street. It belongs to a later phase in the history of the house. Material from these three rooms may represent earlier material from the street rather than vessels belonging to the use of the rooms. The notebook reports that the pottery was much broken. In addition to the sherds from a strainer mentioned in the publication, the notebook lists only a lid with loop handle (**K45.8**) and a tripod leg in gritty blue ware. The boxes produced a good deal of pottery that was not catalogued, including a deep bowl with vertical strokes, a burned krater fragment with multiple-outlined rayed decoration and another with multiple arcs, a bowl with a pinched out spout, and a stirrup jar with a crosshatched motif. Other objects found in the room included a conical stone bead or whorl (373) and a cylindrical terracotta spindle whorl (350).

The pottery is in fragments; there are no nearly complete vessels from this room. The deep bowls or cups look early LM IIIC; **K45.1** with its lozenge with chevron filler and slightly out-turned rim resembles fragments from Archanes of LM IIIA2 date,[117] but similar motifs also occur in early LM IIIC deposits. The two fragments of kraters with spirals (one running, the other buttonhook) (**K45.4**, **K45.5**) also look early, as does the slightly concave and raised base of a deep bowl (**K45.3**).

Pottery Catalogue: K 45

Fine Wares

K45.1　Deep bowl or cup (FIG. 4.27). D. rim est. 14. Single fragment from rim. Fine, rather hard, porous, very pale brown (10YR 8/4) fabric. Worn black paint. Worn surfaces. Lozenge with chevron filler. LM IIIC early.

K45.2　Deep bowl or cup (FIG. 4.27). D. rim est. 16. Single fragment from rim with handle scar. Fine, medium-hard, reddish yellow (7.5YR 7/6) fabric. Crackled black paint, streaky inside. No visible decoration on exterior. LM IIIC.

K45.3　Deep bowl or cup (FIG. 4.27). D. base est. 6. Single fragment from base. Fine, soft, porous, reddish yellow (7.5YR 7/6) fabric. Dark red (2.5YR 3/6) paint. Well-preserved surfaces. Monochrome inside and out and on bottom. LM IIIC early.

K45.4　Krater (FIG. 4.27). D. rim est. 22. Single fragment (two sherds) from rim. Fine, soft, reddish yellow (7.5YR 7/6) fabric. Very pale brown (10YR 8/3) slip. Worn black paint. Very worn surfaces, especially on interior. Running spiral. LM IIIC.

K45.5　Krater (FIG. 4.27). Max. pres. H. 6.8. Single fragment from body. Fine, soft, very pale brown (10YR 7/4) fabric. Very pale brown (10YR 8/4) slip. Black paint worn to shadow. Worn surfaces. Buttonhook spiral above bands. LM IIIC early.

K45.6　Stirrup jar (FIG. 4.27). Max. pres. H. 4.5. Single fragment (two sherds) from top, preserving attachment of spout. Fine, soft, reddish yellow (7.5YR 7/6) fabric. Very pale brown (10YR 8/4) slip. Red (2.5YR 4/8) paint. Worn surfaces. Minoan flower and spiral. LM IIIC.

Coarse Wares

K45.7　Tripod tray (FIG. 4.27). H. 4.2; D. base 38–40. Single fragment from rim and base, preserving scar from attachment of leg; missing legs and handles. Coarse, light red (2.5YR 6/8) fabric

116　Andreadaki-Vlasaki and Papadopoulou 2005, 372, fig. 32.
117　Andrikou 1997, 18–9, fig. 9.39–40.

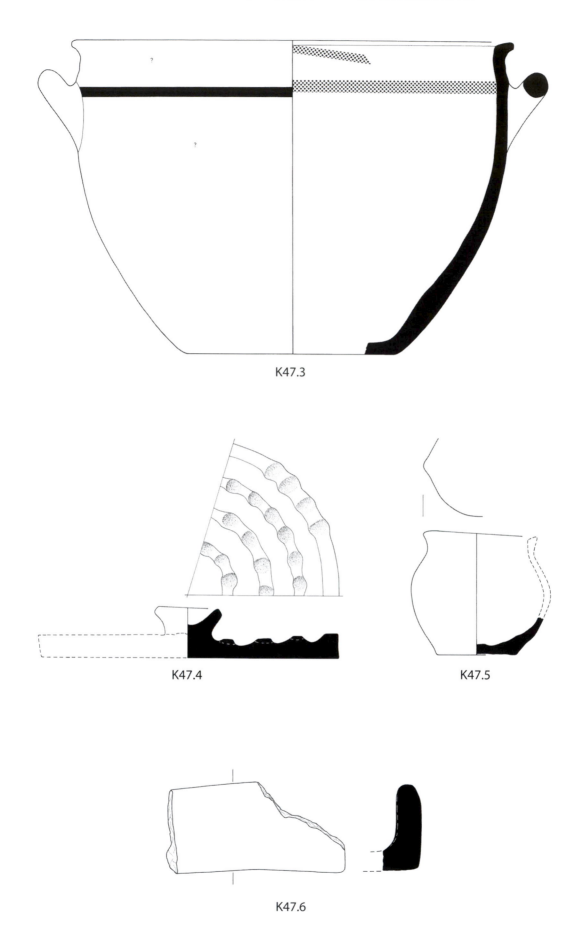

K47.3

K47.4

K47.5

K47.6

*Fig. 4.26. Southern Houses, pottery from K 47 (**K47.3–6**). Scale 1:3.*

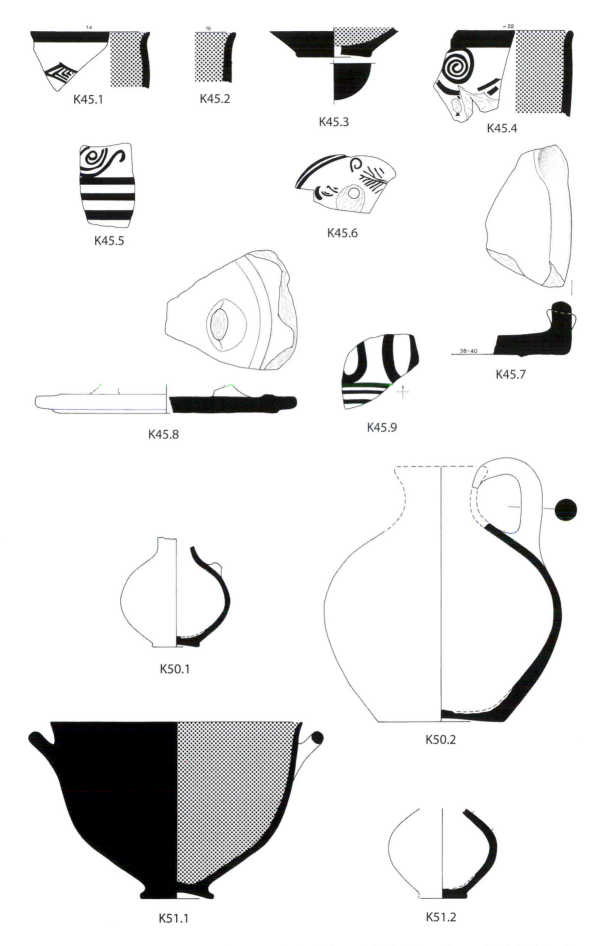

*Fig. 4.27. Southern Houses, pottery from K 45 (**K45.1–9**), K 50 (**K50.1–2**), and K 51 (**K51.1–2**). Scale 1:3.*

with frequent schist and gold mica inclusions (1–2 mm). Burning on rim and base, inside and out. Flat, shallow tray. Rim pushed down as if with finger in one spot. Number difficult to read, probably K 45. LM IIIC.

K45.8   Lid (FIG. 4.27). Max. pres. H. 2.4; D. base 18. Single fragment from rim, preserving one handle attachment. Rim badly chipped. Coarse, light red (2.5YR 6/6) fabric with infrequent schist and mica inclusions (*c*. 1 mm). Burned on underside around edge for 4 mm. Disc lid, with basket handle. Irregular on bottom, flat, but slightly concave around rim. Ridge on top around outside, near rim. For shape, cf. Rethemiotakis 1997, 314, fig. 20 (Kastelli Pediada, Phase 2). LM IIIC.

K45.9   Stirrup jar (PLATE 10 *f*, FIG. 4.27). Max. pres. H. 5; Th. 0.5. Single fragment from body. Coarse reddish yellow (5YR 6/6) fabric with frequent hard black and white inclusions. Very pale brown (10YR 8/4) slip. Worn black paint. Wavy bands or debased octopus above bands. LM IIIC.

Room K 50

Another small chamber built over curving street K 45-50-51, K 50 was entered from K 47. The pottery was reported as usual, but much broken, except for the two catalogued jugs. The notebook records also five pithoi, and in the boxes were fragments of a large jug or jar with crosshatched lozenges and a fine tray fragment. The dish published by Seiradaki was not located.[118] Other objects in the room included a terracotta spool and two terracotta spindle whorls, one biconical (348), the other cylindrical (356). The jug and juglet are of the most common shapes on the site, and do not provide much evidence for function of the room or for its date, but it is interesting that these two small compartments produced only vessels used in drinking and pouring.

Pottery Catalogue: K 50

Fine Wares

K50.1   Juglet (FIG. 4.27). Max. pres. H. 8.8; D. base 3.7. Intact. 90% preserved, including lower handle attachment; missing top of neck, rim, and handle. Fine, soft, white (10YR 8/2) fabric. Base and one side badly burned, and rest may be discoloured from fire. No trace of decoration. LM IIIC.

Coarse Wares

K50.2   Jug (FIG. 4.27). H. est. 20.4; D. base 10; D. rim est. 7.5. Mended from 14 fragments, ten non-joining fragments. 85% preserved, including entire base, handle; missing all of neck and most of rim. Coarse reddish yellow (5YR 6/8) fabric with grey core and frequent small (1 mm) hard angular white and black inclusions, some grey phyllites. Seiradaki Type 3. LM IIIC.

Room 51

The final room of the three small chambers built over the curving street K 45-50-51 had little of note. The notebook records that the pottery was as usual, but all the sherds were small and worn, and there were few pithos fragments. In addition to the deep bowl and jug catalogued below, there were two body sherds from deep bowls, one with a spiral, the other with blob decoration. No other objects were found in the room. The deep bowl looks late, with its rather high concave

foot and handles set high on the body; it finds a parallel at Kommos, where it is dated to LM IIIC, and it is also similar in shape to deep bowls from Phaistos, Knossos, and Khamalevri.[119] The juglet is very similar to the one from K 50, although its base is flat.

Pottery Catalogue: K 51

Fine Wares

K51.1   Deep bowl (PLATE 16 *a*, FIG. 4.27). H. 14.3; D. base 5.8; D. rim 20. Mended from 24 fragments. 50% preserved, including base, one handle; missing half of body and rim, one handle. Fine, rather soft, pink (7.5YR 7/4) fabric. Very pale brown (10YR 8/4) surface. Black to yellowish red (5YR 5/6) paint. Very worn surfaces, except on one fragment. One side discoloured from secondary burning. Monochrome. LM IIIC.

K51.2   Juglet (FIG. 4.27). Max. pres. H. 7.3; D. base 3.9. Mended from two fragments. 85% preserved, including entire base, lower handle scar; missing neck, rim, handle. Fine, soft, very pale brown (10YR 8/3) fabric. Very flaky surfaces. One area of burning on shoulder. No trace of decoration. LM IIIC.

Room K 49

This room, with its two doorways onto streets or squares was interpreted by the excavators as a public structure fronting on square 48.[120] It has a doorway onto the square and possibly another door on the north onto the road (K 54). The pottery was described as usual, and the notebook only adds that all types were present and that there were several examples of a yellow slip on rough red clay. A deep bowl with multiple loops was found in one of the boxes, but not catalogued. Other objects found in the room were two fragments of bronze (345), a conical stone bead or whorl (343), a pierced steatite disc (344),[121] and three cylindrical spindle whorls (340, 341, 342). There was little to indicate anything but an ordinary domestic function, despite the location of this room. The krater with running spirals **K49.1** is unusual, as most kraters have more elaborate and complicated decoration, but parallels can be found from a dump of Phases I–II at Kavousi–*Kastro*,[122] so this vessel may belong to early LM IIIC.

Pottery Catalogue: K 49

Fine Wares

K49.1   Krater (FIG. 4.28). Max. pres. H. 17.6; D. rim est. 33. Partially mended from 86 fragments. 20% of rim preserved, part of handle, body fragments; missing base. Fine, soft, gritty, reddish

---

118   Seiradaki, fig. 6.3.

119   Watrous 1992, 109, fig. 68.1922 (Kommos); Borgna 1997*a*, 278, fig. 6.7 (Phaistos); Popham 1965, 319, fig. 1A (Knossos); Andreadaki-Vlasaki and Papadopoulou 2007, 47, fig. 4.29 (Khamalevri, Phase II).

120   *Karphi*, 81.

121   *Karphi*, pl. 30.4.

122   Mook and Coulson 1997, 360, fig. 32.145.

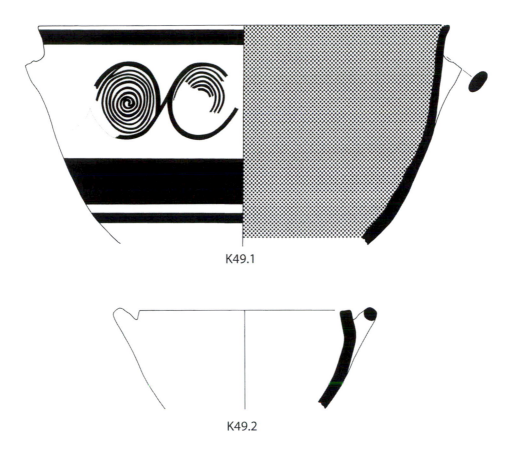

K49.1

K49.2

*Fig. 4.28. Southern Houses, pottery from K 49 (**K49.1–2**). Scale 1:3.*

yellow (7.5YR 7/6) fabric. Very pale brown (10YR 8/4) slip. Black paint. Worn surfaces. Running spirals. LM IIIC early.

Coarse Wares

K49.2   Basin (FIG. 4.28). Max. pres. H. 7.9; D. rim est. 17. Two joining fragments from rim and handle. 20% preserved; missing base. Coarse reddish yellow (5YR 6/8) fabric with frequent red and grey phyllites (1–2 mm). Burned inside and out, particularly on inside. Seiradaki Type 3. LM IIIC.

BROAD ROAD NORTH OF SOUTHERN HOUSES (ROOMS K 52–K 54)

Again, few traces of paving remained in this area, but between K 53 and K 54 was diagonal row of blocks to break the water flow, and the space was interpreted as a road with only a slight gradient.[123] A few blocks were preserved next to Wall 59, and these may have been either remains of the paving or part of an earlier structure. The very fragmentary nature of the pottery recorded from this area supports the identification as a street.

Room K 52

The pottery from this area was much broken, but no other information was provided in either the publication or the notebook; the notebook only says that the pottery is exactly as from K 51. Not much survives except for a few fragments of fine ware. In addition to the catalogued pottery, there was a fragment of a deep bowl with bands and the added disc and base of the false spout of a stirrup jar decorated with a filled curvilinear motif. Objects included two cylindrical spindle whorls (353, 520) and the point of a bone implement (352).

None of the pottery is closely datable, since it is so fragmentary. The deep bowl or cup with spiral and multiple stems (**K52.4**) is like an example from Phaistos.[124] Krater **K52.6** has a good parallel at Kastri in early LM IIIC,[125] while krater **K52.5** resembles one at Kastelli Pediada.[126] Spiral and floral motifs run throughout the settlement history, but these fragments look early in LM IIIC.

---

123   *Karphi*, 83.
124   Borgna 1997*a*, 278, fig. 6.7.
125   *Kastri*, 287, fig. 8t.
126   Rethemiotakis 1997, 312, fig. 15b.

Pottery Catalogue: K 52

Fine Wares

K52.1   Deep bowl or cup (FIG. 4.29). D. rim est. 12–13. Single fragment from rim. Fine, soft, very pale brown (10YR 8/4) fabric and slip. Worn black paint. Fringes or end of Minoan flower. LM IIIC early.

K52.2   Deep bowl or cup (FIG. 4.29). D. rim est. 14. Single fragment from rim. Fine, soft, porous, pink (7.5YR 7/4) fabric. Very pale brown (10YR 8/3) slip. Red (10R 4/6) paint. Spiral. LM IIIC.

K52.3   Deep bowl or cup (FIG. 4.29). D. rim est. 14. Single fragment from rim. Fine, soft, reddish yellow (5YR 7/6) fabric. Very pale brown (10YR 8/3) slip. Red (2.5YR 5/8) paint. Worn surfaces. Curvilinear motif with fringes, flower, or filler. Reserved band on interior. LM IIIC.

K52.4   Deep bowl or cup (FIG. 4.29). Max. pres. H. 4.3. Single fragment from near rim. Fine, soft, reddish yellow (5YR 7/6) fabric. Very pale brown (10YR 8/3) slip. Dark reddish brown (2.5YR 3/4) paint. Worn surfaces. Spiral and multiple stem. LM IIIC early.

K52.5   Krater (FIG. 4.29). Max. pres. H. 4. Single fragment from rim. Fine, soft, reddish yellow (5YR 7/6) fabric. Very pale brown (10YR 8/3) slip. Red (10R 4/8) paint. Worn surfaces. Panelled pattern of crosshatched lozenge with multiple outlines between vertical bands. LM IIIC.

K52.6   Krater (FIG. 4.29). Max. pres. H. 4.6. Single fragment from body. Fine, soft, reddish yellow (5YR 7/6) fabric. White (10YR 8/2) slip. Black paint. Worn exterior surfaces, well-preserved on interior. Panelled pattern with sprays of leafy branches and diagonal bands. LM IIIC.

Area K 53

The pottery was like that from other parts of the street, much broken. None has been preserved. A terracotta conical spindle whorl (355) came from this area.

Area K 54

This area was not a room, but another road linking K 53 to square K 10–K 32 and K 48. In addition to the catalogued pottery, there was also a small fragment of another deep bowl with a spiral and a krater fragment with bands. A fragment of a bronze knife (358), a terracotta cylindrical spindle whorl (357), a conical stone bead (359), and a square pierced fragment of steatite (599) were also found. The pottery is scrappy and small, but includes the usual sort of material found in streets: deep bowls (here with zigzag), kraters (with outlined solid curvilinear motifs), a basin with bands in and out, and a stirrup jar with wavy line or octopus tentacles. The krater (**K54.5**) finds parallels in early LM IIC Knossos.[127] There is nothing that looks late, and most of this material would fit well into early LM IIIC.

Pottery Catalogue: K 54

Fine Wares

K54.1   Deep bowl or cup (FIG. 4.29). Max. pres. H. 5. Single fragment from body. Fine, soft, reddish yellow (7.5YR 7/6) fabric. Very pale brown (10YR 8/3) slip. Worn black to dark red (2.5YR 3/6) paint. Zigzag. LM IIIC.

K54.2   Deep bowl or cup (FIG. 4.29). Max. pres. H. 5.3. Single fragment from body. Fine, soft, reddish yellow (7.5YR 8/6) fabric. Very pale brown (10YR 8/3) slip. Worn black to red (2.5YR 5/8) paint. Multiple stem pattern. LM IIIC.

K54.3   Basin (FIG. 4.29). D. rim est. 28. Single fragment (2 sherds) from rim. Fine, medium-hard, reddish yellow (7.5YR 7/6) fabric. Very pale brown (10YR 8/3) slip. Red (2.5YR 4/8) paint. Well-preserved surfaces. Bands on exterior and interior. Strokes on rim. For shape and banded decoration, cf. Andreadaki-Vlasaki and Papadopoulou 2007, 46, fig. 3.26–27 (Khamelevri, Phase II). LM IIIC.

K54.4   Krater (FIG. 4.29). Max. pres. H. 7.5. Single fragment from body. Fine, soft, reddish yellow (7.5YR 7/6) fabric. White (10YR 8/2) slip. Red (2.5YR 4/6) to very dusky red (2.5YR 2.5/2) paint. Well-preserved exterior surfaces; interior worn. Oulined alternating thick and thin curvilinear bands. LM IIIC.

K54.5   Krater (FIG. 4.29). Max. pres. H. 5.5; Th. 0.45–1.0. Single fragment from body. Fine, medium-hard, reddish yellow (7.5YR 7/6) fabric. Very pale brown (10YR 8/4) slip. Black paint. Well-preserved surfaces. Panelled pattern: vertical scallops with multiple outlines, vertical wavy lines, large half round with multiple outlines. Label is worn; it may also be from K 59. LM IIIC.

Coarse Wares

K54.6   Stirrup jar (?) (PLATE 10 *f*, FIG. 4.29). Max. pres. H. 0.7. Single fragment from body. Coarse reddish yellow (7.5YR 8/6) fabric with frequent large (1–7 mm) red phyllites and hard white angular inclusions. White (2.5Y 8/2) slip. Black paint worn to yellowish red (5YR 5/6). Wavy band above bands, possibly debased octopus. LM IIIC.

BROAD ROAD BETWEEN SMALL SHRINE AND PRIEST'S HOUSE (AREA K 56)

Area K 56

This narrow street ran to the east of the Priest's House and turned west at the north of that building to separate it from the Commercial Quarter. The street may once have continued to the north but was cut off by the construction of the Baker's House. The paving seems to have survived here.[128]

The pottery was unusual only because of the apparent lack of pithos fragments. In addition to the ubiquitous deep bowls, the notebook also records stirrup jars, the spout of spouted jug,[129] two krater bases of Type 3, a lid of Type 4, and a large krater base. Uncatalogued pottery included one handle and one burned body sherd with arcs as filler from deep bowls, a krater fragment, a cooking tray with scalloped rim, a double round horizontal (bucranium) handle,[130] a tripod leg with dints, and a strange fragment that may have come from a chalice or a goddess. Objects found here included a fragment of bronze (413), a conical stone bead (412), and a cylindrical terracotta spindle whorl (361).

---

127   Warren 2007, 341, fig. 6.P2146.
128   *Karphi*, 89.
129   Published in Seiradaki, fig. 9.9, but missing.
130   One of two pictured on Seiradaki, pl. 12a.

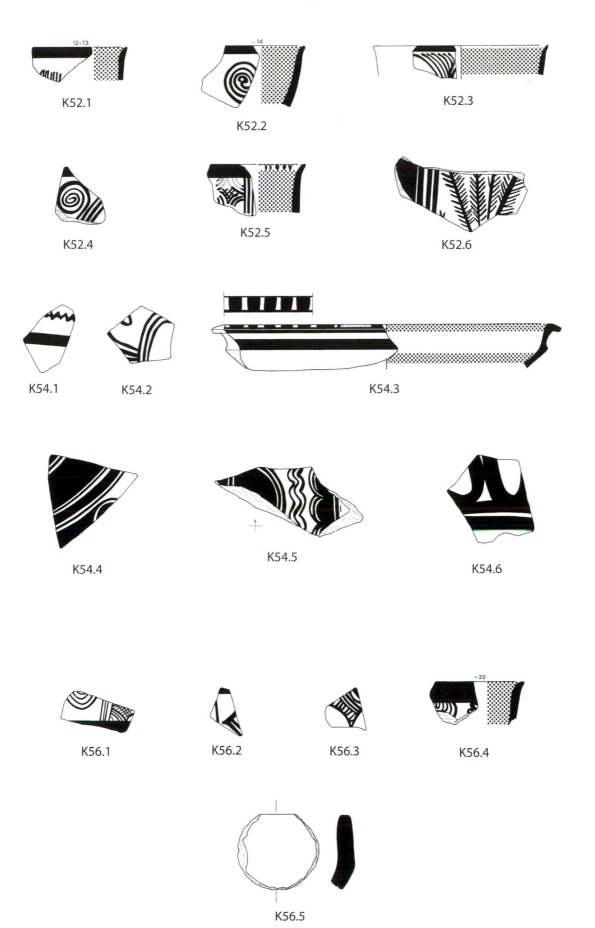

*Fig. 4.29. Broad Road, pottery from K 52 (**K52.1–6**), K 54 (**K54.1–6**), and K 56 (**K56.1–5**). Scale 1:3.*

The preserved pottery is small and worn, as expected from street deposits. The deep bowl with hatched lozenge may be early LM IIIC (the motif is common in Kastri), but the fragment of the filled lozenge (**K56.3**) finds parallels with material from the latest LM IIIC at Karphi.

Pottery Catalogue: K 56

Fine Wares

K56.1 Deep bowl or cup (FIG. 4.29). Max. pres. H. 2.7. Single fragment from body. Fine, medium-hard, very pale brown (10YR 7/4) fabric. White (10YR 8/2) slip. Worn black paint. Well-preserved surfaces. Panelled pattern: multiple pendent loops next to panel with crosshatched lozenges. LM IIIC.

K56.2 Deep bowl or cup (FIG. 4.29). Max. pres. H. 3.2. Single fragment from body, near rim. Fine, soft, porous, very pale brown (10YR 7/4) fabric. Very pale brown (10YR 8/4) slip. Worn brown paint. Worn surfaces. Hatched lozenge. LM IIIC.

K56.3 Deep bowl or cup (FIG. 4.29). Max. pres. H. 3. Single fragment from body. Fine, soft, porous, very pale brown (10YR 7/4) fabric. Very pale brown (10YR 8/3) slip. Dark reddish brown (5YR 3/3) paint. Worn surfaces. Curvilinear pattern with hatching, lozenge? For decoration, cf. Borgna 1997a, 277, fig. 4, top right (Phaistos, LM IIIB–C). LM IIIC.

K56.4 Krater (FIG. 4.29). D. rim est. 22. Single fragment from rim. Fine, soft, reddish yellow (5YR 7/6) fabric. Very pale brown (10YR 8/3) slip. Weak red (10YR 8/3) paint 10R 4/4. Well-preserved surfaces. Arc filler and scalloped edge. LM IIIC.

Coarse Wares

K56.5 Stopper or lid (FIG. 4.29). D. 6–6.5. Single fragment, preserving entire stopper or lid. Coarse, soft, light red (2.5YR 6/8) fabric with infrequent phyllites and hard white angular inclusions. Originally a fragment of cooking dish cut into roughly circular stopper or lid. LM IIIC.

THE SMALL SHRINE (ROOMS K 55, K 57)

This small, two-room building was identified as a minor shrine by the excavators because of its location and contents.[131] It certainly is not a shrine of the goddess with upraised arms, like the Temple, K 15–17, or K 116. Its location off the square (K 32), and road K 54 does suggest a public function, and the snake tube and clay altar suggest a religious function, perhaps similar to that of K 58.[132]

Room K 57

This small room was entered from court K 32, and there was a possible second entrance on the south. The floor of the room was of bedrock, and there was no trace of clay floor or of roofing material, so it was identified as another unroofed shrine. Although the pottery was of the usual sort, there was little fine ware. The notebook adds the following pottery: sherds from two pithoi, one with pinched rope at rim and chevron below, the other with wavy rope between horizontal bands; pithoid jars; tripods; dishes; kalathoi; a scuttle (**K57.5**); a kylix in coarse ware; and a jug with a projection below the spout and braided handle in coarse

red ware. Material from this room found in the boxes but not catalogued includes three body fragments from deep bowls, one with spirals, one with a curvilinear pattern, one with bands; a small medium-coarse jug decorated with a wavy line; a horizontal basket handle; and a coarse bucranium handle with rope decoration. A cooking pot or jar was also not catalogued; 75 fragments from the flat base of this vessel were preserved in a coarse fabric with frequent red and grey phyllites and hard white angular inclusions. The terracotta altar and fragments of a cylindrical stand were also not catalogued.[133] Other objects from this room included three terracotta spindle whorls, two cylindrical in shape (362, 363), one biconical (364).

The pottery from this room was scanty and not closely datable. Of the deep bowl fragments, one (**K57.1**) has a decoration of multiple stems that would fit into any phase of LM IIIC. **K57.2** is a slightly raised and concave base with a spiral painted on the interior; such a design is rare, but can be paralleled on deep bowls from Khania–*Kastelli*,[134] where they seem to come from levels earlier than LM IIIC, and from LM IIIC Kastelli Pediada and Phaistos.[135] The shape of the base looks early. The jar fragment (**K57.6**) finds no parallels among LM IIIC coarse shapes and decoration, and it may represent a later intrusion. The only whole vessel found on the floor was the jug, which, with its linear design, looks very late in LM IIIC; again, no exact parallel can be found. The decoration looks later than that found on the altar, with its alternating arcs, filled triangles, and horns of consecration. The altar may have religious significance, as suggested by its horns of consecration and the animal figurines on the top, but it also is related to the less elaborate fenestrated stands found in other LM IIIC sites, Kavousi–*Vronda* in particular.[136]

Pottery Catalogue: K 57

Fine Wares

K57.1 Deep bowl or cup (FIG. 4.30). Max. pres. H. 4.5. Single fragment from rim. Fine, soft, reddish yellow (7.5YR 7/6) fabric. Very pale brown (10YR 8/3) slip. Black paint. Worn surfaces. Multiple stems. LM IIIC.

K57.2 Deep bowl or cup (PLATE 10 *e*, FIG. 4.30). D. base 4.5. Single fragment preserving half of base. Fine, medium-soft, reddish yellow (7.5YR 7/6) fabric. Very pale brown (10YR 8/3) slip. Red (2.5YR 4/8–5/8) paint. Band on exterior of base, spiral on interior. LM IIIC.

---

131 *Karphi*, 84.
132 Day 2009, 144.
133 The altar has been published in *Karphi*, pl. 34; Young 1938, 235, fig. 12, left; Gesell 1985, pl. 150. Gesell will provide a detailed description of this unusual piece with new photographs and drawings.
134 Kanta 1997, 86, figs. 1.2, 1.6.
135 Rethemiotakis 1997, 316, fig. 24; Borgna 2003, 448, fig. 22.62 (on a cup).
136 *Kavousi IIA*, figs. 41, 60, 96.

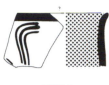

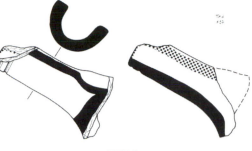

K57.1   K57.2   K57.3

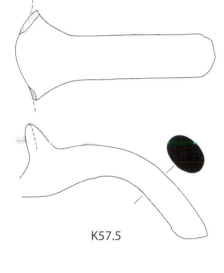

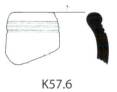

K57.4   K57.5

K57.6

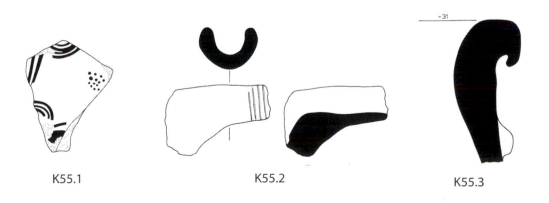

K55.1   K55.2   K55.3

Fig. 4.30. *Small Shrine, pottery from K 57* (**K57.1–6**) *and K 55* (**K55.1–3**). *Scale 1:3.*

K57.3   Tankard or spouted jug (FIG. 4.30). Max. pres. L. 9.5. Single fragment preserving entire spout. Fine, soft, reddish yellow (7.5YR 8/6) fabric. Very pale brown (10YR 8/4) slip. Black paint. Two grooves at end of rim, black bands outlining spout inside and out. LM IIIC.

K57.4   Jug (PLATE 16 *b*, FIG. 4.30). Max. pres. H. 14.4; H. rest. 19.5; D. base 6.5; D. rim est. 6.8. Restored from 13 fragments. 60% preserved, including base and lower body, lower and upper handle attachments, tiny piece of rim; missing nearly all of neck and rim, much of handle. Fine, soft, pink (7.5YR 7/4) fabric with tiny red inclusions and some mica. Pink (7.5YR 7/4) slip. Black paint. Worn surfaces on lower body, well-preserved on upper body. On shoulder: half medallions separated by filled pendent triangles. Hatching between outermost outlines of medallion, with filled triangle at apex; next two outlines filled; in centre is pendent crosshatched triangle between two filled upright triangles, with loops in corner and filler strokes. Publication: Seiradaki, pl. 5d, bottom, second from right (labelled K 11); Young 1938, 235, fig. 12 right, top left. LM IIIC.

Coarse Wares

K57.5   Scuttle (FIG. 4.30). Max. pres. L. 15.2. Single fragment preserving part of rim and entire handle, with tip broken off. Coarse reddish yellow (5YR 7/6) fabric with red, black, and white inclusions (1–2 mm). Rim pushed in at handle attachment. Incisions on interior of rim. LM IIIC.

K57.6   Jar or basin (FIG. 4.30). Max. pres. H. 4. Single small fragment from rim. Coarse, light red (10R 6/8) fabric with frequent small (<1 mm) white inclusions. Decorated with three grooves below rolled rim. LM IIIC.

Room K 55

The second room of the small shrine was on a higher level, and there must have been steps leading up to it from K 57. It had no independent entrance. The excavators mention a buttress in the southeast corner of the room, and it is possible that this was a small platform, like those found at Kavousi–*Vronda*.[137]

Little was found in the room. The publication mentions the neck of a jug with a projection below the spout, and Seiradaki illustrates a one-handled jug of Type 9;[138] it could not be located. The pithoid jar published by Seiradaki is actually the pithos catalogued below (**K55.3**).[139] The notebook adds the following information. There were sherds from three pithoi: one of reddish clay with a serpentine rope pattern and an overhanging rim with pinched rope below (perhaps pithos **K55.3**), one with a similar rope pattern and

darker clay, and one of red clay with oblique strokes incised on bands. There were also three pithoid jars, tripods, kalathoi, and dishes, one with upright sides and finger dents at rim. Two deep bowl fragments were found in the boxes but were too small to catalogue; one was decorated with a spiral, the other of very soft fabric had an undetermined curvilinear motif. Also found in the room was a bronze chisel (411),[140] a pierced schist plaque (360),[141] and a cylindrical terracotta spindle whorl (374).

Nothing found in this room seems to have anything to do with ritual. The function of the room remains a mystery, although it may have served as a storage chamber. The pottery is not datable, nor is there enough to suggest that this was a deposit left on the floor when the settlement was abandoned.

Pottery Catalogue: K 55

Fine Wares

K55.1   Krater (FIG. 4.30). Max. pres. H. 9; Th. 1.0. Single fragment from body. Fine, soft, very pale brown (10YR 7/4) fabric. Very pale brown (10YR 8/4) slip. Red (10R 5/8) to dark red (10R 3/6) paint. Well-preserved surfaces. Spirals (?) and patch of dots. LM IIIC.

Coarse Wares

K55.2   Tankard or spouted jug (FIG. 4.30). Max. pres. H. 5.5; L. spout 8.9. Single fragment from spout. Coarse light red (2.5YR 6/6) fabric with frequent small (<1 mm) hard white angular inclusions and phyllites. Traces of creamy yellow slip. Horizontal spout that may come from a jug or a tankard. Four grooves on outside edge. LM IIIC.

K55.3   Pithos (FIG. 4.30). Max. pres. H. 11; D. rim est. 31. Single fragment from rim. Coarse, soft, reddish yellow (5YR 7/6) fabric with frequent, small, well-sorted inclusions: schist, phyllites, quartzite, and hard angular white inclusions. Sampled KAR 06/79. Publication: Seiradaki, fig. 22.2 (as pithoid jar). LM IIIC.

---

137 *Kavousi IIA*, 95, pl. 16A–D.
138 Seiradaki, fig. 9.9.
139 Seiradaki, fig. 2.2.
140 *Karphi*, pl. 28.2.
141 *Karphi*, pl. 30.3.

5

The Southwest Quadrant

The Priest's House (Rooms K 58–K 61, K 80), Central West Quarter (Rooms K 66–K 69, K 81–K 88, K 96, K 97, K 100), the Southern Shelters (Rooms K 62–K 65, K 90–K 95, K 98, K 99), and Broad Road (Areas K 101, K 103, K 105, K 111)

THE PRIEST'S HOUSE (ROOMS K 58–K 61, K 80)

The excavators saw this building as second to the Great House in size and complexity.[1] They dubbed it the 'Priest's House' for two reasons. In the earlier stages of the settlement's development, the building had direct access to the Temple through the street that once ran between K 52 and K 72, which was later cut off by the construction of the Baker's House. The small room K 58, which produced ritual equipment, was built up against its south wall and was therefore interpreted as belonging to the building, although not directly accessible from any of the rooms. More recently, Nowicki suggested how this building might have functioned as an ordinary domestic unit,[2] although it is almost as large as the Great House, and if not religious in nature was still likely to have been an elite building. Wallace's restudy of the architecture of this house indicated that modifications were made to the structure over the life of the settlement; she suggested that either there were two houses later joined together by a doorway knocked in the wall between K 61 and K 80, or that K 80 was added on after K 61.[3] The largest room (K 61) was entered on its long side from the street (K 56). This room gave access to either the large room K 80 or the smaller room K 60, through which K 59 could be reached. Room K 58 was backed up against K 80, but this small room was apparently not accessible from the building; Wallace was unable to confirm this fact based on the existing evidence on the site.[4] The size of the building and the finds from it suggest that it was the dwelling of an elite individual or family, and like the Great House it was situated close to religious structures: the small room with offering stands (K 58) and the Small Shrine (K 55–57) across the street.

Room K 58

Room K 58 was not connected to the main part of the building, and the only entrance into it was from the street (K 52). It appears to have had a public function, one possibly controlled by the inhabitants of the Priest's House. Ritual objects were found in the southeast corner. The notebook records the following coarse pottery, which was much as usual: many pithoi, but without rims; at least eight kalathoi, four of Type 1,

four more like Type 1 but with plain bases; tripod legs; a jar of Type 7; several dishes of Type 6; and a small jar of red ware with a white slip. The fine ware is said to have been found below the level of the coarse ware and of the cult objects, and the notebook lists eight bowls of Type 1 (the rounded deep bowl), six with painted decoration; a bridge-spouted bowl; a stirrup jar of Type 2; a small krater of Type 1; a cup of Type 1; the base of cup in blue ware; one very upright base; and a triple handle. No pottery other than the pieces catalogued below was found in the boxes. Objects found in this room, in addition to the two stands, included only a fragment of bronze (416) and two terracotta spindle whorls, one conical (414), the other cylindrical (415).

This is a peculiar assemblage, and it is unfortunate that the rest of the pottery was not preserved. The fine wares were at lower level and may represent material earlier than that in use at the time of the abandonment of the settlement. What is preserved are two unusual stands, one kalathos (out of eight found), a scuttle, and a small cup that was once attached to another vessel. The combination of stands, kalathoi, and scuttles also occurred at the shrine at Kavousi–*Vronda*,[5] where they were found associated with terracotta statues of goddesses with upraised arms, as is customary. The stands were probably used to hold kalathoi containing offerings. The stands themselves are both unusual; one is rectangular, the other round but with only two round horizontal handles in place of the many vertical ones that usually wind up the sides of these vessels. If this room was indeed a shrine, it did not house the same sort of ritual activities as the others at Karphi (the Temple, K 15–17, K 116, K 106); offerings were apparently made on the stands, but not in the presence of the goddess, represented by her terracotta images.[6]

1   *Karphi*, 84.
2   Nowicki 1999, 149–50.
3   Wallace 2005, 243.
4   Wallace 2005, 244.
5   Gesell, Day, and Coulson 1995, 79–80; Gesell, Glowacki and Klein forthcoming.
6   Day 2009, 144.

The small size of the room suggests that the ritual activities carried on in it were not intended for the large groups that could be accommodated in the Temple and the open area outside it.

Pottery Catalogue: K 58

Fine Wares

K58.1   Miniature cup (PLATE 16 *c*, FIG. 5.1). H. 4.1–4.4; D. base 4.3; D. rim 3.8. Complete; mended from two fragments. Fine light red (2.5YR 6/8) fabric with grey phyllite and hard white angular inclusions; surface still encrusted with sediment. Flat base, but broken as if attached to another vessel; hole worn through centre. LM IIIC.

Coarse Wares

K58.2   Kalathos (PLATE 16 *d*, FIG. 5.1). H. 7.5; D. base 4.4; D. rim 15.6. Intact except for small bit of rim and restored; rim chipped. Coarse, rather hard, red (10R 5/6) cooking pot fabric with frequent large (up to 4 mm) phyllite and hard white angular inclusions. Surface mottled black, but not burned. Much of surface still coated with sediment. Rim flattened on top with small ledge on interior. LM IIIC.

K58.3   Scuttle (FIG. 5.1). Max. pres. L. 14.5. Single fragment preserving part of rim and entire handle, chipped at end. Coarse red (10R 4/8) fabric with grey (N4/) core and large (2–3 mm) phyllite inclusions. S-curved handle, round in section. Rim pushed in by handle; knob on interior of rim where pushed in. Dint at end. Publication: Seiradaki, pl. 12b, middle, second from right. For shape of handle with dint, cf. *Kastri*, 290, fig. 11t. LM IIIC.

K58.4   Cylindrical stand (PLATE 16 *e*, FIG. 5.1). H. 38.5; D. base 20–21; D. rim 12.5–13.5. Mended from five fragments. 85% preserved, including full profile and one handle; missing 25% of rim and upper body, one handle (preserved in original publication). Coarse red (2.5YR 5/8) fabric with frequent red phyllites (1–5 mm), black, grey, and hard white angular inclusions, and micaceous schist. Surfaces almost entirely gone or still coated with sediment. Base has two mouldings on exterior, large ledge on interior. Nearly cylindrical profile; ridge below outward thickened rim. Two round horizontal handles placed asymmetrically on mid body. Rim has unfinished look, as though something was once attached. Ridging on interior. Publication: *Karphi*, pl. 35.7 middle; Gesell 1976, 257, pl. 43, fig. 16; Gesell 1985, fig. 149. LM IIIC.

K58.5   Stand (PLATE 16 *f*, FIG. 5.1). Max. pres. H. 25; L. 18.5; W. 16. Mended from seven fragments. Entire base preserved and attachments for three handles, two on one side, one on other. Coarse red (2.5YR 5/8) fabric with frequent large phyllites (1–3 mm) and rounded white inclusions, chaff voids. Rectangular stand, with ledge around bottom, irregular hole in base. At least three elliptical vertical handles on side, beginning at bottom. Publication: *Karphi*, pl. 35.7, right; Gesell 1985, fig. 148; Gesell 1976, 257, pl. 43, fig. 17. LM IIIC.

Room K 61

Room K 61 was the largest and main room of the complex. It was entered from the street (K 56) on the east over a high threshold.[7] The floor was of clay over bedrock, with carbonised wood in the cracks in the rock that may represent the remains of earlier structures. A low bench made up of flat stones lay along the west wall over the carbon, and also over earth. Although no traces were found of interior supports, there was ample roofing clay to show that the room was roofed. The room may originally have been wider; the wall that runs under K 83 and K 84 may represent an earlier wall for K 61.

There were three deposits in the room, one above the roofing debris, one on the floor, and a lower deposit below the floor. These deposits were listed separately in the notebook, but in the publication the material from above the floor and the floor were put together. The pottery has been marked only as K 61, so it is difficult to determine from which layer any individual fragment came.

Above floor the pottery was recorded as usual. Coarse ware included fragments of two or three pithoi, a number of pithoid jars, a basin of Type 4, a jug of Type 6, a red pyxis of Type 2, a jar neck with a vertical handle made of three cylinders (preserved in one of the boxes, but not catalogued), and an incised vertical handle. Fine wares were as usual, but there were no pyxides. Objects from this layer included three fragments of bronze (427, 428, 513), a conical stone bead or whorl (431), two conical terracotta spindle whorls (429, 430), and antler of red deer, horns of ox, and goat, as well as a boar's tusk.

The floor deposit included sherds of pithoi, a jar of Type 1, and tripods of Types 2 (possibly **K61.15**) and 3 in coarse ware. Fine wares included a pyxis of Type 2 (possibly **K61.12**), a stirrup jar of Type 5, a dish of Type 7 with horizontal handles, and a basin of Type 5 with horizontal handles. The pyxis **K61.12**, cooking mug **K61.14**, deep bowl **K61.2**, and krater **K61.11** came from this deposit, according to their labels. Other objects included bones.

Below floor the pottery was of usual types but was much broken. The notebook mentions a small grey kalathos (probably **K61.10**), and a bridge spout, possibly the spouted bowl **K61.9**. Other objects from this layer included a cylindrical terracotta spindle whorl (432), 19 terracotta spools, and a piece of yellow colouring material.

Most of the catalogued pottery is simply labelled K 61 and could come from any of the three strata. In addition to the vessels listed below, the boxes produced two deep bowl fragments (one with a spiral with tangents, one with fringed filler pattern), another possible deep bowl, and a rim with a dentil design.

The preserved pottery does not give much hint as to its date, and there is the additional problem of not knowing whether a vessel came from below the floor, was resting on it, or was above the floor in the roofing debris. The lower deposit contained for certain the spouted bowl (**K61.9**) and the kalathos (**K61.10**). The shape of the side-spouted bowl, with its fringed multiple loops finds parallel in LM IIIC Phaistos and Khalasmenos.[8] The 19 terracotta spools suggest that

---

7   *Karphi*, 84–5.

8   Borgna 2003, 452, pl. 26.5.1; Tsipopoulou 2004, fig. 8.13.92-225; for the shape, see also Catling 1968, 127–9, fig. 9.37.

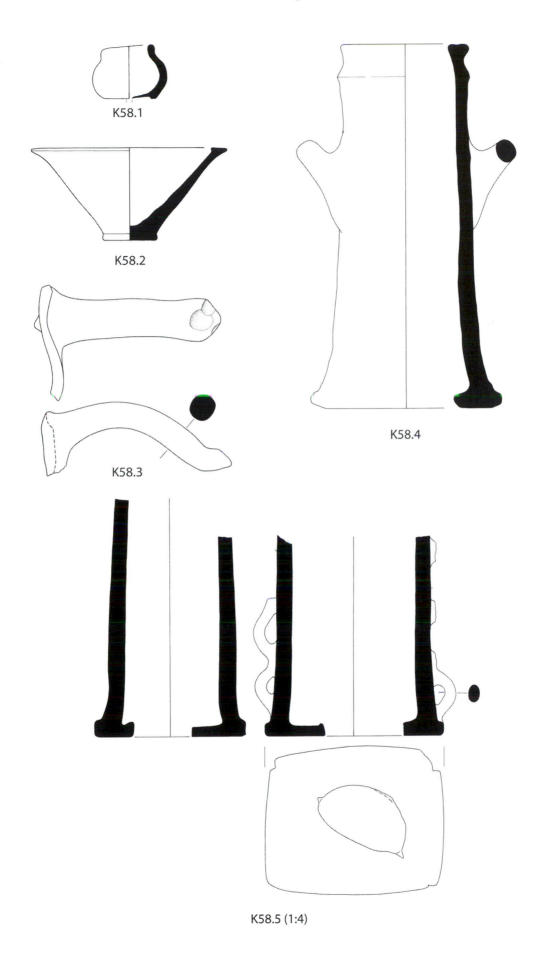

K58.1

K58.2

K58.3

K58.4

K58.5 (1:4)

*Fig. 5.1. Priest's House, pottery from K 58 (**K58.1–5**). Scale 1:3 unless otherwise indicated.*

there might have been a loom in this room in its earliest phase and that weaving may have gone on here.

On the floor was the tripod cooking pot (**K61.15**), which is a typical LM IIIC shape with a close parallel at Knossos;[9] the Type 2 pyxis (**K61.12**) and the deep bowl with multiple loops (**K61.2**) also came from the floor. There is nothing that can securely be identified as being from the upper deposit, but the fine fragments (**K61.3–8**) may have come from here. The hatched interlocking ovals of **K61.6** is an earlier LM IIIB motif,[10] and the goblet stem may also be early. The excavators suggested that many of the pithoi, which were found on the roofing material, were used both for catching rainwater and as chimneys.[11] The rest of the pottery is not clearly datable, but fits in well into LM IIIC.

Pottery Catalogue: K 61

Fine Wares

K61.1   Deep bowl (FIG. 5.2). Max. pres. H. 8.5; D. rim est. 19.5. Once mended from four joining fragments. 33% of rim and upper body preserved, one handle; missing base. Fine light brownish grey (10YR 6/2) to light grey (10YR 7/2) fabric, totally burned. Black paint. Worn surfaces. Sharply carinated body. Panelled pattern: pendent triangle with strokes as filler in corners, leaf pattern in centre. For the shape cf. *Khania II*, pl. 35.71-P 0739. LM IIIC.

K61.2   Deep bowl (FIG. 5.2). Max. pres. H. 8.3; D. rim est. 16. Partially mended from five joining fragments; one non-joining sherd. 25% preserved, including one handle. Fine, soft, very pale brown (10YR 7/4) fabric. White (10YR 8/2) slip. Crackled black paint worn to shadow. Sampled KAR 06/13. Worn surfaces. Large multiple loops with filler. LM IIIC.

K61.3   Deep bowl or cup (FIG. 5.2). D. rim est. 16. Single fragment (two sherds) from rim. Fine, porous, sandy, very pale brown (10YR 8/3) fabric. Very pale brown (10YR 8/3) slip. Black paint worn to brown shadow. Panelled pattern, with curvilinear multiple motif and U-pattern.

K61.4   Deep bowl or cup (PLATE 1 b, FIG. 5.2). D. rim est. 17–18. Single fragment from rim. Fine, medium-hard, very pale brown (10YR 7/4) fabric. Very pale brown (10YR 8/3) slip. Black paint. Well-preserved surfaces. Large loops with fringed arcs as filler, possibly the same design as on **K61.2**. LM IIIC.

K61.5   Deep bowl or cup (FIG. 5.2). D. rim est. 12–13. Single fragment (three sherds) from rim. Fine, medium-soft, pink (7.5YR 7/4) fabric. Very pale brown (10YR 8/3) slip. Black to red (2.5YR 4/6) paint. Double-outlined horizontal ovals. LM IIIC.

K61.6   Deep bowl or cup (PLATE 10 d, FIG. 5.2). D. rim est. 15. Single fragment from rim. Fine, soft, porous, reddish yellow (7.5YR 7/6) fabric. White (10YR 8/2) slip. Red (10R 5/6) paint. Well-preserved surfaces. Hatched interlocking ovals with dots ('kissing fishes'). Publication: Seiradaki, fig. 21m. LM IIIB/C.

K61.7   Deep bowl or cup (FIG. 5.2). D. rim est. 12. Single fragment from rim. Fine, soft, very pale brown (10YR 7/3) fabric. Very pale brown (10YR 8/3) slip. Worn black paint, streaky on interior. Buttonhook spiral. LM IIIC early.

K61.8   Goblet (FIG. 5.2). Max. pres. H. 2.9. Single fragment from stem. Fine, soft, reddish yellow (5YR 7/6) fabric. Very pale brown (10YR 8/3) slip. Worn red (10R 4/8) paint. Worn surfaces. Short stem with central hole. Painted arcs on underside of base. Horizontal stripes on exterior of base. LM IIIC.

K61.9   Spouted bowl (FIG. 5.2). D. rim est. 16. Single fragment from rim, preserving part of spout. Fine, soft, porous, reddish yellow (5YR 7/6) fabric with some mica. Very pale brown (10YR 8/3) slip. Black paint worn to shadow. Worn surfaces. Shallow bowl

with bridge spout. Fringed spirals or loops. Strokes on top of rim. Bands on interior. LM IIIC early.

K61.10   Kalathos (FIG. 5.2). H. 6.5; D. base 5.4; D. rim 12. Mended from eight fragments. 70% preserved, including full profile; missing 75% of rim and upper body. Fine light brown (7.5YR 6/4) fabric with frequent tiny hard white inclusions. Surface slightly lighter, but not slipped. Traces of black to brown paint. Very worn surfaces. Whole vessel burned uniformly (misfired?) Very crude bevelled base with added blobs of clay. Incised grooves on top of rim. Large V-pattern or zigzag painted on exterior. Blob on interior of rim. Publication: Seiradaki, pl. 4d, second from left. LM IIIC.

K61.11   Krater (FIG. 5.2). Max. pres. H. 4.8. Single fragment from body. Fine, soft, reddish yellow (7.5YR 7/6) fabric. Very pale brown (10YR 8/4) slip. Red (10R 4/8) paint. Worn surfaces. Multiple pendent loops. LM IIIC.

Medium-Coarse Wares

K61.12   Pyxis (PLATE 17 a, FIG. 5.2). H. 11.6; D. base 10.8; D. rim 9.6. Intact. 95% preserved; missing chips in rim and one handle restored. Medium-coarse light red (2.5YR 6/6) fabric with frequent sharp black, hard white angular, and schist inclusions. Surfaces almost totally gone. Once decorated, but design too worn to make out. LM IIIC.

K61.13   Miniature jug (FIG. 5.2). Max. pres. H. 4; D. base 3.5. Intact. 90% preserved, including handle scar; missing rim and handle. Medium-coarse red (2.5YR 5/6) fabric with frequent small red inclusions. LM IIIC.

Coarse Wares

K61.14   Cooking jug (FIG. 5.2). H. 7.8 (with handle 8.2); D. base 5.3; D. rim 6.5. Mended from eight fragments. 75% preserved, including full profile, entire base, and handle; missing most of rim. Coarse friable, Dark grey (10YR 4/1) fabric with large white angular inclusions, calcareous inclusions, and dark phyllites. Completely burned or misfired. Cf. Warren 1982–83, 80, fig. 44, left (Knossos). LM IIIC.

K61.15   Tripod cooking pot (PLATE 17 b, FIG. 5.2). Max. pres. H. 13; D. base 9; D. rim 11.2. Mended from 11 fragments. 75% preserved, including nearly complete profile, one leg without tip, entire base; missing two legs, part of one handle, 75% of rim. Coarse reddish yellow (5YR 6/6) fabric dark grey at core, with phyllites and hard white angular inclusions. Much of surface burned. Dint at top of leg, where it attaches to body. Base scored in crisscross fashion where legs attached. LM IIIC.

Room K 60

This small room was entered on same level as the main room K 61. The notebook reports that there was pottery, but it was very broken, including some pithos sherds, at least two dishes of Type 6, two or three tripods, and a little fine ware, mostly from bowls. Nothing has been preserved from this room.

Room K 59

Room K 59 was entered on the same level as the main room K 61 from K 60. The pottery was reported as the

---

9   Cadogan 1967, 264, fig. 5.15.
10   Hallager 2000, 174, n. 343.
11   *Karphi*, 83.

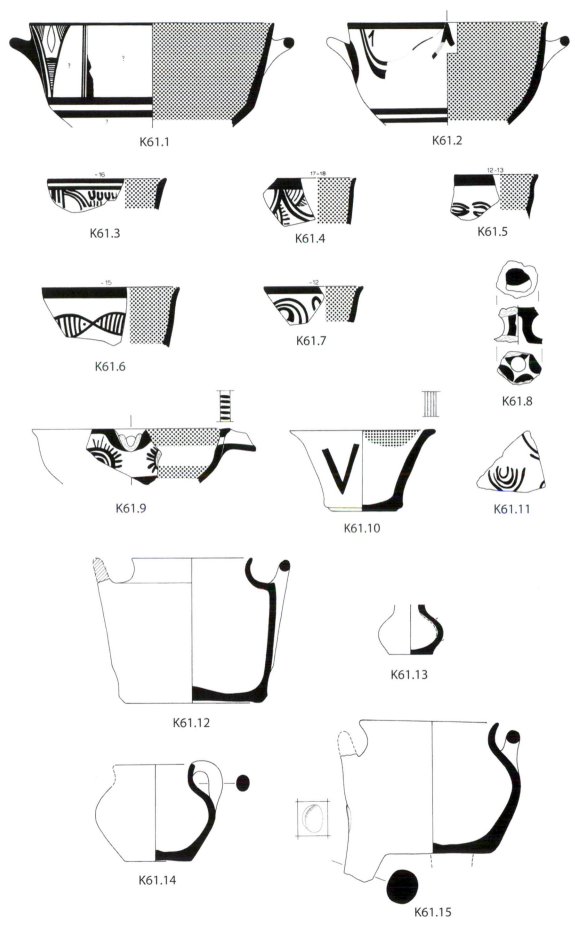

*Fig. 5.2. Priest's House, pottery from K 61 (**K61.1–15**). Scale 1:3.*

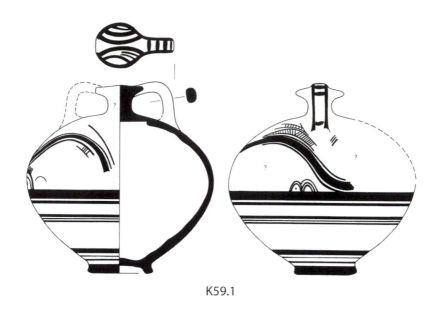

K59.1

*Fig. 5.3. Priest's House, pottery from K 59 (**K59.1**). Scale 1:3.*

usual, but it was much broken and scattered, with only a few fragments from any vessel. The notebook records the following pottery: a pithos sherd with multiple triangles (like one from K 58), the twisted vertical handle from a large jar, a tripod leg with two dints, the handle from a kalathos, a little fine ware mostly from bowls, at least two krater bases, a stirrup jar neck, and a tubular spout (spouted jars 1 or 2). In addition to the octopus stirrup jar catalogued below, there was also a fragment of a plain deep bowl in one of the boxes. Objects included a fragment of bronze (417) and some animal bones and horns.

There is not enough preserved from this room to give a date or particular function. The octopus stirrup jar should date to early in the LM IIIC period.

Pottery Catalogue: K 59

Fine Wares

K59.1   Stirrup jar (PLATE 17 *c*, FIG. 5.3). H. 15.5; D. base 5.2; max. D. 15. Partially mended from 30 fragments, five non-joining fragments. 75% preserved, including entire base, nearly full profile, false spout, one handle; missing one handle, spout, 25% of upper body. Fine, soft, very pale brown (10YR 7/3) fabric with tiny black inclusions. Very pale brown (10YR 8/4) slip. Red (2.5YR 5/8) paint. Very worn and laminating surfaces. Top made separately and added as disc. Possibly octopus decoration. Outlined tentacles, with hatching and fringed loops. Arcade pattern on false spout. Oblique strokes on handles. Bands below. LM IIIC.

Room K 80

This rather larger room was reached from K 61, but it was at a higher level (some 0.6 m) and required a step.[12] Some flat slabs found above the roofing were interpreted as having projected from the roof as eaves. The excavators suggested that the roof of this room

rose above its neighbours and possibly had a clerestory.[13] There was a ledge along west wall that rose 1.45 m above the floor level. The wall behind the bench showed traces of plaster. The remains of pithoi were more numerous than in K 61.[14] The notebook reports that the sherds in front of the door (i.e. in K 61) were higher than elsewhere.

The notebook records the following coarse pottery from the pithos area: at least eight pithoi, two of Type 2 and one each of Types 10, 11, 12, 13, 14, and 15, all with chevron and rope patterns, one with stacked triangles; pithoid jars of Types 7 and 8; a tripod pithos;[15] a large jar or jug; a very large spouted dish; several dishes of Type 6; seven or more kalathoi, three of Type 1, two like Type 1 but with plain base, one of Type 3; a small kalathos; a dish of Type 2;[16] a tripod rim of Type 3 and tripod legs; a large red stirrup jar; a smaller stirrup jar of Type 2; a large basin of Type 4; two scuttle handles; a small pyxis (**K80.8**); a lid (**K80.7**); and a large krater of Type 8. The finer pottery was mostly found below the level of the coarse ware, and included three pyxides of Type 1; three stirrup jars, one Type 1, two Type 2, one with a dotted bivalve shell pattern; a krater of Type 3 and smaller one of Type 1; the base of a jar of Type 2; a ridged kylix stem; and several small bowls of Type 1, one of blue ware, one with a pattern (possibly an uncatalogued body fragment from one of

---

12   Wallace 2005, 243; Pendlebury (*Karphi*, 85) thought it needed a stepladder.
13   *Karphi*, 85.
14   *Karphi*, pl. 21.4 illustrates some of these vessels *in situ*.
15   Seiradaki, pl. 2b.
16   Seiradaki, fig. 6.2; pl. 3c right.

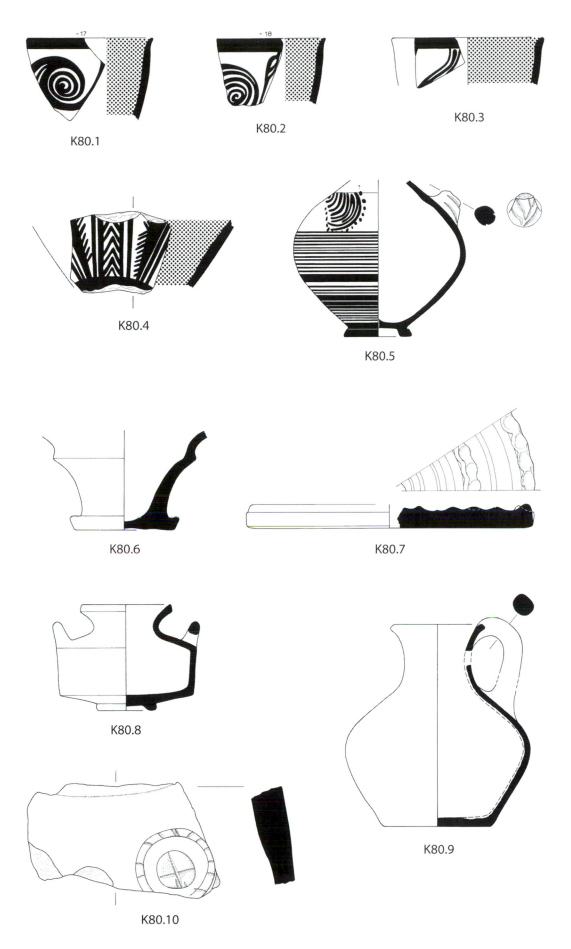

*Fig. 5.4. Priest's House, pottery from K 80 (**K80.1–10**). Scale 1:3.*

the boxes with a ladder pattern). The kylix is probably an uncatalogued one found in one of the boxes, and the stirrup jar has been identified with an unlabelled jug (**K80.5**). The following published vessels were not located: a nearly complete pithos,[17] pithos fragments,[18] a basin,[19] and a tripod pithos.[20]

Objects found in the room included three conical stone beads (460, 461, 462), a crescent-shaped stone inlay (459),[21] and a round stone object (458).[22]

Clearly, this room was used for storage, probably among other functions. The fine ware may have come from an earlier phase of the building, but the preserved pieces do not give much indication of date. Two fragments probably from the same deep bowl have spiral motifs, but they are not closely datable. The kylix, with its fringed and panelled decoration does not look particularly early in LM IIIC. Both the carinated pyxis and the kalathos are of unusual shape, although the kalathos finds a parallel in Khamalevri of early LM IIIC date.[23]

Pottery Catalogue: K 80

Fine Wares

K80.1   Deep bowl or cup (FIG. 5.4). D. rim est. 17. Single fragment from body. Fine, medium-hard, porous, reddish yellow (7.5YR 7/6) fabric. Glossy, very pale brown (10YR 8/4) slip. Very worn black paint. Running spiral. Possibly the same as **K80.2**. LM IIIC.

K80.2   Deep bowl or cup (FIG. 5.4). D. rim est. 18. Single fragment from rim. Fine, soft, sandy, very pale brown (10YR 7/3) fabric. Thin, worn, very pale brown (10YR 8/3) slip. Worn black paint. Spiral and some other motif. Possibly same as **K80.1**. LM IIIC.

K80.3   Deep bowl or cup (FIG. 5.4). D. rim est. 12. Single fragment from rim. Fine, medium-soft, reddish yellow (7.5YR 7/6) fabric. Very pale brown (10YR 8/3) slip. Dark reddish brown (5YR 3/3–3/4) paint. Well-preserved surfaces. Multiple stems. LM IIIC.

K80.4   Kylix (PLATE 11 *e*, FIG. 5.4). Max. pres. H. 5.7. Three joining, one non-joining fragments from body, near stem. Fine, medium-soft, reddish yellow (7.5YR 7/6) fabric. Very pale brown (10YR 8/3) slip. Crackled black paint. Sampled KAR 06/22. Very flaring body; may rather be from a tankard. Panelled pattern: vertical chevrons between vertical bands with fringed solid elements (half rounds?) on either side. LM IIIC.

K80.5   Jug (PLATE 17 *d*, FIG. 5.4). Max. pres. H. 12.5; D. base 5.4. Mended from eight fragments, nine non-joining fragments. 85% preserved, including base, most of body, lower handle attachment; missing neck, rim, upper handle. Fine, soft fabric, laminating. Burned grey inside and out. Black paint. Very worn surfaces. Ring base with knob in centre of interior. Round handle with slashed chevron pattern. Dotted whorl shell on shoulder, narrow bands below. LM IIIC.

Coarse Wares

K80.6   Kalathos (FIG. 5.4). Max. pres. H. 8; D. base 8.3. Mended from five fragments, one non-joining fragment. Entire base preserved; missing rim and upper body. Coarse reddish yellow (5YR 6/6) fabric with frequent phyllites and hard white angular inclusions (1–2 mm). Sampled KAR 06/67. Some possible light burning on interior near preserved top. Publication: Seiradaki, fig. 7.7. LM IIIC.

K80.7   Lid (FIG. 5.4). H. 1.5–1.9; D. rim 23. Two joining fragments preserving *c.* 15% of body; missing knob. Coarse light red (2.5YR 6/6) to red (2.5YR 5/6) fabric with frequent hard angular white inclusions (*c.* 1 mm) and gold mica. Sampled KAR 06/82. Bottom burned black all over. Disc lid. Ridge around top of rim with finger impressions as decoration, and another one farther in; concentric ridges alternating with grooves. Publication: Seiradaki, pl. 12a, bottom, right. LM IIIC.

K80.8   Carinated pyxis (PLATE 17 *g*, FIG. 5.4). H. 8.5; D. base 5.8; D. rim 7.2. Mended from four fragments. 75% preserved, including entire base, one handle, and full profile; missing 75% of rim, one handle, body fragments. Coarse brown (7.5YR 5/4) fabric with large (2–6 mm) red phyllites and gold mica inclusions. Burned all over base and much of upper body. Worn and flaky surfaces. Possible traces of black paint. Imported? Fabric and shape unusual. Ring base. Squared body with sharp carinations near base and on shoulder. Possibly painted. Publication: Seiradaki, fig. 12.7, pl. 7b, bottom, middle. For the shape, cf. *RMDP*, 567–9, fig. 209.333 (straight-sided alabastron, Perati LH IIIC early). LM IIIC.

K80.9   Jug (FIG. 5.4). Max. pres. H. 13; H. est. 16.8; D. base 8.6; D. rim est. 7.6. Restored from five fragments. 85% preserved, including entire base, handle; missing 95% of neck, 80% of rim. Coarse red (2.5YR 5/6–5/8) fabric with frequent grey phyllite and schist inclusions (1–2 mm). Surfaces still coated with sediment. LM IIIC.

K80.10   Pithos (FIG. 5.4). Max. pres. H. 8.2. Single body fragment. Coarse red (2.5YR 5/6) fabric with grey core and large (up to 5 mm) schist, phyllites, and hard white angular inclusions. Decorated with medallion with raised rope-slashed ridge around outside, knob in centre with incised X-pattern. LM IIIC.

CENTRAL WEST QUARTER (ROOMS K 66–K 69, K 81–K 88, K 96, K 97, K 100)

The excavators distinguished four groups of buildings in this block.[24] None of the buildings was large or had large rooms, like those found in the centre and eastern part of the site. All the rooms, however, produced a larger amount of bronze than usual and many bone pins. One building (K 85, K 87, K 69) was identified as a possible shrine because of the animal figurines found in it.

Building K 66-67-68-81

This building is composed of three rooms, with a fourth long and narrow room (K 66) that may have served as the entrance to the complex. The precise relationship among the various rooms is difficult to determine because of the lack of doorways connecting them. Only one doorway exists, that between K 67 and K 81.[25]

---

17   Seiradaki, pl. 1a.
18   Seiradaki, fig. 1.10–13.
19   Seiradaki, fig. 6.2, pl. 3c, right.
20   Seiradaki, pl. 2b.
21   *Karphi*, pl. 30.3.
22   *Karphi*, pl. 30.4.
23   Andreadaki-Vlasaki and Papadopoulou 2007, 45, fig. 2.28 (Khamalevri).
24   *Karphi*, 89–92.
25   *Karphi*, 90.

Nothing in the rooms distinguishes them or suggests functions; they seem to be domestic establishments. The amount of bronze found in this building is unusual and may suggest greater wealth than indicated by the pottery or architecture. Also unusual are the bone pins from K 67 and K 81; such objects are rare at Karphi, but many of the rooms of this quarter produced them. The surviving pottery includes some unusual pieces that may indicate the level of wealth, such as the elaborately decorated basket kalathos (**K68.11**), or the date of abandonment, like the LM IIIC–SM wavy band cup (**K81.1**). Also of interest is the round-bottomed tripod (**K68.14**), a type of cooking vessel that has been interpreted as influenced by mainland types.[26]

Rooms K 66–K 68 (Surface)

The surface material from over these three rooms was kept separate in the publication. Part of a conical stone bead (433) and a fragment of a steatite pestle (494) were found on the surface. A fragment of a fine cup, the spout of a stirrup jar in blue ware, and a tripod with five small holes where the leg attaches were found in the boxes, but not catalogued.

Room K 66

This long and narrow room was perhaps an entrance passage into the building, and it may have given access over a raised threshold, now no longer preserved, to K 67.

The notebook records many fragments of a pithos with chevron pattern and pithoid jars of Types 1 and 2. There was apparently less fine ware than usual, but a fragment of a large kylix of Type 2 or 3 was found. The single preserved sherd, a deep bowl or cup with a buttonhook spiral, is probably early LM IIIC.

Pottery Catalogue: K 66

Fine Wares

K66.1   Deep bowl or cup (PLATE 12 *c*, FIG. 5.5). D. rim est. 13. Single fragment (two sherds) from rim. Fine, soft, reddish yellow (7.5YR 7/6) fabric with tiny black inclusions. Very pale brown (10YR 8/3) slip. Worn black paint. Buttonhook spiral. For decoration, cf. Warren 2007, 337, fig. 2. P251, P253, P285 (Knossos, early LM IIIC); Popham 1965, 326, fig. 6.28 (Knossos). LM IIIC.

Room K 67

The largest room of the building, Room 67, had only a single doorway into Room 81, so it is not clear how it was entered. The pottery included fewer pithos fragments than normal. The notebook mentions a larnax fragment with a handle, a coarse tray with incised lines on the rim, a tripod of Type 1, and a basin of Type 3. Objects found in this room included a bronze stylus-shaped instrument (522), a circular base of schist (435), a conical terracotta spindle whorl (437), a terracotta spool, and part of a bone pin (521),[27] as well as a lump of green mineral (436).

The material found in the room suggests a normal domestic function, although perhaps with less storage than usual. The catalogued deep bowl, krater, and kalathos were fragmentary, not whole vessels that may have been on the floors at the time of abandonment. The deep bowl or cup (**K67.1**) finds a parallel at Sybrita/Thronos of early LM IIIC date,[28] and although it has no close parallels, the krater (**K67.3**) also is early LM IIIC; it is close in shape to a krater from Khania of LM IIIB2/C date,[29] while the decoration finds parallels at early LM IIIC Khamalevri.[30]

Pottery Catalogue: K 67

Fine Wares

K67.1   Deep bowl or cup (FIG. 5.5). Max. pres. H. 3.5. Single fragment from rim. Fine, medium-soft, very pale brown (10YR 7/4) fabric. White (10YR 8/2) slip. Dark red (2.5YR 3/6) paint. Well-preserved surfaces. Pendent multiple loops or multiple stems. LM IIIC early.

K67.2   Krater (FIG. 5.5). D. rim est. 30. Three joining fragments from rim. Fine, hard, reddish yellow (7.5YR 7/6) fabric. Very pale brown (10YR 8/4) slip. Red (10R 5/6) paint. Very well-preserved surfaces. Medallion with rosette inside; petals have multiple outlines. Publication: Seiradaki, fig. 26b. LM IIIC early.

K67.3   Kalathos (FIG. 5.5). Max. pres. H. 2.5. Single fragment from rim. Fine, soft, very pale brown (10YR 7/4) fabric. Very pale brown (10YR 8/4) slip. Worn red (2.5YR 4/8) paint. Very worn surfaces. Strokes on top of rim. LM IIIC.

Room K 81

Room K 81 was reached from Room K 67 down a steep step. There was a rock ledge on two sides of the room. The pottery recorded in the notebook includes the following coarse wares: a pithos rim of Type 1, a kalathos of Type 2, a dish of Type 4 with a horizontal handle, and a coarse sherd with white on dark decoration. Fine wares came mostly from deep bowls, but also included a bowl with wavy line (perhaps the cup **K81.1**), a basin of Type 6 with dark concentric circles inside the base, a krater sherd with U-pattern, a base with ridges at the bottom, and the spout of a jug. Uncatalogued pottery included five deep bowl rims, one with spiral and stacked scale pattern, the others with horizontal curving bands, curvilinear motifs, and plain surface, and other body fragments, one with a spiral. The boxes also included three stirrup jar fragments with fringed or filled motifs and narrow bands enclosed between thicker bands and a coarse jar or jug with a curvilinear filled motif. Objects included a stone Neolithic axe (464),[31] a twisted bronze fibula

---

26   Borgna 1997*b*, 200.
27   *Karphi*, pl. 28.4.
28   Prokopiou 1997, 379, fig. 20b.
29   *Khania II*, pl. 41.84-P 0719.
30   Andreadaki-Vlasaki and Papadopoulou 2007, 46, fig. 3.23 (Phase Ib).
31   *Karphi*, pl. 30.2.

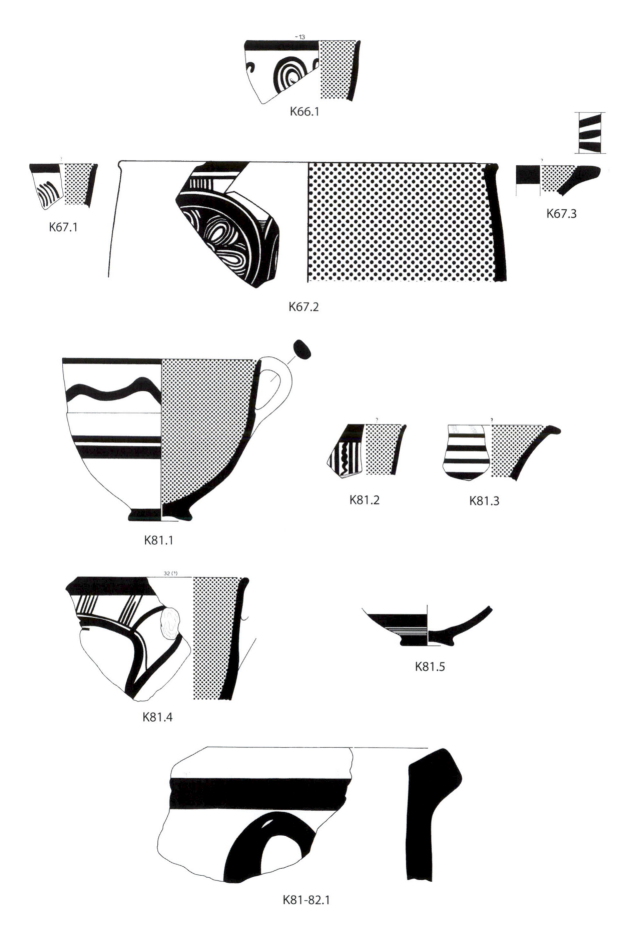

Fig. 5.5. Central West Quarter, Building 1, pottery from K 66 (**K66.1**), K 67 (**K67.1–3**), K 81 (**K81.1–5**), and K 81-82 (**K81-82.1**). Scale 1:3.

(474),[32] a bronze plaque incised with spirals and dots (475),[33] a fragment of bronze (463), a biconical terracotta spindle whorl with impressed circles (473), and two bone pins (476, 477).[34]

From the surface over Rooms 81 and 82 came fragments of pithoi, one a rim of Type 14, the other a body sherd with impressed circles. There was also a strange double-ended object that the excavators thought might have been used in cult. Two larnax fragments are mentioned in the publication; one is catalogued below, while the other may be the flat plaque-like object with the rim of a pithos found in one of the boxes. The boxes also produced a possible figurine fragment from this deposit.

The cup (K81.1) is nearly complete and should be thought of as belonging to the final use of the room. It is an interesting shape, looking forward to the wavy band cups so familiar in Subminoan,[35] but without the bell shape and high foot. This example is more like those from LM IIIC contexts at Knossos, where they are not particularly late.[36] It is extremely large; there are other similar large cups from Karphi (K79.1, K115.1), and one from Kavousi–*Vronda*,[37] but they are rare, and their function is uncertain. The other pottery, a deep bowl, a kalathos, a krater, and some sort of closed vessel are LM IIIC types, but not closely datable.

Pottery Catalogue: K 81

Fine Wares

K81.1 Cup (FIG. 5.5). H. 13 (with handle 13.3); D. base 5.2; D. rim 16. Restored from 19 fragments. 70% preserved, including full profile and handle. Fine, very soft, reddish yellow (5YR 7/8) fabric with tiny white inclusions. Very pale brown (10YR 8/4) slip. Red (10R 5/8) paint. Rather well-preserved surfaces. Tall, slightly carinated rim. Wavy band on rim, bands below. LM IIIC late–SM.

K81.2 Deep bowl or cup (FIG. 5.5). Max. pres. H. 4. Single fragment from rim. Fine, medium-hard, very pale brown (10YR 7/4) fabric. Very pale brown (10YR 8/3) slip. Washy brown paint. Well-preserved surfaces. Panelled pattern: vertical wavy line between vertical bands. LM IIIC.

K81.3 Kalathos (FIG. 5.5). Max. pres. H. 4.5. Single fragment from rim. Fine, soft, reddish yellow (7.5YR 7/6) fabric. White (10YR 8/2) slip. Worn black paint. Worn surfaces. Strokes on rim, bands on body. LM IIIC.

K81.4 Krater (FIG. 5.5). D. rim est. 32. Two joining fragments and one non-joining from rim and handle attachment. Fine, soft, very pale brown (10YR 8/4) fabric; handle is coarser, with inclusions of dark grey phyllites (1 mm). Very pale brown (10YR 8/4) slip. Worn dusky red (2.5YR 3/2) paint. Very worn surfaces. Curvilinear motif with oblique strokes as filler; loop around handle. LM IIIC.

K81.5 Closed vessel (FIG. 5.5). D. base 4.4. Two joining fragments preserving entire base and much of lower body. Fine, soft, porous, reddish yellow (7.5YR 7/6) fabric. White (10YR 8/2) slip. Red (2.5YR 4/6) paint. Worn surfaces. Probably from jug or stirrup jar. Narrow bands between wide bands. LM IIIC.

Pottery Catalogue: K 81–82

Coarse Wares

K81–82.1 Larnax (FIG. 5.5). Max. pres. H. 10.8. Single fragment from rim. Coarse, reddish yellow (5YR 6/6) fabric, bluish grey (5B 6/1) at core, with phyllites and hard white angular inclusions. Fugitive yellow (10YR 8/6) slip. Black paint. Surfaces very worn, and paint and slip come off easily; surfaces still partly coated with sediment. Decorated with loop, possibly octopus or wavy band. LM IIIC.

Room K 68

Room K 68 was a small room, which the excavators thought was entered by a stepladder from Room K 67.[38] It may have been a separate establishment. It had a hearth or oven at the south end between the wall and an outcrop of bedrock, where there were many signs of burning.

Many pithoi were found in the room, one with a serpentine rope pattern. The notebook mentions part of the same tripod found in Room K 67 (possibly K68.14) and a large red stirrup jar (K68.13). Fine ware included two pyxides (K68.11–12), as well as two kraters, one of Type 1. Included in the boxes but not catalogued were the rims of two deep bowls, one with loops and vertical strokes, the other with bands, as well as numerous body sherds from deep bowls with monochrome decoration, oblique strokes, spiral, and multiple curves with dots. The boxes also produced a krater fragment with a curvilinear motif and a fragment from the top of a stirrup jar. Objects included a steatite disc with 'degenerate' Minoan characters (438)[39] and a bronze ring (439).[40]

While the fragments (K68.3–7) may represent earlier material ground into the floor of the room, the rest of the vessels are nearly complete and probably constitute a floor assemblage for the room just before its abandonment. The fragments of deep bowls or cups look early, including the use of quirk, Minoan flower, and multiple ovals. K68.3, with its floral motif of dotted half circles with streamers on either side, is yet another variation on the tricurved streamer motif that so often includes a hatched or crosshatched motif in the centre. The linear pattern on K68.4 can be paralleled from a Phase II krater from Kastelli Pediada, so it is probably early LM IIIC.[41] The fringed motifs and use of the U-pattern on the kraters suggest a date toward the end of the early LM IIIC period.

The nearly complete pots include two fine deep bowls, one with a wavy line, the other with a buttonhook spiral. In shape and decoration K68.1 can be paralleled

---

32 *Karphi*, pl. 29.2.
33 *Karphi*, pl. 29.1.
34 *Karphi*, pl. 28.4.
35 See, for example, Warren 1982–83, 85, fig. 60a–b; Sackett (ed.) 1992, pl. 43.1; D'Agata 2007, 111, fig. 11a.41/5.
36 Warren 1982–83, 84, fig. 54.
37 Day and Glowacki forthcoming, Building N, Room N3: N3 P1.
38 *Karphi*, 89.
39 *Karphi*, pl. 30.4.
40 *Karphi*, pl. 29.2.
41 Rethemiotakis 1997, 324, fig. 35.

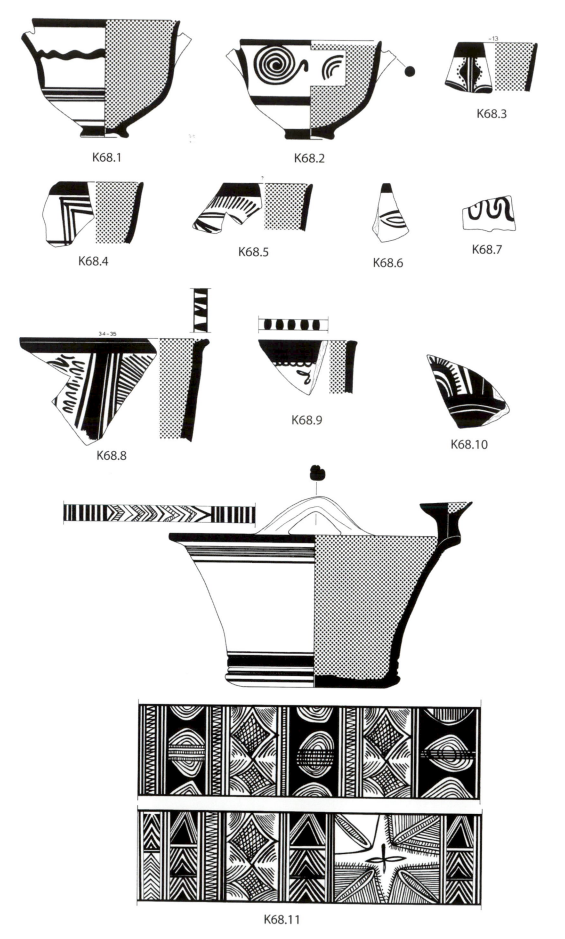

*Fig. 5.6. Central West Quarter, Building 1, pottery from K 68 (**K68.1–11**). Scale 1:3.*

by an example from early LM IIIC Kavousi–*Vronda*,[42] as also can **K68.2**.[43] The buttonhook spiral appears early in LM IIIC and continues in use, and the use of a reserved band on the interior of the rim also appears throughout the period. The elaborately decorated basket kalathos (**K68.11**), however, is clearly a late LM IIIC piece, as may be the decorated pyxis with linear decoration (**K68.12**); the latter may have been decorated with birds, but is too worn to be certain. The tripod (**K68.14**) is unusual, but not unknown at Karphi: a tripod round-bottomed bowl. The decoration of the legs with two dints on either side of a groove with an incised slash, is also uncommon; the piece may not be local, as its fabric is a bit odd for Karphi, and the shape is inspired by mainland types.[44] The coarse stirrup jar (**K68.13**) is of the usual type.

Pottery Catalogue: K 68

Fine Wares

K68.1 Deep bowl (FIG. 5.6). H. 9.6; D. base 3.9; D. rim 12. Partially mended from 30 fragments. 75% preserved, including full profile and handle attachments; missing handles. Fine, rather soft, reddish yellow (7.5YR 7/6) fabric. Very pale brown (10YR 8/3) slip. Red (10R 5/6) paint. Sampled KAR 06/14. Well-preserved surfaces. Wavy band; bands below. For shape, cf. *Kastri*, 295, fig. 15.P27; Kanta 1997, 105, fig. 4.12 (Kommos). LM IIIC early.

K68.2 Deep bowl (FIG. 5.6). H. 8.1; D. base 3.9; D. rim 11.3. Partially mended from 15 fragments. 60% preserved, including base, part of rim, part of one handle, full profile; missing one handle, most of rim. Fine, very soft, sandy, very pale brown (10YR 7/3) fabric and slip. Black paint. Sampled KAR 06/16. Possibly burned or misfired. Buttonhook spirals; reserved band on interior of rim. Cf. Popham 1965, 326, fig. 6.29. LM IIIC early.

K68.3 Deep bowl or cup (FIG. 5.6). D. rim est. 13. Single fragment from rim. Fine, soft, porous, very pale brown (10YR 8/4) fabric and slip. Worn black paint. Dotted half rounds with streamers or leaves — tricurved streamer? LM IIIC.

K68.4 Deep bowl or cup (FIG. 5.6). Max. pres. H. 5. Single fragment from rim. Fine, soft, porous, reddish yellow (7.5YR 7/6) fabric. Very pale brown (10YR 8/3) slip. Black paint. Worn surfaces. Multiple horizontal and vertical bands meeting at right angles. LM IIIC.

K68.5 Deep bowl or cup (FIG. 5.6). Max. pres. H. 3.8. Single (two sherds) fragment from rim. Fine, soft, reddish yellow (7.5YR 7/6) fabric. Very pale brown (10YR 8/4) slip. Worn black paint. Minoan flower. LM IIIC early.

K68.6 Deep bowl or cup (FIG. 5.6). Max. pres. H. 4.7. Single fragment from rim. Fine, soft, reddish yellow (7.5YR 7/6) fabric. Very pale brown (10YR 8/3) slip. Black paint worn to brown shadow. Worn surfaces. Horizontal multiple ovals. For motif, cf. **K61.5**. LM IIIC.

K68.7 Deep bowl or cup (FIG. 5.6). Max. pres. H. 2.7. Single fragment from body. Fine, porous, reddish yellow (7.5YR 7/6) fabric. Very pale brown (10YR 8/3) slip. Worn black paint. Quirk. LM IIIC early.

K68.8 Krater (FIG. 5.6). D. rim est. 34–35. Single large fragment (3 sherds) from rim. Fine, soft, reddish yellow (5YR 7/6) fabric. White (10YR 8/2) slip. Worn red (10R 4/8) paint. Worn surfaces. Horns of consecration (?) with U-pattern in centre and rays to one side. Strokes on top of rim. LM IIIC.

K68.9 Krater (FIG. 5.6). Max. pres. H. 4.2. Single fragment from rim. Fine, soft, reddish yellow (5YR 7/6) fabric. Very pale brown (10YR 8/3) slip. Black paint. Well-preserved surfaces.

Scallops hanging from rim, tiny quatrefoil below. Strokes on top of rim. For shape and scalloped decoration, cf. Warren 2007, 341, fig. 6.P2146 (Knossos, later LM IIIC early). LM IIIC.

K68.10 Krater (FIG. 5.6). Max. pres. H. 5. Single fragment from body. Fine, soft, reddish yellow (5YR 7/6) fabric. Very pale brown (10YR 8/3) slip. Red (10R 4/8) paint. Very worn surfaces. Multiple upright loops with fringe. LM IIIC.

K68.11 Kalathos (HM 11053) (PLATE 17 *e–f*, FIG. 5.6). H. 12.1 (with handle 15.2); D. base 14; D. rim 23–23.5; D. rim of cup 4.2. Restored from many fragments. 90% preserved, including base, full profile, handle, and excrescent cup; missing body fragments. Fine, soft, yellow (10YR 7/6) fabric with tiny black and white inclusions. Black (5YR 3/1) to reddish brown (2.5YR 4/4) paint, streaky and flaking. Well-preserved surfaces. Many fragments burned. Three incised lines around base, incised lines at base of rim. Elaborately painted panelled decoration. Side A: stacked horns of consecration with multiple loops inside and surrounded on both sides with vertical panels of zigzags between panels of a crosshatched vertical lozenge chain with arc fillers. Side B: crosshatched vertical lozenge chain with arc fillers, surrounded by triangles with multiple outlines and chevrons and quatrefoil pattern fringed and with filled corners. On top of rim chevrons with hatching. Publication: Seiradaki, fig. 7.6, pl. 4a. LM IIIC late.

K68.12 Pyxis (PLATE 17 *h*, FIG. 5.7). H. 15; D. base 17; D. rim 13.6. Mended from 33 fragments, seven non-joining fragments. 80% preserved, including entire base, full profile; missing tops of handles, body fragments, and 15% of upper body. Fine, very soft, reddish yellow (7.5YR 7/6) fabric. Very pale brown (10YR 8/3) slip. Red (2.5YR 4/8) paint. Burned on one side, patch of burning on other. Panelled pattern. One side has dark outlined panels, one curving. Other side has possible birds. LM IIIC late.

Coarse Wares

K68.13 Stirrup jar (FIG. 5.7). Max. pres. H. 36.7; D. base 14; Max. D. 36.6. Partially mended from 25 fragments, 20 non-joining fragments. 66% preserved, including most of base and lower body, spout, both handles; missing false spout. Coarse, reddish yellow (5YR 7/6) fabric, grey (N 6/) at core, and frequent phyllites and hard white angular inclusions (1–2 mm). Possible very pale brown (10YR 8/4) slip. Some fragments burned. LM IIIC.

K68.14 Tripod cooking pot (FIG. 5.7). Max. pres. H. 24; D. rim est. 34–36. Once mended from 37 fragments. 75% preserved, including base and part of all three legs, 75% of rim and upper body, one handle and part of another, full profile except for tips of legs; missing large portion of base. Coarse very pale brown (10YR 7/4) fabric, grey (5Y 6/1) at core, with frequent phyllites, black basalt and hard white angular inclusions (1–2 mm). Rounded bottom. Two dints on tops of legs where attach to body, one groove with incised line down centre. LM IIIC.

Building K 82-83-84-86-88

This group of rooms included two (K 86, K 88) that were apparently built over an earlier square.[45] Two

---

42 *Kavousi IIA*, fig. 26.B4 P13; see also Andreadaki-Vlasaki and Papadopoulou 2007, 46, fig. 3.6 (Khamalevri, Phase I); 50, fig. 7.15–16 (Phase Ib).

43 *Kavousi IIA*, fig. 37.B7 P5, Andreadaki-Vlasaki and Papadopoulou 2007, 46, fig. 3.1 (Khamalevri, Phase I).

44 Betancourt 1980, 3 (Type B); Borgna 1997*b*, 201, fig. 11.5b (Lefkandi).

45 *Karphi*, 90.

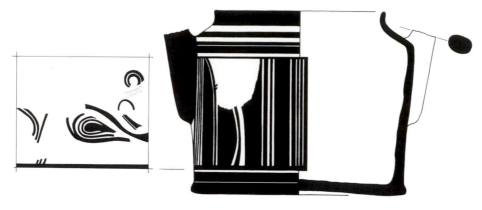

K68.12

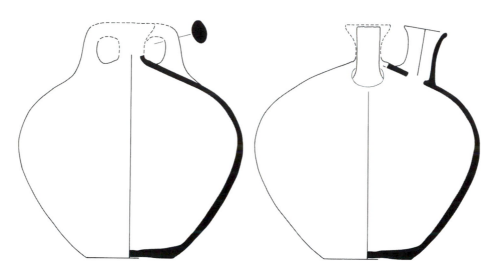

K68.13 (1:6)

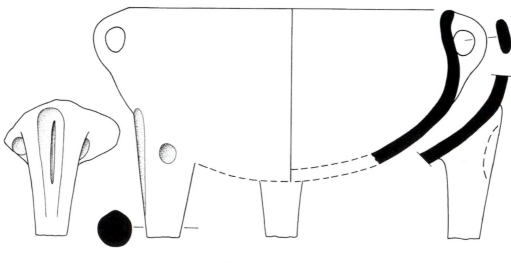

K68.14 (1:4)

*Fig. 5.7. Central West Quarter, Building 1, pottery from K 68 (**K68.12–14**). Scale 1:3 unless otherwise indicated.*

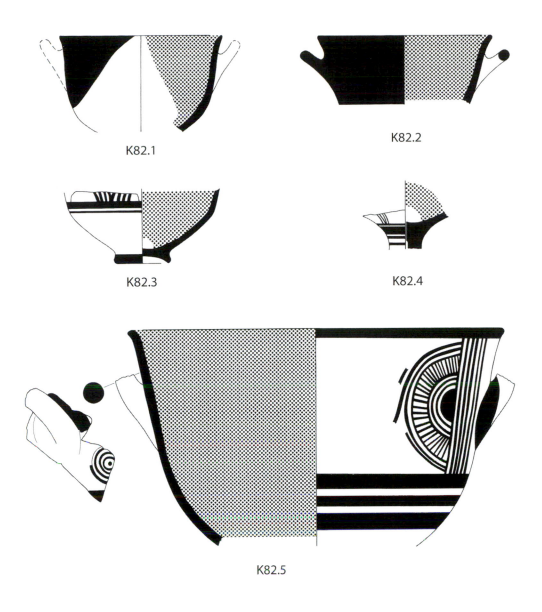

*Fig. 5.8. Central West Quarter, Building 2, pottery from K 82 (**K82.1–5**). Scale 1:3.*

others (K 83, K 84) have earlier walls under them, and they also seem to have been later additions. The relationship of K 82 and K 83 to the other rooms is uncertain. The architectural evidence suggests that the building was a later addition, carved out of space from the Priest's House (K 61) and the square. The extant pottery confirms the idea that this group was a late addition, as there is nothing that belongs to the earlier phases of LM IIIC, except the stirrup jar from K 83. At least three of the rooms produced bronze objects (K 82, K 83, K 88), and two of them had bone pins (K 82, K 83), like so many of the rooms in this quarter.

Room K 82

Room K 82 was a small room with a bedrock bench, possibly remains of an earlier wall, along the west wall. The setback in its northwest corner may show the position of a door. The pottery was very broken, and included pithoi of Types 14 and 15, now missing.[46] The notebook also lists in coarse wares dishes of Types 1 and 4 and a tripod of Type 1, and in fine wares two blob bowls (**K82.1**, **K81.2**), a bowl with wavy lines, the vertical handle of a bowl like that in K 81, krater sherds, and fragments of a stirrup jar. Uncatalogued pottery includes four body fragments from stirrup jars bearing crosshatched triangles or bands, two deep bowls, one with a spiral motif and the other possibly plain, a possible tankard fragment with bands, and a large jug or jar with broad and narrow bands. Objects found in the room included a bronze ring (481)[47] and bronze fragments (479, 480), a conical stone bead (482), and a bone pin fragment (478).

---

46   Seiradaki, fig. 1.14–15.
47   *Karphi*, pl. 29.2.

The pottery is not closely datable. The deep bowl fragments, one with blob decoration, one monochrome, and one with a linear outlined motif could date anywhere in the period. **K82.3** has a reserved disc and a rather high foot, which may indicate a late date; it is carinated, while the other deep bowls are rounded. **K82.1** finds a parallel at Khamalevri dating to early LM IIIC,[48] but also resembles a much later one at Sybrita/Thronos.[49] Such a combination of shapes and decorations can be found throughout LM IIIC.[50] The fragment of a decorated kylix is too small to make its shape certain, but the use of the reserved disc on the interior may indicate an earlier date; all of the later examples (especially the better preserved ones) at Karphi are without this feature, which does appear in the K 76 deposit (LM IIIC early). The krater, with its half medallion with strokes, and possibly a spiral finds no close parallels in decoration, but its rather shallow S-curved profile is similar to other kraters at Karphi that may indicate an early date (e.g. **K49.1**, **K79.3**).

Pottery Catalogue: K 82

Fine Wares

K82.1   Deep bowl (FIG. 5.8). D. rim est. 13. Mended from three fragments. 15% of rim and part of one handle preserved; missing base. Fine, very soft, very pale brown (10YR 7/4) fabric. Black paint. Very worn exterior surfaces, well-preserved on interior. Blob decoration. LM IIIC.

K82.2   Deep bowl (FIG. 5.8). D. rim est. 14. Single fragment from rim, preserving handle. Fresh break on handle. Fine, soft, porous, very pale brown (10YR 7/4) fabric. Dull, streaky red (10R 4/8) paint. Monochrome or blob decoration. For shape, cf. Andreadaki-Vlasaki and Papadopoulou 2007, 49, fig. 6.2 (Khamalevri, Phase II). LM IIIC.

K82.3   Deep bowl or cup (FIG. 5.8). Max. pres. H. 5.8; D. base 4.5. Two joining and one non-joining fragments from base and lower body. Fine, soft, reddish yellow (7.5YR 6/6) fabric. White (10YR 8/2) slip. Black paint. Well-preserved surfaces. Multiple outlined motif. Reserved disc on interior. Band around edge of underside of base. LM IIIC.

K82.4   Kylix (FIG. 5.8). Max. pres. H. 2.6. Single fragment from top of stem and bottom of body. Fine, soft, reddish yellow (5YR 7/6) fabric. Very pale brown (10YR 8/3) slip. Crackled black paint. Stem pierced nearly to bowl. Multiple stems. Bands on stem. Reserved disc on interior. LM IIIC.

K82.5   Krater (FIG. 5.8). Max. pres. H. 17.2; D. rim est. 30.2. Large fragment from handle and rim (12 sherds), two non-joining rim fragments, non-joining fragment of handle (three sherds). Fine, very soft, pink (7.5YR 7/4) fabric. Very pale brown (10YR 8/3) slip. Red (2.5YR 4/8) paint. Worn surfaces. Panelled design: next to handle half circle, with solid centre and hatching between outer circles; on other side, possibly spiral (although this fragment may be from a second krater). LM IIIC.

Room K 83

The excavators thought that Room K 83 was a very low room to judge from the position of the door onto its roof from K 85, and it had earlier walls below the floor.[51] The plan shows a small structure in the northwest corner that may have been a hearth or oven, but it is not mentioned in either the publication or the notebook.

The notebook lists the following coarse pottery: pithos rims of Types 5 and 8; pithoid jars of Types 2, 3, 7, 11; tripod legs of Types 1–3, one of white ware with dark paint; a dish of Type 6; a kalathos of Type 4; a one-handled jug of Type 3; two basins of Types 6 and 7; the base of a cup of Type 1 and the rim of a cup of Type 2. Fine pottery listed included a krater base of Type 1. The following objects were also found in the room: a fragment of bronze (496), a bone pin (483),[52] a pierced circular bone lid (535), a conical stone bead (536), pumice, and yellow colouring matter.

The pottery from the room is scanty but unusual. The decoration on the deep bowl (**K83.1**) finds close parallels on kraters at Khania and Khamalevri of early LM IIIC date,[53] but the shape, with its ring base, looks later. The stirrup jar (**K83.2**), with its lively fringed octopus, may have been produced early in LM IIIC; it is different from the other octopus stirrup jars from Karphi and has a more naturalistic octopus. A close parallel can be seen on a stirrup jar from Kritsa.[54] The decoration on the pithos (**K83.4**) is most unusual.

Pottery Catalogue: K 83

Fine Wares

K83.1   Deep bowl (FIG. 5.9). H. 10; D. base est. 5; D. rim 14.8. Fifteen fragments preserving entire base, half of rim and body, one handle attachment. 55% preserved, including full profile; missing handles. Fine, very soft, reddish yellow (7.5YR 7/6) fabric with many voids (some still with a spongy yellow substance in them) and a few hard grey inclusions. Thick, creamy, very pale brown (10YR 8/3) slip. Black to reddish brown (2.5YR 4/4) paint. Well-preserved surfaces. Tricurved streamer (?) with alternating arcs in centre. Number is worn, but probably K 83. LM IIIC.

K83.2   Stirrup jar (PLATE 18 *a*, FIG. 5.9). Max. pres. H. 17.7; max. D. 21–22. Partially mended into four large fragments (19 sherds, 18 sherds, 7 sherds, 11 sherds); 49 non-joining fragments. 50–55% preserved, including profile from top of jar to near base. Base preserved, but does not join. Missing handles, spout, and false spout. Fine, soft, reddish yellow (5YR 6/6) fabric. White (10YR 8/2) slip. Worn red (2.5YR 5/8) paint. Surfaces worn, laminating, and flaking. Two octopods with fringed tentacles, crosshatched lozenges at top of head, quatrefoils (four curving bands emanating from circle with dot, joined in pointed end). Scalloped edge on lower band. LM IIIC early.

Coarse Wares

K83.3   Lid (FIG. 5.9). Max. pres. H. 1.6. Single fragment from rim. Coarse red (2.5YR 5/8) fabric with frequent red and grey phyllites (1–2 mm), hard white angular and black inclusions.

---

48   Andreadaki-Vlasaki and Papadopoulou 2007, 48, fig. 5.11.

49   D'Agata 2007, 110, fig. 9.20/2, which she dates to her SM II period.

50   Hallager 2000, 142.

51   *Karphi*, 90.

52   *Karphi*, pl. 28.4.

53   *Khania II*, pl. 39.71-P 0908, 71-P 0735; Andreadaki-Vlasaki and Papadopoulou 2007, 50, fig. 7.21.

54   Kanta 1980, fig. 136.1; Paschalides 2009, fig. 69.

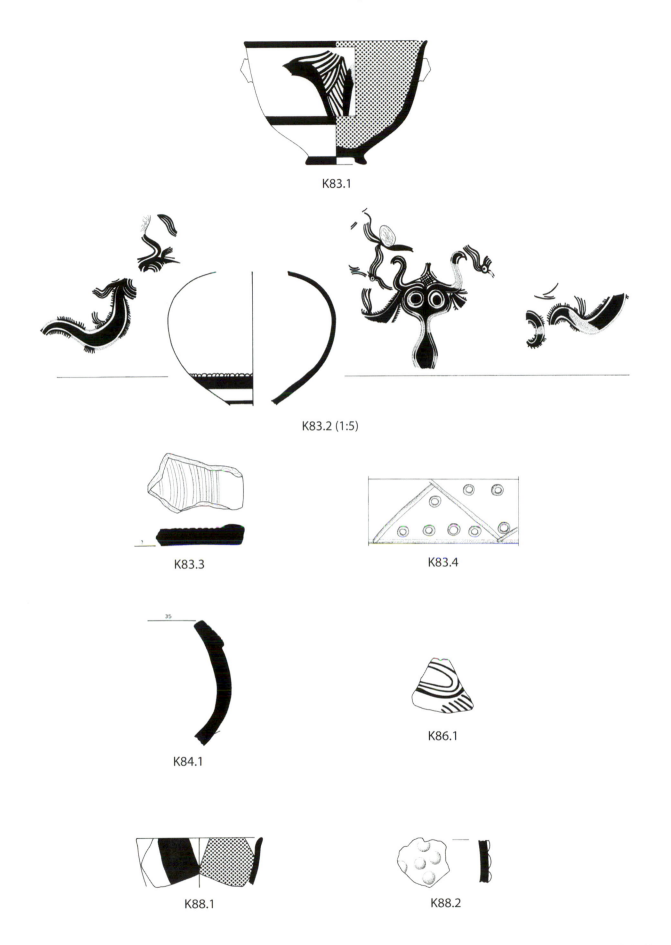

K83.1

K83.2 (1:5)

K83.3

K83.4

K84.1

K86.1

K88.1

K88.2

Fig. 5.9. *Central West Quarter, Building 2, pottery from K 83 (**K83.1–4**), K 84 (**K84.1**), K 86 (**K86.1**), K 88 (**K88.1–2**).*
Scale 1:3 unless otherwise indicated.

Burned on underside in a 5 cm band around outside edge. Decorated with concentric grooves. LM IIIC.

K83.4   Pithos (PLATE 18 *b*, FIG. 5.9). Two non-joining fragments from body. Coarse light red (2.5YR 6/8) fabric with frequent schist, mica, and hard white angular inclusions. Raised band with triangles and impressed circles. LM IIIC.

Room K 84

Room K 84 was another small room with earlier walls below the floor. Stone steps may have led up to Room K 85. According to the notebook, pottery from this room included a large pithoid jar of Type 3 and 3 others of Types 3, 7, and 11; a small sherd of a pithos rim of Type 6; tripod legs; several dishes of Types 1–6; basins of Types 2 and 3; a small jar of Type 3; a kalathos with impressed circles; a tripod with incurving rim (**K84.1**); small bowls of Types 1 and 2; and two small 'egg cups'. Objects included pumice and animal bones. The only surviving pottery is a fragment of a tripod bowl with an incised rim; although the round bottom is not unusual, the rim treatment is otherwise unattested at Karphi.

Pottery Catalogue: K 84

Coarse Wares
K84.1   Tripod bowl (FIG. 5.9). D. rim est. 35. Single fragment (four sherds) from rim, including part of handle or leg scar. Coarse, red (2.5YR 5/8) fabric with phyllites and hard white angular inclusions. Sampled KAR 06/63. Burned toward bottom of exterior. Grooves on exterior band of rim. LM IIIC.

Room K 86

Room 86 was a later addition, built over the earlier square. It was suggested that it acted like corridor to K 84.[55] The notebook records the following pottery: pithos fragments, one with chain moulding around base; a pithoid jar of Type 3; a dish of Type 6; tripod legs; a basin of Type 7; the ridged base of a jar; and deep bowls. Uncatalogued pottery includes deep bowl fragments with outlined curvilinear and filler motifs, a cup, a huge false spout from a coarse stirrup jar, and a large jug or jar with bands. No objects were recorded, but the notebook mentions animal bones. The single catalogued fragment, a krater with a Minoan flower motif, is small and not datable.

Pottery Catalogue: K 86

Fine Wares
K86.1   Krater (FIG. 5.9). Max. pres. H. 4.2. Single fragment from body. Fine, soft, rather porous, very pale brown (10YR 8/3) fabric. Very pale brown (10YR 8/4) slip. Dark reddish brown (2.5YR 3/4) paint. Worn surfaces. Multiple oblique loops and fringe, possibly Minoan flower. LM IIIC.

Room K 88

This room was also built over the former square; the excavators thought that it resembled K 58, but without

cult objects; that is, it is a small room with a single entrance open to the square or street.[56] The notebook records the following pottery from the room: a pithos rim of Type 8; pithoid jars of Types 3 and 10; a jar of Type 3; dishes of Type 6; tripod legs; basins of Types 1, 2, and 6; a krater of Type 1; bowls of Types 1 and 2; a stirrup jar of Type 2; and a one-handled jug of Type 3. Uncatalogued pottery included fragments from two deep bowls, one decorated with multiple pendent loops, the other with a fringed, outlined curvilinear motif. A bronze blade (497),[57] a fragment of iron (498), and animal bones are also said to come from this room. There is nothing that suggests anything other than ordinary domestic use. The date of the material is not clear, although the fragment of a cup with blob decoration may indicate an early LM IIIC date;[58] the vessel is similar to examples from Khamalevri of Phase Ib.[59]

Pottery Catalogue: K 88

Fine Wares
K88.1   Cup or deep bowl (FIG. 5.9). D. rim est. 10. Single fragment from rim, one non-joining body fragment. Fine, very soft, reddish yellow (7.5YR 7/6) fabric. Very pale brown (10YR 8/3) slip. Dark reddish brown (2.5YR 2.5/4) paint. Blob decoration. LM IIIC.

Coarse Wares
K88.2   Body fragment (FIG. 5.9). Max. pres. H. 3.5. Single fragment (two sherds) from body. Coarse reddish yellow (7.5YR 6/6) fabric with frequent schist (1–2 mm) and hard white angular inclusions. Very pale brown (10YR 8/3) slip. Decorated with five knobs in no apparent order. LM IIIC.

Building K 85-87-69

These rooms were possibly connected to those in House K 82-83-84-86-88 by stone steps in the west wall of K 84, no longer preserved, but seen in the profusion of fallen stone.[60] This small, three-room building may have served a religious purpose. Two of the rooms (K 85, K 87) produced figurines; human and animal figurines were found in K 85, and a large terracotta horse in K 87; a hut urn came from K 69. This material is very different from that found in the Temple or the other shrines or religious buildings on the site, to judge from the nature of the ritual material found within. No goddesses with upraised hands were recorded, nor any snake tubes, or pinakes; there was only a single kalathos

---

55   *Karphi*, 90.
56   *Karphi*, 90.
57   *Karphi*, pl. 28.2.
58   Cups with blob decoration characterise the early LM IIIC deposits in Building B at Kavousi–*Vronda*; *Kavousi IIA*, fig. 25.
59   Andreadaki-Vlasaki and Papadopoulou 2007, 46, fig. 3.19.
60   *Karphi*, 90.

from Room K 87. Whatever religious observances occurred in the building, they were not the same as those involving the large terracotta goddesses with upraised arms (as in the Temple, the Great House Shrine, or K 116), or offering on stands (as in K 58 and possibly the Small Shrine), or libations (as in K 27).[61]

Room K 85

Room 85 contained ritual objects and has been identified as a shrine.[62] It contained a small ledge in its west wall on which the ritual objects may have stood. It was connected to both K 87 and K 69.

The publication mentions pottery in large quantities. Seiradaki illustrates a large coarse amphora with rope-twisted handles as coming from this room,[63] but this identification is probably an error; the vessel shown on this plate matches one that is labelled as coming from K 70. The notebook adds the following list of coarse vessels from the room: a pithos of Type 2, pithoid jars of Type 3, legs of four tripods, a jar of Type 1, a dish of Type 6, a tripod dish, a trefoil scuttle, two kalathoi of Types 1 and 3, a basin of Type 3, a large stirrup jar (**K85.13**), new types of basin, dish, and jar. Fine pottery included two pyxides of Types 1 and 2 (**K85.5–6**), two kraters of Types 3 and 2, a kylix base (**K85.3**), two stirrup jars of Type 2 and one of Type 7 (possibly **K85.9**), and several small bowls. Also listed were a fragment perhaps from a mould, a twisted handle, and a cup of Type 2. In addition to the catalogued pottery, the boxes produced the following fragments from this room: a deep bowl decorated with a vertical fringed panel, a burned rope-twisted handle of jug (probably the one mentioned in the notebook), and a large jar or jug with two wavy lines above three bands on the shoulder.

An unusual array of objects came from K 85, as well. There was a bronze ring (505),[64] a conical stone bead (506), a steatite disc (512), a flat stone tool, and a rectangular bone tube with punctuated decoration (507).[65] Of great interest were the many terracotta figurines found in the room, including the head of a female figure (515),[66] the torso of a figurine (504), another torso of a figurine that may originally have been in a kalathos (514),[67] the head of a large hollow bull figurine (516),[68] and a smaller similar bull's head (517). Such a collection of figurines has not been found elsewhere in any room in the settlement and indicates an unusual function. The room next door (K 87) produced more animal figurines. The notebook also mentions pumice and animal bones. Finally, the corner of a rectangular vessel with punctuated design, like the stand or altar found recently at Khalasmenos, was found in one of the boxes (PLATE 9 *h*).

The preserved pottery represents an uncommon assemblage. The carinated stirrup jar (**K 85.9**) is of an unusual type; although the shape is not unknown on Crete,[69] it is more common on the mainland.[70] This example may be an import or made in imitation of

mainland style. The juglet (**K85.7**) has a close parallel from Khalasmenos, possibly from a ritual context,[71] and another similar example came from K 96 (**K96.2**). One of the pyxides (**K85.5**) is similar to examples from Kastri,[72] while the decoration of the other, with its double row of running spirals, is without parallels, except on krater **K26.5**. The flask (**K85.8**) is another unusual shape; only one certain example of this shape comes from Karphi, from tomb M 16, which has SM–PG material (**M16.2**). This example lacks the decoration that was standard on the SM flasks, and more closely resembles LM IIIB examples.[73] The shape finds parallels from LH IIIB1 on the mainland.[74] The large coarse stirrup jar with incised decoration (**K85.13**) is also highly unusual, finding its best parallels farther to the west on Crete at Sybrita/Thronos.[75] The tray or basin (**K85.12**) is an unparalleled shape, and the basin or krater (**K85.10**) is also unusual. The possible religious function of the room is not evident from the rest of the pottery, which seems to include vessels for storage and cooking.

Pottery Catalogue: K 85

Fine Wares

K85.1 Deep bowl or cup (PLATE 1 *h*, FIG. 5.10). D. rim est. 17. Single fragment from rim. Fine, soft, porous, white (2.5Y 8/2) fabric. Worn black paint, streaky on interior. Multiple pendent loops hanging from rim band. LM IIIC.

K85.2 Deep bowl or cup (FIG. 5.10). D. rim est. 12. Single fragment from rim. Fine, soft, porous, reddish yellow (7.5YR 7/6) fabric. Very pale brown (10YR 8/3) slip. Worn black paint. Worn surfaces. Fringed spiral or multiple loops. LM IIIC.

K85.3 Kylix (FIG. 5.10). Max. pres. H. 5.7. Single fragment from top of stem and bottom of bowl. Fine, soft, reddish yellow (7.5YR 7/6) fabric. Black paint. Pierced stem with grooves at attachment of body. Monochrome stem. LM IIIC.

K85.4 Krater (FIG. 5.10). D. rim est. 29. Single fragment from rim. Fine, soft, reddish yellow (7.5YR 8/6) fabric. Very pale brown (10YR 8/3) slip. Red (2.5YR 4/8) paint. Worn surfaces. Outlined curvilinear decoration, loop near rim. LM IIIC.

61 Day 2009, 146.
62 Gesell 1985, 81–2.
63 Seiradaki, fig. 8.4.
64 *Karphi*, pl. 29.2.
65 *Karphi*, pl. 28.4.
66 *Karphi*, pl. 32.2.
67 *Karphi*, pl. 32.2.
68 *Karphi*, pl. 32.2.
69 Kanta 1980, 248, 152, fig. 125.11 (Episkopi, LM IIIB–C).
70 Mountjoy 1986, 107, fig. 131.1 (Vourvatsi, LH IIIB1); see also Kanta 1980, 136–7, fig. 55.2, 4 (Kritsa, LH IIIB, imported from mainland).
71 Tsipopoulou 2005, 115, fig. 8.4 no. 98-71-1.
72 For shape, see *Kastri*, 289, fig. 10j and Kanta 1980, fig. 54.4–5 (Kritsa).
73 Kanta 1980, 63–4, fig. 28c.
74 Mountjoy 1986, 108.
75 Prokopiou 1997, 376, fig. 17.6.

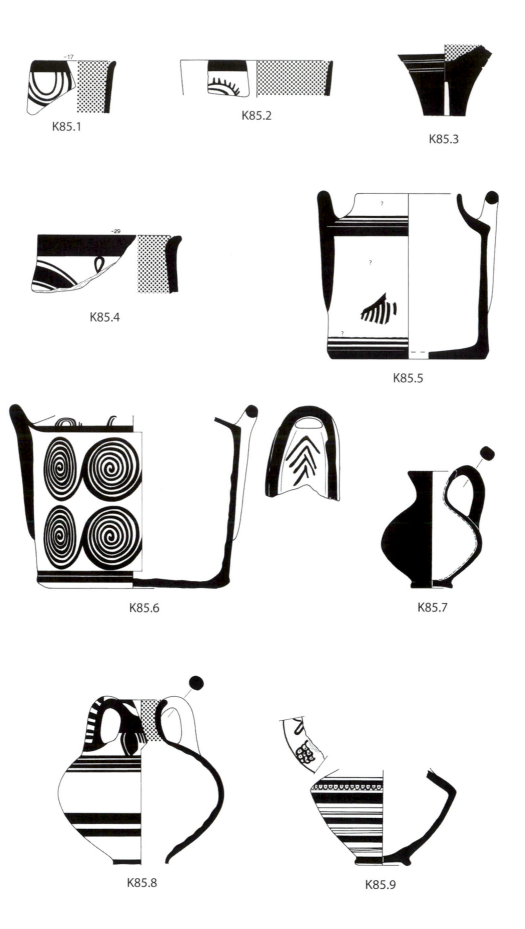

*Fig. 5.10. Central West Quarter, Building 3, pottery from K 85 (**K85.1–9**). Scale 1:3.*

K85.5   Pyxis (PLATE 18 *c*, FIG. 5.10). H. 13.3 (with handles 13.5); D. base 13; D. rim 8.5. Partially mended from 26 fragments, 26 non-joining fragments. 50% preserved, including entire base, full profile, one handle; missing second handle. Fine, soft fabric, burned to very pale brown (10YR 7/4). Black paint. Very worn surfaces. Curvilinear motif with arc filler. LM IIIC.

K85.6   Pyxis (FIG. 5.10). Max. pres. H. 14.7. D. base 15.3. Fifteen joining fragments from base, two large fragments from upper body and shoulder (seven sherds). 45% preserved; missing rim. Fine, soft, porous, reddish yellow (5YR 7/6) fabric with grey (5Y 7/1) core. Very pale brown (10YR 8/3) slip. Black to red (2.5YR 4/8) paint. Two rows of running spirals; multiple upright loops on shoulder. Chevrons between and below handles. LM IIIC.

K85.7   Juglet (PLATE 18 *d*, FIG. 5.10). H. 9.4 (with handle 9.8); D. base 3.4; D. rim 3.9. Intact except for half of rim, which is restored. 95% preserved. Fine light brown (7.5YR 6/4) fabric. Yellowish red (5YR 4/6) paint. Surfaces covered with sediment. Monochrome? LM IIIC.

K85.8   Flask or amphora (FIG. 5.10). Max. pres. H. 13.5; Max. D. 13.2. Twenty-one joining fragments. 75% preserved; missing base. Sherds found in two separate boxes, and never joined. Fine, medium-soft, reddish yellow (7.5YR 7/6) fabric. Very pale brown (10YR 8/3) slip. Weak red (10R 4/4) paint. Well-preserved surfaces. Burned, especially on bottom. Heavy wheel ridging on interior. Leaf pattern with multiple outlines on shoulder. Bands below. Strokes on handle. LM IIIC.

K85.9   Stirrup jar (FIG. 5.10). Max. pres. H. 8; D. base 4.5; max. D. 11.7. Two large fragments, one of base (three sherds), one of top and side (21 sherds), fragment of spout. 10% preserved, including most of base, beginning of one handle attachment; much of profile can be reconstructed. Missing neck, false spout, handles. Fine, soft, porous, very pale brown (10YR 7/3) fabric. White (10YR 8/2) slip. Black paint worn to shadow. Bands on lower body, alternating thick and three thin. Dotted scallop below carination. On shoulder, stack of dotted scale pattern and quatrefoil. LM IIIC.

Medium-Coarse Wares

K85.10   Krater (FIG. 5.11). H. 13; D. base 9; D. rim est. 20. Partially mended from 30 fragments, four non-joining fragments. 75% preserved, including full profile, most of base, one handle; missing much of lower body and second handle. Medium-coarse, light reddish brown (5YR 6/4) fabric with infrequent small (<1 mm) schist and mica inclusions. Burned on one side around handle (after breaking). LM IIIC.

Coarse Wares

K85.11   Tray (FIG. 5.11). Max. pres. H. 3.6. Single fragment from rim to near base, preserving handle. Coarse, light red (2.5YR 6/8) fabric with frequent schist, red phyllites, and hard angular white inclusions (2–3 mm). No burning. For shape, cf. Borgna 1997*b*, 196, fig. 5.2 (Phaistos); *Khania II*, pl. 46.78-P 0515. LM IIIC.

K85.12   Tray or basin (FIG. 5.11). H. 9.4; D. base 35; D. rim 42.4. Mended from 26 fragments, with another large fragment (six sherds) and 14 non-joining fragments. 70% preserved, including full profile, both handles, half of base. Coarse reddish yellow (5YR 6/6) fabric with frequent large (2–4 mm) schist, phyllites, and hard white angular inclusions. Surface smoothed and mottled. Burned all over. Base irregular in places, as though a tripod, but no evidence for legs. Dints at handle attachments. LM IIIC.

K85.13   Stirrup jar (FIG. 5.11). Max. pres. H. 8.4; D. false spout 8.4. Three fragments preserving top of false spout and two lower handle attachments of stirrup jar. Coarse light red (2.5YR 6/6) fabric with large (2–4 mm) phyllite inclusions. Burned on top and one side, blackened on interior. Very large stirrup jar. False spout has large, irregular hole (d. 2.7) through centre. Incised decoration: incisions around rim of false spout, on edges and down centre of

handle. Publication: Seiradaki, pl. 12b, top, second from left (handle); pl. 12b, bottom, right, top. LM IIIC.

K85.14   Jar (FIG. 5.11). D. rim est. 32. Single fragment from rim (recently broken) preserving one handle. Coarse, soft, reddish yellow (7.5YR 6/6) fabric with grey core and small infrequent inclusions. Surface blackened by fire inside and out. LM IIIC.

Room K 87

Room 87 was a small room entered from K 85, and it had an unusual rock table at its southern end, on which, according to the notebook, stood animal figurines. Pottery included a pithos of red fabric without its rim, two tripods or jars of Type 3, dishes of Types 1 and 6, and at least two fine kylikes, along with a jug with beaded decoration (**K87.1**). The boxes produced a small cylindrical object with ridges and a tile or rectangular object, neither of which was catalogued. The incised jug (**K87.1**) is highly unusual and finds parallels from religious contexts at Syme Vianno[76] and at Enkomi on Cyprus, where it has been seen as an import;[77] a similar example came from Afrati.[78] D'Agata dated this jug to late LM IIIC or SM I;[79] the height of the foot, particularly in comparison to the examples from Syme and Enkomi, suggests a date in late LM IIIC.

Of great interest was the large, hollow horse figurine[80] and fragment of another animal figurine apparently found on the table (556). This may have been an area for ritual observance; the figurines are reminiscent of animal figurines from the Piazzale dei Sacelli at Ayia Triada, which produced a greater quantity and variety.[81] Horse and bovine figurines, but solid and not wheel-made, were also found resting on a corner platform in Building D at Kavousi–*Vronda*,[82] where they apparently served as objects of domestic devotion. If K 87 was a shrine, then it was of an unusual type for Karphi.

Pottery Catalogue: K 87

Fine Wares

K87.1   Jug (HM 11072) (PLATE 18 *e*, FIG. 5.12). H. 22.3 (with handle 22.5); D. base 6; D. rim est. 6.5. Restored from numerous fragments. 65% preserved, including nearly complete profile; missing all of rim, much of handle, 25% of body. Fine, soft, pink (7.5YR 7/4) fabric and slip. Black to brown paint. Worn surfaces. Round vertical handle has added coil of clay to make it look twisted. Incised plastic decoration on shoulder: pattern of oblique lines

---

76   Kanta 1991, 497, fig. 31.

77   Dikaios 1969, pl. 106.5; Pilides 1997, 210, fig. 1; Stampolides and Karetsou 1998*a*, 74.39; D'Agata 2005, 10–1, fig. 8.

78   Stampolides and Karetsou 1998*a*, 74.40; Kanta and Karetsou 1998, 165, fig. 9.

79   D'Agata 2005, 10.

80   *Karphi*, pl. 32.1.

81   D'Agata 1997, 85–99.

82   Gesell, Day and Coulson 1995, 71–3; *Kavousi IIA*, 97–8, pl. 16 E–F, fig. 69.

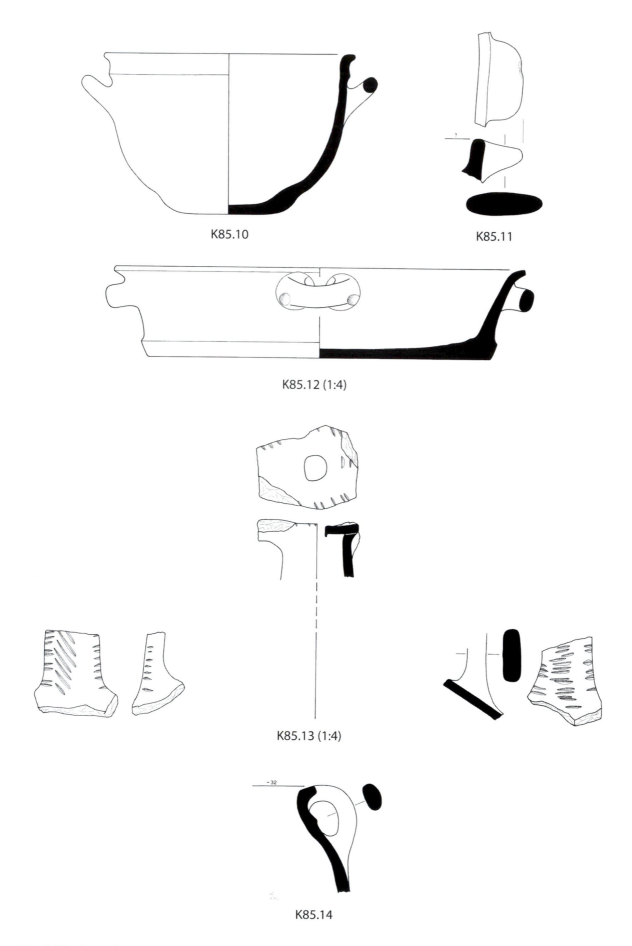

K85.10

K85.11

K85.12 (1:4)

K85.13 (1:4)

K85.14

Fig. 5.11. Central West Quarter, Building 3, pottery from K 85 (**K85.10–14**). Scale 1:3 unless otherwise indicated.

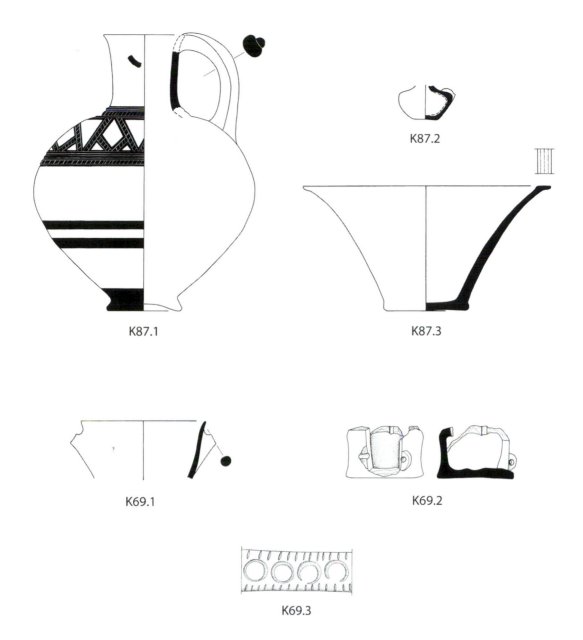

*Fig. 5.12. Central West Quarter, Building 3, pottery from K 87 (**K87.1–3**) and K 69 (**K69.1–3**). Scale 1:3.*

making lozenges. Ridge at base of neck and another below shoulder also incised with oblique slashes. Painted bands on base and lower body, and plastic decoration also painted. Publication: Seiradaki, fig. 9.10, pl. 5a, middle; Stampolides and Karetsou 1998, 74.38; D'Agata 2005, 10–1, fig. 8. LM IIIC.

Medium-Coarse Wares
K87.2   Miniature jug (FIG. 5.12). Max. pres. H. 2.8; D. base 2. Intact. 95% preserved, including lower handle attachment; missing rim and top of handle. Medium-coarse, light red (10R 6/8) fabric with small white and grey inclusions. LM IIIC.

Coarse Wares
K87.3   Kalathos (PLATE 18 *f*, FIG. 5.12). H. 10; D. base 6.8; D. rim 20. Restored from ten fragments. 80% preserved, including entire base and full profile; missing 25% of rim. Coarse red (2.5YR 5/8) fabric with frequent large (2 mm) phyllites and hard angular white inclusions. Burning on interior bottom and on rim. Three incised grooves on top of rim. LM IIIC.

Room K 69
Entered from K 85, this small room had a platform of rock left in its northwest corner. A door to the east was thought to have led to the roof of K 81 and K 82. The pottery from this room was listed as being usual, and it included the rims of at least nine pithoi, none of which survives today;[83] the notebook further records that the pithoi had all the usual patterns. The other coarse ware was in small fragments and included three pithoid jars, a jar, a tankard spout, and a bowl with knobs on the shoulder. Fine ware included a bowl with blob design like that from A1, two kylix bases of Types 1 or 2, and

---

83   Seiradaki, fig. 1.1–9.

a lid of Type 5. Uncatalogued sherds include the medium-coarse blue ware spout from a tankard with incisions on the rim mentioned in the notebook, a small cup rim, a handle with a knob at the top, and a burned stirrup jar fragment with a solid triangle and dots. The large number of pithoi suggests that the room had a primary function of storage, and except for the hut urn (**K69.2**), there was no trace of the religious equipment found in the other rooms. The preserved pottery is not closely datable. The deep bowl shape could fit anywhere in LM IIIC, as could the blob or monochrome decoration. Hut urns are not closely datable. The presence of so many pithoi (9) suggests that the room was used primarily for storage. The surviving pithos fragment (**K69.3**) bears an unusual design for Karphi of impressed circles between rows of incised strokes; a similar design is found on a pithos from the West Magazines at Knossos.[84]

Objects included a bronze blade with rivet holes (448),[85] an iron fragment (449), a stone implement (440),[86] the fragment of a steatite bowl (441), three conical stone beads (442, 443, 444), and three conical terracotta beads or whorls (445, 446, 447).

Pottery Catalogue: K 69

Fine Wares

K69.1   Deep bowl (FIG. 5.12). D. rim est. 10. Single fragment (two sherds) from rim, including handle attachment. Fine, hard, greenish grey (5G 6/1) blue ware fabric. Black paint. Blob or monochrome decoration. LM IIIC.

Coarse Wares

K69.2   Hut urn (PLATE 18 *g*, FIG. 5.12). Max. pres. H. 4.2; D. base 6.2. Mended from six fragments. 70% preserved, including base and one handle; missing most of roof. Coarse, red (2.5YR 5/6) fabric totally burned. No decoration. Publication: Mersereau 1993, 31–2, fig. 20.12. LM IIIC.

K69.3   Pithos (FIG. 5.12). Two non-joining fragments from body. Coarse light red (2.5YR 6/6) fabric, grey at core, with some phyllites and frequent hard white angular and black inclusions. Raised band with impressed circles and small incised strokes at top and bottom. Publication: Seiradaki, pl. 12a, second row, left. LM IIIC.

Building K 96-97-100

The final building in the Central West Quarter consists of a three-room structure entered at the north from the Broad Road (K 103). This door was later blocked.

Room K 96

This small room had a paving in its southeast corner on which stood a small pithos with a rope-slashed ridge at the base of the neck and a band with chevron pattern around the middle,[87] in shape very similar to the small pithos from K 26. The pottery included very little fine ware, but at least three pithoi, one of Type 7 and two others, all now missing.[88] Also included in the list of pottery in the notebook were two kalathoi of Type 1

and a dish of Type 7 with horizontal handles, as well as a krater with a scale pattern (**K96.1**). A flat, rounded, shallow object with horned projections found in the boxes is labelled K 96. Other objects included a possible bronze sword (500)[89] and a boar's tusk.

Pottery Catalogue: K 96

Fine Wares

K96.1   Krater (FIG. 5.13). D. rim est. 23. Single fragment from rim, two body fragments. Fine, soft, reddish yellow (5YR 7/6) fabric. White (10YR 8/2) slip. Red (10R 4/8) paint. Scale pattern. LM IIIC.

K96.2   Juglet (PLATE 18 *h*, FIG. 5.13). Max. pres. H. 6; D. base 2.8. Restored from three fragments. 75% preserved, including entire base (though chipped), most of lower body, and base of neck; missing neck, rim, and handle. Fine, very soft and porous, pink (7.5YR 7/4) fabric with tiny black inclusions and some mica. Dull red-brown paint on lower body. Very worn surfaces. Monochrome? For shape, cf. **K85.7**. LM IIIC.

Room K 97

The pottery from this small room included a large number of pithos sherds,[90] and it may have been used primarily for storage. Other coarse ware recorded in the notebook included the possible base of a larnax, a pithoid jar of Type 11, dishes of Types 5 and 6, a jar of Type 3 or 6, a kalathos of Type 1 and tripods, one with slashed decoration. The fine ware was very fragmentary: a handle with incised chevrons, a doubly pierced lug, a small reddish lid of Type 3, a pyxis of Type 9 (*sic*) of soft pink clay, and a large upright red base that may be from another pyxis. The boxes produced the following uncatalogued fine vessels: three handles from deep bowls, one with a spiral motif, one with curved filler, and three body fragments from deep bowls, one with a panelled design, the others with fillers; there was also a jug or stirrup jar with wavy lines on the shoulder. Objects included a bronze knife with rivet holes (518)[91] and a whetstone (519).

Most of the pottery looks early LM IIIC. The deep bowl with lozenge chain (**K97.1**) recalls similar examples from Khamalevri, Kastelli Pediada, Phaistos and Knossos.[92] Krater **K97.5** also finds parallels in the

---

84   Christakis 2005, fig. 18c.

85   *Karphi*, pl. 28.2.

86   *Karphi*, pl. 30.1.

87   Pictured *in situ*, *Karphi*, pl. 21.3 and Seiradaki, pl. 1c.

88   Seiradaki, fig. 1.17–8.

89   *Karphi*, pl. 29.2.

90   Seiradaki, fig. 1.19–20.

91   *Karphi*, pl. 28.2.

92   Andreadaki-Vlasaki and Papadopoulou 2007, 47, fig. 4.29 (Khamalevri, Phase II); Rethemiotakis 1997, 319, fig. 28af (Kastelli Pediada); Borgna 1997*a*, 280, fig. 15; 2003, 435, fig. 9.82 (Phaistos, LM IIIB–C); Popham 1965, 324–6, fig. 6.36 (Knossos).

K96.1

K96.2

K97.1

K97.2

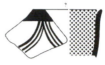

K97.3

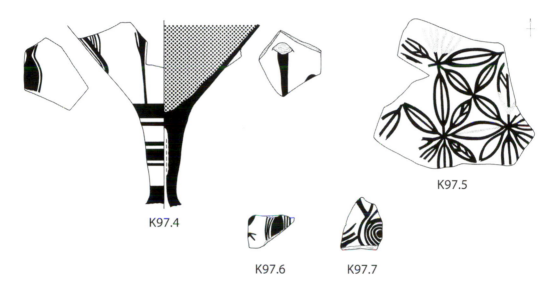

K97.4

K97.5

K97.6

K97.7

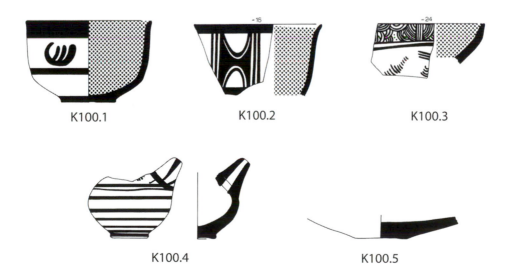

K100.1

K100.2

K100.3

K100.4

K100.5

*Fig. 5.13. Central West Quarter, Building 4, pottery from K 96 (**K96.1–2**), K 97 (**K97.1–7**), and K 100 (**K100.1–5**). Scale 1:3.*

early LM IIIC deposits at Kavousi–*Vronda*.[93] Of interest is the rather large kylix, which may have been used in drinking rituals.[94]

Pottery Catalogue: K 97

Fine Wares

K97.1 Deep bowl or cup (FIG. 5.13). Max. pres. H. 4.7. Single fragment (three sherds) from rim. Fine, medium-hard, reddish yellow (5YR 7/6) fabric with some flakes of mica. Very pale brown (10YR 8/3) slip. Red (10R 5/8) paint. Worn surfaces. Hatched lozenge chain. Cf. LM IIIC.

K97.2 Deep bowl or cup (FIG. 5.13). Max. pres. H. 3.6. Single fragment from rim. Fine, medium-soft, porous, very pale brown (10YR 7/4) fabric. White (10YR 8/2) slip. Crackled black paint. Exterior surfaces worn, interior well-preserved. Multiple curved stems. LM IIIC. For decoration, cf. **K38.5**. LM IIIC.

K97.3 Deep bowl or cup (FIG. 5.13). Max. pres. H. 3.7. Single fragment from rim. Fine, soft, reddish yellow (5YR 7/6) fabric. Very pale brown (10YR 8/3) slip. Black to red (10R 4/8) paint. Worn surfaces. Multiple pendent loops. LM IIIC.

K97.4 Kylix (FIG. 5.13). Max. pres. H. 14.5. Once mended. Two large fragments, one from stem (three sherds), one from lower body (four sherds), and three non-joining body fragments, including lower handle attachment. Base, rim, and handles missing. Fine, very soft, reddish yellow (5YR 7/6) fabric. Very pale brown (10YR 8/4) slip. Red (10R 4/8) paint. Tall pierced stem. Slight bulge in middle of stem. Curvilinear motifs with arc fillers, possibly body of octopus. LM IIIC.

K97.5 Krater (FIG. 5.13). Max. pres. H. 11.7. Large fragment (four sherds) from body. Fine, very soft, micaceous, reddish yellow (5YR 7/6) fabric with tiny red inclusions. Very pale brown (10YR 8/3) slip. Paint almost entirely worn off. Very worn surfaces. Floral pattern with interlocking leaves. LM IIIC.

K97.6 Krater (FIG. 5.13). Max. pres. H. 2.6. Single fragment from body. Fine, soft, reddish yellow (7.5YR 7/6) fabric. Very pale brown (10YR 8/3) slip. Red (10R 4/8) paint. Solid upright oval with multiple outlines, floral motif (?). LM IIIC.

K97.7 Closed vessel (FIG. 5.13). Max. pres. H. 4. Single fragment from body. Fine, very soft, reddish yellow (5YR 7/6) fabric, grey (5Y 6/1) on interior. White (10YR 8/2) slip. Red (2.5YR 4/6) paint. Worn surfaces. Spiral and fringes. LM IIIC.

Room K 100

This room was once entered from K 103 through a doorway, later blocked, but the excavators suggested the possibility of steps also leading up into street K 105.[95] A ledge lay on the north side, and there may have been a door to the roof of K 87. The pottery was recorded as usual, but with few pithos sherds and the coarse ware was much broken. Fine ware included bowls, at least three pyxides (one of Type 3) a spouted jug, a two-handled jug of Type 1, a krater base of Type 1 in flaky stone-like clay, and a flat base. A fragment of a stirrup jar with filler arcs between curved streamers was found but not catalogued. Objects from the room included a pierced stone spool (541), two bone implements (542, 543),[96] and a four-sided stone pounder (610).[97]

The preserved pottery is scanty, but the two deep bowls or cups look early; Hallager suggested that **K100.2** is actually of LM IIIB:2 style,[98] although its reserved band indicates a date in LM IIIC. Kanta labelled the motif on **K100.1** a sea snail pattern, which

she believed began in LM IIIA and continued into LM IIIC.[99] The kylix (**K100.3**) can be paralleled by an example from K 106 (**K106.16–17**). The thelastron (**K100.4**) is of an unusual shape, being much squatter than normal; a similar shape (**K.28**) without a findspot was found in the boxes.

Pottery Catalogue: K 100

Fine Wares

K100.1 Cup or deep bowl (FIG. 5.13). H. 6.5; D. base 4.3; D. rim 10. Full profile preserved; missing handle(s). Fine, soft, reddish yellow (5YR 7/6) fabric. Very pale brown (10YR 8/4) slip. Worn light red (2.5YR 6/8) to red (2.5YR 5/8) paint. Worn surfaces. Pattern of three combs or sea snail. Publication: Seiradaki, fig. 21k. LM IIIC early.

K100.2 Deep bowl or cup (PLATE 10 *d*, FIG. 5.13). D. rim est. 16. Single fragment from rim. Fine, rather hard, reddish yellow (7.5YR 7/6) fabric. White (10YR 8/2) slip. Worn red-brown paint. Very worn surfaces. Double axe. Publication: Seiradaki, fig. 21g. LM IIIB/C.

K100.3 Kylix (PLATE 18 *i*, FIG. 5.13). D. rim est. 24. Single fragment from rim. Fine, rather porous, soft, reddish yellow (7.5YR 7/6) fabric. Very pale brown (10YR 8/3) slip. Dusky red (10R 3/4) paint. Well-preserved surfaces. On rim, alternating arcs; curvilinear motifs below. Publication: Seiradaki, fig. 22c (mislabelled K 106). LM IIIC.

K100.4 Thelastron (PLATE 18 *j*, FIG. 5.13). Max. pres. H. 6.6; D. base 3. Partially mended from five fragments. 80% preserved, including entire base, spout; missing neck, rim, handle. Fine, rather sandy, very pale brown (10YR 8/4) fabric and slip. Dull black paint. Bands on lower body, bands around and down spout. Motif on shoulder, only fringed edge preserved. LM IIIC.

Coarse Wares

K100.5 Base (FIG. 5.13). D. base 4.4. Single fragment preserving entire base. Coarse red (2.5YR 5/6) fabric with infrequent hard white angular inclusions (1–2 mm). Burned inside. Small base, almost horizontal sides; open shape? LM IIIC.

THE SOUTHERN SHELTERS (ROOMS K 62–K 65, K 90–K 95, K 98, K 99)

The Southern Shelters were thought to be amongst the earliest remains on the site, interpreted as housing for the first inhabitants of the site that were later used as animal shelters.[100] Architecturally, there is little to describe; they were simply walled up crevices in the bedrock. The pottery from these rooms is for the most part too fragmentary and scanty to give either a firm date for the use of these rooms or to help determine their function.

93 *Kavousi IIA*, figs. 27, 95.
94 Day and Snyder 2004.
95 *Karphi*, 90.
96 *Karphi*, pl. 28.4.
97 *Karphi*, pl. 30.1.
98 Hallager 2000, 174 n. 343.
99 Kanta 1980, 126, fig. 53.10.
100 *Karphi*, 92.

Rooms K 62–K 65

The notebook lists the pottery from all these rooms together. The only coarse pottery mentioned is a lid of Type 1 in coarse buff clay. There was much fine ware, but it was very fragmentary; most came from bowls of Types 1–3. Other fine ware included two kylix stems, some stirrup jars, some kraters (**K62.1**, **K62.2**), a small trough spout, a spout as from tankard of Type 1 but with four holes making a strainer, and a rim with beading below, both in very soft buff clay, perhaps from the same vessel. There were no obvious pyxis sherds.

Room K 62

Deep bowl fragments with vertical strokes and an uncertain motif that were found in the boxes are labelled as coming from this room. Other objects from K 62 included the head of a bronze stud (419),[101] a bronze awl (420), a conical stone bead (418), and the head of a terracotta figurine (421).

Pottery Catalogue: K 62

Fine Wares

K62.1   Krater (FIG. 5.14). Max. pres. H. 13.5; D. rim est. 38. Two joining fragments and one non-joining from rim. Fine, soft, light red (10R 6/6) fabric. Very pale brown (10YR 8/4) slip. Black paint. Panelled decoration: bird with dotted outline, fringed wings. Publication: Seiradaki, fig. 25g. LM IIIC.

K62.2   Krater (FIG. 5.14). Max. pres. H. 8.2. Single fragment from body. Fine, very soft, light red (10R 6/6) fabric. Very pale brown (10YR 8/4) slip. Worn black to dark red (10R 3/6) paint. Loops with fillers of arcs and strokes. For decoration, cf. Borgna 1997a, 278, fig. 6.8 (Phaistos, deep bowl). LM IIIC.

Room K 63

A strainer spout found in one of the boxes may be the same vessel mentioned in the notebook under K 62–K 65. The only other object found in this room was the hoop of a bronze fibula (422).[102]

Room K 64

A fragment of bronze (425) and two conical stone beads (423, 424) were found in this room.

Room K 65

A stirrup jar top with a large hole through the centre is labelled as coming from K 65.

Rooms K 90, K 91, K 95

Material from these three rooms was recorded together in the notebook. Coarse ware included the leg of a tripod pithos (as from K 80), some pithos fragments with chevron design, pithoid jars of Types 3 and 8, a large number of tripod legs, several dishes of Type 6, several one or two-handled jugs, three basins of Types 2 and 4, 2 two large kraters of Type 1, four stirrup jars of Type 2, two kalathoi of Type 1, several small bowls (one with a side spout), and a one-handled jug with knobs (possibly **K90.3**). Fine pottery included a small dish of Type 8, a pyxis of Type 1, a small lid of Type 1, a stirrup jar of Type 2, and several bowls of Types 1 and 2 (**K90.1**). Also listed were 15 terracotta spools, pumice, animal bones, and human teeth. The human remains suggest a burial in the vicinity. The spools may have come from a loom in one of the rooms, as there were so many of them.

Room K 90

The boxes produced at least two deep bowl rims, one with scallops and loops, the other with arcs or loops, and a body fragment from a deep bowl with arc filler. In addition to pottery, a bronze fragment (469), two Neolithic stone axes (465, 466),[103] a terracotta bull's head (467), and a conical spindle whorl (468) were also found.

Pottery Catalogue: K 90

Fine Wares

K90.1   Deep bowl or cup (FIG. 5.14). D. rim est. 13–14. Single fragment from rim. Fine, medium-hard, reddish yellow (7.5YR 7/6) fabric. Very pale brown (10YR 8/3) slip. Red (2.5YR 5/8) paint. Worn surfaces. Multiple stems (?). LM IIIC.

K90.2   Kylix (FIG. 5.14). D. rim est. 11. Single fragment from rim. Fine, soft, micaceous, very pale brown (10YR 8/3) fabric and slip. Paint black worn to brown. Very worn surfaces. Carinated body. Horizontal floral spray. LM IIIC.

Coarse Wares

K90.3   Amphora (PLATE 19 a, FIG. 5.14). Max. pres. H. 15; D. base 7.6. Restored from numerous fragments. 80% preserved, including entire base and handle attachments; missing rim and handles. Coarse light brown (7.5YR 6/4) fabric with frequent large phyllite inclusions. Surface very smooth, almost burnished, and cracked. Burned on one side near bottom. Three knobs on each side on shoulder. Publication: Seiradaki, pl. 5c, bottom right (labelled K 80), fig. 8.5 (labelled K 80). LM IIIC.

Room K 91

The pottery from this room was listed with that from K 90 and K 95. A pithos of Type 16 was published by Seiradaki as being from this location, but it was not found.[104] A deep bowl with a curvilinear motif from K 91 appeared in the boxes. Also found were the following objects: the hooked end of a bronze pin (471),[105] a conical stone bead or whorl (470), and a biconical terracotta spindle whorl (472).

---

101   *Karphi*, pl. 29.1.
102   *Karphi*, pl. 29.2.
103   *Karphi*, pl. 30.2.
104   Seiradaki, fig. 1.16.
105   *Karphi*, pl. 29.2.

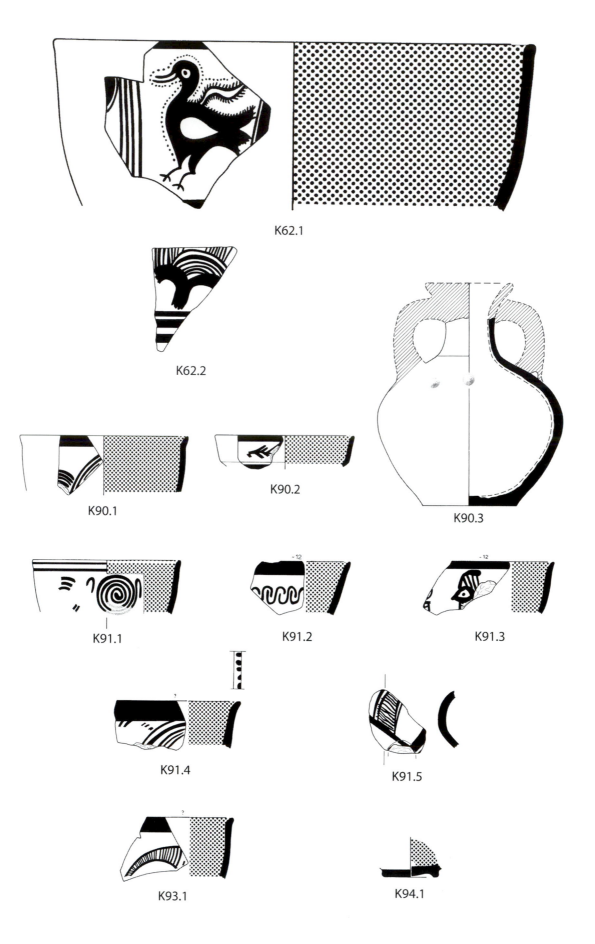

*Fig. 5.14. Southern Shelters, pottery from K 62 (**K62.1–2**), K 90 (**K90.1–3**), K 91 (**K91.1–5**), K 93 (**K93.1**), and K 94 (**K94.1**). Scale 1:3.*

The deep bowl fragments all look early; the buttonhook spiral and quirk are motifs that appear early and are less popular in late LM IIIC. The possible bird on deep bowl **K91.3** may also indicate an earlier LM IIIC date. Bird-shaped rhyta like **K91.5** are known in LM IIIB and later in Subminoan, but are not common in LM IIIC; this example looks like the more naturalistically decorated LM IIIB examples, where the design tries to simulate the markings on the bird's body rather than being schematic or geometric renderings.[106] These early sherds, then, support the excavators' idea that these shelters were in use early in the settlement's history, although they are not necessarily the earliest examples found at Karphi.

Pottery Catalogue: K 91

Fine Wares

K91.1   Deep bowl or cup (FIG. 5.14). D. rim 11.9. Six joining fragments from rim. Fine, soft, reddish yellow (5YR 7/6) fabric. Very pale brown (10YR 8/4) slip. Worn red (2.5YR 4/8) paint. Worn surfaces. Buttonhook spirals below double band at rim. Reserved band on interior of rim. For motif, cf. Andreadaki-Vlasaki and Papadopoulou 2007, 46, fig. 3.1 (Khamalevri, Phase I); Popham 1965, 326, fig. 6.28–29 (Knossos). LM IIIC.

K91.2   Deep bowl or cup (FIG. 5.14). D. rim est. 12. Single fragment from rim. Fine, very soft, reddish yellow (7.5YR 7/6) fabric. Yellow (10YR 8/6) slip. Black paint. Very worn exterior surfaces. Quirk. For motif, cf. Popham 1965, 325, fig. 5.18 (Knossos); Rethemiotakis 1997, 320, fig. 29 (Kastelli Pediada, LM IIIC early); *Khania II*, pl. 35.84-P 0222 (LM IIIC early). LM IIIC.

K91.3   Deep bowl or cup (FIG. 5.14). D. rim est. 12. Single fragment from rim. Fine, soft, porous, very pale brown (10YR 8/4) fabric and slip. Worn black paint. Head of bird or human. LM IIIC.

K91.4   Krater (FIG. 5.14). Max. pres. H. 3.7. Single fragment from rim. Fine, soft, very pale brown (10YR 8/4) fabric and slip. Worn black paint. Spiral (?). Strokes on rim. LM IIIC.

K91.5   Bird vase, possibly a rhyton (FIG. 5.14). Max. pres. H. 4.5. Single fragment from body, with scar from leg (?) Fine, soft, reddish yellow (7.5YR 7/6) fabric. White (10YR 8/2) slip. Reddish yellow (5YR 6/8) paint. Worn surfaces. Irregular shape, perhaps a bird vase. Hatching between bands. LM IIIC.

Room K 95

Nothing is recorded as being from this room. One sherd, catalogued with the material from K 45, may have come from here; it was difficult to distinguish between the numbers 95 and 45.

Rooms K 92 and K 93

The pottery from these two rooms was listed together in the notebook and included the following: tripod legs, a dish of Type 6, a small tray, a lid of Type 1, a pyxis of Type 1, a one-handled jug, and several small bowls of Types 1 and 2.

Room K 92

Only a conical stone bead or whorl (613) is recorded as coming from this room.

Room K 93

In addition to the catalogued sherd, a deep bowl base was found in the storerooms from this room. Other objects included: three fragments of bronze needles (485), part of a bone handle (484),[107] and a conical stone bead or whorl with a compass-drawn rosette on the base (486).

Pottery Catalogue: K 93

Fine Wares

K93.1   Deep bowl (FIG. 5.14). Max. pres. H. 5. Single fragment (two sherds) from rim. Fine, very soft, reddish yellow (7.5YR 7/6) fabric. Very pale brown (10YR 8/3) slip. Red (2.5YR 5/8) paint. Worn surfaces. Curvilinear motif with hatching between lines. One fragment says K 93, but emended to 43?; other fragment emended to 13. For the motif, cf. Rethemiotakis 1997, 321, fig. 32 (Kastelli Pediada). LM IIIC.

Room K 94

The notebook records the following pottery: a pithos of Type 1, tripod legs, several dishes of Type 6, small bowls of Types 1 and 2, fragments of two large kraters, and several kylix stems. The basin illustrated by Seiradaki as being from K 94 was not found.[108] Other objects from this room included a conical stone bead (487), antler of red deer, animal bones, and pumice.

Pottery Catalogue: K 94

Fine Wares

K94.1   Deep bowl or cup (FIG. 5.14). D. base 4.5. Single fragment from base. Fine, soft, porous, pink (7.5YR 7/4) fabric. Very pale brown (10YR 8/3) slip. Dusky red (10R 3/3) paint. Well-preserved surfaces. Ring base. Band on exterior. Reserved disc on interior. LM IIIC.

Room K 98

The notebook lists the following pottery: a pithos of Type 8, the rim of a tripod of Type 3, tripod legs, a jar of Type 1, a dish of Type 6, a basin of Type 3, a kalathos of Type 1, a krater of Type 1, two kylix base fragments, a stirrup jar, and several small bowls of Types 1 and 2. A square stone tool was also found here.

Room K 99

The notebook records the following pottery from this room: a large tripod of Type 3, two basins (one of Type 3), a kylix stem, and a small bowl or cup. No pottery was found from this room.

---

106 Kanta 1980, 44, fig. 11.4 (Nirou Khani, LM IIIA); Stampolides and Karetsou 1998a, 77 no. 46.
107 *Karphi*, pl. 28.4.
108 Seiradaki, fig. 5.6.

BROAD ROAD (AREAS K 101, K 103, K 105, K 111)

The plan shows this area as paved; although it was preserved better than any of the other roads on the site, most of the paving blocks had washed away, leaving only the steps or water-breaks.[109] Thus, the material found here probably comes from beneath the level of the paving, and indeed it is consistent with deposits from streets and earlier rubbish dumps elsewhere, including a great number of small fragments, mostly from fine vessels.

Area K 101

No pottery was recorded for this room in the publication. In the notebook, the pottery from K 101 was put together with that from K 103 and K 111 (the divisions among the areas being arbitrary). The notebook records pithoi: rims of Types 8, 10, 14, 18; a base with chain moulding; and body fragments with various patterns, including diagonal slashes, vertical slashes, X-pattern, chain, and rope. Other coarse wares included: pithoid jars of Types 3, 7, 9, 10; several jars of Type 2; dishes of Type 1 with horizontal handle and Type 6 with a spout; tripod legs; basins of Types 1, 2, 3, and 7; two krater bases of Type 3; several two-handled jars or jugs; a kalathos of Type 1; and three bowls, two of Type 1 and one of Type 2. Fine wares included two jars of Types 2 and 8, several krater fragments, bowls of Types 1 and 2, two stirrup jars of Type 2, a pyxis of Type 2, a small cup of Type 2, and a tankard spout of Type 1. The forequarters of a terracotta bull figurine with broken legs (611) were also recorded as found here, as well as a sherd from an altar and one from a goddess.

A number of fragments from K 101 were found in the boxes, but were not catalogued, either because they were too small or worn or because they did not clearly fit into the category of pottery. A list of these fragments includes the following: a round, horizontal double handle, rather like a bull's head (bucranium);[110] krater body fragments, one with fringed motif, one with spiral under handle, one with an upright leaf; krater rim fragments, one with a reserved band on top of the rim, three with fringed motifs on the exterior; two rims, two handles, and a body fragment with multiple upright loops from deep bowls; two stirrup jar fragments; a fine tile fragment; a square or rectangular object, possibly the 'altar' mentioned in the publication; a sherd with incised ridges; and a vertical jug handle.

The pottery is made up of small fragments of fine ware, mostly from cups or deep bowls and kraters. The cups or deep bowls have a variety of motifs, including blob, quirk, tricurved streamer, multiple pendent loops, multiple oval with dot, spiral, and flower. The blob decoration of **K101.3** seems to occur throughout Karphi, although it is particularly prevalent in the dumps under the Great House and Baker's House. Cups

with blob decoration characterise the early LM IIIC deposits at Kavousi–*Vronda*, as well.[111] The quirk is a common LM IIIC motif, and the unusual example on **K101.4**, more like an S-pattern, can be paralleled at Kastelli Pediada and Kastrokephala.[112] The tricurved streamer of **K101.2** finds parallels in early LM IIIC deposits at Sybrita/Thronos, Kastelli Pediada, and Khamalevri.[113] The multiple oval motif of **K101.6** is found on a variety of vessels at Karphi, and it also appears in the dump of phases I and II at Kavousi–*Kastro*.[114] The flower and multiple pendent loops of **K101.1** appear in a variety of contexts at Karphi, and this example resembles those found at Mikre Koprana (**K149.3**). Overall, there seems to be a good deal of material that looks early in LM IIIC.

Pottery Catalogue: K 101

Fine Wares

K101.1   Deep bowl or cup (FIG. 5.15). D. rim est. 15. Single fragment from rim. Fine, soft, rather porous, very pale brown (10YR 8/4) fabric and slip. Black paint. Surfaces very worn, especially on exterior. Multiple pendent loops. LM IIIC.

K101.2   Deep bowl or cup (FIG. 5.15). D. rim est. 16.5. Single fragment from rim. Fine, soft, porous, reddish yellow (7.5YR 7/6) fabric. Very pale brown (10YR 8/4) slip. Black paint worn to brown shadow. Worn surfaces. Tricurved streamer. LM IIIC.

K101.3   Deep bowl or cup (FIG. 5.15). D. rim est. 11. Single fragment from rim. Fine, very soft, yellow (10YR 8/6) fabric. Streaky worn black paint. Probably a cup. Blob decoration inside and out. LM IIIC.

K101.4   Deep bowl or cup (FIG. 5.15). D. rim est. 11. Single fragment from rim. Fine, very soft, reddish yellow (7.5YR 7/6) fabric. Very pale brown (10YR 8/3) slip. Red (10R 5/8) paint. Worn surfaces. S-pattern or quirk. Tiny reserved band on interior of rim. LM IIIC.

K101.5   Deep bowl or cup (FIG. 5.15). Max. pres. H. 4.7. Single fragment from rim. Fine, very soft, reddish yellow (7.5YR 7/6) fabric. Very pale brown (10YR 8/3) slip. Black paint worn to brown. Worn surfaces. Tailed spiral above tricurved streamer. LM IIIC.

K101.6   Deep bowl or cup (FIG. 5.15). Max. pres. H. 4.1. Single fragment from body. Fine, soft, porous, very pale brown (10YR 7/4) fabric. Very pale brown (10YR 8/4) slip. Worn, streaky black paint. Concentric ovals with dot in centre. LM IIIC.

K101.7   Deep bowl or krater (FIG. 5.15). D. rim est. 20. Single fragment from rim. Fine, soft, reddish yellow (7.5YR 7/6) fabric. Very pale brown (10YR 8/3) slip. Worn paint, once dark red (10R 3/6). Worn surfaces. Minoan flower. LM IIIC.

K101.8   Krater (FIG. 5.15). Max. pres. H. 6.3. Single fragment from body. Fine, soft, reddish yellow (7.5YR 7/6) fabric. Very

109   *Karphi*, 93.

110   Published in Seiradaki, pl. 12a, third row, left.

111   *Kavousi IIA*, fig 25.

112   Rethemiotakis 1997, 320, fig. 29; Kanta and Karetsou 2003, 153, fig. 3E (early LM IIIC).

113   Prokopiou 1997, 379, fig. 20g; Rethemiotakis 1997, 315, fig. 23e; Andreadaki-Vlasaki and Papadopoulou 2007, 48, fig. 5.2 (Phase Ib).

114   Mook and Coulson 1997, 358, fig. 30.118.

*Fig. 5.15. Broad Road II, pottery from K 101 (**K101.1–11**) and K 103 (**K103.1–3**). Scale 1:3.*

pale brown (10YR 8/3) slip. Black to dusky red (10R 3/4) paint. Well-preserved surfaces. Dotted curved streamers (octopus tentacles?) Dots painted in first, then many of them were covered over with paint. Publication: Seiradaki, fig. 22d (labelled a kylix). LM IIIC.

K101.9   Basin (FIG. 5.15). Max. pres. H. 3.5. Single fragment from rim. Fine, soft, reddish yellow (7.5YR 7/6) fabric. Very pale brown (10YR 8/3) slip. Very worn reddish brown paint. Very worn surfaces. Bands on exterior. LM IIIC.

Medium-Coarse Wares
K101.10   Stirrup jar (?) (FIG. 5.15). Max. pres. H. 4.6. Single fragment from body. Medium-coarse, soft, reddish yellow (5YR 7/8) fabric with hard black and white inclusions. Pink (7.5YR 8/4)

slip. Black paint. Well-preserved surfaces. Curvilinear motifs, possibly a debased octopus. LM IIIC.

Coarse Wares
K101.11   Pithos (FIG. 5.15). Single fragment from body. Coarse reddish yellow (5YR 6/8) fabric with infrequent small phyllites, and hard white and black angular inclusions. Raised band with two rows of circular depressions. Publication: Seiradaki, pl. 12a, second row, second from left. LM IIIC.

Room K 103

Pottery found and not catalogued included two fragments of kraters, one with an outlined rayed design, the other with bands, and fragments of three stirrup jars, one with fringes, one with filler, and one with an uncertain design. There is nothing narrowly diagnostic in terms of date; all the sherds look LM IIIC and are consistent with a date early in that period.

Pottery Catalogue: K 103

Fine Wares

K103.1 Deep bowl or cup (FIG. 5.15). D. rim est. 12. Single fragment from rim. Fine, soft, very pale brown (10YR 7/4) fabric. White (10YR 8/2) slip. Black to dark brown (7.5YR 3/2) paint. Curvilinear motif with hatching between curved bands. LM IIIC.

K103.2 Deep bowl or cup (FIG. 5.15). Max. pres. H. 4.3. Single fragment from body, near rim. Fine, very soft, very pale brown (10YR 8/3) fabric and slip. Worn black paint, streaky on inside. Zigzag below rim band. LM IIIC.

K103.3 Krater (FIG. 5.15). Max. pres. H. 9; Th. 0.6–0.7. Single fragment (2 sherds) from body. Fine, porous, very pale brown (10YR 7/4) fabric. Very pale brown (10YR 8/4) slip. Black to red (2.5YR 5/8) paint. Worn surfaces. Vertical, outlined, crosshatched lozenge chain. For motif, cf. Rethemiotakis 1997, 312, fig. 15b (Kastelli Pediada). LM IIIC.

Room K 105

The following pottery was recorded in the notebook as from this area: a pithos rim of Type 12, tripod legs, several dishes of Type 6, several small bowls of Types 1 and 2. Animal bones were also noted. No pottery was preserved.

Room K 111

No pottery was specifically recorded from this area, but the publication mentions a conical stone bead or whorl. Among the fragments in the boxes was the arm of a goddess with upraised arms, mentioned also in the publication.

6
The Northwest Quadrant

The Commercial Quarter (Rooms K 77–K 79, K 89, K 112, K 116), the Eastern Cliff Houses (Rooms K 75, K 110, K 118, K 119), Broad Road and Square (Area K 117), the Western Cliff Houses (Rooms K 102, K 106, K 113–K 115, K 120, K 121, K 126), the Northern Shelters (Rooms K 104, K 107–9, K 122–125, K 127), and the Summit (K 128, K 129)

THE COMMERCIAL QUARTER (ROOMS K 77–K 79, K 89, K 112, K 116)

The excavators thought that these rooms formed a single unit, rather like a shop,[1] and the plan shows all of the rooms connected. Rooms K 79 and K 89 contained only a few traces of roofing along the sides, so they were thought to be open courtyards, an interpretation strengthened by the presence of stone paving in both. The quantity of broken fine ware, similar to that from other open spaces in the settlement, further supports the idea that they were open spaces. K 79 led directly into a large room, labelled K 112 and K 78; room K 78 was at a lower level and required a step down, so was considered a separate unit. The long and narrow room K 77 was entered from K 78 through a doorway toward the end of the long wall, preserving maximum privacy. These rooms seem to have been for ordinary domestic use. K 116, a room entered through K 89, however, seems to have been separate and may have had a different function.[2] It has been identified as a possible shrine because of the statues of goddesses with upraised arms found in it, and it also seems to have been used very late, judging from the pottery of very early SM style.

Room K 79

Little roofing material was found in this room and that only around edges. It also had a 'tarrazza' paving, suggesting that it was probably open. The floor level was uneven, but was much lower than that in K 89.

The published pottery included a pithos of Type 21, which is now missing.[3] The notebook lists pottery from K 79 together with that from K 89, and most of the extant fragments are given the K 79-89 designation. Seiradaki also published the fragments of a tankard or pyxis[4] and a krater with bird decoration[5] as being from K 79; both of these were inscribed with the identification K 79-89 and so they have been catalogued with the pottery from K 79-89. Found in the boxes but not catalogued were a long handle with a plastic attachment, a fine handle with incised chevron decoration,[6] and the ridged body sherd from a tubular vessel. Coarse wares found in the boxes included a pithos fragment with impressed circles and a tripod leg with incisions.

Objects from K 79 included two bronze pins with twisted heads (503),[7] the base of a stone vase (533), the head probably from a human figurine (501), and a cylindrical terracotta spindle whorl (502).

The pottery identified as being from this room (as opposed to that from K 79-89) is quite fragmentary, and it probably does not represent a floor deposit. The large cup (K79.1) has parallels in K 115 and K 81 and looks very much like the SM wavy band cups from early SM Knossos and Sybrita/Thronos.[8] The krater fragment (K79.2) with its fringed whorl shell or filler finds many parallels in LM IIIC, some of them early in the period;[9] the shape is unusually shallow and resembles more the deep bowls to which it is close in size. The trays and tripod trays are similar to other examples from the site and from other LM IIIC sites. Of interest are the lugs on two of the trays and the rim of the third, which has been pushed in by fingers to make a wrinkled edge or spit stand.

Pottery Catalogue: K 79

Fine Wares

K79.1   Cup (FIG. 6.1). Max. pres. H. 7.5. Single fragment (2 sherds) from rim, preserving handle. Fine, soft, porous, reddish yellow (7.5YR 7/6) fabric with some red phyllite inclusions. Very pale brown (7.5YR 7/6) slip. Black to red (2.5YR 4/8) paint. Very worn surfaces. Very large cup. Large wavy band in handle zone, with drip under handle. Cf. **K81.1**. LM IIIC late–SM.

K79.2   Krater (FIG. 6.1). D. rim est. 26. Large fragment (two sherds) from rim, two non-joining rim fragments, two fragments

---

1   *Karphi*, 88–9.
2   Day 2009, 142–3.
3   Seiradaki, fig. 1.21.
4   Seiradaki, fig. 22b.
5   Seiradaki, fig. 25b.
6   Possibly the one illustrated in Seiradaki, pl. 12b, top row, second from the right.
7   *Karphi*, pl. 29.2.
8   Warren 1982–83, 85, fig. 60a–b (Knossos, early SM); D'Agata 2007, 111, fig. 11a.41/5 (earliest SM).
9   Rethemiotakis 1997, 319, fig. 28ai (Kastelli Pediada).

K79.1

K79.2

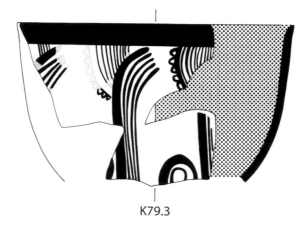

K79.3

K79.4

K79.5

K79.6

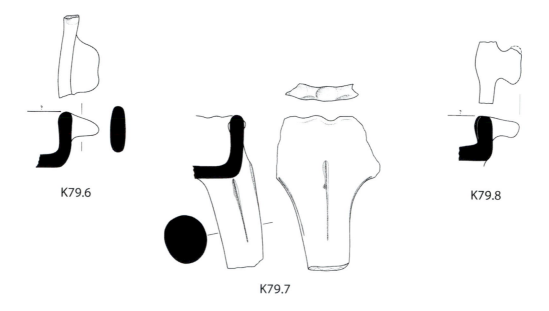

K79.7

K79.8

Fig. 6.1. *Commercial Quarter, pottery from K 79 (**K79.1–8**). Scale 1:3.*

from handle and handle attachment; one lower body fragment may be from another vessel. Fine, very soft, reddish yellow (7.5YR 7/6) fabric. Creamy, thick, very pale brown (10YR 8/4) slip. Worn black paint on top of slip. Worn surfaces. Fringed bivalve shell (?) above multiple bands. LM IIIC.

K79.3 Krater (FIG. 6.1). D. rim est. 22. Eight joining fragments from rim. Fine, very soft, reddish yellow (5YR 7/6) fabric with some infrequent but large phyllite inclusions. White (10YR 8/2) slip. Red (10R 4/8) paint. Worn surfaces. Multiple stems with arc fillers and scallops. Curvilinear motifs. Label is unclear; may also be K 72. LM IIIC.

K79.4 Kalathos (FIG. 6.1). D. rim est. 15. Single fragment from rim. Fine, porous, reddish yellow (7.5YR 7/6) fabric. White (10YR 8/2) slip. Worn black paint. On rim, hatched triangles or zigzags. Bands on exterior and interior. For shape and decoration, cf. **K68.11** basket kalathos; for shape, cf. Andreadaki-Vlasaki and Papadopoulou 2007, 46, fig. 3.14 (Khamalevri). LM IIIC.

K79.5 Pyxis (FIG. 6.1). D. base est. 11–12. Single fragment from base. Fine, soft, reddish yellow (5YR 7/6) fabric. White (10YR 8/2) slip. Worn black paint. Very worn surfaces. Curvilinear decoration. LM IIIC.

Coarse Wares

K79.6 Tray (FIG. 6.1). H. 4.5. Single fragment from rim and base preserving full profile and one handle. Coarse red (10R 5/6) fabric with frequent schist and hard white angular inclusions (1–2 mm). Burning on exterior on top of handle and the surrounding surfaces. Single finger impression on rim. Lug handle. LM IIIC.

K79.7 Tripod tray (FIG. 6.1). Max. pres. H. 12.2; D. base est. 36–38. Single fragment preserving most of one leg, full profile; missing tip of leg. Coarse red (2.5YR 5/8) fabric with frequent schist inclusions (1–2 mm). No burning. Three deep slashes, one vertical, two oblique, on leg; finger impressions on rim. LM IIIC.

K79.8 Tripod tray (FIG. 6.1). Max. pres. H. 3.6. Single fragment from rim and base, preserving full profile and handle, including scar from leg; missing legs. Coarse light red (2.5YR 6/8) fabric with grey core and schist inclusions (1–2 mm). No burning. LM IIIC.

Room K 89

As with K 79, little roofing material and part of a pavement caused it to be interpreted as an open space. Although this area was open to K 79, it was 55 cm higher than K 79 and the excavators suggested it could be reached from K 79 by a step.[10] It is not clear why the excavators decided to combine the material from these two rooms, as in general they were careful to record the individual find spots. There was a large, stone-built oven in the southwest corner, similar to the one in the Baker's House, but smaller. The identification as an oven is not certain, however, since it contained no burned clay lining. The publication listed the pottery as usual. Seiradaki published a small jug of Type 5 from this room, but it could not be located.[11] There were few objects found in the area; only a pierced schist plaque (614) is mentioned.

Rooms K 79 and K 89

The notebook lists pottery from K 79 and K 89 together and provides additional information about what was found in these two sections of the courtyard. Coarse ware included at least four pithoi of Types 2, 5, 8, and 21, one with impressed circles; four pithoid jars of Types 3, 7, 8, and 10; the base of a jar of Type 7; a large jar of unknown type; tripod legs as usual; a tripod dish with crinkled rim (**K79.7**); several dishes of Types 1–6, the latter with spout and holes; a scuttle handle; two basins of Type 7; two kalathoi of Types 1 and 2; a large stirrup jar of Type 2; the base of a krater of Type 3; a lid of Type 1; and a small bowl of Type 2 with holes at the base of the handle. Fine wares included a tankard of Type 2 with beaded edges and double axe pattern (**K79-89.24**), a stirrup jar of Type 2, two pyxides of Type 3, a cup like that from Atsividero 3 (**K79-89.1**), several krater fragments of Type 1, small bowls of Types 1 and 2, a kylix stem, an 'egg cup', and a twisted triple handle. In addition, there was a great deal of fragmentary fine ware in the boxes that was not catalogued. From deep bowls came two rims with spiral decoration, two handles, and seven body fragments: two decorated with pairs of spirals, one with multiple lines, three with filler motifs, and one with bands. Other open shapes included a carinated kylix with curved strokes on the rim and a krater with fringed motif. Closed vessels included four stirrup jar fragments with spirals, fillers, and fringed motifs and a large stirrup jar. There were various types of handles from different vessels as well, including the vertical handle of a jug, a fine rope-twisted handle from a small vessel, and a handle on the interior of an open vessel. The notebook also records for this area the hand of a goddess, a terracotta spool, and two flat stone tools, as well as animal bones and a deer antler.

The catalogued pottery consists chiefly of fine fragments from deep bowls and kraters; very little coarse ware has been preserved. The blob cup (**K79-89.1**) is a very simple shape that finds few parallels at Karphi; blob cups, however, are common in other LM IIIC sites, and at Kavousi–*Vronda*, they characterise the earlier phase of the settlement.[12] A substantial amount of deep bowl **K79-89.2** has been preserved, and it may have been in use just before the abandonment; the decoration and shape of the foot, however, places it in early LM IIIC. The decoration of upright multiple loops is common on LM IIIB deep bowls at Knossos and in vessels from early LM IIIC deposits.[13] The decoration also continues into the later phases of LM IIIC at Kavousi–*Kastro*.[14] It may be significant that **K79-89.2** has both reserved band and

10   *Karphi*, 88.
11   Seiradaki, fig. 9.5.
12   *Kavousi IIA*, fig. 26.
13   Popham 1970*b*, pl. 47e, 50a (Knossos, LM IIIB); *Kastri*, 287, fig. 8:o; 288, fig. 9m (LM IIIC early); Warren 2007, 342, fig. 7.P183 (Knossos, LM IIIC early).
14   Mook and Coulson 1997, 362, fig. 37.150 (Kavousi–*Kastro*, Phase III).

disc on the interior. A similar motif of horizontal multiple loops can be seen on **K79-89.9** with parallels in early LM IIIC Kavousi–*Kastro* and at Knossos.[15] The shape of **K79-89.3** finds parallels in the earlier phases at Kavousi–*Kastro*.[16] The large fragment of a cup or deep bowl (**K79-89.4**) also seems early, as it has a similar shape to vessels at Phaistos;[17] the unusual form of Minoan flower on this vessel has no parallel. **K79-89.5** has a panelled pattern with vertically placed half-rounds that is very common in LM IIIC.[18] Finally, the multiple stemmed spiral motif of **K79-89.12** derives from LM IIIB motifs and is found on a number of early LM IIIC vessels.[19] On the other hand, the fragment of a cup or deep bowl (**K79-89.13**) may have come from a wavy band cup of late LM IIIC. There are no parallels for the kylix fragments, but the fringed motif of **K 79-89.14** puts it squarely into the fringed style of LM IIIC. There are a large number of kraters represented, all of them done in pleonastic style with fringes and fillers. Of particular interest is krater **K 79-89.18**, which was published by Seiradaki, but new fragments were found of the panel that the bird faces; the scalloped edges of the panel find parallels on kraters from a number of sites.[20] The base of a kalathos or tankard (**K 79-89.24**) has a butterfly or double axe pattern that is common, particularly on early LM IIIC pottery. The decoration on fragments of a closed vessel, probably a stirrup jar (**K79-89.28**), is close to a stirrup jar from Khania, and it may have been imported from West Crete.[21] The face on the possible rhyton (**K79-89.29**) is most closely paralleled by an example from Phaistos; such vases are rare, occurring only in the LM IIIB–SM periods, and the known examples are from the Mesara.[22]

The large amount of fine decorated pottery, especially of so many kraters, may simply be a result of chance; dumps often produce many fragments of fine vessels for drinking and mixing, if that is what the deposit represents. It is also possible that the kraters and cups were used in rituals related to the small shrine of the goddess with upraised arms (K 116) and that they were discarded in the court outside. They may, in fact, have functioned in outdoor rituals of the goddess that may have involved parading her statues.[23]

Pottery Catalogue: K 79–89

Fine Wares

K79-89.1   Cup (FIG. 6.2). H. 7 (with handle 7.7); D. base 4.3; D. rim 9.8. Mended from three fragments. 25% preserved, including full profile, entire base, handle. Fine, soft, very pale brown (10YR 8/3) fabric with tiny black inclusions. White (10YR 8/2) slip. Streaky black paint. Blob decoration inside and out. LM IIIC early.

K79-89.2   Deep bowl (FIG. 6.2). H. est. 9.7; D. base 4.2; D. rim 13. Two large fragments, one from rim and handle (seven sherds), one from base (two sherds), and one non-joining fragment from near base. 50% preserved; missing half of rim and body, one handle and part of other. Fine, soft, reddish yellow (7.5YR 7/6) fabric with tiny black inclusions. Very pale brown (10YR 8/4) slip. Black to light red (2.5YR 6/6) paint. Exterior worn, interior surfaces well-preserved. Upright multiple loops. Interior has both reserved band

at rim and reserved disc in base. Irregular blob of paint on underside. Some joining fragments from K 112. For decoration, cf. **K147.1**. LM IIIC early.

K79-89.3   Deep bowl (FIG. 6.2). D. rim est. 13. Single fragment from rim, preserving one handle. Fine, very soft, reddish yellow (5YR 7/6) fabric. Black paint, very worn. Very worn surfaces. Decorated, but too worn to make out motif. LM IIIC early.

K79-89.4   Cup or deep bowl (FIG. 6.2). D. rim 14. Single fragment (four sherds) preserving 10% of rim and body, including handle attachment; missing base and handles. Fine, fairly hard, very pale brown (10YR 8/3) fabric and slip. Crackled black paint, rather well-preserved. Minoan flower. For shape, cf. Borgna 1997*a*, 278, fig. 6.2 (Phaistos, LM IIIC); for decoration, Popham 1965 pl. 86b–c (Knossos, LM IIIB). LM IIIC early.

K79-89.5   Deep bowl or cup (FIG. 6.2). D. rim est. 10. Single fragment (five sherds) from rim. Fine, soft, reddish yellow (7.5YR 7/6) fabric. Very pale brown (10YR 8/3) slip. Dull, streaky brown paint. Panelled pattern: two half-rounds on either side of vertical. LM IIIC early.

K79-89.6   Deep bowl or cup (FIG. 6.2). D. rim est. 16. Single fragment from rim. Fine, medium-hard, reddish yellow (7.5YR 7/6) fabric. White (10YR 8/2) slip. Black paint worn to brown shadow. Well-preserved surfaces. Alternating arcs, curvilinear pattern. LM IIIC.

K79-89.7   Deep bowl or cup (FIG. 6.2). D. rim est. 17. Single fragment from rim. Fine, medium-soft, reddish yellow (7.5YR 7/6) fabric. Very pale brown (10YR 8/3) slip. Black paint. Worn exterior surfaces, well-preserved on interior. Filler arcs. LM IIIC.

K79-89.8   Deep bowl or cup (FIG. 6.2). D. rim est. 14–15. Single fragment from rim. Fine, rather hard, porous, very pale brown (10YR 8/4) fabric. Black paint. Well-preserved surfaces. Quirk. For decoration, cf. Popham 1965, 325, fig. 5.18–9 (Knossos, LM IIIC); Popham 1970*b*, 200, fig. 3.42 (Knossos, LM IIIB); Borgna 1997*a*, 278, fig. 6.5 (Phaistos, LM IIIC). LM IIIC early.

K79-89.9   Deep bowl or cup (FIG. 6.2). D. rim est. 15. Single fragment from rim. Fine, soft, reddish yellow (7.5YR 7/6) fabric. White (10YR 8/2) slip. Black paint. Well-preserved surfaces. Multiple loops set horizontally. LM IIIC early.

K79-89.10   Deep bowl or cup (FIG. 6.2). D. rim est. 15. Single fragment from rim. Fine, medium-soft, reddish yellow (5YR 7/6) fabric. White (10YR 8/2) slip. Red (2.5YR 4/8) paint.

15   Mook and Coulson 1997, 358, fig. 30.117 (Kavousi–*Kastro*, Phases I–II); Popham 1965, 325, fig. 5.26 (Knossos).

16   Mook and Coulson 1997, 359, fig. 31.122 (Phases I–II).

17   Borgna 1997*a*, 278, fig. 6.9 (Phaistos, LM IIIB–C).

18   Popham 1965, pl. 82b, bottom right, where it is called a wavy border; Borgna 1997*a*, 278, fig. 6.1 (Phaistos); *Kastri*, 287, fig. 8q; Mook and Coulson 1997, 344, fig. 8.23 (Kavousi–*Kastro*, Phase II); *Khania II*, 140, fig. 31, pl. 36.84-P 0717; Rethemiotakis 1997, 323, fig. 34a.

19   Rethemiotakis 1997, 315, fig. 23f (Kastelli Pediada, later phase); *Kastri*, 288, fig. 9v, w; Popham 1965, 329, fig. 8.56 (Knossos); Watrous 1992, 109, fig. 68.1920 (Kommos LM IIIB–C); *Khania II*, pl. 36.84-P 0411.

20   Prokopiou 1997, 377, fig. 18f (Sybrita/Thronos); Borgna 1997*a*, 289, fig. 24 (Phaistos).

21   *Khania II*, pl. 38.71-P 0731.

22   Rethemiotakis 1998, 167, pl. 34–6 (rhyton from Moires, vase from Gortyn, face cup from Phaistos — all LM IIIB–SM); Koehl 2006, 84, fig. 4.74, pl. 8.

23   Prent 2005, 189 n. 134.

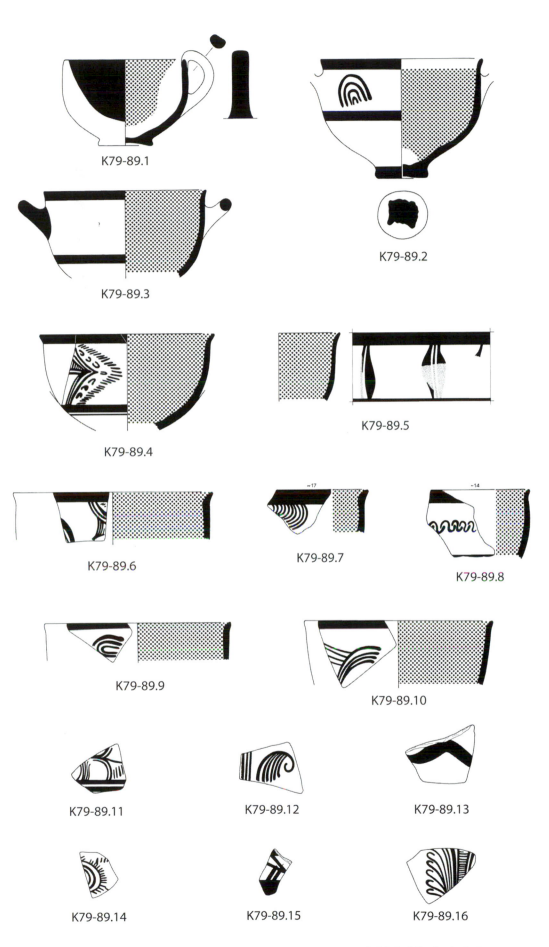

K79-89.1

K79-89.2

K79-89.3

K79-89.4

K79-89.5

K79-89.6

K79-89.7

K79-89.8

K79-89.9

K79-89.10

K79-89.11

K79-89.12

K79-89.13

K79-89.14

K79-89.15

K79-89.16

*Fig. 6.2. Commercial Quarter, pottery from K 79-89 (**K79-89.1**–**16**). Scale 1:3.*

Well-preserved surfaces. Multiple stems and strokes, possibly alternating multiple arcs. For decoration, cf. Andreadaki-Vlasaki and Papadopoulou 2007, 47, fig. 4.1 (Khamalevri, Phase Ib). LM IIIC.

K79-89.11　Deep bowl or cup (FIG. 6.2). Max. pres. H. 3.7. Single fragment from body. Fine, medium-soft, very pale brown (10YR 8/3) fabric and slip. Worn red (2.5YR 4/8) paint. Minoan flower. For motif, cf. Popham 1965, 328, fig. 7.45 (Knossos). LM IIIC early.

K79-89.12　Deep bowl or cup (FIG. 6.2). Max. pres. H. 4. Single fragment from body. Fine, medium-soft, reddish yellow (7.5YR 7/6) fabric. Very pale brown (10YR 8/3) slip. Black paint worn to brown shadow. Worn exterior surfaces, well-preserved on interior. Multiple stemmed spiral in panel. LM IIIC.

K79-89.13　Deep bowl or cup (FIG. 6.2). Max. pres. H. 4.4. Single fragment from body. Fine, very soft, reddish yellow (7.5YR 7/6) fabric. Very pale brown (10YR 8/3) slip. Worn red-brown paint. Very worn surfaces. Wavy band. Possibly a wavy band cup like **K79.1** (or the same cup). Late LM IIIC–SM.

K79-89.14　Kylix or deep bowl (FIG. 6.2). Max. pres. H. 3.6. Single fragment from body. Fine, soft, reddish yellow (7.5YR 7/6) fabric. Very pale brown (10YR 8/3) slip. Black paint worn to brown shadow. Worn surfaces. Fringed spiral. LM IIIC.

K79-89.15　Kylix ? (FIG. 6.2). Max. pres. H. 3.8. Single fragment from body, near rim. Fine, soft, reddish yellow (7.5YR 7/6) fabric. Very pale brown (10YR 8/3) slip. Black paint worn to brown shadow. Worn surfaces. Chevrons. LM IIIC.

K79-89.16　Kylix (FIG. 6.2). Max. pres. H. 4.4. Single fragment from body. Fine, soft, reddish yellow (5YR 7/6) fabric. Very pale brown (10YR 8/3) slip. Red (10R 4/8) paint. Worn surfaces, but very smooth. Vertical hatched band in centre, with outline and multiple hooked stems coming out of centre like flower. LM IIIC.

K79-89.17　Basin (FIG. 6.3). D. rim est. 24. Single fragment (three sherds) from rim, including handle attachment. Fine, medium-soft, reddish yellow (5YR 7/6) fabric. White (10YR 8/2) slip. Red (2.5YR 5/8) paint. Flattened rim, ridge below with horizontal handle. Bands on exterior and interior. Bands around outer edge of rim. For shape and decoration, cf. Andreadaki-Vlasaki and Papadopoulou 2007, 46, fig. 3.26–27; 47, fig. 4.16 (Khamalevri, Phase Ib). LM IIIC.

K79-89.18　Krater (PLATE 19 *b*, FIG. 6.3). Max. pres. H. 12.8; D. rim est. 35–36. Large fragment (four sherds) from rim, three non-joining fragments. Fine, soft, reddish yellow (5YR 7/6) fabric with tiny white inclusions and some mica. White (10YR 8/2) slip. Black paint. Worn surfaces. Panelled decoration: bird beside vertical bands with scalloped edge, panels of solid squares alternating with crosshatched squares with dots. Publication: Seiradaki, fig. 25b (part with bird). LM IIIC.

K79-89.19　Krater (FIG. 6.3). D. rim est. 38–40. Three joining and one non-joining fragment from rim. Fine, soft, reddish yellow (5YR 7/8) fabric with a few red phyllite and white carbonate inclusions. Very pale brown (10YR 8/3) slip. Black paint worn to dark red (2.5YR 3/6). Fringed curvilinear motifs (spirals?), other curvilinear motifs with scallops and arc filler. Strokes on top of rim. Unusual fabric, possibly imported. LM IIIC.

K79-89.20　Krater (FIG. 6.3). Max. pres. H. 4.8. Single fragment from rim. Fine, soft, reddish yellow (5YR 7/6) fabric. Very pale brown (10YR 8/4) slip. Dark brown (7.5YR 3/2) paint. Worn surfaces, especially on interior. Fringed multiple pendent loops, above crosshatched motif with scalloped edge. LM IIIC.

K79-89.21　Krater (FIG. 6.3). D. rim est. 32. Single fragment (two sherds) from rim. Fine, soft, porous, sandy, very pale brown (10YR 7/4) fabric with tiny black inclusions. Creamy, thick, very pale brown (10YR 8/3) slip. Worn black paint, well-preserved on interior. Unusual shape with body curving in to rim. Stacked chevrons, fringed curvilinear pattern. Strokes on top of rim. LM IIIC.

K79-89.22　Krater (FIG. 6.3). D. rim est. 26. Single fragment (two sherds) from rim. Fine, soft, reddish yellow (5YR 7/6) fabric. Very pale brown (10YR 8/3) slip. Black paint worn to shadow. Very worn surfaces. Filled medallion and floral spray. LM IIIC.

K79-89.23　Krater (FIG. 6.3). Max. pres. H. 7.2. Single fragment from rim. Fine, medium-soft, very pale brown (10YR 8/3) fabric and slip. Black paint. Well-preserved surfaces, especially on interior. Outlined curvilinear motif, oblique bands with scalloped edge, regiments of short strokes. Strokes on rim. LM IIIC.

K79-89.24　Pyxis (FIG. 6.3). Max. pres. H. 4.3; D. base 15. Single fragment (two sherds) from base. Fine reddish yellow (5YR 7/6) fabric with rare inclusions (up to 1 mm). Very pale brown (10YR 8/3) slip. Black paint. Well-preserved surfaces. Uncertain shape. Identified as a tankard by Seiradaki, but interior not painted; possibly a pyxis or basket kalathos. Base has ridge with oblique incisions. Double axes with horizontal scallops between blades. Publication: Seiradaki, fig. 22b. LM IIIC.

K79-89.25　Stirrup jar (FIG. 6.3). Max. pres. H. 3.5. Single fragment (two sherds) from top, preserving handle attachment. Fine, soft, reddish yellow (7.5YR 7/6) fabric. White (10YR 8/2) slip. Black paint worn to shadow. Very worn surfaces. On top, fringed pattern (Minoan flower?) and stacked arcs. On shoulder, alternating arcs. LM IIIC.

K79-89.26　Jug (FIG. 6.3). D. rim est. 12. Single fragment from rim, preserving part of handle attachment. Fine, rather hard, porous, reddish yellow (7.5YR 7/6) fabric. White (10YR 8/2) slip. Red (2.5YR 4/8) paint. Band at rim. Band below rim on interior. For shape, cf. Warren 2007, 343, fig. 8.P169 (Knossos, early LM IIIC). LM IIIC.

K79-89.27　Jug (FIG. 6.3). D. rim est. 7. Single fragment from rim. Fine, rather soft, reddish yellow (5YR 7/6) fabric. White (10YR 8/2) slip. Black paint, worn to shadow. Worn surfaces. Wavy band on neck. Band on interior below rim. LM IIIC.

K79-89.28　Closed vessel (FIG. 6.3). Max. pres. H. 6.5. Two fragments from body. Fine, soft, very pale brown (10YR 8/4) fabric and slip. Black paint worn to dark brown (7.5YR 4/4). Well-preserved surfaces. Closed vessel, probably a jug or stirrup jar. Interlocking multiple arcs with crosshatched lozenges. Imported? Publication: Seiradaki, fig. 26c (one of fragments). LM IIIC.

K79-89.29　Face rhyton (FIG. 6.3). Max. pres. H. 4.5. Single fragment from side of face with ear. Fine, soft, very pale brown (10YR 7/3) fabric. White (10YR 8/2) slip. Worn black paint. Cylindrical head, with plastic ear attached and some surface modelling for cheeks. Painted decoration on face: short oblique strokes; arcs behind ear. LM IIIC.

Coarse Wares

K79-89.30　Stirrup jar (FIG. 6.3). Max. pres. H. 8.2; Th. 1.0. Single fragment from body. Coarse reddish yellow (7.5YR 7/6) fabric with frequent red and grey phyllites and hard white angular inclusions. White (10YR 8/1) slip. Very dark greyish brown (10YR 3/2) to dark yellowish brown (10YR 3/4) paint. Wavy band above bands, possibly debased octopus. LM IIIC.

Room K 112

The first actual room in the building, K 112 was entered from K 79. K 78 may have been part of the same room, but it was at a lower level.[24] The notebook records the following information about the pottery found here. Coarse wares included the following: six

---

24　*Karphi*, 88–9.

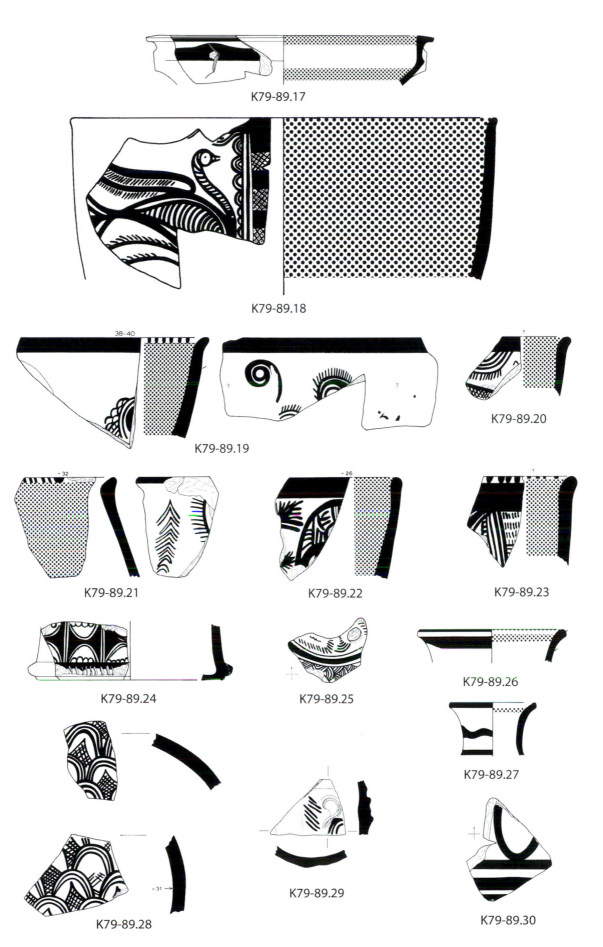

K79-89.17

K79-89.18

K79-89.19

K79-89.20

K79-89.21

K79-89.22

K79-89.23

K79-89.24

K79-89.25

K79-89.26

K79-89.27

K79-89.28

K79-89.29

K79-89.30

*Fig. 6.3. Commercial Quarter, pottery from K 79-89 (**K79-89.17–30**). Scale 1:3.*

pithoi of Types 5, 8, 12, 14, 17, 18; two pithoid jars of Types 3 and 9; the base of jar of Type 7; a Type 1 kalathos; dishes of Types 1–6; basins of Types 1 and 7; tripod legs; and a small tankard spout. Fine wares included several bowls of Types 1 and 2, a pyxis of Type 2, and a kylix stem. Objects found in the room included a bronze knife with rivet holes (548),[25] a flat stone tool, and a terracotta spool.

It is clear that the room was used for storage and probably also for cooking. There is almost no fine ware, and the single sherd that is preserved has a fringed crosshatched triangle. The trays are of the usual sort, with finger impressions on the rim.

Pottery Catalogue: K 112

Fine Wares

K112.1   Closed vessel (FIG. 6.4). Max. pres. H. 4. Single fragment from body. Fine, soft, chalky, very pale brown (10YR 8/4) fabric. White (10YR 8/2) slip. Black paint, worn to dark brown (7.5YR 3/2). Worn surfaces. Jug or stirrup jar. Crosshatched, fringed triangle. LM IIIC.

Coarse Wares

K112.2   Tray (FIG. 6.4). Max. pres. H. 4.1; D. rim est. 33. Single fragment from rim. Coarse, hard red (10R 5/6) fabric with schist and mica inclusions (1–2 mm). Mottled red and black surface. Traces of burning. Rim pinched out to form crude spout (or finger impression). LM IIIC.
K112.3   Cooking dish or tray (FIG. 6.4). D. rim est. 30. Single fragment from rim to near base. Coarse, hard, red (2.5YR 5/8) fabric with frequent schist, phyllite, and hard white angular inclusions (1–2 mm). No burning. Finger impressions on rim. LM IIIC.
K112.4   Basin or pithos (FIG. 6.4). D. base est. 15–16. Large fragment (two sherds) from base. Coarse red (2.5YR 5/8) fabric with large (2–5 mm) schist and phyllite inclusions. Burned on exterior. Overhanging ledge near bottom. Label unclear, may also be from K 102. LM IIIC.
K112.5   Pithos (FIG. 6.4). Single fragment from body. Coarse, soft, reddish yellow (5YR 6/8) fabric with frequent phyllites, hard angular black and white inclusions. Raised band with impressed ovals, with short strokes above and below. LM IIIC.

Room K 78

K 78 may have been part of the same room as K 112. To enter Room K 78, one had to step down from K 112. The pottery is reported as being much broken, and it included fragments from four kraters, including one with bird decoration from K 76 and K 77 and one with a tree from K 75.[26] The notebook adds that there was also a pyxis sherd, a krater in gritty clay, another krater with a white slip, and some fragments of kylikes. Although there was a good deal of pottery preserved in the boxes from K 78, none of it was considered worth cataloguing and drawing. It included a deep bowl handle and a fragment with a hatched circle or spiral, kraters with filler motifs or curved strokes below the rim, a large jug or jar with a debased octopus design, a coarse jug or jar with a wavy band or debased octopus, and a vertical elliptical handle in blue ware. Few objects

were found in the room; only a bronze stylus-shaped rod (499) is recorded.

Room K 77

The floor of K 77 was at two levels, with a rock ledge in the northwest corner. The jar stand along the north wall may have been a fireplace, but there was no sign of burning.

The pottery was listed in the publication as usual, and mentions fragments of a krater with a bird decoration, of which the larger remaining part came from K 76;[27] These fragments were not located. The notebook added the following information about the pottery. There were some pithos sherds, many pithoid jars of Type 1, a two-handled jug of Type 1, a scuttle of Type 1, a lid of Type 1, a tripod of Type 4, a bowl, sherds from a 'tree' krater (the same as one in K 75), and fine ware mostly from bowls. Several sherds found in the boxes were not catalogued. These included a large strap handle, a tiny fragment from a kylix with vertical strokes on the rim, and a body sherd from a jug with filler ornaments on the shoulder. The pottery gives little suggestion as to the possible uses of the room, but it is interesting that there are joins with pieces from K 78 and from the neighbouring K 76, an area which contained a large amount of fragmentary pottery, possibly indicating that this room was built over earlier material that also underlay the street K 76. The tankard or mug finds a parallel in one of the Ta Mnemata tombs (**M4.7**). The open vessel may be a krater, and its decoration does not find any parallels. The other fragments are from jars or stirrup jars with wavy lines, possibly from transport stirrup jars.

Objects from the room included the following: part of a bronze rectangular rod (495), a bone pin (494),[28] and two conical stone beads or whorls (457, 534); the notebook adds that there were no obvious animal bones.

Pottery Catalogue: K 77

Fine Wares

K77.1   Mug or tankard (PLATE 22 *e*, FIG. 6.4). D. rim est. 17. Single fragment from rim. Fine, soft, porous, reddish yellow (7.5YR 7/6) fabric. Red (2.5YR 4/8) paint. Beaded decoration on rim. Monochrome. Cf. **K121.7**, **M4.7**. LM IIIC.
K77.2   Krater (?) (FIG. 6.4). Max. pres. H. 7.5. Single fragment from body, near rim. Fine, soft, very pale brown (10YR 7/4) fabric with tiny white inclusions. White (10YR 8/2) slip. Black paint faded to yellowish red (5YR 4/6). Worn surfaces. S-shaped curve to body. Possibly large deep bowl or krater. Interlocking spirals. Publication: Seiradaki, fig. 25e. LM IIIC.

---

25   *Karphi*, pl. 28.2.
26   *Karphi*, 88–9.
27   Probably the one pictured on Seiradaki, fig. 25a.
28   *Karphi*, pl. 28.4.

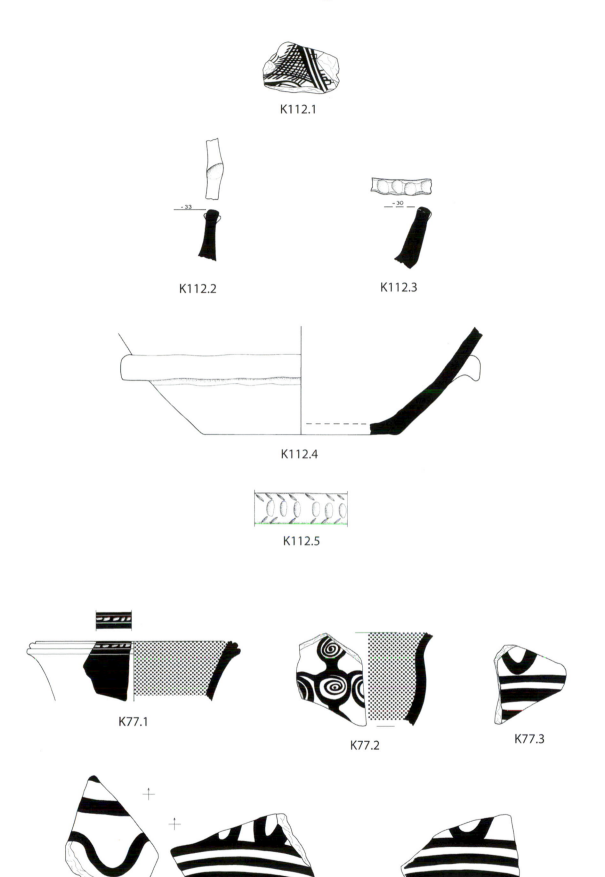

Fig. 6.4. *Commercial Quarter, pottery from K 112 (**K112.1**–5) and K 77 (**K77.1**–5). Scale 1:3.*

Medium-Coarse Wares

K77.3   Stirrup jar (FIG. 6.4). Max. pres. H. 6; Th. 1.3. Single fragment from body. Medium-coarse, medium-soft, porous, reddish yellow (7.5YR 7/6) fabric with frequent tiny white inclusions. White (10YR 8/2) slip. Reddish brown (2.5YR 4/4) paint. Worn surfaces. Wavy band above bands, possibly debased octopus. Publication: Day 2005, 435, fig. 1.6. LM IIIC.

Coarse Wares

K77.4   Stirrup jar (PLATE 10 *f*, FIG. 6.4). Max. pres. H. 9.5; Th. 0.7. Two non-joining fragments from body, one from near neck. Coarse, soft, light red (2.5YR 6/8) fabric with grey phyllites and hard white angular inclusions (1–4 mm). Thick, creamy, very pale brown (10YR 8/4) slip. Dark red (10R 3/6) paint. Well-preserved surfaces. Wavy band, possibly a debased octopus design. Publication: Day 2005, 435, fig. 1.4. LM IIIC.

K77.5   Stirrup jar (FIG. 6.4). Max. pres. H. 6; Th. 0.8–1.1. Single fragment from body. Coarse reddish yellow (5YR 7/6) fabric with frequent phyllite and carbonate inclusions (1–4 mm). Thick very pale brown (10YR 8/4) slip. Very dark greyish brown (10YR 3/2) paint. Well-preserved surfaces. Wavy band above bands, perhaps debased octopus. Day 2005, 435, fig. 1.5. LM IIIC.

Room K 116

This small square room had a rocky floor and a ledge along the north side, on which may have stood the terracotta goddesses found in the room.[29] The publication mentions fragments of at least two goddesses, while the notebook says that there were three, two in white (i.e. buff), the third in red fabric. Fragments of a terracotta plaque were also found. Some of the fragments of terracotta figures of goddesses with upraised arms found in the boxes may come from this deposit, but none of these was labelled. There were no snake tubes found in the room with the goddesses. The other objects found in the room are ordinary domestic items: a grinder (607), a whetstone (627),[30] and three cylindrical terracotta spindle whorls (624, 625, 626).

The pottery included more whole fine vessels than general. In addition to the catalogued fine ware, there were at least three stirrup jars and six or more pyxides, including one of Type 4 with a small cup on the rim, here identified as a pyxis with no find spot written on it (**K116.2**). The kylix base published by Seiradaki as coming from this deposit could not be found.[31] Coarse ware was said to be as usual, and Seiradaki published a scuttle as coming from this room, which could not be located.[32] The notebook lists additional coarse ware from K 116. There were at least two pithoid jars with rims of Type 25 [*sic*], one with vertical, the other with horizontal handles, and a casual sherd from Type 21. Also found were four or more kalathoi of Types 1 and 2, another scuttle of Type 1, tripods, and a coarse vat. Fine ware included a bowl with dark bands (**K116.7**) Additional sherds from the boxes included a blue ware rim pinched to form spout (possibly the Type 8 blue ware jug mentioned in the notebook) and a lug handle.

Two elements of this deposit stand out. First of all, it seems to be a small shrine of the goddess with upraised arms, since there were fragments of two or possibly three terracotta figures.[33] Although there was also part of a plaque, the deposit lacked the snake tubes or offering stands that regularly accompanied such figures.[34] Second, the pottery that has been preserved seems to be among the latest found on the site, especially the stirrup jar (**K116.4**),[35] amphora (**K116.3**), and pyxis (**K116.1**).[36] The jug (**K116.6**) is of a standard LM IIIC shape, with parallels at Knossos and on the mainland.[37] Similarly, the jar finds a good parallel in early LM IIIC Kastelli Pediada.[38] The stirrup jar (**K116.4**) with its high foot, however, looks later. The shape finds parallels at mainland and Cretan sites of late LM IIIC–SM date,[39] but it is also close to a stirrup jar from a tholos tomb at Vasiliki which has been dated to EPG;[40] the Karphi example, however, lacks the conical knob and the linear design on the shoulder still curves somewhat, so it should be earlier. The decoration of crosshatched triangles is found on many LM IIIC and SM stirrup jars, but usually in connection with other motifs; the use of bands on the neck of the spout instead of horizontal strokes makes it look earlier than SM, but that may be a result of local variation, rather than an indicator of date. A date early in SM seems indicated. The small amphora (**K116.3**) also looks late, although it is not certain whether the vessel is a jug, flask, or amphora. A similar decoration on a larger amphora can be found in the Knossos North Cemetery of SM date.[41] Finally, it is interesting to note the presence of the blue ware deep bowl (**K116.5**), since a large number of misfired deep bowls were also found in close connection with the Temple (K 1); it is possible that these misfired vessels had some specific ritual association.

---

29   *Karphi*, 88–9.

30   *Karphi*, pl. 30.3.

31   Seiradaki, fig. 18.4.

32   Seiradaki, fig. 8, lamp 1.

33   Day 2009, 142–3.

34   See, for example, the contemporary LM IIIC shrines at Kavousi–*Vronda* (Day 1997, 401–2), Vasiliki–*Kephala* (Eliopoulos 1998, 301–13) and Khalasmenos (Tsipopoulou 2001, 2009).

35   *RMDP*, 292–3, fig. 100.241 (Epidauros Limera, LM IIIC–SM import).

36   For the general decoration, cf. Mook 1993, 158, 345, fig. 89.P2.20 of earliest LM IIIC date; for the vertical chevron panel, cf. *Kastri*, 289, fig. 10j.

37   Cadogan 1967, 262, fig. 3.12 (Knossos, Kephala tholos); Warren 2007, 343, fig. 8.P169, P197 (Knossos); Mountjoy 1986, 142, fig. 176.2 (Mycenae, LH IIIC early).

38   Rethemiotakis 1997, 310, fig. 11c.

39   For decoration, cf. *RMDP*, 292, fig. 100.241–2 (Epidauros Limera and Pellana, Late LH IIIC–SM). For shape and decoration, Coldstream and Catling 1996, 163, fig. 112.3 (SM).

40   Tsipopoulou, Vagnetti and Liston 2003, 95, fig. 8.5, 15.5 (EPG).

41   Coldstream and Catling 1996, 88, fig. 84.16 (SM); 165, pl. 165.1.

Fig. 6.5. *Commercial Quarter, pottery from K 116 (**K116.1–8**). Scale 1:3.*

The evidence from the pottery, then suggests that K 116 was in use when the SM style was just being introduced, and possibly after much of the rest of the settlement had gone out of use. It may be that this shrine is a late one, in use at the very end of the settlement's history, perhaps when other areas or shrines had been abandoned. The presence of the oven just outside in K 79-89, however, together with the very fragmentary state of the goddess statues, suggests that at the end the room was not being used for ritual practices.

Pottery Catalogue: K 116

Fine Wares

K116.1   Pyxis (PLATE 19 *c*, FIG. 6.5). H. 8.6; D. base 11.9; D. rim 8.7. Mended from 16 fragments, one non-joining fragment. 80% preserved, including full profile; missing fragments of base and body, tops of handles. Fine, soft, reddish yellow (7.5YR 7/6) fabric. Very pale brown (10YR 8/3) slip. Black paint, now worn to brown shadow. Worn surfaces. Burned on one side. Panelled decoration: vertical chevrons between vertical bands; solid, outlined vertical loop with strokes as filler — all between vertical bands. Publication: Day 2009, 143, fig. 12.6. LM IIIC late.

K116.2   Basket kalathos (FIG. 6.5). H. 15 (with handles 18.5); D. base 14.8; D. rim 21.8. Partially mended from 30 fragments. Full profile, most of rim, both handles, excrescent cup, and most of base preserved; missing centre of base and much of middle of body. Fine, very soft, light red (2.5YR 6/8) fabric. Very pale brown (10YR 8/3) slip. Reddish brown (2.5YR 4/4) paint. Burned grey on interior and on patches of body. Surfaces coated with sediment, but when cleaned entire surface comes off. Type 6 kalathos. Elliptical basket handles on rim, with excrescent cup next to one handle. Once decorated, but surfaces too badly preserved to make out. No label with find spot. LM IIIC.

K116.3   Jug or amphora (FIG. 6.5). Max. pres. H. 6.5; Max. pres. D. 12. Five joining fragments from top, including most of shoulder, lower neck, and one handle. Fine, medium-soft fabric, burned to light grey (2.5Y 7/2). Worn crackled black paint. Vertical panel of crosshatching, with tailed spiral; arc filler between tail of spiral and panel. Bands below. Publication: Day 2009, 143, fig. 12.6. SM.

K116.4   Stirrup jar (HM 11069) (PLATE 19 *d*, FIG. 6.5). H. 12; D. base 3.6; max. D. 9. Intact, except for rim of spout and 33% of base, which are restored. Fine, soft, very pale brown (10YR 8/4) fabric. Dark yellowish brown (10YR 3/4) to dark brown (7.5YR 3/2) paint. False spout slightly tilted back. Crosshatched triangles on shoulder, bands on body. Publication: Seiradaki, fig. 22k, pl. 6a, left (labelled K 23); Day 2009, 143, fig. 12.6. SM.

Medium-Coarse Wares

K116.5   Deep bowl or cup (PLATE 19 *e*, FIG. 6.5). Max. pres. H. 7; D. rim 10.6–14. Eight joining fragments. 65% preserved, including nearly complete profile; missing base and handles. Medium-coarse, rather hard, blue ware fabric, reddish yellow (5YR 6/8) to greenish grey (5BG 5/1) with infrequent large (1–1.5 mm) hard white inclusions. Misfired. Shape is totally wonky. Publication: Day 2009, 143, fig. 12.6. LM IIIC.

K116.6   Jug (PLATE 19 *f*, FIG. 6.5). H. 16.8 (with handle 17); D. base 8.7; D. rim 7.8. Nearly complete; restored from four fragments. 95% preserved; missing small piece of rim. Medium-coarse reddish yellow (5YR 5/6) fabric with infrequent fine inclusions (up to 2 mm). Very worn surfaces. Burned. Publication: Day 2009, 143, fig. 12.6. LM IIIC.

K116.7   Jar (PLATE 20 *a*, FIG. 6.5). H. 19.3–19.5; D. base 12.5; D. rim 15.8. Restored from 38 fragments. 80% preserved, including full profile, both handles; missing rim and body fragments. Medium-coarse light reddish brown (2.5YR 6/4) fabric with red and grey phyllites (1–2 mm). Thick, creamy, very pale brown (10YR 8/4) slip. Black paint, red in a few places. Well-preserved surfaces. Burned on upper body on one side, before broken. Wavy band in handle zone, bands below; oblique strokes on handles. Interior has band near rim and splatters of paint. Publication: Seiradaki, fig. 3.10, pl. 1e, right; Mountjoy 2007, 232, fig. 4.5; Day 2009, 143, fig. 12.6. LM IIIC.

Coarse Wares

K116.8   Lid (FIG. 6.5). H. 3.5; D. base 9.9; D. knob 3. Complete except for a few chips. Coarse light red (2.5YR 6/6) fabric with red and grey phyllites (1–2 mm), schist, and mica. Patch of burning on bottom. Flat disc with bevelled edges, concave knob on top. LM IIIC.

THE CLIFF HOUSES, EASTERN BLOCK (ROOMS K 75, K 110, K 118, K 119)

The excavators had little to say about this building except that it was unclear how the rooms were entered.[42] Only the foundations of the northern walls were preserved, almost at the level of the street that ran alongside them to the north.

Room K 75

This room may have been entered from the street K 72 on the east. The pottery was listed as usual, and mention was made of two pyxides, one of Type 7 (**K75.10**) and one of Type 5 with a crosshatched butterfly (**K75.9**). The only pottery illustrated in Seiradaki, a cooking dish[43] and an amphora,[44] were both missing. The notebook provides the following additional information on the pottery. There were sherds from at least three pithoi and another in buff clay with chain and chevron patterns; jars of all types; tripods and basins; kalathoi, including one with base of Type 1 and rim of Type 3; dishes of Types 6 and 4; a lid of Type 1 but with incised lines only, a large red vessel, two-handled jugs of Type 3, and a scuttle of Type 1 (**K75.13**). Fine ware included a bowl, the two pyxides, and sherds from a krater with an orange 'tree' design (**K75.7**). Among the pottery found in the boxes but not catalogued were fragments of deep bowls (three with spirals, one with another curvilinear motif), a jug with a rope in the middle of the handle, a small burned jug with vertical strokes on the neck, a large burned jug with vertical strokes on the shoulder, a fine pithoid jar with a chevron on a ridge below the rim, and a coarse lid with ridges. Objects from the room included a bronze barbed arrowhead (454),[45] a fragment of bronze (489), a burnished black bone pin (488), a conical stone bead

---

42   *Karphi*, 93.
43   Seiradaki, fig. 6.6, pl. 2g.
44   Seiradaki, fig. 8.3.
45   *Karphi*, pl. 29.1.

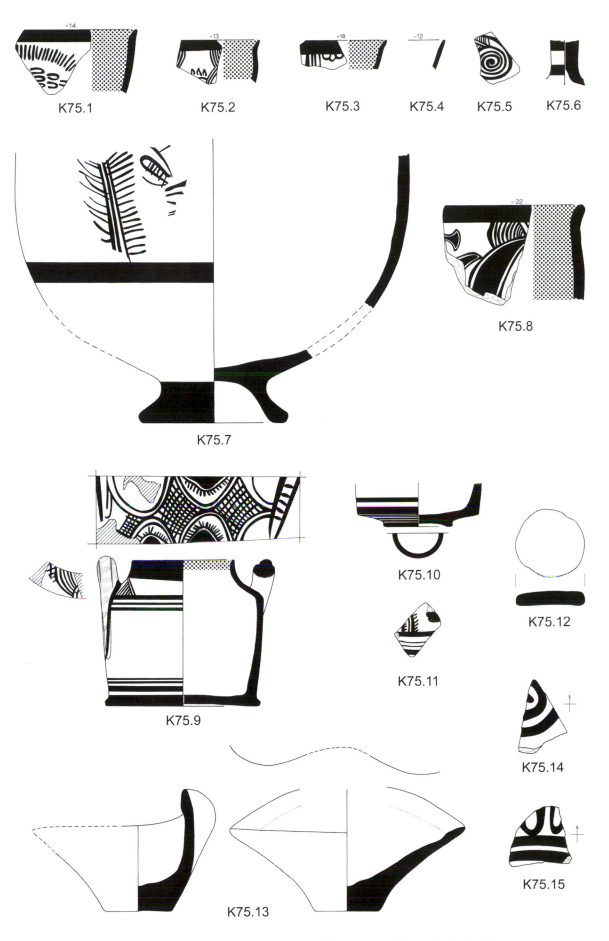

K75.1

K75.2

K75.3

K75.4

K75.5

K75.6

K75.7

K75.8

K75.9

K75.10

K75.11

K75.12

K75.13

K75.14

K75.15

Fig. 6.6. *Eastern Cliff Houses, pottery from K 75 (**K75.1–15**). Scale 1:3.*

or whorl (453), an obsidian core (452), and a large terracotta spool. The notebook also mentions ox horns from this room.

Much of the fine ware is in small fragments and may have been ground into the floor rather than being in use at the time of abandonment. Deep bowl or cup fragments have Minoan flower, arcs, scallops and panel, spiral, and blob or monochrome decoration; all motifs that were popular throughout LM IIIC. **K75.1**, however, has a type of Minoan flower that is common in early LM IIIC.[46] One of the kraters (**K75.7**) has a close parallel for its decoration from Kastelli Pediada from the later part of early LM IIIC.[47] The other (**K75.8**) shows a double axe between horns of consecration, a not uncommon motif.[48] The pyxis (**K75.9**) has a good LM IIIC fringed style decoration, as does also the stirrup jar fragment (**K75.11**). The carinated pyxis (**K75.10**) is one of only two found on the site. The two stirrup jar fragments (**K75.14–15**) are probably left over from earlier phases of occupation; the number of fragments was not sufficient to suppose that an actual stirrup jar still stood in the room at the time of abandonment (as was the case in K 110). The material from the room suggests an ordinary domestic function, with a krater, pyxides, and a scuttle in use at the time of abandonment. The bronze arrowhead suggests that the inhabitants had a greater level of wealth than the pottery might indicate.

Pottery Catalogue: K 75

Fine Wares

K75.1   Deep bowl or cup (PLATE 1 *i*, FIG. 6.6). D. rim est. 14. Single fragment from rim. Fine, medium soft, porous, sandy, very pale brown (10YR 8/3) fabric and slip. Worn dark brown (7.5YR 3/2–4/4) paint. Worn surfaces, especially on interior. Minoan flower with U-pattern in centre. LM IIIC early.

K75.2   Deep bowl or cup (FIG. 6.6). D. rim est. 13. Single fragment (2 sherds) from rim. Fine, porous, pink (7.5YR 7/4) fabric. Very pale brown (10YR 8/3) slip. Black paint worn to shadow. Worn exterior surfaces, well-preserved on interior. Alternating arcs and scalloped edging. LM IIIC.

K75.3   Deep bowl or cup (FIG. 6.6). D. rim est. 18. Single fragment from rim. Fine, soft, reddish yellow (5YR 7/6) fabric. Very pale brown (10YR 8/3) slip. Black paint worn to shadow. Very worn surfaces. Metopal pattern with scallops hanging from rim band. LM IIIC.

K75.4   Deep bowl or cup (FIG. 6.6). D. rim est. 12. Single fragment (2 sherds) from rim. Fine reddish yellow (7.5YR 7/6) fabric. Worn red-brown paint. Monochrome or blob decoration. LM IIIC.

K75.5   Deep bowl or cup (FIG. 6.6). Max. pres. H. 4.1. Single fragment from body. Fine, soft, porous, reddish yellow (7.5YR 7/6) fabric. Very pale brown (10YR 8/3) slip. Black to red (2.5YR 4/8) paint. Worn surfaces. Spiral with filler of short strokes. LM IIIC.

K75.6   Kylix (FIG. 6.6). Max. pres. H. 3.6. Single fragment from stem. Fine, medium-hard, reddish yellow (5YR 7/6) fabric. Very pale brown (10YR 8/3) slip. Dark reddish brown (2.5YR 3/4) paint. Well-preserved surfaces. Stem has deep circular depression in centre, but is not pierced. Bands. LM IIIC.

K75.7   Krater (FIG. 6.6). Max. pres. H. 12.5; D. base 12. Large fragments from base (five sherds) and body (five sherds), 80 body

fragments. Fine, chalky, very soft reddish yellow (7.5YR 7/6) to pink (7.5YR 8/4) fabric. White (10YR 8/2) slip. Weak red (2.5YR 4/2) to red (2.5YR 4/6) paint. Very worn surfaces. Pedestal base is coarser, with rather frequent inclusions. Crude design of fringed multiple vertical bands, hatched loop next to it; possibly panelled decoration. Once probably painted inside, but paint gone. Possibly the krater mentioned in the notebook as joining with sherds from K 76. LM IIIC.

K75.8   Krater (PLATE 2 *a*, FIG. 6.6). D. rim 22. Single fragment from rim. Fine, medium-hard pink (5YR 7/4) fabric. White (10YR 8/2) slip. Crackled black paint, worn in places to shadow. Well-preserved surfaces. Double axe between horns of consecration, with arc filler. LM IIIC.

K75.9   Pyxis (PLATE 20 *b*, FIG. 6.6). H. 11.7 (with handles 12); D. base 12.4; D. rim 8.2. Restored from 20 fragments. 80–85% preserved; missing parts of handle and body. Fine, soft, porous, pink (7.5YR 7/4) to light brown (7.5YR 6/4) fabric with some tiny sand-sized inclusions. Red (2.5YR 5/6) paint. Worn surfaces on one side, better-preserved on other. Burned on one side. Handles round and slashed. Crosshatched lozenges with fringed, outlined, solid loops in between; on shoulder, hatched triangles and alternating arcs. Publication: Seiradaki, fig. 24e, pl. 7b, bottom right (mislabelled K 124). LM IIIC.

K75.10   Pyxis (FIG. 6.6). D. base 5. Single fragment from base. Fine, soft, reddish yellow (5YR 7/6) fabric. Very pale brown (10YR 8/3) slip. Yellowish red (5YR 5/8) paint. Worn surfaces. Carinated body. Bands. Cf. **K80.8**. LM IIIC.

K75.11   Stirrup jar (FIG. 6.6). Max. pres. H. 4.2. Single fragment from shoulder, preserving handle scar. Fine, soft, reddish yellow (5YR 7/6) fabric. Very pale brown (10YR 8/4) slip. Red (2.5YR 4/8) paint. Well-preserved surfaces. Probably stirrup jar. Fringed multiple upright loops. LM IIIC.

Medium-Coarse Wares

K75.12   Stopper or lid (FIG. 6.6). D. 5.5. Intact. Medium-coarse blue ware fabric, reddish yellow (7.5YR 6/6) on surface, greenish grey (5G 5/1) at core, with grey phyllites and hard white angular inclusions. Fragment of pot cut down into rough circle to use as stopper. LM IIIC.

Coarse Wares

K75.13   Scuttle (FIG. 6.6). H. 6.7–9.9; D. base 5.3. Mended from six fragments. 60% preserved, including entire base and part of rim where handle pushed in; missing handle and part of rim. Coarse reddish brown (5YR 5/4) fabric, burned grey (N5/), with frequent schist (1–7 mm) and hard white angular inclusions. Probably burned in firing. Groove on interior of rim. LM IIIC.

K75.14   Stirrup jar (FIG. 6.6). Max. pres. H. 5.9; Th. 0.6. Single fragment from body. Coarse, hard, reddish yellow (5YR 7/6) fabric with very frequent red and grey phyllites (1–2 mm). Very pale brown (10YR 8/4) slip. Dark reddish brown (5YR 3/2) paint. Very worn surfaces. Spiral, part of debased octopus? LM IIIC.

K75.15   Stirrup jar (FIG. 6.6). Max. pres. H. 4.5; Th. 0.6. Single fragment from body. Coarse very pale brown (10YR 7/4) fabric with frequent limestone and hard white angular inclusions. Very pale brown (10YR 8/4) slip. Worn black paint. Very worn surfaces. Wavy band above bands, possibly debased octopus. LM IIIC.

---

46   Popham 1965, 327–8, fig. 7.42, pl. 85f.
47   Rethemiotakis 1997, 324, fig. 35.
48   Rethemiotakis 1997, 322, fig. 33a; Warren 2007, 340, fig. 5.P307 and P662; Popham 1970a, 193, fig. 3.1–4 for some examples on LM III pottery.

Room K 110

There was no obvious entrance into this room, and the excavators suggested that it may have been entered from the north.[49] The plan shows an unexplained line down the middle of the room; possibly this represents a line of bedrock or a change in elevation of the floor. Pottery was listed as usual, but the fine ware included fewer deep bowls and more pyxides than was customary. The publication lists at least six pithoi and six pithoid jars, a jar with a medallion design (**K110.18**) along with a large stirrup jar with octopus design (**K110.16**) and a large pyxis in red ware with white slip (**K110.5**) with its lid (**K110.7**). The notebook adds at least four kalathoi (**K110.12–15**), tripods, and a knobbed jug. Fine ware included four stirrup jars (**K110.9–10**), one with a very flat shoulder, and a fluted bowl (**K110.2**). In addition to the catalogued pottery, the boxes produced fragments of deep bowls decorated with strokes on the rim or filler motif on body, or made of blue ware, and a fragment of a stirrup jar with bands. Objects found in the room included a piece of a bronze blade (525) and another bronze fragment (526), a bone handle (524),[50] a conical stone bead or whorl (527), a pierced slate plaque (529),[51] a MM steatite bowl and lid (530)[52] with a fragment of obsidian in it (531),[53] a circular stone disc (532),[54] a stone rubber (528), a conical terracotta spindle whorl (523), and more than 50 terracotta spools. This large number of spools suggests that there may have been a loom set up in this room, if spools were indeed another form of loomweight.[55]

The preserved pottery from K 110 constitutes one of the most interesting assemblages from Karphi, since so many nearly complete vessels were preserved, and there were few small fine sherds. The material certainly represents a group of vessels that were in use at the same time and at the end of the building's history. The fluted or moulded bowl (**K110.2**) is unique, and may have been made in imitation of palatial blossom bowls, which it resembles. The other deep bowl (**K110.1**) bears a decoration of multiple pendent loops and a lozenge with alternating strokes, similar to an example from the Kephala tomb at Knossos of very late LM IIIC date, but more organised.[56] There are more pyxides than usual, and **K110.5** is the largest example found on the site; with its large conical lid (**K110.7**), it begins to resemble later burial pyxides, like those from the Knossos North Cemetery.[57] The fringed pleonastic style decoration, however, leaves no doubt that this piece belongs to LM IIIC, and it has a close parallel in size and shape to a LM IIIC example from Vrokastro.[58] The jug (**K110.8**), while unusual in shape, finds a parallel in LM IIIC levels at Katalimata Khalasmenos.[59] None of the material in the room looks particularly early, but none of it postdates LM IIIC; the latest piece is probably the stirrup jar **K110.9**, which with its fringed decoration is still in LM IIIC and not yet SM; the other stirrup jar (**K110.10**), with its fringed multiple loops

finds many parallels among LM IIIC stirrup jars.[60] A large number of coarse kalathoi are preserved. Three show extensive burning on the interior (**K110.12, 13, 15**), suggesting that they held burning matter, perhaps coals, while the fourth (**K110.14**) is burned on the exterior and top of the interior; perhaps it held unburned matter at the bottom, possibly oil for a lamp. Finally, the tripod bowl (**K110.21**) is of a unique type for the site, although known elsewhere on Crete.[61] The huge coarse octopus stirrup jar (**K110.16**) is the sort represented by fragments from all over the site; it was probably used for storage and may have been produced in an earlier phase, since these jars when broken do not seem to have been replaced. There are no parallels for the jar (**K110.20**). The coarse lid (**K110.19**) was burned on one side on the bottom and was probably used for cooking; it finds a close parallel at Phaistos.[62] The incense burner or firebox (**K110.17**) was one of only two found on the site (a fragment was also found in the material from the temple), and there are no parallels from LM IIIC. This may have been an earlier example that was kept as an heirloom. It is a standard type for the Neopalatial era, examples having been found in numerous sites on Crete and in the islands.[63]

Pottery Catalogue: K 110

Fine Wares

K110.1   Deep bowl or cup (PLATE 1 *i*, FIG. 6.7). D. rim est. 15. Single fragment (three sherds) from rim. Fine, burned, very pale brown (10YR 7/3–7/4) fabric and slip. Black paint. Hatched lozenges with multiple pendent loops hanging from rim. LM IIIC.

K110.2   Deep bowl or cup (PLATE 20 *c*, FIG. 6.7). Max. pres. H. 10.6; D. base 5.5. Partially mended from eight joining and one non-joining fragments. 35% preserved, including half of base and 66% of lower body; missing rim and any handles. Fine, soft, very pale brown (10YR 7/3–7/4) fabric, burned or misfired, with tiny white inclusions. Black paint. 'Fluted' sides: arcade pattern or

49   *Karphi*, 93–4.
50   *Karphi*, pl. 28.4.
51   *Karphi*, pl. 30.3.
52   *Karphi*, pl. 30.1.
53   *Karphi*, pl. 30.1.
54   *Karphi*, pl. 30.4.
55   Bruun-Lundgren and Wiman 2000, 177, Type 5; Evely 2000, 502; Rahmstorf 2005.
56   Cadogan 1967, 260, fig. 2.11.
57   Coldstream and Catling 1996, pl. 215.52, for example.
58   Kanta 1980, fig. 51.8.
59   Coulson and Tsipopoulou 1994, 85, fig. 19.4; Nowicki 2008, 101, fig. 52.KP 282.
60   Kanta 1980, fig. 71.4, 5, 7 (Praisos), fig. 73.2 (Zakros); Cadogan 1967, 263, fig. 4.2 (Knossos, Kephala tholos, early LM IIIC); Preston 2005, 101; D'Agata 2007, 106, fig. 1.3. Another uncatalogued fragment of a stirrup jar from K 16-17 bears the same decoration.
61   Betancourt 1980, 3 (Type B).
62   Borgna 1997*b*, 196, fig. 5.5.
63   Or fireboxes see Georgiou 1980; 1986, 4–22, esp. pl. 3.66 of Type I.

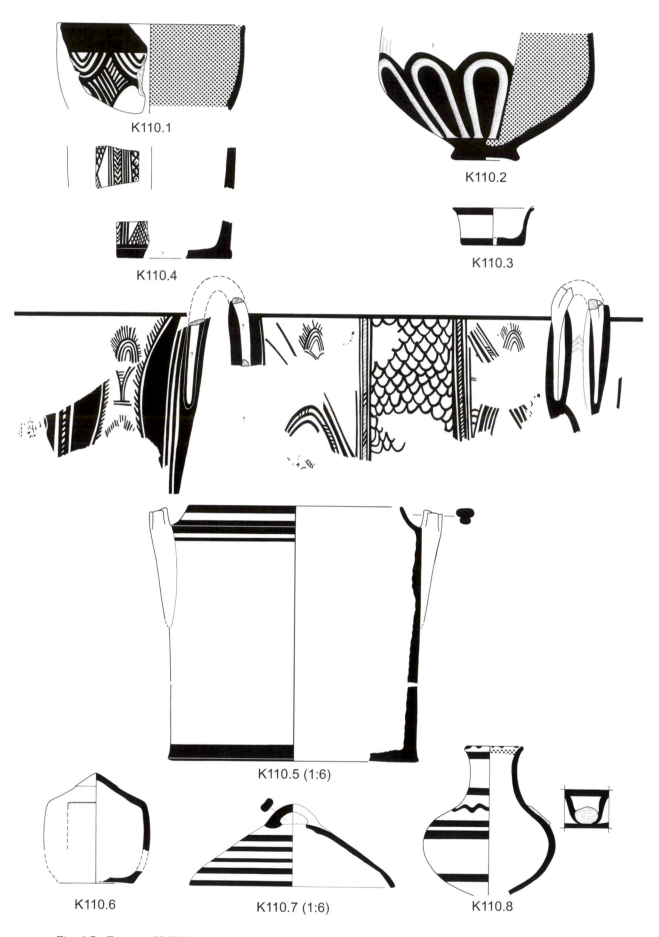

*Fig. 6.7. Eastern Cliff Houses, pottery from K 110 (**K110.1–8**). Scale 1:3 unless otherwise indicated.*

imitation of stone blossom bowl. Monochrome. Not published, but mentioned by Seiradaki.[64] LM IIIC.

K110.3 Kalathos (FIG. 6.7). H. 3. D. base 5.2; D. rim 6.5. Single fragment preserving full profile and 30% of vessel; missing handle. Fine greenish grey (5G 6/1) blue ware fabric with many voids. Black paint. Traces of handle on rim. Bands. LM IIIC.

K110.4 Pyxis (FIG. 6.7). Max. pres. H. 3. Two fragments, one from base, one from body. Fine, soft, light grey (10YR 7/2) fabric. Black paint. Worn surfaces. Burned. Panelled pattern: crosshatched hourglasses, vertical chevrons, vertical chain with dots. LM IIIC.

K110.5 Pyxis (FIG. 6.7). H. est. 40.5; D. base 40; D. rim est. 34. Partially mended from 77 fragments, 15 non-joining fragments. 90% preserved, including full profile; missing tops of handles. Fine, soft, reddish yellow (5YR 6/6) fabric with infrequent phyllites, hard white and yellow spongy inclusions. White (10YR 8/2) slip. Black to red (2.5YR 5/6) paint. Worn surfaces. Slashed handles. Panelled decoration. Side A: scale pattern with hatched vertical bands on either side and multiple hatched loops, both pendent and upright with fringed arc filler. Side B: fringed horns of consecration with fringed upright multiple leaves between horns. Vertical chevrons within one of handle attachments. LM IIIC.

K110.6 Hut urn (FIG. 6.7). Max. pres. H. 6.2; D. base est. 6. Two large non-joining fragments, one from top (eight sherds), one from base (two sherds). 20% preserved; missing most of body, base, doors, and handles. Fine, soft, light brown (7.5YR 6/4) fabric with black core. Light brown (7.5YR 6/4) slip. Blackened from burning inside and out on one side. Laminating surfaces. Small cone on apex. Not decorated. Publication: Mersereau 1993, 32–3, fig. 21.13; Hägg 1990, 99, fig. 7,105. LM IIIC.

K110.7 Lid (FIG. 6.7). H. 13.4; D. rim 32.8. Partially mended from 31 joining fragments, three non-joining. 95% preserved, including most of rim and handle; missing pieces of top. Fine, soft, porous, reddish yellow (5YR 7/6–6/6) fabric. White (10YR 8/2) slip. Black paint. Burned on one side. Domed lid with elliptical basket handle on top and slightly flattened rim. Heavy ridging on interior. Bands. For shape and decoration, cf. *Khania II*, pl. 44.70-P 0472. LM IIIC.

K110.8 Jug (PLATE 20 *d*, FIG. 6.7). Max. pres. H. 12; D. rim 4.7. Mended from 21 fragments. 85% preserved, including most of body and neck; missing base and handle. Fine, soft, grey (5Y 5/1) fabric. White (2.5Y 8/2) to light grey (2.5Y 7/2) slip. Black paint. Worn surfaces. Wavy band in shoulder zone. Bands on lower and middle body, neck. Short strokes on rim. Loop under handle. LM IIIC.

K110.9 Stirrup jar (PLATE 20 *e*, FIG. 6.8). H. 12.4; D. base 3.8; max. D. 11.8. Restored from three fragments. 90% preserved; missing one handle, rim of spout, one body fragment. Fine, very soft, porous, very pale brown (10YR 8/3) fabric with sand-sized inclusions. Black paint. Worn surfaces. Spout is nearly vertical and touches false spout. False spout has slight conical knob. Shoulder decorated with triangles in fringed half medallions with solid centres and stroke filler. Strokes on top of handles, spiral on top of false spout. LM IIIC late.

K110.10 Stirrup jar (PLATE 20 *f*, FIG. 6.8). Max. pres. H. 12; max. D. 12.4. Partially mended from 17 fragments, 11 non-joining fragments. 30% preserved, including nearly entire top; missing top of false spout and upper parts of handles, half of spout, some of body, entire base. Fine, soft, pink (7.5YR 7/4) fabric. Very pale brown (10YR 7/4) slip. Black paint. Almost entirely burned, particularly around spout. Very worn surfaces. Top made separately and added on as disc with ledge of clay at joint. Fringed multiple upright loops, bands. LM IIIC.

Medium-Coarse Wares

K110.11 Pyxis (FIG. 6.8). H. 13.8; D. base 16; D. rim 12.2. Numerous fragments. 95% preserved. Medium-coarse reddish yellow (5YR 6/6) fabric with red phyllites and small, hard, white inclusions (1–3 mm). Interior grey from burning, and part of exterior burned. Extremely worn surfaces. Possibly once decorated, but too worn to tell. Not labelled, but found with other objects from K 110. LM IIIC.

Coarse Wares

K110.12 Kalathos (FIG. 6.8). H. 7.2; D. base 6; D. rim 17.2. Three joining fragments. 50% preserved, including half of base, body and rim (almost sliced in half). Coarse light red (2.5YR 6/6) fabric with frequent large (1–2 mm) red phyllite and hard white angular inclusions. Burned on bottom of interior, top of exterior. Heavy ridging on interior. Groove on top of rim. Cf. **K110.13**. LM IIIC.

K110.13 Kalathos (FIG. 6.8). H. 7.7; D. base 6; D. rim 17.2. Mended from three fragments. 60% preserved, including full profile, half of base and body, 70% of rim. Coarse red (2.5YR 5/6) fabric with large (1–2 mm) red and white inclusions. Sampled KAR 06/09. Burned on interior entirely; patches of burning on exterior. Flat base with groove around underside. Groove on top of rim. Cf. **K110.12**. LM IIIC.

K110.14 Kalathos (FIG. 6.8). H. 10.9; D. base 8; D. rim 22.8. Two large fragments (six sherds each) preserving much of base and full profile. 60% preserved. Coarse red (2.5YR 5/6) to reddish yellow (5YR 6/6) fabric with large schist (4 mm), red phyllites, hard white angular inclusions, and mica. Severe burning on exterior of base and most of rim; on interior, burning on upper body, not on base. String marks on base. Three grooves on interior of rim. Label unclear; may be from K 101 or K 121. LM IIIC.

K110.15 Kalathos (PLATE 20 *g*, FIG. 6.8). H. 8.3–9.4; D. base 5.3; D. rim 17. Mended from six fragments, two non-joining fragments. 75% preserved, including entire base and full profile. Missing 25% of rim and upper body. Coarse light red (2.5YR 6/8) fabric with frequent grey phyllites and hard white angular inclusions (1 mm). Sampled KAR 06/06. Whole interior burned and patches of exterior. Heavy ridging on interior. LM IIIC.

K110.16 Stirrup jar (FIG. 6.9). H. est. 54.4; D. base 18; max. D. est. 44.8. Not mended. 146 fragments, preserving 75% of vessel; missing centre of base, much of false spout, most of spout. Very coarse reddish yellow (5YR 7/6) fabric with frequent carbonates, sharp oblong, angular grey, and hard red angular inclusions. Very pale brown (10YR 8/4) slip. Paint black on one side, red (2.5YR 4/8) on other. Burned in patches. Very worn surfaces. Octopus with spiral eyes, two rows of wavy lines for tentacles, possibly ending in spirals. Publication: Day 2005, 435, fig. 1.1. LM IIIC.

K110.17 Incense burner or firebox (FIG. 6.10). Max. pres. H. 4.6. Single fragment from domed bottom with holes (fresh breaks around edges suggest there was once more). Coarse red (2.5YR 5/6) cooking pot fabric with frequent large inclusions. Black from burning on interior and over much of exterior; burned all the way through to core. Domed bottom with holes pierced from outside in; large central hole in centre. Publication: Seiradaki, pl. 12a, third row, third from right. LM IIIC.

K110.18 Pithos or jar (FIG. 6.10). Max. pres. H. 7.5. Single large fragment from body. Coarse reddish yellow (5YR 6/6) fabric with frequent schist and hard white angular inclusions (2–3 mm). Burned inside and out. Decorated with knob with incised X-pattern. Cf. **K80.10**. LM IIIC.

K110.19 Lid (PLATE 20 *h*, FIG. 6.10). H. 5.8; D. 23.7. Restored from nine fragments. 99% preserved; missing chips from rim. Coarse red (2.5YR 5/6) fabric with red phyllites and hard white

---

64 Seiradaki, 21.

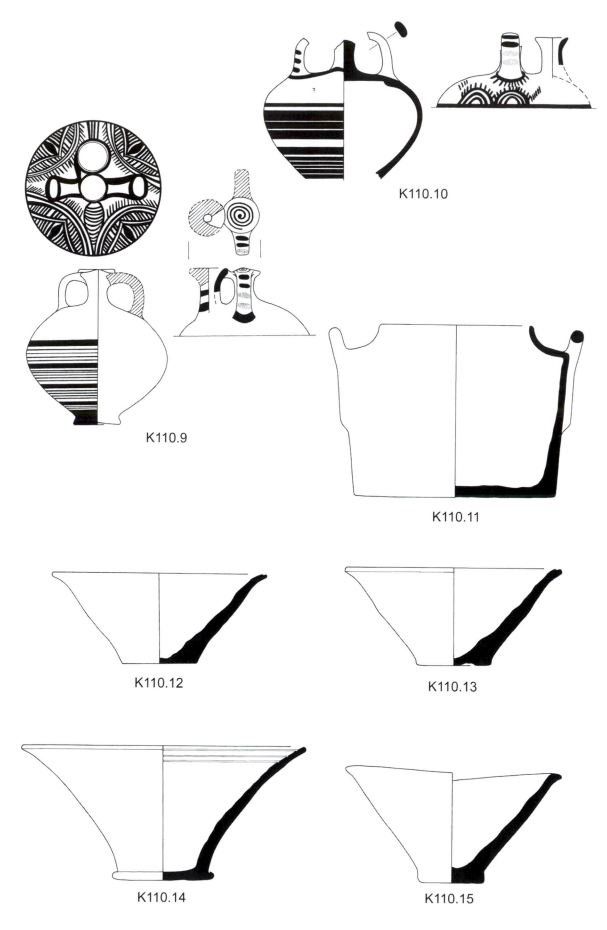

*Fig. 6.8. Eastern Cliff Houses, pottery from K 110 (**K110.9–15**). Scale 1:3.*

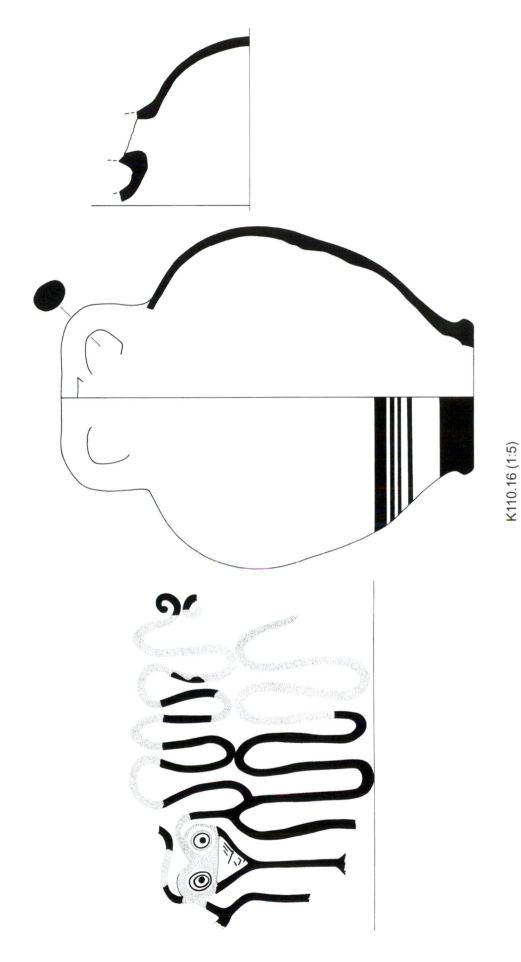

K110.16 (1:5)

*Fig. 6.9. Eastern Cliff Houses, pottery from K 110 (**K110.16**). Scale 1:5.*

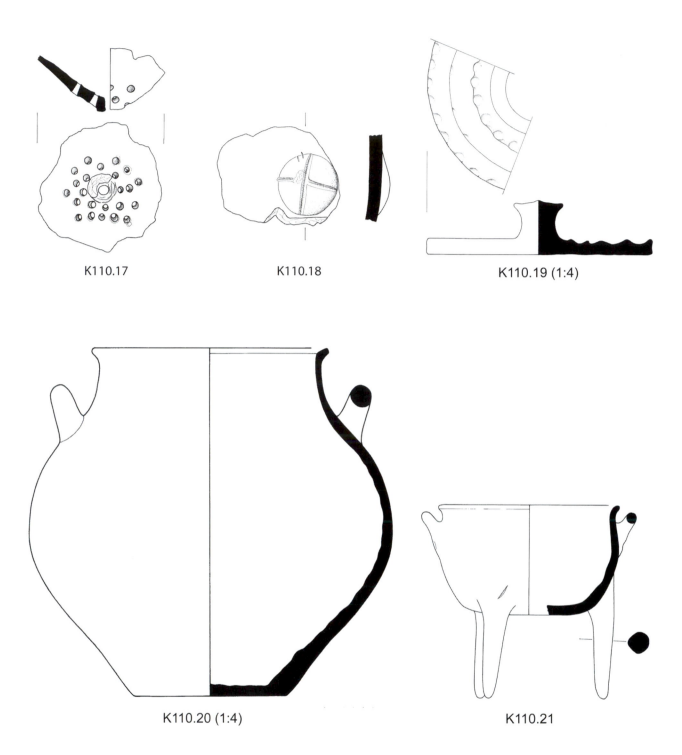

K110.17   K110.18   K110.19 (1:4)

K110.20 (1:4)   K110.21

*Fig. 6.10. Eastern Cliff Houses, pottery from K 110 (**K110.17–21**). Scale 1:3 unless otherwise indicated.*

angular inclusions. Mottled red and black surfaces. Bottom burned on one side. Flat disc with central knob; knob has conical protrusion. Raised bands with finger impressions. For shape and decoration, cf. Warren 2007, 339, fig. 4.P1983. LM IIIC.

K110.20   Jar (FIG. 6.10). H. 36.5; D. base 16; D. rim 14.2. 38 joining and seven non-joining fragments. 80% preserved, including full profile; missing pieces of upper body and rim. Coarse light red (2.5YR 6/8) fabric with frequent phyllites, hard red, hard black, and hard white angular inclusions, some soft spongy yellow inclusions (2–4 mm). Very pale brown (10YR 8/3) surface. Red

(2.5YR 4/6) paint. Surfaces coated with sediment. Flat base, squat globular body, short, wide neck; rim offset and blunted on end. Round horizontal handles on shoulder. Heavy ridging on interior. Bands or monochrome. LM IIIC.

K110.21   Tripod cooking pot (FIG. 6.10). H. 15.4; D. rim est. 14.2. Mended from ten fragments. 50% preserved, including full profile, all three legs, half of base, 33% of rim, one handle. Coarse yellowish red (5YR 4/6–5/8) fabric with infrequent grey and hard white angular inclusions. Burned. Open bowl with tall legs, round in section. LM IIIC.

Room K 118

The excavators mentioned that a stone halfway along the north wall may have been a threshold, and that there was only a step between K 118 and K 119. No pottery has been catalogued from this room, and the publication only comments that there was little fine ware. The notebook, however, lists the following pottery: three pithoi of Types 3, 8, and 10; a pithoid jar of Type 8; tripod legs; at least five dishes, two of Type 1, three of Type 6 with spout and holes; a large krater of Type 3; a basin of Type 7; a kalathos of Type 1; small bowls of Types 1 and 2; and a small egg cup. Two rim fragments of deep bowls were found in the boxes, one with a spiral, the other with a fringed pendent multiple loop hanging from the rim, and two tiny burned stirrup jar fragments. Objects found in the room included a pierced schist plaque (612), five flat and two round stone tools, and animal bones. An ordinary domestic function and a date in LM IIIC seem indicated.

Room K 119

This room may have been entered from K 117. No pottery has been preserved from it, but the publication states that there was little fine ware, all apparently from bowls. The notebook adds that the rim and handles of tripod of Type 1 and several dishes of Types 1–6 were also found.

BROAD ROAD AND SQUARE (AREA K 117)

This narrow continuation of the Broad Road (K 56) between K 61 and K 79 was originally a large square that was later reduced in size, and its exit uphill to the west was apparently blocked by the construction of K 86 and K 88; its northern section was labelled K 117.[65]

The published pottery includes the base of a bowl with compass-drawn circles.[66] The notebook adds the following coarse wares: at least three pithoi, one of Type 9 and two of Type 10; a pithoid jar of Type 8; four tripods, two of Type 2, two of Type 3; tripod legs; several dishes of Type 6; two bases of jars or basins; and a small two-handled jug of Type 3. Fine wares included several bowls of Types 1 and 3, a large krater of Type 3, and an animal head handle.[67] There was only one other object, a terracotta spool (547). In addition to the three deep bowls catalogued below, there was another with multiple strokes and a fragment of a stirrup jar with multiple-outlined rayed decoration. The deep bowls or cups are similar in design and shape to those found in K 101. The identifiable motifs of multiple pendent loops and flower seem to be found both in earlier LM IIIC deposits and later ones.

Pottery Catalogue: K 117

Fine Wares

K117.1   Deep bowl or cup (FIG. 6.11). D. rim est. 13. Single fragment from rim. Fine, soft, reddish yellow (7.5YR 7/6) fabric.

Very pale brown (10YR 8/3) slip. Worn brown paint. Worn surfaces, especially on interior. Multiple pendent loops from rim. LM IIIC.

K117.2   Deep bowl or cup (FIG. 6.11). D. rim est. 12–13. Single fragment from rim. Fine, porous, reddish yellow (7.5YR 7/4) fabric. White (10YR 8/2) slip. Very worn red-brown paint. Minoan flower. LM IIIC.

K117.3   Deep bowl or cup (FIG. 6.11). Max. pres. H. 3.5. Single fragment from rim. Fine, medium-hard, very pale brown (10YR 7/3) fabric. Very pale brown (10YR 8/3) slip. Worn, streaky black paint. Floral spray? LM IIIC

THE WESTERN CLIFF HOUSES (ROOMS K 102, K 106, K 113–K 115, K 120, K 121, K 126)

Rather better preserved than the Eastern Block of the Cliff Houses, this block was divided into three separate buildings.[68] The architecture of rooms K 113, K 114, K 120, and K 121 has been restudied by Wallace.[69]

House K 113-114-120

This was a three-room house on the eastern side of the block, with entrances from the road K 117 on the east and the road K 111 on the south and from the north from the Cliff Road. All the rooms were connected by doorways, none of them on the axis of the building. Room K 113 was open to streets from two sides, but the two entrances were probably not in use at the same time; the door leading into K 114 is not in line with either. Hence, the activities in K 114 would not be visible from either entrance into K 113. The door in the north wall of K 114, however, is aligned with the door leading out from K 120 into the Cliff Road. There were traces of earlier walls that ran under K 120 and K 121, and it seems that K 120 and K 114 were built at the same time to replace this earlier structure, then K 113 and even later K 121 were added on; if this is so, then the pits with carbonised material found in K 113 may have been the remains of an open activity area that existed before K 113 was constructed.[70] According to Wallace's observations, these structures were all built after K 102-106-115.[71]

Room K 113

The room had many entrances, but they were not all used at the same time. Originally the room was connected to K 114 and the square underlying K 89. When K 86 was built, blocking the exit of the Broad Road, a new door into the room from K 111 was constructed on the south. The excavators observed that the floor of K 113 was lower than the street K 111, and

65   *Karphi*, 89.
66   Pictured in Seiradaki, fig. 14.4, but not located.
67   Possibly one of the two pictured in Seiradaki, pl. 12a.
68   *Karphi*, 94–6.
69   Wallace 2005, 229–33.
70   Wallace 2005, 229.
71   Wallace 2005, 229.

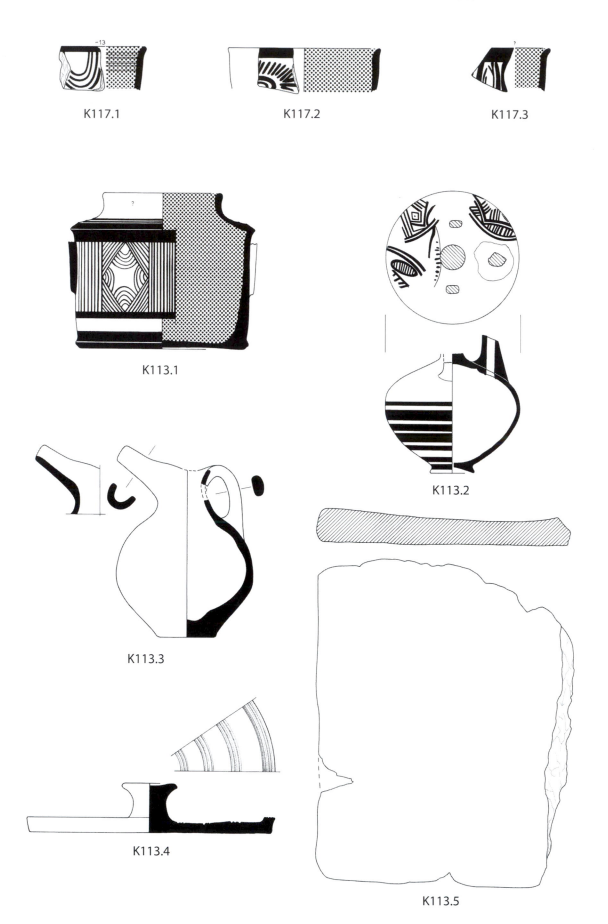

*Fig. 6.11. Broad Road, pottery from K 117 (**K117.1–3**) and Western Cliff Houses, Building K 113-114-120, pottery from K 113 (**K113.1–5**). Scale 1:3.*

this discrepancy in levels suggested that the doorway was a later feature. The room contained a stone column base, and a second one was suggested; Wallace believed that these could have been stands for pithoi, like those at Kavousi–*Vronda*.[72] There were many pits filled with charcoal in the floor, one of which was under the 'column base'. The excavators thought that these were the remains of the earliest habitation of the site and compared them to the remains of fires made by 'two Albanian murderers and the sheep-stealer of Ida'.[73] Traces of a plaque floor were also observed, possibly remaining from an earlier use of the area as a paved open court or square.

The pottery was described as usual, although the fine ware was much blackened with fire. In addition to the pottery catalogued below, the notebook also lists the following: three pithoi, one of Type 8, two of Type 22; three pithoid jars, two of Type 3, one of Type 12; several tripod legs; a large jar of Type 3; a large stirrup jar of Type 2 and a smaller one with a hole through its false spout; two kalathoi of Types 1 and 4; a lid of Type 1 (**K113.4**); several bowls of Types 1 and 2; a large, flat baking board (**K113.5**); and a spouted bowl. The fine ware included a pyxis of Type 2 (**K113.1**), a stirrup jar of Type 2 (**K113.2**), a spouted jug (**K113.3**), and a bowl of Type 2. The cooking dish pictured in Seiradaki was not located.[74] Included in the boxes, but not catalogued, was a vertical handle with a knob on top, also mentioned in the notebook. The following objects were listed as coming from this room: a globular stone bead (549), a rectangular whetstone (604), two flat stone tools, a cylindrical terracotta spindle whorl (605), and animal bones, including a red deer antler.

Most of the preserved pottery from this room is nearly complete and represents what was in use at the time of the abandonment. The list of pottery from the notebooks suggests the normal array of cooking and storage vessels. The coarse lid (**K113.4**), burned all over the bottom, must have been used in cooking, and the flat terracotta slab (**K113.5**) may also have been used in cooking, as the entire surface is blackened except for a roughly circular patch in the centre; it may have been used, as the excavators suggested, as a baking board.[75] This type of thick, flat, terracotta slab is not known (or at least published) from other LM IIIC sites or from Crete at all, and all the Karphi examples come from the Western Cliff Houses, with the exception of one whose find spot is unknown.

There was very little fine ware, and especially few examples of drinking vessels; the ubiquitous deep bowl was almost entirely absent from this room. Possibly the room was used for cooking and storage, but not eating and drinking. The three fine pieces found here included a pyxis, a spouted jug, and a stirrup jar. The pyxis (**K113.1**) is of the usual shape but has a rather more angular shoulder than usual; its linear decoration rather than the more elaborate figured or fringed motifs generally found on pyxides at Karphi makes it appear

of late date. The stirrup jar (**K113.2**) is of good LM IIIC type, although poorly preserved, and its decoration of half medallions with hatched ovals is similar to several LM IIIC stirrup jars from Crete and Rhodes.[76] The spouted jug (**K113.3**) is a highly unusual shape for Karphi, although Seiradaki's Type 9 jug is a variation on the shape. Similar jugs come from LM IIIA and LM IIIB, and there is a parallel from Khalasmenos of LM IIIC.[77]

Pottery Catalogue: K 113

Fine Wares

K113.1 Pyxis (PLATE 21 *a*, FIG. 6.11). H. 12.5; D. base 13.6; D. rim 9.6. Mended from 54 fragments, ten non-joining fragments. 60% preserved, including full profile, nearly all of base and lower body, both lower handle attachments; missing tops of handles, much of upper body. Fine, soft, pink (7.5YR 7/4) fabric. White (10YR 8/2) slip. Black paint worn to red shadow (2.5YR 5/6). Almost totally burned, so that in places decoration is negative. Panelled decoration: lozenge with multiple arcs in corners, strokes filling in rest of panel, between multiple thin bands. LM IIIC.

K113.2 Stirrup jar (PLATE 21 *b*, FIG. 6.11). Max. pres. H. 6; D. base 3.5. Two large fragments, one from top (ten sherds), one from base (six sherds), and seven non-joining fragments. Missing false spout and handles. Fine, soft, grey (2.5Y 7/2) fabric. Black paint. Burned? Very flaky surfaces. Top made as separate disc and added on. Bands on lower body. On shoulder, half medallion with multiple-outlined hatched ovals and filler, multiple lozenge. LM IIIC.

Medium-Coarse Wares

K113.3 Spouted jug (FIG. 6.11). H. 15.3; D. base 4.7. Once mended from 31 fragments, now broken, and pieces are missing. 85% preserved, including full profile; missing only rim and pieces of body. Medium-coarse, soft, reddish yellow (5YR 7/6) fabric with infrequent clay pellets and hard grey inclusions (1–2 mm). Sampled KAR 06/41. Worn and flaky surfaces. Mottled with burning inside and out. LM IIIC.

Coarse Wares

K113.4 Lid (FIG. 6.11). H. 4; D. base 19.2; D. knob 4.5. Complete. Mended from seven fragments. Coarse light red (2.5YR 6/6) fabric with frequent large (1–3 mm) red phyllites and hard angular white inclusions. Entire bottom burned. Flat disc with concave knob in centre, ridge around outside edge. Decorated with groups of concentric grooves. LM IIIC.

K113.5 Cooking slab (PLATE 21 *c*, FIG. 6.11). Max. pres. L. 25.7; max. pres. W. 20; Th. 1.8–2.7. Eleven joining fragments and one non-joining, preserving two edges. Coarse red (2.5YR 5/6)

---

72 Wallace 2005, 229; Day and Glowacki forthcoming.

73 *Karphi*, 94–5.

74 Seiradaki, fig. 6.7.

75 *Karphi*, 95.

76 Kanta 1980, 71, fig. 121. 4 (Kera); 138, fig. 121.7 (Kritsa), fig. 97.7 (Rhodes).

77 Kanta 1980, 103, fig. 37.10 (Ayia Triada, LM IIIB); 185, fig. 72.9 (Adromyloi, LM IIIB); 166, fig. 108.2 (Myrsini); 165, fig. 109.2 (Myrsini, LM IIIA); 109–10 fig. 127.1–7 (Kalokoraftis, LM IIIA–B); Tsipopoulou 2004, 110, fig. 8.4.93-116.

fabric with very frequent schist inclusions (1–2 mm). Sampled KAR 06/43. Entire upper surface burned, except for roughly circular area in centre. Flat, rectangular object, with slight curve to upper surface. LM IIIC.

Room K 114

There was nothing unusual in this small room, except for a jar stand in the northwest corner. The pottery listed in the notebook included sherds from at least two pithoi with rims of Type 22, a pithoid jar of Type 1, the base of a basin of Type 4, at least four tripods, six kalathoi of all types, two jars of Type 3, a coarse stirrup jar, two pyxides of Type 3, one with accompanying lid (**K114.3–5**). Seiradaki mentions a third pyxis in addition to the two catalogued examples,[78] but the notebook only lists two, and only two have been found. Objects included a bronze spearhead (550)[79] and a cylindrical terracotta spindle whorl (606).

As with K 113, the preserved vessels from this room are nearly complete and probably represent what was in use in the room at the time of abandonment, although the inhabitants may have removed finer and more portable vessels, and there may have been later disturbance. No deep bowls are represented here. Instead, there are two drinking vessels: a small conical cup and a monochrome carinated cup. The monochrome cup (**K114.2**) is an unusual shape for Karphi, although it can be paralleled by examples from Khania (where it is also unusual) and Khamalevri.[80] Conical cups are very rare at Karphi, as in most LM IIIC contexts; **K114.1** is similar to one from Ta Mnemata Tomb 16 (**M16.1**). The two pyxides are quite different from one another. **K114.3** is of Type 2, with slashed handles. The decoration is quite uncontrolled, but the elements of spirals and fringed tricurved streamers and panels of chevrons are all LM IIIC date. **K114.4**, with its elegant depiction of two birds on either side of a double axe standing in horns of consecration, presents a marked contrast. It is of Seiradaki's Type 6, with handles beginning at the base and rising above the rim, and it has an interesting fringed and tasselled chevron between the handles. It is only one of two pyxides found with their accompanying lids, and this one is a simple flat lid (**K114.5**) with elaborate decoration of concentric circles with leaves arranged in a zigzag pattern and bands and dots on the sides. The two stirrup jars are also quite different; the small stirrup jar (**K114.6**) is of the usual shape, but its decoration is too poorly preserved to determine. The large stirrup jar (**K114.7**) is more akin to the coarse storage stirrup jar, although it is of fine fabric. It is globular, with a large flat base, and it has a concave disc that is pierced in the centre. A similar stirrup jar was found at Khania,[81] where it was seen as an import from Knossos. The jug with knobbed decoration (**K114.9**) is in shape like many of Karphi jugs, and the use of knobs as decoration is also common on the site. As for the coarse ware, in addition to the storage and

cooking vessels listed in the notebook, there was also a cooking jug (**K114.10**) with pinched out rim that from the extensive burning found on it must have been put directly in the fire frequently.

Pottery Catalogue: K 114

Fine Wares

K114.1 Conical cup (FIG. 6.12). H. 3.7–3.8; D. base 2; D. rim 7.1. Mended from six fragments. 75% preserved, including base; missing 60% of rim and upper body. Fine, hard light red (2.5YR 6/6) fabric with gold mica inclusions. Black paint. Sampled KAR 06/17. Burning or blackening on one side of exterior. Monochrome. LM IIIC.

K114.2 Cup (PLATE 21 *d*, FIG. 6.12). H. 7.8–8.5; D. base 3.5; D. rim 12. Mended from 18 fragments. 85% preserved, including full profile, entire base, and handle; missing 33% of rim, body fragments. Fine, soft, reddish yellow (7.5YR 7/6) fabric. Black to strong brown (7.5YR 4/6) paint. Well-preserved surfaces. Monochrome (?). LM IIIC.

K114.3 Pyxis (PLATE 21 *e*, FIG. 6.12). H. 17; D. base 14.6; D. rim 11–12. Complete; mended from three fragments. Fine, soft, pale yellow (2.5Y 7/4) fabric with tiny black inclusions. Very pale brown (10YR 7/3) slip. Black paint. Well-preserved surfaces with pitting. Deeply slashed round handles; bevelled base. Very crude decoration. Side A: double spiral with fringed tricurved streamer, vertical line with loops, wavy bands above. Side B: panelled pattern with vertical chevrons, scalloped edges, and stacked spirals. Pairs of spirals under handles. Publication: Seiradaki, pl. 7b, top right (mislabelled K 115). LM IIIC.

K114.4 Pyxis (HM 11057) (PLATE 21 *f*, FIG. 6.12). H. 10.5 (with handles 12.3); D. base 14; D. rim 12.7–13. Restored from numerous fragments. 75% preserved, including full profile; missing 25% of base, 50% of rim, tops of handles. Fine, medium-soft, pink (7.5YR 8/4–7/4) fabric; handle grey (10YR 5/1) at core. Very pale brown (10YR 8/4) slip. Black (5YR 2.5/1) paint worn to very dusky red (2.5YR 2.5/2). Well-preserved surfaces. Two holes pierced through walls on one side. Side A: horns of consecration with birds on either side and double axe in centre; two birds are different in details. Between handles, fringed multiple chevron with curved tail. Dots around base. Side B: dots and scallops hanging from upper band, otherwise too worn to distinguish. Strokes on handle. Rim painted on interior. Publication: Seiradaki, figs. 12.6, 24 a2; pl. 7a, left. LM IIIC.

K114.5 Lid (PLATE 21 *f*, FIG. 6.12). H. 2.2; D. rim 14.2–.3. Restored from 20 fragments. 90% preserved; missing 20% of sides. Fine, medium-soft, reddish yellow (7.5YR 7/6) fabric. Very pale brown (10YR 8/4) slip. Red (2.5YR 5/6–4/6) paint. Hole pierced through centre. Decorated on top with concentric circles: solid centre; reserved leaves on dark background, alternating in oblique angles; outer circle has outlined leaves alternating in oblique angles. Sides have alternating bands and rows of dots. Publication: Seiradaki, figs. 12.6, 24 a1; pl. 7a, left. LM IIIC.

K114.6 Stirrup jar (PLATE 21 *g*, FIG. 6.13). Max. pres. H. 9.8; D. base 3.5. Intact. 90% preserved, including lower part of handles, base of spout, and false spout; missing spout, false spout, and rest of handles (glue on spout suggests once preserved). Fine, soft,

---

78 Seiradaki, 18.

79 *Karphi*, pl. 29.1.

80 *Khania II*, 105, pl. 34.84-P 0698, LM IIIB:2/C; Andreadaki-Vlasaki and Papadopoulou 2007, 50, fig. 7.23 (Phase II).

81 *Khania II*, 163, pl. 50.71-P 0736/0763/0779/77-P 0719.

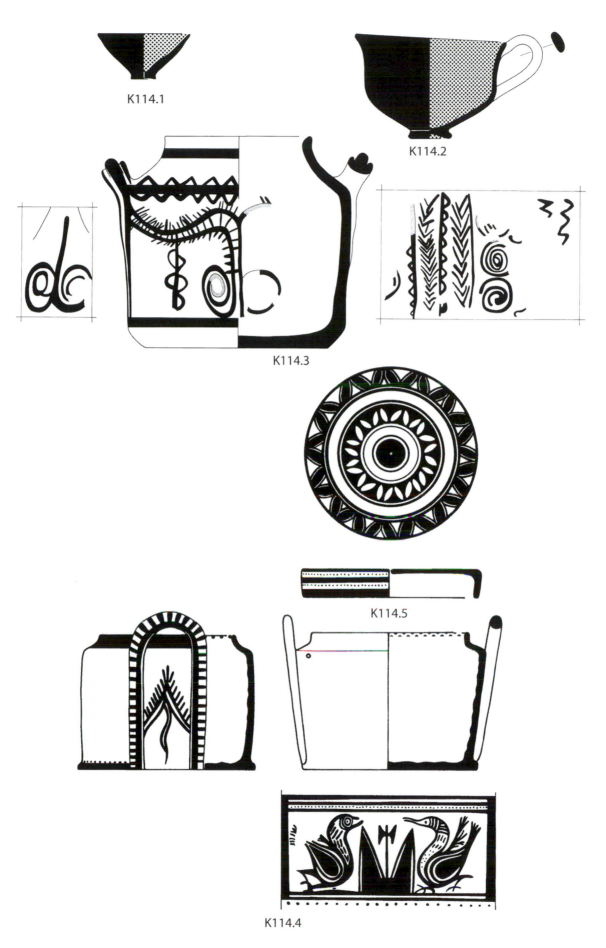

K114.1

K114.2

K114.3

K114.5

K114.4

*Fig. 6.12. Western Cliff Houses, Building 1, pottery from K 114 (**K114.1–5**). Scale 1:3.*

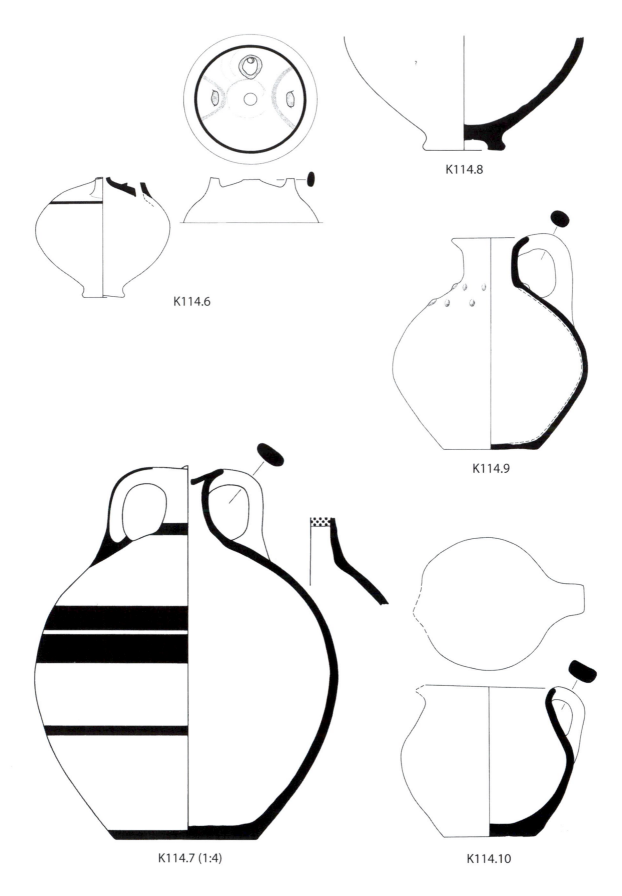

*Fig. 6.13. Western Cliff Houses, Building 1, pottery from K 114 (**K114.6–10**). Scale 1:3.*

porous, reddish yellow (7.5YR 7/6) to yellow (10YR 7/6) fabric with tiny black inclusions and a few larger grey and white ones. Possible lighter slip, but worn surfaces. Black paint. Loops on top around handles. LM IIIC.

K114.7   Stirrup jar (FIG. 6.13). H. 39; D. base 14.7; max. D. 32. Partially mended from 92 fragments, 60 non-joining fragments. 75% preserved, including entire base and lower body, full profile, most of false spout, part of spout, one handle; missing most of spout and second handle. Fine, very soft, very pale brown (10YR 7/4) fabric with infrequent hard angular white and black inclusions (1–2 mm). Worn black paint. Very worn and chalky surfaces. False spout is hollow and slightly concave, with hole pierced through it, like coarse stirrup jars. Bands. LM IIIC.

Medium-Coarse Wares

K114.8   Closed vessel (FIG. 6.13). Max. pres. H. 9.3; D. base 6.5. Mended from four joining fragments, preserving entire base and 33% of lower body. Medium-coarse, reddish yellow (7.5YR 7/6) fabric with greenish grey (5GY 6/1) core and frequent tiny black inclusions. Grey (5Y 6/1) paint. Ring base. Monochrome. LM IIIC.

K114.9   Jug (HM 11062) (PLATE 22 *a*, FIG. 6.13). H. 16.9 (with handles 17.3); D. base 7.5. D. rim 6.2. Nearly complete except for much of rim, which restored. Intact except for handle. Medium-coarse, reddish yellow (5YR 7/6–7.5YR 7/6) fabric with infrequent, small (<1 mm) phyllites and hard black inclusions. Surfaces either worn or still coated with sediment. Body cracked under handle down to base. Burned patch under handle. Two rows of knobs, one at base of neck, and the other slightly lower. Publication: Seiradaki, fig. 9.11; pl. 5a, right. LM IIIC.

Coarse Wares

K114.10   Cooking jug (PLATE 22 *b*, FIG. 6.13). H. 11.8–12.3; D. base 7.5; D. rim 10.6–11.2. Restored from 13 fragments. 95% preserved; missing only tiny fragment of rim and spout. Very coarse reddish brown (2.5YR 5/4) fabric with large (1–3 mm) frequent phyllites and hard white inclusions. Very burned, inside and out, except for a few patches around handle (handle itself burned). Rough and irregular surfaces. Rim pinched out opposite handle to form spout. LM IIIC.

Room K 120

This room had a stone platform in the southwest corner, possibly part of the earlier wall that also ran under K 121. A wall may have once divided the room into two.[82] The pottery was described as usual, but there was little fine ware and no pyxides. The notebook mentions sherds from a pithos of Type 21, three fine bowl or krater handles, a kylix stem of Type 1, and three stirrup jars, one of Type 6. One of these stirrup jars is **K120.4**, another no doubt to be identified as a fragment with a hole in the top found in one of the boxes but not catalogued. Another may be the one pictured in Seiradaki,[83] which was missing. There were many objects from this room: a bone pin (603),[84] a conical stone bead or whorl (601), a Neolithic stone axe (629),[85] a pierced schist whetstone (630)[86] and a pierced schist disc (649), one cylindrical (602) and one conical (650) terracotta spindle whorl, and a terracotta spool.

The material from this room is consistent with a domestic function, but many of the vessels seem to have been fragmentary, perhaps debris broken and ground into the floor rather than a floor deposit. Of the two fragments from deep bowls or cups, **K120.1** is an unusual type, without rim band and with a combination of multiple pendent loops and multiple stems that recalls an example from Phaistos;[87] it may be an import into Karphi, possibly from the Mesara. The stirrup jar fragment (**K120.4**) has fringed decoration. The kylix (**K120.3**) is the very large type found in LM IIIC and possibly associated with drinking rituals.[88] It has the deep conical body with carination just below the rim that is so typical of the kylikes of this date at Karphi and elsewhere in east Crete. The decoration of a large outlined motif, possibly an octopus, is common on LM IIIC kylikes and kraters.[89]

Pottery Catalogue: K 120

Fine Wares

K120.1   Deep bowl or cup (PLATE 2 *g*, FIG. 6.14). D. rim est. 13–14. Single fragment (three sherds) from rim; fresh breaks suggest there were other fragments. Fine, medium-hard, porous, very pale brown (10YR 7/4) fabric. Very pale brown (10YR 8/4) slip. Worn dark reddish grey (5YR 4/2) to reddish brown (5YR 4/4) paint. Multiple stem motif with pendent multiple loops. Imported? LM IIIC.

K120.2   Deep bowl or cup (FIG. 6.14). Max. pres. H. 4. Single fragment from rim. Fine, soft, reddish yellow (7.5YR 7/6) fabric. White (10YR 8/2) slip. Black to reddish brown (5YR 4/4) paint. Worn surfaces. Multiple pendent loops. Reserved band on interior of rim. LM IIIC.

K120.3   Kylix (FIG. 6.14). D. rim est. 25.6. Four joining fragments from lower body, three non-joining fragments from lower body, and one rim fragment. Fine, medium-soft, reddish yellow (5YR 7/6) fabric. Very pale brown (10YR 8/4) slip. Black paint. Worn surfaces. Strokes on rim. Outlined curvilinear motif on body with a dot. LM IIIC.

K120.4   Stirrup jar (FIG. 6.14). Max. D. 9.4. Large fragment (ten sherds) from top and three non-joining fragments. Top, including spout, half of false spout and one handle; missing part of other handle, entire lower body and base. Fine soft, very pale brown (10YR 8/4) fabric. Worn black to brown paint. Spout bent back to touch false spout. Fringed curving bands, multiple triangles, groups of dots. Outlined handles. LM IIIC.

Outside K 120: The Cliff Road

The area outside K 120 and to the north was also considered a street, the so-called Cliff Road. Pottery was much broken, as with all the street areas.[90] The

---

82   Wallace 2005, 229.

83   Seiradaki, pl. 6f.

84   *Karphi*, pl. 28.4.

85   *Karphi*, pl. 30.2.

86   *Karphi*, pl. 30.3.

87   Borgna 1997a, 281, fig. 19 (spirals, not loops) and 278, fig. 6.7. It dates to LM IIIC.

88   Day and Snyder, 2004.

89   Rethemiotakis 1997, 310, fig. 11b; 322, fig. 33a, c; Borgna 1997a, 291, fig. 35; Warren 2007, 341, fig. 6. P2469; *Kavousi IIA*, fig. 22.

90   *Karphi*, 96.

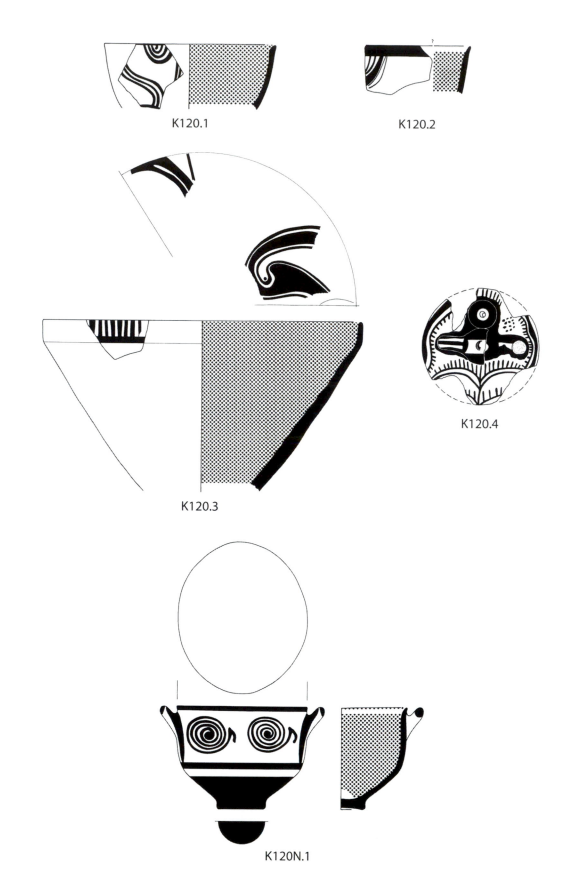

K120.1

K120.2

K120.3

K120.4

K120N.1

Fig. 6.14. Western Cliff Houses, Building 1, pottery from K 120 (**K120.1–4**) and area outside K 120 (**K120N.1**). Scale 1:3.

publication mentions a complete stirrup jar of Type 2, and a pithoid jar of Type 1. The notebook adds that there were a few other fragmentary sherds. The only preserved vessel is a deep bowl decorated with buttonhook spirals and both reserved band and disc on the interior. The shape, with its rather low foot, and high set handles, looks early LM IIIC; it finds parallels at Kastri[91] and in the early deposit at Kavousi–*Vronda*.[92] The buttonhook spiral is a common motif, but this particular variant with sharply angular hooks is not known elsewhere.

Pottery Catalogue: Outside K 120

Fine Wares

K120N.1   Deep bowl (PLATE 22 *c*, FIG. 6.14). H. 8.2; D. base 3.8; D. rim 10.3–12. Complete; mended from two fragments. Fine pink (7.5YR 7/4) to reddish yellow (7.5YR 7/6) fabric with tiny black inclusions. Dull black paint. Misfired or burned. Well-preserved surfaces. Buttonhook spirals. Reserved band on interior of rim, reserved disc on interior of base. Bottom of base painted. Publication: Seiradaki, pl. 10a, top, second from right (mislabelled K 20). LM IIIC.

Room 121

A second building was identified by the excavators in Room 121, a single room structure, but Wallace has suggested that it was part of K 113-114-120, built after the other rooms and after K 102-106-115.[93] The entrance into the room is not clear, although the notebook suggests that it may have been from the north. At the east end, below the floor were wall foundations that continued the line of the west wall of Rooms K 113–K 114. East of this earlier wall, the deposit went down 85 cm deeper than the area over it or to the west. Wallace's investigations suggest that the lower walls belonged to an earlier room of similar location and dimensions to K 120 and that there had been an earlier activity area to the south represented by the sub-floor in K 113.[94]

There was much pottery. In addition to the vessels catalogued below, the publication and notebook record the following coarse pottery: ten pithoi of Types 1, 2, 3, 5, 8, 9, 16, 18, 20, and 24; two tripod pithoi; five pithoid jars, two of Type 8, and one each of Types 1, 3, and 7; a jar base of Type 6; tripod legs; dishes, several of Type 6, two of Type 1; a basin of Type 7; four kalathoi of Type 1; a krater of Type 1; two large stirrup jars of Type 2; and four one-handled jugs of Type 3. Fine wares included a pyxis of Type 2; a kylix of Type 1, a jar of Type 3; two stirrup jars of Type 2 (**K121.10**), a beaded tankard (**K121.7**), a cup of Type 1, and several bowls of Types 1 and 2. There were numerous fragments in the boxes that were not catalogued, including a kylix of Type 1, a burned pyxis of Type 2, the base of a jug or stirrup jar with bands, a burned jug with knobs, and a burned juglet with incised grooves at the base of the neck. The basin pictured in Seiradaki was not located.[95] Objects from this room included part of a bronze blade

(598), a conical stone bead or whorl (596), a schist whetstone (595), a pierced stone disc, and a conical terracotta spindle whorl (597). The notebook also records animal bones and pumice.

There was clearly an extraordinary amount of pottery in this room, much of it involved with storage (ten pithoi, two tripod pithoi, five pithoid jars, and two large storage stirrup jars). Some cooking also occurred, as well as other domestic functions. The two tripod cooking pots catalogued from the room (**K121.13–14**) were unusually small; they are of the variety with a single vertical handle.[96] The basin (**K121.12**) is an unusual type, but a similar example came from Khalasmenos.[97] Of the nearly complete fine ware, the stirrup jar (**K121.10**) is a good LM IIIC type, although not the most common type at Karphi. The neck and false spout are larger than usual, though the body is the familiar globular shape. The half medallion with wavy hatched leaves above a dotted multiple triangle and the fringed antithetic spirals with filler, as well as the quatrefoils and trefoils find parallels on other LM IIIC stirrup jars.[98] The shallow bowl (**K121.5**) is also an uncommon shape, but it has parallels at Kastri and Khamalevri.[99] The small spouted shallow bowl (**K121.6**) is also unusual, and it is uncertain what these two bowls were used for. The rest of the fine ware is fragmentary and may represent earlier pieces ground into the floor or associated with the earlier structure; there is nothing that is not LM IIIC, although **K121.2** finds its closest parallels in LM IIIB Knossos,[100] and **K121.3** is similar to an LM IIIB deep bowl from Phaistos.[101] The decoration on kraters, tankards, and jug find parallels elsewhere on the site and cannot be dated too closely. The quatrefoil leaf decoration on krater **K121.8** is similar to that on a krater from Phaistos.[102]

---

91   *Kastri*, 295, fig. 15.P27.

92   *Kavousi IIA*, fig. 26.B4 P13; Day 1997, 396, fig. 3.1.

93   Wallace 2005, 229.

94   Wallace 2005, 229.

95   Seiradaki, fig. 5.10.

96   A good parallel comes from Kavousi–*Vronda*: Gesell, Coulson and Day 1991, 166, fig. 6.4 from Building I. See also Warren 1982–83, 80, fig. 44, right; 2007, 342, fig. 7.P170, P171 (Knossos).

97   Coulson and Tsipopoulou 1994, 74, 9.5.

98   For the medallions, see Kanta 1980, 138, fig. 121.7 (Kritsa); for the antithetic spirals see Kanta 1980, 173, fig. 118.7 (Tourtouli).

99   *Kastri*, 294, fig. 14.P3, Andreadaki-Vlasaki and Papadopoulou 2007, 45, fig. 2.20 (Khamalevri, Phase Ia).

100 Popham 1965, 326, fig. 6.34 and pl. 85c–d; Popham 1970*b*, pl. 47b, pl. 51a, c.

101 Borgna 1997*a*, 279, fig. 10.

102 Borgna 2003, pl. 34.29.

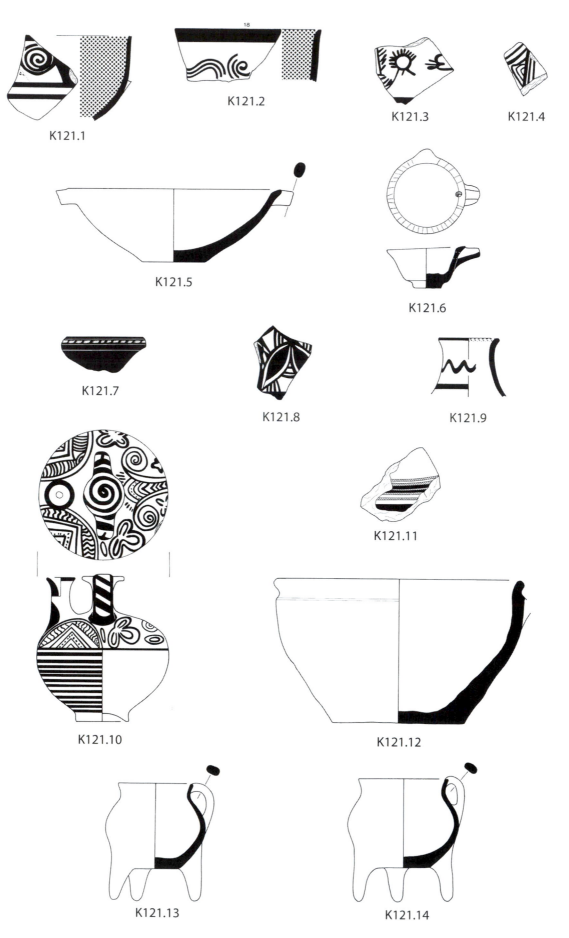

*Fig. 6.15. Western Cliff Houses, pottery from K 121 (**K121.1–14**). Scale 1:3.*

Pottery Catalogue: K 121

Fine Wares

K121.1 Deep bowl (PLATE 1 *a*, FIG. 6.15). Max. pres. H. 7; D. rim est. 11. Single fragment from body near rim, preserving one handle attachment. Fine, soft, yellow (10YR 7/6) fabric. Very pale brown (10YR 8/3) slip. Black paint. Well-preserved surfaces. Possibly burned. Spiral. LM IIIC.

K121.2 Deep bowl or cup (FIG. 6.15). D. rim est. 18. Single fragment from rim. Fine, soft, porous, very pale brown (10YR 8/4) fabric. White (2.5Y 8/2) slip. Very worn black paint. Multiple stemmed spirals. Cf. **K38.1**. LM IIIB/C.

K121.3 Deep bowl or cup (FIG. 6.15). Max. pres. H. 4.5. Single fragment from body. Fine, soft, reddish yellow (5YR 7/6) fabric. White (10YR 8/2) slip. Worn black paint. Very worn surfaces. Fringed circle (bird?), other fringed motifs. LM IIIC.

K121.4 Deep bowl or cup (FIG. 6.15). Max. pres. H. 4.3. Single fragment from body. Fine, soft, very pale brown (10YR 7/4) fabric. Very pale brown (10YR 8/2) slip. Worn brown paint. Worn surfaces on exterior, well-preserved on interior. Panelled pattern with multiple loops or chevrons. LM IIIC.

K121.5 Shallow bowl (FIG. 6.15). H. 5.9; D. base 5.1; D. rim 17.1. Partially mended from 12 fragments. 35% preserved, including entire base and full profile, part of one handle. Fine, soft, reddish yellow (5YR 7/6) fabric with tiny black inclusions, especially in base. Very pale brown (10YR 8/3) slip. Possibly painted, but only a few traces remain. Monochrome? LM IIIC.

K121.6 Miniature spouted bowl (PLATE 22 *d*, FIG. 6.15). H. 3–3.3; D. base 2.3; D. rim 6.3. Mended from several fragments; 95% preserved; edges chipped. Fine, very soft, light red (10R 6/8) fabric. Very worn surfaces. Incised stokes on top of rim. Publication: Seiradaki, fig. 14.6; pl. 4d, left. LM IIIC.

K121.7 Tankard (PLATE 22 *e*, FIG. 6.15). Max. pres. H. 3. Single fragment from rim. Fine, soft, porous, reddish yellow (7.5YR 7/6) fabric. Red (2.5YR 4/8) paint. Beaded design on rim. Monochrome. Cf. **K77.1**, **M4.7**. LM IIIC.

K121.8 Krater (FIG. 6.15). Max. pres. H. 5.8; Th 0.5–0.6. Single fragment from body. Fine, soft, reddish yellow (5YR 7/6) fabric. Very pale brown (10YR 8/4) slip. Red (10R 5/8) paint. Filled outlined quatrefoil with arc fillers between leaves. LM IIIC.

K121.9 Jug (FIG. 6.15). D. rim 4.8. Five joining fragments preserving entire neck and rim. Fine, soft, reddish yellow (5YR 7/6) fabric with voids where inclusions have burned out. Very pale brown (10YR 8/3) slip. Dark red (2.5YR 3/6) paint. Wavy line on neck, interior band at rim. LM IIIC.

K121.10 Stirrup jar (HM 11068) (PLATE 22 *f*, FIG. 6.15). H. 11.7; D. base 4.2; max. D. 10.6. Nearly complete; restored from *c.* five fragments. 95% preserved. Fine, medium-soft, very pale brown (10YR 7/3) to light grey (2.5Y 7/2) fabric, where burned. White (10YR 8/1) slip. Crackled black worn to shadow. Worn surfaces. Burned on one side, so much that decoration has become negative image. Multiple thin bands on lower body. On shoulder: half medallions on either side of spout, with multiple triangles filled with dots and ovals filled with arcs or wavy lines; on other side, spiral volutes with chevron or arc fillers and dots, multiple-outlined trefoil and quatrefoil motifs. Spiral on top of false spout. Oblique strokes on handles. Publication: Seiradaki, fig. 22i; pl. 6a, right (mislabelled K 26). LM IIIC early.

K121.11 Stirrup jar (FIG. 6.15). Max. pres. H. 5.8. Single fragment from body. Fine grey (5Y 5/1) fabric, very burned. Glossy slip, burned black. Dark red (2.5YR 3/6) paint. Bands. LM IIIC.

Coarse Wares

K121.12 Bowl or basin (FIG. 6.15). H. 11.2; D. base 10–11; D. rim 20. Mended from 18 fragments, two non-joining fragments. 65% preserved, including most of base, body, rim; missing handles,

but one handle attachment preserved. Coarse, porous, white (10YR 8/2) fabric with frequent schist (1–2 mm) and hard white angular inclusions. Burned on one side. LM IIIC.

K121.13 Tripod cooking pot (PLATE 22 *g*, FIG. 6.15). H. 9.5; D. rim 6. Restored from three fragments; body intact, two legs separate. 95% preserved; missing one leg and chips from rim. Coarse yellowish red (5YR 5/8) fabric with frequent, large (1–3 mm) hard white, black and grey phyllite inclusions. Burned on bottom, lower body, and legs; may be burned inside, but interior still coated with sediment. Legs round in section. Publication: Seiradaki, pl. 4d, second from left. Cf. **K121.14**. LM IIIC.

K121.14 Tripod cooking pot (FIG. 6.15). H. 9.9 (with handle 11); D. rim 7.2. Mended from five fragments. 90% preserved, including two legs, handle, and full profile; missing one leg, chips from rim. Coarse red (2.5YR 5/6) fabric with frequent large hard white angular and hard black inclusions and some gold mica; dark grey at core. Surface blackened from fire; some of surface still coated with sediment. Legs round in section. Cf. **K121.13**. LM IIIC.

House K 102-106-115-126

This four-room house included two roofed cellars (K 102 and K 115) and a large room (K 106) that may have served as another area for ritual observances. K 126 may have been the entranceway into the building. Wallace suggested that K 102-106-115 predated the later phase of K 120.[103]

Room K 102

This room was said to have been a roofed cellar, probably reached by ladder from K 106.[104] The publication mentions a tripod pithos and a kalathos base with olive pits found in the room. The notebook adds a long list of contents, including the following: pithos rims of Types 1, 3, 7, and 17; a pithos base with chevrons and chain pattern; pithoid jars, two of Type 3, two of Type 7, one new type; two jars of Type 3 and one of Type 7; tripod rims of Types 2 and 3 and usual legs; dishes, one of Type 1 with wavy rim and horizontal handles, several of Type 6; two basins of Types 7 and 10, one of Type 4 without handles; and bowls of Types 1 and 2. Fine pottery included a white pyxis of Type 2 and several bowls of Types 1 and 2.

Fragments of deep bowls from this deposit are preserved in the boxes: a rim fragment with multiple upright loops, body fragments with fringed motifs and a spiral, and a handle fragment with a curvilinear motif. A cooking tray with a pushed-in lug at the rim was also found in one of the boxes. Objects from the room included 16 whole terracotta spools and fragments of 22 others, suggesting the presence of a loom or storage of a loom here. The notebook also records animal bones and pumice from this room.

The preserved pottery is very fragmentary and probably represents material broken earlier and ground

103 Wallace 2005, 229.
104 *Karphi*, 95.

into the floor. The deep bowl or cup (**K102.1**) looks LM IIIC, but it is not more closely datable. Ordinary functions of storage, food preparation, and cooking seem to have gone on, along with weaving.

Pottery Catalogue: K 102

Fine Wares

K102.1   Deep bowl or cup (FIG. 6.16). D. rim est. 10. Single fragment from rim. Fine, soft, reddish yellow (7.5YR 7/6) fabric. Very pale brown (10YR 8/3) slip. Worn black to red (10R 5/8) paint. Upright multiple oval. LM IIIC.

Coarse Wares

K102.2   Jar (FIG. 6.16). D. rim est. 25. Single fragment from rim. Coarse, reddish yellow (5YR 6/6) fabric with very frequent schist inclusions (2–4 mm) and hard white angular inclusions. Sampled KAR 06/60. Possible burning on exterior. LM IIIC.

Room K 106

This larger room was probably roofed, although roofing material was found only along the north. It contained a rectangular, stone-lined pit 15 cm deep. According to the notebook, at least six pithoi were found of Types 5, 6, 7, 8, 17, and 18 with the usual designs, along with a wavy moulding and impressed circles, and one quadruple handle with holes at the base. Other coarse wares listed included three pithoid jars of Type 3, two jars of Types 3 and 7, a tripod of Type 1 and other legs, at least three tripod dishes, two dishes of Type 1, one with a handle, and four of Type 6, a small jar of Type 4, a basin of Type 7, a kalathos of Type 3, two stirrup jars of Type 2, two one-handled jugs of Type 3, a bowl of Type 2, and a scuttle handle. Fine wares included a blue bowl of Type 1 (**K106.11**), three stirrup jars of Type 3, several bowls of Types 1 and 2, a kylix stem (**K106.18**), and a cup of Type 1 (**K106.1**).

A good deal of pottery was found in the museum that was not catalogued, including fragments of a deep bowl with reserved band and spiral, and other deep bowls with spirals, pendent multiple loops, and a fringed motif. There were also krater fragments with scalloped edges on the rim band, dotted hatched curvilinear motifs, crosshatched lozenge or triangle, and groups of strokes on the rim. Uncatalogued stirrup jar fragments had bands or filler ornaments. Also found were a cup, a jug with rolled handle and snake (?) attachment, a kalathos with excrescent cup, a small cylindrical vessel, a possible tile, a pithos handle (?), a small jug with wavy line on shoulder, a jug handle, and a large vertical jug handle with a groove down the middle.

A variety of objects was found in the room, including a good deal of bronze: two fragments of wire (537), a drop pendent or earring (539),[105] a curved knife (540),[106] a ring (554),[107] a votive double axe (555),[108] a rod (553), and a fragment (538). The rod has been identified as belonging to a bronze rod tripod or four-sided stand.[109] Also found were the head of a terracotta statuette (559),[110] the body of an animal figurine (609), and two

sherds from cult objects, perhaps to be identified with two unusual hollow pyramidal objects that were found and not catalogued. A pierced stone plaque (608) was also found, and the notebook adds that animal bones and pumice came from this deposit.

Gesell has identified Room K 106 as a possible shrine.[111] The bronze double axe suggests ritual activity, as does the fragment of a terracotta statuette (which because of the size would seem to be from a figurine rather than a statue of goddess with upraised arms). The hollow pyramidal objects may also have had a ritual function, possibly parts of horns of consecration, like those from Ayia Triada and Patsos.[112] Nevertheless, this is not the same sort of religious area as the Temple or even K 116. Certainly it is not a shrine of the goddess with upraised arms, which regularly has associated snake tubes and plaques, although the basin or stand fragment may indeed belong to a snake tube. It is rather more like rooms K 85–K 87, with its combination of animal and human figurines.[113]

The other pottery resembles an ordinary domestic assemblage, including much cooking ware. The tripod (**K106.25**) is the sort found most commonly at Karphi and other LM IIIC sites.[114] The octagonal leg (**K106.26**), which probably comes from a tripod, is unique. The trays and tripod trays also are typical of LM IIIC assemblages; tray **K106.23** has finger or spit impressions on the rim, as often occurs on trays at Kavousi–*Vronda*, Phaistos, Khalasmenos, Kastri, and Kastrokephala.[115] The tripod tray **K106.24** is unusual only in that it has an elliptical leg rather than the usual round leg, and there are three parallel vertical strokes on the leg for decoration, in place of the usual dint or deep incision.[116] The scuttle handle with its knobs is unique.

The fine wares consist of small fragments that could as easily have been in the floors during the use of the room. The only nearly complete vessel was the miniature cup (**K106.1**). The deep bowls or cups have

---

105   *Karphi*, pl. 29.1.

106   *Karphi*, pl. 28.2.

107   *Karphi*, pl. 29.2.

108   *Karphi*, pl. 29.1.

109   Hoffman 1997, 100; the stylistic date for this Cypriote type is early 12th century.

110   *Karphi*, pl. 32.2.

111   Gesell 1985, 81–2.

112   D'Agata 1997, 90–2, figs. 9–13; Kourou and Karetsou 1994, 113–5, pls. 85–86, 88–89, figs. 29–30.

113   Day 2009, 146–7.

114   *Kastri*, 299, fig. 17.P9; Borgna 1997*b*, 194, fig. 3.1c (Phaistos); Tsipopoulou 2004, 113, fig. 8.7.95-397 (Khalasmenos).

115   Day *et al.* forthcoming (Kavousi–*Vronda*); Borgna 1997*b*, 196, fig. 5.3 (Phaistos); Tsipopoulou 2004, 113, fig. 8.7.97-30 (Khalasmenos); *Kastri*, 290, fig. 11n; Kanta and Karetsou 2003, 159, fig. 10 (Kastrokephala).

116   For tripod trays cf. Borgna 1997*b*, 196, fig. 5.3 (Phaistos).

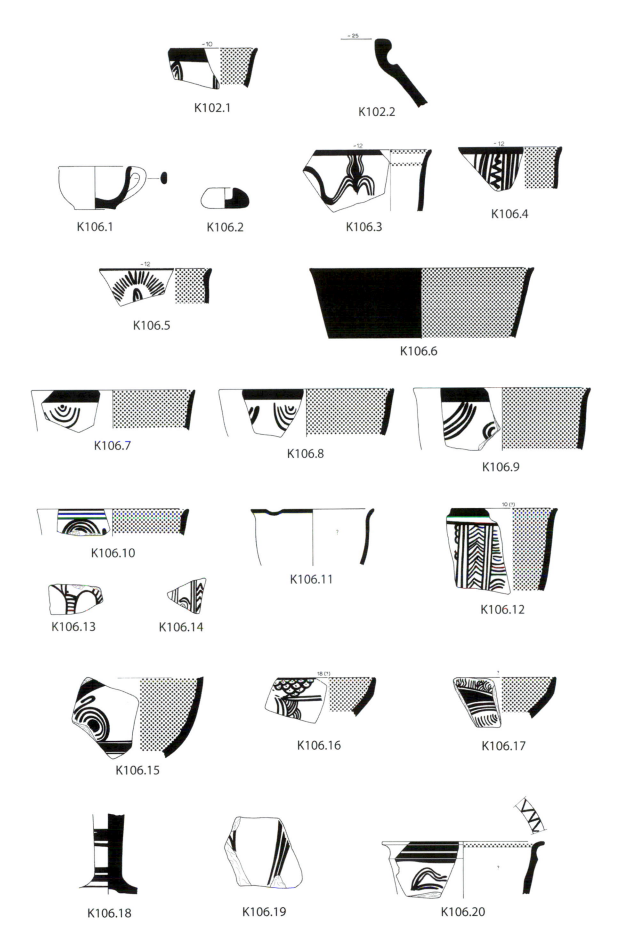

Fig. 6.16. *Western Cliff Houses, Building 2, pottery from K 102 (**K102.1–2**) and K 106 (**K106.1–20**). Scale 1:3.*

the usual LM IIIC patterns, including multiple pendent loops, panel designs with zigzag, upright Minoan flower, button-hook spiral; some are monochrome. All these motifs appear from the earliest phase of LM IIIC. The most unusual decoration is on **K106.3**, which has a tricurved streamer with a floral motif and two interior bands instead of the usual monochrome interior. This piece may well have been imported, possibly from the mainland. There were several kylix fragments, at least two of them from a carinated kylix (**K106.16–17**). The preserved stem (**K106.18**) is not pierced.

Pottery Catalogue: K 106

Fine Wares

K106.1   Miniature cup (FIG. 6.16). H. 3.5; D. base 3.3; D. rim 5.8. Intact. 65% preserved, including handle missing 33% of body and 50% of rim. Fine, soft, light red (2.5YR 6/8) fabric with some black inclusions. Surfaces still coated with sediment. LM IIIC.

K106.2   Finger pot (FIG. 6.16). H. 1.6; max. D. 3.7. Intact. Fine reddish yellow (7.5YR 7/6) fabric. Shaped like spindle whorl, but with circular depression in centre. LM IIIC.

K106.3   Deep bowl or cup (FIG. 6.16). D. rim est. 12. Single fragment (two sherds) from rim. Fine, medium-hard, porous, very pale brown (10YR 7/3) fabric with tiny black hard inclusions. Very pale brown (10YR 8/3) slip. Worn black paint. Worn surfaces. Tricurved streamer with floral head. Interior unpainted except for two bands at rim. Possibly imported. LM IIIC.

K106.4   Deep bowl or cup (FIG. 6.16). D. rim est. 12. Single fragment from rim (glue on edges indicates were originally others). Fine, soft, porous, yellow (10YR 8/6) fabric. Very pale brown (10YR 8/3) slip. Worn reddish yellow (5YR 6/6) paint. Worn surfaces. Panelled pattern with wavy line between vertical lines. For decoration, cf. Popham 1965, 322, fig. 3.3 (Knossos?). LM IIIC.

K106.5   Deep bowl or cup (FIG. 6.16). D. rim est. 12. Single fragment from rim. Fine, medium-hard, very pale brown (10YR 8/4) fabric. Creamy very pale brown (10YR 8/3) slip. Worn red (2.5YR 5/8) paint. Upright Minoan flower. For decoration, cf. Andreadaki-Vlasaki and Papadopoulou 2007, 50, fig. 7.11 (Khamalevri, Phase Ib); Kanta and Karetsou 2003, 153, fig. 3B (Kastrokephala, early LM IIIC). LM IIIC early.

K106.6   Deep bowl or cup (FIG. 6.16). D. rim est. 18. Single fragment from rim. Fine, medium-hard reddish yellow (7.5YR 7/6) fabric. Thick red (10R 4/6) paint. Well-preserved surfaces. Blob or monochrome decoration. LM IIIC.

K106.7   Deep bowl or cup (FIG. 6.16). D. rim est. 13. Single fragment from rim. Fine, medium-hard, reddish yellow (7.5YR 7/6) fabric. White (10YR 8/2) slip. Worn black paint. Multiple pendent loops, not attached to rim band. For decoration, cf. **K106.8**; Andreadaki-Vlasaki and Papadopoulou 2007, 46, fig. 3.3 (Khamalevri, Phase I). LM IIIC early.

K106.8   Deep bowl or cup (PLATE 1 h, FIG. 6.16). D. rim est. 14. Single fragment from rim. Fine, soft, very pale brown (10YR 7/4) fabric. Very pale brown (10YR 8/4) slip. Red (10R 4/8) paint, dark reddish brown (2.5YR 2.5/4) on interior. Worn surfaces. Multiple pendent loops, not attached to rim bands. Cf. **K106.7**. LM IIIC.

K106.9   Deep bowl or cup (FIG. 6.16). D. rim est. 14. Single fragment from rim. Fine, soft, porous, white (2.5Y 8/2) fabric and slip. Black paint. Worn surfaces. Multiple pendent loops, spiral (?). LM IIIC.

K106.10   Deep bowl or cup (FIG. 6.16). D. rim est. 12. Single fragment from rim. Fine, soft, reddish yellow (7.5YR 7/6) fabric.

White (10YR 8/2) slip. Red (10R 4/8) paint. Worn surfaces. Buttonhook spiral. Three bands on rim. LM IIIC.

K106.11   Deep bowl or cup (FIG. 6.16). D. rim 10. Single fragment from rim and body. Fine, hard, dark greenish grey (5BG 4/1) blue ware fabric. Black paint. Either rim warped or pinched out to form spout. Band on rim, possibly painted on interior. LM IIIC.

K106.12   Deep bowl or cup (FIG. 6.16). D. rim est. 10. Single fragment from rim. Fine, very soft, reddish yellow (7.5YR 7/6) fabric with tiny black inclusions. Very pale brown (10YR 8/3) slip. Black paint worn to shadow. Panelled pattern with scalloped edges, vertical chevrons, arcs. LM IIIC.

K106.13   Deep bowl or cup (FIG. 6.16). Max. pres. H. 2.5. Single fragment from body. Fine, soft, very pale brown (10YR 8/4) fabric and slip. Black paint. Well-preserved surfaces. Curvilinear motif with hatching. LM IIIC.

K106.14   Deep bowl or cup (FIG. 6.16). Max. pres. H. 2.7. Single fragment from body. Fine, soft, porous, very pale brown (10YR 7/4) fabric. White (10YR 8/2) slip. Black paint worn to shadow. Very worn surfaces. Panelled pattern with chevrons, arc fillers. LM IIIC.

K106.15   Deep bowl or cup (FIG. 6.16). Max. pres. H. 6.3. Single fragment from body. Fine, medium-soft, reddish yellow (7.5YR 7/6) fabric. Very pale brown (10YR 8/4) slip. Worn red (2.5YR 5/8) paint, especially on interior. Buttonhook spiral and curvilinear ornament. Label unclear, could also be K 100. LM IIIC.

K106.16   Kylix (PLATE 18 i, FIG. 6.16). D. rim est. 18. Single fragment from rim. Fine, soft, reddish yellow (7.5YR 7/6) fabric. Very pale brown (10YR 8/3) slip. Reddish brown (5YR 4/4) to yellowish red (5YR 4/6) paint. Worn surfaces. On rim, pendent stacked scale pattern with dots. Multiple arcs below. May be same vessel as **K106.17**. LM IIIC.

K106.17   Kylix (PLATE 18 i, FIG. 6.16). Max. pres. H. 3.3. Single fragment from rim. Fine, soft, reddish yellow (5YR 7/6) fabric. Very pale brown (10YR 8/3) slip. Red (2.5YR 4/8) paint. Well-preserved surfaces on exterior, worn on interior. Alternating arcs on rim. Below is solid curvilinear motif with multiple outlines, arc filler. May be same vessel as **K106.16**. LM IIIC.

K106.18   Kylix (FIG. 6.16). Max. pres. H. 6.5. Single fragment from stem, preserving part of base; missing edge of base. Fine, soft, reddish yellow (7.5YR 7/6) fabric. White (10YR 8/2) slip. Dull black paint. Worn surfaces. Tall stem, not pierced. Foot has circular depression in centre. Bands on stem. LM IIIC.

K106.19   Kylix (FIG. 6.16). Max. pres. H. 5.7. Single fragment from body, near stem. Fine, soft, very pale brown (10YR 8/3) fabric and slip. Dark reddish brown (5YR 3/2–3/4) paint. Multiple stems. LM IIIC.

K106.20   Basin (?) (FIG. 6.16). D. rim est. 13. Single fragment from rim. Fine, medium-hard pink (7.5YR 7/4) fabric. Very pale brown (10YR 8/4) slip. Worn black paint. Unusual shape; ridge suggests fine basin, but it looks deep. Multiple streamers (?). Zigzag on rim. LM IIIC.

K106.21   Basin or stand (FIG. 6.17). D. rim est. 28. Single fragment from rim, preserving handle scar; almost identical fragment from K 115, probably from same vessel. Fine, soft, chalky light grey (2.5 Y 7/2) fabric with frequent tiny black inclusions. Heavy rim with two ridges below. Unusual shape; may be a basin or more likely the base of a stand or snake tube, like **M8.5**. Monochrome? LM IIIC.

Coarse Wares

K106.22   Scuttle (FIG. 6.17). Max. pres. L. 10. Single fragment preserving end of handle. Coarse red (10R 5/6) fabric with infrequent schist inclusions (2–3 mm). Mottled black and red surface. S-curved handle, round in section. Dint at end. Two pairs of knobs on top. Publication: Seiradaki, pl. 12b, middle, third from right. LM IIIC.

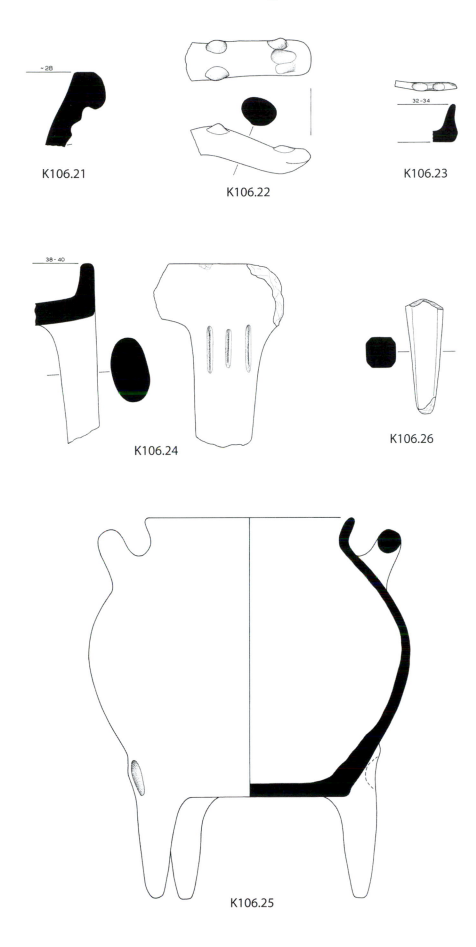

K106.21

K106.22

K106.23

K106.24

K106.26

K106.25

*Fig. 6.17. Western Cliff Houses, Building 2, pottery from K 106 (**K106.21–26**). Scale 1:3.*

K106.23   Tray (FIG. 6.17). H. 3.1; D. base est. 32–34. Single fragment preserving full profile. Coarse red (10R 5/6) fabric with frequent schist inclusions (1–2 mm). Hard mottled surface on interior, burned on exterior; no burning on bottom. Finger impressions on rim. LM IIIC.

K106.24   Tripod tray (FIG. 6.17). Max. pres. H. 13; D. rim est. 38–40. Single fragment preserving most of leg and full profile; tip of leg, handles missing. Coarse red (2.5YR 5/6) cooking fabric with very frequent inclusions of angular chunks. Surface smoothed and mottled red and black. No traces of burning. Three vertical slashes on leg. Publication: Seiradaki, pl. 12b, middle, left. LM IIIC.

K106.25   Tripod cooking pot (FIG. 6.17). H. 30.6; D. base est. 17; D. rim est. 16.8. Partially mended from 55 fragments, six non-joining fragments. 75% preserved, including all legs, full profile, and both handles; missing 20% of body, 50% of rim. Coarse reddish yellow (5YR 6/6) fabric with red phyllites, hard white angular and hard grey inclusions. Sampled KAR 06/53. Base and legs burned in patches; exterior of body totally burned. Dints at top of legs. LM IIIC.

K106.26   Tripod (FIG. 6.17). Max. pres. H. 9.1. Single fragment preserving one leg. Coarse red (2.5YR 4/6) fabric with frequent large (1–2 mm) phyllite and hard white angular inclusions. Surface smoothed and cracked. Octagonal in section (or square with bevelled edges). Publication: Seiradaki, pl. 12b, second row, fourth from right. LM IIIC.

Room K 115

This small room, like K 102, was identified as a roofed cellar, and the excavators thought it was reached by ladder from K 106. In addition to the pottery catalogued below, the notebook records the following coarse wares: four pithoi of Types 1, 2, 14, and 15 and a base with impressed circles (**K115.19**); two pithoid jars of Types 3 and 9; tripod legs; several jars of Type 3; a dish of Type 6; two stirrup jars of Type 2; a jar or jug; krater bases of Types 1 and 2; several bowls of Types 1 and 2; and a small tripod pithos. Finer pottery listed in the notebook included two one-handled jugs, a spouted jug, a scuttle, four painted jars of Type 2, a small kylix of Type 2, a large burned pyxis of Type 2 with lily pattern (**K115.7**), a bowl of Type 1 with a 'Melian imp' (**K115.2**), a kylix of Type 2 (**K115.5**) and another smaller one, a stirrup jar of Type 2, a bowl or krater with scale pattern, several bowls of Types 1 and 2, and a hut urn (**K115.8**). The uncatalogued fragments found in the boxes also included the end of a possible bird vase, a kylix base, an excrescent cup with horns, three stirrup jars decorated with strokes, fringes, and scale pattern, a large jug or jar with a quatrefoil floral motif, and body fragments from the same or other jugs. One jug, decorated with bands and published in Seiradaki was missing.[117] Few objects were found in the room, only a bronze stylus-shaped implement (551) and a bronze arrowhead (552);[118] animal bones were recorded in the notebook.

The preserved pottery from this room is made up of nearly complete vessels and constitutes a good assemblage for the end of the settlement's history. It looks very late in LM IIIC. The skyphos or krateriskos (**K115.4**) is unique for the settlement, and although

the shape appears on the mainland as early as LH IIIC early,[119] it is rare on Crete until later (SM or PG). This example does not look as late as those found in Ta Mnemata Tomb 17, which are narrower and have higher, more conical feet. This may be one of the earliest examples of what becomes a standard shape in SM. The huge cup (**K115.1**) with its zigzag pattern may also be late; a cup of similar size and shape was found at Kavousi–*Vronda*.[120] The pyxis (**K115.7**) has fringed patterns with a bird and possibly a double axe, but it is more careless than usual, possibly a sign of a later date. The large kylix (**K115.5**) with its fringed decoration, however, is still within the LM IIIC tradition; it has the typical carinated profile and a bulbous stem that is not pierced all the way up. The deep bowl (**K115.2**) has both a reserved band and disc and an unusual 'gremlin' or 'scorpion' decoration; the shape is reminiscent of a deep bowl from Sybrita/ Thronos, which is dated to early SM.[121] The bowl (**K115.6**) is highly unusual in shape, although another similar bowl was found without any find spot; they may be related to the mainland spouted bowl shape of LH IIIC.[122] The stirrup jar (**K115.9**), with its filled medallions is more reminiscent of the octopus style stirrup jars and looks earlier in LM IIIC, and its shape is nothing like the later SM to PG style. The three jugs (**K115.10**, **12**, **14**) are all very similar in shape and they are not narrowly datable. The amphora (**K115.15**) finds parallels in LM IIIC Kastri, Khania, and Khalasmenos.[123] The jar (**K115.16**) is a type that appears elsewhere at Karphi, but it was not found commonly at other LM IIIC sites.

As an assemblage, this group is interesting. Some storage obviously was going on in the room, to judge from the numerous pithoi and pithoid jars, and possibly the coarse stirrup jars and amphora. Cooking wares were also found (both tripods and dishes), along with coarse kraters that might have been used in the preparation of food. Thus the room seems to have been used for multiple domestic functions. The fine wares suggest that eating and especially drinking also went on in the room. The hut urn may have served a religious function, but the use of these small items is still a matter for debate, and this single item cannot be used to

---

117   Seiradaki, pl. 5c, bottom middle.
118   *Karphi*, pl. 29.1.
119   Mountjoy 1986, 124.
120   Day and Glowacki forthcoming.
121   D'Agata 1999, 202, fig. 13.41.1.
122   Similar to a spouted cup from Lefkandi (*RMDP*, 713, fig. 273.63, LH IIIC Middle) and Melos (*RMDP*, 918, fig. 373.144 — with wavy band. LH IIIC early.
123   *Kastri*, 296, fig. 16. P31 (actually P28) P 25; *Khania II*, 91, pl. 49.87-P 0020/0029/0379, of LM IIIB2; Tsipopoulou 2004, 110, fig. 8.4.96-358.

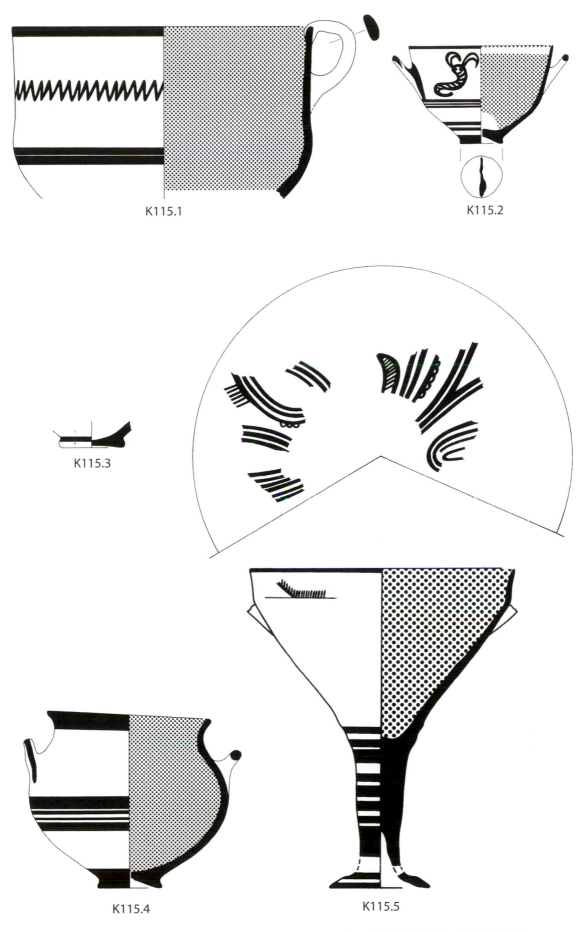

*Fig. 6.18. Western Cliff Houses, Building 2, pottery from K 115 (**K115.1–5**). Scale 1:3.*

suggest a primarily religious function for the room, although its association in the same building as a possible shrine or cult centre is suggestive.

Pottery Catalogue: K 115

Fine Wares

K115.1 Cup (FIG. 6.18). D. rim 24. Partially mended from five fragments from rim and handle. Fine, soft, pink (5YR 7/4) fabric. White (10YR 8/2) slip. Worn black paint. Worn surfaces. Zigzag between bands. LM IIIC late.

K115.2 Deep bowl (HM 11059) (PLATE 22 *h*, FIG. 6.18). H. 8; D. base 3.4; D. rim 11.6. Restored from several fragments. 80% preserved, including entire base, both handles; missing parts of rim and body. Fine, soft, pale brown (10YR 6/3) fabric with infrequent tiny black and white inclusions. No slip. Dark brown (7.5YR 4/2) to very dark grey (10YR 3/1) paint. Misfired or burned. Scorpions or gremlins, two on each side. Reserved band on interior of rim, reserved disc on base. Drip on underside of base. Publication: Seiradaki, fig. 21.l; pl. 10a, top, second from left. For shape, cf. **K120N.1**. LM IIIC late.

K115.3 Deep bowl or cup (FIG. 6.18). D. base est. 5. Single fragment from base. Fine, soft, reddish yellow (7.5YR 7/6) fabric. Very pale brown (10YR 8/3) slip. Black paint. Very worn surfaces. LM IIIC early.

K115.4 Skyphos or krateriskos (PLATE 22 *i*, FIG. 6.18). H. 13.6–14.4; D. base 5; D. rim 12.5–13. Restored from 25 fragments. 75% preserved, including base, full profile; missing much of rim and part of one handle. Fine soft, very pale brown (10YR 7/3) fabric burned to light grey (10YR 7/2), with some sand-sized black inclusions. Black paint. Very worn surfaces. Burned; negative decoration on one side. Very irregular in shape, but possibly due to restoration. Once decorated, but too worn to distinguish anything but bands. Publication: Seiradaki, fig. 14.8. For the shape, cf. *RMDP*, 731, fig. 282.15 (Skyros, LH IIIC, early); *Kastri*, 295, fig. 15.P23. SM.

K115.5 Kylix (FIG. 6.18). Max. pres. H. 23.4; D. base 8; D. rim 21. Once mended from 40 fragments. 60% preserved, including entire stem and lower body, one set of handle attachments, fragment of base, large fragment of rim; missing both handles, 75% of upper body and rim. Fine, soft, chalky, reddish yellow (5YR 7/6) to white (10YR 8/2) fabric. Black paint. Very worn surfaces. Possibly misfired in kiln. Fringes on rim. Hatched and scalloped curvilinear motifs. For the stem, cf. Andreadaki-Vlasaki and Papadopoulou 2007, 47, fig. 4.24 (Khamalevri, Phase II). LM IIIC late.

K115.6 Bowl (FIG. 6.19). Max. pres. H. 17; D. rim est. 20. Mended from 26 fragments, but broken. 70% preserved, including profile down to base; missing base and handles. Fine, very soft, reddish yellow (5YR 7/6) fabric. Pink (7.5YR 8/4) slip. Yellowish red (5YR 4/6) paint. Very worn surfaces. May have had a spout. Wavy bands on rim and below rim, alternating with bands. Bands on interior, one drip. Publication: Seiradaki, pl. 10a, top left. LM IIIC.

K115.7 Pyxis (PLATE 23 *a*, FIG. 6.19). H. 18.8; D. base 19.4; D. rim 12.5. Restored from 21 fragments. 90% preserved; missing fragments of rim, base, and upper body. Fine, light grey (10YR 7/2) fabric with sand-sized black inclusions. Black paint. Very worn surfaces. Burned all over, but especially on base, where decoration has turned negative. Panelled pattern. Side A: double axe (?) with multiple loops in centre, bird and flower on one side, loop filled with chevrons and multiple loops on other. Side B: curvilinear design with fringes and spirals. Chevrons under handles, strokes on top of handles. Publication: Seiradaki, pl. 7b, top left (mislabelled K 114). LM IIIC late.

K115.8 Hut urn (PLATE 23 *b*, FIG. 6.20). H. 8.6; D. base 7.1. Mended from numerous fragments. 95% preserved; missing one handle, part of threshold, and two fragments of roof. Fine, soft, light

red (2.5YR 6/6) fabric, slipped and burnished. No burning. Two pierced lugs on either side of doorway made separately and added on. Very wide (0.06) doorway. No decoration. Publication: Mersereau 1993, 33–4, fig. 22.14; Hägg 1990, 99, fig. 8, 105.8. LM IIIC.

K115.9 Stirrup jar (PLATE 23 *c*, FIG. 6.20). H. 15.2; D. base 5; max. D. 15.7. Restored from 25 fragments. 85% preserved; only missing body fragments. Fine, soft, reddish yellow (5YR 6/6) fabric with tiny infrequent black inclusions. Pink (7.5YR 8/4) slip. Paint crackled and dark brown, now only a shadow. Well-preserved surfaces on top, less so further down. Short spout, tilted back to touch false spout. On shoulder: half medallions with ovals filled with wavy lines creating triangles with arc fillers. Arcs, fringes, scalloped edges, and dots as fillers. Horizontal stripes on handles, circle on false spout. LM IIIC early.

K115.10 Jug (FIG. 6.20). H. 23.5; D. base 9; D. rim 7.2. Nineteen joining fragments from top, two joining fragments from base and lower body, nine non-joining fragments. 75% preserved, including full profile, entire base, and handle. Fine, hard, reddish yellow (7.5YR 6/8) fabric with infrequent soft red inclusions and grey phyllites (1 mm). Traces of white (10YR 8/2) slip and red paint. Very worn surfaces. LM IIIC.

K115.11 Closed vessel (FIG. 6.20). D. base 3.4. Large fragment from base. Fine, soft, reddish yellow (7.5YR 7/6) fabric. Very pale brown (10YR 8/3) slip. Red (10R 4/8) paint. Worn surfaces. Tall raised concave base. Bands with hatching between two pairs. LM IIIC.

Medium-Coarse Wares

K115.12 Jug (HM 11067) (FIG. 6.20). H. 19.5; D. base 7.5; D. rim 7.4. Partially restored from numerous fragments. 75% preserved, including full profile; missing 80% of base and fragments of body. Medium-coarse, very pale brown (10YR 8/3) fabric with frequent inclusions and voids. Very pale brown (10YR 8/3) slip. Worn red (2.5YR 5/8) paint. Rather worn surfaces. Shape: Seiradaki Type 3. Concentric circles, hand drawn, on shoulder; bands below; circle on each side and one opposite handle. Handle solidly painted. Publication: Seiradaki, pl. 5a, left (misidentified as from K 23). For shape, cf. *Kastri*, 296, fig. 16.P16. LM IIIC.

Coarse Wares

K115.13 Scuttle (PLATE 23 *d*, FIG. 6.21). Max. pres. H. 4.6. Three joining fragments from rim, with handle attachment; 12 other non-joining fragments. 10% preserved, including part of rim and handle; missing base. Coarse red (2.5YR 5/8) fabric with red phyllites, schist (1–3 mm), and hard white angular inclusions. Sampled KAR 06/81. No traces of burning. Seven incised lines beneath rim on interior. LM IIIC.

K115.14 Jug (FIG. 6.21). H. est. 20; D. base 6. Fourteen fragments, including base and lower body, rim and handle. 30% preserved, including entire base, handle with neck and rim. Very coarse yellowish red (5YR 5/6) to reddish yellow (5YR 6/6) fabric with frequent red and grey phyllites and hard white angular inclusions. Surfaces still coated with sediment. Nearly all burned grey (5Y 5/1). LM IIIC.

K115.15 Amphora (FIG. 6.21). H. 28.8; D. base 8.7; D. rim 10.4. Once mended from 54 fragments. 75% preserved, including one handle, full profile; missing parts of upper body and rim, one handle, most of base. Coarse, medium-hard and well-levigated pink (7.5YR 7/4) fabric with small (<1 mm) hard white angular inclusions. Surface wiped, not slipped, very pale brown (10YR 8/3) in colour. Red (2.5YR 4/6) paint worn to shadow. Much of surface still coated with sediment. Bands, with possible wavy band on lower body. LM IIIC.

K115.16 Jar (PLATE 23 *e*, FIG. 6.21). H. 15.2; D. base 12; D. rim 13. Restored from eight fragments. 95% preserved; missing only one handle. Coarse very pale brown (10YR 8/3) fabric with frequent

K115.6

K115.7

Fig. 6.19. *Western Cliff Houses, Building 2, pottery from K 115 (**K115.6**–7). Scale 1:3.*

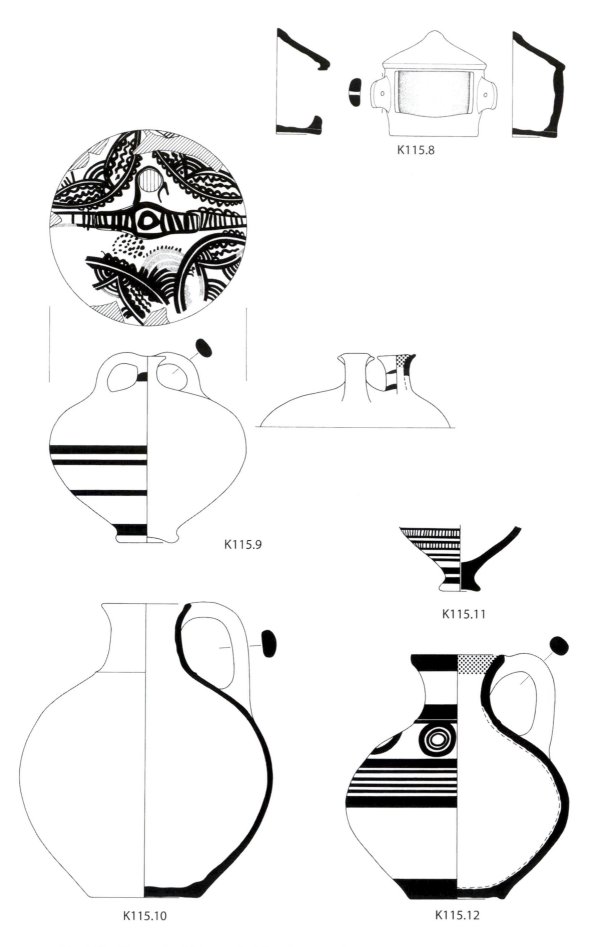

K115.8

K115.9

K115.11

K115.10

K115.12

*Fig. 6.20. Western Cliff Houses, Building 2, pottery from K 115 (**K115.8–12**). Scale 1:3.*

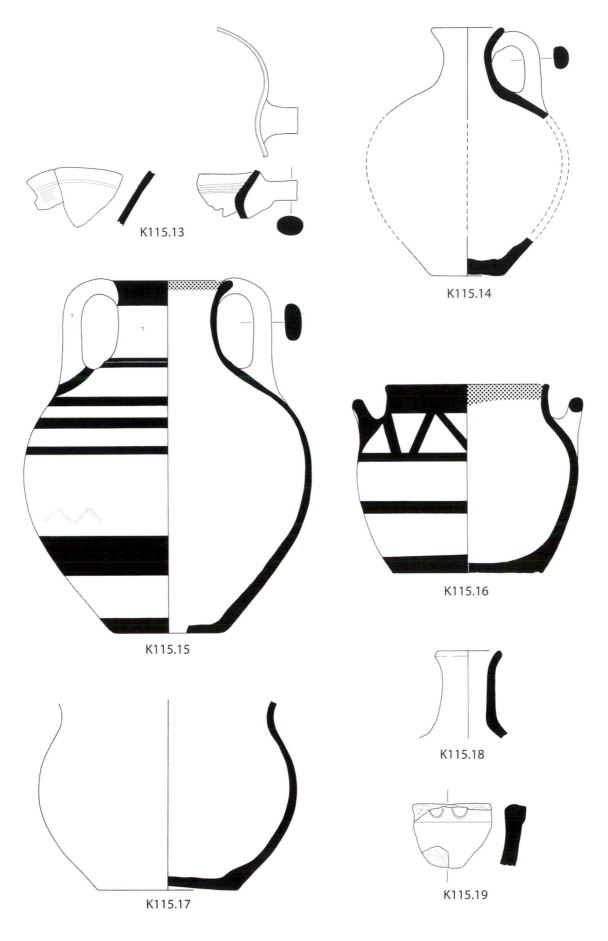

*Fig. 6.21. Western Cliff Houses, Building 2, pottery from K 115 (**K115.13–19**). Scale 1:3.*

inclusions of hard, rounded black stone (1–7 mm), and some hard white angular inclusions. Very pale brown (10YR 8/3) slip. Crackled black paint. Large zigzag on shoulder; bands below. Publication: Seiradaki, pl. 1e, left (mislabelled K 15). LM IIIC.

K115.17   Jar (FIG. 6.21). Max. pres. H. 15.3; D. base 10.4 Large fragment from base (seven sherds), five body fragments, preserving entire base, 75% of lower body, profile to neck; missing rim and handles. Coarse pink (7.5YR 7/4) to reddish yellow (7.5YR 7/4) fabric with frequent phyllites, hard white angular and hard black inclusions. Surfaces still coated with sediment. LM IIIC.

K115.18   Stirrup jar (FIG. 6.21). Max. pres. H. 7; D. rim 5.3. Two fragments from spout. Coarse pink (7.5YR 7/4) to reddish yellow (7.5YR 7/6) fabric with frequent phyllites, hard white angular and hard black inclusions. LM IIIC.

K115.19   Pithos or basin (FIG. 6.21). Max. pres. H. 4.8. Single fragment from body, probably from near rim. Coarse, soft, reddish yellow (5YR 6/8) fabric with frequent schist and limestone inclusions. Raised band with impressed or incised circles. Could be the joint between two fragments of a pithos, which was then strengthened by adding a band, or it could be from the base of a pithos, as the excavators suggested. LM IIIC.

Room K 126

This room was entered from the north. Its west side was entirely of rock, and it had a narrow entrance into K 106. The pottery was unusual only in being broken and not containing obvious pithos sherds. No actual vessels were preserved. There were two of the baking slabs like one found in K 113, along with one loomweight of a type uncommon at Karphi. Such loomweights do appear at Kavousi–*Kastro*, but in the Geometric Period.[124]

Pottery Catalogue: K 126

Coarse Wares

K126.1   Cooking slab (FIG. 6.22). Max. pres. L. 31; max. pres. W. 20.8; Th. 2.6–3.5. Two joining fragments preserving one finished edge of flat slab. Coarse red (2.5YR 5/8) fabric with very frequent dark grey phyllites (2–3 mm). Surfaces still coated with sediment, but surfaces burned. Flat slab with hole pierced into one side. Underside uneven and rough. LM IIIC.

K126.2   Cooking slab (FIG. 6.22). Max. pres. L. 22; max. pres. W. 18.8; Th. 3.7–4.5. Five joining fragments, no finished edges. Coarse red (2.5YR 5/8) fabric with grey core and frequent schist and hard white angular inclusions (1–2 mm). Sampled KAR 06/42. Surfaces coated with sediment, but where cleaned is burned. Flat slab, but with possible raised edge. May be same as **K126.1**. LM IIIC.

Miscellaneous Objects

K126.3   Loomweight (FIG. 6.22). Max. pres. H. 10.4; L. base 9. Partially mended from six fragments, one non-joining fragment. Most of base and lower body preserved, including part of hole, and one fragment from top. Coarse light red (10R 6/8) fabric with infrequent large red phyllite inclusions. Large pyramidal loomweight with hole pierced through near top. LM IIIC.

THE NORTHERN SHELTERS (ROOMS K 104, K 107–109, K 122–125, K 127)

The rooms known as the Northern Shelters were described as simply spaces created by walling up the bedrock, and there was no coherent plan.[125] None of the spaces had any trace of roofing. They were probably reached from the north or from street K 105. The excavators also thought that they were among the earliest buildings on the site, similar to the Southern Shelters.

Room K 104

This was a tiny room without features. The pottery was listed as usual, but without pyxides or stirrup jars. The notebook adds that there was a pithos of Type 23 without a base, a lid of Type 1, and a small tripod bowl (**K104.1**), as well as fragments of a cylindrical ribbed cult object in red clay and a plaque with raised design in buff clay (**K104.2**). Aside from the tripod catalogued below, the boxes produced only a single sherd with incised ridges, possibly the cult object mentioned in the notebook. Objects included a bronze awl (574) and a conical stone bead or whorl (573). Although no find spot was written on the fragments of the plaque (**K104.2**), they are similar enough to the description in the notebook that they have been catalogued with the material from this room.

Pottery Catalogue: K 104

Medium-Coarse Wares

K104.1   Tripod (FIG. 6.23). D. base est. 18. Single fragment from base, preserving one leg. Medium-coarse, soft, reddish yellow (5YR 6/8) fabric with frequent sand-sized white and black inclusions. Grey surface, possible traces of black paint. Flat base with small elliptical leg. Possibly decorated. LM IIIC.

Coarse Wares

K104.2   Plaque (PLATE 23 *f*, FIG. 6.23). Max. pres. H. 6.3. Two joining fragments from edge; one non-joining fragment from body. Coarse, reddish yellow (5YR 6/8) fabric, light grey (5Y 6/1) at core, with infrequent small (1–2 mm) schist and hard white angular inclusions. Very pale brown (10YR 8/3) slip. Black paint. Flat plaque with raised ridge around exterior. Plastic decoration of animal hooves, on painted background; body fragment has plastic decoration of animal legs. LM IIIC.

Room K 107

K 107 and K 108 were on the same level and shared an alignment, with a possible door between. That they belonged together is suggested by cross-joins between the preserved pottery. The notebook records the following coarse ware: at least four pithoi of Types 3, 5, 8, and 14; two pithoid jars of Types 3 and 8; a jar with sharp neck and horizontal handles; the usual tripod legs; four dishes, two of Type 1, one with a handle, and two of Type 6; a krater; two kalathoi of Types 1 and 3; a large pyxis of Type 1; a one-handled jug, a double twisted pithos handle, and a flat clay slab with handles (**K107.10**). Fine wares included two small jars of Type

---

124 Lee Ann Turner (personal communication).
125 *Karphi*, 96–7.

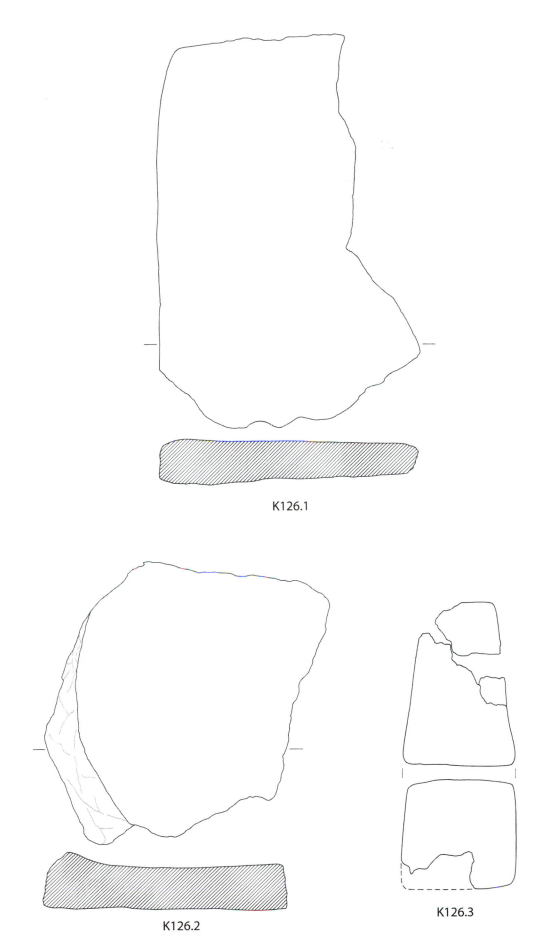

K126.1

K126.2

K126.3

*Fig. 6.22. Western Cliff Houses, Building 2, pottery from K 126 (**K126.1–3**). Scale 1:3.*

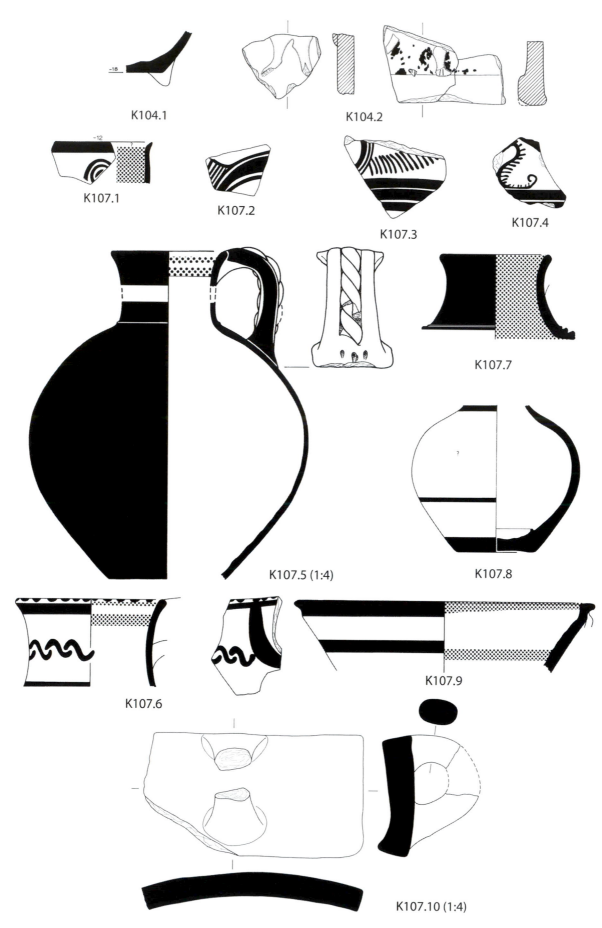

Fig. 6.23. Northern Shelters, pottery from K 104 (**K104.1–2**) and K 107 (**K107.1–10**).
Scale 1:3 unless otherwise indicated.

3, a small cup of Type 1 and one of Type 7; two kraters of Type 1 one with octopus pattern (**K107.4**), a small basin of Type 7 (**K107.9**); a stirrup jar of Type 2, a kylix stem, the neck of a jar or jug with 'running-dog' pattern (**K107.6**), small bowls and a triple handle. More pottery was found in the boxes but was not catalogued. Fine wares included deep bowl fragments with multiple pendent loops or dotted curvilinear patterns, a stirrup jar fragment with a spiral, and a jug or cup handle. Coarser fabrics included a cylindrical ridged vessel and a huge rope-twisted pithos handle with incised chevrons (doubtless the double twisted pithos handle mentioned in the notebook). Objects from this room included a rectangular stone bead (545), a stone grinder (575)[126] a cylindrical terracotta spindle whorl (544), a terracotta spool, and antler of red deer. The notebook mentions also animal bones and pumice from the room.

The material from the room was of little use either for dating the structure or for determining its function. The large coarse stand was probably used for cooking. There were few deep bowl fragments, and a larger number of fine jugs than normal. The red monochrome jug (**K107.5**) may have been in use at the time the room was abandoned, as so much of it was preserved; it is an elegant and unusual vessel, with its rope-twisted handle.

Pottery Catalogue: K 107

Fine Wares
K107.1   Deep bowl or cup (FIG. 6.23). D. rim est. 12. Single fragment from rim. Fine, soft, reddish yellow (7.5YR 7/6) fabric. Very pale brown (10YR 8/3) slip. Worn red-brown paint. Spiral. Possible reserved band on interior of rim. LM IIIC.

K107.2   Deep bowl or cup (FIG. 6.23). Max. pres. H. 4. Single fragment from body. Fine, soft, reddish yellow (7.5YR 7/6) fabric. Very pale brown (10YR 8/3) slip. Dull black paint worn to brown shadow. Worn surfaces. Outlined tricurved streamer with a hatched lozenge in centre. For decoration, cf. Rethemiotakis 1997, 322, fig. 33b (Kastelli Pediada). LM IIIC.

K107.3   Krater (FIG. 6.23). Max. pres. H. 6; Th. 0.75–0.85. Single fragment from body. Fine, soft, porous, very pale brown (10YR 8/4) fabric. White (2.5Y 8/2) slip. Red (2.5YR 4/8) paint. Worn surfaces. Minoan flower. LM IIIC early.

K107.4   Krater (FIG. 6.23). Max. pres. H. 5.2; Th. 0.6–0.85. Single fragment from body. Fine, soft, porous, very pale brown (10YR 8/4) fabric with some tiny grey inclusions. White (2.5Y 8/2) slip. Worn black paint. Worn exterior surfaces, well-preserved on interior. Fringed octopus tentacle. For decoration, cf. Mook and Coulson 1997, 346, fig. 11.32 (Kavousi–*Kastro*, Phase I). LM IIIC early.

K107.5   Jug (PLATE 23 *g*, FIG. 6.23). Max. pres. H. 35; D. rim est. 12.2. Partially mended into three large fragments, one from neck, handle, shoulder, two from body; 60 more non-joining body fragments. 20% preserved, including small part of rim, half of shoulder, entire handle; missing base and most of neck. Fine, soft but clinky, reddish yellow (7.5YR 7/6) fabric. Streaky red (2.5YR 5/8–4/8) to brown paint, unevenly preserved. Large elliptical handle with two twisted coils of clay in centre. Three holes pierced in body at base of handle. Monochrome. Two bands on interior of rim. LM IIIC.

K107.6   Spouted jug (FIG. 6.23). D. rim est. 12.1. Two large fragments (2 sherds each), preserving neck and spout attachment. Fine, rather soft, reddish yellow (7.5YR 7/6) fabric. Very pale brown (10YR 8/3) slip. Black paint worn to brown shadow. Worn surfaces. Spout from rim. Quirk on neck. Bands inside. Strokes on top of rim. Loop under spout. Joining fragments from K 108. For shape, cf. Mook and Coulson 356, fig. 25.82 (Kavousi–*Kastro*, Phase II). LM IIIC.

K107.7   Jug (FIG. 6.23). D. rim est. 9. Single large fragment preserving full profile of neck and handle scar. Fine, soft, reddish yellow (5YR 7/6) fabric. Dull black paint. Worn surfaces. Monochrome. Two grooves (3 ridges) at base of neck. LM IIIC.

K107.8   Jug (FIG. 6.23). Max. pres. H. 11.8; D. base 6.3. Mended from 29 fragments, five non-joining fragments. 80% preserved, including entire base and lower body; missing neck, rim, handle. Fine, very soft, reddish yellow (7.5YR 7/6) fabric. Very pale brown (10YR 8/4) surface. Dark reddish brown (5YR 3/2) paint. Burned on one side. Interior very rough. Bands. For shape, cf. Warren 2007, 341, fig. 6.P3 (Knossos). LM IIIC.

Medium-Coarse Wares
K107.9   Basin (FIG. 6.23). D. rim est. 24. Three large fragments from rim (30 sherds), including handle attachment. 45% of rim preserved. Medium-coarse yellowish red (5YR 5/6) fabric with large (1–2 mm) infrequent grey phyllites. Very pale brown (10YR 8/4) slip. Black paint. Bands inside and out. For shape, cf. *Khania II*, pl. 54.84-P 0415 (kalathos, LM IIIB–C). LM IIIC.

Coarse Wares
K107.10   Stand (PLATE 23 *h*, FIG. 6.23). H. 13; Th. 2.5–3; interior D. 56–58. Mended from three fragments, preserving full profile and most of one handle. Broken at one end and missing centre of handle. Coarse yellowish red (5YR 5/6) fabric dark grey (N4/) at core; frequent hard black and white inclusions (1–2 mm) and large gold mica. Burned on exterior. Slightly curving thick slab of clay with finished edges on bottom and top and elliptical vertical handle. LM IIIC.

Room K 108

According to the notebook, this room had no trace of roofing and may have served as a steep path up to K 109. The notebook lists the following coarse pottery: three pithoi of Types 5, 8, and 10; two pithoid jars of Types 3 and 11; the usual tripod legs; a foot of a tripod pithos; four dishes, one of Type 1, three of Type 6; the base of jar of Type 7; four jars, one of Type 2, three of Type 3; and a kalathos of Type 1. Finer pottery included a stirrup jar of Type 2 with a hole through the false spout, a two-handled jug of Type 3, two kylix stems, and several small bowls of Types 1 and 2. A krater fragment with three bands and vertical strokes and a fragment of a deep bowl with multiple pendent loops were found in the storerooms, but were not catalogued. The pithos rim published by Seiradaki was not found.[127] Other objects from the room included a part of a twisted fibula of bronze (546),[128] a bronze fragment with rivets (578), a bone pin (576),[129] the head of a terracotta figurine (577), and a cylindrical terracotta spindle

126   *Karphi*, pl. 30.3.
127   Seiradaki, fig. 1.23.
128   *Karphi*, pl. 29.2.
129   *Karphi*, pl. 28.4.

*Fig. 6.24. Northern Shelters, pottery from K 108 (**K108.1–8**), K 109 (**K109.1**), K 122 (**K122.1–4**), and K 123 (**K123.1**).*
Scale 1:3 unless otherwise indicated.

whorl (628). The notebook also mentions a piece of metal ore, two pieces of pumice, miscellaneous stone tools, and animal bones.

The preserved pottery is small and scanty. The deep bowl fragments include two that may be early. **K108.1** has a rather neat spiral and a reserved band like those in early IIIC deposits at Kastelli Pediada and Kastri,[130] and in a late LM IIIC context at Kavousi–*Vronda*.[131] **K108.2** is decorated with a tricurved streamer that appears early in LM IIIC and can be paralleled on pottery from Knossos of LM IIIB date.[132] Ring vases like **K108.6** are also uncommon in LM IIIC deposits, and the best parallels for this example come from LM IIIB contexts.[133] The fragment of a closed vessel with crosshatched triangles (**K108.7**), however, is LM IIIC, and looks quite late.

Pottery Catalogue: K 108

Fine Wares

K108.1   Deep bowl (FIG. 6.24). D. rim est. 16. Single fragment (two sherds) from rim, preserving one handle. Fine, soft, reddish yellow (5YR 7/6) fabric. Very pale brown (10YR 8/3) slip. Crackled black paint, worn on exterior, streaky on interior. Spiral. Reserved band on interior. LM IIIC.

K108.2   Deep bowl or cup (FIG. 6.24). D. rim est. 15. Single fragment from rim. Fine, soft, reddish yellow (5YR 7/6) fabric. Thick, glossy, very pale brown (10YR 8/3) slip. Worn red (2.5YR 4/8) paint. Very worn surfaces. Tricurved streamer with multiple loops in centre and petal motif between. For decoration, cf. D'Agata 1999, 195, fig. 7.5.34 (Sybrita/Thronos, early LM IIIC); *RMDP*, 919, fig. 374.159 (Melos, early LH IIIC). LM IIIC.

K108.3   Deep bowl or cup (FIG. 6.24). Max. pres. H. 4.5. Single fragment from rim. Fine, medium-soft, reddish yellow (5YR 7/6) fabric. White (10YR 8/2) slip. Red (2.5YR 4/8) paint. Worn surfaces. Circle and vertical bands. LM IIIC.

K108.4   Deep bowl or cup (FIG. 6.24). Max. pres. H. 5. Single fragment from body. Fine, medium-soft, very pale brown (10YR 8/3) fabric and slip. Red (10R 4/8) paint. Well-preserved surfaces. Panelled pattern with tailed spiral. LM IIIC.

K108.5   Deep bowl or cup (FIG. 6.24). Max. pres. H. 5.2. Single fragment (two sherds) from body. Fine, soft, reddish yellow (5YR 7/6) fabric. Very pale brown (10YR 8/3) slip. Black to red (2.5YR 4/6) paint. Worn surfaces. Panelled decoration with vertical chevrons. For decoration, cf. *Kastri*, 289, fig. 10j (pyxis). LM IIIC.

K108.6   Ring vase (FIG. 6.24). Max. pres. H. 2.6; W. 3.7. Single fragment from top, preserving handle attachment. Fine, medium-hard, reddish yellow (5YR 7/6) fabric. White (10YR 8/2) slip. Red (10R 4/8) paint. Flat top, straight sides, square in section. Round basket handle on top. Bands. LM IIIB.

K108.7   Closed vessel (FIG. 6.24). Max. pres. H. 4.6. Single fragment from body. Fine, soft, white (10YR 8/2) fabric and slip. Black paint, worn to shadow. Worn surfaces. Crosshatched triangle with multiple outlines. LM IIIC.

Coarse Wares

K108.8   Cooking dish (FIG. 6.24). D. rim est. 40. Single fragment from rim. Coarse red (2.5YR 5/8) fabric with frequent schist and phyllites (2–4 mm) and hard white angular inclusions. Sampled KAR 06/61. Smoothed and mottled surface, rough on bottom. No burning. Slightly rounded bottom. Large rim, with ledge at bottom. For shape, cf. Mook 1999, fig. 110.10 (Kavousi–*Kastro*, Phase I). LM IIIC.

Room K 109

This 'room' is simply a space in the bedrock with one wall on the north and no features. The notebook lists the following coarse pottery: two pithoi of Types 1 and 3, the foot of a tripod pithos, two jars of Types 2 and 3, tripod legs, dishes of Types 1 and 6, several basins of Type 3, a krater of Type 1, and several small plain bowls of Type 1. Fine wares included at least three kraters of Type 1, a stirrup jar of Type 2 (**K109.1**), several small bowls of Types 1 and 2, three small jars or jugs, a triple handle, and a pyxis of Type 1. Two fine krater fragments found in one of the boxes were not catalogued. Objects included a bronze awl (564), a bronze hooked pin (565),[134] four conical (563, 569, 570, 571) and one cylindrical (568) stone beads or whorls, a Neolithic axe head (567), two bone instruments (562, 566), the head of a terracotta figurine (560), and two terracotta spindle whorls, one conical (572), the other biconical (561). The notebook reports animal bones from the room.

The stirrup jar (**K109.1**) is probably from an octopus stirrup jar. The motif of outlined tentacle in a field of U-pattern can be found on stirrup jars from Kritsa, Vasiliki, and Sybrita/Thronos of early LM IIIC date.[135]

Pottery Catalogue: K 109

Fine Wares

K109.1   Stirrup jar (PLATE 23 *i*, FIG. 6.24). Max. pres. H. 5.5. Two joining fragments from body. Fine, soft, reddish yellow (7.5YR 7/6) fabric. Very pale brown (10YR 8/4) slip. Black paint worn to shadow. Worn surfaces. Probably stirrup jar. Curvilinear motif (tentacle of octopus?) with arc fillers and a field of U-pattern. LM IIIC.

Room K 122

K 122 was another small space north of K 107, again without any features. The pottery is reported to have been much broken, a feature that elsewhere indicates pottery from a dump or from under the paving of a street or courtyard. The notebook reports a coarse kalathos of Type 3, a large coarse red stirrup jar, fine krater fragments, sherds from a small stirrup jar, and a hut urn with a lug on the door (**K122.4**). Some fragments of the rhyton from K 123 also came from K 122. A jug handle with plastic decoration was found in one of the boxes but not catalogued. A pithos rim

---

130   Rethemiotakis 1997, 315, fig. 23d (Kastelli Pediada); *Kastri*, 288, fig. 9d.

131   *Kavousi IIA*, fig. 39.B7 P21 (Kavousi–*Vronda*).

132   Popham 1970*b*, 198, fig. 2.5 from the Unexplored Mansion at Knossos.

133   Kanta 1980, 162, fig. 64.9, 12 (LM IIIB, Kalo Khorio–*Goula*); 50, fig. 23.12 (Mallia).

134   *Karphi*, pl. 29.2.

135   Paschalides 2009, fig. 69 (Kritsa), 70 (Vasiliki), 71 (Sybrita/Thronos).

published in Seiradaki was not located.[136] Objects from this room included two bronze needles (593, 594), a conical stone weight (591), a conical stone bead or whorl (592), the leg of a terracotta figurine of an ox (590), and a boar's tusk.

The large krater fragment (**K122.3**) with the great loops under the handle finds a parallel at Kavousi–*Vronda*, belonging to the very latest LM IIIC phase.[137] The panelled patterns of the deep bowls also are LM IIIC features. The rhyton, however, has been dated to LM IIIB.[138] Although the conical rhyton was not a popular shape in LM IIIC, it still continued in use, whether as an heirloom item or a vessel of recent manufacture. A good parallel for shape and decoration occurs in LM IIIC contexts at Kastelli Pediada and Khania;[139] another rhyton came from a late LM IIIC context at Kavousi–*Vronda*.[140] It is interesting to note that this rhyton was found in the same context as a hut urn.

Pottery Catalogue: K 122

Fine Wares

K122.1   Deep bowl or cup (FIG. 6.24). D. rim est. 14. Single fragment from rim. Fine, medium-hard, reddish yellow (7.5YR 7/6) fabric. Very pale brown (10YR 8/4) slip. Worn, streaky red-brown paint. Panelled pattern: vertical chevrons between bands; curvilinear motif. LM IIIC.

K122.2   Deep bowl or cup (FIG. 6.24). Max. pres. H. 2.8. Single fragment (two sherds) from body. Fine, soft, reddish yellow (7.5YR 7/6) fabric. Very pale brown (10YR 8/3) slip. Crackled black paint, worn to reddish yellow (7.5YR 6/8). Panelled pattern: leaves or quatrefoil, panel with chevrons. LM IIIC.

K122.3   Krater (PLATE 24 *a*, FIG. 6.24). Max. pres. H. 35; D. rim est. 27. Two large fragments, one from rim and handles (11 sherds), one from lower body (12 sherds); missing base. Fine, soft, porous, reddish yellow (7.5YR 7/6) fabric. Very pale brown (10YR 8/4) slip. Black to red (2.5YR 5/8) paint, worn to shadow. Sampled KAR 06/04. Exterior surfaces worn, interior well-preserved. Deep rounded body. Under handles are loops with tailed loop. Curvilinear pattern, possibly tricurved streamer, with solid centre and multiple outlines; scalloped edges and some arc fillers. For shape, cf. Warren 2007, 340, fig. 5.P307+ P662 (Knossos). LM IIIC.

Coarse Wares

K122.4   Hut urn (PLATE 24 *b*, FIG. 6.24). Max. pres. H. 8; D. base 9.5. Partially restored from 13 fragments; door is separate fragment. 65% preserved; missing centre of base, top of roof and top of door. Coarse red (2.5YR 4/8) cooking pot fabric. Surface smoothed and mottled, eroded or flaked off on top. Bevelled base, straight sides, conical roof. Pierced lugs on either side of door. Pierced lug on door. Publication: Seiradaki, pl. 10a bottom, second from right; Mersereau 1993, 34.15, fig. 23; Hägg 1990, 99, fig. 9, 105–6.9. LM IIIC.

Room K 123

This room was another small space without features. The pottery listed in the notebook included sherds from the same pithos as that found in K 104 with rim of Type 23 and the conical rhyton (**K123.1**).

Pottery Catalogue: K 123

Fine Wares

K123.1   Conical rhyton (PLATE 24 *c*, FIG. 6.24). Max. pres. H. 17.6; max. pres. D. 11.4. Partially restored from nine fragments. Missing base, rim, handle(s). Fine, soft, reddish yellow (5YR 6/6) fabric. Very pale brown (10YR 8/3) slip. Yellowish red (5YR 4/6) paint. Worn surfaces, better preserved on upper part than lower. Elaborately decorated. From top down: birds, panelled design with hatched pendent triangles with long tails on either side of vertical scalloped bands, vertical multiple wavy line. Publication: Seiradaki, fig. 20, right; pl. 10a, bottom right; Koehl 2006, 203, fig. 38.1069. Kanta 1980, 280 suggests that the rhyton could be LM IIIC and certainly is no earlier than LM IIIB. Fragments came from K 122. For the birds, cf. Borgna 1997*a*, 289, fig. 22 (Phaistos, LM IIIC); Adreadaki-Vlasaki and Papadopoulou 2005, 380, fig. 45 (Khamalevri, Phase II). LM IIIC.

Room K 124

This room was like the others. According to the notebook, the coarse pottery included pithos sherds, one rim of Type 2; two pithoid jars of Types 3 and 7; a jar of Type 2; tripod legs; four dishes, one of Type 1, three of Type 6; two bowls of Type 2, and a lid of Type 1 (**K124.9**). Fine pottery included two kraters of Type 1 (**K124.5** and **K124.6** or **7**), two fine stirrup jars of Type 2, and several bowls of Types 1 and 2. In addition to the catalogued pottery the boxes produced fragments of several deep bowls, three with curvilinear patterns (spirals?), one with tricurved motif outlined and with dots, and a krater fragment with a linear decoration. A bronze rod (589), a limestone pounder (579), the spout of an Early Minoan stone bowl (580);[141] three pierced schist discs (581, 582, 651), four bone pins (585, 586, 587, 588),[142] and two terracotta spindle whorls, one cylindrical (584), the other conical (583), were found here. The notebook lists animal bones as well.

Some of the pottery finds parallels in early LM IIIC, and it does not look particularly late.

Pottery Catalogue: K 124

Fine Wares

K124.1   Deep bowl or cup (PLATE 24 *d*, FIG. 6.25). D. rim est. 17. Two large fragments from rim (three sherds each). Fine, medium soft, porous, reddish yellow (7.5YR 7/6) to very pale brown (10YR 7/4) fabric. Very pale brown (10YR 8/4) slip. Red (10R 4/8–5/6) paint. Tricurved streamer with hatched leaf in centre. Publication: Seiradaki, fig. 25c (called a krater and drawn at a wrong stance).

---

136   Seiradaki, fig. 1.22.

137   Day and Glowacki forthcoming.

138   Seiradaki, 28.

139   Rethemiotakis 1997, 315, fig. 23a; *Khania II*, 155, pl. 55.77-P 0080, 84-P 0058.

140   Day 1997, 399, fig. 5.11; *Kavousi IIA*, fig. 23.

141   *Karphi*, pl. 30.1.

142   *Karphi*, pl. 28.4.

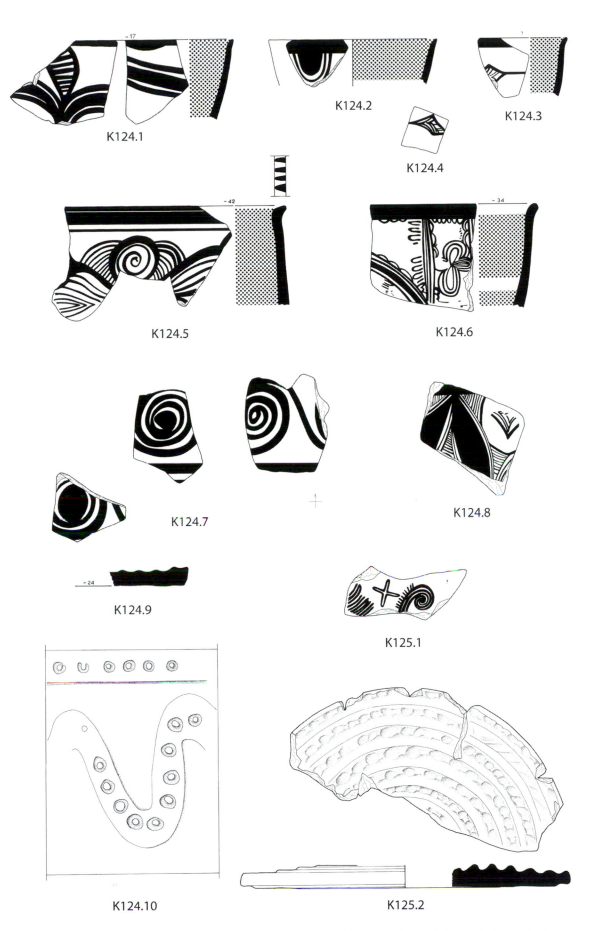

Fig. 6.25. *Northern Shelters, pottery from K 124 (**K124.1–10**) and K 125 (**K125.1–2**). Scale 1:3.*

For decoration, cf. Andreadaki-Vlasaki and Papadopoulou 2007, 48, fig. 5.2 (Khamalevri, Phase Ib). LM IIIC.

K124.2   Deep bowl or cup (FIG. 6.25). D. rim est. 13–14. Single fragment from rim. Fine, very soft, very pale brown (10YR 8/3) fabric and slip. Black paint. Worn surfaces. Multiple pendent loops with solid centre hanging from rim band. Publication: Seiradaki, fig. 21j. LM IIIC.

K124.3   Deep bowl or cup (FIG. 6.25). Max. pres. H. 4.8. Single fragment from rim. Fine, soft, reddish yellow (7.5YR 7/6) fabric. Very pale brown (10YR 8/3) slip. Black paint worn to brown shadow. Worn surfaces. Hatched lozenge chain (?). LM IIIC.

K124.4   Deep bowl or cup (FIG. 6.25). Max. pres. H. 3.3. Single fragment from body. Fine, soft, reddish yellow (7.5YR 7/6) fabric. White (10YR 8/2) slip. Red (2.5YR 5/8) paint. Very worn surfaces. Lozenge filled with chevrons. May be same as **K124.3**. For motif, cf. **K45.1**. LM IIIC.

K124.5   Krater (FIG. 6.25). D. rim est. 40. Large fragment from rim (4 sherds), with fragments missing. Fine, very soft, reddish yellow (5YR 7/6) fabric with tiny white inclusions. Pinkish white (7.5YR 8/2) slip. Red (2.5YR 4/8) paint. Worn surfaces. Double spirals with arc fillers, heart-shaped motifs on either side. Strokes on top of rim. Publication: Seiradaki, fig. 25f (misidentified as from K 109) (some sherds now missing). Cf. *Kastri*, 292, fig. 13. LM IIIC.

K124.6   Krater (FIG. 6.25). D. rim est. 34. Single fragment from rim. Fine, very soft, reddish yellow (7.5YR 7/6) fabric. White (10YR 8/2) slip. Black paint, worn. Very worn surfaces. Panelled pattern: quatrefoil with multiple outlines, with dots and scalloped edges on vertical bands; U-pattern; outlined curvilinear pattern with scalloped edge. LM IIIC.

K124.7   Krater (FIG. 6.25). Max. pres. H. 7.8. Three joining and two non-joining fragments from body. Fine, soft, reddish yellow (5YR 7/6) fabric. Very pale brown (10YR 8/3) slip. Black paint worn to yellowish red (5YR 4/6). Worn surfaces. Running spirals. For decoration, cf. Mook and Coulson 1997, 360, fig. 32.145 (Kavousi–*Kastro*, Phases I–II). LM IIIC.

K124.8   Krater (FIG. 6.25). Max. pres. H. 7.5. Single fragment from body. Fine, soft, very pale brown (10YR 7/4) fabric. White (10YR 8/2) slip. Dusky red (10R 3/2) paint, worn to shadow. Worn surfaces. Filled, outlined leaves with arc fillers. For decoration, cf. **K121.8**; Borgna 2003, fig. 34.29 (Phaistos, LM IIIC). LM IIIC.

Coarse Wares

K124.9   Lid (FIG. 6.25). H. 1.2–1.5; D. rim est. 24. Two joining fragments from rim; missing centre and knob. Coarse red (10R 5/6) fabric, grey at core, with phyllites (1–3 mm) and some hard white angular inclusions. Burned on bottom around edges, in irregular line, 1.5–12.5 cm from edge. Flat disc. Decorated with concentric ridges. Publication: Seiradaki, pl. 12a, bottom, second from left (one fragment). LM IIIC.

K124.10   Pithos (FIG. 6.25). Large fragment (two sherds) from body. Coarse reddish yellow (5YR 7/6) fabric with frequent phyllites and small black inclusions. Raised band with impressed circles. Serpentine ridge with impressed circles. Publication: Seiradaki, pl. 12a, second row, second from right. LM IIIC.

Room K 125

The notebook listed the following coarse pottery from this small space: pithos sherds including one rim of Type 10; several tripod legs; a dish of Type 1; several dishes of Type 6, two with spout and holes; a handle of jar or jug, a lid of Type 1 (**K125.2**), and a scuttle handle. Fine pottery included a large krater with octopus design, a small lid, and bowls of Types 1 and 2. A

fragment of a stirrup jar with a scalloped curvilinear motif was also found in one of the boxes, but was not catalogued. There were apparently no other objects found here.

Pottery Catalogue: K 125

Fine Wares

K125.1   Stirrup jar (FIG. 6.25). Max. pres. H. 4. Single fragment from body, preserving hole and scar for spout. Fine, soft, very pale brown (10YR 8/3) fabric and slip. Paint black worn to shadow. Worn surfaces. Fringed tailed spiral, fringes or arcs, and small quatrefoil. Publication: Seiradaki, fig. 22h (mislabelled K 26). LM IIIC.

Coarse Wares

K125.2   Lid (FIG. 6.25). H. 1–1.8; D. base 26.4. Large fragment from rim (five sherds). 20% preserved; missing central knob. Coarse light red (2.5YR 6/6) fabric with frequent large phyllite inclusions. Sampled KAR 06/02. Flat disc with raised band around underside of rim. Concentric ridges with finger impressions. LM IIIC.

Room K 127

The notebook reports that cult statues were found in crannies of the rocks in this space, but no other information was given, and they were not found. Much pottery was listed, including at least three pithos rims of Types 3, 13, and 23; two pithoid jars of Types 3 and 9; a jar of Type 3; a few tripod legs; two kraters of Type 1; a kalathos of Type 1; four dishes, two of Type 1, two of Type 6; three basins of Types 1, 7, and 12; a jug or jar, perhaps of Type 4; bowls of Types 1 and 2; two stirrup jars of Type 2; a blue tankard spout, and a Byzantine sherd (PLATE 24 *e*). A fragment of a burned blue cooking pot with a rope-slashed ridge, the incised spout of a tankard in blue ware (mentioned in the notebook), and a fine stirrup jar with a dotted loop near the handle were also found in the boxes, but were not catalogued. Objects found in the room included a bronze knife with a curled tang (645),[143] a bronze ring (646),[144] a bronze nail (653),[145] a lump of lead (647), two conical stone beads or whorls (640, 641), a triangular whetstone (648),[146] and a terracotta weight.

The preserved material from the room is small and scrappy. The cup or deep bowl (**K127.2**) finds its closest parallels in LM IIIB cups.[147] **K127.5** could be either LM IIIB or LM IIIC, as the hatched chevron motif is found in both periods.[148] The lozenge with loops as

---

143   *Karphi*, pl. 28.2.
144   *Karphi*, pl. 29.2.
145   *Karphi*, pl. 29.1.
146   *Karphi*, pl. 30.3.
147   Watrous 1992, 71, fig. 44.1196 and pl. 28 (Kommos, LM IIIB); Popham 1970*b*, pl. 49b (Knossos, LM IIIB).
148   Popham 1970*b*, 200, fig. 3.26–28, pl. 47b (Knossos, LM IIIB); *Kastri*, 288, fig. 9f, g; 294, fig. 14.P2; 295, fig. 15.P21; Popham 1965, 326, fig. 6.36 (Knossos, LM IIIC).

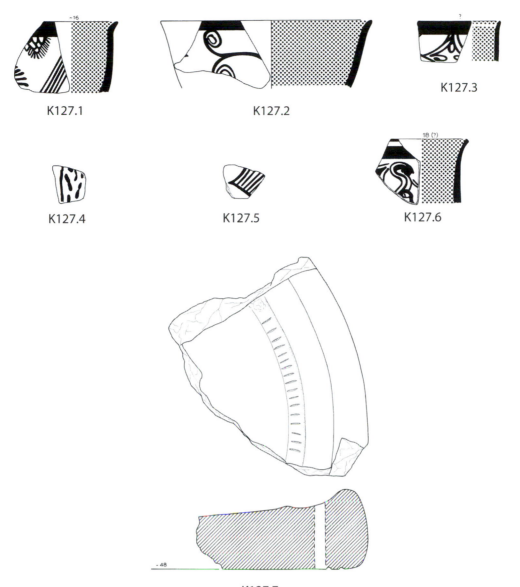

Fig. 6.26. Northern Shelters, pottery from K 127 (**K127.1–7**). Scale 1:3.

filler (**K127.3**) appears on sherds from Kastri and Khamalevri,[149] dated to early LM IIIC.

Pottery Catalogue: K 127

Fine Wares

K127.1   Deep bowl or cup (FIG. 6.26). D. rim est. 16. Single fragment from rim. Fine, rather soft, reddish yellow (7.5YR 7/6) fabric. Very pale brown (10YR 8/3) slip. Very worn paint, only shadow preserved. Pendent stack of loops, with fringe. Fringed motif (flower?) and multiple stems. For fringed stack of loops, cf. Rethemiotakis 1997, 319, fig. 28ab. LM IIIC early.

K127.2   Deep bowl or cup (FIG. 6.26). D. rim est. 18. Single fragment from rim. Fine, medium-soft, porous, reddish yellow (7.5YR 8/6) fabric. Pink (7.5YR 8/4) slip. Black paint, well-preserved on interior, worn on exterior. Curving horizontal stem with two spiral tails. LM IIIB.

K127.3   Deep bowl or cup (FIG. 6.26). Max. pres. H. 3.3. Single fragment from rim. Fine, medium-soft, reddish yellow (7.5YR 8/6) fabric. Very pale brown (10YR 8/3) slip. Worn red (2.5YR 4/8) paint. Lozenge with loops as fillers in corner. Reserved band on interior below lip. Cf. **K76.31**. LM IIIC early.

K127.4   Deep bowl or cup (FIG. 6.26). Max. pres. H. 3. Single fragment from body. Fine, soft, yellow (10YR 8/6) fabric. Very pale brown (10YR 8/4) slip. Red (5YR 4/6) to dark reddish brown (5YR 3/3) paint. Worn surfaces on exterior, well-preserved on interior. Short strokes. LM IIIC.

K127.5   Deep bowl or cup (FIG. 6.26). Max. pres. H. 2.7. Single fragment from body. Fine, rather hard, reddish yellow (7.5YR 7/6)

---

149   *Kastri*, 287, fig. 8j; Andreadaki-Vlasaki and Papadopoulou 2007, 50, fig. 7.3 (Khamalevri).

fabric. Very pale brown (10YR 8/4) slip. Black paint. Worn exterior surfaces, interior well-preserved. Hatched lozenge. LM IIIC.

K127.6   Tankard or mug (FIG. 6.26). D. rim est. 16. Single fragment from rim, but fresh breaks suggest there was more. Fine, medium-hard, reddish yellow (7.5YR 7/6) fabric. Lustrous very pale brown (10YR 8/4) slip. Black paint, worn to shadow. Flared rim, flattened on edge. Curvilinear pattern, possibly a bird or Minoan flower. LM IIIC.

Coarse Wares

K127.7   Potter's wheel (FIG. 6.26). H. 4.5–6.3; D. 48. Single large fragment, preserving 10% of wheel. Coarse reddish yellow (5YR 7/8) fabric with frequent purple-red and some dark grey phyllites. Very pale brown (10YR 8/3) surface. Discoloured on one side, possibly from burning. Flat disc with two grooves on underside, raised rim. Hole pierced through just inside rim. Slightly raised ridge with rope slashing. LM IIIC.

SUMMIT

Rooms 128, 129 'Peak Sanctuary'

The area on top of the peak did not have very well-preserved architecture, but in the crannies were many terracotta figurines, and the area was interpreted as a Middle Minoan Peak Sanctuary. The material from this peak sanctuary has been studied by Alan Peatfield and will not form part of the current study.

Room K 128

This was a square building, mostly rock-cut, which the excavators interpreted as a watch tower. The pottery was as usual, but there was little fine ware. The notebook lists a few sherds from pithoi, but no rims, much broken coarse ware, the rim of a kalathos of Type 2, and a large stirrup jar top of Type 5.

Room K 129

According to the notebook, this room was merely a line of wall between two rocks. The pottery was described as usual, but there were few pithos fragments. The notebook lists many dishes of Type 6, some tripod legs, a few really fine sherds from bowls or cups, some semi-fine from kraters of Types 2 or 3, and two basins of Type 6. From among rocks came small sherds of the usual types along with the following objects: a pierced whetstone (674), two conical stone beads (675, 677), two fragments of lead (667, 668), the tip and fragments of a bronze blade (669, 671), a bronze decorated implement (670),[150] a bronze arrowhead (672),[151] a bronze nail or stud (673),[152] half of a small bone handle (676),[153] two cylindrical terracotta spindle whorls (665, 666), and many fragments of human and animal figurines and miniature vases.[154]

FROM SURFACE OF SLOPES GENERALLY

No pottery was recorded from the slopes, but the following objects were listed: a fragment of an unfinished limestone bowl (127), a fragment of a limestone palette (128), a conical terracotta loomweight (124), two cylindrical terracotta spindle whorls (125, 126), and the head (557) and upper legs of a terracotta statuette (558).

---

150   *Karphi*, pl. 29.1.
151   *Karphi*, pl. 29.1.
152   *Karphi*, pl. 29.1.
153   *Karphi*, pl. 28.4.
154   *Karphi*, pl. 33.1–3.

7

Vitzelovrysis and the tombs

Vitzelovrysis, Ta Mnemata (M 1–17) and Atsividhero (A 1–4)

VITZELOVRYSIS

The area around the Vitzelovrysis Spring was excavated in 1939. There were two separate areas with ancient use: the actual spring and the so-called sanctuary just above the spring.

Vitzelovrysis Spring

On the south side of the spring an ancient retaining wall was well preserved.[1] The pottery from this area consisted of coarse sherds from water jugs of the usual types, and there were no tripod legs. Some fine ware appeared, including a monochrome skyphos and the Protogeometric jug (**V.1**) catalogued below. There were also many terracotta figurine fragments, including four oxen (396), a sheep (397), and the head of a human figurine (398).

It is obvious that the spring continued in use long after the settlement, although perhaps not after the tombs went out of use.

Pottery Catalogue: Vitzelovrysis

Fine Wares

V.1   Jug (PLATE 24 *f*, FIG. 7.1). Max. pres. H. 3.5. Single fragment from shoulder. Fine, soft, reddish yellow (5YR 7/6) fabric. Very pale brown (10YR 8/4) surface. Black paint. Worn surfaces. Ridge of clay on interior, as if top added on to body (like LM IIIC stirrup jars) Concentric, compass-drawn semicircles. PG.

Vitzelovrysis Sanctuary

On the summit immediately above the spring was a small flat area of rock, where many terracotta figurines were found, but no actual building. The area was interpreted as an open air sanctuary, possibly with a sacred tree.[2] There was very little pottery, all said to be of Archaic date. In addition to a disc-headed bronze pin (394), many terracotta figurines were found here, including the head of a human figure (399), part of a Daedalic head (400), part of a plaque with relief (401), a knob that may have come from the headdress of a goddess (402), a fragment of a terracotta relief (403), and seven fragments from animal figurines (404, 405, 406, 407, 408, 409, 410). Six other terracotta figures of animals (116, 117, 118, 119, 120, 121)[3] were either found on the surface in this area or purchased. A terracotta face that was purchased was said to have come from here (375).[4]

TA MNEMATA TOMBS

This large group of tombs lies on the slopes to the south and east of the main settlement, near the Vitzelovrysis spring.

M 1 and M 2

The first two tombs were excavated in 1937.[5] These two seem to have been constructed together, with a single retaining wall built behind them against the hill slope. A low wall at right angles to the retaining wall separated the two tombs. Both tombs were corbelled, but both were rectangular in plan and did not begin to round until the second course.

M 1

This tomb was thought to be the one excavated by Sir Arthur Evans.[6] It had a long dromos that was only one course high and was blocked to that level. The chamber was rectangular and paved with irregular slabs of soft shale. The height of the vault was estimated at 1.25 m, of which 0.30 was below the ground. The number of burials in the tomb is unknown, since no bones were recovered.

In addition to the pottery catalogued below, many sherds from a bathtub larnax with dark-painted decoration were found, along with the rim and handle of a pithos with punctuated decoration, sherds from a stirrup jar, and the rim of a fine basin of Type 6. A handle was found in one of the boxes from M 1. The objects included a bronze pin (100),[7] a conical stone bead or whorl (101), two cylindrical terracotta spindle whorls (102, 103), and the hindquarters of an animal figurine (104).[8]

Although the tomb was not found with its contents intact, at least two of the vessels are preserved and give a range of dates for its use. The kalathos (**M1.1**)

---

1   *Karphi*, 98–9.
2   *Karphi*, 100.
3   *Karphi*, pl. 32.3.
4   *Karphi*, pl. 32.4.
5   *Karphi*, 100–1.
6   *Karphi*, 101.
7   *Karphi*, pl. 28.1.
8   *Karphi*, pl. 32.3.

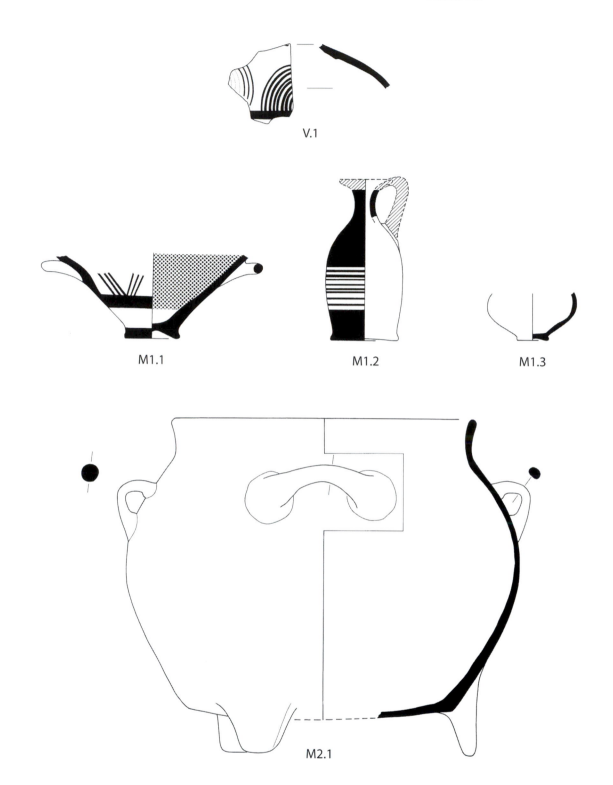

Fig. 7.1. *Vitzelovrysis, pottery from spring (V.1) and Ta Mnemata tombs M 1 (M1.1–3) and M 2 (M2.1). Scale 1:3.*

resembles SM examples from Knossos[9] and Khamaizi–
Phatsi,[10] and the bottle (**M1.2**) has parallels with SM
and PG Athens and LC IIIB Cyprus.[11] The stirrup jar
is too poorly preserved to date. It is not certain whether
the bathtub larnax was used for one of the burials, but
it may well have been; earlier larnakes continued to be
used for burials at the North Cemetery at Knossos.[12]
The date for Tomb M 1 is SM–EPG.

9   A kalathos from the Spring Chamber at Knossos, for example,
    is similar in both shape and decoration; see Sackett (ed.) 1992,
    pl. 49d. Similar decoration is found on amphoriskoi from the
    same deposit, pl. 50c, f.

10 Tsipopoulou 1997, 457, 480, fig. 1.4996.

11 Desborough 1964, 27, pl. 16, for LC IIIB, SM and early PG
    parallels from Athens.

12 Coldstream and Catling 1996, 653.

Pottery Catalogue: M 1

Fine Wares

M1.1   Kalathos (FIG. 7.1). Max. pres. H. 6.8; D. base 4.5. Mended from 13 fragments. 65% preserved, including entire base and lower body, handle attachments; missing both handles and rim. Fine, soft, reddish yellow (7.5YR 7/6) fabric. Very pale brown (10YR 8/3) slip. Red (10R 4/6) paint. Worn surfaces. Multiple triangles or zigzag. Large reserved disc in bottom of interior. SM.

M1.2   Bottle (PLATE 24 *g*, FIG. 7.1). Max. pres. H. 12; D. base 5.4. Intact except for restored rim and handle. 85% preserved; missing rim, handle, part of base, two fragments of body. Fine, soft, pink (7.5YR 7/4) fabric. Worn black paint. Slightly raised base, tall ovoid body, thin neck. Bottom has string marks. Narrow bands on lower body. Publication: Seiradaki, pl. 11b, top right. SM–EPG.

M1.3   Jug or stirrup jar (FIG. 7.1). Max. pres. H. 3; D. base 2. Three joining fragments from base and lower body, large fragment (five sherds) from body; missing top. Fine, very soft, grey (5Y 5/1) fabric. Very burned all through fabric. Surface coated with sediment, so it is difficult to see paint or slip. No traces of decoration. LM IIIC?

M 2

This tomb was much smaller, without a dromos. Like M 1, it was rectangular in plan and was also floored with plaques of soft shale. The vaulting was complete to the capstone, and the door was *c.* 0.50 high. The stones found blocking the doorway were too large to have fit through the door, leading the excavators to suggest that the bodies must have been introduced into the tomb from above. There were three skulls, all at different levels, but all by the southeast corner, along with quantities of snail shells. In addition to the catalogued pottery, the notebook reports a few fine sherds, including one from a stirrup jar. The skyphos illustrated in Seiradaki as coming from M 2 is actually from M 8.[13] Also found in the tomb were an incised fragment of bone (105) and fragments of animal figurines (106, 107).[14]

The only surviving pottery from this tomb is a coarse tripod, an unusual vessel to find in a tomb. It bears no trace of burning. Not only are tripods unusual in a burial context, but the shape of this example is different from tripod cooking pots found in the settlement. It may belong to a later period, but no parallels have been found. It may have been used as a container (perhaps for a child burial or a cremation), but it does not seem to have been used in cooking.

Pottery Catalogue: M 2

Coarse Wares

M2.1   Tripod (FIG. 7.1). H. est. 26.4; D. rim 24. Partially mended from 134 fragments. Less than 50% preserved, including parts of base, one leg and attachment of another, fragments of four handles, pieces of rim. Coarse reddish yellow (5YR 6/8) fabric with frequent red phyllites (1–2 mm) and hard white angular inclusions. Sampled KAR 06/54. Short legs, elliptical in section. Two round horizontal handles, two round vertical handles on shoulder.

M 3

This tomb was located not far from M 1 and M 2.[15] The front was destroyed, but the amount of stone nearby suggests that it originally had a dromos. The tomb was rectangular and had a paved floor raised at the back to form a sort of platform. The tomb was not free-standing but was set into the hill, and the vault reached 1.25–1.50 m. According to the notebook, the human bones of a single individual, including part of a skull were found on the platform along with the two stirrup jars (**M3.1**–2), but the long bronze pin (182)[16] was found in front of the platform. Stirrup jar **M3.2** has LM IIIC parallels for shape and decoration,[17] but the other stirrup jar (**M3.1**) has details that suggest a later date: a higher and larger foot, larger spout and false spout, a cone on top of the false spout, and the linear decoration of multiple triangles. The shape and decoration of this vessel finds parallels at Knossos of SM–EPG date, on imported Minoan stirrup jars at Laconia and Rhodes of late LM IIIC–SM.[18] Since there was apparently only a single burial in this grave, it would appear that one of these stirrup jars was an antique placed in the grave along with a second more contemporary example in SM times. The earlier stirrup jar might also represent remains from an earlier burial in this tomb, a burial from which all other traces had been removed.

Pottery Catalogue: M 3

Fine Wares

M3.1   Stirrup jar (PLATE 24 *h*, FIG. 7.2). H. 12.2; D. base 4.2; max. D. 9.3. Restored from 13 fragments. 95% preserved; missing small pieces of rim and body, half of one handle. Fine, soft, porous, very pale brown (10YR 8/3) fabric with tiny black inclusions. Very pale brown (10YR 8/3) slip. Crackled black paint. Worn surfaces. Type 4. Spout touches false spout. Slight cone on top of false spout. Hatched triangles with dots. Spiral on top of false spout. Oblique strokes on handles. Publication: Seiradaki, pl. 11a, top left. SM.

M3.2   Stirrup jar (PLATE 24 *i*, FIG. 7.2). H. 10.4; D. base 3.2; max. D. 10. Once restored from at least nine fragments, now broken (glue on edges suggests fragments are missing). 60% preserved, including entire base, both handles, spout, and false spout; missing fragments of shoulder and upper body. Fine, medium-hard, pink (5YR 7/4) fabric. Pink (7.5YR 8/4) slip. Dull black paint. Some surfaces well-preserved, others worn and pitted. Type 2. Top made separately as disc and added on. On top: triangles with alternating hatching, stacked scale pattern with dots; on body, zigzag and bands. Circle on top of false spout, bands down edges of handles; horizontal strokes on front of spout. Publication: Seiradaki, fig. 11.2. LM IIIC early.

---

13   Seiradaki, pl. 11b, top left.

14   *Karphi*, pl. 32.3.

15   *Karphi*, 102.

16   *Karphi*, pl. 28.1.

17   Catling 1968, 116–7, fig. 6.24 (LM IIIC); Kanta 1980, 181, fig. 71.4 for zigzag on belly (Praisos, early LM IIIC); for stacked scale triangle, Paschalides 2009, 11, fig. 14 (Tourloti, LM IIIB/C).

18   Coldstream and Catling 1996, 69, fig. 76.20 (SM–EPG); 190–1, fig. 124.186.1 (earliest SM); *RMDP*, 292–3, fig. 100.242 (Epidaurus Limera); 1071, fig. 440.281 (Rhodes).

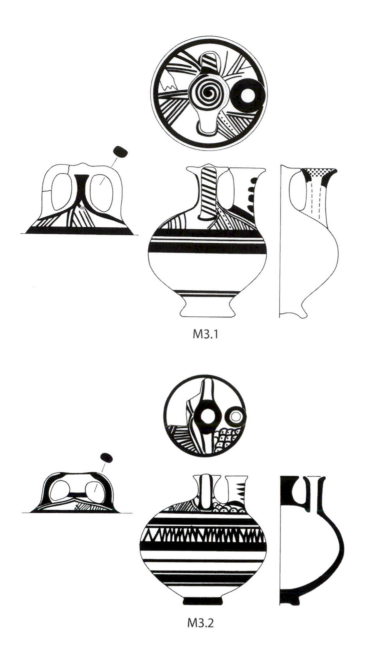

M3.1

M3.2

Fig. 7.2. Ta Mnemata tombs, pottery from M 3 (**M3.1–2**). Scale 1:3.

M 4

Tomb M 4 was excavated in 1938, and it was one of the largest and most impressive of the Ta Mnemata tombs.[19] It was built with the long dromos parallel to the hillside, with a retaining wall at the back. It had a paved floor, and the vault was approximately one metre high. The door was found blocked with a large stone. Within the tomb were pieces of five skulls immediately above the floor, with other bones scattered and disturbed. Outside, between the dromos and the tomb, a rectangular area with walls and a paved floor contained more human bones and sherds, possibly the remains of another burial. East of the retaining masonry was an area of black earth with a few sherds. Much pottery was also found scattered outside the tomb,

particularly to the west; all attests to a good deal of disturbance, either during reuse of the tomb or as a result of robbing.

From inside the tomb came the coarse pyxis (**M4.3**), sherds from a small vessel in red clay with horizontal ribbing (possibly a pyxis), two stirrup jars (**M4.4–5**) and parts of another, and the base of a krater in 'harsh' clay with a dark wash. In addition to these vessels, there were numerous fragments in two separate compartments of one of the museum boxes, one labelled 'M 4 inside tholos, at 1 m', and the other 'M 4 inside tholos, below 1 m'.

19　*Karphi*, 102–3.

The compartment labelled 'M 4 inside, tholos below 1 m' produced many fragments of a thin-walled Hellenistic cup of gritty, clinky, micaceous fabric with ribbing on rim and body.[20] Also from this level were fragments of a small jug or stirrup jar, a deep bowl fragment, two krater fragments, and assorted body sherds. Objects listed in the inventory book as coming from this same deposit were the two bow fibulas (175, 176)[21] and two fragments of an iron nail (178).[22] From the compartment labelled 'M 4, inside tholos, at 1 m' came fragments of another late ribbed vessel of gritty fabric, blue-grey inside, and red on exterior; it had a flat base with incisions on the edge, and a knob above. Also from this deposit were a black-glazed fine rim, a coarse black-glazed overhanging rim, a coarse ring base (D. est. 10) (possibly the base of a krater mentioned above), a painted and coarse rim of micaceous fabric that joins with fragment in the compartment in the box without label. One other compartment in the box had no label, but because of the join may belong to this upper deposit. It contained a black-glazed rim fragment, two ribbed micaceous coarse fragments, a coarse base with tripod attachment and dint, a medium-coarse pedestal base, a PG conical foot, a fine black-glazed ring base, a large jug handle, a small juglet, a deep bowl (?) rim, and assorted body sherds.

The material from outside the tomb was listed in the publication. From the partition outside came bones and fragments of a single vase. Listed as coming from outside the tomb in the publication and notebook were the following: a number of coarse ware sherds, including two from a larnax; two fragments in red clay with ribbing and medallion decoration; fine sherds from stirrup jars; a krater of Type 2 and other krater sherds; a beaded tankard (**M4.7**) and kylix (**M4.6**). The notebook also mentions a few Byzantine fragments, possibly the ribbed wares mentioned above.

The other objects from this tomb were simply listed as M 4. These included a bronze needle with an eyehole (171),[23] part of a bronze ring (177),[24] and three terracotta animal figurines (172, 173, 174), probably bovines.

It is clear that this tomb was in use over a long period of time. Five burials were made in the chamber and one in the space outside. Since no pottery was associated with the exterior burial, no conclusions can be made about its chronological relationship with the burials in the tomb. The presence of so much late material inside the tomb, even at the lowest levels, indicates that the burials were disturbed. The pottery that belonged with the burials inside the tomb is scanty, but suggests a LM IIIC date. Certainly stirrup jar **M4.4** is LM IIIC, and stirrup jar **M4.5** also has the fringed style of IIIC, although the presence of the air hole would make it very late in that period. The shape is peculiar and cannot be easily dated. The deep bowl or skyphos with its blob decoration (**M4.2**) may be late LM IIIC, with parallels at Khalasmenos.[25] The cup (**M4.1**) looks more like the globular one-handled cups that become

popular from the PG on; this example, with its deep shape and thin walls, looks late in the sequence, even Geometric, but the use of blob decoration would suggest an earlier date. The kylix (**M4.6**) and mug (**M4.7**) found scattered outside the tomb may have been deposited when the tomb was opened later on, and they may belong with the burials inside. Both are late LM IIIC types, with parallels in the settlement. The date of the later material found in the tomb is uncertain. The excavators thought it was Byzantine, no doubt because so many of the sherds were ribbed and because of the gritty nature of the clay. The one cup has parallels in Hellenistic pottery, and the black glazed fragments look fourth century to Hellenistic, so the disturbance may have come in that period. The history of the tomb can be reconstructed as follows: it was first used in the late LM IIIC period, and continued in use into PG (cup **M4.1**), perhaps by descendants of the original burying population who had moved elsewhere, or those asserting ownership of the grave and its associations. During this time at least five burials were made. At some point a sixth burial was made outside in the area to the southeast, but whether this was a late burial or the burial of someone not part of the burying group (a different family or class or a later interment) is not clear. Finally, probably in the Hellenistic period (when there was activity also on the site of Karphi in the area of the Great House) people returned, dug out the interior of the tomb, disturbed the bones and some of the pottery, and deposited fragments of their own. Possibly this reuse was related to veneration of ancestors, or perhaps it was simply random destruction of property.

Pottery Catalogue: M 4

Inside M 4, below 1 m

Fine Wares

M4.1 Cup (FIG. 7.3). Max. pres. H. 8; D. base 5.7. Partially mended from eight fragments, preserving most of base and half of lower body; missing rim and handle(s). Fine, medium-hard, very pale brown (10YR 8/4) fabric. Streaky very dark greyish brown (10YR 3/2) paint. Flat, thin base, globular body, possibly a cup. Blob decoration. Publication: Seiradaki, pl. 8e, middle (labelled A1). PG?

M4.2 Deep bowl or skyphos (FIG. 7.3). H. est. 8.2; D. base 4.5; D. rim est. 13.2. Partially mended from five large fragments and handful of smaller ones. Fine, soft, reddish yellow (7.5YR 7/6) fabric, grey (5GY 7/1) at core. Black paint. Very worn surfaces, still coated with sediment. Blob decoration. LM IIIC late.

20 Sackett (ed.) 1992, 98, pl. 78.H9.5; 103, pl. 82.H12.34. Both these vessels have similar shapes, although they are fine wares; both date to the late fourth–early third century.

21 *Karphi*, pl. 28.1.

22 *Karphi*, pl. 28.1.

23 *Karphi*, pl. 28.1.

24 *Karphi*, pl. 28.1.

25 Tsipopoulou 2004, 118, fig. 8.11.95-365.

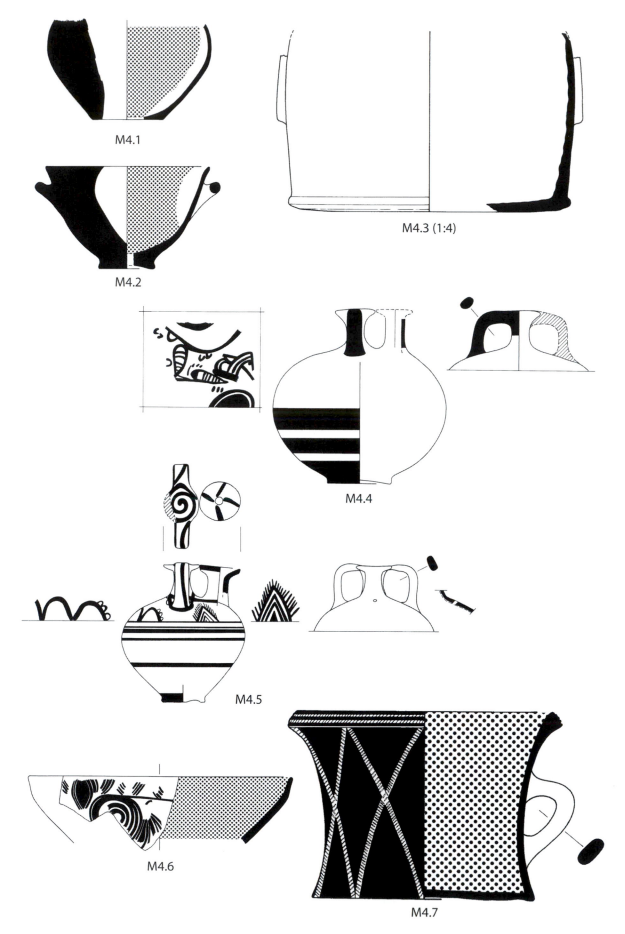

M4.1

M4.2

M4.3 (1:4)

M4.4

M4.5

M4.6

M4.7

Fig. 7.3. Ta Mnemata tombs, pottery from M 4 (**M4.1**–7). Scale 1:3 unless otherwise indicated.

Coarse Wares

M4.3   Pyxis (FIG. 7.3). Max. pres. H. 19.2; D. base est. 30. 23 joining fragments, 54 non-joining fragments. 75% preserved, including entire base and lower body, most of both handles; missing tops of handles and rim. Coarse red (10R 5/8) fabric with frequent schist (2–3 mm) and hard white angular inclusions. Surface mottled black and red. LM IIIC.

Inside M 4

Fine Wares

M4.4   Stirrup jar (PLATE 25 *a*, FIG. 7.3). H. 14; D. base 5.1; max. D. 13.8. Restored from numerous fragments. 70% preserved, including base and full profile; missing 25% of body, one handle, top of spout. Fine, soft, pink (7.5YR 7/4) fabric and slip. Worn red-brown paint. Very worn surfaces. Type 2. Hatched loops, dots, alternating arcs. Bands below. Publication: Seiradaki, pl. 11a, top right. LM IIIC.

M4.5   Stirrup jar (PLATE 25 *b*, FIG. 7.3). H. 11; D. base 3.4; max. D. 9.8. Restored from 15 fragments. Full profile preserved; missing most of centre body, tip of false spout, rim of spout. Fine, soft, porous, light grey (10YR 7/2) to very pale brown (10YR 8/4) fabric. Crackled black paint, worn. Very worn surfaces. Type 3. Large spout tilted to touch false spout. Top of false spout slightly concave. Hole pierced through body at base of false spout. On shoulder: loops with scalloped edges, fringed multiple triangles. Spiral on false spout, pinwheel on interior of spout. Publication: Seiradaki, fig. 11.3, pl. 11a, bottom right. For decoration cf. *RMDP*, 471–3, fig. 172.4 (Ithaca, LH IIIC late, imported from Achaea). LM IIIC late.

Outside M 4, scattered

Fine Wares

M4.6   Kylix (FIG. 7.3). Max. pres. H. 5.5; D. rim 21. Once restored; only four fragments preserved. Fine, very soft, very pale brown (10YR 8/4) fabric. Black paint, worn to shadow. Worn surfaces. Octopus? Multiple-outlined head and topknot, with spiral eye on one side. Publication: Seiradaki, fig. 22e, pl. 10b, middle (shown mended). LM IIIC.

M4.7   Mug (HM 11051) (PLATE 25 *c*, FIG. 7.3). H. 14.8; D. base 17.6; D. rim 21.6. Restored from numerous fragments. 75% preserved, including 75% of base, 66% of rim, and handle. Fine, rather hard, porous, pink (7.5YR 8/4) fabric. Red (2.5YR 5/8) to dark red (2.5YR 3/6) paint, well-preserved on interior, worn on exterior. Monochrome. Decorated with large incised and punctuated X-patterns. Rim incised, alternating plain and beaded. Publication: *Karphi*, pl. 24.6, left; Seiradaki, fig. 13.2; pl. 8d. LM IIIC.

M 5 and M 6

These two tombs were similar to M 1 and M 2, with a retaining wall behind and a wall separating the two.[26] They were not, however, so close together. Much pottery was found outside the two tombs, including much coarse ware of the types found in the settlement. The notebook records that these fragments included tripod legs and pithos sherds with chevron decoration, and a larnax sherd. The notebook and publication also list the following: fine sherds from kylikes, including a base, like those from inside the tomb; an overhanging rim, probably Archaic, and a few fragments of fourth-century glaze. One of the museum boxes had a compartment with sherds and a label identifying them as from M 5–

6 surface. These included a fragment of Classical black-glaze, possibly fourth century; fragments of three small stirrup jars, one carinated, one with a design of fringed multiple upright loops on the shoulder, and a third with a fringed motif. Also in the box were a ring base from a closed vessel, two bases from small jugs or stirrup jars, a cup or jug handle, another handle, and several body fragments. This material may well have been thrown out of the tomb when it was robbed. The LM IIIC sherds suggest that the tomb was in use during the occupation of the settlement of Karphi. Nothing was well enough preserved to catalogue.

M 5

The tomb had a carefully constructed, rectangular chamber with no paving, and it had no dromos. The height of the vault was 1.5 m. Sherds from two kylikes of Types 1 and 2 were found, but no bones.

M 6

This smaller and less well-built tomb was only about a metre high. The back of the masonry was rough and ran into the hillside, so it was not entirely free standing. It had an irregular paving and no dromos. The large blocks found within were too large to have been brought in through the doorway, which was only *c*. 0.50 high. Found inside were sherds from a krater and a few coarse sherds. There were remains only of a single body.

M 7 and M 8

These two tombs were constructed close to one another on the slopes of Mikre Koprana, not too far from M 16 and M 17.[27] There was no retaining wall, because they were parallel to the hillside, but there was a rough wall between the two at approximately right angles.

M 7

The smaller of the two tombs, M 7 was irregular in plan, with a paved floor, and a vault 1.5 m high. The dromos was unlined, and it served as a retaining wall on the east. There were at least two bodies. Sherds from one or more stirrup jars and a kylix of Type 1 were reported, along with two thin bronze discs (183, 184)[28] and a bone needle (371). No pottery was preserved from this tomb. Clearly, the tomb had been disturbed, and there was little to suggest its date; the presence of the kylikes would suggest that it was in use in LM IIIC, however.

M 8

Tomb M 8 was the largest and best-built tomb at Karphi. It was polygonal in plan, with stone paving

---

26   *Karphi*, 103.

27   *Karphi*, 104–5.

28   *Karphi*, pl. 28.1.

and a vault of over 1.5 m. It had a dromos, which was found unfilled, an indication that the tomb had been opened. There were remains of three individuals interred in the tomb. Outside the tomb was a deposit of black earth that ran north of the wall linking M 8 with M 7; this deposit was under a layer of red earth that contained sherds from the robbing of the tomb.

The material from within the tomb included a stirrup jar of Type 6 (**M8.3**), fragments of two large kraters of Types 1 and 2 (**M8.2**), some smaller vessels from near the floor, and pieces of the fenestrated stand (**M8.4**). One of the kraters is preserved (**M8.2**), but the other published in Seiradaki was not found.[29] Objects from inside the tomb included two bronze bow fibulas (157, 158),[30] three bronze rings (159, 160, 161),[31] three spiral hair rings of bronze (162, 163, 164),[32] a bronze implement (166),[33] many small bronze discs with clips at back for attachment (169), a tubular bone bead (165), and a conch shell (181).

The material from the red earth layer outside above 0.85 included sherds from the kraters and other vessels found inside and fragments of a very fine, red-painted kylix that the excavators thought was LM IIIB. One of the boxes had a compartment with sherds from this red layer. In addition to the catalogued fragments, there were at least five bases, seven round handles, one flat handle, and 210 body sherds of the same soft fine fabric. There were no other objects.

The deposit of black earth included a kylix of Type 2 (**M8.8**), many sherds from the fenestrated stand, and some Archaic and later sherds along with the usual fragments. Objects included fragments of two iron needles (167, 168) and three terracotta figurines: the headless figurine of a seated female (170),[34] part of a bovine figurine (179), and a fragment of a female figurine (180).

There were also traces of walls below the two tombs, and associated with these walls were sherds of the usual types, including a few pithos fragments with chevrons, and a few Archaic sherds, one with overhanging rim, one glazed. The head of a terracotta bull figurine was also found.

It is likely that much of the material found outside the tomb was thrown out by tomb robbers and belonged to the burials within; there seem to have been joins between the material found in the red earth outside and that from within the tomb. Fragments of the fenestrated stand also were found both in the tomb and in the black earth outside, along with remains of Archaic and later date. It would appear that there were at least two episodes of reuse when material was removed from the tomb: in or prior to the Archaic period, represented by the black earth, and a later disturbance represented by the red earth. All of the material catalogued below should have come from the three burials made in the tomb. The usual shapes are represented, including skyphos, deep bowl, kylix, krater, cups, stirrup jars, and a thelastron. The fene-

strated stand (**M8.4**) is an unusual vessel to be placed in a burial, and this example finds no definite parallels in the settlement; the shape is, however, popular in late LM IIIC Kavousi–*Vronda*.[35] The pottery is also mixed in date, suggesting a long period of use for the tomb. The kylix (**M8.8**), the stirrup jar (**M8.3**), and the carinated cup (**M8.5**) from outside all are of early LM IIIC date, with shapes or decoration common to that period; the unusual decoration on the kylix finds a close parallel on a krater from Khania,[36] the stirrup jar is similar to an example from Knossos,[37] while the carinated cup resembles examples from the mainland of middle LH IIIC date.[38] The shape of the krater (**M8.2**), with its rather high foot and almost bell-shaped body, looks very late, approaching the Subminoan bell-krater; the decoration, however, appears to be late LM IIIC. The skyphos (**M8.1**) is definitely much later, and finds parallels in either the SM or the EPG period.[39] The date for this tomb would seem to be primarily LM IIIC, with at least one burial later in SM–EPG. The later use, represented by the black earth, included terracotta figurines; perhaps already the tomb was used for ritual, possibly for the veneration of ancestors.

Pottery Catalogue: M 8

Fine Wares

M8.1   Skyphos (PLATE 25 *d*, FIG. 7.4). H. 7.9; D. base 3.5; D. rim 8.2. Mended from 11 fragments. 75% preserved, including entire base, full profile, part of one handle; missing 60% of rim and part of body, tip of one handle. Fine, soft, reddish yellow (7.5YR 7/6) fabric with tiny black inclusions. Black paint. Conical foot, deep bell-shaped bowl. Dipped on exterior. Interior coated. Publication: Seiradaki, pl. 11b, top left (labelled M 2), fig. 14.2 (mislabelled A 3). SM–EPG.

M8.2   Krater (PLATE 25 *e*, FIG. 7.4). H. 26.2–27.2; D. base 10.8; D. rim 30.5. Restored from many fragments, but held together with string. 75% preserved, including entire base and one handle; missing 25% of body and one handle. Fine, rather soft, porous, reddish yellow (5YR 7/6) fabric. Pink (7.5YR 7/4) slip. Black paint, only traces remaining. Very worn surfaces. Panelled decoration, lilies and other motifs with dots and fringes. Publication: Seiradaki, fig. 15.2, fig. 26f; pl. 9d. LM IIIC late.

---

29   Seiradaki, fig. 15.1.

30   *Karphi*, pl. 28.1.

31   *Karphi*, pl. 28.1.

32   *Karphi*, pl. 28.1.

33   *Karphi*, pl. 28.1.

34   *Karphi*, pl. 32.4.

35   Day *et al.* forthcoming.

36   *Khania II*, pl. 39.84-P 0702.

37   Catling 1968, 115–6, fig. 7.23.

38   Mountjoy 1986, 171, fig. 220 (LH IIIC, middle); *RMDP*, 715, fig. 274.71 (Lefkandi, LH IIIC middle).

39   Warren 1982–83, 81, 86, fig. 64 (Knossos, SM); D'Agata 2007, 111, fig. 11a.41/22+2 (Sybrita/Thronos, earliest SM); Boardman 1960, 131, 136, fig. 4. IV.3 (Ayios Ioannis, SM–MPG krateriskos); Tsipopoulou 1997, 458, fig. 2.5052 (Khamaizi–*Phatsi*, EPG).

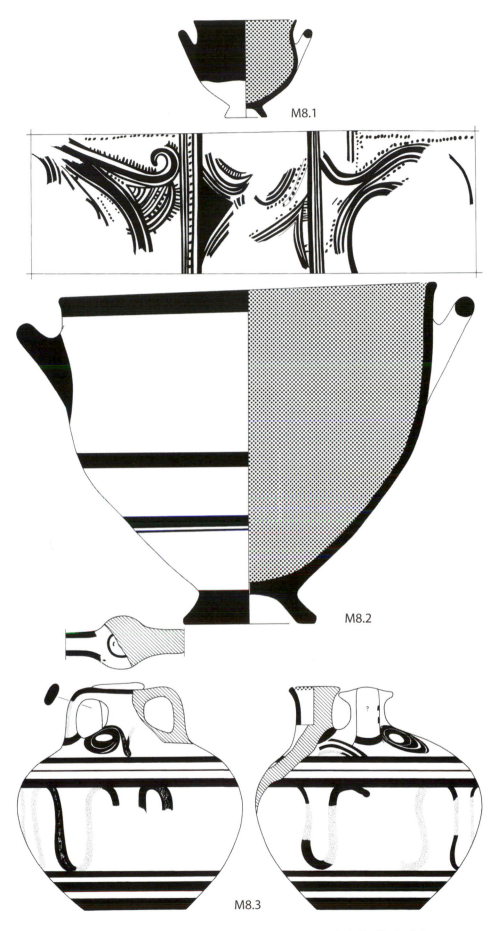

Fig. 7.4. Ta Mnemata tombs, pottery from M 8 (**M8.1**–*3*). Scale 1:3.

M8.3 Stirrup jar (PLATE 25 *f*, FIG. 7.4). H. 18; D. base 8.3; max. D. 18. Restored from numerous fragments. 80–85% preserved, including most of base and full profile; missing half of spout, half of false spout, most of one handle, large body fragment. Fine, soft, reddish yellow (7.5YR 7/6) fabric with tiny black inclusions. Yellowish red (5YR 5/6–4/6) to black paint. Type 2? Spout tilted back to touch false spout. Wavy band or debased octopus decoration on body. Spiral on shoulder. Publication: Seiradaki, fig. 11.6, pl. 11a, top middle. LM IIIC early.

Coarse Wares
M8.4 Fenestrated stand (HM 11049) (PLATE 25 *h*, FIG. 7.5). H. 30.2–31; D. base 20.2; D. rim 17. Restored from *c.* 32 fragments. 80% preserved, including full profile; missing 20% of lower body, 15% of rim. Coarse light red (2.5YR 6/6) fabric with frequent phyllites (1–3 mm) and hard white angular inclusions (2–3 mm). Red (2.5YR 4/8) paint on exterior. Flat open base, squared and outward thickened. Three ridges on base. Roughly hourglass shape, nipped in at the middle. Shoulder rounded, with three ridges. Rim rolled, outward thickened. Fenestrations in two registers, triangular in shape, with points toward centre of vessel. Monochrome. Publication: *Karphi*, pl. 35.7, left. LM IIIC.

Pottery Catalogue: Outside M 8

M8.5 Carinated cup (FIG. 7.5). Max. pres. H. 4.8. Single fragment from body, near rim; possible worn rim fragment and two other non-joining fragments. Fine, chalky, soft, pink (7.5YR 8/4) fabric. Reddish brown (2.5YR 4/4) paint. Monochrome. Outside M8, 0.85. LM IIIC early?
M8.6 Deep bowl (FIG. 7.5). D. rim est. 12. Large fragment (four sherds) from rim and body, including handle. Fine, soft, reddish yellow (5YR 7/6) fabric. Dusky red (2.5YR 3/2) paint. Monochrome. Outside M8, 0.85. LM IIIC late.
M8.7 Deep bowl (FIG. 7.5). D. rim est. 9. Large fragment (four sherds) from rim, including handle attachment, and 13 non-joining fragments. Fine, soft, light red (2.5YR 6/6) fabric. Traces of black paint. Very worn surfaces. Monochrome (?) Outside M8, 0.85. LM IIIC.
M8.8 Kylix (FIG. 7.5). Max. pres. H. 8; D. base 8.5; D. rim 22.4. Large fragments from rim (six sherds) and base (five sherds), 22 fragments from rim and body, including lower handle attachment. 10% preserved; missing stem and handles. Fine, porous, very pale brown (10YR 8/4) fabric. Red (2.5YR 5/8) paint. Well-preserved surfaces. Concave base, pierced. Papyrus pattern with curved solid bands with multiple outlines; filler ornaments of arcs and dots; fragments with scalloped curvilinear motifs. Outside M8. Publication: Seiradaki, fig. 26d. LM IIIC early.
M8.9 Open vessel (FIG. 7.5). D. rim est. 20. Single fragment (two sherds) from rim, five body fragments. Fine, soft, reddish yellow (7.5YR 7/6) fabric. Very pale brown (10YR 8/4) slip. Black paint. Very worn surfaces. Panelled pattern with half round with multiple outlines, hatched lozenge. Deep bowl or kylix. Outside M8, 0.85. LM IIIC early.
M8.10 Basin (FIG. 7.5). D. rim est. 16. Four non-joining fragments from rim. Fine, soft, reddish yellow (5YR 7/6) fabric. Pink (7.5YR 8/4) surface. Black paint. Worn surfaces. Bands on interior. Outside M8, 0.85. LM IIIC.
M8.11 Stirrup jar (FIG. 7.5). Max. pres. H. 6.5. Five joining fragments from lower body. Fine, soft, sandy, pink (7.5YR 8/4) fabric. Red (2.5YR 5/6) paint worn to brown in places. No burning. Solid curvilinear motif with multiple outlines, arc filler, and fringes, possibly an octopus. Publication: Seiradaki, fig. 26e (turned on side). Outside M8. LM IIIC.
M8.12 Thelastron (PLATE 25 *g*, FIG. 7.5). H. 10; D. base 3.1; D. rim 6. Mended from 15 fragments. 60% preserved, including

full profile; missing handle. Fine, soft, pink (7.5YR 8/4) fabric. Very pale brown (10YR 8/4) surface. Black paint. Very worn surfaces. Monochrome. Outside M8. LM IIIC?
M8.13 Jug (FIG. 7.5). Max. pres. H. 8. Single fragment (two sherds) from handle and rim. Fine, soft, pink (7.5YR 8/4) fabric. Crackled black paint. Well-preserved surfaces. Flattened, elliptical handle with two grooves on either side of ridge in centre. Chevrons on handle. Band at rim on exterior. Outside M8.

Tombs M 9–M 15

This group of tombs was located south of Vitzelovrysis, above the pathway.[40] Although there were no links among them, they lie close together and have the same orientation. Tombs 9–12 are on the same level and follow the hill contour, while Tomb 15 lies immediately below M 9, and M 14 lower still, but to the side.

M 9

Tomb M 9 was not entirely free-standing but built into the hillside, and it was without a dromos. It was rectangular in plan and was paved with small stones. It stood only 0.60 high, and the capstone was missing. The bones of at least four human bodies were found in it, including the skulls. The pottery included only a small stirrup jar (**M9.1**) and a coarse jar (**M9.2**). Three bronze pins were also found (378, 379, 380).[41]

There is little to date this grave, and the material from within it cannot be thought of as indicative of the range of grave goods found with four burials. The stirrup jar (**M9.1**) is of an uncommon shape, very squat and with a high foot, and the technique of adding the foot separately as the tops often were on stirrup jars is highly unusual; it finds a parallel in shape at Myrsini of LM IIIC date.[42] The decoration of filled triangles with fringes helps to date this example in late LM IIIC. There are no good parallels for the jar, although its knobbed decoration makes it similar to examples from the settlement.

Pottery Catalogue: M 9

Fine Wares
M9.1 Stirrup jar (FIG. 7.6). Max. pres. H. 10.2; max. D 9.5. Mended from eight fragments; two non-joining fragments from base. 80% preserved, including entire base, part of one handle, and spout; missing top with false spout and handles. Fine, hard, reddish yellow (7.5YR 7/6) fabric. White (10YR 8/2) slip. Black paint. Well-preserved surfaces. Type 1? Foot made separately and added on; ridge of clay where put onto body. On top: triangles with strokes in corners and fringing; bands below. LM IIIC late.

Coarse Wares
M9.2 Jar (FIG. 7.6). H. 29.2; D. base 12; D. rim 19.2. Partially mended from 15 fragments; 49 non-joining fragments. 65%

---

40 *Karphi*, 105–7.
41 *Karphi*, pl. 28.3.
42 Kanta 1980, 171, fig. 116.5.

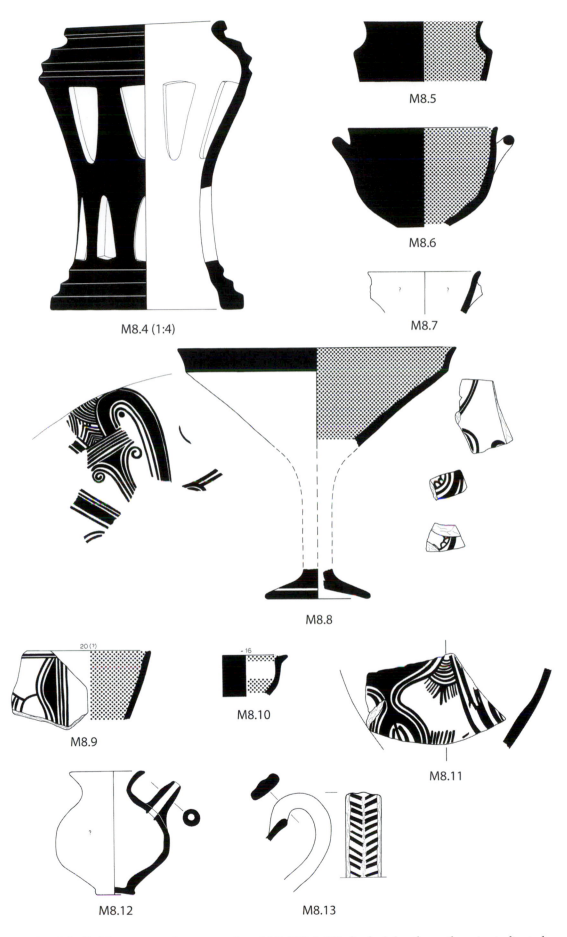

M8.5

M8.6

M8.7

M8.4 (1:4)

M8.8

M8.9

M8.10

M8.11

M8.12

M8.13

*Fig. 7.5. Ta Mnemata tombs, pottery from M 8 (**M8.4–13**). Scale 1:3 unless otherwise indicated.*

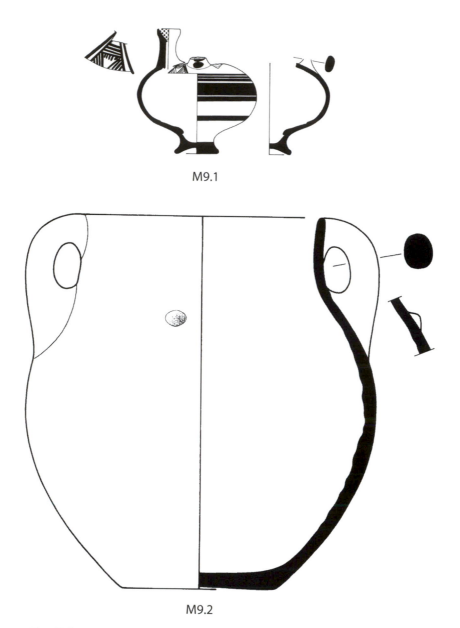

M9.1

M9.2

*Fig. 7.6. Ta Mnemata tombs, pottery from M 9 (**M9.1–2**). Scale 1:3.*

preserved, including full profile, entire base, one handle; missing 75% of rim, most of second handle. Coarse red (2.5YR 5/8) fabric with frequent hard black and white inclusions. Surface badly coated with lime deposit. Some patches of burning. Two knobs on shoulder. LM IIIC.

M 10

M 10 was like M 9, but with upright slabs for door jambs. Square in plan, it had no dromos. It was found with no blocking in the doorway, an indication that it was robbed in antiquity. There were remains of four human bodies and the teeth of a sheep or ox. The publication mentions two small vases, both probably one-handled jugs of Type 1, while the notebook lists one-handled jars of Type 5. No pottery was saved from this tomb. Other finds included a bronze pin (381).[43]

M 11

Like M 9 and M 10 this was a small square tomb, but it had a dromos, of which one wall was preserved on the north.[44] A bit of the paving was left in the southeast. The entrance was not found blocked, indicating that the tomb had been entered and robbed earlier. The remains of two bodies and some animal teeth were found within and quite a bit of other material overlooked by the tomb robbers. In addition to the pottery catalogued below, there were also said to be fragments of a coarse red stirrup jar of Type 5, two

43   *Karphi*, pl. 28.3.
44   *Karphi*, 106.

stirrup jars of Type 2, and one of Type 3,[45] as well as a bowl of Type 1 in very soft clay. Other objects from the tomb included the hoop of a bronze bow fibula (382),[46] two fragments of an iron blade (383),[47] fragments of an iron fibula (384),[48] a cylindrical stone bead (385), and a fragment of rock crystal (386).

The material from this tomb looks very late. The presence of so much iron is an indication that the tomb postdates LM IIIC, when iron was rare. Stirrup jar **M11.5** is of LM IIIC date, to judge by its shape and poorly preserved decoration, and the rhyton with its human head is similar to the LM IIIC example found in the settlement in K 27 (**K27.3**). The bird vase is clearly later, with parallels of SM and PG date, but it is most similar to an example from Axos.[49] Stirrup jar **M11.4** finds its closest parallels in shape and decoration in Knossos tombs of PG date, but also has parallels elsewhere.[50] The thelastron may also be similar in date, as it resembles an EPG example from the Knossos area.[51] A date of EPG would be likely for the later of the two burials in this grave.

Pottery Catalogue: M 11

Fine Wares

M11.1   Rhyton (PLATE 26 *a*, FIG. 7.7). Max. pres. H. 7.9. Eleven joining fragments and three non-joining fragments of top of rhyton, including top of head, both ears, chin, handle and neck; missing eyes. Fine, very soft, pink (7.5YR 7/4) fabric. Very pale brown (10YR 8/3) slip. Very worn surfaces. Neck and top in form of human head, with collar at base of neck; one vertical, elliptical handle on back of head to shoulder. Cf. **K27.3**. LM IIIC late.

M11.2   Bird vase (PLATE 26 *b*, FIG. 7.7). H. 8; L. 12. Intact. Complete except for one chip from rim. Fine, soft, reddish yellow (5YR 7/6) fabric. Glossy very pale brown (10YR 8/4) slip. Brownish black paint. Well-preserved surfaces. Three small knobs for legs. Bird-shaped body, spout like that on stirrup jar; elliptical basket handle on back. Two air holes through body on back on either side of front handle attachment. Alternating hatched triangles on body. Horizontal bands on back. Short strokes on handle. Publication: Seiradaki, fig. 20, left; pl. 11b, bottom middle. SM.

M11.3   Thelastron (PLATE 26 *c*, FIG. 7.7). Max. pres. H. 9.2; D. base 3.3; D. rim est. 3.4. Large intact fragment preserving all of base and body, most of handle; second fragment from rim. 80% preserved; missing most of rim, end of spout. Fine, soft, pink (7.5YR 7/4) fabric with tiny black inclusions. Very pale brown (10YR 8/3) slip. Black paint. Blob decoration. Publication: Seiradaki, fig. 10.3, pl. 11b, bottom, second from right. EPG.

M11.4   Stirrup jar (PLATE 26 *d*, FIG. 7.7). H. 16.5; D. base 4.9; max. D. 11.5. Restored from 23 fragments. 90% preserved; missing rim of spout and body fragments. Fine, soft, reddish yellow (5YR 7/6) fabric with tiny black inclusions. Very pale brown (10YR 8/3) slip. Black paint. Very worn and eroded surfaces. Conical foot, ovoid body. Spout nearly vertical, and touches false spout. False spout has concave top. Hole pierced through body at base of false spout. Bands below; on shoulder multiple triangles. Vertical stripes on handles. Publication: Seiradaki, pl. 11e, bottom, second from left. SM–EPG.

M11.5   Stirrup jar (FIG. 7.7). Max. pres. H. 7. Mended from 19 fragments. 40% preserved; missing base and lower body, one handle. Fine, soft, reddish yellow (5YR 6/8) fabric. Very pale brown (10YR 8/4) slip. Very worn paint. Worn surfaces. Type 2. Whole top made separately and added as disc, with ridge of clay at

joint. Curvilinear ornaments, fringes, but too worn to make out design. LM IIIC.

M11.6   Stirrup jar (PLATE 26 *e*). H. est. 13; D. base est. 5. Mended from several fragments. Fine, soft, very pale brown fabric. Very worn surfaces. Publication: Seiradaki, fig. 11a, bottom left.

M 12

This tomb was similar to the others, but much more ruined.[52] It was square inside for two courses, and it lacked both a paving and a dromos. The doorjambs were like those in M 10. The thelastron came from the entrance. Inside were found a conical stone bead or whorl (387) and the remains of four human bodies.

Pottery Catalogue: M 12

Fine Wares

M12.1   Thelastron (FIG. 7.8). Max. pres. H. 9.1; D. base 4. Mended from 16 fragments. 85% preserved, including base and lower body, bottom of spout, handle attachment; missing most of neck and rim, handle. Fine, soft, reddish yellow (7.5YR 8/6) fabric. Very pale brown (10YR 8/4) slip. Red (10R 4/8) paint. Very worn surfaces. Wavy band on shoulder, bands below. LM IIIC?

M 13

Only a circle of rough stones remained of this tholos tomb.[53] It had been totally robbed, and even the bones had been removed. All that survived were fragments of a small vase that the excavators thought was a cup of Type 1, but which looks more like a small juglet or stirrup jar, fragments of two bronze pins (388, 389),[54] and a bronze spiral hair ring (390).[55] The pottery is not datable, but the hair rings are found in post-Bronze Age graves.[56]

Pottery Catalogue: M 13

Fine Wares

M13.1   Stirrup jar or juglet (FIG. 7.8). Max. pres. H. 3; D. base 2.6. Single fragment preserving entire base. Fine, soft, very pale brown (10YR 8/4) fabric. Black paint. Tiny conical foot. Incised or cut slash on underside.

---

45   This stirrup jar was photographed in the Museum in February of 1994, but there was no time to draw it or write a description. Unfortunately, when the author returned in May to finish the work, this stirrup jar could no longer be located.

46   *Karphi*, pl. 28.3.

47   *Karphi*, pl. 28.3.

48   *Karphi*, pl. 28.3.

49   Desborough 1972, pl. ΛΓ΄ 2.34.

50   Brock 1957, 12, pl. 7.40 (SM–EPG); 25–6, pl. 15.218, 219 (PG); 28, pl. 18.245 (developed PG from Tomb VI at Fortetsa; also Coldstream and Catling 1996, 91, fig. 85.45.7 (EPG).

51   Boardman 1960, pl. 37. IV.5, 6 (Ayios Ioannis, EPG).

52   *Karphi*, 106.

53   *Karphi*, 106.

54   *Karphi*, pl. 28.3.

55   *Karphi*, pl. 28.3.

56   Higgins 1996, 542, n. 1096.

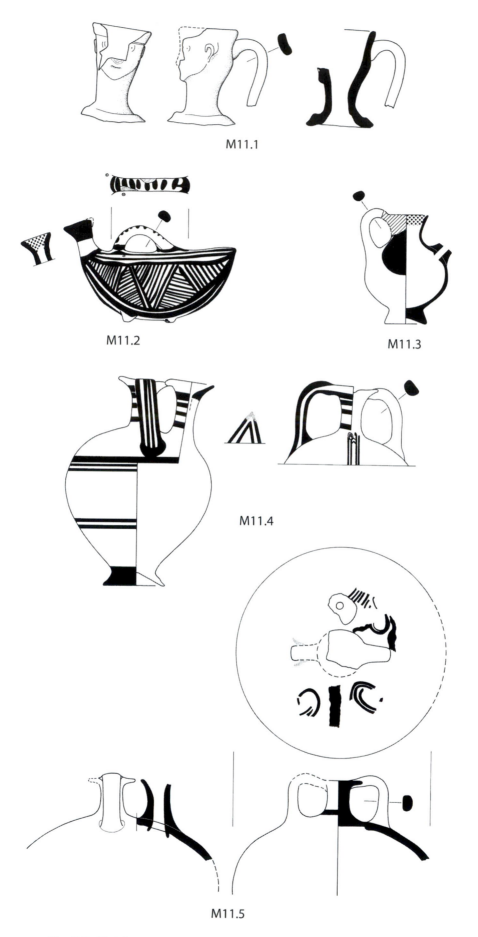

*Fig. 7.7. Ta Mnemata tombs, pottery from M 11 (**M11.1**–5). Scale 1:3.*

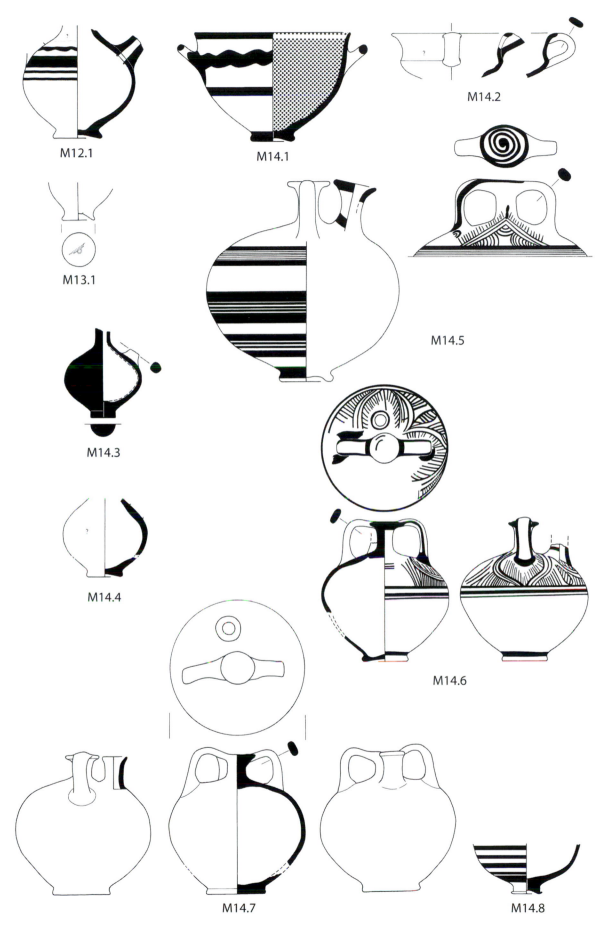

*Fig. 7.8. Ta Mnemata tombs, pottery from M 12 (**M12.1**), M 13 (**M13.1**), and M 14 (**M14.1–8**). Scale 1:3.*

M 14

M 14 is the only tholos at Karphi that was circular inside and out.[57] It was very low, built into the hill at the sides and back, and was possibly covered with earth. It was preserved six courses high, and only the capstone was missing. The dromos was blocked in antiquity, and it had a paved floor. The remains of only a single human body were found within. In addition to the catalogued pottery, a biconical stone bead or whorl (391) came from this tomb.

This tomb may represent the interment of only a single individual and can tell us something about a burial assemblage, although some material may have been robbed out. The assemblage included a deep bowl, a shallow side-spouted bowl, two juglets, and four stirrup jars. The juglets and stirrup jars are most likely to have been present because of their contents, while the deep bowl and spouted bowl may have been either for the use of the dead in the afterlife or the remains of a ritual at the time of the burial. All of the pottery from the tomb is of LM IIIC date. The shape of the deep bowl is not particularly late, with its slightly concave raised base; it is similar to a deep bowl from K 68 (**K68.1**) and finds parallels in early LM IIIC deposits at Kavousi–*Vronda*.[58] The shallow side-spouted bowl is highly unusual; it does appear in LM IIIB and so should be thought of as early in LM IIIC.[59] Two of the stirrup jars have linear fringed decoration that should date in the later part of LM IIIC.

Pottery Catalogue: M 14

Fine Wares

M14.1   Deep bowl (FIG. 7.8). H. 8.9; D. base 3.5; D. rim 12.5. Partially mended from 29 fragments. 60% preserved, including full profile. Fine, soft, reddish yellow (7.5YR 7/6) fabric. Very pale brown (10YR 8/3) slip. Red (10R 4/8) paint. Worn surfaces, but decoration clearly visible. Wavy band; reserved band on interior of rim. LM IIIC early.

M14.2   Shallow side-spouted bowl (FIG. 7.8). Max. pres. H. 3.6; D. rim 9.5. Partially mended from eight fragments. 75% of rim preserved, plus spout and handle; missing base. Rather hard dark grey (N4/) fabric. Burned? Shallow carinated bowl, rim flattened and thickened outward. Bridge spout at rim. Flat vertical handle from rim to carination at right angles to spout. Cf. **K61.9**. LM III B/C.

M14.3   Juglet (PLATE 26 *f*, FIG. 7.8). Max. pres. H. 7.2; D. base 2. Intact; complete except for rim and handle. Fine, very soft, reddish yellow (5YR 7/8) fabric. Brown paint. Monochrome. Publication: Seiradaki, pl. 11b, bottom right. LM IIIC.

M14.4   Juglet (FIG. 7.8). Max. pres. H. 6.2; D. base 2.9. Partially mended into two large fragments (13 sherds), one from base, one from upper body. Entire base preserved, 25% of upper body with lower handle attachment. Fine, medium-hard, light red (2.5YR 6/8) fabric. Very pale brown (10YR 8/4) slip. Red (2.5YR 5/8) paint. Surface burnished. Monochrome. LM IIIC.

M14.5   Stirrup jar (PLATE 26 *g*, FIG. 7.8). H. 16; D. base 4.4; max. D. 15.5. Restored from 28 fragments. 80% preserved; missing 20% of body. Fine, soft, reddish yellow (5YR 7/6) fabric with tiny black inclusions. Very pale brown (10YR 8/3) slip. Worn black paint. Worn surfaces. Type 2. On shoulder is fringed triangle with arcs in angles. Spiral on false spout. Publication: Seiradaki, pl. 11a. bottom middle. LM IIIC late.

M14.6   Stirrup jar (PLATE 26 *h*, FIG. 7.8). H. est. 11.5; D. base 3.7; max. D. 10.2. Mended from 36 fragments. 60% preserved, including entire top, entire base; missing connection between top and base, much of spout. Fine, soft, reddish yellow (5YR 7/6) fabric. Very pale brown (10YR 8/3) slip. Reddish brown (5YR 4/3) paint. Worn surfaces. Type 2. Top made separately and added as disc. Triangles with central hatched leaf and arc and line fillers, multiple outlines with fringes. LM IIIC late.

M14.7   Stirrup jar (FIG. 7.8). H. est. 11.5; D. base 4.7; max. D. 10.8. Partially mended into two large fragments, one from top (14 sherds), one from base and lower body (13 sherds). 65% preserved, including entire base, 75% of top, including spout, false spout, both handles; missing full profile. Fine, soft, reddish yellow (5YR 6/6) fabric. Very pale brown (10YR 8/4) slip. Very worn surfaces. Type 2. Top made separately and added as disc. Probably once decorated, but surfaces too worn to tell. LM IIIC.

M14.8   Closed vessel (FIG. 7.8). Max. pres. H. 4; D. base 2.5. Mended from five fragments, preserving most of base and lower body. Fine reddish yellow (7.5YR 7/6) fabric. Worn dark red (10R 3/6) paint. Very worn surfaces. Raised concave base with little ledge on exterior. Possibly a stirrup jar, thelastron, or jug. Bands. LM IIIC.

M 15

This tomb was rectangular inside and out, and it is unusual because it had no visible entrance and no dromos.[60] It was built into the hill at the back, so it was not free standing. It contained the remains of two human bodies. In addition to the stirrup jar, there were sherds of a large basin of Type 3, a tripod leg with circular impressions at the top, and a small, two-handled cup, probably Archaic in date. This last piece may attest to later activity in or around the tomb.

Pottery Catalogue: M 15

Fine Wares

M15.1   Stirrup jar (FIG. 7.9). Max. pres. H. 8.2; D. base 3.8; max. D. 9. Once mended from eight fragments, two non-joining fragments. 50% preserved, including entire base and 75% of lower body, one fragment of upper body with lower handle attachment; missing spout, false spout, handles, top. Fine, soft, reddish yellow (7.5YR 7/6) fabric. Very pale brown (10YR 8/3) slip. Red (2.5YR 4/6) paint. Well-preserved surfaces. Type 2? Bands below. On shoulder, multiple triangles and hatched verticals. LM IIIC late.

M 16 and M 17

These two tombs lie on the slopes of Koprana, north of M 7 and M 8. They were probably built together, as the hillside was cut back to receive them.

57   *Karphi*, 106–7.

58   Day 1997, 396, fig. 3.2.

59   A good parallel but with a different handle can be found in Catling 1968, 128–9, fig. 9.37 of possible LM IIIB date.

60   *Karphi*, 106–7.

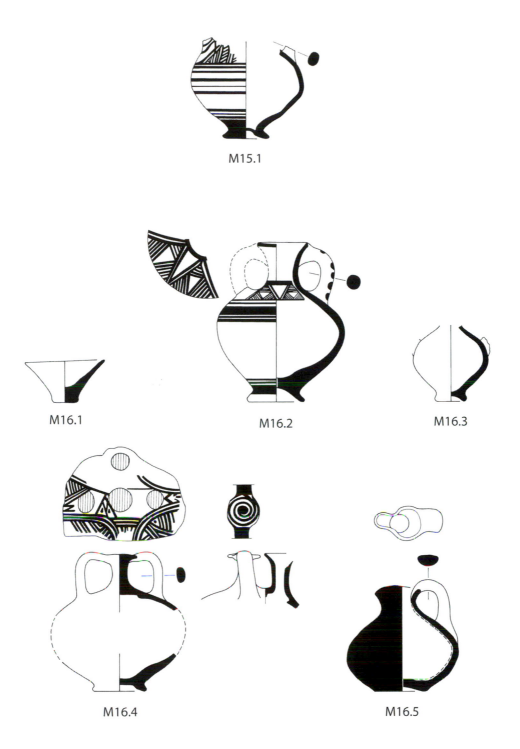

*Fig. 7.9. Ta Mnemata tombs, pottery from M 15 (**M15.1**) and M 16 (**M16.1–5**). Scale 1:3.*

M 16

Tomb M 16 was a very tall (H. 2.00), paved, free-standing structure, rectangular in plan and with a dromos.[61] The entrance was found blocked, with three slabs over it. There were remains of four bodies, including bits of human skull under the lintel and above the stone closing the tomb. There were also bones from dog, sheep, and ox. In addition to the catalogued vases, the tomb produced fragments of two stirrup jars of Type 2 with feet of Type 7 and sherds of a small vase in red clay with a white slip, probably a spouted jug of Type 1 (i.e. a thelastron). The conical cup (**M16.1**), called a miniature kalathos, was found almost directly under the paving.

It is fairly certain that this tomb had been robbed, as it contained little pottery for the number of burials. The stirrup jar (**M16.4**), with its dotted ovals in

---

61   *Karphi*, 107.

medallions and fringed motifs looks late in early LM IIIC. The other stirrup jars mentioned may also be as early; they are of the same general shape, but apparently from the description had flat bases. The flask (**M16.2**), on the other hand, is of SM date, with many parallels; the shape seems to have travelled.[62] Its fabric is so hard and well-fired that it looks out of place at Karphi and was probably an import, most likely from Knossos. The oinochoe (**M16.5**), however, looks even later, although no exact parallels can be found for its shape.[63] The tomb, then, seems to have been in use over a long period of time, from the middle of LM IIIC down at least to SM and possibly even later.

Pottery Catalogue: M 16

Fine Wares

M16.1   Conical cup (FIG. 7.9). H. 3.3; D. base 2; D. rim 6.4. Intact and complete except for chips missing from rim. Fine, very soft, light red (2.5YR 6/6) fabric with tiny white inclusions. Surfaces either laminating or coated with sediment. Publication: Seiradaki, fig. 7.5, pl. 11b, bottom left. LM IIIC?

M16.2   Flask (PLATE 26 *i*, FIG. 7.9). H. 12.7; D. base 4.6; D. rim 4.1. Mended from ten fragments. 95% preserved, including entire base, full profile, one handle, second handle attachment; missing one handle, part of neck and rim, fragment of body. Fine, hard, reddish yellow (7.5YR 7/6) fabric. Very pale brown (10YR 8/3) slip. Reddish brown (2.5YR 4/4) paint. Well-preserved surfaces. Probably an import. Triangles on shoulder with vertical strokes filling angles. Bands on mid body and lower body. Publication: Seiradaki, fig. 22:l; (mislabelled stirrup jar). SM.

M16.3   Amphora (FIG. 7.9). Max. pres. H. 6; D. base 3.6. Three joining and one non-joining fragment. 50% preserved, including base, both lower handle attachments; missing neck, rim, and handles. Fine, soft, reddish yellow (5YR 6/6) fabric with tiny white inclusions. Very worn surfaces. LM IIIC?

M16.4   Stirrup jar (FIG. 7.9). H. est. 11 (with handles 11.2); D. base 4.2. Two large fragments, one from top (3 sherds), one from base (2 sherds) and one non-joining body fragment. 30% preserved, including base, both handles, false spout, and most of spout. Fine, very soft, reddish yellow (7.5YR 7/6) fabric with grey (5Y 6/1) to light grey (5Y 7/1) core. Red (2.5YR 5/8) paint. Top made separately as disc and added on; ridge of clay where joined. Medallions with hatched ovals with dots and other filler motifs; spiral on false spout. LM IIIC early.

Coarse Wares

M16.5   Oinochoe (PLATE 26 *j*, FIG. 7.9). H. 8.5 (with handle 8.9); D. base 4.2; D. rim 2.2–3.7. Restored from five fragments. 90% preserved; missing several body fragments. Coarse light reddish brown (5YR 6/4) fabric with frequent large (2–3 mm) phyllite and hard white angular inclusions. Red (10R 5/6) paint. Most of surface worn or heavily encrusted with lime. Monochrome. Publication: Seiradaki, pl. 11b bottom, second from left. PG?

M 17

M 17 was also tall (H. 1.75), rectangular in plan, and free standing.[64] It had a dromos, and the entrance was found blocked. The remains of three human bodies were found within, along with bones of horse, sheep/goat, and ox.

The publication gives the following pottery in addition to the vessels catalogued below: three stirrup jars, one of Type 1 with a foot of Type 7 and spout of Type 4; two small bowls of Type 2; and a one-handled jug of Type 1, but with a flat lip. To this list the notebook adds a one-handled jar of Type 5 with a rim of Type 4; a two-handled jug of Type 1 with flat lip; the decorated base of large basin of Type 3; the rim of a basin of Type 6; and part of the base of a tripod of Type 3. Other objects included a bronze ring (392)[65] and the hoop of a bow fibula (393).[66]

Only two shapes are represented in the extant pottery: the krateriskos and the thelastron. There are two types of krateriskos; the first (**M17.1**) is found in a single example and is highly unusual, with its flat rim and two vertical handles from rim to body. A similar vessel can be found at Sybrita/Thronos of late LM IIIC date, but it lacks the flattened rim of the Karphi vessel and the wavy line decoration, and it has no base.[67] **M17.1** also resembles a White-painted I amphora from Kaloriziki on Cyprus that has been dated to CG Ia,[68] or CG II (950–850 BC).[69] The other krateriskoi (**M17.2–4**) are of the belly-handled type. There may be two of these rather than three; there were many fragments that included at least two bases, and possibly **M17.2** and **M17.4** are fragments of the same vessel. At any rate, these find parallels in SM contexts at Khamaizi–*Phatsi* and in EPG tombs in Knossos.[70] The thelastron (**M17.6**) has a close parallel in SM tombs at Knossos, as well.[71] The last use of this tomb would seem to have been EPG.

Pottery Catalogue: M 17

Fine Wares

M17.1   Krateriskos (PLATE 27 *a*, FIG. 7.10). H. 9.3–9.7; D. base 4.5; D. rim 8.1. Restored from 12 fragments. 75% preserved, including entire base, full profile, both handles; missing 25% of

---

62   For shape and decoration, Tsipopoulou 1997, 476, fig. 15.4969 (Khamaizi–*Phatsi*, MPG); *RMDP*, 193–4, fig. 60.464; (SM import); Hood, Huxley and Sandars 1958–59, 242, fig. 28. VI A 3 (Gypsades, SM). For shape, Coldstream and Catling 1996, 87–8, fig. 83.13, 14, 17; 165, fig. 117.121.1, 5 (Knossos, SM).

63   Tsipopoulou 1997, 471, fig. 13.4960 (LG) and 4962 (PGB) (Khamaizi–*Phatsi*).

64   *Karphi*, 107.

65   *Karphi*, pl. 28.3.

66   *Karphi*, pl. 28.3.

67   D'Agata 1999, 201, fig. 12.20.1.

68   Benson 1973, pl. 46.K334.

69   Steel 1996, 296.

70   Tsipopoulou 1997, 478, fig. 17.4983, 4984 (Khamaizi–*Phatsi*, SM–PGA); 458, fig. 2.5055, 5051, 5023 (Khamaizi–*Phatsi*, PGA); Coldstream and Catling 1996, 247, fig. 141.114 (EPG).

71   Coldstream and Catling 1996, 165, fig. 117.121.7 (SM).

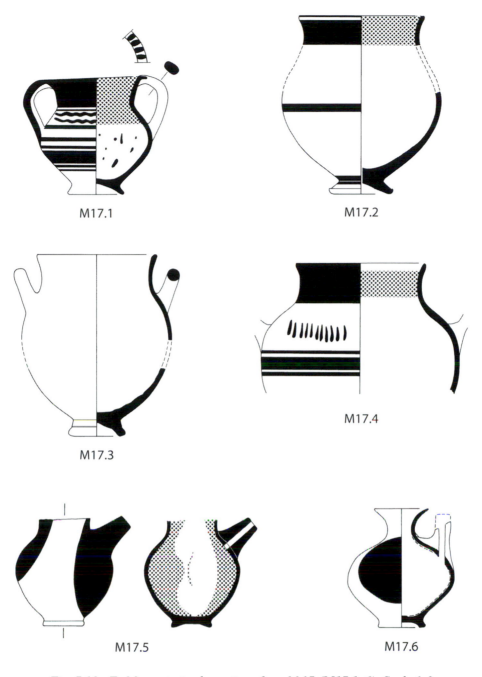

*Fig. 7.10. Ta Mnemata tombs, pottery from M 17 (**M17.1–6**). Scale 1:3.*

rim, much of neck and upper body on one side. Fine, rather soft, light red (2.5YR 6/6) fabric with tiny white and black inclusions. Pink (5YR 7/4) slip. Black paint. Well-preserved surfaces. Shoulder zone has two horizontal wavy bands; bands below. On rim, short strokes. Interior of neck painted; splatter pattern on interior. Publication: Seiradaki, fig. 14.7; pl. 11b, top, third from left. LM IIIC late–SM.

M17.2　Krateriskos (FIG. 7.10). H. est. 14.5; D. base 5; D. rim est. 10. Partially mended from eight joining fragments; three fragments from rim or near rim do not join. 10% preserved. Fine, rather hard, reddish yellow (7.5YR 7/6) fabric. Black (?) paint. Conical foot with small ledge on top, deep bell-shaped body, flaring rim. Bands on lower body, body, and rim; interior of rim painted. SM–EPG.

M17.3　Krateriskos (FIG. 7.10). H. est. 14.5; D. base 4.5; D. rim est. 9.2. Four large fragments, two from rim, one from base,

one from handle (18 sherds). 20% of vessel preserved? Fine, rather hard, reddish yellow (7.5YR 7/6) fabric. Very pale brown (10YR 8/4) surface. Possible paint on very worn surfaces. Conical foot, deep bell-shaped body, flaring rim. Possibly monochrome. SM–EPG.

M17.4　Krateriskos (FIG. 7.10). Max. pres. H. 10.4; D. rim 10.4. Mended from eight fragments. 40% preserved, including most of rim and upper body, one handle attachment; missing base, handles. Fine, rather porous, very pale brown (10YR 8/3) fabric with tiny black inclusions. Very pale brown (10YR 8/3) slip. Black paint. Worn surfaces, but paint well-preserved in places. Tall neck, flaring rim; round horizontal handles on shoulder. Vertical strokes on shoulder above bands. Interior of neck painted; reserve band at top. Publication: Seiradaki, fig. 14.9, pl. 11b, top, second from left. For shape and decoration, cf. Sapouna-Sakellarakis 1990, 83–4, fig. 35a (Phythies). SM–EPG.

M17.5   Thelastron (PLATE 27 *b*, FIG. 7.10). Max. pres. H. 8.8; D. base 3.3. Intact. 70% preserved; missing rim and handle. Pick hole in one side. Fine, rather soft, white (10YR 8/2) fabric. Very pale brown (10YR 8/4) slip. Black paint. Well-preserved surfaces. Blob decoration, inside and out. Publication: Seiradaki, pl. 11b, top, second from right. LM IIIC?

M17.6   Thelastron (PLATE 27 *c*, FIG. 7.10). H. 9.5; D. base 3.8; D. rim 4.3. Intact. 90% preserved including entire base (chipped); missing handle, most of rim, tip of spout. Fine, soft, reddish yellow (5YR 6/6) fabric with tiny black inclusions. Reddish yellow (7.5YR 8/6) slip. Dull brown to black paint. Blob decoration. Publication: Seiradaki, fig. 10.4; pl. 11b, top, third from right. SM.

TOMBS AT ASTIVIDHERO

The other cemetery lies to the east of Karphi, near the spring at Atsividhero. There were four tombs, two set close together (A 2, A 3), and two standing alone (A 1, A 4). The cemetery did not last as long as the Ta Mnemata cemetery, and there is no material from the tombs that dates to the period after the settlement was abandoned. Whatever the nature of the later activity at Ta Mnemata, whether SM–PG burials or later activities perhaps involving rituals in the Archaic or Classical Periods, there is no evidence for it in the Atsividhero tombs.

A 1

Tomb A 1 stood alone.[72] It was a rectangular, paved tholos tomb that ran into the hill at the back and had no dromos. The door was found still blocked, but although it looked undisturbed, the bones were not articulated and the pottery was found up against the wall, so the tomb was doubtless robbed in antiquity. There were remains only of one human body. Two cups illustrated as coming from this tomb were not found,[73] nor was the stirrup jar.[74] A small bowl mentioned in the notebook also was missing. The only other object from the grave was a conical stone bead or whorl (150). The cup (**A1.1**) finds a parallel at Khalasmenos of late LM IIIC date, while the juglet (**A1.2**) is similar to one from Katalimata.[75]

Pottery Catalogue: A 1

Fine Wares

A1.1   Cup or deep bowl (FIG. 7.11). H. 7.5; D. base 4.6; D. rim 10. Mended from two joining fragments. 50% preserved, including full profile and one handle attachment; missing handle. Fine, soft, reddish yellow (5YR 7/6) fabric. White (10YR 8/2) slip. Red (10R 4/6) to black paint. Rather well-preserved surfaces. Blob decoration with drip on interior. LM IIIC late.

A1.2   Juglet (FIG. 7.11). H. est. 9.5; D. base 3.6; max. D. 9. Partially mended into two large fragments, one from top (22 sherds), one from base (3 sherds); 18 body sherds. 75% preserved, including entire base, 75% of upper body, part of neck and handle; missing full profile and rim. Fine, soft, reddish yellow (5YR 7/6) fabric. Very pale brown (10YR 8/3) slip. Laminating surfaces, heavily coated with sediment. Bands, but rest too worn to tell. LM IIIC.

A 2 and A 3

These two tombs formed a pair.[76] There was no retaining wall, and both were built into the hill; they were separated by a wall of shaped blocks.

A 2

The east side of this tomb had disappeared. It was rectangular and paved with water-proof clay. It had a dromos that was paved with stones. There were fragments of only three small vases found inside, and only a few and much damaged bones. There is too little preserved pottery to suggest a date for the burial (s) in the tomb. The beaded tankard resembles those from M 4 and from K 77 and other places in the settlement, so it can be attributed to LM IIIC. The deep bowl base is high and very late, approaching the conical foot of SM, but probably still within LM IIIC.

Pottery Catalogue: A 2

Fine Wares

A2.1   Deep bowl (FIG. 7.11). D. base 3.8. Base and six body fragments. Fine, soft, reddish yellow (5YR 6/6) fabric with tiny black inclusions and mica. Very worn surfaces. Tall, raised concave base. LM IIIC late.

A2.2   Mug or tankard (FIG. 7.11). D. rim est. 20. Once mended from seven fragments. 50% of rim preserved; missing body, base, and handle. Fine, soft, reddish yellow (7.5YR 7/6) fabric. Very pale brown (10YR 8/4) surface. Black paint worn to dark reddish brown (5YR 3/3). Worn surfaces. Beaded decoration on rim, probably monochrome inside and out. Cf. **M4.7, K77.1**. LM IIIC late.

A 3

Tomb A 3 was circular and paved with stones; its dromos had been blocked in antiquity. There were many bones, but they were much damaged, and there were no objects. Inside the tomb six vessels were found. The cup (**A3.1**) and deep bowl (**A3.3**) are examples of the carinated shape found in LM IIIC, and the use of blob decoration can be found in all phases of LM IIIC; these examples both have drips on them. The monochrome deep bowl or cup (**A3.4**) cannot be closely dated, but certainly looks LM IIIC. The miniature cup (**A3.2**) and stirrup jars fit into LM IIIC as well.

---

72   *Karphi*, 108.

73   Seiradaki, fig. 14 cup 2; pl. 8e, top and pl. 8e middle.

74   Seiradaki fig. 11.1, pl. 11a, bottom, second from right.

75   Coulson and Tsipopoulou 1994, 75, fig. 10.3; 85, fig. 19.4; Nowicki 2008, fig. 52.KP 282.

76   *Karphi*, 108.

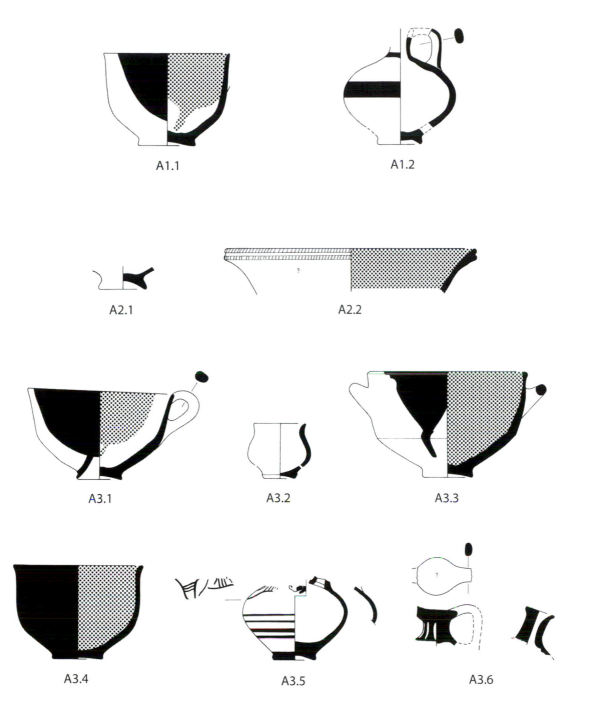

*Fig. 7.11. Atsividhero tombs, pottery from A 1 (**A1.1–2**), A 2 (**A2.1–2**), and A 3 (**A3.1–6**). Scale 1:3.*

Pottery Catalogue: A 3

Fine Wares

A3.1 Cup (PLATE 27 *d*, FIG. 7.11). H. 6.8–7.3; D. base 3.6; D. rim 11.8. Mended from five fragments. 95% preserved; missing one fragment from upper body and rim. Fine, soft, reddish yellow (7.5YR 7/6) fabric. Red (2.5YR 5/6) paint. Well-preserved surfaces. Carinated body. Blob decoration inside and out, with drip connecting them inside and on bottom. Blob decoration extends to underside of base. Publication: Seiradaki, fig. 14 cup 1; pl. 8e, bottom. LM IIIC.

A3.2 Miniature cup (FIG. 7.11). H. est. 4.5; D. base 2.8; D. rim 4.2. Five non-joining fragments preserving 50% of vessel, including rim and base. Fine, soft, reddish yellow (7.5YR 7/6) fabric with infrequent small (<1 mm) grey and white inclusions). Laminating surfaces. Not labelled, but found with A3 material. Publication: possibly Seiradaki, pl. 8e, top (labelled A1). For shape, cf. Warren 2007, fig. 337.P1919 (Knossos, LM IIIC early). LM IIIC.

A3.3 Deep bowl (FIG. 7.11). H. est. 8.5; D. base 4.1; D. rim 12.5. Partially mended from 13 fragments. 50% preserved, including entire base, 33% of rim and one handle; missing much of rim, second handle. Fine, medium-soft, reddish yellow (7.5YR 7/6) fabric. White (10YR 8/2) slip. Red (10R 4/8) paint worn to brown shadow. Well-preserved surfaces. Raised concave base. Carinated body. Blob decoration on exterior with drip, monochrome interior. LM IIIC.

A3.4   Cup or deep bowl (FIG. 7.1). H. 7.5; D. base 4; D. rim 10.4. Mended from ten fragments and glue marks indicate that there were others. 40% preserved, including full profile; missing handle(s) and much of rim. Fine, soft sandy, very pale brown (10YR 7/3) fabric. Worn red to brown paint. Surfaces very worn. Monochrome. LM IIIC.

A3.5   Stirrup jar (FIG. 7.11). Max. pres. H. 6.6; D. base 3.5; max. D. 8.4. Mended from four fragments, preserving half of base and 60% of body. Fine, soft, reddish yellow (5YR 6/6) fabric. Very pale brown (10YR 8/3) slip. Black paint worn to shadow. Worn surfaces. Curvilinear motif on shoulder, bands below. LM IIIC.

A3.6   Stirrup jar (FIG. 7.11). Max. pres. H. 4. Fragments of false spout, one handle, spout. Fine, soft, reddish yellow (5YR 6/6) fabric. Very pale brown (10YR 8/3) slip. Black paint worn to shadow. Worn surfaces. Slightly concave disc on false spout. Vertical bands on neck of false spout. LM IIIC.

A 4

This tomb ran alongside the hill and was free-standing.[77] It was rectangular in plan and has a long dromos that was found blocked. The entrance was not blocked, but there was a pithos partly in the entrance chamber. There were remains of one human body, but they were much disturbed, and the excavators thought the tomb had been robbed soon after the burial was made. Pottery included fragments of a large pithos with chevron decoration, sherds of a stirrup jar in soft pink clay, and bases of two cups or bowls in similar clay. None has been preserved.

---

77   *Karphi*, 108–9.

8

Vases from uncertain contexts

Many fragments and vessels were stored with the Karphi pottery that did not have room or tomb numbers written on them, and some did have worn numbers that were no longer legible. The best-preserved and most important of these have been catalogued below. Some of the uncatalogued coarse wares were sampled petrographically. These include a basin (sampled KAR 06/18), two bases of cylindrical vessels or snake tubes (sampled KAR 06/20–21), and five pithoi (sampled KAR 06/74–76, KAR 06/78, KAR 06/80).

Pottery Catalogue

Fine Wares

K.1   Cup (FIG. 8.1). H. est. 11.5; D. base est. 5.5. Four joining fragments from base, one handle fragment, three non-joining body fragments; once restored, with glue and plaster on the edges. Fine, rather soft, light red (2.5YR 6/6) fabric with pink (5YR 7/4) surface. Red to brown paint. Very worn surfaces. Wheelmarks inside and out. Monochrome, including bottom. No label; found with pyxis from K 147. PG?

K.2   Deep bowl (FIG. 8.1). Max. pres. H. 11.4; D. base 6.2. Mended from six fragments. 40% preserved, including entire base, profile up to rim, one handle; missing entire rim and other handle. Fine, medium-soft, very pale brown (10YR 8/3) fabric. Black paint. Totally burned. Monochrome. No label. LM IIIC late.

K.3   Deep bowl (FIG. 8.1). D. rim est. 8. Single fragment (two sherds) from rim, preserving one handle; glue on edges suggests that there once was a base. Fine, very soft, very pale brown (10YR 8/3) fabric. Worn red (2.5YR 5/6) paint. Monochrome. Labelled Karphi 1937. LM IIIC.

K.4   Deep bowl (FIG. 8.1). D. rim est. 14. Single fragment from rim, preserving handle attachment. Fine, medium-hard, very pale brown (10YR 7/3) fabric. Very pale brown (10YR 8/4) slip. Black paint, flaky on interior. Quirk or buttonhook spiral. Worn label, possibly K 33 or K 53. LM IIIC early.

K.5   Deep bowl or cup (FIG. 8.1). D. rim est. 17. Single fragment from rim. Fine, soft, reddish yellow (7.5YR 7/6) fabric. Very pale brown (10YR 8/3) slip. Black paint. Worn surfaces. Curvilinear motif with fringes. No label. LM IIIC.

K.6   Deep bowl or cup (FIG. 8.1). D. rim est. 14. Single fragment from rim. Fine, medium-hard, pink (7.5YR 7/4) fabric. White (10YR 8/2) slip. Red (2.5YR 5/8) to dark reddish brown (2.5YR 3/4) paint. Hatched lozenge or chevrons? Interior unpainted except for band at rim. Imported from mainland? Label worn, possibly K 95 or K 45. LM IIIC.

K.7   Deep bowl or cup (FIG. 8.1). D. rim est. 13–15. Two joining fragments from rim. Fine, soft, very pale brown (10YR 7/4) fabric. Very pale brown (10YR 8/3) slip. Very worn brown paint. Poorly preserved surfaces. Crosshatched lozenge with horizontal 'tail' and loop. Label unclear; may be from K 12 or K 124. LM IIIC.

K.8   Deep bowl or cup (FIG. 8.1). D. rim est. 12. Single fragment from rim. Fine, soft, reddish yellow (7.5YR 7/6) fabric. Very pale brown (10YR 8/3) slip. Worn red (10R 4/8) paint. Quirk.

No label. For decoration, cf. Rethemiotakis 1997, 318, fig. 27r, s (Kastelli Pediada). LM IIIC early.

K.9   Deep bowl or cup (FIG. 8.1). Max. pres. H. 4. Single fragment from rim. Fine, very soft, yellow (10YR 7/6) fabric. Very pale brown (10YR 8/3) slip. Worn black paint. Quirk. No label. LM IIIC early.

K.10   Deep bowl or cup (FIG. 8.1). D. rim est. 14. Single fragment from rim. Fine, soft, very pale brown (10YR 8/3) fabric and slip. Worn black paint. Loops. No label. LM IIIC.

K.11   Deep bowl or cup (FIG. 8.1). D. rim est. 11. Single fragment from rim. Fine, soft, very pale brown (10YR 7/4) fabric. Very pale brown (10YR 8/4) slip. Black paint worn to brown shadow. Blob decoration. No label. LM IIIC early.

K.12   Deep bowl or cup (FIG. 8.1). Max. pres. H. 5.4. Single fragment from rim. Fine, soft, reddish yellow (7.5YR 6/6) fabric. Very pale brown (10YR 8/4) slip. Very worn surfaces. Three rows of knobs. No label. LM IIIC.

K.13   Deep bowl or cup (FIG. 8.1). Max. pres. H. 2.4. Single fragment from body. Fine, medium-hard, reddish yellow (5YR 7/6) fabric. White (10YR 8/2) slip. Black paint. Well-preserved surfaces. Hatched leaves with multiple loops between. No label. LM IIIC.

K.14   Deep bowl (FIG. 8.1). D. base 3.7. Single fragment from base. Glue on edges suggests that there once were additional pieces. Fine, soft, reddish yellow (7.5YR 7/6) fabric. Very pale brown (10YR 8/4) surface. Very dark greyish brown (10YR 3/2) paint. Worn exterior surfaces, well-preserved on interior. Band on exterior, reserved disc on interior. Labelled Karphi 1937. LM IIIC.

K.15   Kylix (PLATE 27 e, FIG. 8.1). Max. pres. H. 6.8; D. rim 14.5. Restored from 23 fragments. 75% preserved, including nearly complete profile, both handles; missing base, most of rim and upper body. Fine, soft, very pale brown (10YR 7/3) fabric. Black paint. Very worn surfaces. Burned. Tall pierced stem. Octopus on body. Publication: Seiradaki, fig. 10b, left (already without known provenience); Mountjoy 2007, 232, fig. 4.1. No label. For shape and decoration, cf. *Kavousi IIA*, fig. 22. B3 P3–4 (Kavousi–*Vronda*, LM IIIC late). LM IIIC late.

K.16   Kylix (FIG. 8.1). Max. pres. H. 6.9. Single fragment from stem. Fine, soft, reddish yellow (7.5YR 7/6) fabric. White (10YR 8/2) slip. Dull worn black paint. Worn surfaces. Tall, pierced stem, narrower at bottom. Bands. No label. LM IIIC.

K.17   Mug or tankard (PLATE 11 d, FIG. 8.1). D. rim est. 19. Two joining fragments from rim. Fine, soft, reddish yellow (7.5YR 7/6) fabric. Very pale brown (10YR 8/3) slip. Worn red (10R 4/8) paint. Very worn surfaces. Flaring rim. Beaded decoration on rim. Painted outlined pendent dotted triangles. Curvilinear motif below. No label. Cf. **K28.2**, **K23.8** (to which it may belong). LM IIIC.

K.18   Bowl (FIG. 8.2). D. rim est. 19.5. Partially mended from 39 fragments. 20% preserved, including rim and part of handle, body almost to base. Fine, soft, light reddish brown (5YR 6/4) fabric. Very pale brown (10YR 8/3) slip. Black to reddish brown (5YR 4/4) or yellowish red (5YR 4/6) paint. Worn surfaces. Handle at rim, probably horizontal strap handle. May have been spouted. Bands inside and out; wavy band on rim. No label. Cf. **K115.6**. LM IIIC.

K.19   Krater (FIG. 8.2). D. rim est. 38. Single fragment from rim. Fine, very soft, very pale brown (10YR 7/4) fabric. Very pale

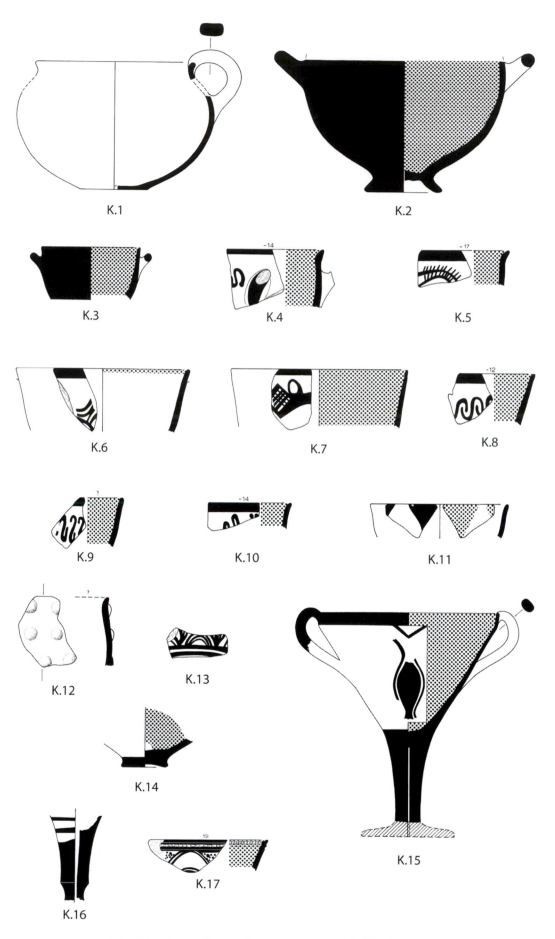

Fig. 8.1. Pottery from unknown contexts (K.1–17). Scale 1:3.

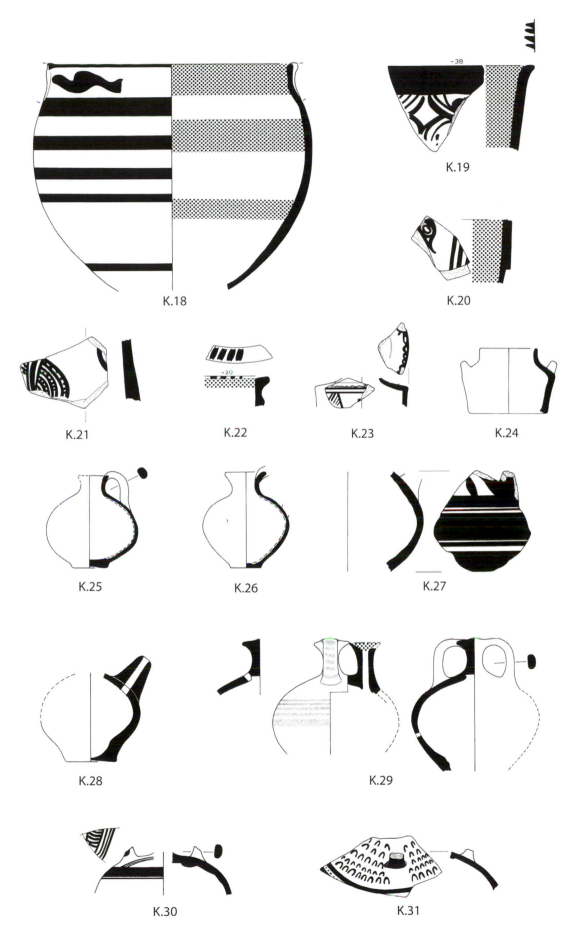

*Fig. 8.2. Pottery from unknown contexts (**K.18–31**). Scale 1:3.*

brown (10YR 8/3) slip. Black paint. Worn surfaces. Curvilinear motif, arc fillers. No label. LM IIIC.

K.20   Krater (FIG. 8.2). Max. pres. H. 5. Single fragment from body. Fine, quite hard, strong brown (7.5YR 5/6) fabric. Very pale brown (10YR 8/4) slip. Dusky red (10R 3/4) paint. Laminating surface. Head of bird. No label. LM IIIC.

K.21   Krater (FIG. 8.2). Max. pres. H. 4.7. Single fragment from body. Fine, medium-hard, reddish yellow (5YR 7/6) fabric. Glossy pink (7.5YR 8/4) slip. Worn black paint. Arcs with dots as filler. Number worn off of sediment, possibly K 79-89. LM IIIC.

K.22   Basin (FIG. 8.2). D. rim est. 20. Single fragment from rim. Rather fine soft, reddish yellow (7.5YR 7/6) fabric with some hard grey inclusions (up to 2 mm). Black paint. Worn surfaces. Strokes on rim, band on interior. Number worn, last digit 5.

K.23   Pyxis (FIG. 8.2). D. shoulder carination 7–8. Single fragment from shoulder. Fine, soft, reddish yellow (5YR 6/8) fabric. Very pale brown (10YR 8/3) slip. Worn red (2.5YR 4/8) paint. Very worn surfaces. Hatched triangles on body, scallops on shoulder. No label. LM IIIC.

K.24   Miniature pyxis (PLATE 27 *f*, FIG. 8.2). H. 5.2; D. base 6.3; D. rim 4.7. Mended from three fragments; full profile preserved. Missing tops of handles and base. Fine greenish grey (5G 5/1) blue ware fabric where burned, reddish yellow (5YR 6/6) where not burned. Black paint. Worn surfaces. No label. LM IIIC.

K.25   Juglet (FIG. 8.2). H. 7.3 (with handle 7.8); D. base 3; D. rim 3. Intact. 95% preserved, including handle; missing most of rim. Fine, soft, reddish yellow (5YR 6/8) fabric with tiny white and black inclusions and larger grey phyllite and hard white angular inclusions. Red to brown paint. Worn surfaces, and still much covered with sediment. Probably once decorated. Label worn; possibly K 115 or K 145. LM IIIC.

K.26   Juglet (FIG. 8.2). H. 7; D. base 2.5; D. rim 3.3. Partially restored from five fragments; missing most of base, all of handle, and fragments of lower body. Fine, soft, light red (2.5YR 6/8) fabric with tiny black sharp inclusions and silver mica. Worn and flaky surfaces. Possible red paint. Burned patches on body, sometimes surfaces almost vitrified. Raised base, ovoid-biconical body. Small neck with flaring rim. Monochrome or blob decoration. Wrapped in paper labelled 'Karphi'. LM IIIC.

K.27   Jug (FIG. 8.2). Max. pres. H. 8; max. D. est. 12. Single fragment (four sherds) from body, from near base to near neck, including handle attachment. Fine, medium-hard grey (2.5Y 6/2) fabric. Red (2.5YR 5/6) paint. Burned or misfired. Floral or curvilinear design on shoulder, broad bands below. Label unclear; may be from K 12, K 24, K 29, or K 124. Cf. **K85.8**. LM IIIC.

K.28   Thelastron (FIG. 8.2). Max. pres. H. 8.5; D. base 4. Mended from seven fragments, one non-joining sherd. 80% preserved, including entire base and spout; missing top of one side, rim and handle. Fine, soft, dark grey (5Y 4/1) fabric with voids. Black paint. Worn surfaces. Totally burned. No label. LM IIIC.

K.29   Stirrup jar (FIG. 8.2). Max. pres. H. 7.6. Partially mended from eight fragments; one non-joining fragment from near base. Top preserved, including false spout, both handles, most of spout. Fine, soft, light red (2.5YR 6/6) fabric. Yellow (10YR 8/6) slip. Worn red-brown paint. Spout bent back to touch false spout. Top added as separate disc. Hole pierced through walls of top, just below false spout. Low cone on false spout. Bands, horizontal bands on handles. Found with pottery from Ta Mnemata tombs. LM IIIC.

K.30   Stirrup jar (FIG. 8.2). Max. pres. H. 3.7; max. pres. D. 10.9. Single fragment from top, preserving base of false spout, both handle attachments. Fine, rather hard, very pale brown (10YR 7/3) fabric and slip. Black to brown paint. Well-preserved surfaces. Burned uniformly, possibly misfired. Top added as separate disc. Half medallion with hatched oval. No label. LM IIIC.

K.31   Stirrup jar (FIG. 8.2). Max. pres. H. 3.5. Single body fragment, including one handle attachment. Fine, soft, reddish

yellow (5YR 7/6) fabric. Very pale brown (10YR 8/3) slip. Black paint. Top added on as disc; ridge of clay joining it to body preserved. Groups of U-pattern on shoulder; alternating bands and rows of dots below. No label. Cf. Andreadaki-Vlasaki and Papadopoulou 2005, 385, fig. 49:93/3/645 (Khamalevri, Phase I–II). LM IIIC.

K.32   Fenestrated stand (PLATE 27 *g*, FIG. 8.3). Max. pres. H. 13.3; max. pres. Th. 3.8. Mended from three fragments; broken on one side. Fine, soft, pale brown (10YR 6/3) fabric with infrequent schist inclusions (1–2 mm). Worn black paint. Worn surfaces. Burned or fired to uniform grey colour. Rectangular or square in shape on flat base. Rectangular 'pillar' at corner, then two flat plaques with horns of consecration; second plaque is larger than the first. Broken, but could be room for a third plaque, forming a sort of tripartite arrangement. Possibly an 'altar' like the one from K57. Monochrome. No label. Publication: Day 2009, 145–6, fig. 12.9. Cf. Eliopoulos 2004, 87, fig. 6.8 (Vasiliki–*Kephala*). LM IIIC.

K.33   Snake tube (PLATE 27 *h*, FIG. 8.3). Max. pres. H. 18.8; D. base 18.5. Partially restored from 14 fragments. Most of base and two lowest handle attachments preserved. No upper body or rim. Fine, rather soft, reddish yellow (7.5YR 6/6) fabric with tiny black and white inclusions (<1 mm). Very worn surfaces. Base has projecting ledges inside and out. Ridged base with vertical handles just above topmost ridge; at least two sets of handles. No label. LM IIIC.

Medium-Coarse Wares

K.34   Cup (FIG. 8.3). H. 9; D. base 4.2; D. rim 11.8. Mended from three fragments, two non-joining fragments. 75% preserved, including entire base, full profile, non-joining handle. Medium-coarse fabric, totally burned black, with some white inclusions. No label, but possible fragments found with stirrup jar from K 147. For shape, cf. Andreadaki-Vlasaki and Papadopoulou 2007, 50, fig. 7.23 (Khamalevri, Phase II). LM IIIC.

K.35   Jug (FIG. 8.3). Max. pres. H. 6.5. D. base 4.7. Partially mended from three fragments, 15 non-joining fragments. Entire base preserved and half of lower body; missing neck, rim, handle. Medium-coarse yellowish red (5YR 5/6) fabric with infrequent phyllites and hard white angular inclusions. Much of exterior burned. No label. Cf. **K3.13**. LM IIIC.

K.36   Stirrup jar (PLATE 27 *i*, FIG. 8.3). H. 22.3; D. base 9.5; max. D. 21. Restored from 30 fragments. 75% preserved; missing body fragments, rim of spout. Medium-coarse light red (2.5YR 6/8) fabric with frequent small black inclusions (<1 mm). Very worn and pitted surfaces. Top of short false spout slightly concave and pierced in centre; spout tilted back almost to touch false spout. No label. LM IIIC.

Coarse Wares

K.37   Kalathos (FIG. 8.3). H. 10.8 (with knob 11.4); D. base 6.2; D. rim 22.8. Eight joining and three non-joining fragments. 75% preserved, including full profile. Very coarse, crumbly, yellowish red (5YR 5/8) fabric with frequent large (2–3 mm, up to 5 mm) phyllite and schist inclusions. Small amount of burning on sides of interior. Flat on top, with at least two knobs preserved. No label. For shape, cf. Day, Coulson and Gesell 1986, 380, fig. 13.37, pl. 84c (Kavousi–*Vronda*, Building E, Room E1); Gesell 1999, pl. 62a, c (Kavousi–*Vronda*). LM IIIC.

K.38   Kalathos (FIG. 8.3). Max. pres. H. 8.5; D. base 5.2. Single fragment preserving entire base and part of lower body; missing rim. Coarse reddish yellow (5YR 6/6) fabric with frequent red phyllites (1–2 mm) and hard white and black inclusions; one large piece of quartz (6 mm). Base rough on bottom with string marks. No label; in box with kalathoi from K 2 and 3. LM IIIC.

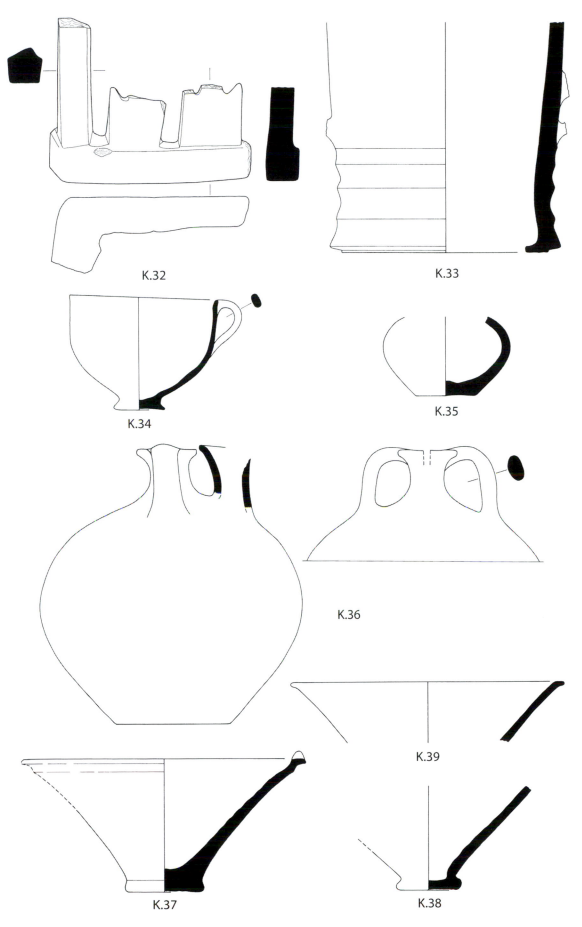

*Fig. 8.3. Pottery from unknown contexts (**K.32–39**). Scale 1:3.*

K.39   Kalathos (FIG. 8.3). D. rim est. 22. Mended from five fragments from rim, but fresh breaks indicate more once preserved. Very coarse yellowish red (5YR 5/6) fabric with frequent phyllites and hard white angular inclusions. Burned inside and out. No label. For shape, cf. Andreadaki-Vlasaki and Papadopoulou 2007, 51, fig. 8.15, 23 (Khamalevri, Phases Ib and II). LM IIIC.

K.40   Krater (PLATE 27 *j*, FIG. 8.4). Max. pres. H. 19.7; D. rim est. 28. Mended from 15 fragments, eight non-joining fragments. 50% preserved, including much of rim and both handles. Base fragment preserved, but does not join. Coarse light red (2.5YR 6/8) fabric with grey core and frequent red and grey phyllites. Surface mottled dark grey, burned on exterior around handle. Lower body is crumbly and laminating. Rounded bottom with added ring of clay to form ring base. No label; found with material from K 2. LM IIIC.

K.41   Lid (FIG. 8.4). H. 16–22; D. est. 26–28. Single fragment from rim; missing knob handle. Coarse red (10R 5/6) fabric with hard black and white inclusions and gold mica (1–2 mm). No burning. Flat disc lid. Raised ridges, one on rim with finger impressions, then plain ridge, then another with finger impressions. Label worn; K_2, perhaps K 52 or K 62. Cf. **K44.9**, possibly from same vessel. LM IIIC.

K.42   Lid (FIG. 8.4). Max. pres. H. 1.4. Single fragment from rim. Coarse red (10R 5/6) fabric with infrequent schist inclusions (up to 3 mm). Hard, smoothed upper surfaces. No burning. Slightly concave, but basically flat disc. Incisions around rim and groove with finger impressions; then incised chevrons and short strokes, incised groove. No label. Publication: Seiradaki, pl. 12a, bottom, second from right. For shape and decoration, cf. Andreadaki-Vlasaki and Papadopoulou 2005, 378, fig. 43.94/3/301. LM IIIC.

K.43   Lid (FIG. 8.4). Max. pres. H. 1.3; D. rim est. 20–22. Single fragment from rim; missing centre knob. Coarse red (10R 5/6) fabric with frequent schist and phyllite inclusions (1–3 mm). No burning on bottom. Flat disc. Raised rope-slashed band at rim, two more concentric raised rope-slashed bands. No label. LM IIIC.

K.44   Jug (FIG. 8.4). Max. pres. H. 5.4. Single fragment from handle. Coarse light red (2.5YR 6/8) fabric with frequent phyllites (2–3 mm) and hard angular white inclusions. Elliptical vertical handle with two twisted coils in centre, creating a rope handle. No label; found with cylindrical stand from K1. LM IIIC.

K.45   Stirrup jar (FIG. 8.4). Max. pres. H. 7.9. Partially mended from eight fragments, including spout, false spout and both handles. Eleven non-joining body fragments. Coarse reddish yellow (5YR 6/8–7.5YR 6/8) fabric, grey (5YR 5/1) just under surface, with frequent hard black and white inclusions (1–2 mm). Black paint? Very worn surfaces. Spout angles back to touch false spout. Top of false spout pierced and concave. Once decorated? No label. LM IIIC.

K.46   Stirrup jar (PLATE 28 *a*, FIG. 8.4). H. 16; D. base 7.5; max. D. 15.7. Nearly complete; intact except for 25% of rim of false spout. 95% preserved. Rather coarse, yellowish red (5YR 5/6) fabric with large (2–3 mm) inclusions: roughly grey siltstone and hard black and white inclusions; possible lighter slip on one side, but too worn to tell. Worn surfaces. Blackened by fire on one side. Large spout, tilted back and almost touching false spout. False spout pierced in centre and concave. Probably decorated but worn. No label. LM IIIC.

K.47   Cooking jug (FIG. 8.4). Max. pres. H. 6.1; D. rim est. 8. Mended from seven fragments from rim and upper body; glue marks on bottom suggest that there was once a base, now missing. 50% preserved, including part of handle; missing 25% of rim and lower body, base. Coarse yellowish red (5YR 5/8) to red (2.5YR 5/8) cooking pot fabric with frequent schist inclusions (1–3 mm). Sampled KAR 06/70. Burned inside and out except for one side of exterior. No label. For shape, cf. Borgna 1997*b*, 197, fig. 7 right (dipper from Phaistos). LM IIIC.

K.48   Cooking jug (FIG. 8.4). H. 10 (with handle 10.2); D. base 10.2; D. rim 13.2. Two large fragments, one from base (three sherds), one from rim and handle (four sherds). 35% preserved, including entire base, half of rim, one handle. Coarse reddish yellow (7.5YR 6/6) fabric, grey (5Y 5/1) at core, with frequent large (2–3 mm) phyllites, angular hard white inclusions, and soft yellow inclusions (1–3 mm). No label; found with material from Rooms K 2 and K 3. LM IIIC.

K.49   Cooking dish (FIG. 8.4). Max. pres. H. 2.6. Single fragment (three sherds) from rim to base. Coarse red (2.5YR 5/8) fabric with frequent schist and hard white angular inclusions (2–3 mm). Burned on exterior. No label; found with scuttle from K 115. LM IIIC.

K.50   Snake tube (FIG. 8.5). Max. pres. H. 6.5. Three fragments from body, one with handle attachment, all with glue on edges, but not joining. Coarse, soft, very pale brown (10YR 8/4) fabric with oblong black inclusions (1–2 mm). Cylindrical, with at least one vertical handle. No label; found with pithos **K26.14** and fragments from K 1. LM IIIC.

K.51   Plaque (FIG. 8.5). Max. pres. H. 10.6. Single body fragment. Coarse very pale brown (10YR 8/3) fabric with frequent black and white inclusions (2–3 mm). White (2.5Y 8/2) slip. Black paint. Decorated with parallel bands, rows of dots, and some larger curvilinear design. No label. LM IIIC.

K.52   Cooking slab (FIG. 8.5). Max. pres. L. 24.3; max. pres. W. 20.8; max. pres. H. 3. Five joining fragments, preserving two edges. Coarse light red (2.5YR 6/8) fabric with frequent schist (2–4 mm) and hard white angular inclusions. Circular area of burning in centre. Flat slab with raised edge, groove around underside of edge. No label. Cf. **K 113.5**, **K126.1–2**. LM IIIC.

K.53   Pithos (PLATE 28 *b*, FIG. 8.5). Max. pres. H. 27; D. base est. 42; D. rim est. 48. Two boxes of fragments from same pithos. Perhaps 50% preserved, including half of base, most of rim, two handles from near rim, two more from near base. Coarse red (2.5YR 5/8) to yellowish red (5YR 5/8) fabric, dark grey at core, with frequent phyllites, schist (1–3 mm), and hard white angular inclusions. Slightly raised base with hole pierced through walls near bottom. Horizontal raised bands with double row of finger impressions. Rope-slashed serpentine bands between horizontal bands; at least three rows of rope pattern preserved from body, another from handle zone. Ridge with impressed circles below rim. Dint at lower handle attachments. No label. LM IIIC.

K.54   Pithos (FIG. 8.6). Max. pres. H. 13; D. rim est. 23. Single fragment from rim and upper body, preserving one handle. Coarse yellowish red (5YR 5/8) fabric with very frequent phyllites and schist (2–3 mm) and hard angular white inclusions (1 mm and less). Outward thickened rim with ridge below. No label. LM IIIC.

K.55   Pithos (FIG. 8.6). Max. pres. H. 28.8; D. rim est. 36. Large fragment from rim, preserving upper body and part of one handle. Coarse light red (5YR 6/6) fabric with frequent grey phyllites (2 mm) and some schist. Burned on one side. Ridge decorated with finger impressions. Plain raised band below. No label. LM IIIC.

K.56   Pithos (FIG. 8.6). Max. pres. H. 11; D. rim est. 34. Single fragment from rim. Coarse reddish yellow (7.5YR 7/6) fabric with phyllites, soft green and hard white angular inclusions. No label. LM IIIC.

K.57   Pithos (FIG. 8.6). Max. pres. H. 13; D. rim est. 38. Single fragment from rim. Coarse light red (2.5YR 6/8) fabric, dark grey at core, with some phyllites and frequent hard white angular inclusions. No label. LM IIIC.

K.58   Pithos (FIG. 8.6). Max. pres. H. 9; D. rim est. 39. Single fragment from rim. Coarse red (2.5YR 5/8) fabric with phyllites. Surface mottled black and red. No label.

K.59   Pithos (FIG. 8.6). D. rim est. 41. Small fragment from rim. Coarse yellowish red (5YR 5/6) fabric with frequent phyllite inclusions. No label. LM IIIC.

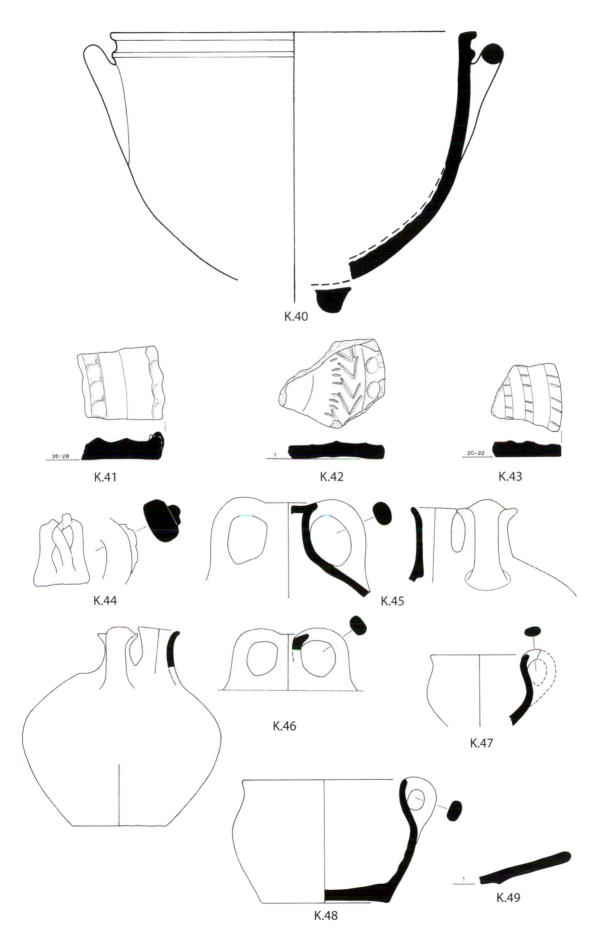

*Fig. 8.4. Pottery from unknown contexts (**K.40–49**). Scale 1:3.*

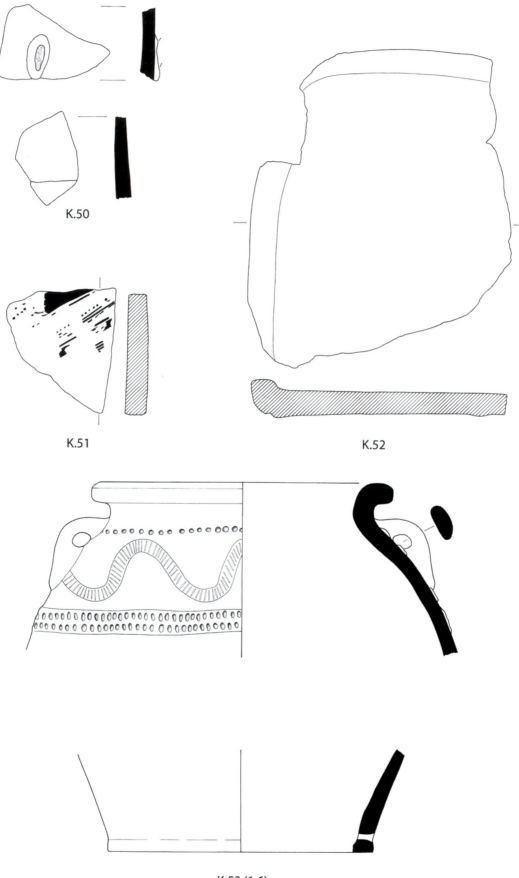

K.50

K.51

K.52

K.53 (1:6)

Fig. 8.5. Pottery from unknown contexts (**K.50–53**). Scale 1:3 unless otherwise indicated.

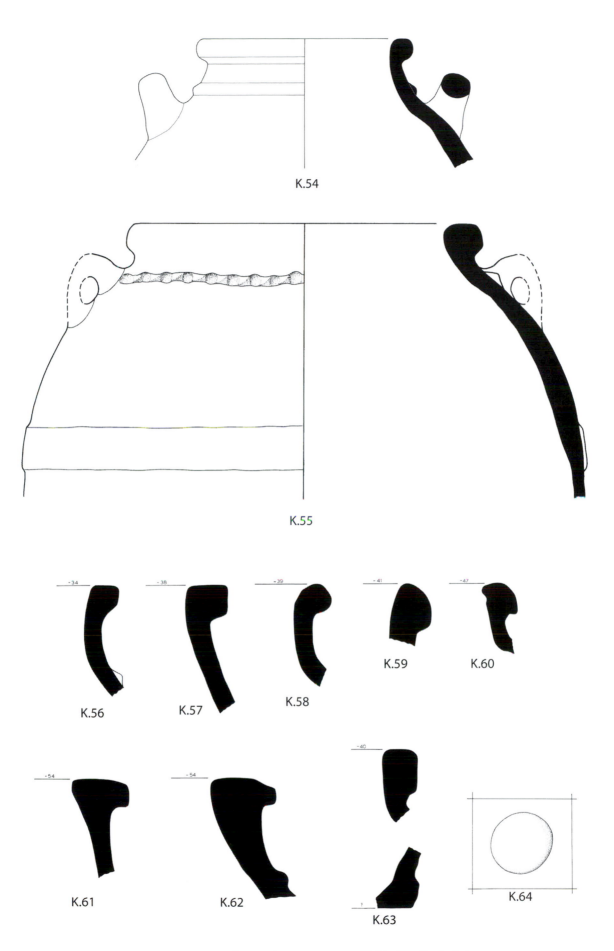

K.54

K.55

K.56

K.57

K.58

K.59

K.60

K.61

K.62

K.63

K.64

*Fig. 8.6. Pottery from unknown contexts (**K.54–65**). Scale 1:4.*

K.60   Pithos (FIG. 8.6). Max. pres. H. 7; D. rim est. 47. Single fragment from rim. Coarse light red (2.5YR 6/8) fabric, grey at core, with frequent phyllites and hard angular white inclusions. No label. LM IIIC.

K.61   Pithos (FIG. 8.6). Max. pres. H. 10.5; D. rim est. 54. Single fragment from rim. Coarse very pale brown (10YR 8/3) fabric with frequent red phyllites. No label. LM IIIC.

K.62   Pithos (FIG. 8.6). D. rim est. 54. Entire box of fragments from single pithos. Coarse reddish yellow (7.5YR 8/6) fabric with frequent red and grey phyllites and schist (2–3 mm) inclusions. Sampled KAR 06/66. Raised band with chevrons. No label. LM IIIC.

K.63   Pithos (FIG. 8.6). D. rim est. 40; D. base est. 40. Entire box of fragments from single pithos. Fragments of rim and base preserved and decorated body fragments. Coarse red (2.5YR 6/8) fabric with very frequent schist inclusions (2–5 mm). Raised bands with incised chevrons, raised band with incised oblique strokes. No label. LM IIIC.

K.64   Pithos (FIG. 8.6). Single fragment from body. Coarse light red (2.5YR 6/6) fabric, dark grey at core, with frequent schist and other phyllites, and hard white angular inclusions. Burned on exterior. Thinner walls, may be cooking pot. Raised circle. No label. Publication: Seiradaki, pl. 12a, second row, right (?). LM IIIC.

9

Pottery analysis

Seiradaki published the Karphi pottery by shapes, without distinguishing between fine and coarse wares, providing a typology within each shape, and finally discussing the decoration separately. In the following discussion, the pottery will be categorised by shape, beginning with open shapes and moving to closed shapes, small vessels first, then larger ones. Within each shape, an attempt will be made to consider the fine, medium-coarse, and coarse examples of each shape separately, since there may have been functional or chronological differences between a fine shape and its coarse or medium-coarse counterpart. Within the fine wares, I will treat decorated wares, including monochrome decoration, separately from the few plain wares that survive. Cooking vessels, which constitute a particular class of pottery at Karphi, will be considered together after the other vessels, and finally there will be a section on a few terracotta objects that do not readily fall into the category of pottery. With a few exceptions, the terminology for the shapes conforms to those established by Hallager.[1]

FABRICS

Fine wares

Not much can be added to Seiradaki's descriptions of the fine fabrics. She distinguished only two general categories, regular buff wares, and the misfired pottery known as blue ware.

Regular buff fine wares

As Seiradaki noted,[2] the fabrics of the regular buff-coloured wares are all soft, and I have chosen to categorise their hardness as follows:

Very soft: comes off easily on the fingers.
Soft: easily scratched with a fingernail, comes off on the fingers if rubbed.
Medium soft: still can be scratched with a fingernail, but does not rub off on the fingers.

Occasionally, there is a fragment of harder fabric (medium-hard) or even one that is impervious to the fingernail (hard). Such fabrics are probably not local; where one has been tested petrographically (**K38.1**) it seems to be an import, and a number of fragments of hard fabric look imported also on the basis of decoration or style, like **K21.1**, which has a mainland motif, or **K46.2**, **K106.3**, and **K.6**, which have interior bands instead of monochrome paint. The softness of the fabric

is most likely to have been a result of the conditions under which the pottery was fired, rather than stemming from the clay itself; it may simply be due to low firing temperatures in the kiln. The presence of so many misfired vessels in blue ware at Karphi suggests that the potters did not have good control over their firing conditions. Many of the fragments of harder fabric are decorated with motifs that belong to early LM IIIC, so there may also have been a change over time. Soft fabrics, however, are a regular feature of LM IIIC pottery, particularly in east Crete; similar fabrics can be found at Kavousi and Khalasmenos, and probably at other LM IIIC sites as well. Soil conditions may also have contributed to the softness of the fabrics; sometimes joining pieces of the same vessel appear to have rather different fabrics, perhaps because they were buried in different types of soil. Such was the case also at Kavousi.[3]

The fabrics are well levigated, generally with few inclusions. Frequently, a fabric may have visible tiny black or white sand-sized inclusions. Two fabrics are most common. The first is a soft fabric of reddish yellow (5YR 6/6, 5YR 7/6, 7.5YR 7/6) with a distinct very pale brown slip (10YR 8/3–8/4). The second is a more porous soft very pale brown (10YR 8/3–8/4) to pale yellow or light grey (2.5Y 7/2–8/2) fabric with a thin slip of the same colour or no slip at all. Other common fine fabrics include a soft light red (2.5YR 6/8) to red (2.5YR 5/8, 10R 6/6) fabric, usually with a thick creamy very pale brown slip; this fabric sometimes comes with tiny black or white inclusions, and when thick often has a grey core. Another common fabric is reddish yellow and micaceous (5YR 7/6–7.5YR 7/6) often with tiny red phyllites, or small white or black inclusions. This fabric varies from the usual soft to hard. Other fabrics are represented by single examples and may be imported. Petrographic analysis of the fine wares, although limited, has shown a remarkable consistency in the fine fabrics, and the two most common types seem to be identical petrographically.

All of the decorated fine wares have dull to glossy paints in black, red, or brown.[4] Many of the paints were

---

1   Hallager 1999*b*.
2   Seiradaki, 2.
3   Day *et al.* forthcoming.
4   I am using the term paint for the dark-coloured decoration, although it is technically incorrect; rather the 'paint' is a form of slip.

thick and crackled, but have worn off to a mere shadow. Often the decoration is difficult to discern; sometimes one can only see where the paint has worn off and left the surface less glossy than the slip. The colour of the paint seems to be determined by the firing conditions, varying from black (fired under reducing conditions) to red (fired under oxidising conditions). The surfaces have worn badly, making the original appearance of the vessel uncertain. The secondary burning of so much of the pottery has also changed the original colour, and it is difficult to know what was intended or even originally produced. Sometimes the surface has been so badly burned that the slip has turned black and the paint is a paler colour (like a negative photographic image).

Plain fine wares are not common at Karphi, where most of the fine wares bear painted or incised decoration. There may originally have been more plain wares, but if so, few have been saved.

Blue wares

Vessels in a fabric called blue ware by the excavators show signs of having been misfired in the kiln; the shapes are often irregular. A large number of these vessels are in fine fabrics, often harder than normal due to overfiring, but occasionally soft. They often have tiny white inclusions and are porous, as if small inclusions have burnt out leaving voids. These blue ware vessels are not, in fact, blue in colour, but range from grey to dark grey (5Y 5/1, 5Y 4/1, 5Y 6/1, N5/1, 5G 6/1), sometimes with a bluish cast (5B 5/1, 5B 4/1, 5 BG 4/1, 5BG 5/1).

Medium-Coarse Wares

Medium-coarse is a difficult category that includes pottery that has more obvious inclusions than the fine wares, but not sufficient or large enough inclusions to be thought of as coarse. Usually, such pottery is thin-walled and looks in drawings as though it were fine. At Karphi, this group occurs in two types: misfired 'blue ware' and other wares that resemble either the fine buff wares or the redder coarse wares. The blue wares (four examples) often have hard white angular inclusions and phyllites, and they are grittier than the finer blue wares. The other fabrics are similar to those found in coarser varieties, but with fewer or smaller inclusions. Phyllite fabrics with hard white angular inclusions are most common, often of reddish yellow colour (5YR 5/6, 5YR 6/6, 5YR 7/6; 7.5YR 7/6), occasionally light reddish brown (2.5YR 6/4). Some micaceous fabrics also appear in light reddish brown (5YR 6/4) to red (2.5YR 5/8) colour. Other fabrics contain small hard angular black or white inclusions, sometimes both; these range in colour from light red (10R 6/8, 2.5YR 6/6) to yellowish red (5YR 5/6–5/8) or reddish yellow (5YR 6/8), although several have been burned, making colour determination difficult. In addition, there is a very soft light red (2.5YR 6/6) fabric with frequent tiny white carbonate inclusions and a fabric in which the inclusions have fired out, leaving only voids.

Coarse Wares

Something can be added to the observations made by Seiradaki about the different coarse fabrics that make up the Karphi pottery, based on macroscopic examination and petrographic analysis. The most common and doubtless local coarse fabrics in non-cooking wares generally have inclusions from the phyllite series, including schist, and nearly always have hard, white, angular inclusions that can be identified as quartz and/or quartzite; they can also have small hard black inclusions and often contain silver or gold mica. Petrographically, these are the fabrics defined as group 1. They most often come in light red (2.5YR 6/6), red (2.5YR 5/6–5/8), and reddish yellow (5YR 7/6) colour, and the larger vessels frequently have a grey core. This fabric type includes a wide variety of vessel shapes, including those for storage, transport, working, and pouring, as well as for some ritual vessels; kalathoi and pithoi are most common shapes. Some of these phyllite fabrics look like those from Kavousi, particularly Type IV (a cooking fabric also used on many coarse vessels) and Type X/XI.[5]

Another common fabric type is represented by flysch fabrics containing igneous rocks, especially basalt, along with the phyllites and quartzites; petrographically, these are fabric groups 3 and 4. They occur most often in lighter colours, often reddish yellow (5YR 6/6–6/8, 5YR 7/6, 7.5YR 6/8, 7.5YR 7/6–8/6) but occasionally in red (2.5YR 5/6–5/8) or light red (2.5YR 6/6–6/8). This fabric type was used for pithoi, storage jars, and stirrup jars, as well as ritual vessels, including goddesses and snake tubes. There is a great variety of other phyllite fabrics, usually occurring in single examples that include carbonates, siltstones, soft green inclusions, and chaff voids.

Some fabrics were used primarily for cooking vessels, although many of the coarse vessels also occur in these same fabrics (especially kalathoi). Cooking wares vary little in colour, primarily red (10R 5/6–5/8, 2.5YR 4/6–4/8, 2.5YR 5/6–5/8), but also light red (10R 6/8, 2.5YR 6/6), reddish yellow (5YR 6/6–7/6), and yellowish red (5YR 4/6, 5YR 5/6–5/8). Nearly all cooking vessels are of phyllite fabrics with hard white angular inclusions and/or gold or silver mica. Shapes include tripods, dishes, lids, jugs, kalathoi, and scuttles. Almost all cooking vessels tested petrographically are of group 1; those that actually came into direct contact with the fire (cooking dishes, jugs, cooking pots, and tripods) more often in group 1b, while

---

5   Haggis and Mook 1993; Mook 2005, 171; *Kavousi IIA*, 163–7.

cooking slabs and lids are more commonly of group 1a. Two unusual types identified petrographically are, however, phyllite fabrics.

SHAPES

Cup (FIG. 9.1)

As Seiradaki observed, cups are comparatively rare at Karphi,[6] although they may have been more common than they appear. Cups are similar to bowls in shape, and the two can be distinguished only by the handles; the cup has a single vertical handle, while bowls have two horizontal handles. If the handles are not preserved, certainty in identification of the shape is difficult. Watrous's observation that at Kommos the two shapes can be distinguished by the rim diameters does not seem to hold true for Karphi.[7] If there is no clear indication about which shape is represented, the vessel has been classed as a deep bowl or cup (or cup or deep bowl, if the evidence seems to indicate that it is more likely to be a cup than a deep bowl). In general, the comparative paucity of cups has been found to be a common feature of LM IIIC assemblages and contrasts with earlier periods.[8]

Seiradaki recognised two types of cups: Type 1 is carinated, while Type 2 is deep and rounded, with a rather small mouth.[9] Both of these types are based on examples from the Atsividhero tombs, but Type 2 vessels appear in the settlement (**K12.1**, **K26.1**, **K48.1**, **K58.1**, **K148.1**). To these can be added five additional shapes. First is a cup similar to Type 1, but rounded instead of carinated (**K114.2**). The second type is a simple curved cup rising from a small base with a vertical lip (**K79-89.1**, **K106.1**, and possibly **K73.1**, **K23.33**, and **K12.17**). The third type is a deep cup with a tall carinated rim (**K81.1**). The fourth type is a large cup with a deep rounded body (**K79.1**, **K115.1**), and the fifth is the conical cup (**K114.1**).

Most common cups are Type 2, and the rounded cup. The least common is the deep cup with tall carinated rim; only a single certain example occurs (**K81.1**), a very late piece, with parallels at Knossos of LM IIIC date, which already anticipate the SM wavy line cup.[10] The foot of this example from Karphi, while rather high, is not yet the conical shape of SM–PG times on Crete. The large cup with deep rounded body is unusual for its size (the rim diameter is 24); it might better be called a mug, except that the term is already used for another shape. Its function might be analogous to the very large kylikes in use throughout the settlement. At the other end of the size scale, several very small cups are preserved (**K106.1**, **K58.1**), some of which may have been attached to larger vessels. The conical cup is also rare, represented by a single example from the settlement (**K114.1**) and one from the tombs (**M16.1**); this scarcity is not unusual and conforms to the situation observed in other LM IIIC sites.[11] The shallow cup, found in LM IIIC Khania,[12] is not found at all among

the vessels that can be securely identified as cups, although several may be represented among the sherd material (e.g. **K76.37–38**). One cup from unknown context (**K.1**) has a shape more akin to Geometric monochrome globular cups and may have come from one of the tombs. One MM cylindrical ribbed cup was found in the rubbish dump under K 17 (**K17.10**).

Rounded cups are most like the deep bowls, and without a handle it is almost impossible to distinguish them from the bowls. Additional possible cups of this type include **K100.1**, **K79-89.4**, **K76.7**, **K48.3**, **K88.1**, **K76.11**, **K.11**, and **K101.3**; all of these vessels have smaller rims than normal for deep bowls (8–10 instead of the more usual 12–14), and **K100.1** has a squatter profile that looks more like a cup. **K76.12** may come from a Type 2 cup.

In all cases where the handle has been preserved, it rises slightly above the rim. Handles are usually elliptical, although on a few examples they are nearly round. Bases are nearly always raised and concave underneath. The only exception to this rule is **K.1**, which has a flat base; this is another indication that this cup is later than the settlement pottery.

The vessels clearly identifiable as cups have a very limited range of decoration: blob decoration (**K79-89.1**, possibly **K73.1**), wavy line (**K81.1**, **K79.1**), zigzag (**K115.1**, **K26.1**), and monochrome (**K114.1–2**, **K12.1**, **K.1**); one may be plain (**K12.17**). Possible cups (**K100.1**, **K 79-89.4**, **K76.7**) add a 'comb' pattern, a Minoan flower, and pendent multiple loops; all the other possible cups have blob decoration. The limited range of known decoration may make identification of cups easier; if the decoration falls outside this range, the fragment is perhaps more likely to come from a deep bowl. Of the four examples decorated with zigzags or wavy lines, two have rim bands and a pair of bands on the lower body; one has a band below the rim.

A possible shallow cup shape may be seen in **K76.37–38**. If these rim fragments are from cups rather than bowls, they would constitute another type, one found also at Khania.[13] Both are decorated with blob pattern.

Cups also occur in the tombs, most commonly in the Atsividhero tombs. There was one of Type 1 (**A3.1**), one of Type 2 (**A3.2**), two probable cups of the rounded type (**A1.1**, **A3.4**), and one conical cup (**M16.1**). A deep

6   Seiradaki, 20.
7   Watrous 1992, 140–1; the same phenomenon was observed by Kanta 1997, 87 for Khania–*Kastelli*.
8   Kanta 1980, 266; Hallager 2000, 138.
9   Seiradaki, 21–2, fig. 14.
10   Warren 2007, 339, fig. 4.P896 (LM IIIC, possibly a mainland import); Warren 1982–83, 85, fig. 60 (SM).
11   Kanta 2003, 171.
12   Hallager 2000, 137.
13   *Khania II*, pl. 34.87-P 0011.

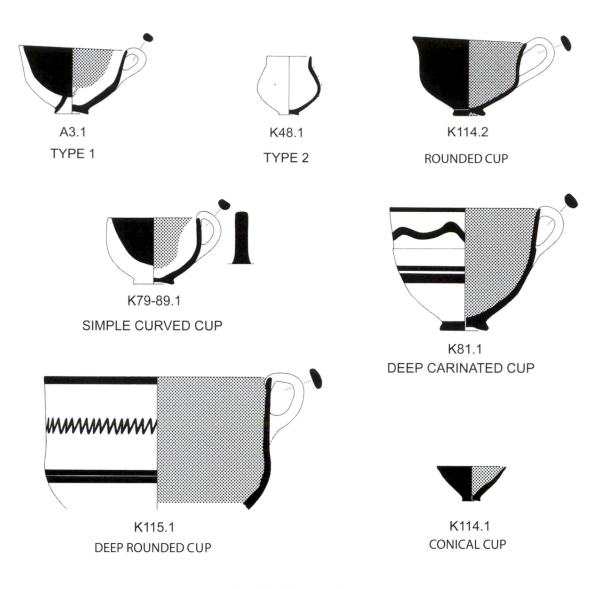

Fig. 9.1. Cups. Scale 1:4.

globular cup came from M 4 (**M4.1**), and an unusual carinated cup from M 8 (**M8.5**). Most of these cups were decorated with either blob or monochrome decoration. Two have surfaces that are laminated or coated with sediment, making identification of the decoration impossible (**A3.2**, **M16.1**).

There are few chronological indicators in the cups; no shape or decoration seems to belong to a particular phase of LM IIIC at the site. This is in keeping with what is known about cups elsewhere on Crete.[14] Carinated cups of Type 1 with blob decoration have been identified elsewhere as late LM IIIC or SM,[15] although an example does appear at Sybrita/Thronos in early LM IIIC.[16] As with the deep bowl, there may be a tendency for the foot to become higher during the period, but a low foot is not a necessary indication that the vessel is early. The use of the zigzag is found throughout LM IIIC, although it seems to appear with greater frequency on deep bowls or cups from earlier dumps on the site (especially K 76); the zigzag is also

the most common decoration on deep bowls from Kastri, which should date in the first half of LM IIIC.[17] Blob decoration is found in the pottery from the early dumps and street deposits at Karphi, but it also appears on nearly complete vessels abandoned on the floors of the settlement and in the Atsividhero tombs. Blob decoration is found in all three phases of the Kavousi–Kastro settlement,[18] and was particularly common in late deposits at Khania, which still date to early LM IIIC.[19] Blob cups are found in greatest quantity in the earlier LM IIIC deposits in Building B at Kavousi–

14　　Hallager 2000, 138–9.
15　　Mountjoy 2007, 224.
16　　D'Agata 1999, 190, fig. 5.3.17.
17　　*Kastri*, 286.
18　　Mook and Coulson 1997.
19　　Hallager 2000, 141.

Vronda,[20] while monochrome cups and deep bowls appear in all phases. The cup with wavy line (**K81.1**) resembles the later SM wavy-line cups[21] and may date to very early SM; wavy line cups, however, do have a long history and go back to the early LM IIIC deposits, as at Khamalevri.[22]

There are only two examples of cups in the medium-coarse category (**K23.21**, **K.34**). Both are of the rounded type, and **K23.21** is blue ware. Neither shows any sign of decoration.

Deep bowl (FIG. 9.2)

The deep bowl is the single most common fine shape encountered at Karphi, and it is nearly ubiquitous. Seiradaki presents nine different types of bowls in her publication,[23] but only two are true deep bowls (Types 1 and 3). Type 2, which comes from Ta Mnemata Tomb 8, might better be called a skyphos, the closest example at Karphi to the bell skyphos so popular in SM–PG times elsewhere on Crete;[24] it is discussed below (pp. 265–6). Type 4 is only a base with a baggy globular body; it was not found, and there are no other similar bases preserved in the material. Type 5 might be categorised as a kantharos, but there seems to have been only a single example made out of coarse ware, and it was not located; the shape is very similar to the krater from K 23 (Seiradaki Type 4), although smaller. Type 6 is a miniature shallow spouted bowl, and is dealt with below. The other types (Types 7, 8, 9) are all varieties of the shape known as the krateriskos, and are discussed below.

Of the two types of deep bowls identified by Seiradaki, Type 1 has a deep rounded body that rises straight to the rim, with either vertical or flaring sides. The foot is raised and concave underneath, and the handles are set high on the body, although not as high as on Type 3. Type 3 is similar, but has a body that is carinated or nearly so, and the handles are set higher; the carination is not always clear and does not always show up on the drawings. It also appears in two varieties: one type has nearly vertical sides, while on the other type the sides are more flaring. The rounded deep bowl is more prevalent than the carinated variety among the nearly complete examples, and among the rounded varieties, those with the flaring sides outnumber those whose sides rise vertically. Mountjoy's suggestion that there is a gradual development of the Cretan deep bowl over LM IIIC from vertical sides to outward leaning and finally to carinated sides,[25] cannot be substantiated by the pottery from Karphi, where the different types seem to occur together in all deposits.

Nearly all of the deep bowls can be put into these two categories, although there is a great variation in the types of rims and bases, and in the position of the handles; these same two major types have also been recognised at Khania.[26] One example (**K38.1**) is unusual in having an almost S-curved profile, and its height is much smaller in proportion to the diameter than is customary; the difference may reflect an earlier

date, suggested by the stemmed spiral motif with parallels on LM IIIB pottery, or place of manufacture, as is suggested by petrographic analysis. Seiradaki also mentioned another possible type, represented by a bowl with fluted sides, that she thought might have had metallic prototypes, but unfortunately she was unable to locate it for the 1960 publication.[27] This is certainly the unique deep bowl **K110.2**, which resembles the arcade pattern of a stone blossom bowl and is close to Type 3.

Rim diameters for deep bowls vary from 8–20, but most have diameters from 12–14; some of the smaller examples may actually be cups. Bowls with rim diameters greater than 20 have been classed as kraters. Deep bowls show a variety of rims. Nearly all of the bowls are the lipless variety, the majority what Mountjoy would classify as flaring lipless;[28] the rest are straight or vertical lipless. A few examples have real lips, or have rims that are thickened on the interior below the rim. One variant of the lipless rim is oblique on the interior (e.g. **K27.1**, **K120.1**, **K46.1**) and resembles an example from Phaistos;[29] these may not have been produced locally,[30] or the unusual rim may indicate a chronological or functional difference.

Bases vary little in size, ranging from 3.4–6; the majority fall within 4–5.5. Bases are nearly always raised and they are concave underneath. The few raised flat bases come from areas below streets or from the few lower deposits that were identified (**K76.25**, **K17.15**, **K12.9**), so must be thought of as an early

---

20 Day 1997, 400, fig. 6.3–5; *Kavousi IIA*, fig. 25.

21 For example, Warren 1982–83, 83, fig. 60.

22 Andreadaki-Vlasaki and Papadopoulou 2007, 51, fig. 8.32.

23 Seiradaki, 21.

24 In essence, the 'skyphos' is a development from the Bronze Age deep bowl, and should be thought of as the same shape. Modern scholarship, however, generally is split between those who work on Bronze Age material and refer to deep bowls, and others who work on material from PG on who call the shape the skyphos. SM specialists generally speak of skyphoi, rather than deep bowls, since it is in this period that the bell-shaped, high-footed skyphos first appears. The two shapes and the two terms should not be thought of as implying a particular group of people (i.e. pre-Greeks or non-Greeks using deep bowls, Greeks using skyphoi).

25 Mountjoy 1999*b*, 512.

26 Hallager 2000, 139; she calls them carinated bowls and deep bowls. A third type of bowl recognised at Khania is a one-handled bowl characterised by a conical profile and lipless rim that Hallager believes is similar to FS 242.

27 Seiradaki, 21.

28 Mountjoy 1986, 201.

29 Borgna 1997*a*, 278, fig. 6.1; see also D'Agata 1999, 192 and parallels cited in n. 19. She thinks this is a cup, rather than a deep bowl.

30 A similar one also appears at Kommos, and this may be a Mesara type; see Watrous 1992, fig. 68.1921.

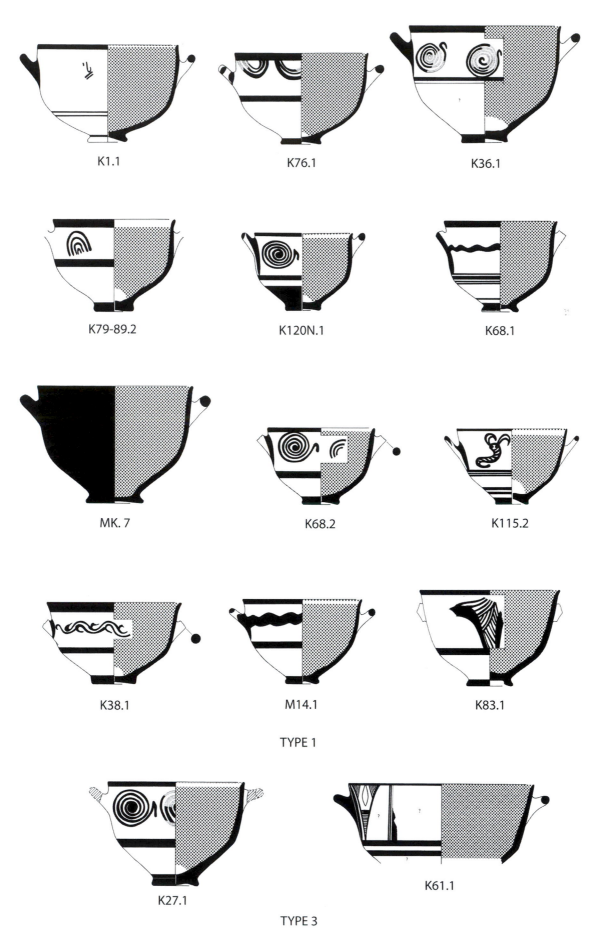

K1.1

K76.1

K36.1

K79-89.2

K120N.1

K68.1

MK. 7

K68.2

K115.2

K38.1

M14.1

K83.1

TYPE 1

K27.1

K61.1

TYPE 3

Fig. 9.2. Deep bowls. Scale 1:4.

feature. Feet vary in height and in the depth of the concavity; it would appear that there was a development from the flat-bottomed raised base to a progressively more concave raised base during the history of the settlement.[31] A few feet are so concave that they approach the later conical foot of SM and PG date, including **K82.3** and **K115.2**, and these should be amongst the latest examples in the settlement. The true conical foot, however, is not found in the settlement pottery, but is present on several vases from the tombs, particularly on krateriskoi and stirrup jars; **K.2** also has a conical foot, but its context is uncertain and it may also come from the tombs. Sometimes the base has a torus moulding (**K76.19**, **K76.21**), or is rounded in profile (**K79-89.2**, **K68.2**, **K23.58**, **K12.28**); both of these features may be early, as examples appear in lower deposits or dumps. Occasionally, there is a true ring base (**K12.10**, **K37.1**, **K68.1**, **K76.24**, **K83.1**, and **K94.1**). Ring bases have been seen as a Mycenaean or Mycenaeanising element in LM IIIC pottery,[32] but none of the Karphi examples is obviously imported, and they may imitate a Mycenaean type. At least two examples come from early deposits, a fact that suggests that such types, while rare, do occur throughout the settlement's history.

There were seven fine deep bowls in blue ware (**K1.1–3**, **K23.56**, **K106.11**, **K69.1**, **K132.1**), three of them from the Temple area; the only medium-coarse blue ware bowl (**K116.5**), with a very warped profile, is similar to the examples in finer wares. All of these with preserved bases have rather high concave feet, and they look late. Most seem to have been intended as carinated, but their shapes have become so warped that it is difficult to tell how these could have served a useful function. Some of the fine deep bowls in blue ware that do not seem obviously to be painted may have been plain. Since the surfaces are so often damaged, however, it is impossible to be certain.

The deep bowls from the tombs are similar in type to those found in the settlement. Only one is definitely of the carinated type (**A3.3**) and is decorated with blob decoration; another may be **M8.6**, which is monochrome. The others are of the rounded type with flaring sides (**M14.1**, **M8.7**). Of the three bases, all are raised and concave, **M14.1** and **A3.3** rather low, **A2.1** high.

A miniature cup or finger pot was found in K 106 (**K106.2**); this was very crude, little more than a small disc with a finger impression in the centre.

Decoration

Nearly all of the bowls are monochrome-painted on the interior, except for those which have blob decoration on both interior and exterior. Only four examples were found with plain interiors with painted rim band or (more occasionally) bands: **K.6**, **K106.3**, **K46.2**, **K12.2**, and possibly **K76.14**; these may be imported from outside Crete, as indicated by the fact that their fabrics are harder than usual.[33] Seventeen examples of

decorated deep bowl rims (*c.* 6%) have reserved bands on the interior, of which four at least also have reserved discs. Few come from the early deposits, but of the 13 nearly complete decorated examples of the deep bowl, seven have the reserved band, indicating that this feature was popular at the end of the settlement's history, whenever it was introduced into Crete; the deep bowl from M 14 (**M14.1**) also shows the reserved band. The reserved band on the deep bowl is one of the clear indications of LM IIIC date, but there has been much controversy about the precise date of its appearance in Crete,[34] and although the Karphi material does not help to determine when it came into use, it can show the popularity of the reserved band throughout the LM IIIC period until the end.

The reserved disc occurs in the bottom of fourteen deep bowls, or roughly 32% of the total number of preserved bases. Reserved discs appear on seven of the 13 nearly complete vessels, suggesting that the motif was popular at the end of LM IIIC at Karphi, although its appearance in several bowls in the K 76 deposit suggests that it was found in the earlier phases as well. There is only one example of a base with a spiral or concentric circles on the interior (**K57.2**); this may be an early feature, as at Khania–*Kastelli*.[35] There is some variety in the treatment of the underside of the bases. The underside of most bases was left unpainted, but they can be monochrome-painted (**K45.3**, **K76.20**, **K120N.1**), have a band around the outer edge (**K40.4**, **K76.19**, **K76.21**), a spiral or circle (**K76.22**), or a blob or line (**K79-89.2**, **K115.2**).

The exterior surfaces of deep bowls are decorated in the following three ways: with motifs, with blobs, or monochrome. Decorated bowls show a wide variety of motifs. Usually LM IIIC deep bowls have been categorised as being either of the open style, with a few isolated motifs, or the close style, characterised by the use of many patterns that cover the entire surface of the vessel.[36] Other scholars prefer the term 'fringed style' for this elaborate Cretan style of LM IIIC, but that term causes problems because fringes are used as a decorative element in other pottery periods, and because some of this style of pottery in LM IIIC comes

---

31   This tendency toward a higher and more concave foot can be observed in deep bowls on the mainland in LH IIIC; see Mountjoy 1986, 205.

32   Kanta 1997, 87–8.

33   The exception is **K12.2**, which has the same soft fabric as found in local fine ware; the slip, however, is of a higher quality than is customary.

34   The most recent discussions of this phenomenon has been Mountjoy 1999*b*, 512–3; 2007, 224.

35   Kanta 1997, 88.

36   See, for example, Mook and Coulson 1997, Prokopiou 1997, Rethemiotakis 1997.

without fringes.[37] Mountjoy has pointed out the problems of using the term 'close style' for Cretan pottery, and like her, I have preferred Schachermeyr's term 'pleonastic style' for the heavily decorated type of pottery.[38] The majority of deep bowls are decorated with the simple motifs of the open style; under 10% are done in the pleonastic style, with multiple motifs, fringes, and/or fillers, generally on bowls whose rim diameters are larger than the usual range, that is, greater than 14. It would seem that there is a correlation between the size of the deep bowl and the type of decorative scheme employed; the larger bowls tend to be more elaborately decorated, while the smaller examples generally are decorated in the simple open style. This correlation can also be seen in the fact that kraters are more often decorated in the pleonastic style than in the open style.

The decorative zone for deep bowls lies between a band on the rim and one or more set below the handles. The vast majority of bowls have a rather wide rim band. Only six bowls have no rim band at all (**K120.1**, **K38.2**, **K23.35**, **K138.1**, **K23.1**, **K32.1**). The absence of the rim band can also be found on deep bowls from Knossos and Phaistos, probably dating to early LM IIIC.[39] Three other deep bowls have a double or triple band at the rim (**K91.1**, **K61.3**, **K106.10**), an unusual feature, but not without parallels on LM IIIC pottery.[40]

The bottom of the decorative zone is marked off by one (15 examples), two (13 examples), three (two examples) or more (one example) bands. There seems to be no chronological distinction among these types of bands. The base always has a band. Only one deep bowl has a solidly painted lower half: **K120N.1**.

The motifs employed on deep bowls are many and varied. Seiradaki published a selection,[41] some typical (e.g. fig. 21a, b, c, e, f, g, i), others uncommon (e.g. fig. 21d, h, i, k, l, m, n).[42]

Spirals

The spiral comprises the most common recognisable motif on decorated deep bowls (14%), and there are several varieties. The buttonhook spiral is most common (FIG. 9.3 a), appearing on at least 15 examples (**K27.1**, **K29.1–3**, **K29.7**, **K31.6**, **K32.1**, **K32.9**, **K36.1**, **K61.7**, **K66.1**, **K68.2**, **K76.4**, **K91.1**, **K106.10**, **K106.15**, **K120N.1**, and possibly **K44.1**), including four of the nearly complete vessels, and three from street deposits. Three of the four nearly complete deep bowls with buttonhook spirals also have reserved bands and three have reserved discs. The buttonhook spiral is one of the hallmarks of the LM IIIC,[43] and the motif occurs on deep bowls at every site with early LM IIIC (Kastri, Knossos, Khamalevri, Khania, Kastelli Pediada, and Kavousi–Kastro). At late LM IIIC sites such as Khalasmenos and Kavousi–Vronda, however, the motif does not seem so popular, if it appears at all. At Karphi it appears in two forms, one with a rounded hook, the other with an angular hook. The two can appear together in the same

deposits, and there is no apparent chronological difference. Less popular are running spirals (FIG. 9.3 b), which appear on only seven examples (**K80.1–2**, **K43.5**, **K147.2–3**, **K147.7–8**). Other forms of spiral appear on at least 20 other deep bowls (**K12.4**, **K23.4**, **K23.38**, **K29.6**, **K29.9**, **K31.7**, **K32.2**, **K38.3**, **K39.1**, **K41.1**, **K52.2**, **K52.4**, **K75.5**, **K101.5**, **K107.1**, **K108.1**, **K108.4**, **K121.1**, **K127.2**, **K143.1**).

Multiple loops or concentric semicircles[44]
Also popular at Karphi are multiple loops (13%); most of these look like loops, rather than an attempt at freehand semicircles. These are most often found in pendent form (FIG. 9.3 c), either hanging from the rim or rim band (**K23.72** — fringed, **K43.3**, **K61.2**, **K76.1**, **K76.6**, **K85.1**, **K97.3**, **K101.1**, **K117.1**, **K120.2**, **K124.2** — with solid centre), **K148.3**, **K149.3**, **K149.5–6**), or hanging in the middle of the decorative field (**K12.24**, **K17.11**, **K32.3**, **K32.5**, **K44.2**, **K71.1**, **K76.7–8**, **K106.7–8**, **K149.4**). When hanging from the rim band, the multiple loops can occur with other patterns: alternating with multiple stems (**K31.5**, **K120.1**), with filled lozenge (**K110.1**), or with a flower (**K73.3**). Less frequently, the loops appear upright (FIG. 9.3 d), floating in the empty field (**K29.8**, **K40.1**, **K43.6**, **K79-89.2**, **K147.1**) or attached to the lower band (**K149.12**). **K76.29** has alternating pendent and upright loops, a motif that finds parallels at Khamalevri in early LM IIIC.[45] Multiple loops can also appear lying horizontally on their sides (**K79-89.9**).

Multiple loops can be found on pottery from all phases of LM IIIC.[46] The pendent loops not attached to the rim appear in early deposits at Knossos, at Kastri, Kastelli Pediada, and Khamalevri.[47] Upright loops

37   Hallager and Hallager 1997, 330–1.
38   Mountjoy 1999b, 513; see Schachermeyr 1979, 206.
39   Popham 1965, 322, fig. 3.4; 325, fig. 5.18; 326, fig. 6.31.
40   See, for example, *Kastri*, 287, fig. 8a, e, f; 288, fig. 9a, d, n; Rethemiotakis 1997, 321, fig. 31k (Kastelli Pediada); Borgna 2003, pl. 3.5, 12.111, 14.130; Andreadaki-Vlasaki and Papadopoulou 2005, 371, fig. 30 (Khamalevri, Phase I).
41   Seiradaki, fig. 21.
42   Fig. 21b is illustrated upside down; fig. 21d was not located.
43   Hallager 2000, 141–2; Popham 1965, 327; Andreadaki-Vlasaki and Papadopoulou 2005, 279.
44   This motif is called either multiple loops or concentric semicircles. Most of the examples found at Karphi are so crudely made that calling them concentric semicircles gives a false impression of their regularity. They are therefore called multiple loops in this discussion.
45   Andreadaki-Vlasaki and Papadopoulou 2005, 368, fig. 23 (Phase I).
46   Hallager 2000, 141.
47   Popham 1965, 325, fig. 5.25, 27 (Knossos); *Kastri*, 295, fig. 15.P27; Rethemiotakis 1997, 309, fig. 10i (Kastelli, Phase I); Andreadaki-Vlasaki and Papadopoulou 2007, 49, fig. 6.10 (Khamalevri, Phase II); 52, fig. 9.3 (Khamalevri, Phase I).

Fig. 9.3. Motifs on deep bowls.

appear in early LM IIIC at Kastri and in late LM IIIC at Kavousi–*Kastro*.[48] Alternating pendent and upright loops appear early as well at Knossos, Khamalevri, Kastelli Pediada, and Phaistos.[49] The less common horizontally-placed multiple loops may be an early feature; they appear on bowls from early deposits at Kavousi–*Kastro*, and at Knossos.[50] Thus, all these variations would appear to belong to early LM IIIC. There are, however, few parallels for the pendent loops that hang from the rim and which is the most common form of the motif at Karphi, so this variation may be more popular in the later phases of LM IIIC; the occurrence of this motif in the Kephala tholos at Knossos supports this idea, although it seems to belong to an earlier phase of LM IIIC than much of the tomb material.[51]

Panelled patterns
Panelled patterns are also common on the deep bowls (11%), and they come in several varieties, including

butterfly or double axe and half medallion (Popham's wavy border,[52] Hallager's panelled pattern).[53]

The butterfly or double axe pattern (**K23.5**, **K29.5**, **K40-41.2**, **K73.2**, **K76.33**, **K100.2**, **K144.1**) (FIG. 9.3 *e*)

---

48 *Kastri*, 287, fig. 8:o; Mook and Coulson 1997, 360–2: fig. 37.150; it also appears in the dump deposit on the Kastro, 358, fig. 10.117, of mixed date, Phases I–II and possibly III.

49 Warren 2007, 342, fig. 7: P183 (Knossos); Andreadaki-Vlasaki and Papadopoulou 2005, 368, fig. 23 (Khamalevri, Phase I); Rethemiotakis 1997, 309, fig. 10c (Kastelli, Phase I); Borgna 2003, 441, fig. 15.164 (Phaistos, late LM IIIB).

50 Mook and Coulson 1997, 358, fig. 30.117 (Kavousi–*Kastro*, Phases I–II); Popham 1965, 325, fig. 5.26 (Knossos).

51 Cadogan 1967, 281, fig. 2.8; for the redating of this and several other vessels in the tomb, see D'Agata 2007, 101, table 3; Preston 2005.

52 Popham 1970*b*, 199–200, fig. 3.40.

53 Hallager 2000, 140, fig. 31.

probably originated in the double axe, but by LM IIIC was exploited as a decorative pattern and may have lost its explicitly religious meaning, although more realistic double axes are illustrated on larger vessels in pleonastic style, often in association with horns of consecration (see below under kraters). The motif is often shown with outlines, sometimes multiple outlines, and/or with filler motifs. Hallager suggested that the motif is a LM IIIB one,[54] but it is certainly found on LM IIIC pottery at Knossos, Sybrita/Thronos, and Kavousi–*Vronda*.[55]

Another variation on the panelled pattern has a group of vertical lines with a half medallion or wavy border (**K31.1**, **K79-89.5**) (FIG. 9.3 *f*). Such a pattern can be found on deep bowls from nearly every LM IIIC site.[56] A single example is also found in the Karphi graves on a possible deep bowl or tankard (**M8.9**).

At least three deep bowls have a panel with a quatrefoil leaf pattern on one side (FIG. 9.3 *h*) (**K23.51**, **K31.4**, **K46.4**), similar to examples from Kastri and Kavousi–*Kastro* of early LM IIIC date, and from Petras and Knossos of advanced LM IIIB date.[57] These vessels would date early in the LM IIIC period.

Other panelled patterns have various motifs in the centre between vertical bands: chevrons (**K106.12**, **K106.14**, **K108.5**, **K122.1–2**) (FIG. 9.3 *g*), wavy lines (**K21.2**, **K76.35**, **K81.2**) or zigzags (**K106.4**), crosshatching (**K23.6**, **K56.1**), horizontal bars (**K43.4**), and triangles with alternating strokes (**K39.1**, **K31.4**). Other panelled patterns have combinations that include scallops (**K75.3**), triangles with strokes in the angles (**K61.1**) and U-pattern with a curvilinear motif (**K61.3**). Other panelled patterns are too worn or fragmentary to make out (**K23.37**, **K76.27**, **K121.4**).

Panelled patterns are varied and common on the deep bowls from Karphi. No nearly complete bowls are decorated with panelled patterns, and they occur most frequently on small fragments, suggesting that the motif was more common in the earlier phases of the settlement, but that its popularity had waned towards the end. Only one large fragment of a deep bowl that might have belonged with the final use was decorated with a panelled pattern that was worn but included triangles with strokes in the angles and an oval in the centre (**K61.1**); this is also an unusual shape, with sharply carinated sides and a very flaring straight rim, and it may not represent the local style.

Multiple stems (FIG. 9.3 *i*)
There are many examples (8%), almost all fragmentary, of the use of multiple stems, probably in a variety of arrangements (**K33.1**, **K38.5**, **K39.2**, **K46.2**, **K52.3**, **K57.1**, **K67.1**, **K79-89.10**, **K79-89.12**, **K80.3**, **K90.1**, **K97.2**, **K106.9**, **K147.4**, **K149.1**, **K149.9**). Occasionally these are angular (**K31.5**, **K68.4**). Sometimes the multiple stems meet in arcs (**K76.2**); these have parallels in deep bowls from Khania of LM IIIB:2/C style and from Pit 5 at Sybrita/Thronos of very early

LM IIIC date.[58] One example has multiple stems alternating with loops (**K120.1**). **K31.2** has multiple stems with U-patterns between them; a similar U-pattern can be found on a fragment from Amnisos.[59] Multiple-stemmed spirals appear on three bowls (**K38.1**, **K43.1**, **K121.2**); this motif is common in LM IIIB,[60] but also exists in early LM IIIC at Knossos.[61] Multiple stems alternating with spirals appear on **K29.6**.

Multiple stems are used as a decorative device on deep bowls of all phases of LM IIIC, and the motif does not seem to be a reliable chronological indicator.

Quirk (FIG. 9.3 *j*)
The quirk is a popular pattern at Karphi (5%), as on other LM IIIC sites (**K11.1**, **K28.1**, **K29.4**, **K32.7–8**, **K68.7**, **K76.15**, **K76.17**, **K79-89.8**, **K91.2**, **K101.4**, **K.4**, **K.8**, **K.9**). Many of the examples come from street or court deposits, and nearly all are small fragments, so the motif may have been more popular in the earlier phases than later LM IIIC. Some of the examples have smaller rim diameters and may be cups, rather than bowls, but it is also possible that the motif was more popular for smaller vessels than for the larger ones. The motif appears in a variety of forms, from a tight S-shape to a looser running motif, but it never seems to occur, as elsewhere, in a form which is closer to alternating semicircles, and which is more common on the mainland.[62]

Minoan flower
The Minoan flower is also popular (5%), and distinctive (FIG. 9.3 *k*). It is most often placed lying vertically (**K12.19**, **K38.4**, **K43.2**, **K46.1**, **K68.5**, **K75.1**, **K76.28**, **K76.32**, **K79-89.4**, **K79-89.11**, **K117.2**, **K147.9**), but in one case stands upright (**K106.5**). The interior of the flower is shown with a V-pattern, loops, or multiple U-pattern. One example (**K79-89.4**), more likely a cup than a bowl, has a more elaborate interior arrangement with hatching between bands. One example may be a

---

54 Hallager 2000, 174, n. 343.

55 Popham 1965, 323, fig. 4.7–9 (Knossos); D'Agata 1999, 199, fig. 10.36.19 (krater of late LM IIIC date, Sybrita/Thronos); Prokopiou 1997, 377, fig. 18e (on a krater from Sybrita/ Thronos); Day *et al.*, forthcoming.

56 *Kastri*, 287, fig. 8q; Mook and Coulson 1997, 344, fig. 8.23 (Kavousi–*Kastro*, Phase 1I); Borgna 1997*a*, 278, fig. 6.1 (Phaistos); *Khania II*, 140, fig. 31, pl. 36.

57 *Kastri*, 287, fig. 8m; Mook and Coulson 1997, 352, fig. 18.55, 63 (Kavousi–*Kastro*, Phase II); Tsipopoulou 1997, 220, fig. 18d 91.144.2; Popham 1964, 14.11, pl. 8a.

58 *Khania II*, 110, pl. 36.80-P 0446; D'Agata 1999, 194–5, fig. 7 (Sybrita/Thronos).

59 Kanta 1980, fig. 15.12.

60 Popham 1970*b*, pl. 51a, c.

61 Warren 2007, 338, fig. 3.P2143.

62 Popham 1965, 327.

Mycenaean flower (**K21.1**), like an example from Khania.[63] Additionally, some of the small fragments with fringed decoration may come from Minoan flowers. An example of an upright Minoan flower may have been a floral spray or tree (**K48.2**).

A number of fragments with the Minoan flower motif come from lower deposits, from beneath later streets (K 76, K 117) or from courtyards (K 79-89), where they are most likely to represent earlier material that was discarded. None of the nearly complete deep bowls has this motif, and it is likely that it was more popular in the earlier phases of LM IIIC than later on. Certainly the motif appears in the early LM IIIC deposits at Knossos, Kastelli Pediada, Kastrokephala, Khamalevri, Kavousi–*Kastro*, and Khania,[64] but not in the late LM IIIC deposits at Khalasmenos and Kavousi–*Vronda*.

Lozenge

Hatched and crosshatched lozenges (FIG. 9.3 *l*) are quite common (4%), although not as popular as at Kastri; From the fragmentary nature of the material, it is often impossible to tell if the motif was a lozenge chain or simply isolated lozenges, so the two motifs are here taken together. Hatched lozenges are the more common, in a chain (**K24.1**, **K97.1**) or isolated (**K56.2**, **K124.3**, **K127.5**, **K147.5–6**). The lozenge-and-loop pattern found at other sites only decorates a single deep bowl at Karphi (**K.7**), and the lozenge is cross-hatched. Other filled lozenge patterns are also found, probably not in chains, one with crosshatching (**K149.13**), two with chevrons (**K45.1**, **K124.4**), one with loops (**K127.3**), two with alternating strokes (**K56.3**, **K110.1**). A hatched lozenge, perhaps part of a chain, appears on deep bowl or tankard **M8.9**, along with a half medallion. Crosshatched (**K149.10**) or hatched (**K107.2**) lozenges also appear as the central pattern in tricurved streamer motifs.

The hatched lozenge is a particularly common motif in early LM IIIC deposits, appearing at Kastri, Khania, Khamalevri, Kavousi–*Vronda*, and Phaistos.[65] Similarly, the lozenge filled with loops also seems to be an early feature, for it is popular at Kastri.[66] The lozenge filled with loops, however, is used in a panelled pattern with scalloped edges on the dress of one of the goddesses from the Temple, which was still in use at the end of LM IIIC, whenever the statue was made.[67] At Karphi there are no nearly complete vessels with filled lozenges, only fragments, so it would appear to have gone out of popularity in late LM IIIC.

Zigzag

The zigzag is not as popular at Karphi as at other LM IIIC sites, and only six examples exist (**K23.36**, **K54.1**, **K76.14**, **K76.16**, **K103.2**, **K138.1**), the last in two registers. The motif appears in fragments from lower deposits and streets, but not on nearly complete vessels, suggesting that it was a popular motif in the earlier phases of the settlement. This fits with the pattern that

can be observed elsewhere; the motif appears in the Knossos deposit, which contains material that seems to be early LM IIIC.[68] It is the most common motif in LM IIIC Kastri, and is popular on deep bowls from the earlier LM IIIC deposits in Building B at Kavousi–*Vronda*.[69] The motif is equally popular on cups, and many of the fragments with zigzag may come from cups rather than bowls. Related to the zigzag is the zone of short strokes found on **K3.2**. This has a close parallel at Phaistos.[70]

Wavy band

The wavy band (FIG. 9.3 *m*) is found on one nearly complete deep bowl from the settlement (**K68.1**) and another from the tombs (**M14.1**), which also has a reserved band. Three other fragments (**K12.2**, **K23.3**, **K79-89.13**) may be from cups or deep bowls, the last resembling the large cup **K81.1**.

The wavy band appears on deep bowls in early LM IIIC at Khania, Knossos, and Phaistos,[71] but this thick wavy line may be a feature of late LM IIIC deep bowls and cups. It survived as a dominant form of decoration on the SM 'wavy-line' cup.[72]

Tricurved streamer

The tricurved streamer appears on at least seven examples of the deep bowl (FIG. 9.3 *n–o*). Where the central motif is still preserved, it can be a crosshatched (**K149.10**) or hatched (**K107.2**) lozenge, a hatched loop (**K124.1**), alternating strokes (**K83.1**), or a floral motif (**K106.3**, **K68.3**). **K108.2** may also be a tricurved streamer, or a variation on the multiple stem motif; it is similar to **K150.1** and finds a close parallel at Sybrita/

63 *Khania II*, 141, fig. 31, pl. 35.80-P 0524.
64 Popham 1965, 327–8 (Knossos); Rethemiotakis 1997, 317, fig. 26h–i, k–n, p (Kastelli); Kanta and Karetsou 2003, 153, fig. 3B (Kastrokephala); Andreadaki-Vlasaki 2005, 371, fig. 31 (Khamalevri, Phase I–II); 373, fig. 34 (Phase I); 2007, 47, fig. 4.27–8 (Phase I); Mook and Coulson 1997, 344, fig. 8.13 (Kavousi–*Kastro*, Phase I); 352, fig. 18.66, 69 (Phase II); *Khania II*, 141, fig. 31, pl. 35.80-P 0524.
65 *Kastri*, 287, fig. 8i; 294, fig. 14.P2; 295, fig. 15.P21; *Khania II*, 141, pl. 36.70-P0160 (+70-P 0906); Andreadaki-Vlasaki and Papadopoulou 2005, 370, fig. 29 (Khamalevri, Phase I); 2007, 47, fig. 4.29 (Phase II); Day 1997, 396, fig. 3.5 (Kavousi–*Vronda*, early LM IIIC; Borgna 2003, 435, fig. 9.82 (Phaistos, LM IIIB late); 436, fig. 10.102; 443, fig. 17.181.
66 *Kastri*, 287, fig. 8j.
67 Rethemiotakis 1998, 22.19, fig. 56.
68 Popham 1965, 325, fig. 5.21–3.
69 *Kastri*, 286; *Kavousi IIA*, fig. 25. This material from the earlier deposits in B4 and B7 seems to be contemporary with Phase II on the Kastro, or early, but not the earliest LM IIIC.
70 Borgna 2003, 435, fig. 9.88.
71 *Khania II*, 141, pl. 35.77-P 0477; Popham 1965, 324 (Knossos); Borgna 2003, 443, fig. 17.180 (Phaistos).
72 Warren 1982–83, 85, fig. 60.

Thronos in early LM IIIC.[73] Hallager has suggested that the tricurved streamer is a motif that comes into the Cretan ceramic repertoire early in LM IIIC, and that it becomes dominant in the latest LM IIIC deposits.[74] This may be the case at Karphi as well, as one of the nearly complete deep bowls is decorated with this motif (**K83.1**); it finds parallels, however, on a krater from Khania and a deep bowl from Phase II at Khamalevri of early LM IIIC date.[75] The tricurved streamer with hatched or more commonly cross-hatched lozenge like **K149.10** is very common in later LM IIIC contexts; it appears at Kavousi–*Vronda* and at Phaistos.[76] **K106.3** may be an import; its motif with a floral head, does not occur elsewhere on the site.

Bivalve shell

The bivalve shell motif (**K23.59**, **K32.4**, **K43.7**) is not common, and it is almost certainly early, appearing only in early deposits under floors or in streets. The motif is found on LM IIIB pottery,[77] and when it does appear in LM IIIC contexts, it is generally considered transitional LM IIIB/C.[78] **K38.2** has a variation on the bivalve shell that is similar to examples from Knossos and Kastri.[79]

Multiple-outlined ovals

This motif is found on a number of vessels, where the ovals are set at an angle or horizontally (**K12.21**, **K44.3**, **K61.5**, **K68.6**, **K101.6**). Multiple-outlined ovals appear commonly on LM IIIC pottery at Khania.[80] **K44.3** may be a floral motif, as it is set close to upright, and there are other motifs on either side. **K12.21** has a solid centre. A variant has upright ovals (**K32.6**, **K76.13**), on one of which two small dots have been placed, making it look like a face with eyes (FIG. 9.3 *p*). Similar motifs can be found at Kastri and Kastelli Pediada, both of early LM IIIC date.[81]

Hatched ovals

There is only a single preserved example of this motif on deep bowls, although it appears regularly on stirrup jars. On bowls it consists of a chain of hatched ovals with dots at the end, a combination that looks like kissing fishes (**K61.6**).

Antithetic spirals

This motif, which is common on other LM IIIC pottery in central and western Crete,[82] is not frequent at Karphi. There may be a single example of its use on **K39.1**.

Other

A number of other motifs occur, but only one or two times. Chevrons appear in horizontal bands on two deep bowls (**K76.26**, **K149.7**). A chevron shell decorates **K76.30**. Stacked pendent loops or scale pattern appear on two examples, one fringed (**K127.1**), the other not (**K40.3**). The gremlin or imp (**K115.2**) appears on a nearly complete vessel and may be thought of as a late

decoration. Another fragment may bear a human or bird head (**K91.3**). A variant of the comb motif (**K12.18**, **K100.1**) appears on two vessels, although one of them is probably a cup. Many other fragments bear fringed decoration (**K61.4**) or filler arcs (**K31.3**, **K33.1**, **K74.1**, **K75.2**, **K76.3**, **K76.34**, **K79-89.7**, **K148.2**, **K149.8**).

Blob decoration

Blob decoration appears on deep bowls as well as on cups. Nine blob bowls or cups exist from the settlement, of which two have preserved handles, so they are clearly deep bowls (**K82.1**, **K22.1**), while others may be and from their shapes are more likely to be, cups (**K48.3**, **K76.11**, **K88.1**, **K101.3**, **K.11**). **K76.12** is almost certainly a cup, probably of Type 2. On all the other uncertain examples, the rim diameter is always much smaller than normal, ranging from 8–11, so this decoration may have been considered appropriate to smaller open vessels (as can be seen also from its use on juglets and small feeding bottles). A blob-decorated deep bowl came also from Atsividero (**A3.3**), and the later skyphos from Ta Mnemata (**M4.2**) is also decorated with blobs. The blob decoration is created by dipping the vessel into the paint, coating one side, and then holding that side and dipping the other side into the paint. This sometimes results in a drip towards the base, as can be seen on **A3.3**.

Blob decoration seems to be found in all phases of LM IIIC. The prevalence of this form of decoration in the deposit from K 76, where there is much very broken fine ware that may represent dump of earlier material under the later room, suggests that it was in use early in the settlement's history. Its use in the tombs both at Ta Mnemata and at Atsividhero indicates that it was also employed in the late phases of LM IIIC, since none of these tombs seems to contain early material.

Monochrome deep bowl

A number of deep bowls are apparently decorated with a monochrome wash inside and out (**MK.7**, **K23.34**, **K51.1**, **K82.2**, **K.2–3**). When the vessel is represented by only a single small fragment, it is impossible to tell if it was monochrome-painted or the painted part of a

73 D'Agata 1999, 195, fig. 7.5.34.

74 Hallager 2000, 141; 2007, 190.

75 *Khania II*, 39.71-P 0908, 71-P 0735; Andreadaki-Vlasaki and Papadopoulou 2007, 50, fig. 7.21.

76 Gesell, Coulson and Day 1991, 166, fig. 6.5; Borgna 2003, 442, fig. 46.172.

77 Popham 1970*b*, 198, fig. 2.11; pl. 49a, 50a.

78 Gesell, Day, and Coulson 1995, 118, fig. 22.2.

79 Popham 1965 329–30, fig. 8.50; he thinks this may be influenced from the mainland. *Kastri*, 288, fig. 9h.

80 Hallager 2000, 140–1.

81 Rethemiotakis 1997, 317, fig. 26g (Kastelli Pediada); *Kastri*, 288, fig. 9q.

82 Popham 1965, 322–3, figs. 3–4; Hallager 2000, 141.

blob decoration or even whether it was a deep bowl or cup (**K23.52–53**, **K23.55**, **K106.6**). A monochrome deep bowl was also found outside one of the Ta Mnemata tombs (**M8.6**), and a cup or deep bowl came from Atsividero (**A3.4**). The presence of so many monochrome fragments in the lowest deposit in Room K 23 suggests that the monochrome bowl or cup was popular early in the settlement history. Two of the monochrome vessels from the floor deposits elsewhere are nearly complete, showing that this style of decoration was also used at the very end of the LM IIIC, an idea that is given support by the appearance of monochrome decoration in the tomb deposits (**M8.6**, **A3.4**).

Shallow bowl (FIG. 9.4)

Seiradaki has only one example of a shallow bowl in her typology: Bowl Type 6.[83] This is a spouted bowl, of which only two examples could be found: the miniature one illustrated (**K121.6**) and a larger decorated one from K 61 (**K61.9**), which is a smaller version of FS 294 and is not common on Crete. Spouted bowls or cups do appear at Kourtes and Adromyloi with transitional LM IIIB–C material, at Milatos in LM IIIA–C,[84] and at Knossos, perhaps in the transitional period between LM IIIB and LM IIIC.[85] In LM IIIC the shape appears at Khalasmenos and Phaistos.[86] This example, with its fringed upright multiple loops is clearly LM IIIC. There are no good parallels for the shape or decoration of the miniature variety **K121.6**, although its profile does resemble FS 252, which has a carination very low on the body. Since this example has a lug at right angles to the spout rather than a handle, the parallel is not great. FS 252 does appear in LH IIIC contexts on Rhodes and Kephallonia.[87]

Only a single example of a shallow bowl exists in plain ware, a carinated side-spouted bowl from Ta Mnemata (**M14.2**). The shape is similar to FS 295, a shallow angular bowl, but there are no close parallels on Crete or the mainland. The base of this bowl is missing, but it is shallow and very angular, with a tall flaring rim above the carination, a single flat handle from the rim to carination, and at a right angle to the handle is a spout. The fabric of this vessel is also highly unusual, since it is a uniform dark grey throughout, and it may have been burned.

A second type of shallow bowl has no spout and has horizontal flat handles pinched out below the rim (FS 296) (**K121.5**, **K17.17**). This shape is uncommon on Crete, although it is a well-known mainland type. On the mainland it seems always to be plain, but both of the Karphi examples have traces of paint. A similar plain bowl, but of earlier date, comes from Kastri.[88] A deeper variety of the shape has been found in early LM IIIC deposits at Kavousi–*Vronda* and at Khalasmenos of late LM IIIC;[89] both of these examples were decorated with blob decoration. The poor preservation of **K121.5** makes it difficult to ascertain if there was decoration or if it was plain, while **K17.17**

is too small to determine the decoration. Plain shallow bowls are rare on Crete, although several do appear in Khania.[90] Rim fragments **K76.37–38** may also come from shallow bowls; they are decorated with blobs.

A shallow bowl fragment from K 23 (**K23.62**) may be one of the above types or may constitute another type. It has a nearly carinated profile and is apparently plain or monochrome. Another possible bowl type is **K33.3**. This is a very shallow bowl and may be a krater base that has been so smoothed down that the edges look finished.[91] It has a conical foot with a torus moulding on it, and short sides, with a rim that has been flattened on top and slopes down inward. It is monochrome painted. Possibly it was originally a krater base that was then smoothed and reused as a bowl or even a lid.

Skyphos (FIG. 9.4)

From the Ta Mnemata tombs come two examples of a shape that might be termed a skyphos rather than a deep bowl. **M4.2** is similar to a deep bowl in shape, but it is much more flaring in profile. It is decorated with blob decoration and is similar to a bowl of late LM IIIC date from Khalasmenos.[92] Somewhat easier is **M8.1** (Seiradaki's Type 2 bowl), which is similar to several SM–EPG skyphoi.[93] Of note here is the deeper, more bell-shaped profile, the conical foot, and the dipped decoration, which is related to the earlier blob decoration but done in a different fashion. Here the vessel is held at the base, and the whole piece is dipped into the paint.

Skyphos/krateriskos (FIG. 9.4)

Seiradaki's Type 8 bowl is represented by a single example from K 115 (**K115.4**). The shape is highly unusual, and it does not look like the later krateriskoi from M17 (**M17.2–4**). That it is meant to be an open shape can be seen from the monochrome-painted interior. The krateriskos shape came into use on the

83   Seiradaki, 21, fig. 16.6.

84   Kanta 1980, 88, fig. 24.3 (Kourtes); 186, pl. 72.6 (Adromyloi); 125, fig. 53.11 (Milatos).

85   Hood, Huxley and Sandars 1958–59, 242, fig. 28.VII.10, VI.1.

86   Tsipopoulou 2004, fig. 8.13.92-225; Borgna 2003, 452, pl. 26.5.1.

87   *RMDP*, 463–4; 1060–1061.

88   *Kastri*, 294, fig. 14.P3.

89   *Kavousi IIA*, fig. 26.B4 P21; Coulson and Tsipopoulou 1994, 85, fig. 19.3.

90   Hallager 2000, 157.

91   Seiradaki published it as a krater: fig. 16.8.

92   Tsipopoulou 2004, 118, fig. 8.11.95-365.

93   Warren 1982–83, 81, 86, fig. 64 (Knossos, SM); Boardman 1960, 132, 136, fig. 4 IV.3 (Ayios Ioannis, SM–MPG krateriskos); Tsipopoulou 1997, 458, fig. 2.5052 (EPG).

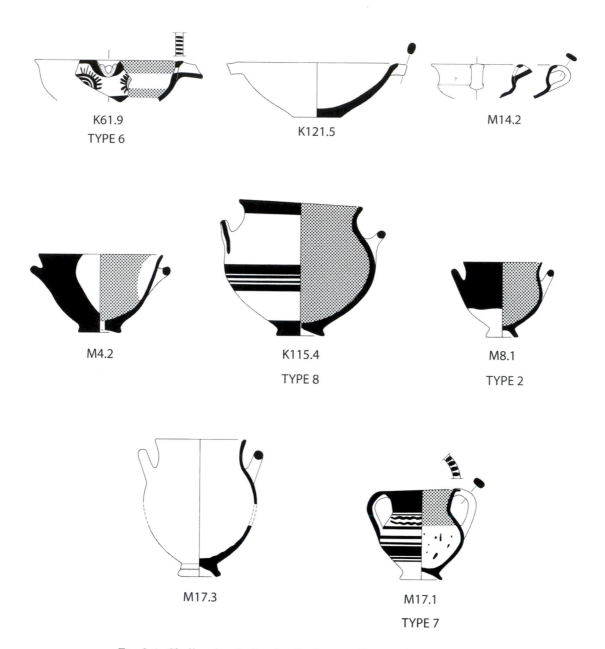

K61.9
TYPE 6

K121.5

M14.2

M4.2

K115.4
TYPE 8

M8.1
TYPE 2

M17.3

M17.1
TYPE 7

Fig. 9.4. Shallow bowls, bowls, skyphos, and krateriskoi. Scale 1:4.

mainland as early as LH IIIB, although it did not become popular until LH IIIC.[94] The shape of **K115.4** is very globular, with a deeply concave foot, and it finds no parallels on Crete; the closest example is a krateriskos from Kastri.[95] A somewhat similar shape can be found from Skyros.[96] Both of these parallels are true krateriskoi and are more closed shapes than the Karphi example. **K115.4** is certainly later than most of the other pottery from the Karphi settlement, and it is datable to the earliest stages of SM.

Krateriskos (FIG. 9.4)

There are only four examples of the krateriskos at Karphi, and they come only from a single tomb.[97] **M17.1** (Seiradaki's Type 7 bowl) is highly unusual; it has two elliptical vertical handles from rim to shoulder

instead of the usual round horizontal handles on the shoulder and a high conical foot and a very tall neck with an unusual flattened rim that is decorated with

94   Mountjoy 1986, 124.
95   *Kastri*, 295, fig. 15.P23.
96   *RMDP*, 731, fig. 282.15 (LH IIIC, early).
97   The same shape can be called either a krateriskos or an amphoriskos; the term krateriskos suggests that this was primarily an open shape, while labelling the shape amphoriskos indicates that it was a closed shape. The Karphi examples seem to be sufficiently finished on the interior to be counted as open shapes, even though they are not monochrome painted inside. The term krateriskos will therefore be used here.

strokes. The interior is half painted, and the lower half has splatters of paint, making it difficult to determine if the piece was meant to be an open or a closed shape. Hallager suggested that the vessel is actually an amphoroid krater, to which it is similar in handles and rim type, an idea that seems plausible.[98] Kanta dated it to advanced LM IIIC and cited Cypriote parallels,[99] and it may be an import or imitation of a Cypriote shape.[100] A similar example has recently been found at Sybrita/Thronos of late LM IIIC date; it has the same sort of handles and a similar shape and decoration (including the splatters on the interior), but the rim is much simpler.[101] While the Karphi example may indeed belong to the late LM IIIC, it was found with other material that dates as late as EPG, so it does not necessarily have to have such an early date; the Cypriote parallels would also support a later date.

Seiradaki's Type 9 bowl is another form of krateriskos, this one better known. Only two or three examples exist, all from M 17 (**M17.2–4**). Seiradaki's drawing is either a composite drawing of **M17.4** and **M17.2** or the vessel was broken up after it was drawn. Similar examples can be found in SM and EPG tombs on Crete.[102] Common features include the high conical foot, deep S-shaped body and tall rim, with two round vertical handles on the shoulder.

Kylix (FIG. 9.5)

The kylix was not found in great quantity, but nearly every major room produced one or two; a few examples came from the larger Ta Mnemata tombs, but not from the Atsividhero tombs.[103] Seiradaki distinguished four types of kylix.[104] Type 1 was the most common, and is illustrated by an example from M4 (**M4.6**), which unfortunately has subsequently been broken and lost what had been preserved of its stem and handles. It is a large kylix with a bowl carinated just below the rim, twisted handles, and probably a tall stem. Seiradaki suggested that the handles for this type were more regularly plain, and that the stems most often had a bulge in the middle, like Types 2 and 3;[105] **K115.5** and **K.15** may be more representative examples of Type 1. Type 2, which is smaller, has a tall stem with a bulge and a deep bowl carinated at the top and two regular vertical elliptical handles. The illustrated example (**K3.4**) has subsequently lost its stem, and the bowl seems to rise to a straight rim, without the carination found on Type 1, but with a slight ridge at the top of the lower handle attachment. Type 3 is also a large kylix with a tall bulged stem and a ridge at the point where the stem attaches to the body. It has a deep hollow on the foot, but the stem itself is not pierced. The body is conical and Seiradaki restores a plain flaring rim, although she suggests that it may have had a carination, like Type 1, and it certainly had handles like the others. Type 4 is represented only by a base from K 116, and it could not be located; Seiradaki described it as having a more splayed foot than usual.

Few of the feet are preserved. Of the four surviving examples, one is rounded on top and concave underneath (**K115.5**), one is more conical and concave underneath (**K7.1**), one is flaring and totally hollow up to the bowl (**K9.2**), and one is quite flat with a small depression in the centre (**K106.18**). The miniature version from K 25 (**K25.1**) is similar to the last variety. Base diameters range from 7–8.5, and the rim is usually 2.5 to 3.5 times the diameter of the base.

The stems either have a bulge in the centre or are straight, and the two types occur in about equal numbers. Kanta and Mountjoy suggested that the bulging stem is a feature of late LM IIIC kylikes,[106] but it seems to be no certain chronological indicator at Karphi. A nearly complete vessel (**K115.5**) from a clearly late LM IIIC context has the bulging stem, and this would seem to support Kanta's idea. Both types can be found together in the same deposit, however, as in K 9.

The majority of the stems were pierced in the Cretan fashion;[107] of the preserved stems, ten were pierced (**K9.2**, **K17.16**, **K32.11**, **K82.4**, **K85.3**, **K97.4**, **K115.5**, **K140.1**, **K.15–16**) and six were not (**K7.1**, **K9.1**, **K12.12**, **K75.6**, **K106.18**, **K131.3**); **K3.4** may or may not have been pierced. The type of piercing varies. Some stems are pierced only about a third of the way up and become progressively narrower before stopping (**K115.5**). Most are pierced all the way up with a thin hole (**K12.12**, **K32.11**, **K82.4**, **K85.3**, **K97.4**, **K.15–16**,). A few are pierced with a very wide hole (**K9.2**, **K140.1**, **K17.16**); in the case of **K9.2**, the oblique lines left on the interior of the stem by the potter's wheel are still visible.

Stems were made separately and added onto the bowl. In several instances the vessel has broken at the point where the two were attached (**K3.4**, **K140.1**) showing how the bowl and top of the stem were scored at an oblique angle to make the attachment more secure, a feature illustrated by Seiradaki.[108] Sometimes at the point of attachment an extra ridge of clay was added for strength (**K7.1**, **K115.5**), and occasionally incisions were added for a decorative effect (**K85.3**).

The bowls of the kylikes are deep, although some of Type 1 have shallower bowls (**K131.1**, **M4.6**). Rims

---

98   Hallager 2000, 150.

99   Kanta 1980, 274.

100   Benson 1973, pl. 46.K334.

101   D'Agata 1999, 201, fig. 12.20.1k

102   Tsipopoulou 1997, 478, fig. 17.4983, 4984 (Khamaizi–
      Phatsi, SM–PGA); Coldstream and Catling 1996, 247, fig.
      141.114 (Knossos, EPG).

103   Seiradaki, 25.

104   Seiradaki, 26, fig. 18.

105   Seiradaki, 25–6.

106   Kanta 1980, 264; Mountjoy 2007, 223.

107   For a discussion of the piercing of stems, see Kanta 1997, 95.

108   Seiradaki, pl. 12b, bottom row, second from left.

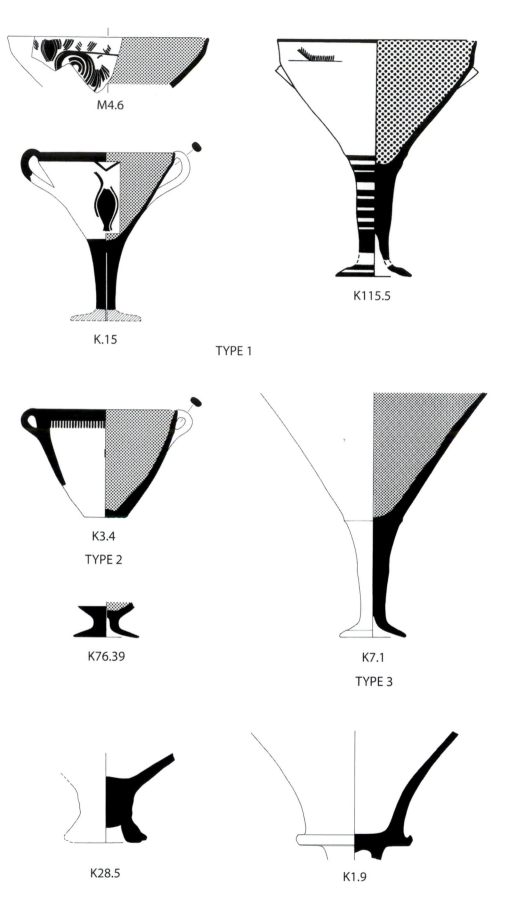

Fig. 9.5. Kylikes, goblets, and chalice. Scale 1:4.

are generally vertical or slightly flaring from a carination just below the lip (12 out of 17), or at least these are the rims that are most easily identified as kylix rims. Occasionally another type of rim appears, one that is more flaring (**K43.9**, **K76.40**, **K90.2**), and sometimes with thickening on the interior (**K131.2**); one kylix (**K3.4**) has no carination and is lipless. The rim diameters range from 11–27 (not including the miniature example). These fall into two groupings, a smaller variety with rim diameters from 11–18 (nine examples), and a larger variety with rim diameters from 21–27 (six examples).

Kylikes are generally elaborately decorated; one example may be monochrome (**K23.63**), but there are no certain examples that are plain. The stem is usually banded (**K75.6**, **K82.4**, **K97.4**, **K106.18**, **K115.5**, **K140.1**, **K.16**), but can be solidly painted (**K85.3**, **K12.12**, **K.15**). Occasionally the decoration covers the entire body of the kylix, but the rim above the carination most often bears a special decoration, usually strokes (**K9.3**, **K11.3**, **K120.3**, **MK.1**), sometimes fringes (**K106.17**, **K115.5**), a band (**K.15**, **M8.8**) or scallops (**K131.1**); strokes appear below the wide rim band on **K3.4**. **K100.3** has alternating arcs on the rim, while **K106.16** has a triangle of scale pattern with dots, and **K90.2** bears a floral branch. Most of the decoration on the body is elaborate, with outlined vertical elements rising from the stem and curving out over the surface of the bowl; few kylikes are well enough preserved to show the entire pattern. A typical pattern for LM IIIC kylikes can be seen on **K.15**, which has an outlined bulbous element that may represent the body of an octopus, outlined, and probably with tricurved streamers for tentacles coming out at the top; a similar motif is known from Kavousi–*Vronda* and other LM IIIC deposits at Vrokastro, Kritsa, and Kastelli Pediada.[109] Similar patterns may occur on **K9.1**, **K97.4**, **K131.1**, **K140.1**, and possibly **MK.1** and **K120.3**. **K43.8** has what is perhaps a tricurved streamer with hatching in the centre. **K131.3** is decorated with hatched lozenge and loops. Fragments identified as kylikes from their profiles are decorated with the following: a panelled pattern with a vertical chevron band and fringed outlined triangular motifs (**K80.4**), quatrefoil leaf with wavy border (**K32.12**), horizontal chevron band (**K79-89.15**), fringed spiral (**K79-89.14**), floral 'hooks' on either side of a hatched pattern (**K79-89.16**), and dotted curvilinear pattern (**K72.1**). Of the two kylikes from the tombs, **M4.6** may have an octopus decoration, with alternating arcs on the rim; the spirals may represent the eyes on either side of the topknot. **M8.8** is highly unusual, with a formalised pattern that may originally derive from a Mycenaean flower motif or represent a stylised octopus. A similar design can be found on a LM IIIC krater from Khania.[110]

The interiors of kylikes are always monochrome coated. No examples were found with a reserved band. Two fragments had reserved discs (**K32.11**, **K82.4**).

Since the reserved disc was never found on the nearly complete examples from late LM IIIC, it may be an earlier feature; at least one of the two examples was from an early street deposit (K 32).

The kylix is certainly a shape that was introduced into Crete from the mainland in LM II, and it was popular as a drinking vessel throughout the LM III period; its development has been the subject of much study.[111] The shape is popular at Karphi, but does not occur as frequently as the deep bowl. LM IIIC kylikes tend to be larger than those of earlier periods, as is also the case at Kavousi–*Vronda* and Khalasmenos in late LM IIIC.[112] The size of these vessels and the fact that they appear in nearly every large house complex suggests their use in elite drinking rituals; the greatest number come from the Great House.[113]

Champagne cup (*footed cup or goblet*) (FIG. 9.5)

Despite Hallager's rational discussion of the proper name for this shape,[114] I have chosen to keep the highly descriptive (if misleading) name of 'champagne cup'. While it is not an accurate term, it has been so widely used that most scholars immediately visualise the shape, with its flaring base, short stem, and simple body with a single handle. There are only three certain examples found at Karphi, where the shape does not seem to have been popular. These are always fragments from the bases and stems, and no rims or bodies have been recognised. Two of the stems are monochrome coated (**K12.11**, **K76.39**), while one is decorated with vertical blobs of paint on the stem, painted arcs on the underside, and a blob on the interior (**K61.8**).

At Kavousi–*Vronda*, this shape was more popular in the earlier part of LM IIIC, and had nearly disappeared by the end of the period,[115] and the same may be the case at Karphi, to judge from the relative paucity of nearly complete examples, and the fact that two of the examples of the shape came from deposits with a great deal of early material; some of the blob-decorated cup rims found in these early deposits may come from champagne cups.

Goblet or chalice (FIG. 9.5)

One stem from an unusual coarse goblet or chalice was found in a room in the Southern Houses (**K28.5**). This

109 Day 1997, 399, fig. 5.2; *Kavousi IIA*, fig. 22.B3 P3; Hayden 2003, 33, fig. 8.53; (Vrokastro); Popham 1969, pl. 64f (Kritsa); Rethemiotakis 1997, 315, fig. 23g, h (Kastelli Pediada).
110 *Khania II*, 147, pl. 39.84-P 0702.
111 Popham 1969; Hallager 1997a.
112 Day 1997, 399, fig. 5; Day and Snyder 2004, 72–3, fig. 5.11; Tsipopoulou 2004, 121, fig. 9.13.94-180.
113 Day and Snyder 2004, 71–3.
114 Hallager 1997a, 18–9.
115 Day and Snyder 2004, 73.

has a base with a groove on the bottom, a wide, short, solid stem, and a flaring body. Coarse goblets are not otherwise known on the site, nor are there any close parallels. It may have been a chalice, but does not look like the preserved examples of the type.

Chalice (FIG. 9.5)

A large, coarse, open vessel with a stem was found in the Temple, and it has been called a chalice (**K1.9**). Unfortunately, it is broken on top and bottom, so the entire shape is not certain. It has a hollow stem and a thick ridge with a hook on the top at the joint of the stem to the body. The body is flaring, much like the bodies of coarse kalathoi. A similar chalice was also found in the Shrine at Kavousi–*Vronda*,[116] and smaller and shallower, shape is known from Gazi.[117] Fragments of two other possible small chalices, occurred in the material saved from the Temple. The chalice shape looks like a kalathos on a stem. Its function is uncertain, but in earlier periods the chalice form (a tall cylindrical or slightly flaring handleless cup on a stem) was found in ritual settings. Chalices were common at Kato Symi in the Proto- and Neopalatial levels,[118] where they have been interpreted as vessels reserved for offerings to the divinity.[119] Indeed, a chalice can be seen held by the seated figure, probably a divinity, approached by genii on the Tiryns gold ring. The only two certain examples found from LM IIIC come from shrines or temples (Karphi and Kavousi–*Vronda*), so the shape may have served a ritual function involved with the worship of the goddesses with upraised arms.

Mug and tankard (FIG. 9.6)

Seiradaki indicated that tankards were rare at Karphi, and she thought that they may have served a religious function.[120] She observed that like pyxides, the vessels were allowed to harden before cut off from the stand, by which it is assumed that she means the marks of cutting them off the stand were clear on the bases. She did not distinguish between mugs (FS 226), which do not have spouts, and the spouted tankards.[121] When the vessel is fragmentary, it is difficult to distinguish between the two. Hallager's observation that tankards are generally larger than mugs does not necessarily hold at Karphi, where one of the preserved tankards is a miniature. Since it is impossible to distinguish the two without the spout, they are considered together, though they probably served different functions.

Seiradaki distinguished three types, all in fine wares; the shape was rare in medium-coarse and coarse wares. Type 1 is a large tankard, Type 2 is a mug from Ta Mnemata 4, and Type 3 is a miniature tankard from K 17; these represent the only three nearly complete mugs or tankards from the site. Tankards of Types 1 and 2 are similar in shape, with a large base, concave profile, and wide rim; on **K26.4** the rim and base diameters are approximately the same, while the miniature tankard

(**K17.1**) has a rim larger than its base. In both cases the handle is set opposite to the spout, which is a bridge spout. On both tankards the handle rises from the rim to the base (**K26.4**) or mid body (**K17.1**). **K26.4** has a rim that has been described as 'beaded;' that is, it was thickened, then cut twice so that the clay fanned out, and the resulting ridges on the rim were then cut crossways into small beads or pillow shapes. Two additional spouts from the Small Shrine (**K55.2**, **K57.3**) may be from tankards, since they resemble the shape of the tankard spout and have incisions on the end of the spout like **K26.4**. Mug **M4.7** is similar in shape to the tankards, although the base is a bit smaller than the rim. It has a similar flat base and concave profile, and the treatment of the rim is identical to that of **K26.4**. The elliptical handle, however, is placed in the middle of the body of the vessel, not from the rim to body or rim to base. Other fragments identified as mugs or tankards also have beaded rims (**K23.8**, **K28.2**, **K77.1**, **K121.7**, **K.17**, **A2.2**), although some show differences. In the case of three rims (**K23.8**, **K28.2**, **K.17**) the flaring pointed rim has not been thickened, and incisions were made inside and outside to produce a ridge that was then beaded. Base fragment **K23.10** is more straight-sided than usual, but its shape is similar to mugs from the mainland.[122] Body fragment **K23.9** may come from a tankard or mug; it has a similar concave profile, probably from near the base. All the mugs or tankards, with the exception of K 17, which is a miniature variety, have rims that measure between 17 and 21.

The painted decoration of the mugs and tankards is varied. Tankard **K26.4** has the most elaborate decoration, with panels of different motifs, including chequerboard, tree of solid outlined ovals with dots and hatching between each oval, two butterfly or double axe patterns stacked one on top of the other with multiple outlines, a field of zigzags under the handle, and a complex 'sail' pattern that has vertical, horizontal, and oblique elements between the sails, each surrounding a set of upright chevrons. This elaborate decoration is reminiscent of several of the large pyxides (e.g. **K22.3**, which also has the sail pattern); a similar example found in the Psychro cave may have come from Karphi.[123] Most of the mugs and tankards are not so elaborately decorated. Three of the rim fragments have the same painted decoration on the rim (**K23.8**, **K28.2**, **K.17**) with a series of rather curvilinear triangles pendent from

---

116   Gesell, Glowacki and Klein forthcoming.
117   Kanta 1980, fig. 9.4, called a stemmed bowl.
118   Lebessi and Muhly 1990, 324–5, figs. 10–1.
119   Lebessi and Muhly 1990, 327.
120   Seiradaki, 19–20.
121   Hallager 2000, 153–4 for the distinction.
122   *RMDP*, 576–7, fig. 213.368-70 (Perati, LH IIIC early).
123   Watrous 1996, 41, pl. 25a–b.

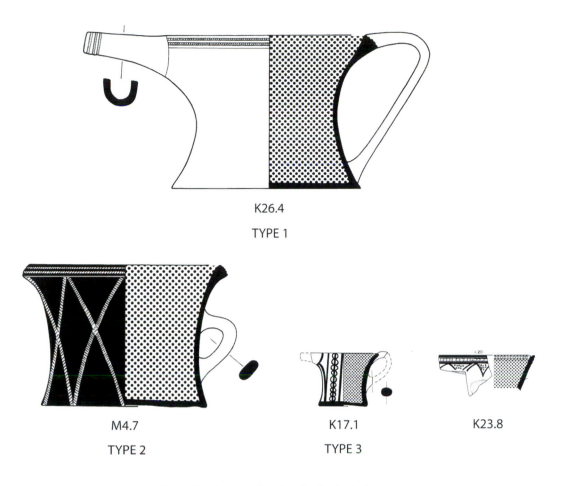

K26.4

TYPE 1

M4.7

TYPE 2

K17.1

TYPE 3

K23.8

Fig. 9.6. Mugs and tankards. Scale 1:4.

the rim and filled with dots; some other curvilinear motif is below. Such a decoration is not paralleled elsewhere on Crete, but it does appear on a krater from the mainland of middle LH IIIC date.[124] **K23.9** has solid triangles with multiple outlines. The miniature tankard **K17.1** has panels with a vertical chain pattern, very simple as befits its size. Alternating arcs decorate the lower portion of **K23.10**; this motif goes back to LM IIIA but is also popular in LM IIIB.[125] At least three and possibly four of the mugs or tankards seem to be monochrome. Mug **M4.7** also has an additional motif of large incised X's which were then beaded. The closest parallel to this decoration, which was then monochrome painted, is jug **K87.1**. Tankards and mugs are always monochrome painted inside.

The function of tankards and mugs is uncertain, but clearly tankards were used for pouring, and their elaborate decoration suggests a uses in formal or public situations. Mugs may have been used for drinking and the large decorated examples may have served a function in elite drinking rituals similar to the oversized kylikes and cups.

Kalathos (FIGS. 9.7, 9.8)

There are few fine kalathoi from Karphi (FIG. 9.7), although the shape is found throughout the settlement in coarse wares. Of Seiradaki's seven types of kalathoi, only types 5 and 6 occur in fine wares: Type 5 is here identified as a conical cup (**M16.1**) and has been discussed above (p. 255), and Type 6 is a basket kalathos (**K68.11**), of which only four definite examples were found at Karphi: the elaborately decorated vessel with an excrescent cup (**K68.11**), two similar examples with excrescent cup (**K116.2**, **MK.3**), and a miniature version in blue ware (**K110.3**).

Other fine kalathoi are without handles and are closer to Type 1 in shape, a simple flaring, handleless, open shape. This type is represented by one nearly complete example from K 61 (**K61.10**) with a bevelled base, a slightly flaring body, and a flattened, outward-thickened rim with incised lines. Several rim fragments may also be of this type, although they are larger and the sides flare more (**K17.18**, **K67.3**, **K79.4**). **K81.3** may also come from a kalathos, but it is so poorly preserved that it is difficult to tell; it may also be the rim of an amphoroid krater.

124 Mountjoy 1986, 174, fig. 224.3.
125 Warren 1997, 163, fig. 13, top right (Knossos, LM IIIA:e); Popham 1970*b*, 198, fig. 2.7 (Knossos, LM IIIB).

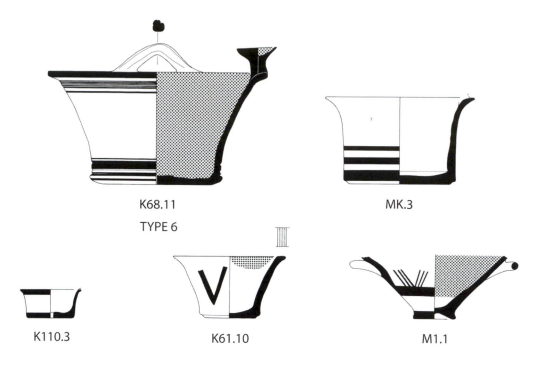

K68.11

TYPE 6

MK.3

K110.3

K61.10

M1.1

Fig. 9.7. Basket kalathos and other fine kalathoi. Scale 1:4.

There is only one example of the later type of kalathos that becomes popular in SM and PG graves on Crete: a very flaring bowl with two round horizontal handles below the rim and a very small raised foot, and it comes from Ta Mnemata (**M1.1**) of SM date. A similar shape from K 26 (**K26.3**) has been reconstructed from many fragments that may not actually go together; the upper part may come from a deep bowl.

All types of fine kalathos are painted on the interior, and they are usually monochrome. **K61.10** apparently has blob decoration on the inside, although the remainder of the paint may have worn off. There is no trace of paint on the interior of **K110.3**. The most elaborate exterior decoration can be found on the Type 6 basket kalathos. A particularly exuberant example is **K68.11**. This vessel has elaborate decoration that includes incision at the base and rim, and strokes and chevrons on the rim itself. The main zone has panelled decoration in which the entire surface is covered in pleonastic style with different motifs, including zigzags, chevrons, vertical crosshatched lozenge chains, vertical rows of butterfly or double axe pattern with multiple outlines, solid triangles with multiple outlines, and a quatrefoil surrounded with hatched and fringed motifs. The whole decorative scheme is similar to that on tankard **K26.4** and pyxis **K22.3**. The decorations on the basket kalathoi **K116.2** and **MK.4** are too worn to determine, and the miniature example (**K110.3**) only has bands. The Type 1 fine kalathoi have much simpler decorations; **K61.10** has a chevron or V-pattern, **K17.18** has an undetermined motif. The rims of **K79.4** and **K67.3** are decorated, the former with hatched triangles and chevrons, the latter with strokes.

The SM kalathos (**M1.1**) has a simple design of multiple triangles; the interior has a reserved disc at the bottom. The underside is not decorated, so this vessel was apparently not designed as a lid.

There are not enough fine kalathoi at Karphi to determine a development during LM IIIC in shape or decoration. The basket kalathos seems to have been more popular at the end of the Karphi settlement, since most of the examples are nearly complete, and no recognisable examples come from earlier deposits or those under streets and courts.

Basket kalathoi and other fine kalathoi do exist in other LM IIIC settlements, but often are represented only by small fragments.[126] They range in date from early to late LM IIIC. Basket kalathoi were found in the early LM IIIC deposits at both Kavousi–*Vronda* and Kavousi–*Kastro*,[127] but there are also examples from late LM IIIC deposits. From the settlement at Khalasmenos come two kalathoi, one from the ritual deposit in sector A,[128] and there is a third from the tholos tomb at Khalasmenos.[129] Two basket kalathoi were said to come from the Ayios Theodoros tomb near Vasiliki, also of LM IIIC date.[130]

126 Hallager 2000, 153.
127 Day and Snyder 2004, 68, fig. 5.6.9; Mook, personal communication.
128 Tsipopoulou 2004, 115, fig. 8.12.95-227, 97-114.
129 Coulson and Tsipopoulou 1994, fig. 18.1; Tsipopoulou 2004, 115–9, fig. 8.12.92-18.
130 Betancourt 1985, 181, fig. 128.

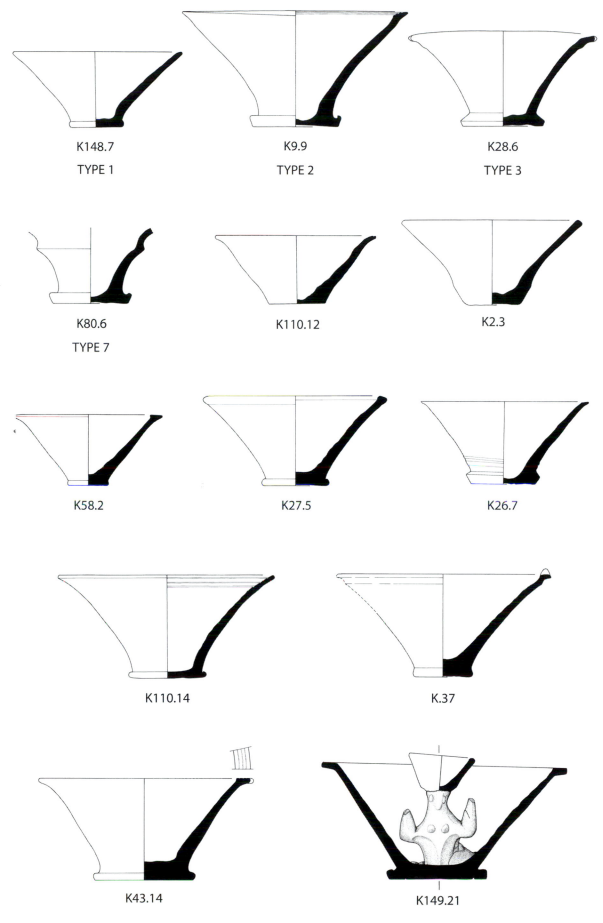

K148.7
TYPE 1

K9.9
TYPE 2

K28.6
TYPE 3

K80.6
TYPE 7

K110.12

K2.3

K58.2

K27.5

K26.7

K110.14

K.37

K43.14

K149.21

Fig. 9.8. Coarse kalathoi. Scale 1:4.

The function of the fine kalathos is uncertain; the shape appears in both domestic and funerary contexts, as at Khalasmenos. The basket kalathos with excrescent cup may have served a ritual function; perhaps some small and special offering was placed in the tiny cup. For other kalathoi, the function is less clear, but the elaborate decoration of these vessels suggests that they were used for display, possibly in elite rituals; indeed, a basket kalathos was found in the early deposits in Building B at Kavousi–Vronda, which may represent the remains of an elite drinking ritual.[131] The later type of kalathos of SM–PG is encountered most often in graves, where it may have held an offering made to the dead.

The coarse kalathos (FIG. 9.8) without handles is one of the most common coarse ware shapes, and certainly one of the most easily recognisable. Of the seven types of kalathoi distinguished by Seiradaki, only four are coarse handleless kalathoi (Types 1–3, 7).[132] Type 4 has a handle and a lug and is more like a basin in profile; it exists only in a single example from the Temple (**K1.12**) and is discussed below under coarse basins. The kalathos shape is simple and has few variations, generally in the treatment of the rim and the base; it resists easy typological distinctions. The base is small (5–10.5), the sides flare out sharply, so that the rim is generally about three times the diameter of the base (15.6–26.6), although the ratio can be as low as 2:1 or as high as 3.7:1. The rim is generally twice the height (2:1–2.2:1), although it can be smaller or larger. The height is most commonly between 8 and 10, but can be as low as 7 and as high as 18. Variation comes in the rim and base treatments, and the four types illustrated incorporate all of these variations. As Seiradaki says, and as is also clear from the notebook, any rim type can occur with any base type.[133]

Bases can be flat (**K3.10–11**, **K110.12–13**, **MK.10**), but more commonly they are raised, either with a simple base (**K2.2**, **K22.7–8**, **K26.8**, **K58.2**, **K110.15**, **K.37**), a bevelled base (**K2.3**, **K26.7**, **K28.6**), a torus moulding (**K27.5**, **K43.14**, **K110.14**, **K148.7**, **K.38**), or a ledge (**K12.5–6**, **K27.4**, **K149.21**); in two cases the base moulding has a hook on it (**K9.9**, **K80.6**). Occasionally, one or more grooves were incised on the underside (**K22.8**, **K26.7**, **K110.13**). Whatever the treatment, the bases are usually very heavy.

Rims also show a great variety: flaring (ten examples) or flattened (15 examples). Flaring rims may have incisions decorating the interior (**K22.8**, **K110.14**, **MK.10**) or have a single notch (**K110.12–13**). Flattened rims may have incisions on top (**K9.9**, **K12.6**, **K27.4**, **K43.14**, **K87.3**), or they may have a ledge on the interior of the rim (**K27.5**, **K58.2**). Flattened rims may also be decorated with knobs on the outer edge (**K28.6**, **K43.14**) or on top (**K.37**), similar to types found at Kavousi–Vronda.[134]

Kalathoi are most often in fabrics used for cooking wares, but occasionally occur in those found in storage vessels. The most common is the phyllite fabric (groups 1a and 1b). The surfaces are often smoothed, almost burnished, and are sometimes mottled red and black; the latter feature is not a slip or painted decoration, but may result from an unknown surface treatment, one that has been observed on cooking wares, kalathoi, and cult equipment at Kavousi–Vronda.[135] Many of the kalathoi (16 out of the 29) show burning, four only on the interior, eleven on both interior and exterior, and only one on the exterior alone. Of those burned both inside and out, five are more heavily burned on the interior, two more heavily on the exterior. It would appear that kalathoi were often used in fire-related activities, and this may explain the use of cooking fabrics that were designed to withstand sudden extremes in temperature. Those kalathoi burned on the interior probably held burning material, while those burned on the exterior may have suffered accidental (set too close to the fire) or deliberate (placed in or near a fire) burning. It seems likely, then, that kalathoi were multi-functional vessels that were designed to hold burning material. They may have been used as lamps, as a few of them show patches of burning on the upper part of the interior that might have been made from a wick floating in the oil that protected the lower portion from burning. They may also have contained charcoal and have been used as scuttles or braziers; in fact, in shape kalathoi resemble scuttles, but without the handle. It is also possible that the kalathoi were used in cooking. Those kalathoi that were unburned may have been used as ordinary containers, or as offering vessels. A kalathos from K 102 contained olive pits, for example, possibly indicating a household function.[136] At any rate, kalathoi were frequent in nearly every context at Karphi.

Seiradaki suggested that kalathoi, while they were used for household purposes, were in favour for religious offerings,[137] and there is some evidence to support a ritual function. Large numbers occurred in five rooms that were in or adjacent to possible ritual areas: seven in K 27 with the two rhyta and eight next door in K 26; seven in K 80 of the Priest's House, which was associated with K 58 with its stands and eight kalathoi. On the other hand, according to the notebook the largest deposit of kalathoi (10) came from K 3, which had no religious association, and K 114 produced six kalathoi in a domestic context, although it was across the street from a possible shrine (K 116). The

131 Day and Snyder 2004, 69–71.
132 Seiradaki, 11–2, fig. 7.
133 Seiradaki, 11.
134 Gesell 1999, pl. 62a, c; Day, Coulson and Gesell 1986, 380, fig. 13.37.
135 Day et al. forthcoming.
136 Seiradaki, 11.
137 Seiradaki, 11.

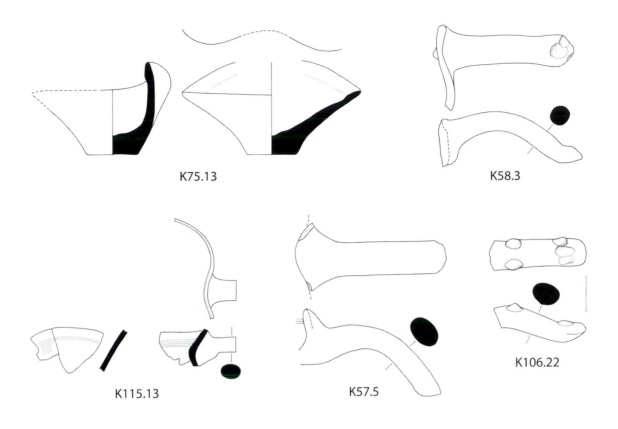

K75.13

K58.3

K115.13

K57.5

K106.22

Fig. 9.9. Scuttles. Scale 1:4.

kalathos from Mikre Koprana (**K149.21**), with its small figure of a goddess with upraised arms, clearly had a religious connection; it showed no signs of burning. Nearly all cult rooms had kalathoi, but no more than were found in ordinary domestic contexts. The Temple produced only a fragment of a kalathos rim with a horned projection, along with its large assortment of goddesses, plaques, and snake tubes. One of the Temple Dependencies (K 38) produced a fragment of a goddess figurine and a kalathos, but these fragments may belong to an earlier deposit underneath or have fallen down from the ritual area above. The Great House Shrine, which also included goddess figures and a snake tube, produced a kalathos. The Small Shrine had a kalathos in one of the rooms, but not the one in which the altar was found. K 116 was also a shrine, with goddess figures and at least four kalathoi. K 85–87 had animal and human figurines, along with several kalathoi, and K 106 also had figurines and a kalathos. Certainly there was no religious area with large numbers of kalathoi, as was the case at Kavousi–*Vronda*, and kalathoi may have been in the religious rooms for domestic as well as ritual reasons.

Kalathoi seem to show the same multitude of functions at other sites as well. Kavousi–*Vronda* produced a kalathos in nearly every house, in addition to the large number in the shrine, and kalathoi occured in both ordinary domestic deposits and in the shrine at Khalasmenos.[138] In other LM IIIC shrines kalathoi served as bowls for burnt or unburned offerings and were placed on top of snake tubes in shrines of the goddess with upraised arms.[139] No coarse kalathoi were found associated with any of the tombs.

Scuttle (FIG. 9.9)

Related to the kalathos is the scuttle, which has a bowl of similar shape, with a handle added. The bases are generally small but thick, as on kalathoi, and the sides flare outward sharply. The single large round or elliptical handle has been pushed into the body at the rim, creating an irregular rim diameter. Scuttles are most often recognised from the distinctive handles; rims and bases can be mistaken for kalathoi, unless enough is preserved to show the irregularity that comes from the attachment of the handle. Seiradaki called vessels of this shape 'lamps',[140] and only distinguished a single type. They were found in many buildings, but never more than one example was found in a room.

Only nine scuttles are preserved, all in coarse fabrics. Seven of these were simply handles (**K2-7.1**, **K17.33**, **K27.6**, **K44.8**, **K57.5**, **K58.3**, **K106.22**), but two also preserved part of the rim (**K115.13**) or body (**K75.13**).

---

138 Day *et al.* forthcoming; Tsipopoulou 2004, 115.
139 Gesell, Coulson and Day 1991, 162; Gesell 1999.
140 Seiradaki, 12, fig. 8.

The most complete example, **K75.13**, had a small, thick, flat base and a flaring body with a straight rim that had a small ledge around the interior; the rim outline was heart-shaped. **K115.13** had a simpler rim, without the inner ledge, but with incisions on the interior near the rim; other rim and handle fragments also had incisions on the interior of the rim (**K2-7.1**, **K57.5**). One rim was rounded and outward-thickened (**K27.6**). Handles were round (**K17.33**, **K44.8**, **K58.3**) or elliptical (**K2-7.1**, **K27.6**, **K57.5**, **K106.22**, **K115.13**). They always curved, sometimes in a single C-curve to rest on the end of the tip (**K57.5**, **K58.3**), more often in a double S-curve, which could be more (**K44.8**) or less (**K27.6**, **K106.22**) curved. Often the end of the handle has a dint (**K17.33**, **K27.6**, **K58.3**, **K106.22**). One example (**K106.22**) also had four knobs or projections on top of the handle. Other scuttle handles found but not catalogued include one with a crude bird's head at the end from the Temple (K 1) and one with spiral fluting found in K 23.[141]

There has been a great deal of discussion of the name and function of these vessels. Evans first called the larger examples of the shape incense burners,[142] but other types of vessels are more demonstrably used for burning aromatics, and this term has been abandoned for the shape. Seiradaki thought they were lamps because of the burning marks. None of the preserved examples, however, showed any traces of burning, although most were only handle fragments, which would not show burning. Of the two that were better preserved, however, one (**K115.13**) was not burned, and the other (**K75.13**) was totally discoloured from fire, possibly in the kiln itself; none of the burning marks suggests that these objects functioned as lamps, and there was no patch of burning near the rim or top where the wick might have rested as in some of the kalathoi. The shape is also called a brazier, but Georgiou accepted the term scuttle as the most precise, and this is the one used here.[143] The name suggests that they may have been used for transporting hot charcoal. All of the examples were made out of cooking fabrics, suggesting that they were fashioned with use in fire in mind. Many of the scuttles were found in contexts that also included ritual equipment. Nearly every shrine of the goddess with upraised hands included a scuttle: one came from the Temple, one from the lower level in K 17 that may have included ritual equipment, and one from K 116. Others were found associated with different kinds of ritual equipment: two scuttles accompanied the rhyta from K 27, one scuttle came from the Small Shrine (K 57), one from K 58 was accompanied by two cylindrical stands, those from K 85 and K 106 were found with animal figurines, and one came from K 79, where there was also some ritual material, possibly associated with K 116. The scuttle mentioned from K 147 may have been used in connection with the kalathos with a goddess figurine in it found next door in K 149, since the two rooms

were connected by a door. Others have more dubious connections with religious activities: one came from K 19, which may have formed part of the Temple Dependencies, and one came from K 80 in the Priest's House, but without associated ritual equipment. Those from K 2-7, K 23, K 44, K 77, K 125, and K 133 have no known connection with ritual. Scuttles have been found in the shrine of the goddess with upraised arms at Kavousi–*Vronda*, so the shape seems regularly to be connected with religious observances.[144] That scuttles also served a more ordinary function can be seen from their appearance in domestic settings, such as K 23, K 77, K 125, K 133, and even K 44, which may have had a public function. In the climate on the high peak of Karphi they may have been needed as portable sources of heat in the colder months.

Krater (FIG. 9.10)

The decorated krater is, after the deep bowl, the most common open shape at Karphi. Seiradaki mentioned that there were regularly 1–3 sherds from kraters in each room, and that there were quite a few restorable examples, indicating the popularity of the shape toward the close of the LM IIIC period.[145] She also mentioned that many krater fragments were found in earlier rubbish dumps, so the shape was clearly popular throughout the history of the settlement. Seiradaki identified ten types of kraters at Karphi. Type 1 is similar to the rounded deep bowl (Type 1) in shape, and Seiradaki indicated that this and Type 3 were the most common;[146] the illustrated example came from one of the Ta Mnemata tombs (M 4), but it could not be located. The low ring base is unusual for the krater, although the rest of the profile finds parallels in the settlement material. Type 2 was represented in the settlement, although the example illustrated is from Ta Mnemata (**M8.2**). It has a high foot and an S-shaped curve to the profile that is not often found on kraters from the settlement. Type 3 was also not located; its very high almost cylindrical foot is most unusual. The handles were placed higher on the body, but otherwise it is not so different from Type 2 in profile. The decoration, seen in the published photograph, seems to consist of rows of double upright loops with horizontal strokes between them.[147] A similar repetitive pattern of loops covering the entire surface of the pot

---

141   Other scuttles (called lamps) were mentioned in the notebook from K 19, K 27, K 77, K 79, K 80, K 116 (pictured in Seiradaki, fig. 8.1), K 125, and K 133; two 'trefoil lamps' were recorded in K 85 and K 147.
142   Evans 1928, 135.
143   Georgiou 1986, 28.
144   Gesell, Glowacki and Klein forthcoming.
145   Seiradaki, 22.
146   Seiradaki, 22.
147   Seiradaki, pl. 11c.

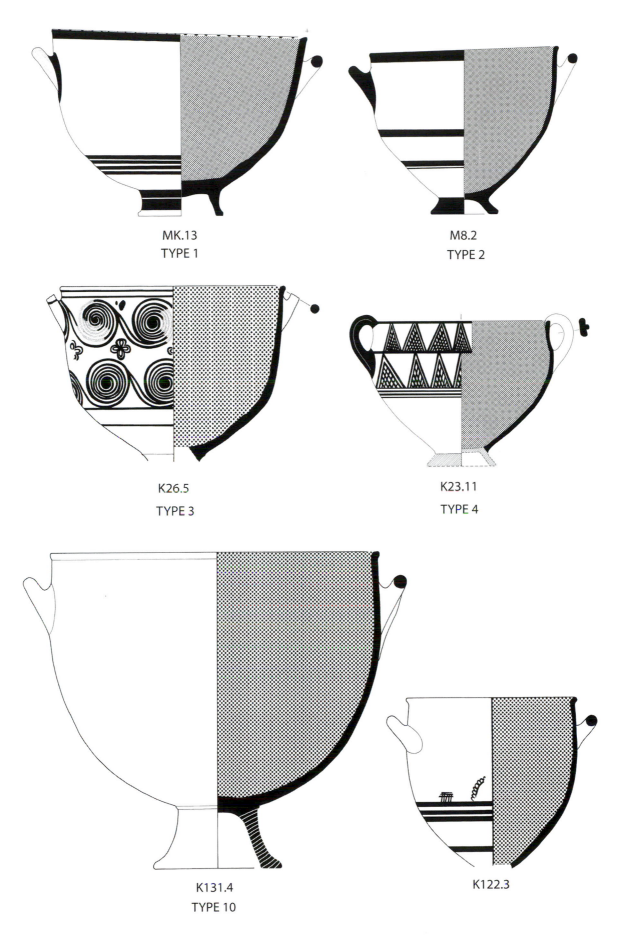

MK.13
TYPE 1

M8.2
TYPE 2

K26.5
TYPE 3

K23.11
TYPE 4

K131.4
TYPE 10

K122.3

Fig. 9.10. Kraters. Scale 1:6.

can be seen in a late LM IIIC krater from Building N at Kavousi–*Vronda*.[148] Type 4 is represented only by a single example, a nearly complete vessel from the floor deposit of K 23 (**K23.11**). The tall offset rim finds no parallels in the rest of the Karphi material, although it is similar to one of the large cups (**K81.1**), and the triple handles are also unique; the base is restored. Types 5–9 were distinguished by their bases, which were the only parts preserved. Type 5 is represented only by a single coarse example, discussed above as a coarse goblet or chalice. Type 6 is a coarse stemmed goblet from K 16 that is probably of Hellenistic date. Type 7 seems to be the base of a champagne cup or goblet, but it was not located; it is similar to the champagne cup base (**K76.39**) discussed above, with its shallow circular depression in the centre. Type 8 is probably what has been identified as a small bowl or saucer (**K33.3**); what Seiradaki took to be a broken edge seems to be finished, and the whole vessel should be turned upside down. Type 9 was not located, nor have any similar bases been preserved in the boxes. Finally, Type 10 is represented only by a single example from K 131 (**K131.4**); it is like Type 3 except that it has double handles and is of extraordinary size; the base is not preserved, but has been restored.

The preserved examples of the kraters seem to fall into three major types: Types 1, 2, and 3; Types 4 and 10 are represented only by single examples. Type 1 is a deep rounded form usually with a low foot, but sometimes with a pedestal base; the body rises straight up to a rim that is vertical or only very slightly flaring. Into this category fall **K132.2** and **MK.13** and perhaps **K62.1**. Type 2, with its S-shaped profile, is represented by **M8.2**, **K49.1**, **K79.2**, **K82.5** and possibly **K79.3**. Type 3 kraters have deeper rounded bodies and a nearly vertical rim; since none of the bases are preserved, it is difficult to know if they have the type of base pictured in Seiradaki. To this type belongs **K26.5** and the more fragmentary **K31.8**, **K43.10**, **K79-89.18**, **K124.6**; a similar shape from Knossos is LM IIIC in date.[149] Type 4 (**K23.11**) is not common either at Karphi or on Crete in general; the closest parallel for its shape appears in Kephallonia,[150] and this vessel may have followed an outside influence or have been an import. **K122.3** represents a different type, with a very deep body and a nearly vertical rim. Finally, there are a number of vessels whose rims seem to turn in; that is, the rim is not the widest part of the vessel, but is narrower than the widest diameter. Included in this type are the following: **K67.2**, **K79-89.21** and **K124.5**; such kraters are also found in LM IIIC Khania.[151]

Few krater bases are preserved, although many have been restored. From the settlement, only the bases of **MK.13**, **K75.7**, **K76.45**, and **K132.2** are preserved, although apparently the foot of the missing Type 3 krater from K 30 was also preserved. All of these are pedestal bases of varying heights. From the tombs, only one base was found, on **M8.2**, and it is similar to **K75.7**.

None of the bases has the holes pierced through them that are found on examples from Kavousi–*Vronda*.[152]

Rim diameters vary from 20 to 55.5, but most of them fall into two groups of either 20–30 or 30–40, the larger slightly more common (20 examples) than the smaller (18 examples). Only three rims fall into the 40–50 category (**K79-89.19**, **K124.5**, **MK.13**), and only a single example (**K131.4**) is larger than 50. The rims themselves show great variety; some kraters are lipless and have pointed rims, like their counterparts on deep bowls, while others have lips that are rolled or flattened on top, usually with a pronounced thickening on the outward edge. Often, but not always, it is the larger kraters that have the rolled or outward thickened rims; the smaller kraters (those with a diameter of less than 30) are more often lipless.

The kraters are always monochrome painted on the interior. There are no examples of a reserved disc on the interior, and only a single example of a reserved band at the rim (**K124.6**). Many of the rims that are flattened on top and/or thickened have reserved bands on top and are decorated with strokes (**K31.9**, **K32.13**, **K52.5**, **K68.8–9**, **K76.42–44**, **K79-89.19**, **K79-89.21**, **K79-89.23**, **K91.4**, **K124.5**, **K148.4**, **MK.13**, **K.19**), or occasionally a wavy line (**K147.13**).

Kraters regularly have more elaborate decoration than any other shape except the pyxis. While there are a few examples of the simple open style, the majority of kraters are elaborately decorated in the pleonastic style. Seiradaki published two figures depicting krater patterns;[153] neither the illustrated bird nor the 'tree' motif could be found.[154] Similarly, the large krater fragment with scroll pattern from K 28 was not located.[155] Several of the illustrations are from shapes other than kraters, including deep bowl, kylix, and stirrup jars.[156]

Few kraters were decorated in the simple style. **K23.11** has two rows of crosshatched triangles and nothing else. This use of very linear style with repetitive motifs can be seen as an indication of very late date, possibly SM, but it also may show that the vessel on which it appears was manufactured elsewhere, perhaps not even on Crete. **K49.1** bears simple running spirals, similar to those found on deep bowls. **K45.4** and **K124.7** also have running spirals. **K26.5** is more complex, with two rows of running spirals connected by double tan-

148   Gesell, Day and Coulson 1995, 90, fig. 7.2; Day and Glowacki forthcoming.
149   Popham 1965, 332, fig. 9.62.
150   *RMDP*, 462, fig. 167.73.
151   *Khania II*, pl. 41.70-P 0155, 84-P0304.
152   Day *et al.* forthcoming.
153   Seiradaki, figs. 25–6.
154   Seiradaki, fig. 25d.
155   Seiradaki, fig. 26a.
156   Seiradaki, fig. 25c, e (deep bowl); Seiradaki, fig. 26d (kylix); Seiradaki, fig. 26c, e (stirrup jars).

gents and small quatrefoils filling the field among them. The designs on the other krater fragments are pleonastic, combining several motifs, with fillers and fringes.

The most elaborately decorated krater, as well as the largest, is **K131.5**. This krater is surely of local inspiration. It is unfortunate that its surfaces are so poorly preserved that the motifs are difficult to identify. One side has two animals, certainly fantastic creatures, on either side of a central motif that may be horns of consecration, with a tree of hatched leaves growing out of the centre, between the horns. The figures have claw-like feet, perhaps of lions, but their bodies look more like those of horses; the right-hand figure in particular has the kind of knobby knees associated with horses. This figure is clearly male, but the one on the left is too poorly preserved to identify its sex. The right-hand figure also has a long fringed tail that appears equine. The bodies of both animals are outlined with dots. Unfortunately, the heads of both animals are poorly preserved; the right-hand creature seems to have a beak, or else the mouth is represented as open. Either the two animals wear elaborate headdresses, or their mouths or beaks are open, with curving fringed fronds growing out of them. The left-hand figure seems to have a tree with oval leaves growing out of its back. It is possible that these are griffins or some other composite animal; they resemble the griffins on the vessel from LH IIIC Lefkandi, with their dotted outlines, claw feet, and headdresses.[157] The other side is also panelled, but the motifs could not be determined. Clearly, nearly all of the available space was filled with fringes, arcs, and small ornaments.

Other kraters also show figured decoration, but they are less elaborate. In addition to the large fragment from K 76 published by Seiradaki and not located,[158] there were at least five kraters depicting birds (**K62.1, KR K79-89.18, K149.14–15, K.20**). Often these birds are arranged in panels with other motifs. The birds usually have fringed wings, and often have a dotted outline. Other creatures are represented; one krater fragment (**K107.4**) depicts the tentacle of an octopus. Several kraters bear floral motifs, including tree (**K75.7, K52.6**), palm (**K149.14**), and Minoan flower (**K86.1, K101.7, K107.3**; possibly **K76.42**). **M8.2** has lilies, arranged on either side of a panelled pattern. Other floral motifs are arranged in patterns over the surface of the pot (**K97.5, K47.1, K121.8, K124.8**). One fragment (**K75.8**) portrays a realistic double axe between horns of consecration.

Most of the kraters have non-figured panelled patterns. **MK.13** has a combination of spirals, ovals with alternating strokes, and fringed, outlined curvilinear motifs. **K148.5** has a combination of scale pattern, chequerboard, and S-pattern, similar to that found on pyxis **K110.5**. **K82.5** is decorated with concentric semicircles with solid centres and hatching between some of the circles. **K124.6** has a panel with a multiple-outlined quatrefoil, and a scalloped curvilinear outlined pattern. Other motifs on fragments include: spirals (**K23.12, K23.15, K23.64–65, K32.15, K45.5, K79-89.19, K91.4, K147.12**); medallions with rosettes (**K67.2**), dotted filled ovals (**K43.10**), and other fillers (**K79-89.22**); stacked chevrons (**K79-89.21**); multiple stems (**K79.3**); dotted zigzag (**K23.13**); crosshatched (**K52.5, K103.3**) or outlined (**K76.43**) lozenges; scale pattern (**K96.1, K148.5**); outlined curvilinear patterns (**K32.13, K54.4–5, K76.42, K85.4, K122.3, K130.1, K148.4**), filled loops (**K31.8**) and wavy borders (**K32.14**). Other krater fragments are too small to determine the overall patterns, but most are decorated with curvilinear motifs, and many have arcs filling spaces, U-motif, fringes, dots, and scalloped edges. One small krater (**K132.2**) is monochrome.

There is no discernable development in the shapes or decorations on the kraters. Krater fragments with elaborate decorative schemes appear in the lower levels of K 12, K 17, and K 23, and in the streets and courts, particularly K 32, K 76, and K 79-89. Whole kraters were found on the floors and represent vessels in use at the end of the settlement's history, and at least one appears in a tomb (**M8.2**). Except for the example from K 23, which may be an import, these late examples look little different from the fragments found throughout.

Kraters are always elaborately decorated and usually made in fine fabrics. Whatever their function, whether as mixing vessels for water and wine as in later Greek culture or something else, they were meant for social display rather than to serve as simple utilitarian vessels. It is not unreasonable to see the kraters as part of the drinking or feasting rituals that may have formed a major element in the social fabric of the Karphi settlement.

Other open shapes

Large spouted (?)bowl (FIG. 9.11)

There are two very similar examples of a large deep bowl decorated with bands and wavy band(s) and possibly spouted (**K115.6, K.18**). This is a shape for which there are no parallels on Crete. It has a tall offset rim and deep rounded body, and it is decorated with a wavy line on the rim and either bands or a wavy line and bands on the body; the interior is also banded. A similar shape, popular in the islands in early LM IIIC was the large spouted cup (FS 249), which appears on examples from Lefkandi, Naxos, Paros, Melos, and Rhodes.[159] The Karphi examples may be variations on that shape and may show some contact with the islands.

157 Mountjoy 2007, 234, fig. 6.

158 Seiradaki, fig. 25a.

159 *RMDP*, 712–3, fig. 273.63 (Lefkandi, LH IIIC early); 918, fig. 373.144 (Melos, LH IIIC early); 935–6, fig. 381.4 (Paros, LH IIIC early to middle); 958–9, fig. 391.64 (Naxos, LH IIIC middle); 1060–1, fig. 434.230 (Rhodes, LH IIIC early to middle).

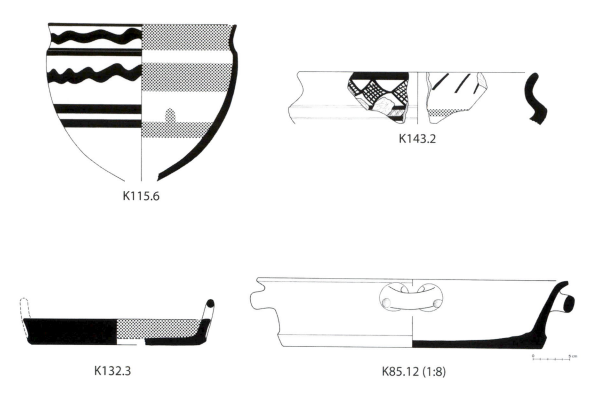

Fig. 9.11. Bowls and basins. Scale 1:4, unless otherwise indicated.

Large carinated bowl (FIG. 9.11)

There is a single example of a large carinated bowl from K 143 (**K143.2**). Decorated with crosshatched lozenge chain, it also has an incised X-pattern below and incisions on the interior, along with bands. Its closest parallel is an unpublished fragment from Kavousi–*Vronda*, which may come either from a LM IIIC context or have been discarded from a later Geometric tomb.

Tray (FIG. 9.11)

There are two examples of the fine tray, Seiradaki's Type 8 dish. This is FS 322, a shape which first appeared on the mainland in middle LH IIIC, but which by late LH IIIC was generally decorated with bands or monochrome paint.[160] The mainland and island examples seem to have more flaring sides and often have double or even triple handles, and they are elaborately decorated. The two examples from Karphi are both monochrome painted, and both have basket handles, but only single ones. **K132.3** is shallow (2.7), with a bevelled flat base and flat rim, similar in shape to coarse cooking trays, but with a handle. **K43.12** is deeper (4.9), similar in shape to a tray from Rhodes of early to middle LH IIIC.[161] Both trays have large diameters (20–28), and they would make excellent shallow serving dishes. Published examples of fine trays with basket handles from other sites have not been found.

Coarse trays not used in cooking are rare. **K85.12** is a unique shape that is either a very shallow basin or a tall tray, but it seems to fit more into the category of tray. It has a wide, bevelled base, a body that spreads to a flaring rim, and a horizontal handle below the rim; the handles display dints at either end.

Basin (FIG. 9.12)

Seiradaki defined a basin as any open vessel, except kalathoi, whose height is between one-third and two-thirds of its rim diameter.[162] She distinguished 11 different types of basins in her publication, including fine, medium-coarse, and coarse wares.[163] She mentioned that sherds from basins were found in most rooms, although they were not as common as pithoi, pithoid jars, jars, and tripods. The shape occurs more often in coarse or medium-coarse wares than in fine wares.

Fine basins are open shapes with very wide diameters, ranging from 13 to 28. Most of the preserved fine examples are of Seiradaki's Types 6 and 7. Fine basins are probably quite deep, although no whole complete profile has been preserved, but they appear

160   Mountjoy 1986, 155, 193.
161   *RMDP*, 1065–6, fig. 436.252.
162   Seiradaki, 9.
163   Seiradaki, 8–9, fig. 5.

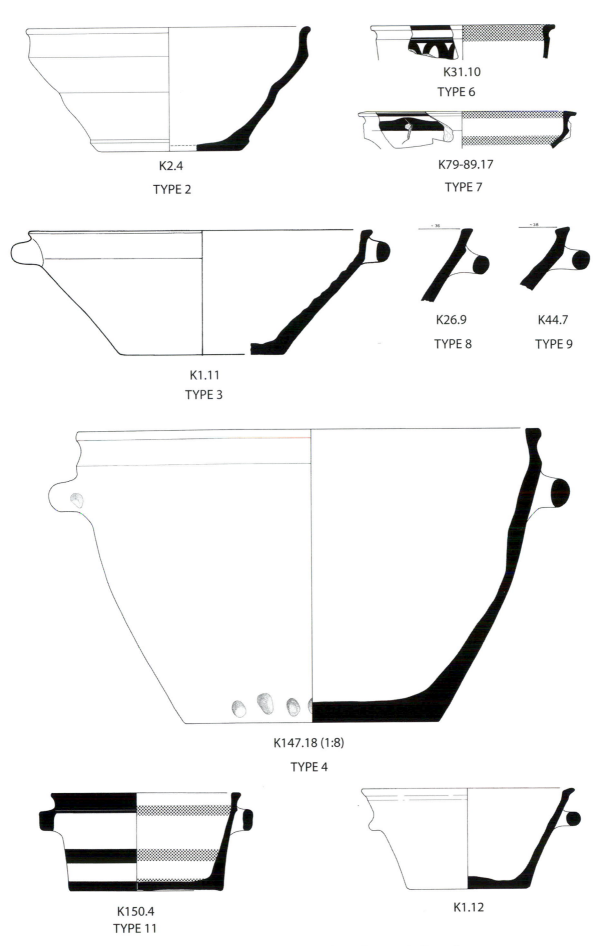

K2.4

TYPE 2

K31.10

TYPE 6

K79-89.17

TYPE 7

K1.11

TYPE 3

K26.9

TYPE 8

K44.7

TYPE 9

K147.18 (1:8)

TYPE 4

K150.4

TYPE 11

K1.12

Fig. 9.12. Basins. Scale 1:4 unless otherwise indicated.

to be shallower than their coarse counterparts. They are characterised by a ridge below the rim, and a flat horizontal handle is attached at the ridge. The rims are flattened on top and thickened outward.

The decoration of fine basins is quite simple. Two examples have strokes on top of the rim (**K54.3**, **K.22**), while one possible basin (**K106.20**) has a zigzag motif. The exteriors have bands (**K54.3**, **K79–89.17**, **K101.9**) or the deep wavy bands that may represent a debased octopus decoration (**K9.6**, **K31.10**). One possible basin (**K106.20**) has a more elaborate decoration of multiple stems, but the precise motif is not certain. The interiors of fine basins have either a single band at the rim (**K9.6**, **K31.10**, **K106.20**, **K.22**) or multiple bands (**K54.3**, **K79–89.17**); only one example has a monochrome interior (**K101.9**). Only one possible basin came from the tombs. A rim fragment found outside Ta Mnemata 8 (**M8.10**) is of similar shape, but lacks the ridge below the flattened, outward thickened rim; it has banded decoration on the interior and monochrome on the exterior. It is smaller than most fine basins (rim diameter is *c.* 16), and it may not be a basin, but a shallow bowl.

Fine basins are rare in LM IIIC deposits elsewhere, although the coarse and medium-coarse varieties are common. A few examples have been found at Kavousi–*Vronda*.[164]

Only one true basin appears in medium-coarse fabric (**K150.4**), and it is published as Seiradaki's Type 11. It has a flat base, slightly concave underneath, and nearly vertical sides rising to the usual flattened and outward thickened rim, with a ridge below it. Two elliptical horizontal handles are attached at the ridge and below. The shape is similar to the basins in fine wares, although perhaps deeper and not as rounded. Like the fine ware examples, it is decorated with bands inside and out, with a large spiral on the bottom of the interior.

Coarse basins are difficult to distinguish from pithoid jars, particularly when only the rim is preserved, as they often have similar profiles; basins, however, are shallower than pithoid jars and generally have horizontal rather than vertical handles. Basins vary a great deal in size, and doubtless also in function. They were part of the kitchen equipment, as they frequently show burning, and they may also have been used in the preparation of food or for other household activities, such as washing.

The coarse lekane or basin usually has a flat base, a ridge below a flattened and outward-thickened rim, and a horizontal handle at the ridge and below. The profiles vary a great deal. Types 1 and 3–6 were said to be frequent, and Type 3 was more common than 8–11. Type 1 has straight sides to the ridge, and the handle is unusually set below the ridge; unfortunately, no vessels of this type were located. Type 2 is most unusual, with two carinations, as if the vessel was made in two sections and the pieces joined; only a single example was found (**K2.4**). Type 3 has more flaring

sides, and the handle is between the ridge and the rim; several examples exist (**K1.11**, **K48.7**), and it is a type found frequently on LM IIIC sites.[165] Type 4 (**K147.18**) is close to being a pithoid jar, as it is just under the limit for a basin; it is similar to examples from Kavousi–*Vronda*, Kastri, Knossos, and Khamalevri.[166] Types 5–7 are only represented by rim fragments and differ in the depth, angle, and decoration of the rim; Type 5 has incisions decorating the rim, while Types 6 and 7 are primarily found in fine wares. Types 8 (**K26.9**) and 9 (**K44.7**) have much thicker walls, a flattened rim that is not thickened outward, and a small ridge at the handle attachment; Type 9 seems to have a more curving profile. Type 10 was not located, but seems to have more of an S-curve. Type 11 only occurs in medium-coarse wares (see above). To these types might be added **K1.12** from the Temple, which Seiradaki categorised as a kalathos of Type 4, but which fits more comfortably into the category of basin; it has a two-pronged lug (imitating horns?) as well as a round horizontal handle, but it lacks the ridge found on most of the basins. It also perhaps has some paint on the rim.

Coarse basins are rarely decorated, but occasionally have incised decoration on the rim (Type 5), a chain of finger impressions around the base (**K147.18**), or the same sort of dint or thumbprints on the handles found on pithoi and pithoid jars (**K147.18**).

Deep basin or bowl (FIG. 9.13)

Another shape found at Karphi but not in any of Seiradaki's charts is a deep and rounded bowl or basin (**K47.3**, **K85.10**, **K121.12**, **K.40**). This shape has the rounded profile of the krater, but lacks the pedestal base generally found on kraters. In two cases (**K47.3**, **K.40**) the ratio of height to rim diameter does not fall within Seiradaki's parameters for basins; they are too deep, but not by much. I have called this shape the deep basin or bowl, rather than creating a new type of basin to add to Seiradaki's eleven types; the profiles seem too different. I have also avoided calling them coarse kraters, since that term implies a certain function that is perhaps erroneous; they are clearly for domestic use, and were not decorated as display items. One was in medium-coarse ware, the others in coarse wares.

---

164 Day *et al.* forthcoming.
165 Tsipopoulou 2004, 117, fig. 8.10.97-5 (Khalasmenos); *Kastri*, 295, fig. 15.P34; Day *et al.* forthcoming (Kavousi–*Vronda*).
166 Gesell, Day and Coulson 1995, pl. 18d (Kavousi–*Vronda*); *Kastri*, 296, fig. 16.P11; Warren 1982–83, 84, fig. 56 — this example, however, is scored on the interior: see the drawing in Warren 2007, 341, fig. 6.P2468 (Knossos); Andreadaki-Vlasaki and Papadopoulou 2005, 37, fig. 39 (Khamalevri); Andreadaki-Vlasaki and Papadopoulou 2007, 51, fig. 8.33 (Khamalevri, Phase II).

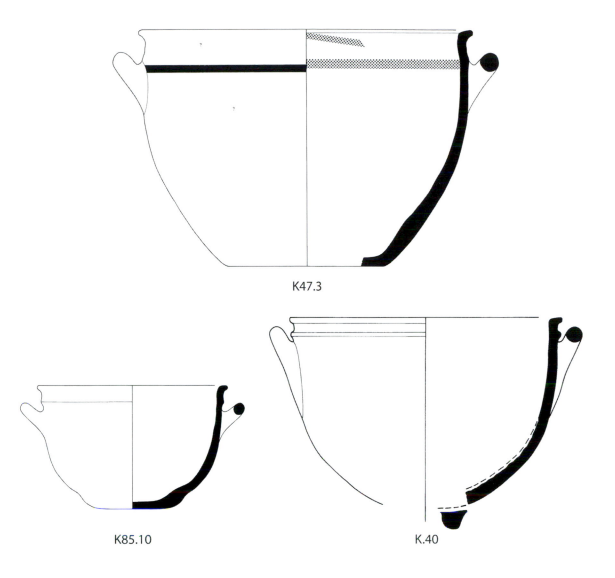

K47.3

K85.10   K.40

Fig. 9.13. Deep basin or bowl. Scale 1:4.

Three have flat bases (**K47.3**, **K85.10**, **K121.12**), while the third (**K.40**) has a rounded bottom to which a ring of clay has been added for a base (now separated). All examples have deep rounded bodies, and two (**K47.3**, **K.40**) have flattened outward thickened rims with ridges below, like the basins; **K121.12** has a rounded rim and no ridge. All have round horizontal handles set below the ridge or rim. **K47.3** has a creamy buff slip and is painted with bands on the interior and exterior. The vessels of this shape may have been used for some of the same purposes as the basins.

Lid (FIG. 9.14)

Seiradaki distinguished seven types of lids. Type 1 is a cooking lid (**K47.4**). Type 2 (**K2.8**) is found only in coarse ware; **K116.8** is similar in shape to Type 2, but has a knob in place of the basket handle, more like the cooking lids. Type 3 (**K1.12**) is a domed lid with a basket handle that also occurs in fine fabrics (e.g. **K110.7**). Types 4 and 5 are like cups with handles inside

the bowl, but neither of the lids illustrated in the typological chart were found; there were, however, several similar examples with interior knobs (**K23.27**, **K29.13**, **K41.2**, **K143.3**). Type 6 is another cooking lid (**K22.9**). Type 7 is the lid illustrated with the pyxis from K 114 (**K114.5**), and there are two other examples (**K28.3**, **K76.53**); this type is shallow, with straight sides, sometimes curving inward, and a wide, flat bottom. A new type, not in the typology is represented by a miniature lid in blue ware from MK 1E (**MK.12**). It resembles an upside-down conical cup with a carination and a slightly knobbed top.

Fine lids were often used to cover pyxides (**K110.7**, **K114.5**), but they are few in number in comparison with the large quantity of pyxides found on the site. The small lids (**K29.13**, **K41.2**, **K143.3**, **MK.12**) would have served as covers for vessels with smaller mouths, perhaps jugs. Lid **K114.5** is the most elaborately decorated, with alternating bands and dots on the sides and concentric circles with solid ovals set obliquely in

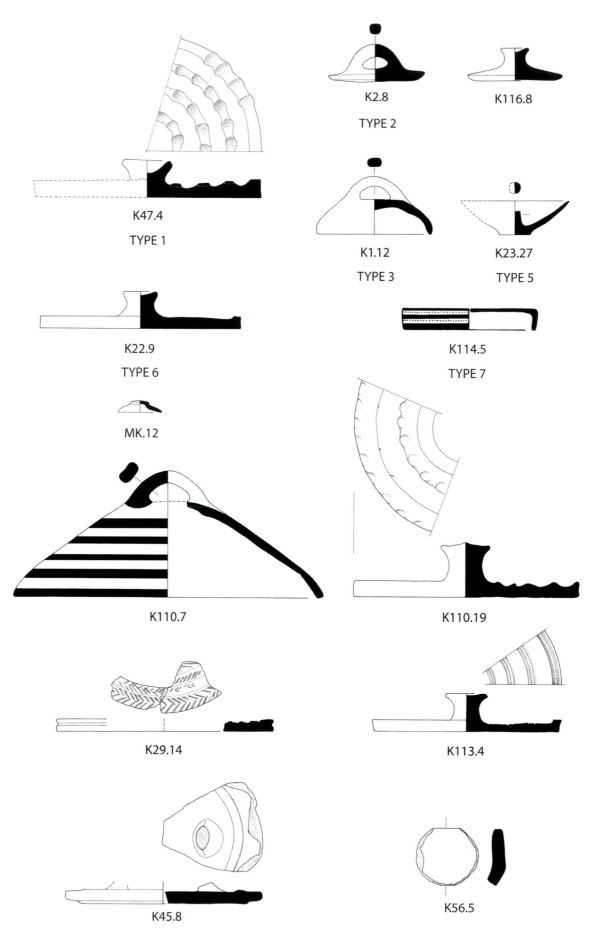

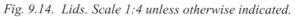

Fig. 9.14. Lids. Scale 1:4 unless otherwise indicated.

a V-pattern on top. Other lids are less elaborately decorated, with bands (**K28.3**, **K110.7**), or monochrome paint (**K41.2**, **K76.53**). Lids **K29.13** and **MK.12** were probably undecorated. Lid **K143.3** is decorated with incised lines around the body.

The coarse lids are all small (9–11.5), made of cooking fabrics, but without evidence of burning. These lids would have been used to cover small-mouthed vessels, like jars or jugs. The cup-like lid with the knob in the centre of the interior would be very practical to place over the mouth of a water jug to prevent any foreign objects from getting in.

A subcategory of lid is the stopper, which is made from a piece of pottery that has been cut into a disc to fit into the mouth of a vessel. Three stoppers were found in the preserved material from Karphi (**K56.5**, **K75.12**, **K76.56**). These are 5.5–6.5 in diameter, and all three have been cut down from other vessels by chipping them around the edges to form a circular disc. **K75.12** is of blue ware, but the other two are of ordinary phyllite coarse wares. **K56.5** was cut down from a cooking dish, and the profile can still be seen; the other two are from body sherds. Such stoppers have also been found in other LM IIIC sites, including Kavousi–*Vronda*.[167] They must have been used for covering or sealing small vessels like jugs or amphoras, and would not have been appropriate for pyxides, jars, or cooking vessels; they would have been created by the householder, not manufactured by a potter.

The majority of lids found on the site, however, were made out of coarse cooking fabrics, many of which show signs of burning; these are designated as cooking lids. They are Seiradaki's Types 1 and 6, flat discs with central knobs. Type 1 lids regularly have applied bands decorated with finger impressions and incisions, while Type 6 lids are without decoration and are a bit thinner (**K22.9**, possibly **K38.8**). Cooking lids are large, with diameters ranging from 19–27. The knob handles are generally concave, but one example (**K110.19**) has a handle with a conical knob on the top. The bottoms of these lids are usually flat and rough, as though formed on the ground or on fabric; the tops are often smoothed and sometimes almost burnished. Occasionally a lid has a projecting ledge on the bottom making it concave (**K38.9**, **K.42**); two examples (**K45.8**, **K125.2**) have a groove around the edge of the underside. The edges are generally straight and vertical, but can be concave (**K110.19**, **K113.4**), rounded (**K29.15**, **K45.8**, **K125.2**, **K.42**), grooved (**K29.14**, **K39.6**) or bevelled (**K22.10**). A raised ridge regularly appears on top at the edge of the rim. The tops are decorated with a variety of concentric ridges with elaborate patterns and incisions, including plain ridges (**K39.6**, **K124.9**), incised concentric circles (**K22.10**, **K83.3**, **K113.4**), incised concentric circles with strokes on the rim (**K19.4**, **K38.9**, **K46.7**), and ridges with strokes (**K.43**), incised chevrons (**K29.14**, **K.42**), and oblique slashes (**K70.3**); these lids are, however, most commonly decorated with

ridges that bear finger impressions: one row (**K29.15**), two rows alternating with grooves (**K44.9**, **K110.19**, **K.41**), two rows alternating with ridges (**K80.7**), four rows (**K47.4**), or even six rows (**K125.2**).

Besides these two types of cooking lids, a third variety exists in at least one, possibly two examples: a flat disc lid with a round or elliptical basket handle (**K45.8**). This type has a flat base, a groove around the outer edge of the underside, and an undecorated ridge on top near the rim. **K2.8**, Seiradaki's Type 2 lid, may have been a cooking lid that once was larger but was broken or deliberately cut down.

Ten examples of the preserved cooking lids are unburned (**K9.10**, **K22.9–10**, **K44.9**, **K46.7**, **K70.3**, **K125.2**, **K.41–43**), while the remainder show a variety of burning patterns (PLATE 12 *f*). Six (**K29.14–15**, **K38.9**, **K39.6**, **K83.3**, **K124.9**) have a burned band around the outside edge of the underside, two (**K31.15**, **K45.8**) are burned everywhere on the bottom except for a band around the outside edge, three (**K80.7**, **K113.4**, **K19.4**) are entirely burned on the bottom, one (**K110.19**) is burned on one side of the bottom, and one (**K47.4**) was burned on the top and one side. Those without burning were probably not used in the cooking process, although they may have been placed on a cooking pot after it had been removed from the fire. The others were certainly used during cooking. Those with burned edges were probably larger than the mouths of the vessels they covered. Those which were totally burned may have been set directly into the fire, perhaps as dampers or like a modern pizza pan.[168] The examples that were burned everywhere except for an edge around the exterior are more difficult to explain. An experimental traditional oven built at Kavousi produced a cooking installation with a hole in top on which a pot might be placed, or it could be sealed off with a lid, and that might result in this pattern of burning.[169] Others were simply selectively burned.

Disc-shaped cooking lids first appeared in Crete in LM IIIC, and they are found in nearly every LM IIIC site.[170] Those from Khania and Khamalevri are of similar size, shape, and decoration to the Karphi examples.[171]

Strainer (FIG. 9.1)

There is one fragment of a strainer that is probably a lid but may be a bowl (**K44.5**). This seems to be an open shape, painted on the interior, with a flat rim painted black and a reserve band just below the rim. It may have been part of another vessel or placed over the spout of a jug, or used as a strainer over another vessel.

---

167 Day *et al.* forthcoming.
168 Hallager 2000, 163.
169 Day, Glowacki and Klein, 2001, 122.
170 Hallager 2000, 163.
171 *Khania II*, pl. 55.77-P 1635; Andreadaki-Vlasaki 2005, 278, fig. 43 Khamalevri, Phase II.

Pyxis (FIG. 9.15)

Pyxides were common at Karphi, although not as ubiquitous as deep bowls and kraters, and they occurred primarily in fine fabrics; a few were medium-coarse. Seiradaki distinguished seven types.[172] Of these, Type 7 might more accurately be called a straight-sided alabastron, and there are only two known examples: the coarse vessel depicted in the publication (**K80.8**) and a fine example, of which only the base is preserved, from K 75 (**K75.10**). The remaining types fall into two basic categories: a cylindrical vessel with sharp incurve at the top and a low collar (Types 1–3, Type 6) and a wide-mouthed cylindrical vessel with basket handles and a ledge around the interior of the rim (Types 4 and 5). Within the first group, the types seem to be determined on the basis of the position of the handles. Type 1 has handles rising on the shoulder, the handles of Type 2 rise from the middle of the sides and to the level of the rim, and Types 3 and 6 have handles that begin at the base and rise high above the rim, those of Type 3 more vertical, those of Type 6 more flared. Types 3 and 6 also have wider mouths. Within the category of wide-mouthed cylindrical pyxides, Type 4 has twisted rope handles and may be rather taller than Type 5, which has plain handles and is shallow. Pyxides of Type 2 are the most common.

The bases of pyxides are generally rough, as though cut from the wheel when slightly hardened and not smoothed off. They are generally flat or slightly concave on the bottom. Occasionally the bases have a groove around the underside, near the outer edge (**K14.1, K22.3, K61.12, K116.2, K134.1**). Bases can be plain (**K8.1, K9.7, K22.2–3, K22.6, K79.5, K110.5, K110.11, K116.1, K147.16, K150.2, K.24**), bevelled (**K2.1, K3.5, K43.13, K76.49, K85.5–6, K114.3, K116.2, K137.1, MK.9**), or made with a projecting ledge (**K22.4, K68.12, K75.9, K79-89.24, K110.4, K113.1, K114.4, K115.7, M4.3**). The bodies of pyxides can be shallow or deep, and they are generally cylindrical until the carination. There is a good deal of variation in the shoulder and rim treatments; the most common shape has a gentle carination with sloping shoulders that rise to a vertical rim. Occasionally (**K22.4, K61.12, K85.5, K110.5, K110.11, K113.1, K137.1, K150.2**) the carination is a sharper and the shoulder almost concave. Types 3 and 6 have more rounded shoulders with a sharply offset collar. Handles vary both in placement and in type. Most common is the round handle that begins at the middle or toward the bottom of the body and rises above the rim (Type 2). Occasionally the handle begins at the base (Types 3 and 6). The handles are generally round, but sometimes they are slashed and fan open, creating a triple handle (**K110.5, K114.3, K115.7**), and they can also be double (**K2.1**). On the cylindrical basket-handled pyxides (Types 4–5), the preserved handles are rope-twisted (**K43.13**), and they are set directly on the flattened rim. A ledge is set on the interior of the rim where a lid

presumably rested. This shape is close to the basket kalathos, but the sides flare less.

Pyxides should be thought of as closed shapes, and the interior is rarely painted; a few examples have splatters on the interior (**K8.1, K134.1**). The exteriors are nearly always decorated in pleonastic style, and along with tankards and kraters bear the most elaborate decoration; medium-coarse examples are painted on top of a creamy yellow slip. The main decorative zone lies on the cylindrical sides of the vessel from base to carination, with a secondary zone on the shoulder. Seiradaki states that the decoration nearly always includes horns of consecration or double axes, but this does not seem to be the case on the preserved examples.[173] Panelled decoration is most common, and only **K85.6** has a different scheme, with its rows of running spirals. Motifs on pyxides include the following: double axe (**K79-89.24, K114.4, K115.7**), horns of consecration (**K14.1, K114.4**), spirals (**K114.3, K115.7, K134.1**), windmills (**K22.3**), hatched or crosshatched lozenges or lozenge and loop (**K37.2, K75.9, K147.16, K.23**), quatrefoil (**K22.2, K22.6**), half medallions or wavy border (**K22.3, K68.12, K110.5, K116.1, K134.1**), chevron panel (**K14.1, K22.3, K22.6, K110.4, K114.3, K116.1**), hatched or crosshatched triangles (**K8.1, K110.4**), bird (**K68.12, K114.4, K115.7**), dotted hatched oval (**K8.1**), fringed bulb (**K14.1**), scale pattern (**K110.5**), alternating arcs or triangles (**K22.2, K22.6, K23.44**), dotted curvilinear pattern (**K22.2**), and fringing (**K14.1, K22.3, K75.9, K110.5, K114.3–4, K115.7, K150.2**). Many pyxides are of very soft fabric and no trace of the decoration still remains. Handles are decorated either with strokes or are solidly painted.

Secondary motifs on the shoulders include hatched triangles (**K22.4, K75.9**), loops (**K8.1, K85.6, K.23**), zigzag (**K114.3**), and oblique or upright strokes (**K40.5, K115.7, K147.16**). Under the handles are designs of spirals (**K114.3**), wavy lines (**K8.1**), chevrons (**K22.4, K85.6, K115.7**), or fringed chevron with tail (**K114.4**).

Pyxides were not often made in coarse wares. Only three examples are known: two are large and plain (**K137.1, M4.3**), one from the settlement and the other from one of the Ta Mnemata tombs. The third is a most unusual shape (Type 7), better identified as a straight-sided alabastron (**K80.8**). It has a ring base, straight sides above a low carination, handles on the sharply carinated shoulder, and a small mouth. The two coarse pyxides from the settlement are both burned and may have stood near the hearth or been used in cooking or the preparation or storage of food.

The distribution of pyxides on the site is instructive. Nearly every house had one, but there were a few areas

172   Seiradaki, 18–9, fig. 12.
173   Seiradaki, 18.

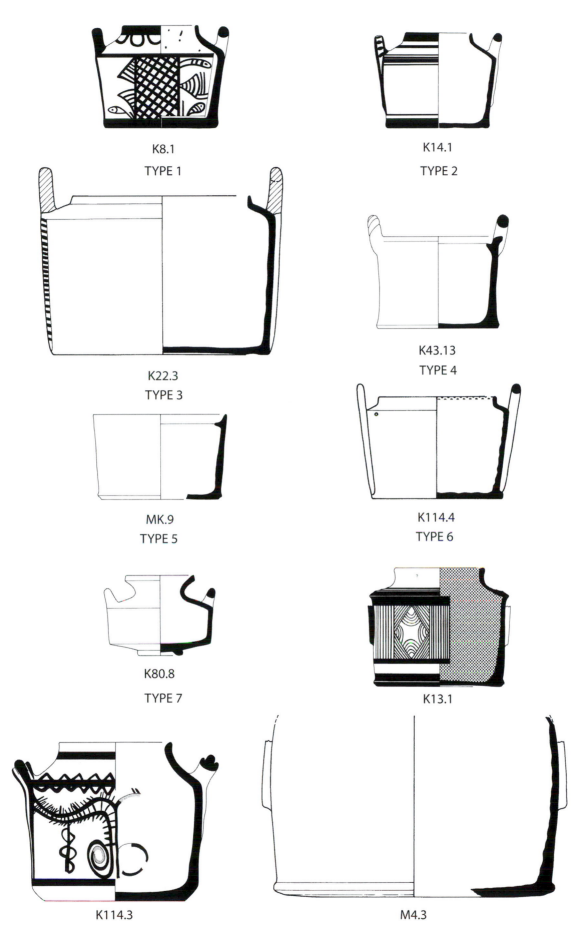

Fig. 9.15. Pyxides. Scale 1:4.

that had dense concentrations of them: the Magazines (8), the Eastern Cliff Houses (5), the Western Cliff Houses (4), the Great House (3), and the Commercial Quarter (3). Seiradaki mentioned three in K 22, and there are four extant examples; K 110 and K 114 were also said to contain three each, K 80 in the Priest's House had four, while K 116 produced as many as six.[174] The presence of pyxides in lower deposits in K 23 and below streets and courts in K 76 and K 79-89 indicates that the shape was present in the early stages of the settlement, and the large number of nearly complete vessels shows that they were popular at the end of the settlement's history, but that the inhabitants did not carry them away when they left.

Because of their frequency at Karphi, pyxides were thought to be one of the most common LM IIIC shapes, but subsequent excavations of LM IIIC sites produced surprisingly few examples.[175] The popularity of the pyxis seems to be a local peculiarity of the Karphi assemblage. The function of these vessels is unknown, but several of them have lids (**K110.5, K114.4**), so they may have served as small boxes for storage of objects or food. It is possible that they were used for storing precious objects (so many of them are elaborately decorated and fine), as suggested by Seiradaki,[176] but they could have been used for storage of food (like modern plastic containers); many of the pyxides show traces of burning, suggesting the possibility that they were placed near the cooking fires. The elaborate decoration suggests that they were meant to impress, and it is likely that they made a statement about the status of the inhabitants on social or ritual occasions. The presence of so many in a room with goddesses with upraised arms (K 116) suggests that they may have also had a ritual function. Pyxides were not found in the tombs, with the exception of **M4.3**, one of the largest found, and it was in coarse ware.

Hut urn (FIG. 9.16)

The hut urns from Karphi have been well published, and only the examples from Mikre Koprana (**MK.12**) and the Great House Shrine (**K16.1**) can be added to the published lists by Hägg and Mersereau.[177] There are nine preserved hut urns from Karphi, including a piece found in K 149 that was inventoried as a terracotta palette, but identified by Hägg as a hut urn door;[178] of the other eight, half are in fine wares (**K33.2, K110.6, K115.8, K147.17**), the other half are coarse (**K16.1, K69.2, K122.4, MK.12**).

The fine hut urns tend to be smaller than those of coarse wares, although the largest and smallest examples are both coarse. All have domed tops and cut-out doorways, and all but one have pierced lugs on either side of the doorways; the doors themselves are missing except in **K147.17** and **K122.4**. Most hut urns are plain, but **K33.2** is monochrome painted and decorated with incised lines. **K115.8** may have been burnished. **K147.17** has small horned projections over the doorway,

possibly representing horns of consecration. Otherwise, the hut urns are devoid of decoration.

The coarse examples of hut urns are similar to the fine ones, except for a greater variation in sizes. At least two of the coarse hut urns are of cooking pot fabric, but this fabric was used for other kinds of pottery at Karphi. One example (**MK.12**) has a green stain on the interior, as if from bronze, possibly from a pin that kept the doorway in place.

Seiradaki noted a similarity in shape to pyxides,[179] and Mersereau believed that the hut urns derived from the pyxis shape, but that the potters adapted the form to create an architectural model.[180] Petrakis, however, has questioned how this similarity in form could reflect a deeper conceptual link between pyxides and hut urns, and has rejected the association.[181] Not noted by either scholar is the great difference in size and decoration between pyxides and hut urns, and if the method of creating the hut urn was derived from the manufacture of pyxides, there seems to be little other connection between the two ceramic forms. Pyxides tend to be large and have elaborate decoration, and their appearance, even with a conical lid, is very far removed from that of the hut urns. Although Seiradaki suggested that hut urns may have been influenced by basketwork cages for birds or small animals, rather than by tholos tombs or granaries, most scholars have seen them as imitating tholos tombs; in fact, Petrakis has suggested that the tholos tomb is the only possible architectural prototype.[182] The tholoi of this period, however, tend to be square or rectangular at the bottom, whereas the hut urns are always round, a fact that diminishes the connection between the two forms. To my knowledge, no one has suggested that hut urns are meant to represent the other common round and corbelled or vaulted structures of the period, namely kilns, and it is difficult to imagine any reason for showing such a mundane architectural form.[183]

---

174 Seiradaki, 18.
175 Nearly every report of a LM IIIC site includes a statement of surprise at the paucity of pyxides. So *Kastri*, 84; Hallager 2000, 153. At Kavousi, the Kastro produced no pyxides (Mook, personal communication) and there were few at Vronda (Day *et al.* forthcoming).
176 Seiradaki, 18.
177 Hägg 1990; Mersereau 1993.
178 Seiradaki, 27, n. 59; Mersereau 1993, 35.
179 Seiradaki, 18, 28.
180 Mersereau, 6–8.
181 Petrakis 2006, 185.
182 Seiradaki, 28; Petrakis 2006, 188.
183 It is true, however, that the goddess figures were fired in such vaulted kilns, such as the one at Kavousi–*Vronda*; see Day, Coulson and Gesell 1989, 104–5. It is interesting to note that the kiln at Vronda is on the outskirts of the community, but quite close to the shrine. At least one cylindrical stand fragment was found within the kiln, and this was misfired, so

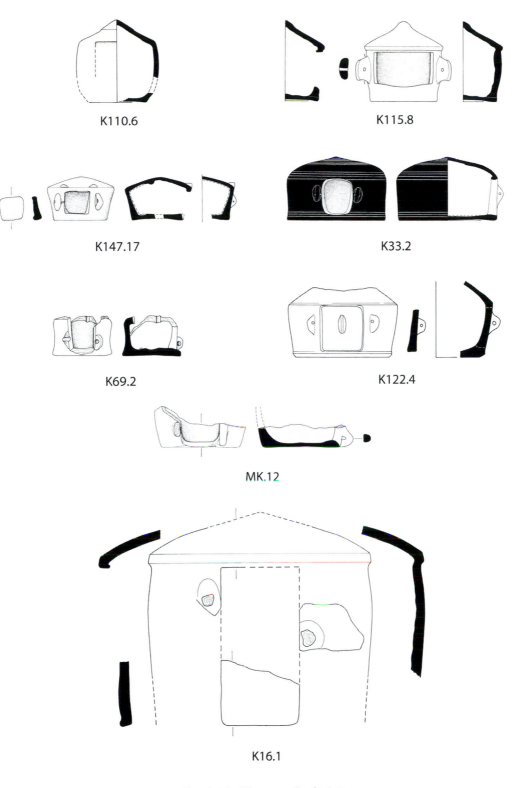

K110.6

K115.8

K147.17

K33.2

K69.2

K122.4

MK.12

K16.1

Fig. 9.16. Hut urns. Scale 1:4.

The function of the hut urns has been hotly debated, and there is little new evidence to add to the discussion here. Mersereau thought that they were household cult objects connected to the worship of the goddess with upraised arms, because of the two later SM and PG models with figures of the goddesses within, but Hallager has challenged that idea for LM IIIC, it is quite likely that the cult equipment was produced at the site and in this particular kiln (as also suggested by the use of mostly local fabrics). If, as Hallager suggests (2009, 119–20), the hut urns are thought of as housing guardian spirits of a workshop, then it is possible that these hut urns could belong to potters.

suggesting that hut urns might have functioned as 'spirit houses' to house the guardian spirits of a household or workshop.[184] Petrakis has used the similarity in form to tholos tombs to suggest that hut urns have an explicit connection with death, perhaps representing the tomb type in which the ancestors of the kin group were buried.[185] At Karphi hut urns are not widespread, a fact which suggests that whatever their use, hut urns were not part of the normal domestic assemblages of the houses. On the other hand, they were not found in any identifiable specialised contexts. Hut urns are totally lacking from the Temple, and they were not found in any room that can be identified as related to the worship of the goddess with upraised arms. The largest hut urn came from K 16, a room that almost certainly was dedicated to the worship of the goddess at some point in its history, as fragments of goddesses and attendant ritual equipment were found in the vicinity; it is not clear, however, if the hut urn and the cult equipment were in use at the same time. No hut urns were found or identified in K 116, which was another shrine of the goddess. No examples were found in either rooms with altars or snake tubes (K57, K 58), nor in the room with the two rhyta (K 27). The hut urn from K 115 may have a religious connection, as human and animal figurines were found in the deposit in the next room (K 106), and similarly the hut urn from K 69 may have a connection with the animal figurines found next door in K 85 and K 87. If hut urns have a religious connection, it is not with the shrines of the goddess with upraised arms, but with smaller and perhaps less formal religious observances that involved animal figurines. At least three of the hut urns were burned to a greater or lesser degree (**K69.2**, **K110.6**, **MK.12**), but none of them shows the kind of burning associated with cooking; they may have contained small oil lamps or had lamps placed next to them. All in all, there is little in the shape and their contexts to suggest a single function for hut urns.

Stirrup jar (FIG. 9.17–9.18)

Stirrup jars occur in abundance at Karphi, both the small, fine, decorated variety (FIG. 9.17) and the large coarse transport or storage stirrup jars (FIG. 9.18). Stirrup jars are among the most common fine closed shapes, both in the settlement and in the tombs. They are also among the most easily recognisable. They occur in all sizes and in all fabrics. Basically there are three types: small fine, decorated stirrup jars (11–20 in height), medium-sized stirrup jars (20–30 in height) in coarse or medium-coarse fabrics, and large coarse stirrup jars (over 30 in height) used primarily for storage and/or transport; all sizes exist in fine fabrics, but the small stirrup jars are confined to fine wares. Seiradaki defined eight different types of stirrup jar, of which five are found in fine wares (Types 1, 2, 3, 4, and 7); Types 5, 6, and 8 are in medium-coarse or coarse fabrics.

Nearly all examples of fine stirrup jars at Karphi were manufactured using a technique recognised as diagnostic of LM IIIC.[186] The base and body of the vessel were thrown but the top with the false spout was made separately as a disc that was then added on to the body with a ridge of clay on the interior to strengthen the join between the two. Two features thought to be typical of later LM IIIC stirrup jars are not common on the Karphi examples. One is the cone top of the false spout, which is seen by Kanta as a feature that is typical of the mature LM IIIC period.[187] Only one stirrup jar from the settlement has a cone on the top, albeit a small one (**K110.9**), and only a single example from the tombs (**M3.1**). A stirrup jar that probably comes from the Ta Mnemata tombs but was unlabelled (**K.29**) also has a cone on top. This feature probably belongs, as Hallager has suggested, to advanced IIIC through SM.[188] The other feature often used as a chronological marker is the air hole close to the neck or handles.[189] None of the stirrup jars from the settlement show this feature, and only two from the tombs (**M4.5**, **M11.4**). The two examples from the tombs date to late LM IIIC (**M4.5**) or SM (**M11.4**), supporting Mountjoy's suggestion that this is a late feature.

Of the types of fine stirrup jars, all of the illustrated examples in the publication are from the tombs, except for Type 7, which only occurs in a single example from the settlement (**K47.2**). The most common shape in both settlement and tombs is Type 2, of which there are numerous examples (FIG. 9.17); the Type 2 stirrup jar has a globular body and ring base. The Type 1 vessel illustrated in Seiradaki was not located, and no certain examples have been found of the shape. Type 3 was confined to a single vessel (**M4.5**), and its chief distinguishing feature was the air hole behind the false spout. Type 4 is short (**M3.1**), with a slight knob on its false spout. Seiradaki's Types 3 and 4 both have larger spouts than those on Types 1 and 2, and often these spouts are angled back to touch the false spout (**M3.1**, **M4.5**, **M11.4**, **K.29**); only one example of a stirrup jar from the settlement shows this feature (**K110.9**), and it also has the knob on top of the false spout, an indication of later date. The pulled-back large spout may thus be another late feature.

---

184   Hallager 2009, 119–20.
185   Petrakis 2006, 204.
186   Popham 1965, 320. The same feature is found in Khania; see Hallager 2000, 144, although she also finds examples from late LM IIIB:2 there. It can also be seen on a stirrup jar from Kastri; see *Kastri*, 289, fig. 10e (KP 26).
187   Kanta 1980, 247; see also Popham 1965, 320, who thinks it is diagnostic of LM IIIC in all phases, and Hallager 2007, 190, who thinks it comes in late in LM IIIC early.
188   Hallager 2000, 146.
189   Mountjoy (2007, 223) sees the airhole as a feature of SM.

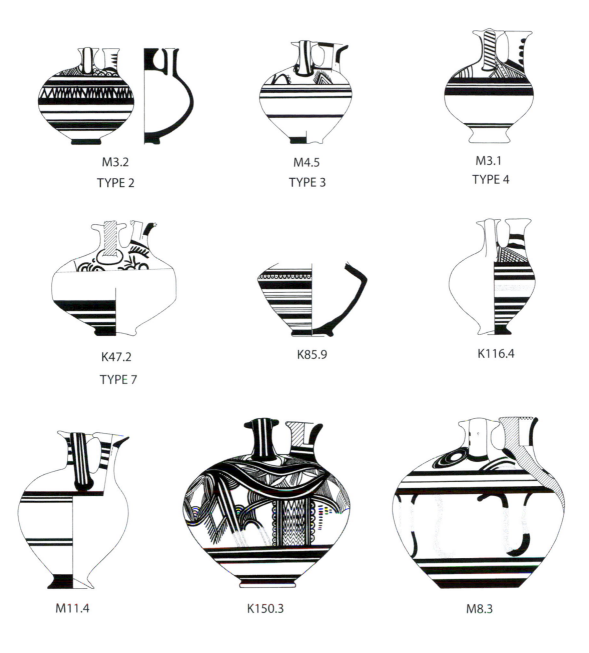

Fig. 9.17. Fine stirrup jars. Scale 1:4.

The straight-sided or carinated stirrup jar (Type 7) is most unusual and exists only in a single example (**K47.2**), although Seiradaki mentions another from K 80. As Kanta observed, the straight-sided stirrup jar is found from LM IIIA on, but is common in LM IIIC;[190] a similar stirrup jar was also found at Khamalevri of early LM IIIC date.[191] An unusual type with angular sides (**K85.9**) finds a parallel at Kritsa of LM IIIB date.[192]

The decoration of the stirrup jars is elaborate. In general, the stirrup jars have bands on the lower body (many small bands, groups of larger bands enclosing small bands, large and small bands in various arrangements).[193] Those with many small lines seem to belong in very early LM IIIC, while those with groups of lines and bands in careful patterns seem to be later,

but earlier than those with broader bands or bands in no pattern. The main decorative field is usually confined to the shoulder or to the shoulder and upper body, although on a few examples there is a secondary field between bands on the middle of the body (**K44.4**, **K85.9**, **K149.18**, **M3.2**), with simple designs of wavy lines, strokes, dotted scallops, and zigzag. This secondary decoration of the sides of stirrup jars is thought to be

---

190 Kanta 1980, 248.
191 Andreadaki-Vlasaki and Papadopoulou 2005, 372, fig. 32.
192 Kanta 1980, 248, fig. 125.3.
193 Mountjoy *RMDP*, 1044 suggests that the use of groups of narrow lines between broad bands is a distinctly Minoan feature.

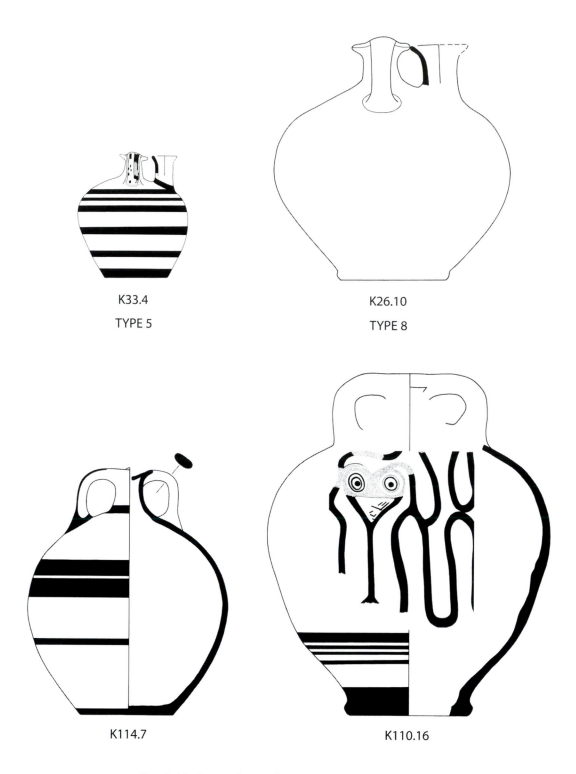

K33.4
TYPE 5

K26.10
TYPE 8

K114.7

K110.16

Fig. 9.18. Large fine and coarse stirrup jars. Scale 1:6.

highly unusual, but it does appear on Mycenaean stirrup jars from LH IIIB1 onwards and there are rare examples on Crete from LM IIIB or early LM IIIC.[194]

Decorative motifs are varied, and most vessels also show filler motifs of fringes, arcs, scallops, and strokes. Very common are half medallions, usually three or four of them, with their rounded edges at the top. These are commonly filled with ovals that are hatched with straight (**K110.9**, **K113.2**) or wavy (**K115.9**, **K121.10**)

lines, sometimes dotted so that they look like fishes (**K38.6**, **M16.4**). The triangular space below can be filled with bulbs and filler (**K110.9**), multiple triangles (**K121.10**), or other motifs. Sometimes the top area of the stirrup jar is filled with crosshatched triangles,

---

194   See Hallager 2000, 146 for a discussion of this feature.

either curving with the profile of the pot (**K72.2**, **K116.4**, **M14.6**), or straight and angular (**M3.1**). The more rigid straight type is found on vessels from the tombs and not in the settlement. Other motifs on stirrup jars include multiple triangles (**M11.4**, **M15.1**), fringed and filled triangles (**M4.5**, **M14.5**), fringed, cross-hatched, and dotted triangles (**K23.19**), multiple upright loops, often fringed (**K16-17.1**, **K75.11**, **K110.10**), dotted scales (**K85.9**, **M3.2**), alternating arcs (**K79-89.25**, **K47.2**), Minoan flower (**K45.6**, **K79-89.25**, **K149.19**), U-pattern (**K109.1**, **K.31**), triangles filled with arcs (**M3.2**, **M9.1**, **M14.5–6**), spirals (**K38.7**, **K125.1**), crosshatched lozenge (**K76.51**), scroll or moustache pattern (**MK.8**), and various other recti-linear and curvilinear patterns.

The exception to this definition of the decorative field can be found on a class of stirrup jars with octopus motifs that cover a large percentage of the surface. In general, these stirrup jars are larger than the ordinary ones, measuring 15.5–20.5 in height instead of the more usual 11–18. All the octopus stirrup jars are from the settlement (**K59.1**, **K83.2**, **K134.3–4**, **K147.14**, **K149.17**, **K150.3**, and possibly **K120.4** and **K109.1**), and none came from the tombs, although the stirrup jar fragment from M 8 (**M8.11**) may have octopus decoration. Three of these octopus stirrup jars are similar (**K134.3–4**, **K150.3**), with the eyes and body of the octopus below the spout, and tentacles that curve around the vessel and end in filled medallions on the back; two of these (**K134.3**, **K150.3**) have also panels of zigzags with scalloped edges and may be from the same workshop or by the same hand. **K83.2** is slightly different and has an octopus with a crosshatched topknot and fringed tentacles. Another type of octopus decoration is represented by two fragments from Mikre Koprana (**K147.14**, **K149.17**) that certainly come from the same vessel and fell on either side of the doorway between the two rooms; these portray the octopus in a more miniature style, with multiple dotted lines for tentacles. Each of these octopus stirrup jars is unique, and while parallels exist on other LM IIIC octopus stirrup jars from Crete and Rhodes, they are not particularly close.[195]

The dating of the octopus stirrup jars still remains a problem, as they seem to appear in both early and late LM IIIC deposits.[196] Of the Karphi examples, **K83.2** is closest to the early LM IIIC examples from Tourloti and Mouliana, and is probably of early date.[197] **K150.3**, **K134.3**, and **K134.4**, however, are much more formally arranged, with more rectilinear filling ornaments and the tentacles ending in filled medallions; they may date later in early LM IIIC or even belong to the middle part of LM IIIC. That so many of the octopus stirrup jars were found nearly complete on the floors of the settlement indicates that they were in use at the end of the period, although they may have been manufactured earlier. They are elaborate and beautiful vessels that probably were high-status objects and they may have

been used or displayed long after the potters who produced them were gone.

Another unusual stirrup jar, both in shape and decoration, is an example from Ta Mnemata tomb 8 (**M8.3**). This is globular, but has a wide flat base instead of the usual ring base or raised concave variety. It has a short, wide spout touching an equally short, wide false spout. Spirals decorate the shoulder, and the body has a large zone decorated with wavy line or debased octopus motif. The shape and decoration are unusual for this period, but a similar coarse example can be found in Oxford, without, however, any good date from context.[198] The Karphi example lacks the air hole in the disc that is so common on coarse examples of the shape.

The decoration of the handles and spouts also shows a good deal of variation. The handles can be barred with strokes (**K23.19**, **K38.6**, **K59.1**, **K72.2**, **K110.9-10**, **K115.9**, **K121.10**, **M3.1**, **K.29**), outlined with vertical bands (**K116.4**, **K134.3**, **K150.3**, **M3.2**, **M14.5–6**), or have a wavy band (**M4.5**), vertical bands (**K120.4**, **M11.4**), or be solid (**M4.4**, **MK.8**). Kanta suggested that the use of loops to outline the handles and spouts was less common in LM IIIC,[199] and indeed it is only found on **K110.9**. The spouts are decorated with single (**M14.5–6**) or multiple bands (**K110.9**, **K115.9**, **K116.4**, **MK.8**, **M11.4**) or with strokes (**M3.1–2**); those with bands generally look late. The top of the disc of the false spout most frequently bears spirals (**K110.9**, **K116.4**, **K121.10**, **M3.1**, **M4.5**, **M14.5–6**, **M16.4**), but also circle(s) (**K115.9**, **MK.8**, **M3.2**, **M8.3**) and arcade patterns (**K38.6**, **K59.1**, **K134.3–4**, **K150.3**), the latter found particularly on the octopus stirrup jars. One example (**M4.5**) also has a pinwheel design on the interior of the spout.

The latest stirrup jars from Karphi are from the tombs; the latest is doubtless **M11.4**, which is probably early in PG, to judge from the parallels for its shape and decoration. It has a true conical foot, an ovoid body, a pulled back spout, and an air hole, although it is missing the cone on the false spout. **K116.4** does not look as late, but certainly is the latest stirrup jar from within the settlement; the foot is not yet conical, but the body is ovoid, and the decoration while linear, still

---

195   For octopus stirrup jars, see Kanta 1980, 255–6 and *RMDP* 1045–51. The closest parallels for **K83.2** are the Kritsa stirrup jar (Kanta 1980, fig. 136.1) and the one from Myrsini (Kanta 1980, fig. 137.2). Elements of decoration found on **K34.3** and **K150.3** find parallels on Minoan jars found at Ialysos; for the use of strokes as filler on the lower part, cf. *RMDP*, pl. 8e, f; for the medallions, cf. *RMDP*, pl. 8b. Paschalidis 2009 publishes several from Tourloti, where they are generally thought to be early LM IIIC.

196   D'Agata 2007, 97. See also Paschalides 2009, 23, n. 207 for a discussion of the dating.

197   Paschalides 2009, 30–6, figs. 36, 52–3, 57, 58.

198   Catling 1968, 115–6, fig. 7.23.

199   Kanta 1980, 257.

curves to fit the space available. **M3.1** may also be late, since it has a rather high foot and a cone on top of the false spout. All the others look LM IIIC. Although stirrup jars occur in both burial and settlement contexts, a greater percentage of the tomb pottery consists of stirrup jars than is the case in the settlement; of the 65 catalogued pots from the graves, 16 are stirrup jars (25%). The stirrup jar seems to have been a major grave offering, whether because of the intrinsic value of the vessel itself or for its contents.

There are two fine stirrup jars that do not fit into the category of small stirrup jars, **K114.7** and **K147.15**. These large stirrup jars (H. 32 and 39) are similar to an example from Khania, which on the basis of the clay analysis is thought to have been imported there from Knossos.[200] The shape of **K147.15** from Karphi is similar, but is squatter and more biconical; the decoration is too worn to determine. It may be an import in Karphi, but it has been so badly burned that it is difficult to determine. **K114.7** is more ovoid in shape, but not as globular as the Khania example; it also has a similar concave top to the false spout. Both Karphi examples are pierced in the centre of the hollow false spout, a feature that is common on coarse stirrup jars.

All of the medium-coarse stirrup jars seem also to be medium in size, although many are simply fragments. Some were decorated, but others were not. They seem to be squat and globular in shape, with wide, flat bases (**K139.1**, **K.36**). Both of the nearly complete examples have large but short spouts and false spouts, and the false spout on one example (**K70.1**) is concave and pierced. The shapes and fabrics are much like those found in coarse wares; the major difference is in the frequency or size of the inclusions. **K23.23** had painted decoration on a creamy slip, but not much was preserved, and all that can be said is that there were arcs used as filler in curvilinear triangles. Several body fragments of medium-coarse fabrics with debased octopus or wavy line decoration were found, and these may well come from stirrup jars (**K23.24**, **K31.13**, **K77.3**, **K101.10**).

Coarse stirrup jars were common (FIG. 9.18). Three of Seiradaki's types are found almost exclusively in coarse fabrics: Types 5, 6, and 8. They tend to be medium-sized (20–30 in height) or large (30–55 in height), although there is one small example (**K.45**) with a height of 16. Coarse stirrup jars tend to have wide flat bases, and be globular or ovoid in shape; only the large stirrup jar from K 26 (**K26.10**) has a raised base. Both the spouts and the false spouts of coarse stirrup jars are short and wide, and the spouts are often tilted to touch or nearly touch the false spouts. Where the false spouts are preserved, they are concave on top, hollow, and pierced through the middle (**K1.13**, **K26.10**, **K33.4**, **K70.1**, **K85.13**, **K.45–46**); Type 6, of which no example was found, had a solid false spout.

Most of the stirrup jars are plain, but a few are decorated. Stirrup jar **K33.4** has painted decoration of

bands, with crude spirals on the shoulder. The very large storage stirrup jar **K110.16** is decorated with an octopus, and the tentacles go around the vessel in two rows. Probably similar to this vessel are the numerous coarse fragments bearing large wavy bands, possibly the tentacles of debased octopods (**K11.11**, **K40–41.1**, **K45.9**, **K54.6**, **K75.14–15**, **K76.54–55**, **K77.4–5**, **K79–89.30**, **K149.22**). **K85.13** has incised decoration: vertical and oblique strokes on the handles, incisions around the edge of the false spout. **K26.10** is monochrome-painted.

Coarse stirrup jars come in a variety of fabrics, like many of the other coarse wares; those tested petrographically, however, are most often in flysch fabrics (Fabric groups 3 and 4) and may not be local.

The evidence from Karphi for the most part seems to support the idea that coarse octopus stirrup jars were popular in the early phases of the settlement's use, but declined toward the end; most of the fragments come from early deposits under streets and courts. The single exception is the nearly complete stirrup jar from K 110, which was certainly being used just before Karphi was abandoned.

Coarse stirrup jars are well known in LM IIIC sites on Crete, and they come primarily from early LM IIIC contexts, such as Khania, Kastri, and Phase I at Kavousi–*Kastro*.[201] Two coarse octopus stirrup jars were found at Kavousi–*Vronda*, but neither comes from a secure late LM IIIC context, and they may be from the earlier LM IIIC period.[202]

Thelastron (FIG. 9.19)

Seiradaki distinguished four different types of side-spouted jugs, represented by only 15 examples in the settlement and five in the tombs.[203] Types 1 and 2 have basket handles. Type 1 is in medium-coarse fabric and has an offset base; it was said to be more common than Type 2. The Type 2 thelastron illustrated is in coarse ware and badly warped from misfiring; no other like it appears in the Karphi assemblages. Types 3 and 4 were rare; Type 3 has a vertical handle opposite the spout, while Type 4 has no handle. Seven nearly complete examples are preserved from the settlement and five from the tombs. Many of the examples are missing the handles, making it difficult to distinguish their types. Those of Type 1 include **K1.7** and **K23.18**, while **K11.6** is the only example of Type 2. **K1.4** and **M11.3** are of Type 3 and **M8.12** and **M17.6** seem to be of Type 4;

200 *Khania II*, 41, 163, pl. 50.71-P 0736/0763/0779/77-P 0719.
201 *Khania II*, pl. 50.71-P 0736/0763/0779/77-P 0719, thought to be an import into Khania; *Kastri*, fig. 15.P24, fig. 16.P6; Mook and Coulson 1997, 319–20, figs. 15, 17.36–7 (Kavousi–*Kastro*).
202 Gesell, Coulson and Day 1991, 151, fig. 3.2; Day 2005, 436.
203 Seiradaki, 14–6, fig. 10.

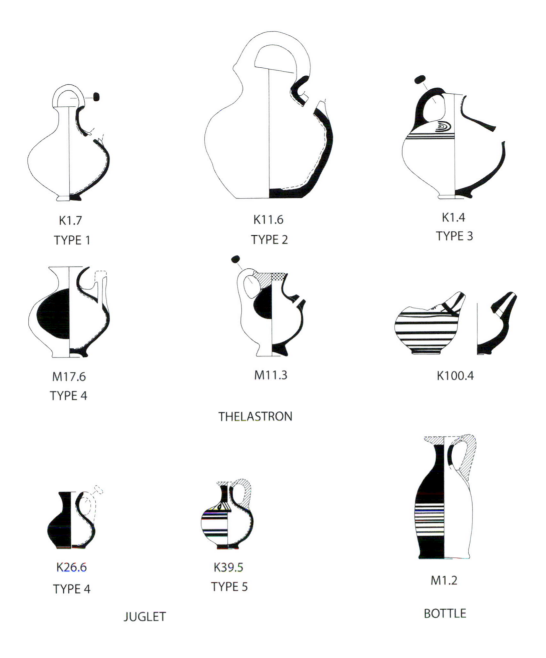

Fig. 9.19. Thelastron, juglets, and bottle. Scale 1:4.

K100.4, **K132.4**, **M12.1**, **M17.5**, and **K.28** have no rim or handles preserved, and it is difficult to determine to which class they belong.

At least two of the thelastra come from the Temple and are misfired blue ware, one fine (**K1.4**), the other medium-coarse (**K1.7**); the others are ordinary fine wares, except for **K11.6**, which is coarse. This vessel is larger than usual; it is misfired into blue ware, and is very warped. While coarse thelastra are even less common than the fine examples, a parallel can be found at Kavousi–*Vronda* of late LM IIIC date.[204]

Most of the finer examples from the settlement have small raised concave bases; **K1.4** has quite a high foot. The thelastra from the tombs all have raised, concave feet; **M17.6** has a real ring base, and **M11.3** has a conical foot. The tombs from which the last two come contain later pottery that is probably PG, and these may belong to the same date. All thelastra have globular bodies, with the spouts set at an angle on the side. The necks are narrow, like juglets, and the rims flare out to a greater or lesser degree.

Thelastra are simply decorated, most commonly with blob decoration, which appears on the examples from the tombs (**M11.3**, **M17.5–6**); one example has a wavy line above bands (**M12.1**), and another is uncertain (**M8.12**). Thelastra from the settlement are decorated

---

204 Day, Coulson and Gesell 1986, 379 and fig. 12.35.

with bands (**K100.4**), monochrome paint (**K23.18**), and in one instance a pattern of horizontal multiple loops (**K1.4**). Others may have been plain, but they are too worn to be certain (**K1.7**, **K132.4**, **K.28**).

The thelastron is often called a feeding bottle, but its precise function is uncertain. The shape is common enough in LM III, and the shape with more globular body and narrow neck, without a rivet at the back of the handle is typical of LM IIIC.[205] It is interesting that the shape appears in both tombs and settlement, but like stirrup jars, there are proportionally more thelastra in the tombs, and the form seems to continue into the later periods in cemetery assemblages.[206]

Juglet (FIG. 9.19)

Very small jugs are treated as a separate category, since they are so different in size and hence probably in function from their larger counterparts. A juglet is any one-handled jug less than 10 in height, with a rim diameter between 2.5–4. Seiradaki includes two types of juglet in her typology for one-handled jugs: Types 4 and 5.[207] Type 4 has a slightly raised base and a wide short neck, while Type 5 has a higher base, is more globular, and has a taller narrower neck, rather like the later lekythos shape; the example illustrated by Seiradaki is said to be from K 89, but no jug from this location was found, and the juglet from K 39 looks much like the illustrated vessel. There are seven nearly complete examples of the juglet from the settlement (**K7.2**, **K22.5**, **K26.6**, **K39.5**, **K85.7**, **K96.2**, **K.25–26**). Three juglets came from the tombs, two from Ta Mnemata (**M14.3–4**), and one from Atsividhero (**A1.2**). Most of these resemble Seiradaki's Type 4, but a few seem to be of Type 5 (**K39.5**, **M14.3**, **A1.2**, **K.25**). These small juglets generally have raised concave bases; the exceptions are **K26.6**, which has a flat concave base and **K.26**, **K51.2**, and **M14.3**, all of which have raised bases that are flat on the bottom. The raised feet can be very low (**K.25**) or high (**K96.2**, **A1.2**). The decoration on juglets is simple; three examples are monochrome (**K26.6**, **K85.7**, **M14.3**), one has blob decoration (**K22.5**), and one has a teardrop between oblique lines above bands (**K39.5**). The others appear to be plain (**K7.2**, **K50.1**, **K51.2**, **K.25**), but given their surface preservation, it is not certain. The plain juglets are similar in shape to the decorated ones and seem to be close to Type 5, although two of them lack rims.

There are two examples of miniature juglets in medium-coarse fabrics (**K61.13**, **K87.2**), one of them possibly a Type 4, the other more carinated and of no known type. Both are squat, with flat bases, and neither has its rim or handle preserved. **K61.13** is probably similar to juglet **K26.6**.

Juglets have been found in LM IIIC contexts at Khania, although they are not common,[208] and they also exist at Kavousi–*Kastro* in Phase II.[209] Although juglets began on the mainland early in LH IIIC,[210] they became popular again in the Late Geometric and Early Orienta-

lising Periods, where they were used as grave offerings. On Crete the juglet appeared in LM IIIB late and continued into IIIC.[211] The juglet **K39.5** looks very much like these later examples in shape and decoration, but it is probably LM IIIC.

Bottle (FIG. 9.19)

There is a single example of this shape, which also might be termed a lekythos, and it comes from one of the Ta Mnemata tombs (**M1.2**). It is a tall, cylindrical shape, with a wide, slightly concave raised base and a narrow neck widening to a very flared rim (restored) with a single vertical handle from rim to shoulder. The vessel is decorated with multiple narrow bands on the lower body, with the base, shoulder, and neck in black monochrome paint. This is clearly not a Minoan shape, and there are no Bronze Age parallels; it seems to be a Cypriote development. The shape is thought to have been introduced into Crete from Cyprus in the early Iron Age, and the closest parallel is an example from Athens dating to the transition from Sub-Mycenaean to PG.[212] The bottle seems to be used primarily as a grave offering, and is only found in tombs in Cyprus, Crete, and the mainland. It should date to SM or EPG.

Jug (FIG. 9.20–21)

One-handled jugs are very common in the settlement at Karphi. Jugs are more plentiful and more varied than amphoras, which show the same shapes but have two handles; it is often difficult to distinguish jugs from amphoras. One to three jugs were found in every room; in a few cases (K 121, K 23) four or more jugs were found in the same room. These jugs come in fine, medium-coarse, and coarse fabrics, and can be decorated or left plain.

Seiradaki distinguished 11 types of jugs (FIG. 9.20).[213] Types 1, 6, and 7 are found chiefly in fine wares, while Types 3, 9, and 11 are primarily in medium-coarse and coarse fabrics. Type 2 is found only in a single example that is medium-coarse. Type 8 is a

---

205 Kanta 1960, 281; Hallager 2000, 154.

206 In addition to the examples mentioned in west Crete by Hallager, there are thelastra also in the tombs in the Knossos area. The North Cemetery produced a close parallel for **M17.5** of SM date: Coldstream and Catling 1996, 302, pl. 165.121.7. Parallels for both **M17.6** and **M11.3** were found at Ayios Ioannis of EPG date (Boardman 1960, pl. 37 IV.5 and 6).

207 Seiradaki, 15, fig. 9.

208 Hallager 2000, 151–2.

209 Mook and Coulson 1997, 355–6, fig. 25.85.

210 Mountjoy 1986, 143 calls the shape a lekythos.

211 Hallager 2007, 190; the narrow-necked variety like **K39.5**, however, she called a lekythos and saw it as a new shape in LM IIIC (Hallager 2007, 192).

212 Desborough 1964, 27–8, pl. 16d.

213 Seiradaki, 14–5, fig. 9.

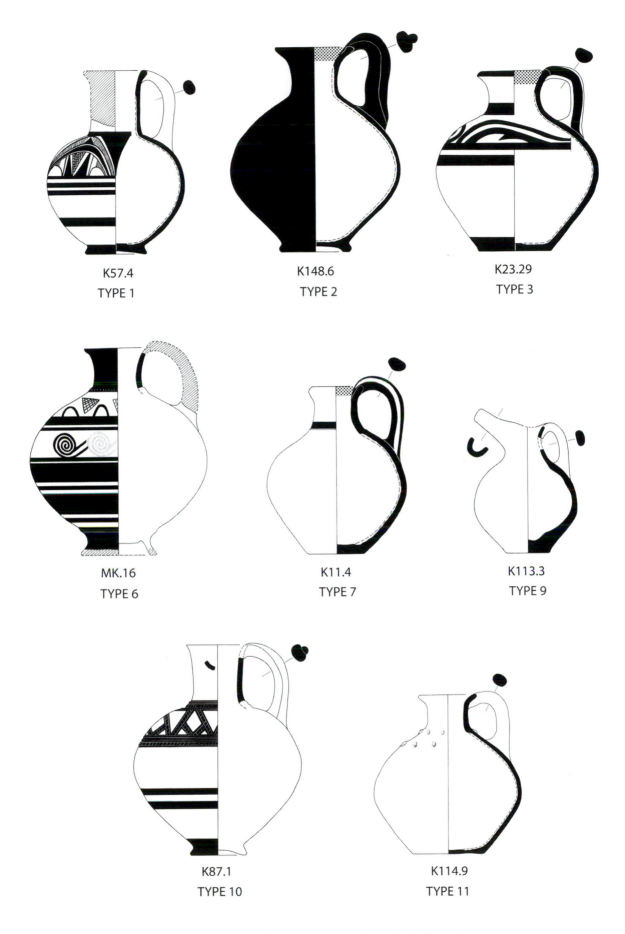

K57.4
TYPE 1

K148.6
TYPE 2

K23.29
TYPE 3

MK.16
TYPE 6

K11.4
TYPE 7

K113.3
TYPE 9

K87.1
TYPE 10

K114.9
TYPE 11

Fig. 9.20. Jugs. Scale 1:4 unless otherwise indicated.

cooking jug, and it is treated below (pp. 318–19). Types 4 and 5 are juglets and have been discussed above (p. 296). There is only a single example each of Types 6 and 10. Type 9 is a spouted jug with a thickening or 'wattle' below the spout. No examples are extant of this type with the 'wattle', but there are several spouted jugs that might be placed in this category (**K113.3**, **K107.6**). The majority of fine jugs fall into three of Seiradaki's types: 1, 3, and 7. All these jugs are cylindrical-necked and wide-mouthed; trefoil mouthed jugs are rare, and none are known in fine wares.

Jugs come in small and large varieties. The small jugs are primarily in fine wares, and they range from 12–14 in height, with rim diameters of 4.7–7 (FIG. 9.21). Few of them have both rim and base preserved. **K31.11** has a ring base. **K110.8** and **K121.9** have tall cylindrical necks with flaring rims. **K12.31**, **K17.19**, and **K79-89.27** all have shorter necks with more flaring rims that look rather like stirrup jar spouts. **K.27** is only a body sherd. The small jugs have simple decoration: wavy lines on the shoulder (**K31.11**, **K110.8**) or on the neck (**K79-89.27**, **K121.9**). **K.27** has alternating broad and narrow bands on the lower body and an oblique solid leaf on the shoulder. The neck of **K17.19** has a band, and the top of **K12.31** is monochrome. The interior can have a band (**K12.31**, **K79-89.27**, **K110.8**, **K121.9**) or a reserved band (**K17.19**); **K110.8** has strokes on top of the rim.

Large cylindrical-necked jugs are more common (FIG. 9.20–21). These are 17.7–22.3 in height, with rim diameters of 6.5–12.2. One of these (**K57.4**) is of Type 1, one of Type 3 (**K23.29**), one of Type 6 (**MK.16**), one of Type 10 (**K87.1**), and two are of Type 7 (**K11.4**, **K107.5**). **K134.5** is a fine version of Type 11. Two jugs do not fall into Seiradaki's types. **K11.5** has a flat base, ovoid body, and tall neck with a flaring rim; it resembles Type 7, but with a wider neck and less globular body. **K3.8** is also unusual; it has a raised concave base, a globular-biconical body, and a very narrow neck (rim diameter 4.5). This vessel was constructed rather like the stirrup jars, with the top thrown separately and added on as a disc, with a ridge of clay inside at the attachment. Other fine jugs are too fragmentary to determine a type (**K3.7**, **K11.7**, **K23.20**, **K23.69**, **K79-89.26**, **K107.7–8**, **K17.7**, **V.1**, **K.44**). Bases are either raised or flat, and ring bases are not uncommon (**K80.5**, **K148.6**, **MK.16**). The bodies are generally globular, and necks cylindrical; sometimes there is a ridge at the juncture of the neck and body, perhaps to strengthen the joint between the neck and body (**K3.8**, **K11.4–5**, **K87.1**, **K107.5**, **K107.7**, **K115.10**, **K116.6**, **MK.16**),[214] and often this ridge is decorated with incisions or is punctuated. Rims are usually simple and flaring; one example (**K148.6**) has a concave depression around the interior of the rim. Handles show a variety of treatments; they can be round or elliptical. At least three jugs have braided handles (**K11.7**, **K107.5**, **K.44**), one is incised with chevrons (**K80.5**), and two have an added coil of clay down the centre (**K87.1**, **K148.6**). One of the most elaborate handles is that on **K107.5** with its twisted coil of clay down the centre; three holes are pierced at the lower attachment, perhaps for more even firing. A similar handle, even with the three holes at the base, can be found on an Archaic jug from Atsalenio at Knossos.[215] Finally, a jug from Ta Mnemata Tomb 8 (**M8.13**) has an unusual ridged handle with painted oblique strokes that looks like a survival from the Neopalatial period.

Large jugs are elaborately or simply decorated. The main field of decoration is the shoulder, with bands on the lower body; a secondary field is the neck. Decoration is most often painted, but on one unusual vase (**K87.1**) there is also incised decoration of beaded triangles with oblique beaded strokes in the lower corners. This piece finds parallels at Kato Symi,[216] Afrati,[217] and Enkomi on Cyprus;[218] in most of these cases, the jugs were found in a context that implied ritual activities.[219] Jug **K57.4** has an elaborate decoration of a half medallion with strokes or solid fillers, and in the centre a pendent crosshatched triangle with two upright solid triangles, loops and filler arcs. Jug **MK.16** has running spirals with double tangents on the body and loops alternating with crosshatched triangles on the shoulder. **K80.5** has a whorl shell with dots. **K23.29** has a curvilinear design of possible spirals with long tails. Other jugs have simpler decoration of necklace (**K23.20**) or curvilinear pattern (**K11.5**). A number of vessels are monochrome (**K107.5**, **K107.7**). One spouted jug has a quirk on the neck (**K107.6**). Finally, there is one jug from the Vitzelovrysis Spring area that has compass-drawn concentric semicircles on the shoulder (**V.1**), certainly a fragment of PG date, possibly from the mainland. The lower body is painted with bands, generally one to three at the middle, and one at the base; sometimes there is another band on the lower body, or several bands, either wide bands alternating with narrow bands (**MK.16**) or narrow bands (**K80.5**). There are also generally bands at the

---

214 As Seiradaki, 13, suggests for amphoras.

215 Kourou and Karetsou 1998, 247, fig. 12.

216 Kanta 1991, 497, fig. 31.

217 Stampolides and Karetsou 1998, 74.40; Kanta and Karetsou 1998, 165, fig. 9.

218 Kanta 1991, 497, fig. 31 (Kato Symi); Stampolides and Karetsou 1998, 74.40; Kanta and Karetsou 1998, 165, fig. 9 (Afrati); Dikaios 1969, pl. 106.5; Pilides 1997, 210, fig. 1; Stampolides and Karetsou 1998, 74 no. 39 (Enkomi). This vessel is seen as an import into Cyprus (Mountjoy 2005, 193–4, fig. 35), and since there are good parallels on Crete, it is likely that the oinochoe came from there.

219 The Enkomi jug was found in association with a shrine of the Horned God (Pilides 1997, 209), the Symi jug was found in a religious site, and the K 87 example was in association with the large terracotta horse figurine.

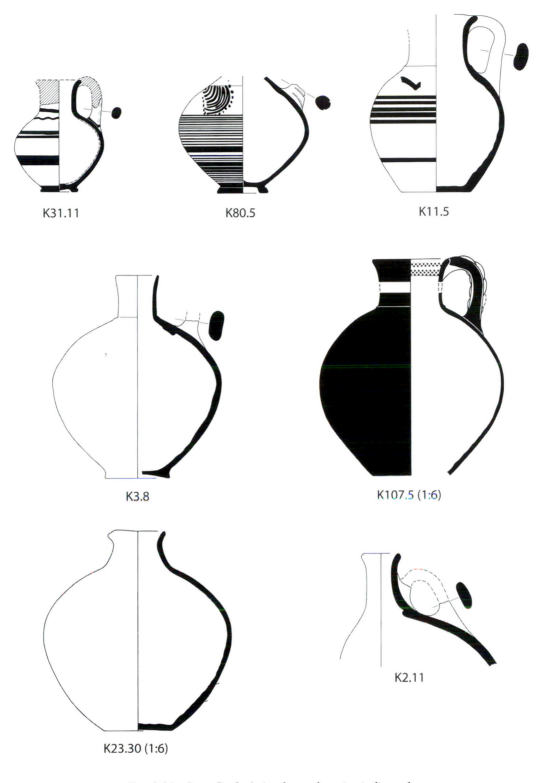

K31.11   K80.5   K11.5

K3.8   K107.5 (1:6)

K23.30 (1:6)   K2.11

Fig. 9.21. Jugs. Scale 1:4 unless otherwise indicated.

neck attachment and at the rim, and a band or bands on the interior of the rim. Handles are decorated with bands (**K11.4**, **K23.29**, **K57.4**) or wavy line (**K11.5**).

Jugs are also found in plain wares, usually the larger varieties. There is only one example of a small jug that is plain (**K134.5**), and this is of Type 11, with knobs on the shoulder, like those in medium-coarse and coarse wares. **K113.3** is also apparently plain, and is unusual

in that it is spouted; it has a small flat base and a globular biconical body and cylindrical neck with flaring rim. **K115.10** is of Type 7, but with a slightly concave rim. A handle with a twisted rope in the centre (**K.44**) from an unknown context may also come from a plain jug.

There are only six jugs in medium-coarse wares. One is painted with concentric circles on the shoulders (**K115.12**). It most closely resembles Type 3, but has a low ring base and a shorter neck. **K114.9** also is decorated, but with two rows of knobs. It is of Seiradaki's Type 11. **K148.6** is Seiradaki's Type 2, and it is monochrome-painted. **K116.6** is plain and has a ridge at the base of the neck. **K.35** is similar to the group of small coarse jugs from K3 (**K3.12–13**). Finally, there is a smaller jug of blue ware (**K23.22**) with impressed circles on the middle of the body; this has a raised concave base and is very squat.

Many large cylindrical-mouthed jugs exist in coarse wares. One is Seiradaki's Type 3 (**K149.23**) with a ridge at the base of the neck, one is of Type 7 (**K44.10**), two are of Type 11, one with knobs (**K114.9**), the other without (**K50.2**). One is of the narrow-necked variety (**K115.14**), another is a wider-mouthed type with a squat, almost biconical, body (**K80.9**). There are also smaller jugs, but since many have lost their necks, their identification is tentative. All of the probable small jugs have flat bases, sometimes slightly concave underneath, and remains of a single handle on the shoulder (**K3.12–13, K23.28**). **K12.8** may come from a jug, but it certainly dates to after the abandonment of the settlement; its closest parallels are Geometric or later.[220]

Finally, there are two jugs with trefoil mouths. One is a very large specimen (**K23.30**) that has a pinched-out rim and a handle very low on the body of the vessel; it may be a hydria, although no vertical handle is preserved. The other is a small version with a true trefoil mouth from one of the Ta Mnemata graves (**M16.5**); it is decorated with monochrome paint. There are no close parallels for this shape, and the trefoil mouth is highly unusual at Karphi, although elsewhere on Crete it appears as early as LM IIIA:2.[221] This may be a late example, as it occurs with a flask (**M16.2**) that dates to SM; the jug may be SM or PG.

Jugs are the basic pouring vessels for the site, and there may be functional differences among the various types. There are few spouted jugs of any type, so there seems to have been little need for careful control of the flow of the liquid. Small jugs and juglets would probably have served for liquids used in smaller quantities, like oil or vinegar. The larger jugs with cylindrical mouths may have been used for water and wine that would have been poured in some quantity. Fine decorated jugs probably functioned as tableware, while the plain fine jugs and the coarse jugs would have been for everyday use of storing water (as in a modern stamnos) or pouring into other vessels.

Amphora (FIG. 9.22)

Amphoras are similar to jugs but have two handles rather than one; if both handles are not preserved, they are difficult to distinguish from jugs. They are not as common as one-handled jugs, and although they are similar in shape to jugs, their variety is not as great. As with jugs, they appear in both fine and coarse wares, and they vary in size from the miniature (**K23.17**), with an estimated rim diameter of 2.85, to the oversize

(**K70.2**), with an estimated rim diameter of 20. Seiradaki distinguished five types.[222] Types 1 and 2 were found in fine wares, while Types 3–5 were primarily in coarse fabrics. Type 1 is represented only in a single example (**K149.20**), and this may be the one published in the typological chart as from K 148; it is close to the Type 1 jug in shape. Type 2 is a miniature amphora from K 23 (**K23.17**). A fine amphora of Type 3 was mentioned in the notebook from K 108. A number of fine examples belong to none of these categories, but have narrower necks and may better be identified as flasks (see below, p. 302). **K149.20** has a ring base, a globular body, and a wide neck. It is decorated on the shoulder zone with a panel of crosshatching with tailed spirals on either side; bands decorate the lower body. **K3.6** may be of the same type, but it is missing the neck, and it is difficult to tell. It has a flat base and globular body.

Fine amphoras are rare in LM IIIC deposits on Crete. The miniature amphora (**K23.17**) finds a parallel in the Kephala tomb at Knossos, probably of very late LM IIIC date.[223] Few others have been found in LM IIIC contexts. A single amphora of medium-coarse fabric comes from the Southern Houses (**K44.6**), and it appears in a misfired blue ware. Like other small amphoras or flasks, it has a rather high ring base, and the round handles run from the neck to the shoulder.

Coarse amphoras were probably used for transportation of liquids and for storage. Seiradaki's Types 3–5 are all in coarse wares, but in addition there is at least one amphora of Type 1 (**K115.15**) in coarse ware which is decorated with bands and a possible wavy line; two more were mentioned in the notebook. Another decorated amphora does not fit into any of Seiradaki's types (**K2.9**), but finds parallels at Kastri, Khalasmenos, Sybrita/Thronos, Kavousi–*Vronda*, and Kommos.[224] It has a wide flat or slightly concave base, a globular body, a narrow neck with a flaring rim and two handles that rise above the rim to the shoulder; this example is decorated with bands, but others often have a tassel ornament. Type 3 only exists in a single example from K 75, which was not located in the museum. It has a cylindrical mouth, flattened rim that is thickened outward, and a triple handle. Hallager has suggested that

220   Mook 1993, 358, fig. 98, P2 99 and P2 100 (Kavousi–*Kastro*, PG–G). See also Coldstream 1960, 162, fig. 5.31 (Geometric) and Sackett (ed). 1992, pl. 75.H3.8, pl. 79.3 (Archaic).

221   Hallager 2007, 190.

222   Seiradaki, 12–4, fig. 8.

223   Cadogan 1967, 261–2, fig. 3.3; D'Agata 2007, 117, fig. 19 categorises this vessel as SM I, while Preston 2005, 102.P82, dates it to LM IIIC (?).

224   *Kastri*, 296, fig. 16.P31, P25; Tsipopoulou 2004, 110, fig. 8.4.96-358 (Khalasmenos); D'Agata 2002, 54, fig. 5 (Sybrita/Thronos, early LM IIIC); Day *et al.* forthcoming; Watrous 1992, 82, fig. 54.1412, 1415 (Kommos, LM IIIB).

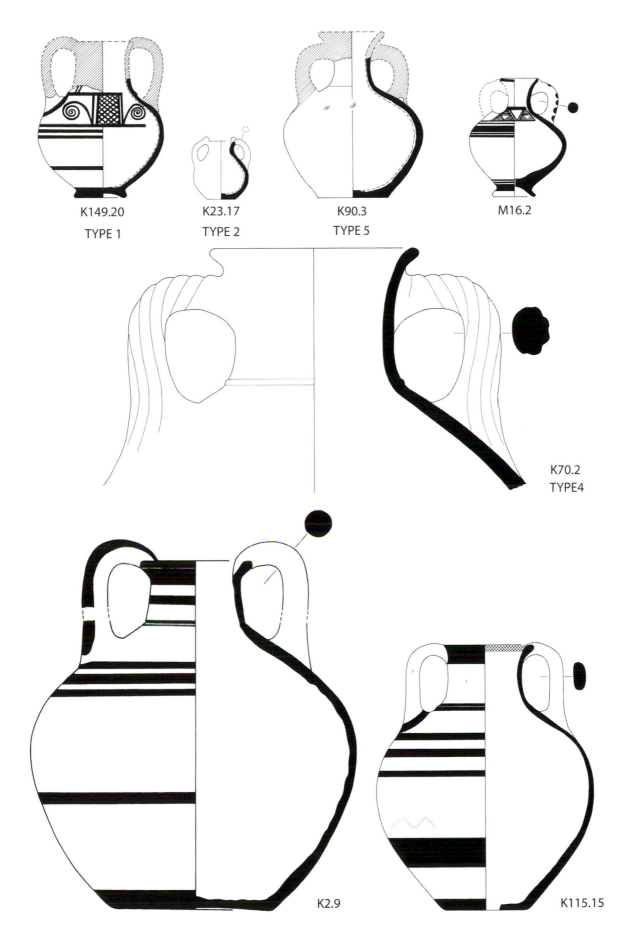

K149.20
TYPE 1

K23.17
TYPE 2

K90.3
TYPE 5

M16.2

K70.2
TYPE 4

K2.9

K115.15

Fig. 9.22. Amphoras. Scale 1:4.

this may be an amphoroid krater, rather than an amphora, on the basis of the rim, but if so, it is the only example of this shape from Karphi.[225] Type 4 is a large amphora with rope-twisted handles, and two examples were found (**K22.11**, **K70.2**); **K70.2** has painted decoration, but only three bands are preserved. D'Agata has suggested that these amphoras with rope-twisted handles should be classed with later SM amphoras, but a very close parallel exists at Kavousi–*Vronda* from a clearly late LM IIIC context.[226] Finally, there are two examples of Type 5, a coarse flat-based amphora with knobbed decoration on the shoulder (**K23.73**, **K 90.3**). Coarse jugs and amphoras with knobbed decoration seem to be particularly popular at Karphi, but do not appear so commonly on other LM IIIC sites.

Although amphoras have a long history on Crete, in LM III they become popular only in LM IIIC, and they eventually replace the coarse transport stirrup jar.[227] The shape appears in early LM IIIC levels at Khania, Kastrokephala, and Kastri, and in late LM IIIC at Kavousi–*Vronda* and Khalasmenos.[228]

Askos (FIG. 9.21)

There is a single example of this shape from Karphi, and it occurs in a coarse fabric (**K2.11**). It has a spout rather like a stirrup jar, but the profile is assymetrical; a single elliptical handle runs from neck to shoulder. As on the stirrup jars, the neck of this vessel was apparently made separately and was added to the body, with extra clay to support the joint on the interior. The vessel has knobbed decoration. The function of this shape is uncertain, but it would have been useful for pouring small amounts of liquids that were stored within in considerable quantity.

Flask (FIG. 9.22)

The flask is a rare shape on Crete, although it appears on the mainland from LH IIIA:2 on.[229] Flasks resemble small amphoras, but they have narrow necks and bear the same relation to amphoras as lekythoi do to jugs. Although the shape appeared perhaps as early as the end of LM IIIB on Crete,[230] flasks were not common in LM IIIC,[231] but were popular in SM times, particularly in graves, where they may have contained oil or perfumed oil. Some of these SM examples are so similar that they seem to have been manufactured by a single workshop,[232] like the example from Ta Mnemata (**M16.2**). It has the high conical foot and handles from rim to shoulder found on those examples from Knossos, and it is decorated in similar fashion with triangles with multiple strokes filling the angles as found there; even the use of bars on the outside of the handles is similar. There are, however, several examples from the settlement which could be classed as horizontal flasks (FS 193). Two of these are clearly decorated (**K85.8**, **K116.3**), while a third is too poorly preserved to tell, but has incised lines at the base of the neck (**K134.2**);

it also has a true ring base. **K85.8** has on the shoulder an upright outlined leaf, while **K116.3** is decorated with a panel of crosshatching, with tailed spirals on either side and filler strokes between the panel and the tail of the spiral; it is similar to the decoration of amphora **K149.20**. Bands decorate the lower part of the bodies of both. On **K85.8** there are bars on the handles, which run from the rim to the shoulder. All of these flasks from the settlement are different from **M16.2**, which has the conical foot typical of SM pottery, and they may be earlier. Another possible flask can be seen in the smaller **M16.3**.

A different type of flask was found in the Great House Shrine (**K18.1**); this may be a lentoid flask, but only part of the neck and shoulder and one handle are preserved. Unusually, it has handles that rise from the shoulder to the base of the neck. A similar handle arrangement can be found on an imported legged flask from Pseira and on a flask from Alalakh in Syria.[233] The Karphi example may be an exotic import.

Jar (FIG. 9.23)

Seiradaki defined as jars 'all vessels with more or less in-curving rims which are too small to be termed pithoi, but which seem to have been used for storage rather than pouring.'[234] Of the ten types of coarse jars distinguished by Seiradaki, some are actually other shapes. Seiradaki Type 2 is a tripod cooking pot (**K1.21**), as it has attachments for feet rather than a simple flat bottom. The type of jar it represents, however, is found: a deep jar with a collar and two (rather than the three on **K1.21**) round vertical handles on the shoulder (e.g. **K11.8**, **K27.8**, **MK.5**). Types 6, 7, and 8 were not found. Type 7, with its straight sides, looks more like a pyxis than a

---

225 Hallager 2000, 150, n. 142.
226 D'Agata 2007, 99; Day and Glowacki forthcoming (Vronda, Building E, Room E1: E1 P119).
227 Day 2005, 436.
228 Hallager 2000, 152 (Khania); Kanta and Karetsou 2003, 160, fig. 11A, D (Kastrokephala); *Kastri*, 296, fig. 16. P25, P31; Day *et al.* forthcoming (Kavousi–*Vronda*); Tsipopoulou 2004, 140. fig. 8.4.96-358 (Khalasmenos).
229 Mountjoy 1986, 80.
230 Hood, Huxley and Sandars 1958–59, 242, fig. 28 VI.A.3. Material from this tomb is said to date to the late LM IIIB:2 period, but it is clearly SM; see D'Agata 2007, 101, table 3.
231 Hallager 2000, 151, n. 150, for examples.
232 Coldstream and Catling 1996, 87–8, fig. 83.13, 14, 17; 165, fig. 117.121.1, 5. A similar example was found at Khamaizi–*Phatsi*, dated to MPG; see Tsipopoulou 1997, 476, fig. 15.4969. A flask found in the Argolid is thought to be a SM import from Crete; see *RMDP*, 193–4, fig. 60.464.
233 Betancourt 1998, 49, fig. 1 (Pseira); 51, fig. 2; Woolley 1955, 324, pl. 112.44c, (Alalakh, level IV, after 1483 to 1370 BC).
234 Seiradaki, 5.

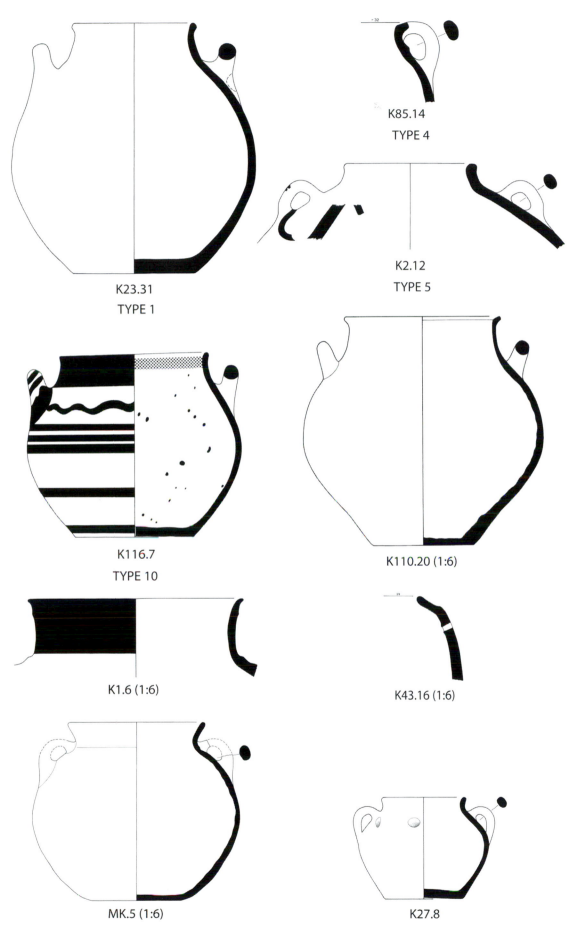

Fig. 9:23. Jars. Scale 1:4 unless otherwise indicated.

jar; Type 8 may have been a cooking dish. Type 9 is actually a larnax (**K81-82.1**). That leaves seven different types of jars in Seiradaki's typology.

Although most jars are in coarse fabrics, there are a few possible fine examples. **K1.6** has a very wide mouth (34.5), tall collar, and a ridge at the attachment of the neck; it stands out as unusual in comparison to the other jar rims and neck and may be an earlier type (LM III), although no precise parallels have been found. **K12.29** is a rim fragment that has a sharply out-turned rim with a band on the interior, showing that it is a closed shape. It has strokes on top that reach down on the exterior of the rim. **K3.9** is also of fine fabric. Although only the top is preserved, it appears to have a rather globular body, with two horizontal round handles set on the shoulder, and a short collar, like Type 5. It may have been decorated, but the surface is too coated with sediment to be certain.

There are three examples of jars in medium-coarse fabrics, and they are all decorated. One is Seiradaki's Type 10, a painted jar (**K116.7**) with a slightly concave base, rounded body, and nearly vertical rim; two round horizontal handles lie on the shoulder. The exterior is decorated with bands: two on the lower body, three just below the handle zone, and a broad band on the neck, and it has a wavy line in the handle zone; the handles are decorated with strokes. On the interior is a reserved band with painted band below, and the rest is covered with splatters. This vessel finds a close parallel in a coarse jar from K 115 (**K115.16**), and in a jar at Kastelli Pediada.[235] **K17.6** is a rim fragment from a closed shape, as it has only a band on the interior of the rim and the rest is left unpainted; the rim is too wide, however, to have been a jug and too sharply out-turned to have come from a krateriskos, so it is here identified as a jar. It has a band at the exterior rim as well as on the interior. **K12.32** is of similar shape, although the mouth is not as wide. The exterior is decorated with bands, and there is no interior decoration.

The majority of coarse examples fit into Seiradaki's Types 1, 2, or 3. Type 1 (**K7.4, K23.31, K110.20**) is a deep jar with a flat base, wide mouth, and horizontal handles on the shoulder; it can also be found in fine wares (**K3.9**).[236] Type 2 (**K11.8, K27.8, MK.5**) is a similar kind of jar, but with a more articulated collar and vertical handles on the shoulder.[237] This type also occurs in LM IIIC deposits at Kastelli Pediada.[238] The vessel representing Type 3 was not located; it has a collar with a vertical handle that rises above the rim to the shoulder. Close to Type 3 is the jar from Ta Mnemata Tomb 9 (**M9.2**); this is not as globular as the pictured example, but it has the knobbed decoration that is found on jars, jugs, and amphoras in the settlement.[239] Type 4 is similar to Type 3, but has a more flaring rim with a ridge below it (**K2.5, K22.12, K85.14**). This type is much like the pithoid jars, except that the body seems to be more rounded. Only one other fragment was recorded in the notebook, from K 71. Type 5 is rather

like Type 2 but has a taller collar and the vertical handles are set farther down on the shoulder. Only one vessel of this type was recognised in coarse ware (**K2.12**), and it was painted; another was found in K 149, according to the notebook. Type 6 is only known from the illustrated example, said to be from K 9, and the fragment was not located.[240] It has a tall vertical rim and a ridge at the attachment of the neck; the handles are round and vertical. Type 7 is an unusual cylindrical jar and may be a pyxis; none was actually found in the boxes; Seiradaki illustrated an example from K 47.[241] There were no examples of Type 8; the one published in Seiradaki was not found, but it looks as though it might have been a cooking dish. Type 9 is a larnax rim. Type 10 is represented by the example from K 115 (**K115.16**), but a medium-coarse example also came from K 116 (**K116.7**).

To these must be added several others that do not fit any of Seiradaki's types. **K43.16** is a most unusual shape, with a rounded body and a rim that seems to be turned in to accommodate a lid fitting over it, rather like some of the pyxides; it is also pierced through the body. A similar jar can be found at Kavousi–*Vronda* of LM IIIC date.[242] **K57.6** also has an in-turned rim that is rolled on top and has incisions below. Finally, **K16.2** in fabric and shape is very out of place in the Karphi assemblage. There are two nearly identical handles preserved, but they do not necessarily go on the same vessel; a base of the same fabric does not seem to go with this rim and handle, and there may be two separate vessels represented, each with a single handle. Parallels for the general shape, the base, and the handles exist in Hellenistic Knossos, although in finer fabrics,[243] but there are enough similarities to suggest that this type is a later Hellenistic intrusion.

---

235 Rethemiotakis 1997, 310, fig. 11c.

236 Examples of Type 1 are recorded from the notebook also from K 61 floor, K 71, K 85, K 98, K 137, and K 149.

237 Others of Type 2 are recorded in the notebook from K 71, K 108, K 109, K 124, K 136, K 139, K 147, K 148, and K 149.

238 Rethemiotakis 1997, 308, fig. 8.

239 Other examples of Type 3 mentioned in the notebook come from the following locations: outside K 23 (two examples, one decorated with knobs), K 71, K 76, K 84 (small), K 97 (may be Type 6), K 102, K 113, K 114 (two examples), K 115, K 108 (three examples), K 109, K 136 (three examples), and K 147.

240 Other fragments of this type were said to have been found in K 121, K 144, and K 150.

241 Others of Type 7 are mentioned in the notebook from K 58, K 74, K 79-89, K 112, K 102, K 106, K 107, K 108, and K 149.

242 Day and Glowacki forthcoming, IC2 P36.

243 Sackett (ed.) 1992, pl. 100.37, a fine, cylindrical kantharos of Hellenistic date; pl. 104.12 (50-28 A.C.). It looks late (Hellenistic or Roman), but there are no precise parallels.

Jars are usually large, but smaller versions do exist; jars range in height from 10.9–36.5, while rim diameters vary from 9–32, with the majority falling between 10 and 19. Bases are generally flat or slightly concave underneath. The bodies are commonly globular, sometimes baggy, as in the case of **K23.31**. Jars are generally collared, although occasionally have a wide flaring rim. Mouths are most often wide so as to make removal of stored goods easier. Only Type 4 has a ridge below the rim (**K22.12**), a feature that appears more commonly on pithoid jars. Handles can be either horizontal on the shoulder or vertical, usually from the rim to the shoulder, but occasionally on the shoulder. Often there are dints at the points where the handle attaches to the body.

Some coarse jars have painted decoration (**K2.12, K115.16**), and the decoration is usually quite simple, consisting of bands or zigzag. Other jars are decorated with knobs, like the jugs and amphoras (**K11.8, K27.8, M9.2**), and occasionally with incised lines (**K57.6, K16.2**), although these incised examples may be later intrusions.

Jars are found at every LM IIIC site, but are often fragmentary and not well published. Type 1 jars, although not as baggy in shape, can be found at Kavousi–*Vronda*, where they are called pitharakia.[244] Jars of shapes like Type 2 appear at Khania, Khalasmenos, and Khamalevri, where they are clearly used in cooking, rather than functioning as storage vessels.[245] Jars of Type 10 appear at several LM IIIC sites, including Khalasmenos and Kastelli Pediada.[246]

Pithoid jar (FIG. 9.24)

Pithoid jars are smaller than pithoi, but like pithoi were used for storage, perhaps temporary storage, as Seiradaki suggested.[247] No complete example is preserved from Karphi, and the shape is known only from rim fragments. The rims of pithoid jars are nearly identical to those found on basins or lekanai, so it is often difficult to distinguish them from basins, unless a good deal of the body or the handles are found; basins have horizontal handles below the rim, while pithoid jars have horizontal handles on or below the ridge. Pithoid jars differ from other forms of jars because they are straight-sided, almost cylindrical vessels.

Seiradaki distinguished ten different types of pithoid jars based on the rims. Type 1 is actually a larnax (**K29.17**).[248] Type 2 is better classified as a pithos; similar rims were recognised in K 66, K 83, and K 107. Type 8 is actually a round-bottomed tripod (**K30.1**).[249] The other types are probably pithoid jars. Most common was Type 3, which has a flat rim, slightly outward-thickened, with a ridge below and a round horizontal handle below the ridge; the ridge on the illustrated piece (**K26.13**) is decorated with a chain pattern.[250] Type 4 has a more rounded rim and ridge below, and there is no handle. The illustrated example from K 24 was not located, and no other examples of

the type were mentioned in the notebook; it may not have been common. Type 5 has a large flat rim with a ridge below, and again the illustrated piece from K 25 could not be found, nor were there any other examples. Type 6 existed only in a single piece (**K8-18.2**), a fragment of a large rim with a double ridge and a chain moulding between. Type 7 had a flat squared rim with a flat ridge far below the rim; the illustrated pithoid jar from K 21 was not located.[251] Type 9 also has a very flat and squared rim, and the illustrated example from K 31 was not located.[252] Type 10 is a large pithoid jar (**K2.14**) with a profile similar to that of Type 9, with a large squared rim, but the rim is sharply undercut, and there is a sharp angle between it and the body; this type has a round horizontal handle below the ridge.[253] The notebook also mentions a Type 11, but there is no indication of what this shape might be.[254] One pithoid jar of Type 12 is listed from K 113, but again, there is no indication of the shape.

Of the few pithoid jars remaining, the majority are large and cylindrical and have rim diameters that range from 25–48, with most examples falling between 40 and 49. The rims are nearly always flattened on top and thickened outward, with a ridge below the rim. There is most often a horizontal handle set at the ridge (Type 1) or below it (Types 3 and 10). The ridge is sometimes decorated (**K8-18.2, K26.13**) with a row of finger impressions or a chain motif, and one example has an incised chevron on the rim (**K29.16**). Other pithoid jars (**K17.8, K17.26–27**) do not quite fit into Seiradaki's typology, although it is difficult to tell since so few examples of the types are preserved.

---

244 Day *et al*. forthcoming.

245 *Khania II*, pl. 45.84-P 0658, 77-P 0872; Tsipopolou 2004, 114, fig. 8.8.96-33 (Khalasmenos); Andreadaki-Vlasaki and Papadopoulou 2007, 46, fig. 3.28; 53, fig. 10.4 (Khamalevri).

246 Tsipopoulou 2004, 112, fig. 8.6.95-71; Rethemiotakis 1997, 2310, fig. 11c.

247 Seiradaki, 5.

248 The notebooks mention other examples with this type of rim from K 66, K 77, K 114, outside K 120, K 121, and K 150.

249 Similar rims were also found in K 72, K 79-89, K 80, K 91, K 117, K 121, K 107, K 118, and K 132.

250 Other examples of Type 3 listed in the notebook include the following: K 79-89, K 84 (2), K 85, K 86, K 88, K 91, K 101, K 102 (2), K 106 (3), K 108, K 113 (2), K 115, K 121, K 124, K 127, K 133, K 135, K 136, K 138 (2), K 139, K 143 (4), K 147 (6), K 148 (2), K 149 (3).

251 According to the notebook, other examples of Type 7 came from K 79-89, K 80, K 83, K 84, K 101, K 102 (2), K 121, K 124, K 143, K 147 (2), and K 149 (2).

252 The notebook lists pithoid jars of Type 9 from the following locations: K 101, K 112, K 115, K 127, K 148, and K 149 (2).

253 Other examples of Type 10 listed in the notebook come from K 72, K 73, K 79-89, K 88, K 101, and K 143.

254 Examples come from K 83, K 84, K 97, K 108, and K 139.

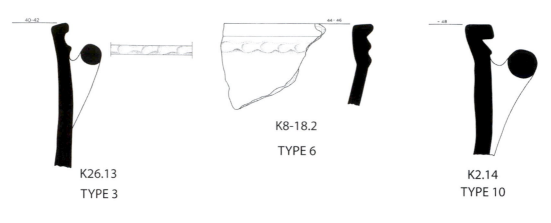

Fig. 9.24. Pithoid jars. Scale 1:4.

The precise function of pithoid jars is uncertain. They are common at LM IIIC sites, and nearly complete examples have been found at Kastelli Pediada, Khalasmenos, and Kavousi–*Vronda*.[255] Seiradaki thought they were used for temporary storage, and this may be correct; the inhabitants may have transferred material from the pithoi, which were used for long-term storage and were difficult to use because of their size, into pithoid jars for immediate use in cooking or eating. The wide mouths suggest a need for easy access, and there is no indication that they ever had lids. In fact, none of the terracotta lids found at Karphi is large enough to have fit a pithoid jar; if the vessels were covered, some other material must have been used, perhaps flat stone discs. There is usually more than one example for each room; perhaps they functioned like canisters for different types of staple supplies. Pithoid jars may also have been used to hold non-food items, like clothing or tools, in much the way pithoi are still used today in traditional Cretan houses. Christakis suggests that pithoi with unrestricted mouths may have been used in processing activities, and the same may be true of the pithoid jars.[256] They would have made excellent chimney pots as well, and if so one would expect to see traces of blackening on the interior.

Pithos (FIG. 9.25–26)

Pithoi were among the most common vessels found at Karphi, and they were easily recognised. Seiradaki reports that pithoi occurred in every room except K 32, K 38, K 50, K 70, K 126, and K 140, and some rooms produced eight or more examples (K 22, K 69, K 80, K 121, K 149).[257] Unfortunately, not many are actually preserved, and only 33 examples have been kept and catalogued. Seiradaki illustrated 23 types, but not one of these could be located, and they may have been discarded on the site. Three nearly complete pithoi were illustrated in photographs, but none of them was found in the museum.[258] All of the fragments illustrated on pl. 12a were located and catalogued. Thus, what is presented here is only a small percentage of the actual

pithoi, although perhaps representative of the total in terms of fabrics, shapes, and decoration.

Seiradaki distinguished twenty-three types on the basis of rim profiles. She indicated that the rim of Type 8 (a simple rounded rim) was the most common, followed by 1, 2, 3, 5, and 14. Types 4, 11, 16, 19, and 20 were rare. Types of pithoi were recorded in the 1939 notebook.[259]

Pithoi are always in coarse fabrics. There are few whole shapes preserved. Two nearly complete vessels from K 80 and K 147 illustrated in the publication are

---

255   Rethemiotakis 1997, 308, fig. 9 (Kastelli); Tsipopoulou 2004, 109, fig. 8.3.92-43 (Khalasmenos); Day *et al.* forthcoming (Vronda, particularly from Building E, Room E7).

256   Christakis 2005, 66–8.

257   Seiradaki, 3.

258   Seiradaki, pl. 1a, b, c.

259   Type 1: K 94, K 102, K 115, K 121, K 109, K 132 (2), K 136, K 149.
Type 2: K 69, K 73, K 74, K 79-89, K 80 (2), K 81, K 85, K 121, K 124, K 148, K 149 (2), K 150.
Type 3: K 69, K 102, K 107, K 109, K 115, K 118, K 121, K 127, K 132, K 143, K 149.
Type 4: K 69, Baker's House, K 138, K 150.
Type 5: K 69, Baker's House, K 75, K 79-89, K 83, K 106, K 107, K 108, K 112, K 121, K 138, K 143.
Type 6: K 69, K 84, K 106, K 147 (2), K 149 (4).
Type 7: K 69, K 96, K 102, K 106, K 137, K 147.
Type 8: K 69, K 79-89, K 83, K 88, K 98, K 101, K 106, K 107, K 108, K 112, K 113, K 118, K 121, K 131, K 139, K 143, K 148, K 149.
Type 9: K 69, K 72, K 73, K 117, K 121.
Type 10: K 80, K 101, K 108, K 117 (2), K 118, K 125, K 137.
Type 11: K 80, K 131, K 132.
Type 12: K 80, Baker's House, K 105, K 112, K 149.
Type 13: K 80, K 127, K 138, K 139.
Type 14: K 80, K 81-82, K 101, K 107, K 112, K 115, K 136, K 139, K 147, K 149, K 150.
Type 15: K 80, K 115, K 138, K 147, K 149.
Type 16: K 121.
Type 17: K 96, K 102, K 106, K 112.

now missing. **K26.14** can be reconstructed and is similar to the example from K 96 published by Seiradaki.[260] There are at least two pithoi that might be restorable, **K.53** (in boxes numbered 10 and 57), the other **K.62** (in the box numbered 7), probably those mentioned by Seiradaki.[261] The rim and base of **K9.11** are preserved, as is the case with another from an unknown context (**K.63**). The base and many body fragments of **K36.2** are preserved. A number of rims come from identifiable contexts, including **K22.13**, **K23.32**, **K24.2**, **K55.3**, and **MK.3**. Other preserved rims have no identifying numbers (**K.54–63**). Very few of the preserved pithos rims correspond to the 23 different types published by Seiradaki; **K.57** resembles Type 19, **K.59** may be Type 7, **K55.3** is Seiradaki's pithoid jar Type 2.

The few preserved bases are all flat (**K.53**), some with a ledge (**K9.11**, **K26.14**, **K.63**), or bevelling (**K36.2**). Base diameters range from 23 to 42, but come in both small varieties (**K9.11**, **K26.14**) and large (**K36.2**, **K.63**). **K.53** has a hole through the walls close to the base, pierced from the outside in.

Few pithoi are sufficiently preserved to show their general shape. Those illustrated by Seiradaki would fall into several different categories. The pithos from K 80 is a piriform shape with a wide mouth and low collar common in LM III.[262] The pithos from K 147 is ovoid in shape, similar to Christakis Form 43.[263] Finally, the smaller pithos from K 96 is globular, with a narrow mouth and high collar, similar to Christakis Form 52 of LM IIIB/C date.[264] **K26.14**, the only preserved pithos that can be completely restored on paper, is a piriform pithos with narrow mouth and high collar.[265]

The preserved pithoi nearly always have restricted mouths and a neck or collar. In general, the smaller pithoi have taller necks. Smaller pithoi have rim diameters that range from 23–35, while the larger varieties run from 36 to 54 in rim diameter, and according to Seiradaki are 75–125 in height.[266] Handles are most often vertical and round, attached at the ridge below the rim and on the shoulder. Two preserved examples (**K26.14**, **K.54**) have round horizontal handles attached below the rim at or below the ridge. The handles, whether vertical or horizontal, often have dints at the attachments (**K9.11**, **K26.14**). Rim profiles vary greatly, and no two are exactly alike. The rims fall into three basic groups: rims that are rolled and thickened outward (**K9.11**, **K23.32**, **K.53**, **K.58**), rims that are flattened on top and thickened outward (**K22.13**, **K24.2**, **K.55**, **K.56**, **K.57**, **K.61**, **K.63**), sometimes with a groove or indentation on the rim (**K.62**), and rims that are flattened, thickened outward, and undercut (**K55.3**, **MK.3**, **K.60**).

Pithoi are elaborately decorated, almost always with incised motifs on horizontal raised bands that run horizontally around the surface of the vessel. These bands were functional, added to strengthen the joint between sections of the pithos that were made

separately. Sometimes the pithos breaks at one of these joints, revealing the scoring that the potter made to piece them together; an example of this technique can be seen on Seiradaki pl. 12b, bottom left. This technique has also been observed on pithoi from the LM IIIC settlement at Kavousi–*Vronda*.[267]

Often a single pithos will have more than one decoration. The most common decoration on the bands is the incised chevron (**K37.3**, **K149.25**).[268] On larger vessels, the chevron band is accompanied by a rope-slashed serpentine moulding that undulates between the applied bands, as on **K37.3**, **MK.3**, and **K.53** and the two missing pithoi shown by Seiradaki.[269] Other decorations on horizontal bands are less common. At least five preserved examples have impressed circles (**K115.19**, **K124.10**, **MK.3**), probably made with a reed.[270] One example has bands with impressed circles and oblique slashes (**K69.3**), like a pithos from the west magazines at Knossos.[271] **K112.5** has a similar combination of oblique slashes, but with finger impressions. A unique example of impressed circles with incised triangles occurs on **K83.4**, and another is listed in the notebook from K 149. Several examples were decorated with an incised X-pattern (**K7.5**; examples recorded in the notebook from K 12, K 101, and K 149).[272] The notebook also mentions examples of vertical slashes from K 2, K 22, and K 101, and two

Type 18: K 96, K 101 K 106, K 112, K 121.
Type 19: K 97.
Type 20: K 97, K 121.
Type 21: K 79-89, K 120, K 133, K 149.
Type 22: K 113 (2), K 114, K 138, K 149 (2).
Type 23: K 91, K 94, K 98, K 104/K123, K 127, K 133, K 138, K 139 (3), K143 (5), K 147 (2), K 148.
In addition, the notebook also lists pithoi of Types 24 and 25, although there is no indication of what distinguished them, nor are there any drawings of them.
Type 24: K 121
Type 25: K 143 (2), K 149.

260 Seiradaki, pl. 1c.
261 Seiradaki, 3, n. 13.
262 Christakis 2005, 16, fig. 19, Form 86.
263 Christakis 2005, 10, fig. 10.
264 Christakis 2005, 13, fig. 14.
265 Christakis 2005, 17, fig. 20, Form 92.
266 Seiradaki, 3.
267 Day *et al.* forthcoming.
268 The notebook lists the following other examples: K 2, K 14, K 15, K 16, K 18, K 22, K 26, K 27, K 28, K 44, K 57, K 73-74, K 75, K 80, K 91, K 102, K 106, K 134, K 147.
269 There are also examples listed in the notebook from K 15, K 18, K 24, K 26, K 36, K 55, K 57, K 68, K 73-74, K 106, K 147.
270 Christakis 2005, 30–1, pl. 18–9, Group 12. The notebook also records examples of impressed circles from K 2, K 79-89, K 81-82, K 106, and K 149.
271 Christakis 2005, pl. 18c.
272 Christakis 2005, 28, fig. 39a, Band 32.

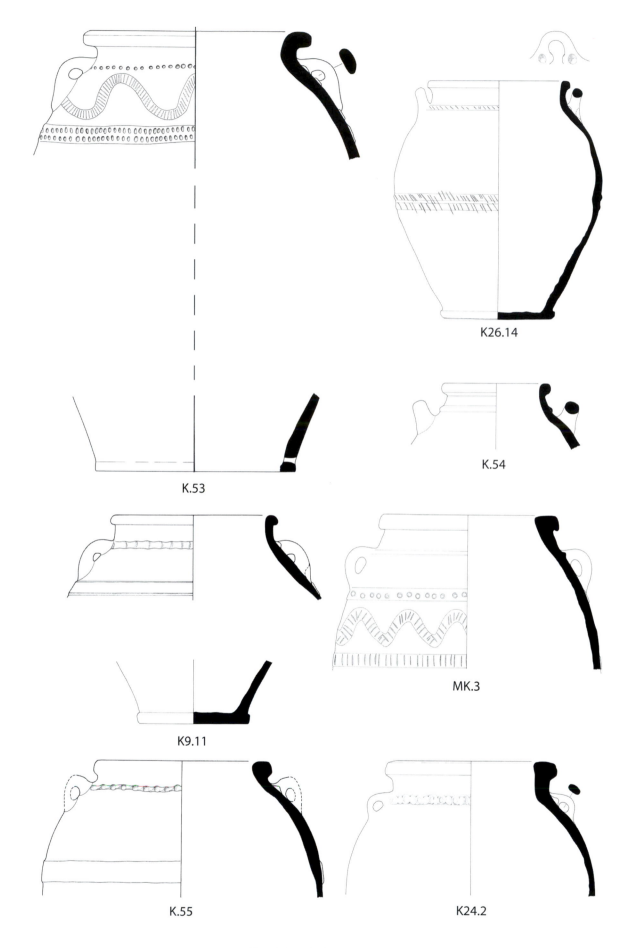

K26.14

K.53

K.54

K9.11

MK.3

K.55

K24.2

Fig. 9.25. Pithoi. Scale 1:8.

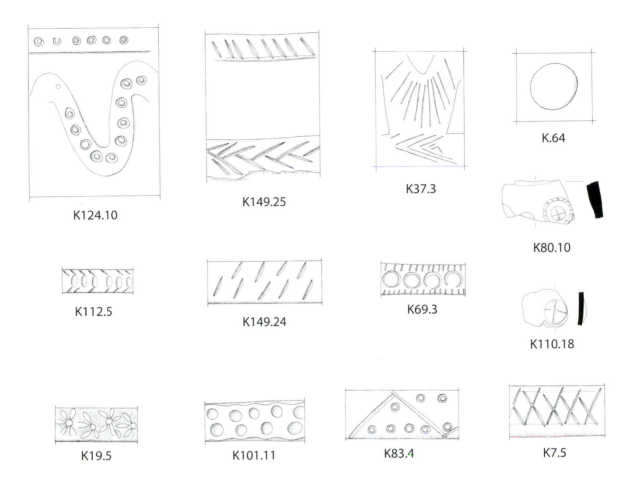

Fig. 9.26. Pithos decorations. Scale 1:4.

are preserved (**K149.25**, **MK.3**).[273] Oblique slashes occur on **K26.14** and possibly **K149.25**, and others are mentioned in the notebook from K 22, K 55, and K 101.[274] Impressed rosettes were found on **K19.5**.[275] Other motifs include crosshatching (K 15), plain bands (**K9.11**, **K.55**; also K 22, K 26), squares (also K 149), alternating triangles (**K83.4**; also K 59, K 149), multiple triangles (K 80), and one or more chains of finger impressions (**K101.11**, **K.53**; also K 15, K 16, K 22, K 26, K 75, K 86, K 101, K 102). Ridges below the rim are often decorated with rope slashing (**K26.14**)[276] or finger impressions (**K9.11**, **K24.2**, **K.53**, **K.55**; also K 16, K 18, K 22, K 33, K 27). Finally, several examples are decorated with bosses, either plain (**K.64**) or with an incised X (**K80.10**, **K110.18**), but not enough is preserved to determine what part of the vessel these bosses decorated. One rim (Type 19) was mentioned by Seiradaki[277] as having a chevron pattern on the outer edge, but generally the rims were left plain.

Pithoi were certainly used for storage, probably of all sorts of material, including foods, liquids, and cloth,[278] but without organic residue analysis we cannot be certain about their contents. The hole in **K.53** suggests that liquid was stored within; perhaps it served as a drain hole to empty out the vessel, like a pithos

from Building B at Kavousi–*Vronda*, which also has a hole in the base.[279] The sizes and shapes (i.e. height or whether the mouth is restricted or open) may have also had a functional differentiation; small pithoi (like **K26.14**) were the most accessible, while the tall pithoi with narrow mouths were less so.[280]

Many of the pithoi found in the settlement may have had a secondary usage, rather than representing storage at the end of the site's use. The upper portions of broken pithoi might have been reused as chimney pots, as was probably the case at Kavousi–*Vronda*,[281] and the bottoms as basins or watering troughs for animals, as

273 Christakis 2005, 27–8, figs. 34–7, Bands 1–8.
274 Christakis 2005, 28, fig. 38, Bands 25–28.
275 Christakis 2005, 30, pl. 19d, Group 12.
276 The notebook lists K 1, K 2-7, K 14, K 16-7, K 57, K 80, K 101.
277 Seiradaki, 4.
278 In traditional field houses in eastern Crete pithoi are used to store anything that rats and other small rodents might get at, so old clothing and bee-keeping equipment are stored in large pithoi, as well as wine; Christakis 2005, 64–7.
279 *Kavousi IIA*, 53, 56, fig. 40.
280 Christakis 2005, 47–8.
281 Day, Glowacki and Klein 2009, 81, 83.

suggested by Pendlebury for a base from the buildings on Mikre Koprana.[282] Hence, calculations of the amount of storage in the rooms and houses at Karphi, such as those by Nowicki, may not be entirely accurate.[283] Without more information on the percentage of nearly complete vessels as opposed to fragments or reused segments, it is impossible to know if a pithos was in use in the room at the time of abandonment or whether there were only fragments from earlier usage or secondary use.

Pithoi are common at all LM IIIC sites, but there is not yet an established typology of the shapes or decorations. Most existing typologies, like that of Seiradaki at Karphi[284] and that at Khania,[285] distinguish the types on the basis of rim profiles, in the absence of large numbers of nearly complete vessels. Rim profiles, however, vary greatly; at Karphi no two are exactly alike. Decoration may be a clearer indicator of LM IIIC date; at Kavousi–*Vronda*, nearly all of the pithoi were decorated with bands, usually with incised chevron motifs, but occasionally with vertical incisions, impressed circles, or finger impressions.[286] The use of chevron bands seems to be ubiquitous in all LM IIIC sites uncovered so far.

Rhyton (FIG. 9.27)

The rhyton is not a common form at Karphi, and only four definite examples are known. Three different types are represented: the conical rhyton (**K123.1**), the piriform rhyton with human head (two examples: **K27.3**, **M11.1**), and a fantastic composite vessel of a cart or chariot decorated with bulls' heads (not catalogued). The conical rhyton **K123.1** was thought by Seiradaki to be an heirloom brought by the first settlers to the site, since it is so unusual but of local clay.[287] Although this piece does look early, it does not necessarily date to LM IIIB;[288] a similar conical rhyton was found at Kastelli Pediada of LM IIIC date.[289] The piriform rhyton is represented by an unusual example from K 27 (**K27.3**). It has a human head as its top, and three handles. The base is missing. The decoration, with its fringed spiraliform motifs and hatched triangles, is certainly LM IIIC. The shape of the body, but not the head, finds a close parallel from Kavousi–*Vronda*, of LM IIIC date.[290] A similar head, probably from another rhyton comes from one of the Ta Mnemata tombs (**M11.1**). K 27 produced a second rhyton, an elaborate composite vessel that depicts a three-wheeled cart or chariot with three bulls' heads on the front and surmounted by a human figure that is driving. It is most likely that the bulls' heads are meant to suggest an ox-drawn cart, and the vessel is extremely elaborate.[291] There is another possible rim fragment of a conical rhyton from K 23 (**K23.16**); the unusual rim finds a parallel at Kommos, which is similar in size.[292]

A fragment of a fine, thin-walled vessel with a human face was found from K79-89 (**K79-89.29**), and it may come from a rhyton in the shape of a human head. Only a small fragment survives from the side of the head, preserving the ear in low relief. In front of the ear is a painted decoration of oblique strokes that may represent hair. It is too fine and thin-walled to be the head of a goddess figure, and is more likely to be from a head rhyton, like the one from Phaistos.[293] It also resembles head vases from Gortyn and Moires;[294] all are of LM IIIC–SM date, and possibly the type was manufactured in the Mesara.[295]

The most recent study of rhyta suggests that they were ritual vessels used for pouring libations, even into the LM IIIC period.[296] They occur rarely in LM IIIC deposits in comparison to the large numbers known from earlier Minoan and Mycenaean contexts. Few of the palatial rhyta, however, were as large and elaborate as the ox-drawn chariot from K 27, a fact that suggests that the ceremony involving the rhyta may have been more public and more meant to impress with elaborate display than was the case in earlier periods.

Bird vase (FIG. 9.27)

Bird vases are rare at Karphi, and in all but one case very fragmentary. There are two types. One is more naturalistic, decorated to imitate a real bird, with wings indicated, and is usually in LM III style; this type was found in the settlement. The other is the more common SM to PG type found only at Ta Mnemata (**M11.2**). There were two fragments of the LM III type catalogued from the settlement (**K28.4**, **K91.5**), and two more mentioned in the notebook or publication (K 115, K 130). **K28.4** may have been a rhyton, but since only a large fragment from the body is preserved, it is difficult to tell. It has wings indicated by an oval with wavy lines, and curvilinear lines with short strokes between them to indicate feathers. **K91.5** has wavy strokes between parallel lines. These pieces are irregular in shape, so they could not have come from stirrup jars, which they otherwise resemble. **K91.5** has an attachment for the foot. They may also be hollow bird figurines, which appear in the middle and last

282 *Karphi*, 69.
283 Nowicki 1999.
284 Seiradaki, 3.
285 Hallager 2000, 24–7.
286 Day *et al.* forthcoming.
287 Seiradaki, 28.
288 So Kanta 1980, 280.
289 Rethemiotakis 1997, 315, fig. 23a; Koehl 2006, 362–3 describes how this vessel may have functioned.
290 Day and Snyder 2004, 72, fig. 5.11.9.
291 Seiradaki, pl. 13; Koehl 2006, 83, pl. 7.71.
292 Watrous 1992, 76, fig. 48.1303.
293 Koehl 2006, 84, pl. 8.74.
294 Rethemiotakis 1998, pl. 34, 35a–b.
295 Rethemiotakis 1998, 167.
296 Koehl 2006, 326.

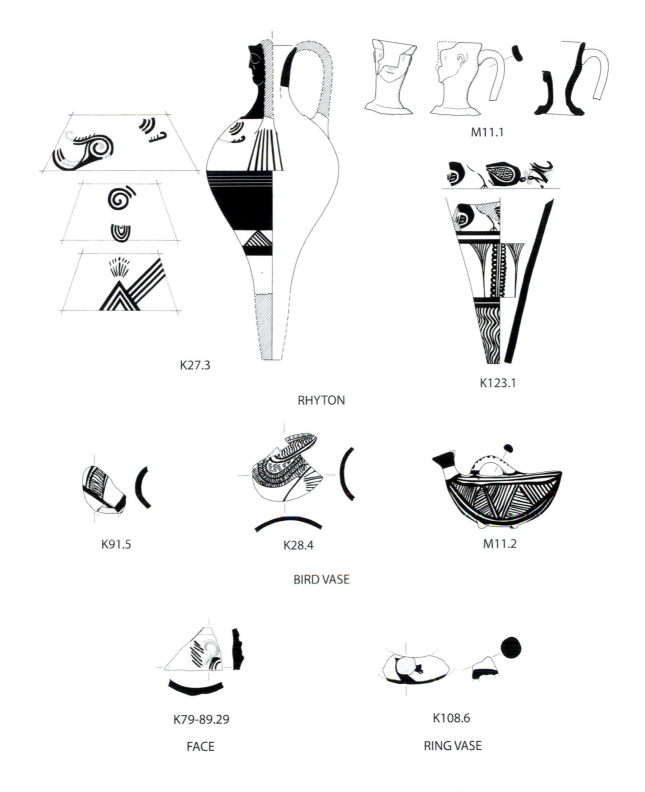

M11.1

K27.3

RHYTON

K123.1

K91.5   K28.4   M11.2

BIRD VASE

K79-89.29   K108.6

FACE   RING VASE

Fig. 9.27. Rhyta, bird vases, head vase, ring vase. Scale 1:4.

stages of LH IIIC on the mainland.[297] Bird vases are not unknown in LM III Crete, and a parallel can be found from Nirou Khani of LM IIIA date.[298] The Karphi examples are probably later in date, although they may be earlier than LM IIIC.

The second type of bird vase is more familiar from SM and PG tombs, and published by Desborough as Type II.[299] It has three small legs, a spout like a stirrup jar, and a basket handle, and it is decorated with alternating hatched triangles, like examples from Axos

---

297 Lemos 1994, 229.

298 Kanta 1980, 44, fig. 11.4; Stampolides and Karetsou 1998, 77 no. 46.

299 Desborough 1972.

and Khamaizi–*Phatsi* of SM date.[300] The function of these bird vases is uncertain, but the later type is regularly found in tomb deposits.

Ring vase (FIG. 9.27)

There is a single example of a ring base (**K108.6**). This is a squared tube with a round basket handle on top. It has painted decoration, which is too fragmentary to determine. Ring vases were never common, but appeared more often in mainland contexts than Cretan ones; on the mainland they were popular in LH IIIC. The type with a square profile seems to be Cretan, and examples can be found in LM IIIB contexts at Mallia, Kavousi–*Khordakia*, and Kalo Khorio–*Goula*.[301] Kanta suggests that the Mallia example may be LM IIIC in date.[302] The function of these vases is uncertain.

Tripod

Only one fine tripod vessel (**K48.6**) was found, and it is fragmentary, preserving an elliptical leg and part of the flat base. **K48.6** is decorated; it has a dint at the top of the leg, with a painted loop around it and bands above. A medium-coarse tripod vessel (**K104.1**) is similar. It has a flat base and short elliptical leg. It was turned a grey colour by smoke or burning, and there is trace of painted decoration, possibly light on dark. The function of these vessels is uncertain.

Cylindrical stand and snake tube (FIG. 9.28)

There are a number of cylindrical stands from Karphi, including the tall cylindrical stands with vertical handles on the sides known as snake tubes;[303] although no complete examples of snake tubes have been published from Karphi, many fragments exist. This category also includes fenestrated cylindrical stands.

Stands are open on both top and bottom. They generally, but not always, have a rim slightly smaller than the base. Bases are bevelled or squared, and there is often a ledge on the interior that has the effect of making the base wider and hence steadier. A ridge or ridges often appear just below the rim, and the rim is flattened on top and thickened outwardly. Stands at Karphi do not usually have painted decoration.

There are several fragments of cylindrical stands in fine wares. One (**K.33**) is possibly a snake tube, as it has vertical round handles on the sides toward the bottom. The lower part of the cylinder is ribbed with three ridges above a bevelled base that has a small ledge around the interior; unfortunately, the top is missing. Fragments of a cylindrical stand made out of fine buff ware were also found among the material from the Temple, but were not restored.

In coarse wares, the only nearly complete cylindrical stand is **K58.4**, and it is an unusual example, as it has two round horizontal handles set midway up the body, rather than multiple vertical handles. **K1.15** has a simpler base, and **K1.14** has a plain rim or base.

Fragments from an uncertain context (**K.50**) show the attachments for handles. Other fragments were found in K 1, the dump outside K 1, outside K 40-41, K 16-17, K 70, K 79, and possibly K 7 and K 87.

Fenestrated stands are rare at Karphi and other LM IIIC sites, although they are found in abundance at Kavousi–*Vronda*.[304] The best and only certain example comes from Ta Mnemata tomb 8 (**M8.4**), and it has no known parallels. The base has three steps, and the body is shaped rather like an hourglass, with triangular cutouts in two rows; the lower row has upright triangles, the upper has pendent triangles. The vessel has a rounded shoulder with three ridges, and a sharply out-turned rim. It is monochrome painted. An unusual rim or base fragment from K 106 and K 115 (**K106.21**) may be from a similar fenestrated stand; with a diameter of 28, it would have been very large.

Cylindrical stands were no doubt used to hold open vessels, both in domestic and in religious contexts, and snake tubes seem to have been purely ritual in function. It is likely that most of the examples from Karphi were used in religious observances, but few examples fit into the canonical category of snake tubes: a cylindrical stand with vertical handles up the side and often a ridged top. This may be due to the fact that few examples were nearly complete, and it may be because the stand fragments were not recognised and kept, except from the Temple.

Square stand or altar (FIG. 9.28)

Square or rectangular stands are related to cylindrical stands, and probably served a similar function. There is only one coarse example known (**K58.5**). This stand is actually rectangular rather than square, and it has an oval opening in the base, with a ledge around on the inside. There is a ledge also on the exterior of the base, and immediately above the vertical elliptical handles begin to snake up the sides, much like a canonical snake tube; the top is missing. A fragment of a square tube from K 34 was also found in one of the boxes.

The excavators identified the fine rectangular stand from K 57 as an altar. It is basically a square box with a round mouth set on top. It has fenestrations of different types and is also elaborately decorated with horns of consecration and alternating arcs, and it has small animal figurines on the shoulder.[305]

No other such elaborate stand has been found, but a fragment with an uncertain find spot may come from

---

300 Desborough 1972, 253, pl. ΛΓ΄ 2.34 (Axos); Tsipopoulou 1997, 462, fig. 5.4897 (Khamaizi–*Phatsi*).

301 Kanta 1980, 51, fig. 23.12; 145, fig. 56.8; 162, fig. 64.12.

302 Kanta 1980, 51.

303 Gesell 1976, 247–59.

304 E.g. Day 1997, 401, fig. 7 (from Building N, Room N5); Day *et al.* forthcoming.

305 This altar is under study by Geraldine Gesell.

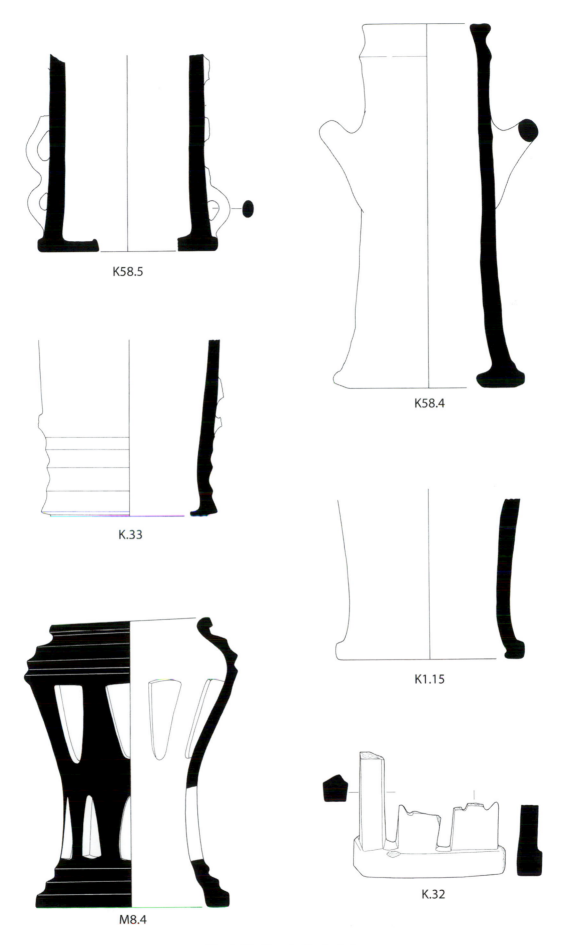

K58.5

K58.4

K.33

K1.15

M8.4

K.32

Fig. 9.28. Stands. Scale 1:4.

a similar object (**K.32**). Only a corner of this object is preserved. It has a base with a raised ledge, and the interior is uneven, like the base of **K58.4**. At the corner is a more or less square pillar with two cut-outs next to it, both of flat objects with horns of consecration on top; the second one is larger than the one toward the corner, and it is likely that there was a third smaller one next to the larger one for balance. It may represent a tripartite shrine on the base of a square stand. The use of the horns of consecration suggests a ritual function. A similar square fenestrated stand without the horns of consecration came from the shrine at Vasiliki–*Kephala*.[306]

A fragment of a possible fine fenestrated stand was found in one of the megaron houses of the Eastern Quarter (**K140.2**). This is a flat, rectangular object finished on both ends and with a slight curve to it. It may have been between the fenestrations on a stand of the sort that is found on other LM IIIC sites, especially Kavousi–*Vronda*.

Finally, fragments of another object may be from an altar or stand from K 85 (PLATE 9 *h*). There are several fragments from the corner of a rectangular open stand, and they are decorated with punctuated designs. A similar object with incisions, rather than punctuated decoration, came from the shrine at Khalasmenos.[307]

Plaque (*Pinax*)

There are many fragments of plaques from Karphi, and while the majority of these are coarse, a few fine examples do exist.[308] One plaque from the Temple is flat, but has a human head on the top.[309] **K17.20** is a fragment of a fine plaque with a raised edge around it. Three non-joining fragments possibly of the same plaque were found in one of the boxes, but without any label (PLATE 28 *c*). These were of fine buff clay with a creamy slip and traces of paint, and they had plastic decoration with punctuated and incised decoration; it is difficult to make out the design, but it may be an animal. These fragments were similar to others of a coarser fabric probably from the Northern Shelters (**K104.2**) with painted reliefs of bovine hoofs and legs. Only one example of a coarse plaque still has paint preserved, and the decoration is not clear (**K.51**); the fragment is from the centre of the plaque and has oblique lines and rows of dots in black paint.

Decorated plaques are rare, but other examples with relief decoration do exist; a plaque from Kannia has two sphinxes on either side of a palm tree,[310] plaques from Kavousi–*Vronda* and Mathia have depictions of the goddess with upraised arms.[311] Painted plaques are not often found, but the painted decoration may have worn off or come off when the sediment was removed, as is often the case with LM IIIC pottery in eastern Crete.

Plaques are common, but few of the extant examples are labelled, and it is impossible to know where they were found. It is likely that they came from the Temple or other ritual places, where we know plaques were

found, but they may not all be from religious contexts. Where the find spots are known, plaques came from rooms identified as shrines, usually accompanying figures of goddesses (K 1), or from dumps that lay below buildings and streets (K 17 lower deposit, K 32, K 70, K 72, K 76). Only one (**K2.13**) is known to come from a non-ritual context.

Elsewhere on Crete, plaques accompanied terracotta figures of goddesses with upraised arms; they were found at Kannia, Kavousi–*Vronda*, Khalasmenos, and Vasiliki–*Kephala*.[312]

Larnax

At least two larnakes were found in the settlement at Karphi, although not recognised in the publication. **K29.17** was published as a pithoid jar rim,[313] the other (**K81-82.1**) was identified as a jar.[314] **K29.17** is better preserved and finds more close parallels. The curve of the rim suggests that it was a bathtub larnax, as does the decoration. The excavators could not have seen the decoration, since the surface was left heavily coated and the decoration was revealed only by careful cleaning. It is difficult to find parallels for the rim

---

306 Eliopoulos 2004, 87, fig. 6.8.

307 Tsipopoulou, 2001, 101, pl. 28e.

308 One box of plaques from the storerooms of the Herakleion Museum contained fragments without identifying numbers. There was a fine thin plaque with a white slip (10YR 8/4) and a wide flat edge, 1.8 wide. The corner of another fine another plaque from K 76 was not catalogued. This was of very soft fabric, 7.5YR 7/6, and it was 2.2 thick, except around the raised edges, where it was 3.3. The ledge around the edge was 1.9 wide. Medium-coarse and coarse plaques included the following: two fragments of a medium-coarse to coarse reddish yellow fabric (5YR 7/8) with very pale brown slip (10YR 8/4), 1.2–1.8 thick; three fragments of flat coarse plaques (2.5YR 6/8) with almost no edge; five fragments of 'oatmeal' fabric, with at least two and possibly three holes pierced in them; and two fragments of another coarse plaque. Finally, there was another fragment of a fabric like **K104.2**. Another unlabelled box in the museum contained much ritual material, including three plaques. One came from K 70; it was a rounded corner, 1.9 thick, with a wide flat ledge, 2.5 wide. It was made of coarse fabric, 5YR 6/8, with hard black and white and gold mica inclusions. Another from K 72 was also a corner, also 1.9 thick, with a narrower edge (1.8) and made from a very coarse fabric, 5YR 6/6 in colour, with large schist inclusions (2–4 mm). Another corner from a plaque from K 32 had a large hole pierced through it. Finally, there was a very coarse red plaque (10R 5/6) with frequent large schist inclusions that had a narrow flat edge 1.2 wide.

309 *Karphi*, pl. 35.1; Gesell 2001, pl. 84a–b.

310 Gesell 1985, pl. 108.

311 Gesell 2001, pl. 82b–c (Kavousi–*Vronda*), pl. 84c–d (Mathia).

312 Gesell 1985, 77; 2004; Tsipopoulou 2001, 101, pl. 28c; 2009, 128–9, figs 11.16–18; Eliopoulos 2004, 87, fig. 6.9.

313 Seiradaki, fig. 2.1.

314 Seiradaki, fig. 3.9.

profile, since few published larnakes are shown with profiles. The fish decoration on the interior, however, is common and finds close parallels on LM IIIB/C larnakes from other east Cretan sites at Piskokephalo, Tourtouli, Pacheia Ammos, and Praisos–*Papoures*.[315] The LM IIIB larnax from Pacheia Ammos has the same sort of rendering of the fish, with gills indicated and several 'fins' on top, but it lacks the wavy lines on the body. Watrous has suggested that bathtubs decorated with fish served a domestic function, and the context of this example in a room and a building that has little but domestic material seems to fit.[316] The other larnax (**K81-82.1**) has a strange angular profile that is too poorly preserved to determine its shape or decoration. It is likely to have been a bathtub larnax as well, and the wavy line on the exterior suggests that it may have been decorated with an octopus.

Fragments of larnakes were also found in the Ta Mnemata tombs. A bathtub larnax is reported from M1, and fragments of larnakes were found outside M4 and outside M5 and 6. Others may have existed in both tombs and settlement, but the fragments were not recognised, since they are easily mistaken for pithoi.

Other utilitarian or industrial shapes

Drain tile

A single fragment of a drain tile was found among the Karphi pottery (**K47.6**). It is a short (6.8 in height) probably U-shaped coarse vessel and is similar to examples found at Kavousi–*Vronda* and Kastri;[317] at both those sites, however, the drain tiles are dated to LM I. Other examples of drain tiles appear in MM deposits at Kavousi–*Vronda*.[318] Drain tiles were used to drain liquids and channel them from one place to another, but there is no indication of how extensive this channelling might have been. It has been suggested that drain tiles were used to take water run off from a flat roof so that it was directed out beyond the wall,[319] and they may have carried water through a parapet arrangement.[320]

Firebox

Only a single example exists of the shape known as an incense burner, censor, brazier or firebox.[321] This is a fragment from the perforated bottom of a capsule made out of cooking pot fabric from K110 (**K110.17**). The vessel is blackened from fire on the interior and much of the exterior, and it is burned all the way through. This example fits into Georgiou's Type I,[322] a type that was in use from the MM III–LM IA through LM III periods, although it does appear as early as the EBA.[323] Fireboxes, however, are not common on LM IIIC sites. This example from the bottom of the vessel has a larger central hole with smaller holes pierced all around it. Georgiou suggested that these vessels were used in heating volatile ingredients in the production of aromatics.[324] This being the only known example from

Karphi, it is possible that it was an antique or that the production of aromatics was very limited.

Miscellaneous shapes

There are several pieces of unknown shape that do not fit into any of the above categories. A lug handle from K 31 (**K31.16**) is squared at the end and pierced, an otherwise unknown shape and piercing. It could come from a tray or a scuttle, but there are no known parallels at Karphi or elsewhere.

Finally, there is a body fragment from K 88 (**K88.2**) that has knobs all over the surface. It is coarse, with schist inclusions, but it is slipped. In decoration it is like the fine bowl from unknown context (**K.12**).

Cooking Pottery

There are six basic shapes in cooking pottery: cooking dishes, trays, jugs, tripod cooking pots, lids, and baking slabs; a few other unusual coarse shapes with evidence for burning are included here as well. All cooking vessels are distinguished by their coarse fabrics and their heavy burning. Cooking dishes are the most ubiquitous form, although few nearly complete examples have been found. Tripod cooking pots are almost as plentiful, easily recognisable from their legs, and cooking mugs and trays are less common. Coarse lids that show evidence of burning also may have been used in cooking. Apparently missing from the Karphi assemblage but common on LM IIIC sites elsewhere are what have been termed cooking jars or amphoras, that is — cooking pots without legs.[325] One example of a cooking jar may be **K23.31**, Seiradaki's example of a Type 1 jar, which is made out of cooking ware fabric and shows burning; it is, however, much larger than usual for such cooking jars. Other cooking jars may have been recorded simply as jars and discarded.

Cooking dish (FIG. 9.29)

Seiradaki included in the category of dishes all vessels whose height is less than one-third of their diameter;[326]

315 Kanta 1980, 177, fig. 66.1–2; 178–9, fig. 65.3–4; 144, fig. 56, 3–4; 182, fig. 73.10.
316 Watrous 1991, 303, n. 109.
317 Day, Coulson and Gesell 1986, pl. 80a (Kavousi–*Vronda*); *Kastri*, 297, fig. 17.P30.
318 Day *et al.*, forthcoming.
319 Renfrew and Cherry 1985, 335.
320 Shaw 2004, 188.
321 Georgiou 1980, 154–8; Georgiou 1986, 8.
322 Georgiou 1980, 124–5.
323 Georgiou 1980, 165.
324 Georgiou 1980, 171.
325 Hallager 2000, 159–60; Tsipopoulou 2004, 115; Yasur-Landau 2006, 51–4; Day *et al.* forthcoming.
326 Seiradaki, 9.

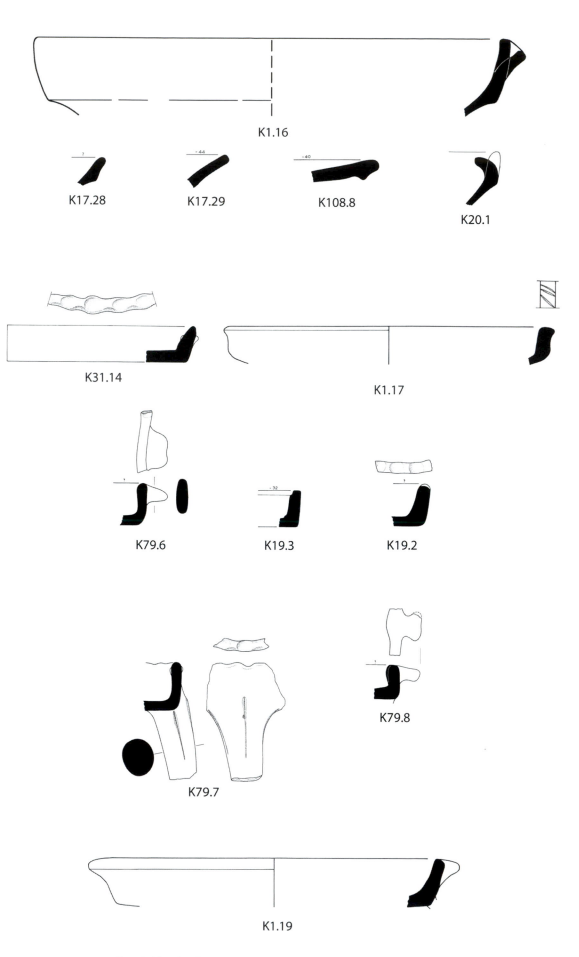

Fig. 9.29. Cooking dishes, trays, and tripod trays. Scale 1:4.

her definition covers shapes distinguished here as dishes, trays, and even a basin. There has been some confusion about the different types of trays and dishes, but the publication of LM IIIC sites has helped to refine the distinctions.[327] Cooking dishes have thin rounded bottoms, without base or legs, thickened rims that are nearly vertical to flaring with a sharp demarcation between base and rim, and roughened bottoms.[328] The bottoms are nearly always missing, probably because they were burned away during use. In Seiradaki's typology, only Type 6 can be identified as a cooking dish. Types 1, 3, 4, 5, and 7 are actually cooking trays, while Type 8 is a fine tray; Type 2 may be a basin, but it was not located and so it is uncertain.

Cooking dishes are very common at Karphi and are easily recognisable. They were found in nearly every room, and none was associated with the tombs.[329] While dishes are common, they are rarely found complete, and the bases are never preserved. One published example preserving about half the vessel from K 75 was not located.[330] Another large fragment came from the Temple (**K1.16**). The rim of this vessel had been pulled out during manufacture, as had also rim fragments **K3.14** and **K18.2**; two other examples (**K2.6**, **K20.1**) had small spouts created by pinching in a section of the rim. Several fragments were pierced (**K2.6**, **K23.25**). Rims can be short (**K17.28**, **K108.8**) or tall (**K.49**), and the angle can go from nearly vertical (**K20.1**, **K23.25**) to flaring (**K2.6**, **K18.2**, **K17.29**, **K.49**), sometimes on the same vessel (**K1.16**, **K2.6**, **K3.14**, K 75). Cooking dishes are very large; rim diameters range from 40 to 52, while the rims vary from 2.5–6.8 in height.

Cooking dishes are always made of very coarse fabrics that were meant to withstand the heat of the fire and extreme and sudden changes in temperature. These vessels were clearly used for cooking, as nearly all of them show extensive burning, usually on the exterior (**K1.16**, **K2.6**, **K3.14**, **K17.28**, **K23.25**, **K18.2**, **K.49**); they are almost never burned on the interior, so most could not have held burning coals for roasting meat, as Seiradaki suggested.[331] Probably these dishes were set directly in the fire, with the rounded bottoms resting in the coals. They could be used like a modern wok for frying.[332] If a large domed lid or another cooking dish was placed on top of them, they could become small ovens;[333] the few cooking dishes that are not burned (**K17.29**, **K20.1**, **K108.8**) may have functioned as lids in this way, and perhaps Seiradaki's missing Type 2 from K 80 was this sort of lid since it closely resembles an example from Kavousi–*Kastro*.[334] Mook has also suggested that dishes may have been turned upside-down and the rounded surface used as a griddle.[335] The creation of outward pouring spouts, as well as the pinched-in spouts suggests that these vessels were used for cooking liquids, but they may have served other functions; folding the rim inward may have provided a convenient lifting device.[336] The holes pierced in some examples could have been for emptying the vessels or for pouring off liquids, but they may also have been used to hold rods to suspend the pot above the fire,[337] although in that case there should be more than one hole; unfortunately, these vessels are so poorly preserved that it is impossible to tell how many holes a single vessel had. A significant feature of the cooking dishes is size; they were extremely large, either for cooking large portions of food, or to create an extensive work surface for cooking different portions of the food under different conditions or at different times.

Cooking tray (FIG. 9.29)

Trays are shallower than dishes and have thick, flat bases and vertical or flaring rims. They are not as common as cooking dishes, but they appear frequently in the settlement, and they are easily recognisable. Usually a full profile is preserved.

In Seiradaki's typology of dishes, there are five coarse trays: Types 1, 3, 4, 5, and 7. Type 1 is wide, with a vertical pointed rim and a large lug on the side; the published example from K 149 was not found, but it seems to be similar to a tray from Khania.[338] Types 3, 4, and 5 vary only in the angle of the sides, but the most frequent is the slightly flared Type 4, which often has finger impressions on the rim and sometimes has horizontal handles. There was only a single example of Type 7, which had the top of its rim incised. The surviving examples of trays fall into these types, and they can either have flat bases or be placed on tripod legs (Seiradaki's Tripod Type 4). There are no certain extant examples of Type 1, although **K1.19** and **K17.30**

327 Betancourt 1980; Borgna 1997*a*; Mook 1999; Hallager 2000, 160; Day *et al.* forthcoming.

328 Mook 1999, 503.

329 Dishes of Type 6 are recorded in the notebook from the following rooms: K 16, K 24 (6), K 58 (several), K 70, K 72, K 73 (many), K 74, K 75, K 79–89, K 80 (several), K 83, K 84, K 85, K 86, K 87, K 88, K 91 (several), K 93, K 94 (several), K 97, K 98, K 101, K 102 (several), K 106 (several), K 107 (2), K 108 (3), K 109, K 112, K 115, K 118 (3), K 119, K 121 (several), K 124 (3), K 125 (several), K 127 (2), K 129 (many), K 132 (3), K 135, K 136 (2), K 138 (3), K 139, (4) K 143 (4), K 147 (8), K 148, and K 149 (12).

330 Seiradaki, pl. 2g.

331 Seiradaki, 9. The same can be said at Khania; see Hallager 2000, 160.

332 Betancourt 1980, 7.

333 Mook 1999, 508.

334 Mook 1999, pl. 110.30, 111c, d.

335 Mook 1999, 508.

336 Mook 1999, 507.

337 Mook 1999, 507.

338 *Khania II*, pl. 46.78-P 0515.

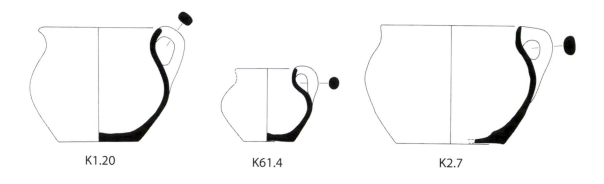

K1.20   K61.4   K2.7

Fig. 9.30. Cooking jugs. Scale 1:4.

may be of this type.[339] Type 3, with its very vertical sides, is represented by the flat-based varieties **K1.18, K19.3, K79.6, K85.11, K106.23, K112.2**); many of the tripod trays have similar profiles (**K21.3, K45.7, K79.7, K79.8, K106.24**).[340] Type 4, with more flaring sides, is represented by **K17.30, K19.2, K31.14**, and **K112.3**, and the notebook adds examples from K 72 and K 75. There are no preserved trays of Type 5, but the notebook records one each from K 97 and K 136 and six from K 149. Similarly, the illustrated example of Type 7 from K 113 was not located, nor were any fragments of this shape recognised in the extant material; the notebook lists two more from K 61 and K 96. Another type, rather like Type 7 was found in K 85 (**K85.12**), but this has been classed with trays (see above, p. 280). Seiradaki's tripod Type 4 was actually a tray. The illustrated example from K 31 was not located, but many others were found (**K21.3, K45.7, K79.7, K79.8, K106.24**); other examples listed in the notebook came from K 10, K 21, K 77, and K 106 (3).

Trays are very shallow; their height varies from 3–5, with the majority being 3.5–4.5. They are very wide, from 30–50 in diameter, the majority 30–40. Trays of Types 3 and 4, whether tripods or flat-based, often have finger impressions on the rim (**K19.2, K21.3, K31.14, K45.7, K79.7, K106.23, K112.3**) or have lugs (**K1.19, K79.6, K79.8, K85.11**). One unusual example (**K1.17**) has incised oblique lines on the rim. The tripod trays have legs that are round (**K21.3, K79.7**) or elliptical (**K106.24**) and are often decorated with vertical slashes (**K79.7, K106.24**) or a dint and oblique slashes forming a V-pattern (**K21.3**). The preserved fragments show no traces of exposure to fire, with the exception of **K45.7**, which is burned on rim and base inside and out. This lack of burning seems unusual, as other tripod cooking pots are clearly used over open fires. Trays without tripod legs show more frequent burning (**K17.30, K31.14, K79.6, K106.23, K112.2**), generally on the exterior. These trays could not have been used to hold burning coals over which spitted meat was placed, for they do not often show burning or discolouration from fire on the interior. They are more likely to have served for warming near the fires or for presentation.

Cooking trays are common in LM IIIC sites in all phases of the period. They appear at Khania, Khamalevri, Sybrita/Thronos, Kastrokephala, Phaistos, Kavousi–*Vronda*, Kavousi–*Kastro*, Khalasmenos, and Kastri.[341] Whatever their function(s), they seem to have served as a regular part of the kitchen equipment throughout the period.

Cooking jug (FIG. 9.30)

Seiradaki's Type 8 jug is a cooking jug. This shape resembles a large cup, with wide, flat base and a collared globular body, with the rim often pinched out opposite the handle to form a spout. A single vertical handle runs from rim to shoulder. There are two different types, one with a flaring rim (**K1.20, K2.7, K11.10, K114.10, K.48**) and one with a narrower mouth and a collar (**K11.9, K47.5, K61.14, MK.5**). The type with the flaring rim is the one illustrated in Seiradaki's typology from K 148, and it was not located. One example from an unknown context (**K.47**) is small and shaped more like a cup; it lacks the pinched out spout, but it was clearly used in the fire and probably belongs in this category; it is similar to a shape which is called a 'dipper' at Phaistos.[342] In all these shapes, the rim and base diameters are nearly the same; the ratio of the rim to base varies from 1:1.1 to 1:1.5 and so does the ratio

339 The notebook records many examples of Type 1 from the following locations: K 84, K 87, K 101, K 102, K 107 (2), K 108, K 109, K 112, K 118 (2), K 119, K 121 (2), K 124, K 125, K 127 (2), K 139 (3), K 143 (5), K 147 (3), K 149 (3).

340 Other examples of Type 3 mentioned in the notebook came from K 67 and K 150.

341 Hallager 2000, 160–1(Khania); Andreadaki-Vlasaki and Papadopoulou 2005, 388; 2007, 33, 37 (Khamalevri); D'Agata 2002, 54, fig. 5 (Sybrita/Thronos); Kanta and Karetsou 2003, 159, fig. 10 (Kastrokephala); Borgna 1997*b*, 193, fig. 5 (Phaistos); Day *et al.* forthcoming (Kavousi–*Vronda*); Mook 1999, 503 (Kavousi–*Kastro*); Yasur-Landau 2006, 54–5 (Khalasmenos); *Kastri*, 285, 290, fig. 11m–o.

342 Borgna 1997*b*, 193, 197, fig. 7.

of the rim diameter to the height. The bases are generally flat (**K1.20**, **K47.5**, **K114.10**, **MK.5**) and occasionally slightly concave underneath (**K2.7**, **K61.4**, **K.48**). The bodies can be shallower (**K2.7**, **K.48**) or deep. Handles are almost always elliptical in shape, although **K61.4** has an almost round handle.

Nearly all of the identified examples show heavy and extensive burning, both on the interior and exterior. On one example (**K114.10**) the entire surface is burned except for the area around the handle. It looks as though cooking jugs were placed directly onto an open fire, possibly to heat water or other liquids. The fact that they were burned on the interior suggests that something other than water was heated in them and that often that liquid material burned. Cooking jugs have not been identified at many LM IIIC sites, but they do occur in some quantity at Kavousi.[343]

Tripod cooking pot (FIG. 9.31)

The most common cooking vessel was the tripod cooking pot. Seiradaki was not certain that these tripods were used for cooking, since she saw little evidence for burning on the legs of the pots.[344] She distinguished seven types, but some of them are not standard tripod cooking pots. Type 4 is a tripod tray and was discussed above (p. 318), and Type 7 is a multiple vessel from K 150 that is the only one of its kind; it will be discussed separately (see below, p. 320). Although Types 5 and 6 are not illustrated on the figure of tripod types, Type 5 is described as looking like krater type 4 (**K23.10**), but shallower and with a rounded base. According to the publication, tripods of this type had square legs, and the type is only represented by the leg **K106.26**; Seiradaki thought it derived from metal prototypes.[345] Type 6 is a tripod jar; three examples from K 43, K 80, and K 137 were illustrated in photos, but not found at the time of publication or drawn.[346] The type is essentially a jar with narrow neck resting on tripod legs. The examples from K 43 and possibly K 80 have painted decoration. **K27.7** may be of this type as well and may be deeper than has been restored. Like the tripod from K 137, it has slashes on the round legs.[347]

Seiradaki stated that Types 1–3 occurred most often and with almost equal frequency. Type 1 is a standard LM IIIC cooking pot, with round legs, deep body with collared neck and round horizontal handles below the neck. Belonging to Betancourt's Type A, it is found in nearly every LM IIIC site.[348] Five examples are preserved (**K14.2**, **K26.11**, **K26.12**, **K61.15**, **K106.25**), and the notebook mentions others from K 33 (2), K 82, K 83, K 119, K 138, and K 147. The tripods of this type are usually large, with rim diameters of about 17–19, although they can be as small as 11 and as large as 22. The legs can be vertical or flare out slightly.

The Type 2 tripod is similar in shape, but has vertical rather than horizontal handles; one-handled (**K1.22**, **K121.13**, **K121.14**) and two-handled varieties (**K23.26**) both exist, and the handles run from rim to shoulder. The one-handled tripods of this type are generally smaller, with rim diameters from 6–10, while the two-handled variety is larger, with an average diameter of 20.[349]

Type 3 is a round-bottomed tripod vessel with vertical handles. The illustrated example from K 16 was not found, but a shallower example came from K 68 (**K68.14**) and there are also fragments of round-based tripods (**K7.3**, **K30.1**, **K84.1**).[350] This may be the shape also that is referred to in the notebook as a tripod lebes. Tripods of this type are open, with very large diameters (35–48). Type 6 is a tripod pithos, illustrated by three photos in the publication, but these examples from K 137, K 80, and K 43 had already disappeared at the time of publication.[351]

In addition to Seiradaki's seven types, there are other shapes. The first is a tripod bowl, more like Betancourt's Type B tripod (**K110.21**). This has tall round legs, a shallow body, a flaring rim and two round horizontal handles below the rim. Another type is represented by the tripod vessel **K1.21** that was categorised by Seiradaki as a Type 2 jar. This is a most unusual vessel; the scars on the edge of the base attest to the attachment of feet. It has three round vertical handles set on the shoulders instead of the usual two handles from rim to neck. It is the only example of this shape, and there are no close parallels.[352] The one tripod from the Ta Mnemata tombs is also unusual (**M2.1**). It has very short legs that are elliptical in section, a globular body, and a wide short collar; round vertical handles alternate with round horizontal handles on the shoulder. No parallels have been found for this shape. Other tripods are known from fragments and may come from any of the above types, including rims **K17.31–32** and legs **K16-17.4**, **K17.9**, and **K140.3**.

With the exception of the octagonal leg **K106.26**, the elliptical leg **K16-17.4**, and the short legs on the **M2.1**, all of the tripod legs from Karphi cooking pots are round in section, whatever their type. This is typical of the LM III period, especially LM IIIC.[353] The legs were

---

343 Day *et al.* forthcoming; Mook forthcoming.
344 Seiradaki, 7.
345 Seiradaki, 7–9.
346 Seiradaki, 9, pl. 2a–c.
347 Other examples of the tripod jar came from K 91, K 102 (both legs), K 121 (2), K 108, K 109, and K 147.
348 Betancourt 1980, 3. For a list of LM IIIC sites that produced this kind of tripod, see Hallager 2000, 158, n. 224.
349 Other tripods of Type 2 were found in K 61, K 83, K 87 (2), K 102, K 132, K 133, K 138, and K 144.
350 According to the notebook, others were found in K 33 (2), K 72 (2), K 83, K 98, and K 99.
351 Seiradaki, 9 n. 15, pl. 2a, b, c.
352 Three-handled jars of this shape but without the legs are common in Neopalatial sites. See Barnard and Brogan 2003, figs. 34–5.
353 Hallager 2000, 158; Betancourt 1980, 5.

made separately and the body and top of the leg roughened or scored by the potter to make attachment easier and more secure, as noted by Seiradaki.[354] Legs often have a dint at the top (**K1.22**, **K14.2**, **K17.9**, **K23.26**, **K26.12**, **K27.7**, **K61.15**, **K106.25**), and sometimes on the side (**K68.14**). Often there are slashes instead of or in addition to the dint (**K140.3**, **K16-17.4**). In addition to the tripods catalogued and kept, the notebook mentions decoration on other tripod legs: dints on examples from K 8, K 12, K 59, incisions on those from K 8, K 79, and K 97. Tripod legs were set quite high on the vessel, except for **M2.1**, where they are small and set on the bottom. This technique of setting the legs higher on the vessel seems to appear in LM III and may have been learned from the mainland.[355]

Nearly all of the tripod cooking pots show evidence of burning, primarily on the exterior, but sometimes on the interior as well (**K1.22**, **K7.3**, **K14.2**). Sometimes the entire pot is quite thoroughly burned (**K1.21**, **K7.3**, **K30.1**, **K61.15**, **K 106.26**), at other times it is burned in patches (**K1.22**, **K23.26**, **K26.12**), and occasionally it shows no burning at all (**K26.11**, **K27.7**).

The different types of tripod cooking pots may indicate functional differences, different places of manufacture, or different dates. Borgna has suggested that the height of the collar on tripod cooking pots is a chronological indicator, the high flaring rim developing from the short everted rim, and this may be the case at Karphi.[356] Although most of the rims are the tall flaring type, two rims from the lower deposit in K17 (**K17.31**, **K17.32**) have small everted rims. Otherwise, there seem to be no chronological distinctions among the various types, all three being found in deposits all over the site and in use when the settlement was abandoned. Likewise, there is no correlation between the fabrics used in the cooking pots and the type of cooking pot; all of the cooking pots appear in a variety of fabrics, so the people of Karphi do not seem to have imported a particular type of cooking pot from a single area. Potters in different communities in LM IIIC Crete were making a variety of cooking pots and were apparently exchanging them with other communities, whether in trade or accompanying exogamous marriages. It is possible that a particular type of cooking pot manufactured at one village was imitated in another.

The round-bottomed Type 3 cooking pot has been seen as reflecting Mycenaean influence.[357] Certainly this type is not common on Crete before LM III, and it is widely found in mainland contexts. The round-bottomed tripod cooking pot does, however, already exist in Neopalatial contexts on Crete, such as Nerokourou.[358] The fact that these Type 3 cooking pots have very wide mouths also suggests that there may be a functional reason for the rounded bottom.[359] Like the position of the tripod feet, the use of round-bottomed cooking pots may have been introduced into Crete from the mainland, but for the feet this probably represents a technological innovation that was adopted because it

produced a more functional product, and with the round-bottomed shape it may have to do with the type of food being cooked or the method of cooking. Round-bottomed cooking pots do not indicate that Mycenaeans were living at Karphi any more than megaron-shaped houses do. The different types of tripod cooking pots probably represent what was needed for the household and might have included a smaller one-handled tripod, a deep Type 1 tripod and a round-bottomed tripod, along with the dishes, trays, jugs, and lids that made up a household assemblage. Only in two instances do we have very different types, one in the Temple, and one in Ta Mnemata 2, and these may have served special functions; the tomb tripod shows no trace of burning. **K1.21** may have been given a special shape because it was used in the preparation of ritual meals or ritual substances.

Cooking jar

There are no certain examples preserved of the cooking jar or amphora shape that has been found on other LM IIIC sites, especially at Khania, Kavousi–*Vronda*, Khalasmenos, Kastri, Phaistos, and Khamalevri.[360] Some might have existed, but from rim and body fragments it is impossible to distinguish these from tripods.

Multiple vessel (FIG. 9.31)

Seiradaki's Type 7 tripod is a unique multiple vessel represented by a single example (**K150.5**). It has small feet that are elliptical in section and a flat base. The outer walls are nearly vertical to a pointed rim, and there is a flattened round handle from rim to leg. Inside is a second vessel, with an incurving profile that rises above the rim of the outer side. Within this smaller bowl is a depression in the bottom. Seiradaki suggested that it might have been something like an EM or MM candlestick or a MM incense burner from Knossos.[361] Its exact purpose is not clear, but the interior is entirely burned, and one side of the exterior, so it was obviously involved in cooking, burning of aromatics, or carrying of burning material.

---

354 Seiradaki, 7.

355 H. Martlew, personal communication.

356 Borgna 1997*b*, 198.

357 Borgna 1997*b*, 200.

358 Kanta and Karetsou 2003, 150.

359 So also Kanta and Karetsou 2003, 150.

360 Hallager 2000, 159–60 (Khania); Day *et al.* forthcoming (Kavousi–*Vronda*); Tsipopoulou 2004, 115; Yasur-Landau 2006, 51–4 (Khalasmenos); *Kastri*, 285, fig. 17.P29; Borgna 1997*b*, 195, fig. 4 (Phaistos); Andreadaki-Vlasaki and Papadopoulou 2005, 388 (Khamalevri).

361 Evans 1921, 578.

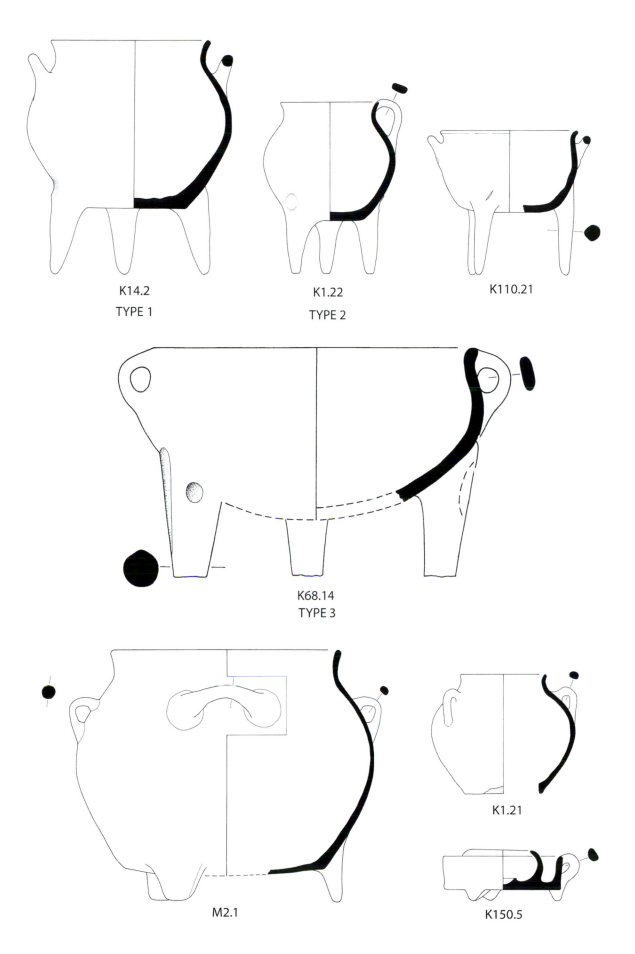

K14.2
TYPE 1

K1.22
TYPE 2

K110.21

K68.14
TYPE 3

M2.1

K1.21

K150.5

Fig. 9.31. Tripod cooking pots. Scale 1:4.

Cooking slab

There are four examples of what is termed a cooking or baking slab. Three of these came from the West Cliff Houses (**K113.5**, **K126.1**, **K126.2**), and the fourth (**K.52**) has no number on it and may belong to one of the other three. These objects are flat slabs of terracotta, 2–4.5 thick, rather like the plaques found in religious contexts, but coarser and thicker. One (**K.52**) has a ridge around the edge, while the others are simply flat, perhaps becoming slightly thicker at the edge. One has a hole pierced through it (**K126.1**). The bottoms are rough, as if made by pressing a slab of clay onto coarse fabric or smooth ground. None of them has been preserved in entirety, so we do not know their measurements. All four are of cooking fabrics with schist or phyllites and quartzite. All show burning; two of them are burned in no discernable pattern, one (**K.52**) has a burned circular patch in the centre, and the last (**K113.5**) is entirely burned with a circular unburned patch in the centre (PLATE 21 c). These slabs may have been used like pizza bricks in an oven to give more diffuse heat, or they may have been used to seal up ovens or large cooking pots. They seem to be limited to a single complex on the northwest side of the settlement. Two fragments of flat slabs found with plaques in one of the museum boxes may also come from cooking slabs, as they were both very burned. There are no known parallels from LM IIIC, but in the Neopalatial artisan's quarters at Mochlos were found a number of 'work slabs' that appear to be similar. These are thought to have been used for metalworking, ceramic production, or food preparation.[362]

Stand

A large slightly curving stand with a vertical round handle was found in the northern shelters (**K107.10**). It shows burning on the interior and may have functioned as a spit stand,[363] or a stand for a cooking jar like those at Khania;[364] it may also have been associated with some other industrial process.

TERRACOTTA OBJECTS

A number of objects found at Karphi were made out of terracotta but were not used as vessels for cooking, storing, or dining. There were many terracotta spindle whorls or beads found in the settlement, and some of these have been preserved. These were discussed in the publication, and nothing new is added here. There are several other objects of terracotta, however, that appeared in the boxes with the pottery, and these are discussed here.

Potter's wheel

A single fragment of a potter's wheel was found at Karphi (**K127.7**). This fragment comes from the rim of a large (D. 48) wheel, and it is pierced vertically just below the rim. The underside has a ridge that is decorated with incised strokes. It belongs to Evely's Type 3C, which is the most common kind of Cretan potter's wheel, although it is a bit larger than usual.[365] Most of the examples of this type are Neopalatial in date, and there are few examples from LM IIIC.[366] Two fragments come from the LM IIIC levels at Khania, both of them of the same Type 3C.[367]

Loomweight

Only a single loomweight was preserved in the boxes in the Herakleion Museum (**K126.3**). It is of an unusual size and pyramidal in shape, with a square base 9 on a side. It is shaped like an elongated pyramid and has a large hole pierced through the walls toward the short top. The shape is not well known on Crete, although examples do occur at Kavousi–*Kastro* of somewhat later date.[368]

Spool (TABLE 9.1)

Spools were very common at Karphi, and a sample of them was saved. Since these spools were not described, drawn, or photographed in the publication, the information about the surviving examples is given here.

Three large and 20 small spools were preserved from Mikre Koprana 1E, without specific room designation (PLATE 4 c). The large spools measure 5.6 in height and 4.3 at either end (3.3 in the middle); they weigh 50–100 g. The smaller spools are 4.1 in height and 3.3 at the ends (2.1 in the middle), and they weigh 20–50 g, the majority of them 30–40 g. Both large and small spools are of the same light reddish brown fabric (5YR 6/4) and all examples are burned on one side. None shows any signs of abrasion or wear.

A number of spools were also preserved from the Southern Houses. Five spools came from K 44 (PLATE 15 c). They are all of the same size, approximately 2.8 high, with diameters at the ends of 2.7 and a diameter at the middle of 2.2. The weights are very close, ranging from 25–35 g. Their fabrics are not as uniform as those from MK1E; colour varies from pale red (10R 6/4) to reddish yellow (7.5YR 6/6–5YR 6/8), and the pale red examples are the only ones that show signs of burning. K 27 also produced seven worn examples of similar shape, all burned, and weighing 50–75 g; a partial example weighed 40 g. Finally, Room K 46 produced two examples weighing 75 g (PLATE 5 c).

---

362 Soles (ed.) 2004, 24–7, fig. 7.
363 Hallager 2000, 162; Georgiou 1983, 78–80.
364 *Khania II*, pl. 77f.
365 Evely 1988, 100–6; 2000, 284–6.
366 Evely 1988, 101.
367 Bruun-Lundgren and Wiman 2000, 179–80.
368 Lee Ann Turner, personal communication.

TABLE 9.1: **Concordance of spools.**

Findspot	Number	Wt. in grammes	H.	Max. D.	Min. D.	Colour
K 2	1	210				black
K 2	2	60				black
K 2	3	75				black
K 21	1	50				
K 21	2	70				
K 22	1	60				
K 22	2	60				
K 23 floor		100				
K 27	1	50				burned
K 27	2	60				burned
K 27	3	50				burned
K 27	4	60				burned
K 27	5	40				burned
K 27	6	60				burned
K 27	7	75				burned
K 44	1	25	2.8–3.0	2.8	2.2	7.5YR 6/6
K 44	2	25	2.8–3.0	2.8	2.2	5YR 6/8
K 44	3	30	2.8–3.0	2.8	2.2	5YR 6/8
K 44	4	25	2.8–3.0	2.8	2.2	10R 6/4
K 44	5	25	2.8–3.0	2.8	2.2	10R 6/4
K 46	1	75				
K 46	2	75				
MK1E	1	100	5.6–5.8	4.5	3.4	5YR 6/4
MK1E	2	50	5.6–5.8	4.5	3.4	5YR 6/4
MK1E	3	100	5.6–5.8	4.5	3.4	5YR 6/4
MK1E	4	25	4.4–4.5	3.3	2.1	5YR 6/4
MK1E	5	0.30	4.4–4.5	3.3	2.1	5YR 6/4
MK1E	6	50	4.4–4.5	3.3	2.1	5YR 6/4
MK1E	7	30	4.4–4.5	3.3	2.1	5YR 6/4
MK1E	8	50	4.4–4.5	3.3	2.1	5YR 6/4
MK1E	9	40	4.4–4.5	3.3	2.1	5YR 6/4
MK1E	10	50	4.4–4.5	3.3	2.1	5YR 6/4
MK1E	11	50	4.4–4.5	3.3	2.1	5YR 6/4
MK1E	12	40	4.4–4.5	3.3	2.1	5YR 6/4
MK1E	13	30	4.4–4.5	3.3	2.1	5YR 6/4
MK1E	14	30	4.4–4.5	3.3	2.1	5YR 6/4
MK1E	15	25	4.4–4.5	3.3	2.1	5YR 6/4
MK1E	16	25	4.4–4.5	3.3	2.1	5YR 6/4
MK1E	17	25	4.4–4.5	3.3	2.1	5YR 6/4
MK1E	18	35	4.4–4.5	3.3	2.1	5YR 6/4
MK1E	19	35	4.4–4.5	3.3	2.1	5YR 6/4
MK1E	20	40	4.4–4.5	3.3	2.1	5YR 6/4
MK1E	21	25	4.4–4.5	3.3	2.1	5YR 6/4
MK1E	22	40	4.4–4.5	3.3	2.1	5YR 6/4
MK1E	23	40	4.4–4.5	3.3	2.1	5YR 6/4

From K 2 came a large spool (PLATE 4 *c*) weighing 210 g, and two small spools weighing 60 and 75 g respectively. These are made of a very coarse fabric that has been burned totally black over most of the surface. The Magazines also produced a few spools. From K 21 came two examples weighing 50 and 70 g. There were two spools from K 22 in different fabrics and with different shapes, both weighing 60 g. From the floor of K 23 came a single spool weighing 100 g and burned black.

Single spools were recorded in the notebook for the following rooms: K 6, K 16, K 67, K 75, K 79, K107, K 112, K 117, and K 120. K 4 and K 26 produced two spools each, and three spools each were found in K 2, K 24, and K 147. Larger numbers were found in other rooms: five in K 22 and in K 139, six in K 44, seven in

K 46, nine in K 23 (2 large, 7 medium), nine in K 148, 15 in K 91, at least 18 in K 150, 19 in K 61, 20 in K 27, 21 in K 136, 23 in Mikre Koprana, 38 in K 102, and 50 or more in K 110.

Spools have been found in many LM IIIC sites, and they have been given various names. At Kastri they were called reels and were thought to be weights suspended by a string tied around the centre.[369] At Khania they were termed bobbins and identified as the most common form of loomweight.[370] Both the settlement and the ceremonial pits at Khamalevri produced examples, as did Khalasmenos, Phaistos, and Sybrita/Thronos.[371] None, however, have been found at either of the Kavousi sites. Often they are said to be made of unfired clay; at Karphi they may originally have been of unfired clay, but all show signs of extensive burning that may have hardened and preserved them.

The function of these spools is still a matter of some debate. Some have thought they might be gaming pieces to be used with kernos stones.[372] At Knossos they were found on top of a kernos stone, and Warren suggested that they may have been used in the depressions of the kernos; the fact that this stone was a reused olive press, however, makes any ritual significance unlikely.[373] They are more likely to have been used in weaving. Barber suggested that they were used with a small portable loom for producing bands or belts,[374] and most scholars now accept spools as a form of loomweights.

The origins of the spool are uncertain; spools seem to have been common in the EBA on the mainland and on Crete, but then disappeared until the end of the Bronze Age.[375] Evely pointed out that spools seem to be a feature of LM IIIC sites, possibly part of a wider Aegean manifestation;[376] indeed, such spools have been found not only in the Aegean, but on Cyprus and in Anatolia and the Levant.[377] Their presence on Crete comes quite early in IIIC, and it is difficult to know if they originated on the island and spread throughout the eastern Mediterranean, or whether they came to Crete from elsewhere; Rahmstorf suggests that they appear earliest on Crete in LM IIIC, and that they may have spread from there to Cyprus.[378] At any rate, spools suggest that Crete is part of a wider milieu in this period.

If spools were indeed used as loomweights, then they seem to represent a new weaving technology introduced into the island in LM IIIC. At Karphi it is reasonable to suppose that the rooms with the larger numbers of spools probably held a loom. It is interesting to note that the weights of groups of spools seem to be so similar, as one would expect for a loom.

369 *Kastri*, 302, 305, fig. 19.46 and 50.
370 Bruun-Lundgren and Wiman 2000, 177.
371 Andreadaki-Vlasaki and Papadopoulou 2005, 359, 392, 389, fig. 54 (Khamalevri); Coulson and Tsipopoulou 1994 80, pl. 10.3 (Khalasmenos); Rahmstorf 2005, 149 (Phaistos and Sybrita/Thronos).
372 Hillbom 2005, 299–302.
373 Warren 1982–83, 73, fig. 58.
374 Barber 1997, 515–9.
375 Evely 2000, 502 for spools in EM Crete. For the origins and history of spools, see Rahmstorf 2003.
376 Evely 2000, 502.
377 Rahmstorf 2005.
378 Rahmstorf 2005, 155.

10

Conclusions

The history and culture of the Karphi settlement

The restudy of the pottery from Karphi provides new evidence for the date and phasing of the Karphi settlement and cemeteries. It is hoped that the presentation of this evidence will also lead to new interpretations of the site, and reconstructions of the life, society, economy, technology, and beliefs of the people of Karphi. A few ideas are suggested here.

Although the material from Karphi has value in determining the dating of the rooms and suggesting the activities that went on in them, it must be recognised that there are limitations to the knowledge it can provide. The pottery and objects may not precisely reflect the whole assemblages that were being used by the inhabitants, because some material may have been removed when the inhabitants left the site, and post-abandonment depositional processes may also have resulted in the movement of some material.[1] If the settlement was abandoned, rather than suffering a single calamity, the inhabitants may have taken with them portable items, and the rooms and buildings may have lain open for a long time before the roofs collapsed and the walls fell in covering what was left in the houses. Thus, the contents of the rooms do not represent all that was in use at the time of abandonment because some objects may have been moved, either by natural processes or human activity, and some material may already have been removed. In addition, so much of the pottery was discarded by the excavators, particularly the coarse wares, that the current view of the ceramic assemblages can give only an incomplete or partial reading of room contents. Even when the notebook gives the types of vessels represented, it does not always indicate whether the vessels were only fragments or were nearly complete, and what was recorded depended on the interests and observations of the ceramic specialist, often made without mending or even washing the pottery. Nevertheless, from what was kept and recorded we can get a picture, however incomplete, of the contents of the rooms and of the date of the material found in them. In this analysis, it is assumed that the sherd material probably reflects earlier usage: vessels that had been broken during the building's history and were ground into floors or pushed up against walls. Whole or nearly complete vessels are interpreted as having been in use at the time of abandonment.

CHRONOLOGY AND PHASING OF KARPHI

The study of the extant pottery by context from Karphi, taking into account more closely dated assemblages from recent excavations, now provides a clearer picture of the history of this settlement. Not all of the material recovered is of the same phase or period, as other scholars have noted. There is a considerable amount of early LM IIIC material and even some of LM IIIB style, a fact that indicates that the settlement was founded at the transition from LM IIIB to LM IIIC, when LM IIIB styles were still in use. Early LM IIIC material abounds throughout the site, generally in fragments, rather than whole vessels. This material is remarkably similar to that found on sites in western, central, and eastern Crete. Despite the fact that this period is usually regarded as marked by regionalism, with refuge settlements in nearly inaccessible locations developing independently and without contact with other communities,[2] there is remarkable homogeneity in the pottery styles, a fact that suggests contact among the various communities on the island. Warren has postulated that the LM IIIC style originated in one place and spread, whether from a single site on Crete or, less likely, from the mainland.[3] Once this style was established, it changed little over a long period of time, and it is difficult at this time to define a middle phase of LM IIIC.

The majority of complete vessels belonged to LM IIIC late, and are similar to those found at Kavousi–*Vronda*, Kavousi–*Kastro*, and Khalasmenos. As suggested by the geographic closeness of these sites, there seems to be little variation among them in terms of style, but the assemblages show preferences for different shapes; the pyxis, for example, is common at Karphi but not elsewhere, while the fenestrated stand is popular at Kavousi–*Vronda*, but not at other sites. Karphi may be lacking in some types of cooking vessels found on the other late LM IIIC sites, in particular the cooking jar or amphora.

---

1   For a discussion of problems involved in depositional processes, see La Motta and Schiffer 1999.
2   Nowicki 2000.
3   Warren 2007, 334.

A few rooms at Karphi contained a small number of nearly complete vessels of early SM date, and it would appear that while the settlement belongs almost entirely to the LM IIIC period, it went out of use when the new SM styles were just developing or being introduced.[4] The graves, however, particularly those at Ta Mnemata, continued to be used down to EPG, long after the abandonment of the settlement, perhaps by the former inhabitants who had moved to nearby Papoura.[5]

A look at material from specific deposits at Karphi is helpful. Much of the earliest material on the site comes from the streets or open courts. These are indicated on the Karphi plan with paving stones, but these pavers were rarely found in place; often, only the lines of the widely-spaced steps indicated that the area was originally paved.[6] Stratigraphically, the fact that the pavers had disappeared from many of the streets and courts before excavation means that much of the pottery found in these areas may have come from below the pavements, although some fragments may have been thrown out as rubbish or washed in from elsewhere.[7] Thus, most of this pottery belonged to the time of or before the construction of the streets and courts, not to the period of final use of the site. The nature of the preserved material from these areas bore out the interpretation that they were not habitation deposits; the pottery came in small fragments and included a high percentage of fine wares. Much of the pottery from these areas was of very early LM IIIC date and gives a picture of the earliest phases of the settlement.

Three roads or public courts produced the earliest material on the site. In K 32, K 76, and the so-called 'Broad Road' (K 101, K 103, K 105, K 111) deep bowls were plentiful and decorated with buttonhook spirals, quirk, comb pattern, Minoan flower, and bivalve shell, all of which are found in LM IIIB or early LM IIIC deposits. The bases of deep bowls and other vessels were either flat or low raised and concave and included none of the higher feet found on the later vessels. The courtyard K 79-89 also produced pottery from an early phase of LM IIIC, although not as early as the fragments from K 76. One exception is the cup **K79.1**, which is one of the latest pieces from the site, anticipating the SM wavy line cup; since the nearby room K 116 shows evidence of continued use into the beginning of SM, this cup may belong with that phase, when court K 89 may have housed a bread oven.

Although there were indeed few stratified deposits, in several rooms the excavators distinguished lower strata that were earlier than the period of abandonment. In K 23 of the Magazines, there were two lower levels, but unfortunately, the preserved pottery consists of small fragments and is not plentiful, so these deposits are not as helpful as they might be. Nevertheless, the deep bowls with low raised or flat bases and one with a bivalve shell look very early in LM IIIC, although perhaps not as early as those from K 76. This evidence accords well with the suggestion made by Pendlebury that the Magazines

were not among the earliest structures at Karphi, but came later than the Great House, Temple, Barracks, and Northern and Southern Shelters.[8]

A large rubbish dump ran under the Great House and the streets outside it to the west (K 12, K 13, K 16-17, K 70, K 72); this dump pre-dated the construction of the later rooms of the Great House and was recognised and kept separate in the boxes by the excavators. The two lower deposits beneath K 12 produced deep bowls that were early in shape (flat and low raised bases) and motifs (Minoan flower, comb). The same rubbish dump was picked up under K 17, where the excavators kept separate pottery from two different layers. The pottery from the upper deposit is small and scrappy, with few diagnostic elements, except for a deep bowl with a low foot. The lower deposit contains a MM ribbed tumbler base, perhaps belonging to the period when the peak sanctuary was in use. The remainder of the preserved pottery is early LM IIIC, including flat deep bowl bases; the plaque fragment suggests that religious equipment was in use in this area in the early stages of the settlement's history.

K 70 was a cellar built over the same rubbish dump, and it may have been a storeroom for a shrine of the goddess with upraised arms in K 15–17, since much ritual equipment was found here. The preserved pottery from K 70 seems to come not from the dump but from the use of the area for storage, as it included a large coarse stirrup jar (**K70.1**) and an amphora with rope-twisted handles (**K70.2**). While all of the material is certainly LM IIIC, the coarse ware cannot be more closely dated.

K 72, part of the street leading up to the Temple, also lay over the rubbish dump. Most of the preserved material seems to come from the final use of the area. The stirrup jar (**K72.2**) found here has some late features; the air hole near the false spout, the tilted spout, and the linear decoration of the vessel point to a very late LM IIIC date.

---

4   B. P. Hallager has recently questioned the existence of Subminoan as a distinct chronological period, citing the lack of sites with evidence for SM pottery stratified between LM IIIC and PG (Hallager 2010). While there is much merit in her argument, at Karphi (and at Kavousi), pottery of a style that is more developed than late LM IIIC but not yet clearly PG does exist, and the term Subminoan still seems appropriate for it. Much of Hallager's evidence from Karphi comes from the tombs, many of which continued in use after the settlement was abandoned in late LM IIIC, and when these pieces are removed from the discussion of LM IIIC, the lack of Subminoan does not seem as clear.

5   Watrous 1982, 20.

6   *Karphi*, 66.

7   In fact, Pendlebury (*Karphi*, 66) even suggested a massive flooding at the end of the settlement's history that took out all of the pavings.

8   *Karphi*, 135.

A few other rooms produced early material. A large amount of LM IIIB style pottery came from K 38 in the so-called Temple Dependencies. Pendlebury believed that the Temple was constructed at the beginning of the settlement, and it is possible that the material from K 38 is evidence for that early use, although its proximity to the rubbish dump found around the Great House suggests that some of this early material may have come from that dump. This room may have been associated with the Great House Shrine (K 15–18), with which it is contiguous. K 68 also produced a good deal of early LM IIIC pottery suggesting that the Central West Quarter may also have been one of the early complexes on the site.

In general, while the small fragments of fine decorated wares found in every room may belong with earlier phases of the building's use, the nearly complete vessels are probably representative of the material from the time of the abandonment of the settlement, and should provide a date for the last use. Some earlier LM IIIC material continued in use, but it is clear that the majority of the pottery from the latest period of occupation of Karphi was late LM IIIC. Nevertheless, a few rooms produced ceramic material that may be termed SM. These are clustered in the northwest part of the settlement, including K 81 in the Central West Quarter, K 115 in the Western Cliff Houses, and K 116 in the Commercial Quarter; the exception is the possible late vessel from the floor deposit in K 23 in the Magazines in the southeast quadrant. Two of the rooms in the northwest were near or in areas with ritual equipment; K 115 was a storeroom associated with a room containing figurines (K 106), and K 116 produced fragments of at least three statues of the goddess with upraised arms. These rooms of ritual importance may have continued in use when other areas of the settlement were abandoned.

A cup from K 81 in the Central West Quarter is probably also very late in date, although not so late as vessels in some of the other deposits just mentioned. **K81.1** is a large cup with a tall offset rim and a wavy line in the centre. It resembles the wavy band cups that are typical of SM deposits at Knossos,[9] although lacking the conical foot and bell-shaped body found on the SM examples.

K 115, a small roofed cellar associated with a room with ritual objects (K 106) also produced many fine nearly complete vessels. The krateriskos (**K115.4**) is unique in the settlement, and although the shape begins as early as early LH IIIC on the mainland, it is rare on Crete until SM or PG. The rest of the pottery is late LM IIIC, including the large cup with zigzag, fringed kylix with bulbous stem, and gremlin deep bowl. The stirrup jar is more reminiscent of earlier LM IIIC.

K 116 was apparently a shrine of the goddess with upraised arms. The pottery is amongst the latest in the settlement, especially the stirrup jar (**K116.4**) and amphora (**K116.3**), both of which look similar to vessels

of SM date. A possible wavy line cup was also found in K 79 (**K79.1**), part of the courtyard outside K 116.

The floor deposit from K 23 included the burned krater (**K23.11**) with its uncommon shape and cross-hatched triangles. It is difficult to know if the vessel is unusual for chronological reasons or because it was an import. The linear decoration suggests that it was later than LM IIIC in style, and it finds parallels from Kephallonia of late LH IIIC date; although the correlations between mainland and Cretan styles in this period are still not fixed, late LH IIIC may have been contemporary with early SM.[10]

The settlement, then, seems to have gone out of use early in SM, before the SM style became fixed or when the potters were just beginning to imitate the new style. Even that late use may have been restricted to a particular area. The tombs, however, must be considered separately, as they are likely to have continued in use for a considerable period of time after the settlement itself was abandoned; the late pottery found within the Ta Mnemata tombs cannot be used to suggest continued inhabitation of the houses into the PG period. Use of a LM IIIC site for continued burials was certainly the case at Kavousi–*Vronda*, where the tholos tombs actually cut into the earlier houses of the settlement and where the material is all later than what was found on the floors of the abandoned houses.[11] At Ta Mnemata SM vessels appeared in M 3 and M 16 (**M3.1, M16.2, M16.5**), while M 1, M 4, M 11, and M 17 contained pottery of the SM–PG phase (**M1.1, M1.2, M4.1, M8.1, M11.2–4, M17.1–4**); M 17 seems to have produced nothing but SM–EPG. The spring at Vitzelovrysis also continued in use, to judge from the one imported PG fragment with compass-drawn concentric semicircles that was found there (**V.1**).

The study of the pottery by context, then, provides some new information about the date of the Karphi settlement. It was founded at the beginning of the LM IIIC period, in the transitional LM IIIB/C phase. Pendlebury assigned the earliest habitation to the Northern and Southern Shelters that lie on the eastern edge of the settlement up the slopes of the hill,[12] where he envisioned the people roofing over clefts in the rock with brushwood and living while they constructed the earliest parts of the city. The earliest real buildings were thought to be Room 9 of the Great House, perhaps the Temple, and the Barracks. The settlement in this phase had a communal rubbish dump picked up under K 12,

---

9   Warren 1982–83, 85, fig. 60; Sackett (ed.) 1992, pl. 50a, b.
10 D'Agata 2007, 95. Hallager 2007, 196, however, questions this correlation.
11 *Kavousi IIA*, 7–8. The situation there may have been different, since it is not certain that any of the tombs were used by the inhabitants of the settlement.
12 *Karphi*, 135.

K 13, K 16, K 17, and K 70. When or before these buildings were completed, the Magazines, Rooms K 42–43, K 47, and the road K 45-51-50 in the Southern Houses, as well as the Eastern Block were apparently constructed. In a later phase, additions were made to the Great House, covering over the dump, and the town was regularised with the Broad Road laid out going up to the Temple, the Square K 48, and the remaining rooms of the Southern Houses constructed, with a new road (K 52, K 54) replacing the road covered over by K 45-51-50. Another square existed where later K 86 and K 88 were built. Finally, there were minor alterations: the blocking of the Temple Road, perhaps another cellar for the Great House (K 70), the enlargement of K 74 and K 71.

This picture painted by Pendlebury depends a good deal on his idea of how communities were planned and developed, with people living in temporary housing while constructing first important public buildings, then constructing the smaller living quarters, and finally laying out the streets. He often made reference to his discoveries at Amarna as providing a model for development, a reasonable approach for his time. Nevertheless, Amarna period Egypt is a model of dubious applicability for LM IIIC Crete, which did not have the same social, political, economic, or religious organisation. The study of the pottery, however, does bear out some of what Pendlebury proposed. Both the Northern and Southern Shelters produced fragments that have parallels in deposits of early LM IIIC, including the rhyton **K123.1**. The rubbish dump was early, and probably was used by the inhabitants of the Great House, and the Temple Dependencies (especially K 38) do provide some of the earliest pottery from the site. The lower material from the Magazines was not as early, suggesting that this building was constructed at a somewhat later date. The LM IIIB/C and early LM IIIC material found in the streets and courts suggest that the layout of the street system and many of the buildings belong to the earliest phases of the settlement.

Pendlebury did not concern himself with the phases of abandonment, yet there is some indication that some areas went out of use before others. The last buildings in use seem to have been the Western Cliff Houses, the area around a possible ritual centre (K 106), as well as a shrine of the goddess, K 116. There is no evidence elsewhere on the site of anything as late as those two rooms, and perhaps the eastern part of the settlement had already been abandoned; it is possible that when the population left Karphi, the site continued to be used seasonally by shepherds or former inhabitants continued to practice their religious observances at the shrines and Temple, where the goddess statues and accompanying ritual material were left behind. The question remains as to why the population left Karphi; despite Pendlebury's insistence that there was no evidence of any catastrophe on the site the pottery shows much burning, possibly caused by contact with the fires in the

houses that must have been used for cooking and warmth, but also perhaps as a result of natural disasters like earthquakes or caused by hostile actions. When the settlement was abandoned, the larger coarse vessels were left behind, but the inhabitants may have taken with them some of their finer drinking and eating vessels; there are few identifiably late LM IIIC deep bowls from the site that are nearly complete. The people also abandoned their statues of the goddesses with upraised arms and ritual equipment, a pattern that can be seen also at Kavousi–*Vronda*, Khalasmenos, and Vasiliki–*Kephala*.[13] While the abandonment of ritual objects seems surprising, it may be that these objects had locational importance and could not be removed from the places with which they were associated. Perhaps elder members of the community or the most devout continued to visit the shrines and temple after the abandonment.

The Ta Mnemata tombs were used even after the last rooms were abandoned and continued for several generations until SM–EPG. The spring at Vitzelovrysis was also visited into PG. After the PG period, however, the cemetery seems to have been abandoned for a long period.

Somewhat surprisingly, later use of the site can also be seen. There was apparently an Archaic shrine at Vitzelovrysis,[14] and a good deal of what seems to be Archaic and Classical pottery was found in and around the Ta Mnemata tombs. It is possible that the tombs became a locus for ancestor veneration, or that the cemetery was used by groups of inhabitants of the Lasithi to assert their claims to power through connections with the past or even to establish territorial claims on the site, as was the case elsewhere.[15] Hellenistic pottery has been found in K 12–K 17, suggesting reuse in the late fourth — third centuries; possibly Karphi was at that time a seasonal settlement. Finally, Byzantine presence is attested by a fragment of glazed pottery from K 127.

FUNCTION OF BUILDINGS AND ROOMS

The excavators assigned names to the various blocks or quarters of the settlement, providing them with designations that reflected their presumed functions. Often these names related to religious practices, like the Temple, the Priest's House, and the Small Shrine. The Great House was thought to be the ruler's dwelling, the Barracks were so called because it was thought that soldiers stayed there to guard the entrance into the site. The Magazines contained a large number of pithoi and other storage vessels, the Baker's House had an oven, and the Commercial Quarter was thought to be shops

---

13   Gesell 2004 (Kavousi–*Vronda*); Tsipopoulou 2001, 2009 (Khalasmenos); Eliopoulos 1998, 2003, 2004 (Vasiliki–*Kephala*).

14   *Karphi*, 100.

15   Day 2011 *b*.

(although K 116 contained religious equipment). Other names were more neutral, simply reflecting the area in which they were located (Southern Houses, Eastern Quarter, Central West Quarter, and so on).

For the most part, the finds, especially the pottery, do not help to determine specific functions for the various buildings or rooms. By using a combination of the notebook and the extant pottery, however, one can reconstruct some of the activities that went on in the rooms, at least those that left archaeologically visible remains. The notebook, while helpful in determining what was in the rooms, must be used with care. The material was recorded with increasing detail, so that in the 1937 and 1938 seasons only general shapes were recorded, but by the 1939 season the actual types of each shape were often given; thus there is greater information about the material from the western part of the settlement and the eastern edge than about that from the centre of the excavated area. In 1939, however, most of the pottery was examined without washing and discarded on the site, so the observations about this material may not be complete. Finally, it is not always clear from the notebook whether the pottery that was mentioned was nearly complete or fragmentary. Thus, when the notebook reports that room K 138 in the Eastern Quarter had five pithoi with different rims, it is not certain that all those pithoi were complete and in use in the room at the time of abandonment, since some may only have been represented by fragments, and the upper portions of pithoi could have been reused as chimney pots. Modern attempts at reconstructing the economy and society of Karphi have taken what is given in the publication and notebooks to suggest numbers of vessels and to reconstruct the amount of storage and other activities that occurred in the rooms and buildings.[16] Nowicki has even produced plans of major buildings at Karphi with circles representing each pithos or storage jar;[17] these seem to be based on a combination of the number of pithoi mentioned in the publication and notebooks together with a calculation of available space, but they are misleading, since we cannot be certain that there were ever that many jars in use in that room at the same time. Nevertheless, the preserved remains do allow us to see typical assemblages and to reconstruct some activities that occurred in the rooms and buildings.[18]

Most of the buildings in the settlement seem to be ordinary domestic establishments, and the rooms within them multifunctional; activities attested in the archaeological record include storage, the preparation and consumption of food, and weaving; other activities can be deduced from the non-ceramic finds. In general, the larger rooms in the buildings showed the greatest number of activities.

Storage

Storage occurred in nearly every room of the settlement; only street/courts K 32, K 50, K 70, and K 140 and Rooms K 38 and K 126 produced no fragments of pithoi or other storage jars. Most rooms had between one and five storage vessels, including pithoi, pithoid jars, tripod pithoi, and coarse stirrup jars; jars have not been included in this count, since many of these may have been used in cooking rather than storage. A few rooms produced exceptionally large numbers of pithoi: nine in K 69, eight each in K 22 and K 80. The rooms with the largest numbers also had many other types of storage vessels: K 149 had 17 pithoi, four tripod pithoi, and seven pithoid jars; next door in K 147 were five pithoi, eight pithoid jars, a tripod pithos, and a stirrup jar; K 121 contained ten pithoi, two tripod pithoi, and five pithoid jars;[19] K 16-17 had six pithoi, eight pithoid jars, and a stirrup jar; K 143 had five pithoi and seven pithoid jars; K 106 contained six pithoi, three pithoid jars, and two stirrup jars; K 110 had three pithoi, six pithoid jars, and a stirrup jar. While there is no evidence for the nature of the material stored within most of these vessels, whether solids or liquids, foodstuffs or other materials, the large coarse stirrup jars almost certainly were used for liquids, whether wine or oil. We can, however, guess that the pithoi were used for long-term storage, while the pithoid jars, being smaller and with wider mouths, would have served for short-term storage.

In general, the rooms with the largest number of pithoi tend to be the largest within the house (e.g. K 147, K 149, K 137, K 139, K 132, K 23, K 44, K 110, K 106), but occasionally storage vessels are numerous in smaller rooms (e.g. K 22, K 26, K 50, K 55, K 71, K 84, K 102, K 115). Large rooms with evidence of storage were not found in the Barracks, the Southern Shelters, or most of the houses in the Central West Quarter. The Temple and its Dependencies also were without major storage facilities. The assemblages of some LM IIIC shrines elsewhere included pithoi, as at Khalasmenos,[20] but others did not, as at Kavousi–*Vronda*.[21] Perhaps at Karphi whatever food was needed for rituals came from the stores of the members of the community.

It is hard to estimate the storage capacities of the houses, since so few pithoi are preserved and the notebook does not provide information on the size of those that were discarded. Basing his interpretation on ethnographic evidence from Lasithi, Nowicki has

---

16 Nowicki 1999, Wallace 2005.

17 Nowicki 1999, figs. 11–2, 14, and 15; these are reproduced in Nowicki 2002, fig. 60.

18 Day 2011*a*.

19 The number of storage vessels for what was interpreted as a single-room structure in K 121 is extraordinary, and it is likely that this room belonged with one of the other buildings in the Western Cliff Houses, probably K 113-114-120; see Wallace 2005, 229.

20 Tsipopoulou 2009, 159–60.

21 Gesell, Glowacki and Klein, forthcoming.

estimated that an average family of five would need the following amount for storage of basic subsistence: for cereals three large pithoi (or 9–12 small), for pulses one large or 1–2 small pithoi, and for olive oil one large or two small pithoi.[22] If he is correct, then either these buildings with large storage capacity housed larger, perhaps extended, families, or the pithoi represent storage of goods beyond what was needed for subsistence.

Cooking

Cooking also went on in many of the rooms, although few hearths were found (only in K 22, K 68, K 83, K 136, K 137, and K 139). Nevertheless, tripod cooking pots, cooking dishes, cooking trays, cooking jugs, and cooking lids were found in nearly all of the rooms of the settlement. Even ritual rooms produced cooking pottery; the Temple had a cooking dish and several tripod cooking pots. A few rooms contained little or no cooking ware, including one of the buildings in the Eastern Quarter (K 137-141), one of the houses of the Southeast Block (K 130-131), and some of the dependencies of the Temple (K 38, K 39). Some of the rooms with large numbers of storage vessels contained few if any cooking wares (K 69, K 80).

Rooms with extraordinary numbers of cooking pots may have served as kitchens: K 138–139 and K 143 for the Eastern Quarter, K 132 for the Southeast House, K 2 for the Barracks, K 19 for the Temple, K 16-17 for the Great House Shrine, K 14 for the Great House, K 31 for the Magazines, K 26–27 for the Southern Houses, K 60 and K 80 for the Priest's House, K 118 for the Eastern Cliff Houses, K 113 and K 121 for one Western Cliff House, K 106 for the other Western Cliff House, and all the rooms for the houses on Mikre Koprana.

Cooking pottery came in a variety of types. In general, cooking equipment included at least one tripod cooking pot and a cooking dish; cooking trays were also common, but cooking jugs and lids were less so. None of the flat-bottomed cooking jars or cooking amphoras found at other LM IIIC sites were identified at Karphi,[23] but some may have been discarded and recorded as jars. It is assumed that the various types of cooking pottery were employed in different kinds of cooking. The tripod cooking pot comes in a variety of shapes and sizes; most are the deep, two-handled collared jars, but smaller tripods with one or two vertical handles, tripod bowls, and round-bottomed tripods also occur. Tripods seem to have been designed to set directly over the fire,[24] and they may have been used for preparing stews or soups; the different shapes for the base may have been designed for cooking different kinds of food. Cooking jugs also show evidence of having been placed in the fire, possibly for heating liquids, which could then be poured through the spout. Trays were probably used for warming near the fire or for serving; they do not show the same degree

of burning as other cooking vessels. The tripod trays from Karphi show no signs of the interior burning that occurred on examples from Khalasmenos that has led to their being identified as grills or portable hearths.[25] The function of cooking dishes is still uncertain. These large, rather shallow vessels had thin rounded bottoms that nearly always were burned so badly that they disintegrated; the rims, however, were very thick, often pulled out or pressed in to form spouts, and sometimes with holes. Dishes may have been used like a Chinese wok for keeping part of the food warm on the sides while the rest was cooking in the bottom. They may also have been used for cooking large quantities of food, perhaps for social occasions. Two cooking dishes were found in the oven of the Baker's House, suggesting that they may have been used in baking. The dishes could be turned into small ovens with the addition of a lid of similar shape.[26] It is also possible that dishes were used in the cheese-making process.[27]

While lids are not generally classed among cooking vessels, many of the LM IIIC lids are made of cooking fabrics and show traces of burning, and they may have been placed over the cooking pots. The most common type of lid is a flat knobbed disc, often elaborately decorated on top. The undersides of these lids show burning in a variety of patterns. Other types of vessels may have been used not in cooking, but in the preparation of food, such as basins; these may have been employed like plastic lekanai today for a variety of purposes, for mixing food but also for washing.

A few rooms had unusual types of cooking vessels in them. K 126, for example, contained at least two large cooking slabs. These may equally have been used for an industrial process such as metalworking or pottery manufacture.

Eating and Drinking

Eating and drinking also seem to have gone on in nearly every room. These activities were most often daily and domestic, involving coarse and simpler fine vessels; the more elaborately decorated shapes, however, may have been used as display items in more social forms of eating

---

22   Nowicki 1999, 156.
23   Yasur-Landau 2006, 54.
24   Yasur-Landau 2006, 51.
25   Yasur-Landau 2006, 54.
26   Mook 1999, 508.
27   It is interesting that no specialised equipment for cheese-making has been identified at Karphi, given the importance that shepherding must have played in the local economy. The site is too high to make ordinary agriculture possible, and olives do not grow in the Lasithi at all. Perhaps the cooking dishes were used to boil milk for making cheese; cheese would have been aged in baskets, which leave no trace in the archaeological record.

and drinking. Feasting may have provided households an opportunity to display wealth, status, or taste in their serving vessels and vessels for consumption.

Communal or public feasting is part of the social fabric of human communities, and doubtless went on at Karphi. Much of the pottery seems to have been decorated with a view to impressing people beyond the household on feasting occasions. It is difficult, however, to know what kinds of feasting occurred from the limited archaeological record, particularly in the absence of any preserved animal bones.[28] Nevertheless, examining the evidence of highly decorated eating and serving vessels, along with cooking facilities can give insights into the feasting practices at Karphi.[29]

The most frequent fine table vessel was the deep bowl, and fragments occurred in nearly every room. The shape is generally thought of as a drinking vessel, but it may also have been used for eating, perhaps for cracked wheat or porridge that may have served as a basic food for the inhabitants.[30] Cups were certainly used for drinking, and like deep bowls could have served for daily and private use or be brought out for social occasions; cups are less common than deep bowls and are also spread around the settlement.

The large and elaborately decorated kylikes and mugs, oversized cups, and even some of the larger deep bowls or small kraters (those with a rim diameter from 18–23) may have functioned in specialised feasting occasions that focused on drinking. Kylikes in general seem to have been employed in feasting occasions in LM II–III Crete, as can be seen on wall paintings.[31] In particular, the LM IIIC kylix can be extremely large, and the shape may have played an important role in elite drinking rituals at both Karphi and Kavousi–Vronda.[32] Kylikes are rarer than other drinking vessels, but they do occur in nearly every building on the site, although not in every room. Several buildings had larger than usual numbers of kylikes: the Great House, the Southeast Block, the Western Cliff Houses, and Building K 85-87-69 of the Central West Quarter. The presence of kylikes in K 106 and K 85, both of which contained figurines of possible ritual significance suggests that these vessels played a role in sacred as well as secular rituals. I have argued elsewhere that the large kylikes found on LM IIIC sites may remain from competitive drinking rituals that helped elites create and maintain power.[33] Although these drinking rituals seem to have gone on in several large houses on the site, more kylikes were found in the Great House than elsewhere. With its accompanying shrine, its architectural refinements like the use of cut blocks in the doorways, and the variety of luxury goods found in its storerooms this building seems to have been marked as one of the most important buildings so far uncovered at the site.

Other types of vessels seem to have been used in festive circumstances, both the drinking rituals and feasting. Kraters were abundant, and while similar in shape to the deep bowls, they are much larger and generally more elaborately decorated. The function of kraters is not certain; the name suggests a large bowl for mixing water and wine in the later Greek fashion, but there is currently no evidence to confirm this association. At Karphi, kraters are often found in association with large kylikes, and may also have been used in the elite drinking rituals, where their elaborate decoration would display the wealth and taste of the owner; a huge and elaborately decorated krater, for example, accompanied the large kylikes found in K 131 in the Southeast Block. Kraters were, however, also found without kylikes and may have been used in other types of feasting rituals, along with mugs and tankards.

Highly decorated pyxides and stirrup jars probably were meant to display the taste, wealth, or status of the owners during social occasions. The pyxis is one of the peculiarities of the Karphi ceramic assemblage; although known at other LM IIIC sites, the shape is not so plentiful elsewhere as at Karphi. Pyxides are among the most highly decorated vessels at Karphi, and whatever their function, they must have been display items. Fine stirrup jars are generally small and have elaborate decoration; the finest examples with octopus motifs. Perhaps they were used as oil containers, impressive during festive dining. The juglet or small amphora may have served a similar use in ordinary domestic circumstances; these rarely carry elaborate decoration. One-handled, cylindrical-mouthed jugs are plentiful, the coarse and undecorated examples used in ordinary domestic context, the more elaborate and fine vessels employed in social or religious circumstances. All of these types of vessels seem to have been spread around the site, suggesting that small-scale feasting occurred regularly in every household.

Cooking vessels also can be useful in determining sites of medium- to large-scale feasting; such vessels should be plentiful and of large size.[34] At Karphi, a few of the buildings seem to have larger than normal cooking assemblages. The houses on Mikre Koprana (K 147, K 149–150), for example, produced large numbers of cooking dishes and tripod cooking pots, along with a large number of storage vessels. Building

---

28   Wallace 2005, 264–70 gives much of the non-ceramic evidence for feasting at Karphi and other LM IIIC sites.

29   Hayden 2001, 46–58.

30   The deep bowl is perhaps analogous to the bowls used for rice or even noodles in Chinese culture, where small amounts of meats and vegetables are placed on top of a bed of rice that forms the staple meals.

31   For example, on the Campstool Fresco from Knossos: Evans 1935, 388, pl. 31.

32   Day and Snyder 2004.

33   Day and Snyder 2004, 73. See also Dietler 1990; Joffe 1998; Arnold 1999.

34   Hayden 2001, 47–8.

K 138-139-140 of the Eastern Quarter also had large numbers of cooking vessels, and even more were found in K 143 to the east of this building, possibly part of the same complex. This building was a megaron type and had a hearth in the centre of the large room; its size suggests that it was an elite building, and it may have been involved in regular feasting activities. Not surprisingly, the Great House also had much cooking equipment, particularly if the material from the Great House Shrine is added into the total. K 26-27-28 produced many tripod cooking pots, and K 106 had a variety, including a large number of cooking trays. Of these buildings, at least two (the Great House and K 106) also produced more than one large kylix. Three of them (the Great House, K 106, and K 27) had evidence for religious activities. While the Temple did not have a large number of cooking vessels, taken with the pottery from K 19 of the Temple Dependencies, there is ample evidence that feasting was at least on occasion a sacred ritual.

What was the nature of the feasting that went on at Karphi? The oversized drinking vessels and the emphasis on elaborate display on feasting pottery suggests that feasting was part of a system of competitive elite status display, possibly the patron-role feasting or diacritical feasting identified by Dietler and Hayden.[35] It is also possible that at least some of the Karphi feasts were aimed at promoting alliances among groups, and some at least had a religious meaning.

Weaving

Some of the other terracotta finds provide evidence for spinning and weaving, including spools, spindle whorls, and a single large weight. Spools were found all over the site, usually one or two to a room, but occasionally they occurred in such large numbers that one can postulate a loom in the room. Many of similar size and weight were found in Mikre Koprana, at least 18 from a single room (K 150). K 136 in the Eastern Quarter had 21 spools, the Southern Shelters produced 15, and in the Southern Houses there were at least 20 in K 27, two in K 26, six in K 44, and seven in K 46. K 23 in the Magazines had nine, with five in K 22 next to it. K 61 in the Priest's House produced 19 spools. K 102 in the Western Cliff Houses had 38, and K 110 in the Eastern Cliff Houses produced over 50. The large pyramidal weight found in K 126 may also have been part of a loom, but only the single example is recorded. Terracotta beads or spindle whorls were also found all over the site, but never more than four of them came from a single room. Clearly the people of Karphi were engaged in spinning and weaving on a domestic scale, and in at least six rooms enough spools (i.e. around 20 or more) were found to suggest that looms were set up: K 27, K 61, K 110, K 102, K 136, and K 150.

Other activities

Other objects give us further information on the activities and functions of rooms. There is little to suggest industrial activity. Although there must have been a potter's workshop, only a single fragment of a potter's wheel was found and no kiln; the large quantity of misfired blue ware vessels found in the Temple, however, may represent wasters from a nearby kiln. Metal hoards have been seen as possible indicators of metallurgical activity,[36] but they may equally well show wealth. The lead run-offs found in K 11 and K 12 of the Great House, however, do attest to some metallurgical activity there.

Religion

Many rooms that produced ritual equipment may have served religious functions, with evidence for varying degrees of private or public involvement and distinctly different kinds of rituals. The ritual areas at Karphi have been recognised and discussed by many scholars, but without taking into account the whole assemblages found in them.[37] The Temple itself was the largest religious area, and doubtless served a public function. The large open area to the east may have been used for community gatherings.[38] K 19, just to the south of the Temple and to the west of the open area produced a good deal of cooking equipment, and it is possible that food preparation for rituals took place in that room. The Temple produced the largest amount of ritual material, including the following: five nearly complete goddesses, fragments of at least four other faces and 40 arms, pieces of a fine buff figure, and attributes from headdresses (birds, discs, palettes, and incised cones). There were also fragments of plaques, one with a head and at least three others, and many cylindrical offering stands, the two catalogued stands and at least ten others. Other shapes included scuttles, a kalathos with horns, an incense burner, a chalice, the base of a rhyton, a possible hut urn, a fenestrated stand, and at least two animal figurines. Other material recorded from the Temple included fine blue ware vessels, and cooking pottery, including tripods and a dish, but no storage vessels. It is not clear whether these objects were all found in association with the goddesses or if they were in one of the other spaces that may have been part of the religious complex. Nevertheless, it is clear that the Temple had the greatest amount and variety of ritual material of all the religious buildings on the site. It is clearly a shrine involving the worship

---

35   Hayden 2001, 57–8; Dietler 2001, 82–8.
36   Wallace 2005, 259.
37   Gesell 1985, 79–82; Prent 2005, 137–49, 193–4; Hallager 2009, 114–6.
38   Rutkowski 1987, 259.

of goddesses with upraised arms and is similar to other contemporary shrines at Kavousi–*Vronda*, Khalasmenos, and Vasiliki–*Kephala*.[39]

The two other possible shrines in which goddess figures have been found at Karphi are not without problems. The Great House Shrine (K 15–18) produced ritual material, including a goddess face, snake tube, and figurines, suggesting that this was another shrine. The area had, however, been disturbed in later periods. Even if this disturbance did not affect the distribution of finds, it is possible that some of the material may have come from the dump under K 16 and K 17, since a plaque fragment was found from the lower deposits in K 17. The other areas built over the dump also produced additional cult equipment, including K 70, but it is unclear if these came from the dump below or were being stored in the storeroom at the time the building went out of use. Other fragments of ritual equipment came from the areas around the Great House: part of a goddess face, a plaque and a kalathos were found in K 38, a room that Pendlebury thought was part of the Temple Dependencies, but contiguous with K 16 and possibly constructed over the dump; it produced very early LM IIIC pottery. The streets and courts around the Great House also had ritual equipment, including K 72 to the north and west and K 32 to the south.

There seem to be three possibilities about this shrine. First of all, the cult material found scattered throughout this area may have been part of the rubbish dump and have nothing to do with Rooms K 15–18. A second possibility is that most of this material may come from a shrine in K 15–18. The third possibility is that there had been a shrine in K 15–18 in an early phase of the settlement's history and remains from it were left in the area before the later K 15–18 shrine was built. The last explanation would account for the apparent presence of cult equipment both below the floors and above the floors of the area. In addition to the ritual equipment, there was evidence for cooking and storage in K 16-17 and in K 18. The association of this ritual building with the Great House suggests that the inhabitants of that dwelling exerted some control over the religious activity in the shrine. If the shrine existed from the beginning, then they always had control and possibly gained status from that association. If the shrine came later, then as Wallace suggested, it may provide evidence that the group in the Great House was asserting its own power by taking over the shrine.[40]

The third shrine of the goddess with upraised arms was located in K 116 of the Commercial Quarter. Three goddesses are recorded from this room, along with part of a plaque, two scuttles, and more than four kalathoi. Outside the small shrine was an open courtyard, K 79-89. K 116 contained some of the latest pottery found in the settlement at Karphi, including a SM stirrup jar (**K116.4**), and this shrine may have been later or continued to be used after all or parts of the rest of the settlement had passed out of use. There is, however, some evidence that the building was no longer a shrine at the end of the settlement's history; the goddesses were so fragmentary that no attempt was made to make them up, and the court outside had been taken over by an oven.

The material from the Temple and two smaller shrines of the goddess with upraised arms have certain features in common. Goddess statues and plaques were found in all three, stands in all but K 116. It is possible that the three shrines were not in use at the same time. K 15–18 may have been in use from early on in the settlement's history, while the shrine in K 116 may have been in use later than most of the rest of the settlement. It is impossible to date the construction or abandonment of the Temple, since so little datable fine ware was found in it. Pendlebury believed that the Temple was one of the earliest buildings constructed on the site, and if K 38 was part of the dependencies of the Temple, which is not at all certain, then his hypothesis is supported by the very early pottery found there. The blue ware vases found in the Temple have high concave raised bases that look rather late in LM IIIC, and if they do belong with the Temple assemblages, they indicate a use in the later part of LM IIIC. The exceptional preservation of the cult equipment also supports the idea that the Temple continued in use until the end of the settlement.

In addition to the shrines of goddesses with upraised arms, there are other areas that produced different types of cult equipment, suggesting different types of rituals.[41] Two rooms have been identified as the location of cult activities on the basis of cylindrical stands or altars found within them. The so-called Small Shrine (K 55, K 57) is so designated because of the elaborate 'altar', and a snake tube found in it. The altar clearly has ritual associations, with the double axes and small animals depicted on it, but its precise function is not certain. Whether it is actually an altar or is simply an elaborate stand is not known, but it does bear some resemblance to cylindrical stands found elsewhere in LM IIIC sites.[42] The snake tube was quite fragmentary. Cylindrical tubes were used to hold offering bowls in religious contexts.[43] Nothing else was found in this building to suggest a religious function. The layout of the building, however, with doorways facing on two large squares, does suggest a public function. Similar

39 Gesell 2004 (Kavousi–*Vronda*); Tsipopoulou 2001, 2009 (Khalasmenos); Eliopoulos 1998, 2003, 2004 (Vasiliki–*Kephala*).

40 Wallace 2005, 260–1.

41 Day 2009.

42 They are particularly common at Kavousi–*Vronda*, where they occur in domestic assemblages (at least one in each building) but without any clear cult association; see Day *et al*. forthcoming.

43 Gesell 1976.

is K 58, a small room off the Priest's House that faced onto a street. Here there were two stands, one cylindrical, one rectangular. Eight kalathoi were also found in the room, possibly used as offering bowls with the stands, but no other ritual objects appeared. If the Small Shrine and K 58 did figure in religious activities, they functioned differently from the shrines of goddesses with upraised arms.

Gesell identified K 27 in the Southern Houses as a cult area based on the two rhyta found in it.[44] Although the piriform rhyton with the human head is portable and thus cannot be used to indicate that ritual activities occurred in the room, the large rhyton in the form of a charioteer and bull's heads is neither easily portable nor of any imaginable function other than ritual. A votive bronze double axe found next door in K 26 may indicate a ritual function for other parts of the building as well. It is difficult to imagine what sort of ritual activity went on in K 27, especially since the room produced so many domestic objects, including 17 pithoi and five tripod cooking pots. The presence of 20 spools suggests that a loom may have been set up in the room as well. At any rate, it is safe to assert that different sorts of cult activity occurred in this room than what went on in the shrines with the goddess figures, since the equipment is so different. There are no other rooms in which more than a single rhyton was found, and few are known at all. Rhyta imply that libations were made into the ground or another vessel. The rhyton is associated with ritual practice from the early stages of Minoan culture, and was especially common in palatial society. Use of these vessels may have involved appeasement of powers believed to reside in or under the earth: deities who regulated the fertility of the earth, those who controlled earthquakes, or those involved with death, even perhaps the dead themselves. The presence of the rhyta along with cooking equipment suggests that the pouring of libations may have been associated with feasting in or around the Southern Houses.

Finally, a number of rooms that contained figurines may also have ritual associations. The figurines, while they are probably religious, do not indicate that the room in which they are found was a community-oriented ritual centre,[45] and figurines appear in many domestic contexts across the site (e.g. K 62, K 90, K 91, K 108, K 109, K 122, K 38, K 140, K 101). There are, however, at least two areas with figurines in association with other objects that indicate religious activity. K 85 and K 87 in the Central West Quarter produced larger animal figurines. In K 85 cult objects are said to have stood on a small ledge in the west wall, and many figurines came from the room, including two or three females, a bull, and the head of a large hollow bull. Possible fragments of a rectangular stand with punctuated design also came from this room. The adjoining room (K 87) contained a large hollow horse figurine and fragments of another animal figurine found on a table of rock. These two rooms, with their

figurines set up on ledges or tables suggest definite ritual activity, but one different from what went on in the shrines of goddesses with upraised arms, or the rooms with the cylindrical offering stands. The building is unusual in the fact that storage was separated from the other activities; K 69 was used for storage (12 storage vessels), but none appeared in the other two rooms, which contained cooking vessels. The hut urn from K 69 seems to have been associated with storage and not involved in the rituals with the animal figurines. A similar assemblage came from K 106 in the Western Cliff Houses. The head of a terracotta statuette, body of an animal figurine, and fragments of unusual shapes that could represent possible altars or horns of consecration were found together with a bronze votive double axe. A rim fragment may come from a snake tube or some other sort of cylindrical stand. Cooking and storage also occurred in the room, and the associated room next door (K 102) had 38 spools and so possibly there was a loom here. That these two groups of figurines associated with stands or altars have religious meaning is quite certain, but we are less sure about the nature of that religious activity. The figurines may be a sign of private devotion rather than any public or community ritual. At any rate these rooms lack the clearly public nature of the shrines of the goddesses with upraised arms or even of the small rooms with offering stands that lie open to major streets.

Since only a small portion of the entire Karphi settlement has been uncovered, it is difficult to make pronouncements about the religious beliefs of the inhabitants or their ritual practices. Nevertheless, it is clear that religion played a major role in the lives of the people of Karphi. The large temple, bigger than the religious buildings of other contemporary settlements,[46] with its many figures of goddesses with upraised arms and open areas for public gatherings outside, seems to have been the central focus of ritual activities, but other smaller shrines with goddess figures scattered throughout the houses, whether all contemporary or not, suggest that ritual was not completely centralised. The presence of special rooms or buildings for offerings on stands and a room housing vessels for pouring libations, perhaps to different deities, indicates different ritual activities scattered

---

44 Gesell 1985, 81.

45 At Kavousi–*Vronda*, for example, two horse figurines and a bovine were found on a platform in the corner of Room 1 of building D, but without any other ritual objects, and they must have been the object of domestic piety, rather than the focus of cult activity in a cult building. See Gesell, Day and Coulson 1995, 71–3.

46 Klein and Glowacki 2009, 157. If indeed all of the rooms of the complex at Vasiliki–*Kephala* belong to the same building, then it would be larger; the actual shrine, however, is quite small; see Eliopoulos 1998, 2003, 2004.

around the site. Finally, the animal and human figurines found in the houses without other ritual equipment suggest the importance of family or private devotion. The presence of cooking equipment in nearly all of the religious buildings indicates that part of the rituals included feasting.

SOCIAL, ECONOMIC, AND POLITICAL ARRANGEMENT OF THE KARPHI SETTLEMENT

Trade and outside contact

Watrous has suggested that Karphi may have been a seasonal settlement, only in use during the summer months, but this seems doubtful.[47] Traditional seasonal settlements do not usually have cemeteries, nor so many nor such varied religious buildings. The organised nature of the settlement plan, with its cobbled streets and courts suggests a level of town planning that would not be in keeping with a village only inhabited during one season.

As both Watrous and Nowicki suggest, the inhabitants of the Karphi settlement were probably involved largely in subsistence farming and herding, and they stored their agricultural produce in storage jars within the rooms of the settlement.[48] The sheer amount of storage suggests that each household kept food and material needs for its own use and the groups were more or less self sufficient; the fact that some of the houses showed greater storage facilities, however, suggests control over a surplus, and many of these buildings also show evidence of larger scale feasting. The economy, then, was quite simple, and there is no internal evidence that the inhabitants lived on the proceeds of brigandage, as suggested by Pendlebury and Watrous.[49]

While there may be a few imported goods found in the settlement, the picture from the pottery is that there was little trade with sites outside the immediate area. Most of the fabrics are local, and only a few vessels seem to have come from other sites on Crete, other islands, or the mainland. Several vessels seem to have been brought to the site from elsewhere on Crete. Petrographic analysis shows that **K38.1** was not of local manufacture, and it shows similarities to vessels from Knossos and the Mesara. **K147.15** resembles a stirrup jar found at Khania, possibly an import from Knossos. The spouted bowls **K115.6** and **K.18** show possible contact with the islands in IIIC. Deep bowls without the interior monochrome coating may come from the mainland (**K12.2**, **K46.2**, **K106.3**, **K.6**, and possibly **K76.14**). Krater **K23.11** is a possible import from Kephallonia. The flask **K18.1** has its closest parallels in Syria and may be an import from the Levant. It is not clear if jug **K87.1** was of local manufacture, although its shape and decoration have similarities to other vessels from the site. A close parallel was found at Syme Vianno, and the presence of a similar vessel at Enkomi may suggest contact between Crete and Cyprus. The carinated bowl **K143.2** may be an import, as it is unusual in shape and decoration, but there are no parallels to suggest where it might have come from. The evidence is scanty, but suggests that Karphi was not entirely isolated and that the inhabitants had connections, whether direct or indirect, with a number of areas of the eastern Mediterranean.

Ethnicity

The ethnicity of the inhabitants has been discussed on numerous occasions. Pendlebury believed that some of the inhabitants of the Karphi settlement were Mycenaeans or mainlanders, while others were Minoans, and other scholars have followed his suggestion.[50] In particular, they have pointed to the megaron-type plans of the building of the Eastern Quarter as an indication that mainlanders lived at Karphi, segregated from the Minoan inhabitants. The megaron-type building continues to be seen as an indicator of Mycenaean inhabitation or mainland influence,[51] although the use of large, rectangular and axial buildings may have as much to do with making symbolic connections to the power and stability of the Mycenaeans as with an indication of ethnicity.[52]

Other features have been seen as indicative of a Mycenaean presence at Karphi. Two types of cooking pots have been seen as introduced into Crete from the mainland. The round-bottomed tripod, in particular, has been seen as a mainland feature in the cooking assemblage.[53] The cooking amphora, which may not appear at Karphi, has also been seen as a mainland type.[54]

Without written documents, we cannot determine the language spoken by the inhabitants of Karphi, but the material found in the settlement does not show differences that can be attributed to varying ethnic backgrounds rather than to different class or status groups or different dates.

---

47 Watrous 1982, 19–20.
48 Watrous 1982, 19–20; Nowicki 1999.
49 *Karphi*, 140; Watrous 1982, 19. It is difficult to know what would constitute archaeological evidence for brigandage, however.
50 Mazarakis Ainian 1997, 219.
51 Tsipopoulou 2005, 324.
52 Whittaker 2005, 338.
53 Borgna 1999, 200.
54 Tsipopoulou 2004, 115.

11

Analysis of Postpalatial pottery from Karphi

Eleni Nodarou and Ioannis Iliopoulos

INTRODUCTION[1]

The destruction of the palaces in the LM IIIB period has been followed by the foundation of new settlements in remote and fairly inaccessible areas across Crete. The publication of LM IIIC sites like Kavousi–*Vronda*,[2] Katalimata,[3] Vasiliki–*Kephala*[4] and Khalasmenos[5] in eastern Crete, Gazi[6] and Karphi[7] in central Crete, as well as the discovery of new sites through survey[8] generated a renewed interest on the character and function of these settlements as well as the economy and structure of the societies inhabiting them.[9]

The new approaches have brought to light aspects of the material culture that can be explored through analysis. The production and distribution of Postpalatial pottery is at the centre of archaeometric analyses, since ceramics of domestic and religious function are found in quantities and in various contexts. Within this framework an analytical project combining thin section petrography and scanning electron microscopy was undertaken for the study of the ritual equipment from Kavousi. It demonstrated the presence of contrasting technologies used by different groups of potters in the area of the Isthmus of Ierapetra during the LM IIIC period.[10]

The combination of thin section petrography and scanning electron microscopy for the study of ancient ceramics has contributed greatly in the understanding of Minoan pottery making traditions and distribution of ceramics.[11] The analytical programme for the Postpalatial pottery from Karphi was put forward in order to assess the following issues:

a) Characterisation and grouping of the pottery fabrics according to their mineralogical and textural characteristics through optical microscopy. The petrographic groups are then compared to the groups that derived from the macroscopic fabric study. This comparison reveals the connection between the visual properties of the final product (variation in colour, texture of the surface, hardness) and its technology of manufacture.

b) Inferences on the raw materials and, thus, on the origin of the pottery used at Karphi on the basis of the mineralogical composition of the ceramic fabrics. The potential correlation between the function of the vessel and the respective clay recipes is also examined as well as the relationship between the fabrics of the domestic vessels and

those of the ritual artefacts (goddess figures and snake tubes).

c) Inferences on the technology of manufacture of the ceramics and more specifically on the firing temperature and kiln atmosphere through the examination of the clay body microstructure using Scanning Electron Microscopy (SEM). The semi-quantitative elemental analysis provided by an Energy Dispersive X-ray Spectrometer (EDS) allows the grouping of samples according to their chemical composition and compare them with those from petrography.

THE PETROGRAPHIC ANALYSIS

Eighty-two samples were selected for petrographic analysis from the Karphi assemblage (for a complete catalogue of the vessels sampled, see TABLE 11.1). The analysis was carried out at the INSTAP Study Center for East Crete using a LEICA DMLP polarising microscope. Among the shapes selected for analysis are included domestic wares as well as ritual objects. The petrographic analysis resulted in the establishment of five fabric groups, four of which are coarse and semi-coarse and one is fine. Detailed petrographic descriptions of the fabric groups are provided at the end of the chapter.

---

1   We would like to thank the 23rd Ephoreia of Prehistoric and Classical Antiquities in Herakleion and the Greek Ministry of Culture for permission to sample the pottery from Karphi for analysis.

2   Day 1997; Gesell, Coulson and Day 1991; Gesell, Day and Coulson 1988; 1995.
3   Nowicki 2008.
4   Eliopoulos 1998.
5   Tsipopoulou 2001; 2004.
6   Marinatos 1937.
7   Day and Snyder 2004; Nowicki 1987.
8   For an overview of the site location and topography, see Wallace 2007.
9   Dickinson 2006; Whitley 1991; Wallace 2003; 2007.
10 Day *et al.* 2006.
11 Wilson and Day 1994; Shaw *et al.* 2001; Papadatos *et al.* forthcoming, to name just a few.

TABLE 11.1: **Concordance of vessels sampled for analysis.**

Sample	Shape	Context	Sample	Shape	Context
KAR 06/ 1	Lid	**K29.14**	KAR 06/ 42	Cooking slab	**K126.2**
KAR 06/ 2	Lid	**K125.2**	KAR 06/ 43	Cooking slab	**K113.5**
KAR 06/ 3	Lid	**K22.10**	KAR 06/ 44	Pithos	K 66
KAR 06/ 4	Krater	**K122.3**	KAR 06/ 45	Snake tube	K 1
KAR 06/ 5	Kalathos	**K3.11**	KAR 06/ 46	Snake tube	K 1
KAR 06/ 6	Kalathos	**K110.15**	KAR 06/ 47	Snake tube	K 1
KAR 06/ 7	Kalathos	**K28.6**	KAR 06/ 48	Snake tube	K 1
KAR 06/ 8	Kalathos	**MK.10**	KAR 06/ 49	Snake tube	K 1
KAR 06/ 9	Kalathos	**K110.13**	KAR 06/ 50	Snake tube	K 1
KAR 06/ 10	Goddess skirt	K 1	KAR 06/ 51	Snake tube	K 1
KAR 06/ 11	Snake tube	K 1	KAR 06/ 52	Snake tube	K 1
KAR 06/ 12	Snake tube	K 1	KAR 06/ 53	Tripod	**K106.25**
KAR 06/ 13	Deep bowl	**K61.2**	KAR 06/ 54	Tripod	**M2.1**
KAR 06/ 14	Deep bowl	**K68.1**	KAR 06/ 55	Stirrup jar	**K150.3**
KAR 06/ 15	Deep bowl	**K38.1**	KAR 06/ 56	Stirrup jar	**K134.4**
KAR 06/ 16	Deep bowl	**K68.2**	KAR 06/ 57	Stirrup jar	**K134.3**
KAR 06/ 17	Conical cup	**K114.1**	KAR 06/ 58	Jar	**K2.12**
KAR 06/ 18	Basin	K?	KAR 06/ 59	Cooking dish	**K20.1**
KAR 06/ 19	Snake tube	K 40-41	KAR 06/ 60	Pithoid jar	**K102.2**
KAR 06/ 20	Snake tube	K?	KAR 06/ 61	Cooking dish	**K108.8**
KAR 06/ 21	Snake tube	K?	KAR 06/ 62	Basin	**K44.7**
KAR 06/ 22	Kylix	**K80.4**	KAR 06/ 63	Tripod bowl	**K84.1**
KAR 06/ 23	Flask	**K18.1**	KAR 06/ 64	Jar	**K43.16**
KAR 06/ 24	Cookpot	K 22	KAR 06/ 65	Pithos	**K36.2**
KAR 06/ 25	Stirrup jar	MK1E	KAR 06/ 66	Pithos	**K.62**
KAR 06/ 26	Blue ware jug	K 28	KAR 06/ 67	Kalathos	**K80.6**
KAR 06/ 27	Stirrup jar	K 12	KAR 06/ 68	Kalathos	**K22.8**
KAR 06/ 28	Stirrup jar	MK1E	KAR 06/ 69	Kalathos	**K12.6**
KAR 06/ 29	Stirrup jar	K 3	KAR 06/ 70	Cooking cup	K 47
KAR 06/ 30	Stirrup jar	K 1	KAR 06/ 71	Jar	**K2.14**
KAR 06/ 31	Snake tube	K 1	KAR 06/ 72	Kalathos	K 26
KAR 06/ 32	Snake tube	K 1	KAR 06/ 73	Kalathos	**K26.8**
KAR 06/ 33	Pithos	K?	KAR 06/ 74	Pithos	K?
KAR 06/ 34	Cookpot	**K27.8**	KAR 06/ 75	Pithos	K?
KAR 06/ 35	Pyxis	**K3.5**	KAR 06/ 76	Pithos	K?
KAR 06/ 36	Askos	**K2.11**	KAR 06/ 77	Pithos	**K9.11**
KAR 06/ 37	Pyxis	**K22.4**	KAR 06/ 78	Pithos	K?
KAR 06/ 38	Tripod	**K23.26**	KAR 06/ 79	Pithos	**K55.3**
KAR 06/ 39	Tripod	**K27.7**	KAR 06/ 80	Pithos	K?
KAR 06/ 40	Pyxis	**K43.13**	KAR 06/ 81	Scuttle	**K115.13**
KAR 06/ 41	Jug	**K113.3**	KAR 06/ 82	Lid	**K80.7**

Coarse and Semi-Coarse Fabrics

The coarse and semi-coarse fabrics incorporate almost 60% of the samples and the majority of the shapes represented in the assemblage. Fabric Groups 1 and 2 are connected with sources of metamorphic rocks whereas Fabric Groups 3 and 4 with raw material from flysch sources.

Metamorphic Fabrics

The majority of the material is manufactured in a range of fabrics where the predominant non-plastic com-

ponent is the low grade metamorphic rock fragments. Two main groups have been identified:

Fabric Group 1

Subgroup (a): Coarse fabric with low grade metamorphic rocks (COLOUR PLATE 1 *a–b*)

Samples:
KAR 06/ 34 (**K27.8**), 54 (**M2.1**): cooking pots
KAR 06/ 42 (**K126.2**), 43 (**K113.5**): cooking slabs
KAR 06/ 33, 44 (K 66), 75, 77 (**K9.11**), 79 (**K55.3**): pithoi
KAR 06/ 71 (**K2.14**): jar

KAR 06/ 63 (**K84.1**): tripod bowl
KAR 06/ 60 (**K102.2**): pithoid jar
KAR 06/ 81 (**K115.13**): scuttle
KAR 06/ 3 (**K22.10**), 82 (**K80.7**): lids
KAR 06/ 7 (**K28.6**), 67 (**K80.6**), 72 (K 26): kalathoi
KAR 06/ 12, 20, 47: snake tubes
KAR 06/ 36 (**K2.11**): askos

This is a coarse red firing fabric, characterised by a red brown to dark brown matrix which ranges from optically moderately active to inactive. The absence of optical activity is indicative of a generally high firing temperature. The non-plastic inclusions are moderately well sorted and they consist of low-grade metamorphic rocks, namely fine grained phyllites in a variety of colours and consistencies, set in a mica rich clay matrix. The other non-plastic components are quartzite, monocrystalline quartz and sandstone. There are also very few to rare clay pellets and mudstone fragments which become common in subgroup (b).

This rock and mineral suite is indicative of the Phyllite-Quartzite series outcropping in the area of the Lasithi plateau[12] (FIG. 11.1). This series has experienced low grade (HP/LT) metamorphism[13] and is composed of phyllites, quartzites, mica-schists and quartzose-feldspar rich meta-sandstones, marbles and chert.[14] The presence of the red clay pellets is indicative of incomplete clay mixing.

The vessels represented in this group serve various functions. The domestic component includes cooking pots, cooking slabs, pithoi, jars and one pithoid jar, lids, kalathoi, and a scuttle. There are also three snake tubes and one askos.

Subgroup (b): Low grade metamorphic rocks, mudstone and pellets (COLOUR PLATE 1 *c*)

Samples:
KAR 06/ 1 (**K29.14**): lid
KAR 06/ 59 (**K20.1**), 61 (**K108.8**): cooking dishes
KAR 06/ 24 (K 22), 39 (**K27.7**), 53 (**K106.25**): cooking pots
KAR 06/ 70 (K 47): cooking cup
KAR 06/ 65 (**K36.2**), 80: pithoi
KAR 06/ 62 (**K44.7**): basin
KAR 06/ 64 (**K43.16**): jar
KAR 06/ 26 (K 28): jug
KAR 06/ 5 (**K3.11**), 6 (**K110.15**), 8 (**MK.10**), 9 (**K110.13**), 68 (**K22.8**), 69 (**K12.6**), 73 (**K26.8**): kalathoi
KAR 06/ 19 (K 40-41), 48: snake tubes
KAR 06/ 35 (**K3.5**): pyxis

This group is compositionally similar to subgroup (a): the main non-plastic components are the same low grade metamorphic rocks but in this subgroup they are poorly sorted and the presence of mudstone fragments, clay pellets and clay striations becomes more prominent. This indicates the use of a different clay recipe, possibly involving the addition of a red clay of alluvial origin. The Lasithi plateau alluvium is a potential source for the red clayey raw material.

As for subgroup (a), the vessels represented in this group also serve domestic and ritual functions: there

are cooking pots, cooking dishes, a cooking cup, kalathoi, a lid, a jug, one basin, one jar, two pithoi, and also two snake tubes, and a pyxis.

Fabric Group 2: Semi-coarse with quartz-rich matrix (COLOUR PLATE 1 *d*)

Samples:
KAR 06/ 32, 50, 51: snake tubes
KAR 06/ 58 (**K2.12**): jar

This is a semi-coarse red firing fabric. The matrix is dark red brown and optically inactive. The dark colour of the groundmass indicates a firing temperature higher than that of Fabric Group 1. This fabric is characterised by densely packed small quartz fragments evenly distributed in a micaceous clay groundmass. The semi-coarse non-plastic inclusions consist of phyllite, quartzite, and chert fragments. The fragments of chert, although not abundant, are consistently present in this fabric and this leads to assign to Fabric Group 2 a different origin from Fabric Group 1. Chert constitutes a component of the low grade metamorphic environment of the Phyllite-Quartzite series but the raw materials as well as the recipe of manufacture of this fabric are different from those of Fabric Groups 1a and 1b.

The vessels represented are three snake tubes and a jar.

Small groups and loners
The samples presented here are also connected with metamorphic sources of raw materials but due to compositional or textural variations were not included in the fabric groups described above.

KAR 06/ 30, 38 (**K23.26**) (COLOUR PLATE 1 *e*)

These samples are characterised by a red firing, coarse fabric set in a mica-rich base clay. The colour of the matrix is dark red brown and it is optically inactive. The non-plastic inclusions are low grade metamorphic and there are also mudstone fragments. This composition is very similar to Fabric Group 1(b) but instead of phyllite in these samples the main metamorphic component is phyllite mica schist. The vessels represented are a stirrup jar and a tripod.

KAR 06/ 18 (COLOUR PLATE 1 *f*)

This is a calcareous fabric. The matrix has a dark greenish brown colour and it is optically inactive. The non-plastic inclusions consist of very fine grained brown metamorphic rock fragments, polycrystalline quartz, sandstone and very little quartz. The presence of rare mudstone fragments indicates a link with the Fabric Group 1b. There are also rare microfossils. The

---

12   I.G.M.E. 1989.
13   Seidel *et al*. 1982; Theye *et al*. 1992.
14   Fassoulas 1999.

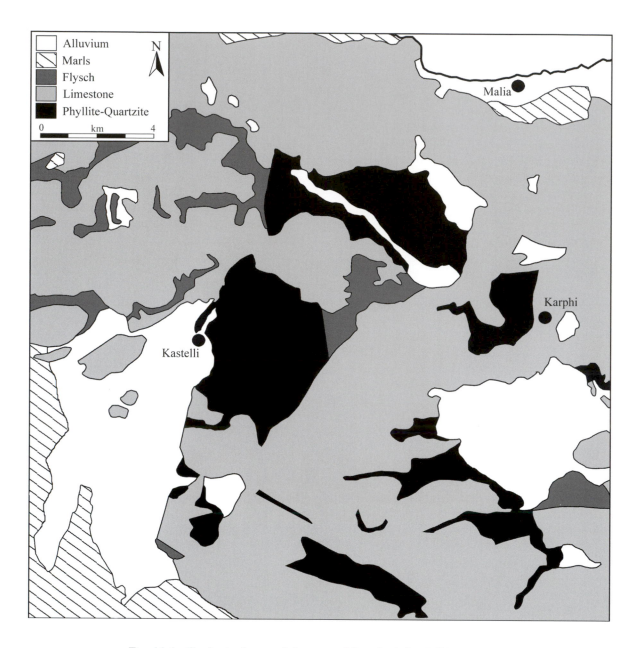

Fig. 11.1. Geological map of the area of Karphi (after I.G.M.E. 1989)

characteristic elongate voids in the groundmass are indicative of tempering with organic material. This fabric is highly calcareous and has no affinity with any of the fabrics encountered in the Karphi assemblage. The raw material used seems to have been a calcareous marl mixed with a non calcareous red clay. The mudstone fragments could provide a link with Fabric Group 1b, i.e. the red non calcareous component could be from the local alluvial deposits. The vessel represented is a basin.

KAR 06/ 21, 46 (COLOUR PLATE 1 *g*)

This sample exhibits also a coarse, red firing fabric characterised by a red brown and optically inactive matrix. The non-plastic inclusions consist primarily of angular quartz grains and smaller quantities of polycrystalline quartz, chert, phyllite, quartzite, sandstone and rare plutonic rock fragments. The raw material for this fabric seems to be connected with an alluvial origin. The vessels represented are snake tubes.

KAR 06/ 2 (**K125.2**), 52 (COLOUR PLATE 1 *h*)

This is a coarse fabric characterised by a yellowish brown matrix which is optically moderately active. The non-plastic inclusions consist of metamorphic rock fragments which bring this group close to Fabric Group 1(a). However, the predominance of quartzite over phyllite as well as the presence of amphibole led to differentiate these samples from the rest of Fabric Group 1(a). The vessels represented are a lid and a snake tube.

Flysch Fabrics

These fabrics are characterised by combinations of non-plastic components which belong to different rock types. Such coexistence of disparate components is attributed to a 'melange'-like lithologic formation or a flysch sequence. All samples of these fabric groups are characterised by a very fine clay matrix which indicates elaboration (levigation or sieving) of the clayey raw material prior to its use. Two main groups have been identified:

Fabric Group 3: Semi-coarse with metamorphic and igneous rock fragments (COLOUR PLATE 2 *a*)

Samples:
KAR 06/ 10: goddess figure (skirt)
KAR 06/ 11: snake tube
KAR 06/ 25, 27 (K 12), 28: stirrup jars
KAR 06/ 74, 76, 78: pithoi

This is a semi-coarse fabric characterised by a very fine brown matrix which is optically inactive. The fineness of the clay indicates refinement (i.e. levigation) of the raw material prior to use. The non-plastic inclusions consist mainly of metamorphic and basic igneous rock fragments, along with rare sandstone fragments. The coarse non-plastic inclusions must have been added in the clay paste as temper.

This rock and mineral suite is connected with flysch deposits. Such outcrops form part of the Tripolis zone and are found at the southern edge of the Lasithi plateau but also in the area of the Pediada, west of the Lasithi plateau. They consist mainly of shales and sandstones with common occurrences of volcanic material of basic composition.[15] There is an ongoing analytical project on the material from the Pediada survey[16] and there seem to be compositional similarities but not exact parallels between Fabric Group 3 from Karphi and the flysch fabrics from Pediada. With the present data it can be suggested that the samples from Karphi constitute the product of a broadly local workshop.

The vessels represented are a goddess figure, a snake tube, three stirrup jars and three pithoi.

Fabric Group 4: Semi-coarse with grey siltstone fragments (COLOUR PLATE 2 *b*)

Samples:
KAR 06/ 29: stirrup jar
KAR 06/ 45, 49: snake tubes
KAR 06/ 66 (**K.62**): pithos

This fabric group displays affinities with Fabric Group 3. It is semi-coarse, characterised by a very fine brown matrix which is optically inactive. The colour of the matrix and the absence of optical activity are indicative of quite high firing. Especially in the case of sample KAR 06/ 29 the matrix is greenish brown and there are rounded bloating pores, both characteristic of high firing temperatures. The non-plastic inclusions consist

primarily of fine grained phyllite-metamorphosed siltstone which has a silvery grey colour. There are also a few quartzite and sandstone rock fragments.

A flysch outcrop might also be the source of the non-plastic inclusions of this fabric group but it is uncertain whether it is of the same origin as Fabric Group 3. The clay matrix of the two groups is very similar but Fabric Group 3 lacks the grey siltstone fragments. Close parallels for Fabric Group 4 have been encountered at the LM IIIC site of Kastrokephala, near Gazi, at the MM building of Gournes on the north coast east of Herakleion,[17] among the Minoan pottery of the wider Pediada region,[18] and in the Early Iron Age assemblage of Knossos.[19] Therefore, there is a possibility that the pottery of Fabric Group 4 may be imported from outside the Lasithi plateau. It remains open to future research and chemical analysis whether all these samples share a common provenance or they were manufactured with similar raw materials.

The vessels represented are a stirrup jar, two snake tubes and a pithos.

Fine Fabrics

One major group and several small groups and loners have been established. They are all characterised by a very fine clay matrix and small non-plastic inclusions which, in most cases, are inconclusive of origin.

Fabric Group 5: Fine red fabric with small quartz fragments (COLOUR PLATE 2 *c*)

Samples:
KAR 06/ 4 (**K122.3**): krater
KAR 06/ 13 (**K61.2**), 14 (**K68.1**), 16 (**K68.2**): deep bowls
KAR 06/ 17 (**K114.1**): conical cup
KAR 06/ 22 (**K80.4**): kylix
KAR 06/ 31: snake tube
KAR 06/ 55 (**K150.3**), 56 (**K134.4**), 57 (**K134.3**): stirrup jars

This is a fine fabric characterised by a reddish brown to greenish brown and optically inactive matrix. The colour of the matrix is indicative of high firing temperatures. The non-plastic inclusions range from common to rare and comprise fragments of angular quartz and biotite mica. Rarer are small fragments of phyllite, chert, and sandstone. There are also dark red brown clay pellets.

Due to the fineness of this fabric it is not possible to make inferences on its provenance. A similar fabric has been encountered in the LM III material from the

15   I.G.M.E. 1989.
16   E. Nodarou, N. and M. Panagiotakis, work in progress.
17   Galanaki *et al.*, forthcoming.
18   E. Nodarou, N. and M. Panagiotakis, work in progress.
19   Boileau and Whitley 2010, 234.

Pediada survey and more specifically from the area around Voni[20] (COLOUR PLATE 2 *d*).

The vessels represented are a krater, three deep bowls, a conical cup, a kylix, a snake tube and three stirrup jars.

Small groups and loners

KAR 06/ 15 (**K38.1**) (COLOUR PLATE 2 *e*)

Fine calcareous fabric characterised by a greenish brown matrix which is optically inactive. The colour of the matrix is indicative of high firing temperature. The non-plastic inclusions consist of a few fragments of angular quartz and some biotite mica. There are also rare microfossils. The presence of the latter is indicative of a marly raw material. There are not any marl outcrops in the broader area of the Lasithi plateau. Outcrops of Neogene marl deposits are found on the north coast in the area of Chersonisos and also in the area of the Pediada (FIG. 11.1). The vessel represented is a deep bowl.

KAR 06/ 23 (**K18.1**) (COLOUR PLATE 2 *f*)

Very fine calcareous fabric characterised by a brown and at parts greenish and optically inactive matrix. The colour of the matrix as well as the rare, small rounded voids is indicative of high firing. The very rare non-plastic inclusions consist of small quartz fragments; there are also a few red clay pellets. This sample may or may not be connected to Fabric Group 5. Its colour is not the reddish brown seen in that group, it seems higher fired and it has significantly less non-plastic inclusions. The fineness of the fabric does not allow any secure provenance assignment. The vessel represented is a flask, a shape that is not common at Karphi. There is a possibility, therefore, that this sample is an import.

KAR 06/ 37 (**K22.4**) (COLOUR PLATE 2 *g*)

Fine calcareous fabric characterised by a dark brown and optically inactive matrix. The non-plastic inclusions are densely packed in the clay matrix and consist of angular quartz fragments and biotite mica along with common fragments of rounded micritic limestone. As for the previous sample, a marly clay must have been used for the manufacture of this vessel. The vessel represented is a pyxis.

KAR 06/ 40 (**K43.13**) (COLOUR PLATE 2 *h*)

Fine fabric characterised by a dark brown matrix which in some areas is optically moderately active, in others it is optically inactive. There are few non-plastic inclusions consisting of small quartz fragments, and rare chert. There are also few dark brown clay pellets. This composition is not diagnostic of origin but the fabric is not common at Karphi. The vessel represented is a pyxis.

KAR 06/ 41 (**K113.3**) (COLOUR PLATE 2 *i*)

Fine fabric characterised by a dark reddish brown micaceous matrix which is optically inactive. There are common non-plastic inclusions consisting of small quartz fragments, rare phyllite and biotite mica laths. There are also few dark brown clay pellets and clay striations which are indicative of incomplete clay mixing. The composition of the fabric is not diagnostic of origin but the fabric is not common at Karphi. The vessel represented is a jug.

ANALYSIS WITH SCANNING ELECTRON MICROSCOPY

A total of ten samples have been submitted for analysis under the Scanning Electron Microscope (SEM) in order to investigate technological aspects relating to the manufacture of the Karphi pottery. Fresh fracture surfaces of sherds coated with gold were analysed at the Laboratory of Electron Microscopy and Micro-analysis of the University of Patras using a JEOL 6300 SEM fitted with an Oxford Energy Dispersive X-ray spectrometer (EDS). The latter allowed us to complement the study of the microstructure with a semi-quantitative chemical analysis of the clay body. An overview of the analytical data is provided in TABLE 11.2. The samples selected are representative of the petrographic groups and the macroscopic fabrics.

The issues examined through SEM/EDS analysis include:

a) the nature of the clays used for the manufacture of the Karphi pottery, i.e. non calcareous red clays or calcareous marly clays, according to the qualitative and semi-quantitative compositional data provided by the EDS.
b) the firing atmosphere as estimated from the microstructure and degree of vitrification of the ceramic body.[21]
c) potential similarities and discrepancies between the petrographic and the SEM groups
d) comparison with published data from a contemporary site at Kavousi, East Crete.[22]

The Analysis

The results of the chemical characterisation were indicative of the nature of the raw materials used for the manufacture of the Karphi pottery. Three groups were formed on the basis of the calcium content in the clay paste: group 1 is low calcareous (CaO<3%), group 2 is calcareous (CaO~5%) and group 3 is highly

---

20   E. Nodarou, N. and M. Panagiotakis, work in progress.
21   After Maniatis and Tite 1981.
22   Day *et al.* 2006.

TABLE 11.2: **Compositional data from SEM analysis.**

	SiO₂	*Al₂O₃*	*TiO₂*	*Fe₂O₃*	*CaO*	*MgO*	*Na₂O*	*K₂O*
KAR 06/ 8	56.23	23.38	1.27	13.36	3.03	0.49	<LLD	2.24
KAR 06/ 10	48.33	12.93	<LLD*	15.74	11.84	9.29	<LLD	1.88
KAR 06/ 19	61.09	25.39	<LLD	10.91	0.90	0.37	<LLD	1.35
KAR 06/ 22	51.57	10.96	1.13	14.16	9.37	10.58	1.16	1.05
KAR 06/ 27	50.00	10.32	0.57	17.03	13.21	7.31	0.56	0.98
KAR 06/ 31	49.75	10.10	1.00	17.28	14.26	6.14	0.44	1.04
KAR 06/ 32	55.43	17.31	1.33	15.46	5.49	2.47	0.59	1.91
KAR 06/ 45	48.37	12.09	0.83	18.12	12.42	5.89	1.25	1.02
KAR 06/ 47	59.63	16.46	1.40	17.71	1.24	1.31	0.33	2.01
KAR 06/ 78	50.75	13.32	1.45	22.67	5.32	4.29	1.31	1.17

* below lower limit of detection

TABLE 11.3: **Concordance of petrography and SEM data.**

Sample	*Shape*	*Petrographic group*	*SEM group*	*Vitrification* *(estim. fir. temp.)*
Kar 06/ 8	Kalathos	F1 metamorphic	Low calcareous	NV (<750°C)
Kar 06/ 19	Snake tube	F1 metamorphic	Low calcareous	NV (<750°C)
Kar 06/ 47	Snake tube	F1 metamorphic	Low calcareous	NV (<750°C)
Kar 06/ 32	Snake tube	F2 quartz rich	Moderately calcareous	V (900–1000°C)
Kar 06/ 78	Pithos	F3 metamorphic + igneous	Moderately calcareous	NV (~800°C)
Kar 06/ 10	Goddess figure	F3 metamorphic + igneous	Highly calcareous	Vc+ (850–1050°C)
Kar 06/ 27	Stirrup jar	F3 metamorphic + igneous	Highly calcareous	IV (750–800°C)
Kar 06/ 45	Snake tube	F4 grey siltstone	Highly calcareous	IV (750–800°C)
Kar 06/ 22	Kylix	F5 fine red with quartz	Highly calcareous	IV (750–800°C)
Kar 06/ 31	Snake tube	F5 fine red with quartz	Highly calcareous	IV (750–800°C)

* NV – no vitrification; IV – initial vitrification; V/Vc+ – extensive vitrification (after Maniatis and Tite 1981)

calcareous (CaO>9%) (FIG. 11.2). Below we present the results of the analysis with SEM and we investigate to what extent the compositional groups relate to the petrographic groups and whether we can detect specific recipes of pottery manufacture. A summary of the SEM results and concordance with petrographic groups is provided in TABLE 11.3.

Low calcareous group

Samples:
KAR 06/ 8, 19, 47 (PLATE 29 *a*)

This is a fairly homogeneous group with low Ca (<3%) and Mg (<0.5%) content. Moreover, in this group the values for Si and Al are the highest among all samples examined. Although we cannot suggest that all three samples derive from the same source, they definitely

represent a similar geological environment which is Ca-poor and rich in Si and Al. This composition is compatible with a clayey raw material emanating from the erosion of the Phyllite-Quartzite series. This result matches the petrographic analysis since all three samples belong to Fabric Group 1 (metamorphic) and the main non-plastic component is phyllite in a mica rich base clay. The microstructure of these samples does not show any development of the clay filaments or any degree of vitrification (NV), and this is indicative of a low firing temperature (below 750°C). The samples represented belong to a kalathos and two snake tubes. The colour of the fired clay ranges from grey (for the kalathos) to orange-red for the surface and grey for the core (for the snake tubes). These colours are indicative of a firing atmosphere which is not entirely oxidising.

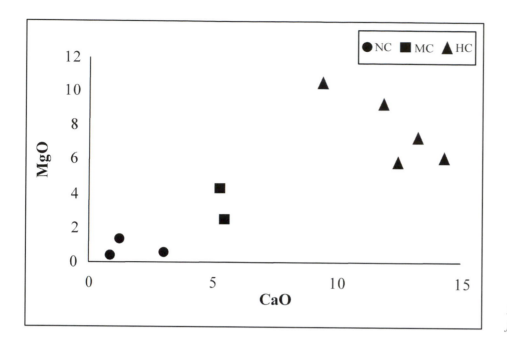

Fig. 11.2. Diagram CaO/MgO for the SEM samples

Moderately calcareous group

Samples:
KAR 06/ 32, 78

These samples have a Ca content slightly above 5.0% which indicates a different origin than the samples of the low Ca group. Similarly moderate are the Mg values (2.5% and 4.3%). The Si and Al components display significantly lower values than those encountered in the low calcareous samples. A clayey raw material containing carbonatic material, of calcareous and dolomitic origin, must have been used.

The microstructure of sample KAR 06/ 32 (PLATE 29 *b*) is indicative of advanced vitrification (V) and the estimated firing temperature is *c.* 900–1000°C. The sample represented is a snake tube and belongs to Fabric Group 2 which is characterised by the predominance of quartz fragments. The colour of the final product is a bright red surface and a grey core which is indicative of a two stage firing, including a phase of oxidation and a phase of reduction.

In sample KAR 06/ 78 (PLATE 29 *c*) the microstructure indicates a non vitrified stage (NV), i.e. a firing temperature of 800°C. The vessel represented is a pithos and belongs to Fabric Group 3 (with metamorphic and igneous rock fragments). The colour of the vessel is buff on the surface and the core and it seems to represent firing in oxidising conditions.

Highly calcareous group

Samples:
KAR 06/ 10, 22, 31, 27, 45

This is a fairly homogeneous group with regard to its chemical composition. The Si and Al values are close to those encountered in the moderately calcareous samples but the Ca content is much higher, ranging from 9% to 15%. The Mg content is accordingly higher, ranging from 6.1% to 10.6%. This compositional variability is associated with differences in the microstructure and the firing temperature of the samples. More specifically,

Sample KAR 06/ 10 (PLATE 29 *d*) has a Ca content of 11.8% and the microstructure indicates extensive vitrification (Vc+). The vessel represented is the skirt of a goddess with upraised hands and belongs to Fabric Group 3 (with metamorphic and igneous rock fragments). The colour of the surface and the core is buff and it represents firing in oxidising conditions. The estimated firing temperature is 850–1050°C.

Samples KAR 06/ 27 and 45 (PLATE 29 *e*) exhibit similar values for the Ca-content (12.4–13.2%) and similar microstructures. The presence of non developed clay filaments indicates a stage of initial vitrification (IV). The samples represented belong to a stirrup jar and a snake tube and they were classified in Fabric Groups 3 and 4 respectively. The colour of the surface and the core is buff and it represents firing in oxidising conditions. The estimated firing temperature is 750–800°C.

Samples KAR 06/ 22 and 31 (PLATE 29 *f*) have high Ca content (9.4% and 14.3% respectively) and are also at the stage of initial vitrification (IV). The samples represented are a kylix and a snake tube and they belong to Fabric Group 5 (fine red with small quartz fragments). The colour of the surface and the core is buff and it represents firing in oxidising conditions. The estimated firing temperature is 750–800°C.

DISCUSSION OF THE ANALYTICAL RESULTS

The petrographic and SEM analysis of selected pottery samples from the settlement of Karphi resulted in a rather consistent grouping according to the nature and technology of manufacture of the ceramic vessels. The samples comprised a range of shapes used for domestic purposes (cooking pots, jars, basins, pithoi, serving vessels), but also transport vessels (such as stirrup jars) and religious objects (goddess figures and snake tubes).

The petrographic analysis confirmed the macroscopic observations on the fabrics used for the Karphi pottery. The coarse and semi-coarse red fabrics form a homogeneous group and are connected in their majority with mica rich clays containing low grade metamorphic rocks (Fabric Group 1). This fabric seems to represent the local component in the Karphi assemblage since there are outcrops of the Phyllite-Quartzite series in the broader area of the Lasithi plateau. In terms of its technology of manufacture this group is very homogeneous: as demonstrated by the study of the microstructure and the semi-quantitative elemental analysis the clay used is Ca-poor and the firing took place in an oxidising kiln atmosphere and under a fairly low temperature. The vessels of this group are mainly used for domestic purposes (cooking and storage) but there are also a few special shapes such as snake tubes.

Another category of semi-coarse, red firing ceramics represented by a small number of vessels are connected with metamorphic rocks (Fabric Group 2). It is impossible to differentiate macroscopically this group from Fabric Group 1 because it has the same red colour and phyllitic inclusions. However, the clay paste and the technology of manufacture are different; the microscopic analysis showed that there is a higher amount of quartz whereas according to the SEM analysis the amount of Ca in the clay paste and the kiln temperature are also higher than in Fabric Group 1. The origin of the raw material is uncertain but the snake tubes included in this group are vessels of special use and not domestic wares as the majority of the vessels in Fabric Group 1.

The buff fabrics (Fabric Groups 3 and 4) are different in appearance, composition and technology of manufacture. They are connected with an environment of flysch deposits, they are manufactured with Ca-rich raw materials and at higher temperatures than the red fabrics. Also, there is compositional variability within the calcareous group, not seen in the red fabrics, indicative either of greater natural variation in the raw materials used and/or of different provenance.

The petrographic analysis demonstrated that, although Fabric Groups 3 and 4 derive from similar geological environments, the clay pastes are different. The SEM analysis confirmed this differentiation and showed that there is also internal variability within Group 3 with the pithos having a lower Ca content and a microstructure indicative of lower firing temperature than the goddess figure and the stirrup jar. This strengthens the argument on the natural variation within the flysch deposits and also the possibility of

Fabric Group 4 not being produced in the broader vicinity of Karphi.

Within the same technological group of the buff wares belong also the samples of Fabric Group 5. These do not contain any diagnostic rock fragments and there cannot be any secure provenance assignment. However, the technological similarity with the coarse buff fabrics provides an indication that they could be part of the same manufacturing tradition.

The presence of material that was not incorporated in any of the major groups is also of interest. The metamorphic small groups and loners are differentiated mainly due to the use of micaceous clay mixes contrary to the main metamorphic group which is not mica rich. This variability is indicative of the use of a multitude of clay sources for the manufacture not only of special vessels such as snake tubes but also of domestic wares. Moreover, there are medium sized semi-coarse containers whose provenance remains open to discussion. Whether imported or local these vessels demonstrate that Karphi received products from many production centres and that there must have been many groups of potters and/or workshops operating in the broader area.

POTTERY PRODUCTION IN CONTEXT

The pattern of pottery production at Karphi as seen from the analysis of selected samples is characterised by common recipes and a similar technology of manufacture for religious objects (such as goddesses with upraised hands and snake tubes) as well as for regular domestic vessels. This is particularly the case for the locally produced pottery of Fabric Group 1 which comprises all kinds of domestic vessels as well as a few kalathoi and snake tubes. The same picture is seen in the buff fabrics. Fabric Groups 3 and 4 comprise pithoi, stirrup jars, as well as ritual implements. It should be noted that stirrup jars are the only vessels that are represented exclusively in the buff wares and are manufactured solely with calcareous raw materials. Considering that they are the transport vessels *par excellence* it could be suggested that some of them may have been imported to Karphi either per se or for their content. Finally, fine Fabric Group 5 was also used for both domestic wares and ritual implements.

The absence of specialised production for the ritual objects matches the picture of the settlement at Kavousi–*Vronda*,[23] and comes in accordance D'Agata's analysis on the LM IIIC cult activities and their social framework.[24] The material evidence available suggests the presence of a socio-political system based on non-centrally controlled autonomous entities sharing a common ideological structure and a religious system

23 Day *et al.* 2006.
24 D'Agata 2001.

with similar codes and symbols. An expression of these common ideologies and practices is to be found in the shared elements of material culture, and the homogeneity seen especially in the clay objects (pottery and religious implements). Goddesses with upraised hands, snake tubes, kalathoi as well as kylikes, deep bowls and pithoi with plastic decoration form part of the pottery repertoire of all LM IIIC sites. However, this homogeneity in religious symbols comes in contrast with the regional differentiations in the architecture and other aspects of material culture as exemplified by a closer comparison between two of the most significant buildings at Karphi and Kavousi respectively.[25] D'Agata attributes this phenomenon to different social and political organisation.[26]

The analysis of the Karphi assemblage demonstrated that this material fits well in the pattern of shared material culture with regional variations, especially when our results are compared to those from the Kavousi project. In both sites an array of recipes is used for the production of religious and domestic ceramic objects but the production is fairly localised. However, the imported ceramics and the variety of imported prestige items such as jewellery and bronzes[27] are indications that Karphi was involved in an active exchange network at small or larger scale during the LM IIIC period.

PETROGRAPHIC DESCRIPTIONS

The petrographic descriptions are based on the descriptive system introduced by I. K. Whitbread (1995). The following abbreviations are used: a: angular, r: rounded, sa: subangular, sr: subrounded, wr: well rounded, tcf's: textural concentration features, PPL: plane polarised light, XP: crossed polars.

Fabric Group 1: Coarse with low grade metamorphic rocks

Subgroup (a) Samples: KAR 06/ 3, 7, 12, 20, 33, 34, 36, 42, 43, 44, 47, 54, 60, 63, 67, 71, 72, 75, 77, 79, 81, 82

Subgroup (b) Samples: KAR 06/ 1, 5, 6, 8, 9, 19, 24, 26, 35, 39, 48, 53, 59, 61, 62, 64, 65, 68, 69, 70, 80

Microstructure
Few meso and macro vughs, single- to close-spaced, very few macro planar voids, single-spaced. Voids and non-plastic inclusions are randomly oriented. The planar voids display preferred orientation parallel to vessel margins.

Groundmass
Homogeneous throughout the section. The colour of the matrix ranges from reddish brown to brown in PPL (×50) and from dark red brown to dark brown in XP. The only exception is sample KAR 06/ 36 which has a dark brown core and a red outer margin (in XP). The micromass ranges from moderately active to optically inactive.

Inclusions
c:f:v $_{10\mu m}$ = 40:55:5 to 25:70:5
Coarse fraction: 3.2–0.25 mm long diameter
Fine fraction: <0.25 mm long diameter
The matrix is relatively fine with sparse large- and small-sized inclusions. Bimodal grain size distribution. The size of the coarse fraction ranges from granules to medium sand. The fine fraction is of medium sand and below. The coarse fraction is moderately well sorted for subgroup (a) and poorly sorted for subgroup (b). The packing of the coarse fraction is single- to open-spaced, that of the fine fraction is double- to open-spaced. It is matrix supported (wackestone texture).

Coarse Fraction
Dominant to common: Metamorphic rock fragments.
a)   There is an impressive variety of phyllites: their colour ranges from golden brown and reddish brown to silvery and grey brown and they are composed of biotite mica, biotite mica and quartz, biotite and muscovite mica. Some fragments display folding of the schistosity while others are in intergrowth with quartzite. Moreover, some grains are stained by black opaques (illmenite?). Size: 3.2–0.2 mm long diameter.
b)   Quartzite, equant to elongate, sa, coarse grained to fine grained, occasionally grading into schist. Size: 2.2–0.2 mm long diameter.
Frequent to common: Monocrystalline quartz, equant and rarely elongate, a-sa. Mode: 0.2 mm long diameter. Size: 1.6–0.2 mm long diameter.
Frequent to few: Mudstone fragments, equant to elongate, a. Their colour is dark red brown and in most cases they do not contain any inclusions. It is only their large size and angularity that differentiates them from the tcf's. Seen only in the samples of subgroup (b). Size: 2.0–0.2 mm long diameter.
Few: Polycrystalline quartz, equant, sa. Size: 0.8–0.2 mm long diameter.
Very few to rare: Sandstone, equant to slightly elongate, sa, composed of monocrystalline quartz, white mica, and biotite set in a reddish brown matrix. Size: 1.4–0.4 mm long diameter.
Very rare to absent: Plagioclase feldspar displaying lamellar twinning.
Epidote.
Chert.

Fine Fraction
Dominant: Biotite mica laths.
Frequent: Monocrystalline quartz.
Common: White mica laths.
Rare: Phyllite fragments.

Textural Concentration Features
Subgroup (a): Very few tcf's, equant, sr-r, ranging in colour from dark red brown to dark brown (in XP). In most cases they are devoid of non-plastics. They are

---

25   Day and Snyder 2004.
26   D'Agata 2001, 348.
27   Day and Snyder 2004, 77.

discordant with the micromass. Size: 0.8–<0.2 mm long diameter. They are clay pellets.

Subgroup (b): Common tcf's, equant to elongate, ranging in shape from a-sa to sr-r. Their colour is dark red brown (in XP) and they are discordant with the micromass. The larger and angular fragments are often surrounded by a void and contain small inclusions consisting of quartz and biotite mica laths.

Fabric Group 2: Semi-coarse with quartz-rich matrix

Samples: KAR 06/ 32, 50, 51, 58

Microstructure
Very few meso vughs, rare planar voids and mega vughs. Voids and non-plastic inclusions are randomly oriented.

Groundmass
Homogeneous throughout the section. The colour of the matrix is brown in PPL (×50) and dark red brown in XP. The micromass is optically inactive.

Inclusions
$c:f:v_{10\mu m} = 15:82:3$
Coarse fraction: 2.4–0.1 mm long diameter
Fine fraction: <0.1 mm long diameter
The matrix is very fine with many small-sized inclusions evenly distributed and sparse large rock fragments. Bimodal grain size distribution. The size of the coarse fraction ranges from granules to very fine sand. The fine fraction is of very fine sand and below. The coarse fraction is poorly sorted. The fine fraction is moderately sorted. The packing of the coarse fraction is single- to open-spaced, that of the fine fraction is single-spaced. It is matrix supported (wackestone texture).

Coarse Fraction
Frequent:
Common to few: Metamorphic rock fragments:
a)   Slate, elongate, very fine grained, grey to grey brown. Size: 2.0–0.4 mm long diameter.
b)   Phyllite, elongate, fine grained, ranging in colour from golden brown to grey. It is composed of quartz, biotite and white mica laths. In some cases it is in intergrowth with quartzite. Some fragments display folding of the schistosity. Size: 2.4–0.4 mm long diameter.
c)   Quartzite, elongate, sa. Size: 1.6–0.2 mm long diameter.
Few: Monocrystalline quartz, equant, a-sa. Size: 1.0–0.1 mm long diameter.
Very few to rare: Chert, equant, sa, composed of fine grained quartz. Size: 0.8–0.2 mm long diameter.

Fine Fraction
Predominant: Monocrystalline quartz.
Dominant: Biotite mica laths.
Very rare: Epidote.

Textural Concentration Features
Very few tcf's, equant, sr-r; their colour is dark red brown and they are optically inactive. They are discordant with the micromass. They are clay pellets. Size: 0.8–<0.1 mm long diameter.

Fabric Group 3: Semi-coarse with metamorphic and igneous rock fragments

Samples: KAR 06/ 10, 11, 25, 27, 28, 74, 76, 78

Microstructure
Very few meso vughs, few to very few meso and macro planar voids. The latter surround in many cases the larger grains and occasionally they are filled with clayey material. Voids and non-plastic inclusions are randomly oriented.

Groundmass
Homogeneous throughout the section. The colour of the matrix is brown in PPL (×50) and dark red brown in XP. The micromass is optically inactive.

Inclusions
$c:f:v_{10\mu m} = 20:72:8$ to 5:93:2
Coarse fraction: 4.8–0.1 mm long diameter
Fine fraction: <0.1 mm long diameter
The matrix is very fine with large-sized inclusions added in the clay mix. Bimodal grain size distribution. The size of the coarse fraction ranges from pebbles to very fine sand. The fine fraction is of very fine sand and below. The coarse and fine fraction are poorly sorted. The packing of the coarse fraction is single- to open-spaced, that of the fine fraction is double-spaced. It is matrix supported (wackestone texture).

Coarse Fraction
Common: Metamorphic rock fragments:
a)   there is a variety of phyllitic material displaying a multitude of colours and textures. Some fragments are reddish brown and very fine grained (slate). There are also coarser ones ranging in colour from golden brown to grey brown and consisting of small fragments of quartz and some biotite mica. Occasionally they also contain opaques. In some cases the phyllite is in intergrowth with quartzite. Size: 4.8–0.4 mm long diameter.
b)   Quartzite, elongate. Size: 2.0–0.1 mm long diameter.
Few: Basalt, equant, sa-sr, containing plagioclase needles and little clinopyroxene in a groundmass consisting partly of interstitial brown glass. Size: 2.8–0.8 mm long diameter.
Monocrystalline quartz, equant, a-sa. Size: 0.8–0.1 mm long diameter.
Very few: Polycrystalline quartz fragments, equant, sa.
Rare: Sandstone, sa-sr, composed of monocrystalline quartz set in an orange brown matrix. Size: 1.6–0.4 mm long diameter.
Very rare to absent: Greenschist, equant, sa, composed of epidote, albite and biotite. Size: 1.8–0.8 mm long diameter. Seen only in sample KAR 06/ 76.
Epidote.

Fine Fraction
Frequent to few: Biotite mica laths.
White mica laths.
Common: Monocrystalline quartz.
Very few: Polycrystalline quartz.

Textural Concentration Features
Very few to rare tcf's, equant, sr-r. Their colour is dark red brown to dark brown (in XP) and they are optically inactive. They are devoid of non-plastics and they are discordant with the micromass. They are clay pellets. Mode: 0.4 mm long diameter. Size: 0.8–<0.1 mm long diameter.

Fabric Group 4: Semi-coarse with grey siltstone fragments

Samples: KAR 06/ 29, 45, 49, 66

Microstructure
Very few meso and macro vughs, very few to rare meso and macro planar voids. Voids and non-plastic inclusions are randomly oriented.

Groundmass
Homogeneous throughout the section. The colour of the matrix is brown in PPL (×50) and dark red brown in XP. In sample KAR 06/ 29 the colour of the matrix is grey in PPL (×50) and greenish brown in XP. In this sample some vughs are circular (bloating pores). In all samples the micromass is optically inactive.

Inclusions
c:f:v $_{10\mu m}$ = 25:70:5
Coarse fraction: 2.8–0.1 mm long diameter
Fine fraction: <0.1 mm long diameter
The matrix is very fine with large-sized inclusions added in the clay mix. Bimodal grain size distribution. The size of the coarse fraction ranges from granules to very fine sand. The fine fraction is of very fine sand and below. The coarse and the fine fractions are poorly sorted. The packing of the coarse fraction is single- to double-spaced, that of the fine fraction is double-spaced. It is matrix supported (wackestone texture).

Coarse Fraction
Frequent: Metamorphic rock fragments.
a) Fine grained siltstone, which is the main component of this fabric. The grains are elongate, their colour ranges from silvery grey to dark grey and they are composed of small fragments of quartz. Some fragments are so fine that no inclusions are visible. Some fragments are metamorphosed. Size: 2.8–0.2 mm long diameter.
b) Quartzite, equant to elongate, sa. Size: 1.8–0.4 mm long diameter.
c) White mica schist, elongate, very rare fragments.
Few: Monocrystalline quartz, equant, sa. Size: 0.6–0.1 mm long diameter.
Rare: Sandstone, equant, sr. Size: 1.0–0.2 mm long diameter.
Very rare to absent: Serpentinite, equant, sr. Size: 0.3 mm long diameter.
Plagioclase feldspar. Size: 0.2 mm long diameter.

Fine Fraction
Common to rare: Biotite mica laths.
Few to very rare: Monocrystalline quartz.
Very rare: White mica laths.

Textural Concentration Features
Very few to rare tcf's, equant, sr-r. There are also clay striations. Their colour is dark red brown to dark brown, almost black (in XP) and they are optically inactive. They are devoid of non-plastics and they are discordant with the micromass. They are clay pellets. Their colour and texture are indicative of the high firing of the fabric. Size: 0.4–<0.1 mm long diameter.

Fabric Group 5: Fine red fabric with small quartz fragments

Samples: KAR 06/ 4, 13, 14, 16, 22, 17, 31, 55, 57

Microstructure
Few meso and macro vughs, rare meso planar voids. Voids and non-plastic inclusions are randomly oriented.

Groundmass
Homogeneous throughout the section. The colour of the matrix is brown in PPL (×50) and dark red brown in XP. The micromass is optically inactive.

Inclusions
c:f:v $_{10\mu m}$ = 2:91:7
Coarse fraction: 0.6–0.1 mm long diameter
Fine fraction: <0.1 mm long diameter
The matrix is very fine with very small non-plastic inclusions. Grain size distribution is almost unimodal. The fineness of the fabric does not allow to differentiate between coarse and fine fraction. The size of the inclusions ranges from coarse to very fine sand and below. The non-plastic inclusions are poorly sorted. The packing is single- to open-spaced. It is matrix supported (wackestone texture).

Fine Fraction
Common: Biotite mica laths.
Few: Monocrystalline quartz, equant, a-sa. Size: 0.4–<0.1 mm long diameter.
Very few: Chert, equant, sa, composed of fine grained quartz. Size: 0.6–<0.1 mm long diameter.
Rare: Polycrystalline quartz, equant, sa.
Very rare: Epidote.

Textural Concentration Features
Very few to common tcf's, equant, sr-r. Their colour ranges from dark red to dark brown and black (in XP). Some fragments are optically active, others are optically inactive. They are devoid of non-plastics and they are discordant with the micromass. They are clay pellets. Size: 0.4–<0.1 mm long diameter.

Bibliography

JOURNALS AND SERIES

AA	*Archäologischer Anzeiger*
Aegaeum	Annales d'archéologies égéenne de l'Université de Liège et University of Texas Program in Aegean Scripts and Prehistory (PASP)
AJA	*American Journal of Archaeology*
AR	*Archaeological Reports*
ArchDelt	*Αρχαιολογικόν Δελτίον*
ArchEph	*Αρχαιολογική Εφημερίς*
BAR–IS	British Archaeological Reports — International Series
BCH	*Bulletin de correspondence hellénique*
BSA	*Annual of the British School at Athens*
CAJ	*Cambridge Archaeological Journal*
CMS	*Corpus der minoischen und mykenischen Siegel*. Berlin 1964–2000; Mainz 2002 –.
JHS	*Journal of Hellenic Studies*
KChron	*Κρητικά Χρονικά*
SMEA	*Studi Micenei ed Egeo-Anatolici*
SIMA	Studies in Mediterranean Archaeology

SHORT TITLES

Ariadne's Threads	A. L. D'Agata and J. Moody (eds.), 2005. *Ariadne's Threads: Connections between Crete and the Mainland in the Post Palatial Period (LM IIIA2 to LM IIIC)*. Scuola Archaeologica Italiana di Atene, Tripodes 3. Athens.
Archaeologies of Cult	A. L. D'Agata and A. Van de Moortel (eds.), 2009. *Archaeologies of Cult: Essays on Ritual and Cult in Crete. Hesperia* Suppl. 42. Princeton.
Crete Beyond the Palaces	L. P. Day, M. S. Mook and J. D. Muhly (eds.), 2004. *Crete Beyond the Palaces. Proceedings of the Crete 2000 Symposium*. INSTAP Prehistory Monographs 10. Philadelphia.
Cyprus-Dodecanese-Crete	V. Karageorghis and N. Stampolides (eds.), 1998. *Proceedings of the International Symposium: Eastern Mediterranean: Cyprus-Dodecanese-Crete 16th–6th c. B.C.* Athens.
Karphi	J. D. S. Pendlebury, H. W. Pendlebury and M. C. Money-Coutts, 1937–1938. 'Excavations in the plain of Lasithi. III. Karphi: A city of refuge of the Early Iron Age in Crete', *BSA* 38: 57–145.
Kastri	L. H. Sackett, M. R. Popham and P. M. Warren, 1965. 'Excavations at Palaikastro, VI', *BSA* 60: 248–315.
Kavousi IIA	L. P. Day, N. L. Klein and L. A. Turner, 2009. *Kavousi IIA. The Settlement at Vronda: Houses on the Summit*. INSTAP Prehistory Monograph 26. Philadelphia.
Khania II	E. Hallager and B. P. Hallager, 2000. *The Greek-Swedish Excavations at the Agia Aikaterini Square Kastelli, Khania, 1970–1987. Volume II. The Late Minoan IIIC Settlement*. Skrifter Utgivna av Svenska Institutet I Athen, 4, XLVII: II. Stockholm.
Late Minoan III Pottery	E. Hallager and B. P. Hallager (eds.), 1997. *Late Minoan III Pottery Chronology and Terminology*. Monographs of the Danish Institute at Athens 1. Athens
LH IIIC Chronology I	S. Deger-Jalkotzy and M. Zavadil (eds.), 2003. *LH IIIC Chronology and Synchronisms: Proceedings of the International Workshop Held at the Austrian Academy of Sciences at Vienna, May 7th and 8th, 2001*. Vienna.
LH IIIC Chronology II.	S. Deger-Jalkotzy and M. Zavadil (eds.), 2007. *LH IIIC Chronology and Synchronisms II. LH IIIC Middle: Proceedings of the International Workshop Held at the Austrian Academy of Sciences at Vienna, October 29th and 30th, 2004*. Vienna.
MELETEMATA	P. P. Betancourt, V. Karageorghis, R. Laffineur and W.-D. Niemeier (eds.), *MELETEMATA. Studies in Aegean Archaeology presented to Malcolm H. Wiener as he enters his 65th year*. Aegaeum 20. Liège and Austin
RMDP	P. A. Mountjoy, 1999. *Regional Mycenaean Decorated Pottery*. Deutsches Archäologischen Institut. Rahden/Westf.
Seiradaki	M. Seiradaki, 1960. 'Pottery from Karphi', *BSA* 55: 1–37.

REFERENCES

Andreadaki-Vlasaki, M., and E. Papadopoulou, 2005. 'The habitation at Khamalevri, Rethymnon, during the 12th century B.C.', in *Ariadne's Threads*: 353–97.

——, 2007. 'Recent evidence for the destruction of the LM IIIC habitation at Khamalevri, Rethymnon', in *LH IIIC Chronology II*: 27–53.

Andrikou, E., 1997. 'Thoughts and considerations on the Mycenaeanisation of Crete motivated by pottery from Archanes', in J. Driessen and A. Farnoux (eds.), *La Crète mycénienne. BCH* Suppl. 30. Athens: 9–22.

Arnold, B., 1999. 'Drinking the feast: alcohol and the legitimization of power in Celtic Europe', *CAJ* 9: 71–93.

Barber, E. J. W., 1997. 'Minoan women and the challenges of weaving for home, trade and shrine', in R. Laffineur and P. P. Betancourt (eds.), *TEXNH. Craftsmen, Craftswomen, and Craftmanship in the Aegean Bronze Age.* Aegaeum 16. Liège and Austin: 515–19.

Barnard, K. A., and T. M. Brogan, 2003. *Mochlos IB. Period III. Neopalatial Settlement on the Coast: The Artisans' Quarter and the Farmhouse at Chalinomouri. The Neopalatial Pottery.* INSTAP Prehistory Monographs 8. Philadelphia.

Benson, J. L., 1973. *The Necropolis of Kaloriziki Excavated by J. F. Daniel and G. H. McFadden for the University Museum, University of Pennsylvania, Philadelphia.* SIMA 36. Göteborg.

Betancourt, P. P., 1980. *Cooking Vessels from Minoan Kommos. A Preliminary Report.* Institute of Archaeology, University of California, Occasional Paper 7. Los Angeles.

——, 1985. *The History of Minoan Pottery.* Princeton.

——, 1998. 'The legged flask from Pseira', in *Cyprus-Dodecanese-Crete*: 49–53.

Boardman, J., 1960. 'Protogeometric graves at Agios Ioannis near Knossos', *BSA* 55: 128–48.

Boileau, M.-C., and J. Whitley, 2010. 'Patterns of production and consumption of coarse to semi-fine pottery at Early Iron Age Knossos', *BSA* 105: 225–68.

Borgna, E., 1997a. 'Some observations on deep bowls and kraters from the "Acropoli mediana" at Phaistos', in *Late Minoan III Pottery*: 273–303.

——, 1997b. 'Kitchen-ware from LM IIIC Phaistos: cooking traditions and ritual activities in LBA Cretan societies', *SMEA* 39: 189–217.

——, 2003. *Il complesso di ceramica tardominoico III dell'acropoli mediana di Festòs.* Studi Archeologia Cretese 3. Padua.

——, 2004. 'Aegean feasting: a Minoan perspective', in J. Wright (ed.), *The Mycenaean Feast.* Princeton: 127–59.

——, 2007. 'LM IIIC pottery at Phaistos: an attempt to integrate typological analysis with stratigraphic investigations', in *LH IIIC Chronology II*: 55–72.

Brock, J. K., 1957. *Fortetsa. Early Greek Tombs near Knossos. BSA* Suppl. 2. Cambridge.

Bruun-Lundgren, M., and I. Wiman, 2000. 'Industrial activities and personal adornment', in *Khania II*: 175–82.

Cadogan, G., 1967. 'Late Minoan IIIC pottery from the Kephala tholos tomb near Knossos', *BSA* 62: 257–65.

Callaghan, P., and A. Johnston, 2000. 'The Iron Age pottery from Kommos', in J. W. Shaw and M. C. Shaw (eds.), *Kommos IV: The Greek Sanctuary.* Princeton: 210–301.

Catling, H. W., 1968. 'Late Minoan vases and bronzes in Oxford', *BSA* 63: 89–131.

Christakis, K., 2005. *Cretan Bronze Age Pithoi: Traditions and Trends in the Production and Consumption of Storage Containers in Bronze Age Crete.* INSTAP Prehistory Monographs 18. Philadelphia.

Coldstream, J. N., 1960. 'A Geometric well at Knossos', *BSA* 55: 159–71.

Coldstream, J. N., and H. W. Catling, 1996. *Knossos North Cemetery: Early Greek Tombs. BSA* Suppl. 28. London.

Coulson, W. C., and M. Tsipopoulou, 1994. 'Preliminary investigations at Halasmenos, Crete, 1992–1993', *Aegean Archaeology* 1: 65–97.

D'Agata, A. L., 1997. 'The shrines on the Piazzale dei Sacelli at Ayia Triadha', in J. Driessen and A. Farnoux (eds.), *La Crète mycénienne. BCH* Suppl. 30. Athens: 85–100.

——, 1999. 'Defining a pattern of continuity during the Dark Age in central-western Crete: ceramic evidence from the settlement of Thronos/Kephala (Ancient Sybrita)', *SMEA* 41: 181–218.

——, 2001. 'Religion, society and ethnicity on Crete at the end of the Late Bronze Age. The contextual framework of LM IIIC cult activities', in R. Laffineur and R. Hägg (eds.), *POTNIA. Deities and Religion in the Aegean Bronze Age.* Aegaeum 22. Liège and Austin: 345–54.

——, 2002. 'Ritual and rubbish in Dark Age Crete: the settlement of Thronos/Kephala (Ancient Sybrita) and the Pre-Classical roots of a Greek city', *Aegean Archaeology* 4: 45–59.

——, 2003. 'Late Minoan IIIC–Subminoan pottery sequence at Thronos/Kephala and its connections with the Greek mainland', in *LH IIIC Chronology I*: 23–36.

——, 2005. 'Cult activity on Crete and Cyprus at the end of the Late Bronze Age and the beginning of the Early Iron Age. What comparative analysis can tell us', in V. Karageorghis, H. Matthäus and S. Rogge (eds.), *Cyprus: Religion and Society from the Late Bronze Age to the End of the Archaic Period.* Möhnesee-Wamel: 1–17.

——, 2007. 'Evolutionary paradigms and Late Minoan III. On a definition of LM IIIC middle', in *LH IIIC Chronology II*: 89–118.

Day, L. P., 1997. 'The Late Minoan IIIC period at Vronda, Kavousi', in J. Driessen and A. Farnoux (eds.), *La Crète mycénienne. BCH* Suppl. 30. Athens: 391–406.

——, 1999. 'A Late Minoan IIIC window frame from Vronda, Kavousi', in *MELETEMATA*: 185–90.

——, 2005. 'Response to Joseph Maran', in *Ariadne's Threads*: 433–9.

——, 2009. 'Ritual activity at Karphi: a reappraisal', in *Archaeologies of Cult*: 137–52.

——, 2011*a*. 'Household assemblages in LM IIIC Crete: the evidence from Karphi', in K. T. Glowacki and N. Vogeikoff-Brogan (eds.), *Stega: the Archaeology of Houses and Households in Ancient Crete from the Neolithic through the Roman Era. Hesperia* Suppl. 44. Princeton.

——, 2011*b*. 'Appropriating the past: Early Iron Age mortuary practices at Kavousi, Crete', in A. Mazarakis-Ainian (ed.), *The 'Dark Ages' Revisited. An International Conference in Memory of William D. E. Coulson. Volos 14–17 June 2007*. Volos.

——, W. D. E. Coulson and G. C. Gesell, 1986. 'Kavousi, 1983–1984: the settlement at Vronda', *Hesperia* 55: 355–87.

——, W. D. E. Coulson and G. C. Gesell, 1989. 'A new Early Iron Age kiln at Kavousi, Crete', *Rivista di Archeologia* 13: 103–6.

——, K. T. Glowacki and N. L. Klein, 2000. 'Cooking and dining in Late Minoan IIIC Vronda, Kavousi', *Πεπραγμένα του Η´ Διεθνούς Κρητολογικού Συνεδρίου*. Herakleion: A3, 115–25.

——, and L. Snyder, 2004. 'The 'Big House' at Vronda and the 'Great House' at Karphi: evidence for social structure in LM IIIC Crete', in *Crete Beyond the Palaces*: 63–80.

——, and K. T. Glowacki, forthcoming. *Kavousi IIB. The Vronda Settlement: Houses on the Periphery*. INSTAP Prehistory Monographs. Philadelphia.

——, H. Dierckx, G. C. Gesell, K. T. Glowacki, N. L. Klein and L. M. Snyder, forthcoming. *Kavousi IIC. The Vronda Settlement: Analysis and Conclusions*. INSTAP Prehistory Monographs. Philadelphia.

Day, P. M., V. Kilikoglou, L. Joyner and G. C. Gesell, 2006. 'Goddesses, snake tubes, and plaques: analysis of ceramic ritual objects from the LM IIIC shrine at Kavousi', *Hesperia* 75: 137–75.

Desborough, V. R. d'A., 1964. *The Last Mycenaeans and their Successors*. Oxford.

——, 1972. 'Bird vases', *KChron* 24: 245–77.

Dickinson, O., 2006. *The Aegean from Bronze Age to Iron Age: Continuity and Change between the Twelfth and Eighth Centuries BC*. London.

Dietler, M., 1990. 'Driven by drink: the role of drinking in the political economy and the case of Early Iron Age France', *Journal of Anthropological Archaeology* 9: 352–406.

——, 2001. 'Theorizing the feast. Rituals of consumption, commensal politics, and power in African contexts', in M. Dietler and B. Hayden (eds.), *Feasts: Archaeological and Ethnographic Perspectives on Food, Politics, and Power*. Washington: 65–114.

Dikaios, P., 1969. *Enkomi. Excavations 1948–1958*. Mainz (1969–1971).

Eliopoulos, T., 1998. 'A preliminary report on the discovery of a temple complex of the Dark Ages at Kephala Vasilikis', in *Cyprus-Dodecanese-Crete*: 301–13.

——, 'Ο Υστερομινωϊκός IIIΓ ομφαλόεις βωμός της Κεφάλας Βασιλικής', in A. Vlachopoulou and K. Birtacha (eds.), *Αργοναύτης. Τιμητικός τόμος για τον καθηγητή Χριστό Γ. Ντούμα*. Athens: 389–408.

——, 2004. 'Gournia, Vronda Kavousi, Kephala Vasilikis: a triad of interrelated shrines of the expiring Minoan age on the Isthmus of Ierapetra', in *Crete Beyond the Palaces*: 81–90.

Evely, R. D. G., 1988. 'The potter's wheel in Minoan Crete', *BSA* 83: 83–126.

——, 2000. *Minoan Crafts: Tools and Techniques. An Introduction. II*. SIMA 92:2. Jonsered.

Evans, A. J., 1921. *The Palace of Minos at Knossos* I. London.

——, 1928. *The Palace of Minos at Knossos* II. London.

——, 1935. *The Palace of Minos at Knossos* IV. London.

Fassoulas, C., 1999. 'The structural evolution of Central Crete. Insight into the tectonic evolution of the south Aegean (Greece)', *Journal of Geodynamics* 27: 23–43.

Galanaki, K., E. Nodarou, C. Papadaki and I. Triantaphyllidi, forthcoming. 'Μινωικό κτίριο στις Γούρνες Πεδιάδος', *Πεπραγμένα του Ι´ Διεθνούς Κρητολογικού Συνεδρίου, Χανιά 1–8 Οκτωβρίου 2006*.

Georgiou, H. S., 1980. 'Minoan fireboxes: a study of form and function', *SMEA* 21: 123–87.

——, 1983. 'Minoan coarse wares and Minoan technology', in O. Krzyszkowska and L. Nixon, *Minoan Society*. Bristol: 75–92.

——, 1986. *Ayia Irini: Specialized Domestic and Industrial Pottery. Keos VI*. Mainz.

Gesell, G. C., 1976. 'The Minoan snake tube: a survey and catalogue', *AJA* 80: 247–59.

——, 1985. *Town, Palace, and House Cult in Minoan Crete*. SIMA 67. Göteborg.

——, 1999. 'Ritual kalathoi in the shrine at Kavousi', in *MELETEMATA*: 263–7.

——, 2001. 'The function of the plaque in the shrine of the goddess with up-raised hands', in R. Laffineur and R. Hägg (eds.), *POTNIA. Deities and Religion in the Aegean Bronze Age*. Aegaeum 22. Liège and Austin: 253–8.

——, 2004. 'From Knossos to Kavousi: the popularizing of the Minoan palace goddess', in A. P. Chapin (ed.), *ΧΑΡΙΣ: Essays in Honor of Sara A. Immerwahr. Hesperia* Suppl. 34: 131–50. Princeton.

——, 2010. 'The snake goddesses of the LM IIIB and LM IIIC periods', in O. Krzyszkowska (ed.), *Cretan Offerings: Studies in honour of Peter Warren. BSA* Studies 18. London: 131–9.

——, W. D. E. Coulson and L. P. Day, 1991. 'Excavations at Kavousi, Crete, 1988', *Hesperia* 60: 145–77.

——, L. P. Day and W. D. E. Coulson, 1988. 'Excavations at Kavousi, Crete, 1987', *Hesperia* 57: 279–301.

——, L. P. Day and W. D. E. Coulson, 1995. 'Excavations at Kavousi, Crete, 1989 and 1990', *Hesperia* 64: 67–120.

——, K. T. Glowacki and N. L. Klein, forthcoming. *Kavousi III: the Shrine at Vronda*. INSTAP Prehistory Monographs. Philadelphia.

Glowacki, K. T., 2004. 'Household analysis in Dark Age Crete', in *Crete Beyond the Palaces*: 125–36.

Hägg, R., 1990. 'The Cretan hut-models', *Opuscula Atheniensis* 18: 95–107.

Haggis, D. C., and M. S. Mook, 1993. 'The Kavousi coarse wares: a Bronze Age chronology for survey in the Mirabello area, east Crete', *AJA* 97: 265–93.

Hallager, B. P., 1997. 'Terminology — the Late Minoan goblet, kylix, and footed cup', in *Late Minoan III Pottery*: 15–44.

——, 2000. 'Late Minoan IIIC pottery', in *Khania II*: 135–74.

——, 2007. 'Problems with LH/LM IIIB/C synchronisms', in *LH IIIC Chronology II*: 189–202.

——, 2009. 'Domestic shrines in LM IIIA2–LM IIIC Crete', in *Archaeologies of Cult*: 107–20.

——, 2010. 'The elusive Late LM IIIC and the ill-named Subminoan', in O. Krzyszkowska (ed.), *Cretan Offerings: Studies in honour of Peter Warren*. *BSA* Studies 18. London: 141–55.

Hatzaki, E., 2005. *Knossos: The Little Palace*. *BSA* Suppl. 38. London.

Hayden, B. J., 1981. 'The development of Cretan architecture from the LM IIIA through the Geometric periods' (unpublished PhD thesis, University of Pennsylvania).

——, 2001. 'Fabulous feasts: a prolegomenon to the importance of feasting', in M. Dietler and B. Hayden (eds.), *Feasts: Archaeological and Ethnographic Perspectives on Food, Politics, and Power*. Washington: 23–64.

——, 2003. *Reports on the Vrokastro Area, Eastern Crete. I. Catalogue of Pottery from the Bronze and Early Iron Age Settlement of Vrokastro in the Collections of the University of Pennsylvania Museum of Archaeology and Anthropology and the Archaeological Museum, Herakleion, Crete*. Philadelphia.

Higgins, R., 1996. 'The jewellery', in J. N. Coldstream and H. Catling (eds.), *Knossos North Cemetery: Early Greek Tombs*. *BSA* Suppl. 28. London: 539–54.

Hillbom, N., 2005. *Minoan Games and Game Boards*. Lund.

Hood, S., G. Huxley and N. Sandars, 1958–1959. 'A Minoan cemetery on Upper Gypsades', *BSA* 53–54: 194–261.

I.G.M.E., 1989. *Geological Map of Greece, Mochos Sheet*, 1:50 000.

Joffe, A. H., 1998. 'Alcohol and social complexity in ancient western Asia', *Current Anthropology* 39: 297–322.

Kanta, A., 1980. *The Late Minoan III Period in Crete. A Survey of Sites, Pottery, and their Distribution*. SIMA 58. Göteborg.

——, 1991. 'Cult, continuity, and the evidence of pottery at the sanctuary of Syme Viannou, Crete' in D. Musti (ed.), *La transizione dal Miceneo all'Alto Arcaismo — dal palazzo alla città*. Rome: 479–505.

——, 1997. 'LM IIIB and LM IIIC pottery phases. Some problems of definition', in *Late Minoan III Pottery*: 83–110.

——, 2003. 'The citadel of Kastrokephala and the date of the Minoan refuge citadels', in *LH IIIC Chronology I*: 167–82.

——, and A. Karetsou, 1998. 'From Arkades to Rytion. Interactions of an isolated area of Crete with the Aegean and East Mediterranean', in *Cyprus-Dodecanese-Crete*: 159–73.

——, and A. Karetsou, 2003. 'The acropolis of Kastrokephala and its pottery', in *LH IIIC Chronology I*: 145–65.

Klein, N., and K. Glowacki, 2009. 'From Kavousi Vronda to Dreros: architecture and display in Cretan cult buildings', in *Archaeologies of Cult*: 253–67.

Kourou, N., and A. Karetsou, 1994. 'Το ιερό του Ερμού Κρανίου στην Πατσός Αμαρίου', in L. Rocchetti (ed.), *Sybrita. La Valle di Amari fra Bronzo e Ferro* I. Incunabula Graeca 96. Rome: 81–164.

——, 1998. 'An enigmatic stone from Knossos: a reused cippus?', in *Cyprus-Dodecanese-Crete*: 243–54.

Koehl, R. B., 2006. *Aegean Bronze Age Rhyta*. INSTAP Prehistory Monographs 19. Philadelphia.

LaMotta, V. M., and M. B. Schiffer, 1999. 'Formation processes of house floor assemblages', in P. M. Allison (ed.), *The Archaeology of Household Activities*. London and New York: 19–29.

Lebessi, A., and P. Muhly, 1990. 'Aspects of Minoan cult. Sacred enclosures: the evidence from the Syme sanctuary (Crete)', *AA* 1990: 315–36.

Lemos, I. S., 2004. 'Birds revisited', in V. Karageorghis (ed.), *Proceedings of the International Symposium 'Cyprus in the 11th Century B.C.'*. Nicosia: 229–37.

Macdonald, C., 1986. 'Problems of the twelfth century B.C. in the Dodecanese', *BSA* 81: 125–51.

Maniatis, Y., and M. S. Tite, 1981. 'Technological examination of Neolithic–Bronze Age pottery from Central and South-East Europe and from the Near East', *Journal of Archaeological Science* 8: 59–76.

Marinatos, S., 1920–21. 'Λαξευτοί μυκηναϊκοί τάφοι Μιλάτου', *ArchDelt* 6: 154–7.

——, 1937. 'Αι μινωικαί θεαί του Γάζι', *ArchEph* 1937: 278–91.

Mazarakis Ainian, A., 1997. *From Ruler's Dwelling to Temples: Architecture, Religion, and Society in Early Iron Age Crete (1100–700 B.C.)*. SIMA 121. Jonsered.

Mersereau, R., 1993. 'Cretan cylindrical models', *AJA* 97: 1–47.

Mook, M. S., 1993. 'The Northwest Building: houses of the Late Bronze and Early Iron Ages on the Kastro at Kavousi, East Crete' (unpublished PhD thesis, University of Minnesota).

——, 1999. 'Cooking dishes from the Kastro', in *MELETEMATA*: 503–08.

——, 2004. 'From foundation to abandonment: new ceramic phasing for the Late Bronze Age and Early Iron Age on the Kastro at Kavousi', in *Crete Beyond the Palaces*: 163–79.

——, 2005. 'The Kavousi fabrics: a typology for coarse pottery in the Mirabello region of eastern Crete', in D. Haggis, *Kavousi I. The Archaeological Survey of the Kavousi Region*. INSTAP Prehistory Monograph 16. Philadelphia: 167–76.

——, forthcoming. *The Pottery from the Kastro*. INSTAP Prehistory Monograph. Philadelphia.

——, and W. D. E. Coulson, 1997. 'Late Minoan IIIC pottery from the Kastro at Kavousi', in *Late Minoan III Pottery*: 337–70.

Mountjoy, P. A., 1986. *Mycenaean Decorated Pottery: A Guide to Identification*. SIMA 73. Göteborg.

——, 1999. 'Late Minoan IIIC/Late Helladic IIIC: chronology and terminology', in *MELETEMATA*: 511–16.

——, 2005. 'The end of the Bronze Age at Enkomi, Cyprus: the problem of Level IIIB', *BSA* 100: 125–214.

——, 2007. 'A definition of LH IIIC middle', in *LH IIIC Chronology II*: 221–42.

Munsell, A. H., 1998 and 2000. *Munsell Soil Color Charts*. Rev. ed. New York.

Nowicki, K., 1987. 'The history and setting of the town of Karphi', *SMEA* 26: 235–56.

——, 1999. 'Economy of refugees: life in the Cretan mountains at the turn of the Bronze and Iron Ages', in A. Chaniotis (ed.), *From Minoan Farmers to Roman Traders: Sidelights on the Economy of Ancient Greece*. Stuttgart: 145–71.

——, 2000. *Defensible Sites in Crete c. 1200–800 B.C.: LM IIIB through Early Geometric*. Aegaeum 21. Liège and Austin.

——, 2002. 'From Late Minoan IIIC refuge settlements to Geometric acropoleis: architecture and social organization of Dark Age villages and towns in Crete', in J. Luce (ed.), *Habitat et urbanisme dans le monde grec de la fin des palais mycéniens à la prise de Milet (494 Av, J.-C.)*. Pallas 58. Toulouse: 149–274.

——, 2008. *Monastiraki Katalimata. Excavation of a Cretan Refuge Site, 1993–2000*. INSTAP Prehistory Monographs 24. Philadelphia.

Papadatos, Y., P. Tomkins, E. Nodarou and I. Iliopoulos, forthcoming. 'The beginning of Early Bronze Age in Crete: continuities and discontinuities in the ceramic assemblage at Petras Kephala, Siteia', in O. Kouka, C. Doumas and A. Giannikouri (eds.), *Proceedings of the International Conference 'The Early Bronze Age in the Aegean: new evidence.'* Athens 2008.

Paschalides, C., 2009. *The Late Minoan III Cemetery at Tourloti near Siteia. The 'Xanthoudidis Master' and the Octopus Style in East Crete*. BAR–IS 1917. Oxford.

Petrakis, V. P., 2006. 'Late Minoan III and Early Iron Age Cretan cylindrical terracotta models: a reconsideration', *BSA* 101: 183–216.

Pilidis, D., 1997. 'Incised wares from Enkomi: possible inferences regarding their connections', *Proceedings of the International Archaeological Conference, Cyprus and the Aegean in Antiquity: From the Prehistoric Period to the 7th century A.D.* Nicosia: 208–16.

Popham, M. R., 1964. *The Last Days of the Palace at Knossos*. SIMA 5. Lund.

——, 1965. 'Some Late Minoan III pottery from Crete', *BSA* 60: 316–42.

——, 1969. 'The Late Minoan goblet and kylix', *BSA* 64: 299–304.

——, 1970*a*. 'A Late Minoan shrine at Knossos', *BSA* 65: 191–4.

——, 1970*b*. 'Late Minoan IIIB pottery from Knossos', *BSA* 65: 195–203.

——, 1992. 'The Sub-Minoan pottery', in L. Sackett (ed.), *Knossos. From Greek City to Roman Colony. Excavations at the Unexplored Mansion* II. BSA Suppl. 21. London: 59–66.

Prent, M., 2005. *Cretan Sanctuaries and Cults: Continuity and Change from Late Minoan IIIC to the Archaic Period*. Leiden.

Preston, L., 2005. 'The Kephala Tholos at Knossos: a study in the reuse of the past', *BSA* 100: 61–123.

Prokopiou, N., 1997. 'Late Minoan III pottery from the Greek-Italian excavations at Sybritos Amariou', in *Late Minoan III Pottery*: 371–400.

Rahmstorf, L., 2003. 'Clay spools from Tiryns and other contemporary sites. An indication of foreign influence in LH IIIC?', in N. Kyparissi-Apostolika and M. Papakonstantinou (eds.), *Η περιφέρεια του μυκηναϊκού κόσμου — The Periphery of the Mycenaean World (2nd International Interdisciplinary Colloquium)*. Athens: 397–415.

——, 2005. 'Ethnicity and changes in weaving technology in Cyprus and the eastern Mediterranean in the 12th century B.C.', in V. Karageorghis, H. Matthäus and S. Rogge (eds.), *Cyprus: Religion and Society from the Late Bronze Age to the End of the Archaic Period*. Möhnesee-Wamel: 143–69.

Renfrew, C., and J. Cherry, 1985. 'The other finds', in C. Renfrew, *The Archaeology of Cult. The Sanctuary at Phylakopi*. London: 299–360.

Rethemiotakis, G., 1997. 'Late Minoan III pottery from Kastelli Pediada', in *Late Minoan III Pottery*: 305–36.

——, 1998. *Ανθρωπομορφική Πηλοπλαστική στην Κρήτη από τη νεοανακτορική έως την υπομινωική περίοδο*. Athens.

——, 2001. *Minoan Clay Figures and Figurines: From the Neopalatial to the Subminoan Period*. Archaeological Society at Athens Library 219. Athens.

——, 2009. 'A Neopalatial shrine model from the Minoan peak sanctuary at Gournos Krousonas', in *Archaeologies of Cult*: 189–99.

Rutkowski, B., 1987. 'The temple at Karphi', *SMEA* 26: 258–79.

Sackett, L. H. (ed.), 1992. *Knossos. From Greek City to Roman Colony. Excavations at the Unexplored Mansion* II. BSA Suppl. 21. London.

Sapouna-Sakellarakis, E., 1990. 'Archanès à l'époque mycénienne', *BCH* 114: 67–101.

Schachermeyr, F., 1979. 'The pleonastic pottery style of Cretan middle IIIC and its Cypriote relations', *Acts of the International Archaeological Symposium 'The Relations between Cyprus and Crete ca. 2000–500 B.C.* Nicosia: 204–14.

Seidel, E., H. Kreuzer and W. Harre, 1982. 'A Late Oligocene/Early Miocene high pressure belt in the external Hellenides', *Geologisches Jahrbuch* E23: 165–206.

Shaw, J. W., 2004. 'Roof drains and parapets in the southern Aegean', *BSA* 99: 173–88.

——, A. Van de Moortel, P. M. Day and V. Kilikoglou, 2001. *A LM IA Ceramic Kiln in South-Central Crete*. Hesperia Suppl. 30. Princeton.

Soles, J. S. (ed.), 2004. *Mochlos IC. Period III. Neopalatial Settlement on the Coast: The Artisans' Quarter and the Farmhouse at Chalinomouri. The Small Finds*. INSTAP Prehistory Monographs 9. Philadelphia.

Stampolides, N., and A. Karetsou, 1998. *Ανατολική Μεσόγειος: Κύπρος–Δωδεκάνησα–Κρήτη 16ος–6ος αι. π. X.* Herakleion.

Steel, L., 1996. 'Transition from Bronze to Iron at Kourion: a review of the tombs from Episkopi-Bamboula and Kaloriziki', *BSA* 91: 287–300.

Theye, T., E. Seidel and O. Vidal, 1992. 'Carphollite, sudoite and chloritoid in low high-pressure metapelites from Crete and the Peloponnese, Greece', *European Journal of Mineralogy* 4: 487–507.

Tsipopoulou, M., 1997. 'Phatsi-Droggara: un dépôt de céramique de la fin de l'Âge du Bronze et du début de l'Âge du Fer provenant de Crète orientale', in J. Driessen and A. Farnoux (eds.), *La Crète mycénienne. BCH* Suppl. 30. Athens: 455–84.

——, 2001. 'A new Late Minoan IIIC shrine at Halasmenos, east Crete', in R. Laffineur and R. Hägg (eds.), *POTNIA. Deities and Religion in the Aegean Bronze Age.* Aegaeum 22. Liège and Austin: 99–101.

——, 2004. 'Halasmenos, destroyed but not invisible: new insights on the LM IIIC period in the Isthmus of Ierapetra. First presentation of the pottery from the 1992–1997 campaign', in *Crete Beyond the Palaces*: 103–24.

——, 2005. '"Mycenoans" at the Isthmus of Ierapetra: some (preliminary) thoughts on the foundation of the (Eteo)Cretan cultural identity', in *Ariadne's Threads*: 303–34.

——, 2009. 'Goddesses for *gene*? The Late Minoan IIIC Shrine at Halasmenos, Ierapetra', in *Archaeologies of Cult*: 121–36.

——, and L. Vagnetti, 2006. 'Late Minoan III evidence from Kritsa, Mirabello', Πεπραγμένα του Θ΄ Διεθνούς Κρητολογικού Συνεδρίου. Herakleion: A1, 201–10.

——, L. Vagnetti and M. Liston, 2003. 'New evidence for the Dark Ages in eastern Crete. An unplundered tholos tomb at Vasiliki', *SMEA* 45: 85–124.

Wallace, S. A., 2003. 'The perpetuated past: re-use and continuity in material culture as evidence for the growth of community identity structures in the Early Iron Age of Crete, 12th to 7th centuries BC', *BSA* 97: 251–77.

——, 2005. 'Last chance to see? Karfi (Crete) in the twenty-first century: presentation of new architectural data and their analysis in the current context of research', *BSA* 100: 215–74.

——, 2007. 'Why we need new spectacles: mapping the experiential dimension in prehistoric Cretan landscapes', *CAJ* 17, 3: 249–70.

——, 2010. *Ancient Crete. From Successful Collapse to Democracy's Alternatives, Twelfth to Fifth Centuries BC.* Cambridge.

Warren, P. M., 1982–83. 'Knossos: stratigraphical museum excavations, 1978–82. Part II', *AR* 29: 63–87.

——, 1997. 'LM III pottery from the city of Knossos: Stratigraphic Museum Extension Site', in *Late Minoan III Pottery*: 157–82.

——, 2007. 'Characteristics of Late Minoan IIIC from the stratigraphical museum site at Knossos', in *LH IIIC Chronology II*: 329–43.

Watrous, L. V., 1982. *Lasithi. A History of Settlement on a Highland Plain in Crete. Hesperia* Suppl. 18. Princeton.

——, 1991. 'The origin and iconography of the Late Minoan painted larnax', *Hesperia* 60: 285–307.

——, 1992. *Kommos III. The Late Bronze Age Pottery.* Princeton.

——, 1996. *The Cave Sanctuary of Zeus at Psychro.* Aegaeum 15. Liège and Austin.

Whitbread, I. K., 1995. *Greek Transport Amphorae: A Petrological and Archaeological Study.* Fitch Laboratory Occasional Paper 4. Oxford.

Whitley, J., 1991. 'Social diversity in Dark Age Greece', *BSA* 86: 341–65.

Whittaker, H., 2005. 'Response to Metaxia Tsipopoulou. "Mycenoans" at the Isthmus of Ierapetra: some (preliminary) thoughts on the foundation of (Eteo)cretan cultural identity', in *Ariadne's Threads*: 335–43.

Wilson, D. E., and P. M. Day, 1994. 'Ceramic regionalism in Prepalatial Central Crete: the Mesara imports from EM IB to EM IIA Knossos', *BSA* 89: 1–87.

Woolley, C. L., 1955. *Alalakh: An Account of the Excavations at Tell Atchana in the Hatay, 1937–1949.* London.

Yasur-Landau, A., 2006. 'The last *glendi* in Halasmenos: social aspects of cooking in a Dark Age Cretan village', *Aegean Archaeology* 7: 49–66.

Young, G. M., 1937. 'Archaeology in Greece 1936–1937', *JHS* 57: 119–46.

——, 1938. 'Archaeology in Greece 1937–1938', *JHS* 58: 217–39.

Index

Afrati 157
altars 4, 43, 74, 134, 155, 166, 246,
 275, 290, 312–14, 333, 334
Ayia Triada 157, 191, 200
amphoras 12, 14, 28, 29, 32, 35, 37,
 44, 60, 71, 73, 84, 87, 88, 90, 97,
 123, 155, 157, 163, 178, 180, 204,
 206, 238, 285, 296, 298, 300–02,
 304, 305, 325, 326, 327, 330, 331;
 see also cooking pottery
amphoriskoi see krateriskoi
animal bones 7, 14, 23, 24, 26, 74, 81,
 82, 138, 142, 154, 155, 163, 165,
 168, 171, 176, 189, 191, 197, 199,
 200, 204, 213, 215, 216, 238, 331
 deer 101, 102, 138, 165, 171, 191,
  213
 goat 23, 81, 138, 238
 horse 238
 ox 138, 182, 238
 sheep 238
Archaic Period 7, 62, 221, 227, 228,
 236, 240, 298, 300, 328
askoi 28, 29, 302, 338, 339
Atsividhero 107, 240–2, 255, 256,
 264, 267, 296

Baker's House 4, 80–2, 171, 306, 328,
 330
Barracks 27–37, 326, 327, 328, 329,
 330
basins 7, 8, 11, 14, 16, 23, 24, 27, 28,
 29, 45, 47, 55, 56, 58, 62, 69, 71, 99,
 101, 102, 107, 108, 112, 121, 123,
 127, 131, 132, 136, 138, 142, 144,
 145, 152, 154, 155, 157, 163, 165,
 166, 167, 171, 174, 176, 180, 189,
 192, 197, 199, 200, 202, 210, 213,
 215, 218, 220, 221, 230, 236, 238,
 243, 246, 274, 280–2, 305, 309, 317,
 330, 338, 339, 340, 345
 deep basin or bowl 199, 282–3
beads 52, 62
 stone 7, 16, 19, 21, 23, 24, 26, 32,
  34, 39, 42, 44, 69, 102, 105, 107,
  123, 127, 130, 132, 138, 144, 145,
  151, 152, 155, 160, 163, 165, 168,
  176, 180, 183, 191, 195, 197, 210,
  213, 215, 216, 218, 220, 221, 233,
  236, 240
 terracotta 44, 332
 see also bone; glass
benches 23, 32, 34, 39, 42, 43, 56, 62,
 66, 115, 138, 142, 151

birds on ritual equipment 44, 276, 332
bird vases 37, 118, 165, 204, 233,
 310–12
blue ware 7, 19, 34, 35, 39, 42, 43, 44,
 45, 50, 52, 56, 58, 82, 90, 95, 99,
 109, 118, 123, 127, 137, 142, 145,
 160, 176, 178, 180, 182, 183, 185,
 200, 202, 218, 246, 253, 254, 257,
 259, 271, 283, 285, 295, 300, 332,
 333, 338
boar's tusk 16, 68, 69, 101, 138, 160,
 216
bone 223
 beads 52, 228
 handles 35, 55, 110, 165, 183, 220
 implements 97, 131, 162, 215
 lid 152
 needle 227
 pins 26, 76, 144, 145, 147, 151,
  152, 176, 180, 195, 213, 216
 sword pommel 88
 tubes 81, 155
bottles 34, 63, 222, 223, 296
bowls 63, 64, 66, 73, 74, 82, 97, 102,
 107, 109, 127, 140, 142, 145, 151,
 154, 155, 159, 162, 163, 165, 166,
 168, 171, 176, 178, 183, 189, 191,
 195, 204, 206, 213, 220, 238, 240,
 243, 255, 285, 315
 carinated 26, 88, 280, 335
 deep 7, 8, 11, 12, 14, 16, 19, 23,
  24, 26, 27, 32, 34, 35, 42, 45, 50,
  52, 53, 55, 56, 58, 60, 62, 64, 65,
  66, 69, 71, 74, 76, 78, 81, 82, 83,
  84, 88, 90, 93, 94, 95, 97, 99,
  101, 102, 103, 104, 105, 107, 108,
  109, 110, 112, 115, 118, 119, 121,
  123, 125, 127, 130, 131, 132, 134,
  136, 137, 138, 140, 142, 144, 145,
  147, 149, 151, 152, 154, 155, 159,
  160, 162, 163, 165, 166, 168, 169,
  171, 172, 176, 178, 180, 182, 183,
  185, 189, 191, 192, 195, 197, 199,
  200, 202, 204, 206, 213, 215, 216,
  218, 219, 225, 228, 230, 233, 236,
  240, 241, 242, 243, 255, 256,
  257–65, 269, 272, 276, 278, 286,
  326, 327, 328, 331, 335, 338, 341,
  342, 346
 shallow 35, 71, 76, 80, 99, 197,
  199, 265, 282
 spouted 137, 138, 140, 191, 197,
  199, 204, 236, 279, 335
 see also tripod bowls

bronze 7, 23, 62, 76, 99, 110, 112, 130,
 132, 137, 138, 142, 144, 145, 147, 151,
 152, 163, 180, 183, 200, 213, 346
 arrowheads 180, 182, 204, 220
 awls 50, 69, 110, 163, 210, 215
 axe 74
 blades 23, 69, 74, 105, 154, 160,
  183, 197, 220
 chisels 62, 136
 daggers 62, 110
 decorated plaques 62, 147
 discs 97, 110, 227, 228
 double axes 110, 112, 115, 200, 334
 earring 200
 fibulae 7, 23, 145, 163, 213, 228,
  233, 238
 hair rings 228, 233
 hook 53
 implements 204, 220, 228
 knives 7, 21, 101, 105, 132, 160,
  176, 200, 218
 nails 62, 69, 218, 220
 needles 32, 62, 102, 165, 216, 225
 pins 19, 163, 169, 215, 221, 223,
  230, 232, 233
 rings 53, 58, 62, 72, 97, 147, 151,
  155, 200, 218, 225, 228, 238
 rods 105, 176, 200, 216
 saws 62, 69
 sickles 62, 69, 97
 spear 192
 sword 160
 stud 163
 tripod 23
 tweezers 76
 vessels 88, 105
 wire 200
Byzantine Period 218, 225, 328

Central West Quarter 4, 144–62, 327,
 329, 331
 Building 66-67-68-81 144–9
 Building 82-83-84-86-88 149–54
 Building 85-87-69 154–60, 331, 334
 Building 96-97-100 160–2
chalices 44, 45, 47, 132, 269–70, 278,
 332
chisels 62, 136
Classical Period 227, 240, 328
Close style see Pleonastic style
closed vessels 12, 47, 52, 58, 62, 64, 66,
 71, 72, 80, 82, 88, 93, 94, 97, 101, 105,
 107, 108, 147, 162, 171, 172, 174,
 176, 195, 206, 215, 227, 236

Commercial Quarter 4, 169–80, 327, 328, 333

cooking 26, 28, 32, 34, 56, 60, 101, 112, 127, 155, 176, 183, 191, 197, 200, 223, 328, 329, 331, 333, 345

cooking fabric 138, 185, 204, 216, 254, 274, 276, 285, 322, 330

cooking pottery 4, 32, 34, 45, 64, 134, 191, 192, 200, 204, 213, 218, 315, 325, 330, 331, 332, 334, 335, 338, 339, 345

  dishes 8, 11, 28, 29, 32, 34, 45, 47, 50, 71, 73, 81, 90, 134, 176, 180, 191, 215, 248, 254, 285, 304, 315–17, 330, 338, 339

  jars/amphoras 118, 315, 320, 322, 325, 330, 335

  jugs 14, 19, 28, 29, 34, 47, 60, 71, 127, 140, 192, 195, 248, 298, 318–19, 330

  lids 29, 50, 53, 55, 59, 66, 73, 127, 142, 144, 152, 171, 176, 180, 183, 186, 191, 210, 216, 218, 248, 283, 285, 330, 339, 340

  mugs/cups 138, 315, 338, 339

  pots 7, 8, 29, 72, 223, 252, 254, 285, 288, 315, 320

  slabs 191, 210, 248, 255, 322, 338, 339

  trays 44, 47, 50, 71, 99, 130, 145, 165, 169, 171, 176, 199, 200, 204, 280, 315, 317–18, 320, 330, 332

  tripod bowls 99, 105, 118, 125, 149, 154, 155, 183, 319, 330

  tripod cooking pots 11, 47, 66, 69, 72, 93, 99, 112, 118, 130, 138, 140, 145, 147, 149, 151, 157, 160, 165, 176, 178, 180, 183, 188, 189, 192, 197, 199, 200, 204, 223, 225, 238, 254, 280, 302, 305, 315, 318, 319–20, 330, 332, 334, 335

  tripod legs 7, 14, 23, 24, 26, 27, 35, 44, 50, 56, 62, 64, 66, 69, 80, 82, 84, 127, 132, 138, 142, 152, 154, 163, 165, 166, 168, 169, 171, 176, 189, 191, 197, 204, 210, 213, 215, 216, 218, 220, 221, 227, 236, 317

courtyards 21, 26, 34, 44, 74, 102, 105, 169, 171, 172, 191, 217, 326, 327, 328, 329, 333, 335

cups 7, 8, 11, 12, 14, 23, 24, 26, 32, 35, 42, 45, 47, 52, 53, 55, 60, 62, 64, 65, 66, 69, 71, 74, 76, 81, 82, 83, 88, 90, 93, 94, 95, 97, 99, 101, 102, 104, 105, 107, 108, 109, 110, 112, 115, 118, 121, 123, 125, 127, 131, 132, 134, 137, 138, 140, 144, 145, 147, 149, 152, 154, 155, 160, 162, 163, 165, 166, 168, 169, 171, 172, 180, 182, 183, 192, 195, 197, 199, 200, 202, 204, 206, 213, 215, 216, 218, 219, 220, 225, 227, 228, 230, 233, 236, 240, 241, 242, 243, 246, 255–7, 259, 262, 263, 264, 265, 271, 278, 279, 283, 285, 326, 327, 331

champagne 64, 76, 80, 102, 269, 278

conical 14, 26, 192, 237, 238, 271, 283, 338, 341, 342

MM cylindrical cup 69, 71

Cyprus 157, 222, 238, 296, 298, 324, 335

decorative motifs on pottery

  alternating arcs 88, 90, 94, 101, 102, 127, 134, 152, 162, 172, 174, 182, 202, 227, 269, 271, 286, 293, 312

  beading 88, 90, 118, 157, 163, 171, 176, 197, 199, 225, 227, 240, 243, 270, 271, 298

  birds 12, 44, 74, 99, 105, 149, 163, 165, 169, 172, 174, 176, 192, 199, 206, 216, 220, 246, 264, 278, 279, 286

  bivalve shells 56, 95, 105, 121, 142, 171, 264, 326

  blobs 14, 32, 65, 76, 78, 80, 81, 84, 87, 93, 94, 95, 107, 108, 130, 140, 151, 152, 154, 159, 160, 166, 171, 172, 182, 202, 225, 233, 240, 241, 242, 243, 246, 255, 256, 259, 264, 265, 269, 272, 295, 296

  chevrons 12, 37, 50, 53, 58, 66, 78, 81, 82, 84, 87, 90, 99, 107, 112, 127, 144, 149, 157, 165, 174, 178, 180, 185, 192, 199, 202, 205, 215, 216, 218, 230, 243, 262, 263, 264, 269, 270, 272, 279, 285, 286, 298, 305

  comb 64, 125, 162, 255, 264, 326

  compass-drawn semicircles 221, 298, 327

  double axes 27, 52, 78, 81, 82, 88, 90, 97, 99, 101, 112, 162, 171, 172, 174, 182, 192, 204, 206, 261, 262, 270, 272, 279, 286, 333

  fish 56, 74, 97, 99, 292, 315

  fringes 7, 11, 12, 15, 21, 23, 37, 39, 58, 64, 66, 72, 74, 80, 82, 84, 88, 90, 95, 97, 99, 102, 107, 108, 109, 115, 118, 121, 125, 127, 132, 138, 140, 142, 144, 145, 147, 149, 152, 154, 155, 162, 163, 166, 168, 169, 171, 172, 174, 176, 182, 183, 185, 189, 191, 192, 195, 197, 199, 200, 204, 206, 213, 218, 219, 225, 227, 228, 230, 233, 236, 238, 243, 259, 260, 263, 264, 265, 269, 272, 279, 286, 292, 293, 310, 327

  gremlin or imp 204, 206, 264

  hatched ovals 74, 191, 263, 279

  horns of consecration 11, 39, 66, 84, 134, 149, 182, 185, 192, 200, 246, 262, 279, 286, 288, 312, 314

  lozenges 16, 53, 82, 159, 191, 263, 279

    hatched or crosshatched 8, 11, 12, 26, 39, 69, 74, 80, 84, 104, 105, 109, 130, 132, 134, 149,

152, 160, 162, 168, 174, 182, 183, 200, 213, 218, 220, 230, 243, 263, 264, 269, 272, 280, 286, 293

    lozenge and loop 8, 78, 218, 219, 263, 286

  elaborate 37, 127, 134, 183, 191, 218, 260

  Minoan flowers 8, 12, 50, 53, 64, 76, 78, 83, 105, 121, 125, 127, 132, 147, 149, 154, 166, 172, 174, 182, 189, 202, 213, 220, 255, 262–3, 279, 293, 326

  monochrome 14, 19, 32, 42, 52, 62, 65, 71, 78, 80, 81, 87, 88, 90, 93, 94, 95, 102, 108, 112, 115, 121, 123, 127, 130, 147, 152, 155, 157, 160, 176, 182, 185, 188, 192, 195, 199, 202, 213, 221, 227, 230, 236, 238, 239, 240, 242, 243, 246, 253, 255, 256, 257, 259, 264–5, 266, 269, 271, 272, 279, 280, 282, 285, 288, 294, 296, 298, 300, 312

  multiple loops 8, 12, 24, 45, 52, 53, 62, 69, 74, 76, 78, 81, 94, 95, 99, 101, 105, 112, 118, 123, 130, 138, 140, 145, 149, 155, 171, 172, 183, 195, 199, 200, 206, 215, 243, 255, 260–1, 265, 296

  octopus 8, 11, 12, 14, 16, 24, 35, 37, 39, 52, 58, 60, 74, 80, 84, 90, 93, 94, 101, 130, 132, 142, 147, 152, 162, 167, 174, 176, 178, 182, 183, 185, 195, 204, 213, 215, 227, 230, 243, 269, 279, 282, 293, 294, 315, 331

  panels 11, 12, 14, 16, 21, 27, 37, 39, 42, 52, 55, 56, 62, 63, 66, 74, 78, 83, 84, 87, 88, 90, 93, 94, 95, 97, 99, 101, 102, 105, 107, 112, 118, 121, 125, 132, 134, 140, 144, 147, 149, 152, 155, 160, 163, 168, 172, 174, 178, 180, 185, 191, 192, 199, 202, 205, 215, 216, 218, 228, 230, 261–2, 263, 269, 270, 271, 272, 279, 286, 293, 300, 302

  quatrefoils 78, 84, 87, 95, 101, 107, 112, 125, 149, 152, 157, 197, 199, 204, 216, 218, 262, 269, 272, 279, 286

  quirks 60, 76, 78, 97, 105, 107, 118, 147, 149, 165, 166, 172, 213, 243, 262, 298, 326

  reserved bands 8, 26, 52, 53, 64, 71, 115, 123, 132, 149, 162, 165, 166, 171, 172, 195, 197, 200, 204, 206, 213, 215, 219, 236, 259, 260, 263, 269, 278, 298, 304

  reserved discs 52, 53, 76, 78, 103, 107, 115, 152, 165, 172, 197, 206, 223, 243, 259, 260, 272, 278

  scales 11, 14, 52, 80, 99, 102, 105, 107, 112, 145, 157, 160, 185, 202, 204, 223, 264, 269, 279, 286, 293

  spirals 7, 8, 11, 12, 14, 16, 21, 32,

34, 37, 39, 50, 52, 53, 55, 58, 62,
74, 76, 78, 81, 84, 88, 90, 93, 94,
95, 97, 99, 101, 102, 105, 118,
119, 123, 127, 130, 132, 134, 136,
138, 140, 144, 145, 147, 151, 152,
155, 160, 162, 165, 166, 171, 174,
176, 180, 182, 185, 189, 192, 195,
199, 200, 202, 205, 213, 215, 216,
218, 227, 230, 236, 238, 259, 260,
269, 279, 282, 286, 293, 294, 298,
302, 310
  antithetic   197, 264
  buttonhook   26, 76, 97, 99, 101,
    103, 105, 107, 115, 123, 127,
    140, 145, 147, 149, 165, 197,
    202, 243, 260, 326
  running   8, 21, 26, 39, 90, 112,
    121, 125, 127, 130, 131, 144,
    155, 157, 218, 260, 278, 286,
    298
  stemmed   14, 99, 101, 105, 107,
    121, 166, 172, 174, 180, 199,
    215, 218, 219, 257, 262, 300,
    302
trees   39, 108, 112, 176, 180, 263,
  270, 278, 279, 314
triangles   11, 16, 21, 27, 52, 55, 56,
  74, 80, 84, 87, 88, 90, 105, 112,
  118, 121, 123, 127, 134, 136, 140,
  142, 149, 151, 160, 171, 176, 178,
  180, 182, 185, 195, 197, 199, 200,
  206, 215, 216, 223, 227, 230, 233,
  236, 238, 243, 246, 262, 269, 270,
  271, 272, 278, 286, 292, 293, 294,
  298, 302, 307, 309, 310, 311, 312,
  327
tricurved streamers   8, 11, 12, 147,
  149, 152, 166, 192, 202, 213, 215,
  216, 263–4, 269
U-pattern   14, 37, 80, 94, 140, 145,
  149, 182, 215, 218, 246, 262, 293
wavy bands   8, 11, 14, 62, 74, 80,
  84, 90, 93, 130, 132, 145, 147,
  149, 169, 172, 174, 176, 178, 180,
  182, 185, 192, 204, 206, 230, 233,
  236, 239, 243, 263, 279, 282, 293,
  294, 327
zigzags   11, 16, 26, 37, 53, 71, 76,
  78, 87, 90, 112, 132, 140, 149,
  168, 171, 192, 202, 204, 205, 210,
  223, 255, 256, 262, 263, 270, 272,
  279, 282, 286, 291, 293, 305, 327
see also pithos decoration
dints   11, 27, 47, 56, 60, 62, 66, 68, 69,
  72, 83, 93, 99, 108, 112, 115, 118,
  132, 138, 140, 142, 149, 157, 200,
  202, 204, 225, 248, 276, 280, 282,
  305, 307, 312, 318, 320
dishes *see* cooking pottery
drinking   24, 34, 39, 56, 58, 130, 162,
  172, 191, 192, 195, 204, 269, 271,
  274, 279, 328, 330–1, 332

Eastern Cliff Houses   4, 180–9, 228,
  332

Eastern Quarter   21–7, 314, 329, 330,
  332, 335
  House K 135-136   21–3
  House K 137-141   23, 330
  House K 138-139-140   23–6, 332
Egypt   1, 74, 328
Enkomi   157, 298, 335

fabrics   335
  definition of   4–5, 253–5, 337–8
  flysch fabrics   254, 294, 338, 341
  metamorphic fabrics   338–40, 341,
    343, 344, 345, 346, 347, 348,
  phyllite–quartzite series   253, 254,
    274, 285, 322, 339, 340, 342, 343,
    345, 346, 347
faience   23, 62
feasting   279, 331–2, 335
figurines   4, 24, 58, 68, 115, 147, 163,
  213, 215, 220, 327, 331, 333, 334
  animal   19, 44, 45, 69, 134, 144,
    154, 155, 157, 166, 200, 216, 220,
    221, 223, 225, 228, 332, 334, 335
  human   11, 34, 154, 155, 169, 200,
    220, 221, 228, 334, 335
fireboxes   16, 183, 185, 315
flasks   66, 73, 155, 157, 178, 238, 300,
  302, 335, 338, 347
flysch deposits   341, 345

Gazi   337, 341
Geometric Period   55, 62, 82, 210, 225,
  255, 280, 296, 300
glass bead   62
goddesses with upraised arms   4, 11,
  14, 43, 44, 45, 53, 56, 68, 71, 73, 74,
  115, 132, 134, 137, 154, 155, 166,
  168, 169, 171, 172, 178, 180, 200,
  221, 326, 327, 328, 332, 333, 334,
  337, 338, 341, 343, 344, 345, 346
Great House   4, 55–67, 97, 104, 105,
  112, 137, 166, 225, 269, 288, 302,
  326, 327, 328, 331, 332, 333
Great House Shrine   55–6, 68–73, 155,
  275, 289, 327, 330, 332, 333
griffins   39, 279
Gypsades   238

hearths   21, 23, 24, 58, 83, 147, 152,
  330, 332
Hellenistic Period   56, 58, 62, 68, 72,
  225, 278, 304, 328
Herakleion Museum   4, 44, 314, 322
horns of consecration   334
human remains   163, 221, 223, 224,
  225, 227, 230, 233, 237, 240
hut urns   7, 11, 19, 44, 52, 68, 102,
  154, 160, 185, 204, 206, 215, 216,
  288–90, 332, 334

imported pottery   34, 60, 74, 78, 83,
  99, 144, 155, 157, 172, 174, 195,
  202, 223, 227, 243, 253, 259, 294,
  302, 320, 327, 335, 341, 342, 345,
  346

incense burners   44, 45, 183, 185, 276,
  315, 320, 332
iron   154, 160, 233
  blade   233
  fibula   233
  nail   225
  needle   228
Isthmus of Ierapetra   337

jars   7, 8, 11, 14, 16, 23, 24, 26, 27, 28,
  32, 34, 35, 45, 47, 50, 52, 53, 60, 62,
  64, 66, 68, 69, 71, 74, 80, 82, 83, 84,
  87, 88, 90, 93, 95, 97, 99, 105, 107,
  109, 115, 119, 121, 125, 130, 134,
  136, 137, 138, 142, 145, 151, 154,
  155, 157, 159, 160, 165, 166, 171,
  176, 178, 180, 183, 185, 188, 189,
  191, 192, 197, 199, 200, 204, 206,
  210, 213, 215, 216, 218, 230, 232,
  238, 254, 280, 285, 302–05, 314,
  319, 329, 330, 335, 338, 339, 345;
  see also cooking pottery
jugs   7, 11, 12, 14, 16, 19, 21, 23, 24,
  26, 27, 29, 32, 34, 35, 37, 44, 50, 52,
  53, 55, 56, 58, 60, 66, 68, 71, 72, 74,
  82, 88, 90, 93, 95, 97, 101, 105, 107,
  109, 119, 123, 125, 130, 132, 134,
  136, 138, 140, 142, 144, 145, 147,
  151, 152, 154, 155, 157, 159, 160,
  162, 163, 165, 166, 171, 174, 176,
  178, 180, 183, 185, 189, 191, 192,
  195, 197, 199, 200, 204, 206, 210,
  213, 215, 218, 221, 223, 225, 227,
  230, 232, 236, 237, 238, 246, 248,
  254, 271, 283, 285, 296–300, 302,
  304, 305, 331, 335, 338, 339, 342;
  see also cooking pottery
juglets   35, 55, 71, 87, 110, 112, 130,
  155, 157, 160, 197, 225, 233, 236,
  240, 246, 264, 295, 296, 298, 331

kalathoi   23, 45, 47, 112, 142, 147,
  152, 154, 172, 185, 213, 271–5, 334
  basket   19, 71, 145, 149, 171, 174,
    180, 200, 271–4
  handleless   7, 11, 14, 19, 29, 34, 42,
    44, 53, 56, 58, 62, 82, 87, 107,
    112, 118, 119, 121, 137, 138, 140,
    144, 145, 155, 159, 160, 165, 166,
    176, 185, 189, 199, 200, 213, 215,
    218, 220, 246, 248, 271, 274–5,
    332, 333, 338, 339, 343, 345, 246
  side-handled   221, 222, 223, 272
Kastelli Pediada   3, 12, 26, 55, 78, 80,
  93, 101, 103, 105, 107, 110, 118,
  121, 123, 125, 130, 131, 134, 147,
  160, 165, 166, 168, 169, 172, 178,
  182, 213, 215, 216, 243, 260, 261,
  263, 264, 269, 304, 305, 306, 310
Kastri, Palaikastro   3, 8, 14, 16, 26, 29,
  34, 35, 39, 45, 52, 53, 56, 64, 66, 71,
  73, 76, 78, 81, 90, 93, 95, 97, 101,
  102, 104, 105, 108, 112, 115, 127,
  131, 134, 138, 149, 155, 171, 172,
  178, 197, 200, 204, 206, 215, 218,

219, 256, 260, 261, 262, 263, 264,
265, 266, 282, 288, 290, 294, 300,
302, 315, 318, 320, 324
Kastrokephala 64, 71, 166, 200, 202,
263, 302, 318, 341
Katalimata 101, 183, 240, 337
Kavousi 3, 5, 23, 72, 253, 254, 285,
312, 319, 324, 326, 337, 342, 346
Kastro 3, 8, 26, 29, 34, 45, 52, 62,
73, 76, 88, 93, 95, 101, 105, 109,
121, 123, 125, 130, 166, 171, 172,
210, 213, 215, 218, 255, 260, 261,
262, 263, 272, 288, 294, 296, 300,
317, 318, 322, 325
Vronda 3, 8, 21, 24, 26, 32, 39, 45,
58, 73, 76, 87, 95, 99, 118, 121,
134, 136, 137, 147, 149, 154, 157,
162, 166, 171, 178, 191, 195, 197,
200, 204, 215, 216, 228, 236, 243,
246, 256, 257, 260, 262, 263, 264,
265, 269, 270, 272, 274, 275, 276,
278, 280, 282, 285, 288, 294, 295,
300, 302, 304, 305, 306, 307, 309,
310, 312, 314, 316, 318, 320, 325,
327, 328, 329, 331, 333, 334, 337,
345
Kephallonia 88, 265, 278
Khalasmenos 3, 45, 66, 87, 138, 155,
178, 191, 197, 200, 204, 225, 240,
253, 260, 263, 265, 269, 272, 274,
275, 282, 300, 302, 305, 306, 314,
318, 320, 324, 325, 328, 329, 330,
333, 337
Khamalevri 1, 3, 8, 12, 14, 39, 45, 47,
50, 53, 66, 76, 78, 84, 87, 99, 112,
118, 127, 130, 144, 145, 149, 152,
154, 160, 165, 166, 171, 174, 192,
197, 202, 206, 216, 218, 219, 246,
248, 259, 260, 261, 263, 264, 282,
285, 291, 305, 318, 320, 324
Khania 2, 3, 8, 12, 16, 21, 26, 45, 52,
60, 66, 76, 80, 88, 90, 99, 103, 105,
109, 110, 123, 140, 145, 152, 157,
165, 172, 185, 192, 204, 213, 216,
228, 255, 256, 257, 260, 262, 263,
264, 265, 269, 278, 285, 290, 294,
296, 302, 305, 310, 317, 318, 320,
322, 324, 335
Kastelli 134, 255, 259
Knossos 1, 3, 8, 11, 12, 14, 16, 26,
39, 45, 52, 53, 62, 66, 69, 76, 78,
81, 88, 90, 93, 97, 101, 103, 105,
107, 110, 115, 121, 123, 125, 130,
132, 140, 145, 147, 149, 160, 165,
169, 171, 172, 174, 178, 183, 192,
197, 202, 213, 215, 218, 222, 223,
228, 233, 238, 241, 255, 260, 261,
262, 263, 264, 265, 267, 271, 278,
282, 294, 296, 298, 300, 302, 304,
307, 320, 324, 327, 331, 335; *see
also* Gypsades
Kommos 29, 53, 78, 90, 115, 125, 130,
149, 172, 218, 255, 257, 300, 310
kraters 8, 11, 12, 14, 19, 21, 26, 27,
34, 35, 37, 39, 42, 53, 55, 58, 60, 62,

63, 64, 66, 68, 69, 71, 74, 80, 88, 90,
93, 94, 95, 99, 101, 102, 105, 107,
110, 112, 118, 121, 123, 125, 127,
130, 131, 132, 134, 136, 137, 138,
140, 142, 145, 147, 149, 151, 152,
154, 155, 157, 160, 162, 163, 165,
166, 169, 171, 172, 174, 176, 180,
182, 189, 195, 197, 199, 200, 204,
210, 213, 215, 216, 218, 220, 224,
225, 227, 228, 243, 246, 248, 257,
260, 262, 264, 265, 269, 271, 276–9,
286, 302, 319, 327, 331, 335, 338,
341, 342
krateriskoi 204, 206, 228, 238, 239,
265, 266–7, 304, 327
Kritsa 53, 125, 152, 154, 191, 197,
215, 269, 291, 293
kylikes 11, 12, 16, 24, 27, 32, 34, 35,
37, 39, 56, 58, 60, 63, 64, 68, 71, 74,
80, 81, 83, 93, 95, 99, 102, 105, 107,
109, 118, 119, 121, 134, 142, 144,
145, 152, 155, 157, 159, 162, 163,
165, 167, 171, 172, 174, 176, 178,
182, 185, 197, 200, 202, 204, 206,
213, 225, 227, 228, 230, 243, 255,
267–9, 271, 278, 327, 331, 332, 338,
341, 342, 343, 344

larnakes 66, 97, 99, 145, 147, 160,
221, 222, 225, 227, 304, 305, 314–15
Lasithi Plateau 335, 339, 341, 342,
345
Late Minoan IIIB 1, 3, 8, 12, 29, 52,
53, 76, 81, 88, 97, 101, 105, 107,
110, 115, 118, 121, 123, 125, 127,
134, 140, 155, 160, 165, 171, 172,
191, 197, 204, 215, 216, 218, 219,
228, 236, 257, 261, 262, 263, 264,
265, 271, 290, 291, 292, 296, 300,
302, 310, 312, 315, 325, 326, 327,
337
Late Minoan IIIB/C 53, 60, 78, 90, 95,
97, 99, 101, 110, 115, 121, 125, 127,
140, 145, 162, 172, 192, 199, 213,
223, 262, 264, 265, 307, 315, 325,
327, 328
lead 60, 62, 218, 220, 332
ledges 43, 56, 142, 145, 155, 162, 176,
178
Lefkandi 39, 149, 204, 228, 279
lids 19, 23, 26, 27, 28, 29, 32, 37, 45,
47, 52, 53, 60, 64, 80, 99, 118, 123,
134, 160, 163, 165, 182, 183, 185,
192, 218, 254, 255, 265, 272, 283–5,
286, 288, 304, 306, 315, 317, 320;
see also cooking pottery
looms *see* weaving
loomweights 68, 115, 183, 210, 220,
322
pyramidal 210, 322, 332
spools 8, 16, 19, 23, 24, 28, 34, 68,
83, 84, 88, 109, 110, 115, 123,
125, 130, 138, 145, 162, 163, 171,
176, 182, 183, 189, 195, 199, 213,
322–4, 332, 334

Lower deposits 62, 64, 66, 68, 69–71,
87, 93–7, 105, 138, 257, 259, 263,
288, 314, 320, 326, 333

Magazines 4, 83–104, 288, 326, 327,
328, 330, 332
Mikre Koprana 4, 7–21, 125, 166, 288,
293, 310, 322, 324, 330, 331, 332
mother of pearl 50, 51
Megaron 21, 23, 55, 56, 320, 332, 335
Mesara 172, 195, 257, 310, 335
Mochlos 319, 322
Mouliana 11, 53, 293
mugs 225, 227, 255, 270–1, 331; *see
also* cooking pottery
mugs/tankards 90, 118, 176, 220, 240,
243, 331
Mycenaeans 99, 259, 263, 269, 292,
310, 320, 335

Naxos 21, 60, 62, 279
Northern Shelters 4, 210–20, 314,
322

olives 199, 330
Open style 259, 260, 278
open vessels 171, 176, 230
ovens 24, 74, 80, 81, 147, 152, 171,
180, 326, 328, 330, 333

Pacheia Ammos 97, 315
Palaikastro *see* Kastri, Palaikastro
Papoura 326
Peak Sanctuary 4, 71, 220, 326
petrographic analysis 337–42
petrographic descriptions 346–8
Phaistos 12, 14, 16, 32, 42, 45, 50, 53,
73, 78, 83, 84, 93, 97, 99, 101, 105,
109, 118, 121, 125, 130, 131, 134,
138, 157, 160, 163, 172, 183, 195,
197, 200, 216, 218, 248, 257, 260,
261, 262, 263, 264, 265, 310, 318,
320, 324
pins 26, 76, 144, 145, 147, 151, 152,
163, 169, 176, 180, 195, 213, 215,
216, 221, 223, 230, 232, 233
pinakes *see* plaques
Piskokephalo 97, 315
pitharaki 19, 305
pithoi 7, 8, 11, 14, 16, 23, 24, 26, 27,
28, 29, 32, 34, 35, 37, 39, 42, 44, 50,
53, 56, 58, 59, 60, 62, 63, 64, 66, 68,
69, 72, 73, 74, 80, 81, 82, 83, 84, 87,
88, 93, 99, 101, 102, 104, 105, 107,
109, 112, 115, 118, 123, 125, 130,
132, 134, 136, 137, 138, 140, 142,
144, 145, 147, 151, 152, 154, 155,
157, 159, 160, 162, 163, 165, 166,
167, 169, 171, 176, 180, 183, 185,
189, 191, 192, 195, 197, 199, 200,
204, 210, 213, 215, 216, 218, 220,
221, 227, 228, 242, 243, 248, 252,
254, 280, 282, 302, 305, 306–10,
315, 319, 328, 329, 330, 334, 338,
339, 341, 343, 344, 345, 346

decoration of pithoi
   circles   32, 68, 72, 147, 154, 160, 210, 248, 307
   chevrons   7, 14, 27, 29, 35, 66, 68, 72, 83, 99, 102, 104, 109, 115, 118, 123, 134, 142, 145, 160, 163, 180, 199, 213, 227, 228, 242, 248, 252, 307, 309, 310
   impressed ovals/finger impressions   7, 11, 16, 27, 44, 50, 60, 68, 84, 109, 154, 166, 170, 171, 176, 200, 204, 218, 248, 307, 309
   oblique slashes   11, 14, 37, 308, 309
   pinched rope/piecrust   74, 83, 84, 102, 109, 115, 134, 136
   rope   7, 23, 35, 44, 66, 80, 104, 109, 115, 118, 142, 144, 161, 166, 248, 307
   rosette   50, 308
   serpentine bands   16, 29, 66, 68, 72, 102, 104, 109, 134, 136, 147, 218, 248, 307
   triangles   11, 142, 154, 309
   vertical slashes   11, 66, 83, 166, 307
   X-pattern   63, 144, 166, 185, 307
   other   307–08
   see also tripod pithoi
pithoid jars   7, 8, 11, 14, 16, 23, 24, 26, 27, 29, 32, 34, 37, 39, 42, 50, 56, 58, 60, 63, 66, 68, 69, 71, 72, 73, 74, 80, 81, 83, 88, 97, 99, 109, 112, 115, 118, 123, 125, 134, 136, 138, 142, 145, 152, 154, 155, 159, 160, 163, 166, 171, 176, 178, 180, 189, 191, 192, 197, 199, 200, 204, 210, 213, 216, 218, 280, 282, 304, 305–06, 307, 314, 329, 338, 339
plaques   28, 29, 43, 44, 45, 53, 56, 71, 73, 74, 76, 105, 107, 115, 136, 147, 178, 200, 210, 221, 248, 275, 314, 322, 326, 332, 333
platform   223
Pleonastic style   66, 110, 172, 183, 259, 260, 262, 272, 278, 279, 286
pot stands   24, 56, 87, 176, 191, 192
potter's wheel   220, 267, 322, 332
Praisos   97, 183, 223, 315
Priest's House   4, 137–44, 274, 276, 288, 328, 330, 332, 334
prodromos   21, 23
Protogeometric Period   1, 44, 45, 55, 62, 93, 155, 178, 204, 221, 222, 223, 225, 228, 233, 238, 239, 243, 255, 257, 259, 265, 267, 272, 274, 289, 293, 295, 296, 298, 300, 302, 310, 311, 326, 327, 328
Pseira   73, 302
Psychro   271
pumice   23, 24, 26, 42, 152, 154, 155, 163, 165, 197, 199, 200, 213, 215
pyxides   11, 16, 19, 23, 24, 26, 27, 28, 29, 32, 34, 35, 39, 56, 58, 66, 80, 81,

82, 83, 84, 87, 93, 94, 95, 104, 109, 110, 115, 119, 121, 125, 138, 140, 142, 144, 149, 157, 160, 163, 165, 166, 169, 171, 174, 176, 178, 180, 182, 183, 185, 191, 192, 197, 204, 206, 210, 215, 224, 227, 246, 272, 278, 279, 284, 286–8, 302, 304, 325, 331, 338, 339, 342

religion *see also* ritual
   religious activities   11, 28, 45, 56, 115, 134, 137, 154, 155, 157, 204, 206, 262, 270, 276, 290, 320, 324, 328, 331, 332, 333, 334, 337
   religious buildings/areas   44, 45, 56, 154, 157, 200, 270, 272, 274, 275, 298, 314, 322, 332, 333, 335
   religious objects   43, 45, 68, 274, 276, 312, 326, 329, 334, 345, 346
rhyta   44, 71, 90, 115, 118, 165, 172, 174, 215, 216, 233, 310, 328, 332, 334
ritual(s) *see also* religion
   activities   43, 45, 172, 180, 199, 200, 228, 236, 240, 298, 327, 328, 329, 332, 334, 335
   elite   24, 34, 39, 56, 58, 162, 195, 269, 271, 274, 279, 288, 331–2
   equipment   43, 44, 45, 56, 68, 71, 73, 115, 137, 154, 155, 157, 160, 276, 290, 314, 326, 327, 328, 332, 333, 334, 335, 337, 345
   function   11, 32, 71, 112, 136, 137, 138, 178, 200, 270, 274, 275, 312, 314, 333, 334, 339
   rooms/areas   330, 332, 333
Rhodes   16, 191, 223, 265, 279, 280, 293
ring vase   215, 312
roads *see* streets
Road House   38
Rooms
   K 1   43–9
   K 2   27–31, 330
   K 3   31–4
   K 4   34
   K 5   34
   K 6   34
   K 7   34–5
   K 8   56
   K 9   56–60
   K 10   105
   K 11   60–1, 332
   K 12   62–6, 326, 327, 328, 332
   K 13   66, 326, 328
   K 14   66–7, 328, 330
   K 15   68, 326, 327, 328, 333
   K 16   68, 326, 327, 328, 329, 330, 333
   K 17   69–72, 326, 327, 328, 329, 330, 333
   K 18   72–3, 327, 333
   K 19   50, 330, 332
   K 20   50
   K 21   83
   K 22   84–7, 329, 330, 332

K 23   87–97, 326, 327, 329, 332
K 24   109
K 25   109
K 26   109–15, 329, 330, 332, 334
K 27   115–18, 330, 332, 334
K 28   118, 332
K 29   97–9
K 30   99
K 31   99–102, 330
K 32   105–07, 326, 329, 333
K 33   102
K 34   102
K 35   102
K 36   102–04
K 37   104
K 38   52, 55, 327, 328, 329, 330, 333, 334
K 39   55, 330
K 40   50–2
K 41   52
K 42   119, 328
K 43   119–22, 328
K 44   123–4, 328, 332
K 45   127–30, 328
K 46   125, 332
K 47   125–7, 328
K 48   107–09, 328
K 49   130–1
K 50   130, 328, 329
K 51   130, 328
K 52   131–2, 328
K 53   132
K 54   132, 328
K 55   136, 329, 333
K 56   132–4
K 57   134–6, 333
K 58   137–8, 334
K 59   140–2
K 60   140, 330
K 61   138–40, 332
K 62   163, 334
K 63   163
K 64   163
K 65   163
K 66   145
K 67   145
K 68   147–9, 327
K 69   159–60, 329, 330, 334
K 70   73, 326, 328, 329, 333
K 71   80–1, 328, 329
K 72   74, 326, 333
K 73   81–2
K 74   82, 328
K 75   180–2
K 76   74–80, 326
K 77   169, 176–8
K 78   169, 174, 176
K 79   169–71, 327
K 79-89   171–4, 326, 333
K 80   142–4, 329, 330
K 81   145–7, 327
K 82   151–2
K 83   152–4, 330
K 84   154, 329
K 85   155–7, 331, 334

K 86   154, 328
K 87   157–9, 334
K 88   154, 328
K 89   171, 326
K 90   163, 334
K 91   163–5, 334
K 92   165
K 93   165
K 94   165
K 95   165
K 96   160
K 97   160–2
K 98   165
K 99   165
K 100   162
K 101   166–7, 326, 334
K 102   199–200, 329, 332, 334
K 103   167–8, 326
K 104   210
K 105   168, 326
K 106   200–04, 327, 328, 329, 330, 331, 332, 334
K 107   210–13
K 108   213–15, 334
K 109   215, 334
K 110   183–8, 329, 332
K 111   168, 326
K 112   174–6
K 113   189–92, 330
K 114   192–5
K 115   204–10, 327, 329
K 116   178–80, 326, 327, 328, 329, 333
K 117   189
K 118   189, 330
K 119   189
K 120   195–6
K 121   197–9, 329, 330
K 122   215–16, 334
K 123   216
K 124   216–18
K 125   218
K 126   210, 329, 330, 332
K 127   218–20, 328
K 128   220
K 129   220
K 130   37–9, 330
K 131   39, 330, 331
K 132   42, 329, 330
K 133   39–42
K 134   35–7
K 135   21, 23
K 136   23, 330, 332
K 137   23, 329, 330
K 138   23–6, 329, 330
K 139   23, 329, 330
K 140   24, 329, 334
K 141   23
K 142   26
K 143   26, 329, 330, 332
K 144   26–7
K 145   27
K 146   37
K 147   7–11, 329, 331
K 148   14–15, 331

K 149   11–14, 329, 331
K 150   14–17, 331, 332
MK   16–22
rubbish pits   53, 56, 62, 66, 68, 69, 71, 73, 74, 76, 80, 166, 255, 256, 259, 261, 264, 276, 312, 314, 326, 327, 328, 333

Scanning Electron Microscopy   337, 342–4
scuttles   7, 35, 42, 44, 45, 50, 72, 88, 102, 115, 118, 123, 134, 136, 137, 138, 142, 155, 171, 176, 178, 180, 182, 200, 202, 204, 206, 218, 254, 274, 275–6, 315, 332, 333, 338, 339
seals   42, 44
shells   44, 52, 53, 88, 107, 125
     conch   68, 119, 228
     cowrie   44
     oyster   58
     snail   223
     triton   44
Shrine   28, 43, 44, 45, 47, 53, 55, 56, 68, 71, 74, 105, 115, 134, 137, 144, 154, 155, 157, 169, 172, 178, 180, 200, 206, 326, 328, 329, 331, 332, 333, 334
skyphoi   69, 221, 223, 225, 228, 257, 264, 265
skyphoi/amphoriskoi   204, 206, 265–6
Small Shrine   4, 104, 105, 134–6, 270, 275, 276, 328, 333, 334
snakes (on pottery)   44, 45, 107, 200
snake tubes *see* stands
Southeast Block   37–42, 330, 331
Southern Houses   4, 109–31, 328, 329, 330, 332, 334
Southern Shelters   4, 162–5, 326, 327, 328, 329, 332
spindle whorls   7, 19, 23, 26, 32, 34, 35, 37, 44, 50, 53, 55, 58, 60, 62, 69, 76, 84, 88, 93, 97, 99, 101, 102, 107, 109, 115, 118, 123, 125, 127, 130, 131, 132, 134, 136, 137, 138, 145, 147, 163, 169, 178, 183, 191, 192, 195, 197, 202, 213, 215, 216, 220, 221, 332
     stone   44
squares   4, 102, 105–06, 107–09, 123, 130, 132, 134, 149, 151, 154, 178, 189, 191, 328, 333
stands   115, 127, 137, 155, 178, 200, 202, 213, 274, 312–14, 334
     cylindrical   45, 47, 134, 137, 138, 248, 276, 280, 312–14, 332, 333, 334
     fenestrated   44, 134, 228, 230, 246, 312–14, 325, 332
     rectangular   24, 137, 138, 155, 200, 246, 312–14, 334
     snake tubes   43, 44, 47, 52, 56, 69, 73, 74, 115, 134, 154, 178, 200, 202, 243, 246, 248, 254, 275, 290, 312, 333, 334, 337, 338, 339, 340, 341, 342, 343, 344, 345, 346

stirrup jars   29, 32, 37, 39, 44, 55, 62, 64, 68, 142, 144, 145, 163, 165, 189, 195, 197, 210, 218, 221, 254, 259, 290–4, 296, 298, 302, 310, 338
     coarse transport/storage   14, 16, 19, 21, 23, 24, 28, 32, 35, 37, 39, 42, 45, 47, 50, 52, 55, 56, 60, 62, 71, 73, 80, 84, 88, 97, 99, 101, 102, 112, 115, 119, 121, 123, 125, 130, 132, 142, 147, 149, 154, 155, 157, 163, 167, 171, 174, 176, 178, 182, 183, 185, 191, 192, 197, 200, 204, 210, 215, 220, 232, 248, 294, 302, 326, 329, 338, 339, 341, 343, 344, 345
     fine   8, 11, 12, 19, 23, 24, 26, 34, 35, 42, 47, 50, 52, 53, 58, 64, 69, 72, 74, 80, 81, 82, 88, 90, 94, 95, 97, 99, 102, 105, 107, 109, 110, 118, 119, 123, 125, 127, 131, 137, 138, 142, 145, 147, 151, 155, 157, 160, 162, 163, 166, 168, 171, 172, 174, 176, 178, 180, 182, 183, 185, 189, 191, 192, 195, 197, 199, 200, 204, 206, 213, 215, 216, 218, 222, 223, 224, 225, 227, 228, 230, 233, 236, 237, 238, 240, 242, 246, 264, 278, 290–4, 326, 327, 331, 333, 335, 338, 341, 342
     octopus   8, 12, 16, 35, 37, 152, 174, 176, 178, 182, 183, 185, 204, 215, 230, 293–4
stone
     discs   7, 26, 102, 183, 197
     inlays   110, 144
     plaques, pierced   171, 183, 189, 200
     tools   155, 165, 171, 176, 189, 191, 215
       axes, Neolithic   88, 97, 101, 109, 145, 163, 185, 215
       obsidian   44, 53, 182, 183
       pestles   63, 145
       pounders   7, 44, 123, 162, 216
       whetstones   7, 16, 21, 23, 42, 160, 178, 191, 195, 197, 218, 220
     weights   50, 52, 216
     vessels   23, 73, 101, 162, 169, 183, 216, 220
     see also beads; seals; spindle whorls
stoppers   35, 37, 80, 134, 182
storage   5, 8, 11, 24, 26, 28, 32, 34, 35, 43, 45, 56, 58, 83, 101, 102, 112, 136, 144, 145, 155, 160, 176, 183, 191, 192, 197, 199, 200, 204, 254, 274, 286, 288, 290, 294, 300, 302, 305, 306, 309, 310, 326, 328, 329–30, 331, 332, 333, 334, 335, 345
storerooms   4, 7, 16, 50, 56, 58, 66, 83, 112, 119, 165, 213, 326, 327, 331, 333
strainers   26, 39, 99, 115, 123, 127, 163, 385
streets   21, 34, 35, 39, 50, 73, 74, 76, 80, 83, 102, 104, 105, 109, 127, 130, 131, 132, 134, 137, 138, 154, 162,

166, 176, 180, 189, 195, 210, 215, 274, 326, 328, 329, 333, 334, 335
Broad Road   105–07, 131–4, 160, 166–8, 189, 326, 328
Cliff Road   189, 195
Temple Road East   52, 73–4, 328
Temple Road West   74–80
street deposits   257, 260, 262, 263, 264, 269, 272, 279, 288, 294, 314
Subminoan Period   1, 14, 45, 62, 74, 88, 90, 112, 145, 147, 152, 155, 157, 165, 169, 172, 174, 178, 180, 183, 204, 206, 222, 223, 228, 233, 238, 239, 240, 255, 256, 257, 259, 263, 265, 266, 267, 272, 274, 278, 289, 290, 296, 300, 302, 310, 311, 312, 326, 327, 328, 333
Summit   220
Sybrita/Thronos   1, 3, 24, 27, 35, 37, 50, 62, 66, 76, 88, 121, 123, 145, 152, 155, 166, 169, 172, 204, 215, 228, 238, 256, 262, 263, 267, 300, 318, 324
Syme Vianno   157, 335
Syria   73, 302, 335

Ta Mnemata   176, 192, 204, 221–40, 257, 264, 265, 267, 270, 272, 276, 282, 286, 290, 293, 296, 298, 300, 302, 304, 310, 312, 315, 319, 320, 326, 327, 328
tankards   23, 69, 74, 88, 90, 94, 109, 110, 112, 118, 136, 144, 151, 159, 160, 163, 166, 169, 171, 172, 174, 176, 197, 199, 218, 225, 240, 262, 263, 270–1, 272, 286, 331

Temple   3, 7, 16, 43–9, 115, 134, 137, 138, 154, 155, 178, 183, 200, 259, 263, 270, 274, 275, 276, 282, 290, 295, 312, 314, 317, 320, 326, 327, 328, 329, 330, 332, 333, 334
Temple Dependencies   4, 50–5, 275, 276, 328, 329, 332, 333
thelastra/feeding bottles   42, 45, 47, 52, 60, 69, 71, 74, 88, 90, 97, 162, 228, 230, 233, 236, 237, 238, 240, 246, 264, 294–6
tholos tombs   78, 183
  A 1   240, 255, 296
  A 2   240, 259, 270
  A 3   240–2, 255, 256, 259, 264, 265
  A 4   242
  M 1   221–3, 272, 296, 315
  M 2   223, 319, 320
  M 3   223, 290, 291, 293, 294
  M 4   176, 224–7, 256, 264, 265, 267, 269, 270, 271, 286, 288, 290, 293, 315
  M 5   227, 315
  M 6   227
  M 7   228
  M 8   228–30, 256, 259, 262, 263, 265, 269, 276, 278, 279, 282, 293, 294, 295, 298, 312
  M 9   230–2, 293, 304, 305
  M 10   230, 232
  M 11   230, 232–3, 290, 293, 294, 295, 296, 310
  M 12   230, 233, 295
  M 13   230, 233
  M 14   230, 236, 259, 263, 265, 293, 296

M 15   230, 236, 293
M 16   155, 192, 236, 237–8, 255, 256, 271, 292, 293, 300, 302
M 17   204, 236, 238–40, 265, 266, 267, 294, 295, 296
Thronos *see* Sybrita/Thronos
tombs   4, 74, 107, 115, 155, 176, 178, 183, 204, 326, 327, 328
Tourtouli   97, 197, 315
trade   320, 335, 346
trays   11, 16, 42, 50, 97, 121, 130, 155, 157, 165, 280; *see also* cooking pottery
tripod bowls   58, 99, 105, 118, 125, 154, 183, 210, 319, 330, 338, 339; *see also* cooking pottery
tripod cooking pots *see* cooking pottery
tripod pithoi   7, 9, 23, 142, 144, 163, 199, 204, 213, 215, 319, 329
trough   7

Vasiliki   178, 272
Vasiliki Kephala   178, 215, 246, 314, 328, 333, 334, 337
Vitzelovrisis   221
Vrokastro   183, 269

weaving   23, 27, 115, 140, 183, 199, 200, 324, 329, 332, 334
Western Cliff Houses   4, 189–210, 288, 327, 328, 329, 330, 331, 332, 334
  House K 113-114-120   189–96, 329
  House K 121   197–9
  House K 102-106-115-126   199–210
wood   66, 138

PLATE 1

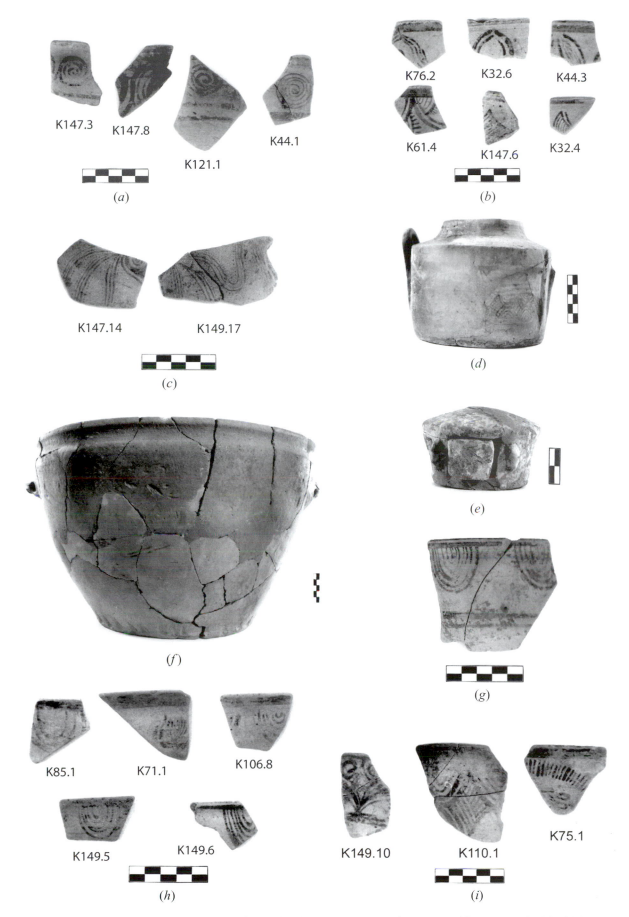

*(a) Fragments of deep bowls; (b) fragments of deep bowls; (c) stirrup jar fragments; (d) pyxis **K147.16**; (e) hut urn **K147.17**; (f) basin **K147.18**; (g) deep bowl **K149.3**; (h) deep bowl fragments; (i) deep bowl fragments.*

PLATE 2

K75.8

K149.14

K47.1

(a)

(b)

(c)

(d)

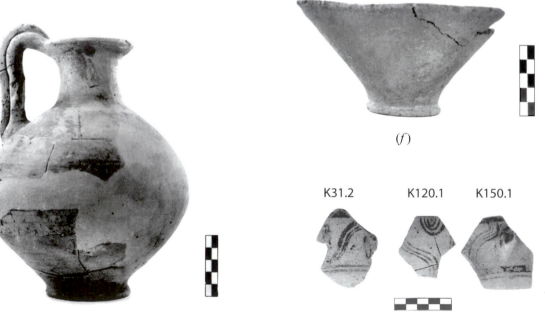

(e)

(f)

K31.2   K120.1   K150.1

(g)

*(a) Krater fragments; (b) amphora **K149.20**; (c) kalathos **K149.21**; (d) jug **K149.23**; (e) jug **K148.6**; (f) kalathos **K148.7**;
(g) deep bowl fragments.*

PLATE 3

(a)

(b)

(c)

(d)

(e)

(f)

*(a) Pyxis **K150.2**; (b–d) stirrup jar **K150.3**; (e) basin **K150.4**; (f) multiple vessel **K150.5**.*

PLATE 4

(a)

(b)

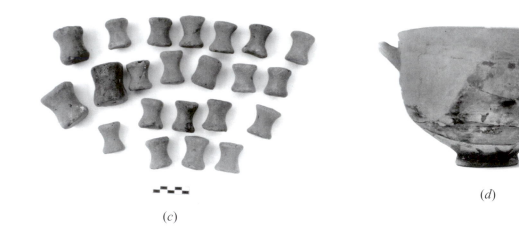

(c)

(d)

(e)

(f)

*(a) Pithos **MK.2**; (b) cooking jug **MK.4**; (c) MK spools; (d) deep bowl **MK.6**; (e) stirrup jar **MK.7**; (f) hut urn **MK.11**.*

PLATE 5

(a)

(b)

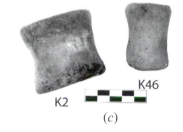

K46

K2

(c)

(d)

(e)

(f)

(g)

K7.5

K19.5

(h)

*(a) Krater **MK.13**; (b) jug **MK.15**; (c) spools (K 2, K 46); (d) kalathos **K2.3**; (e) cooking jug **K2.7**; (f) pithos **K2.15**; (g) kalathos **K3.10**; (h) pithos fragments.*

PLATE 6

*(a) Pyxis **K134.1**; (b) stirrup jar **K134.4**; (c–d) krater **K131.4**; (e) K 1 goddess fragment; (f) K 1 goddess fragments; (g) K 1 goddess fragment.*

PLATE 7

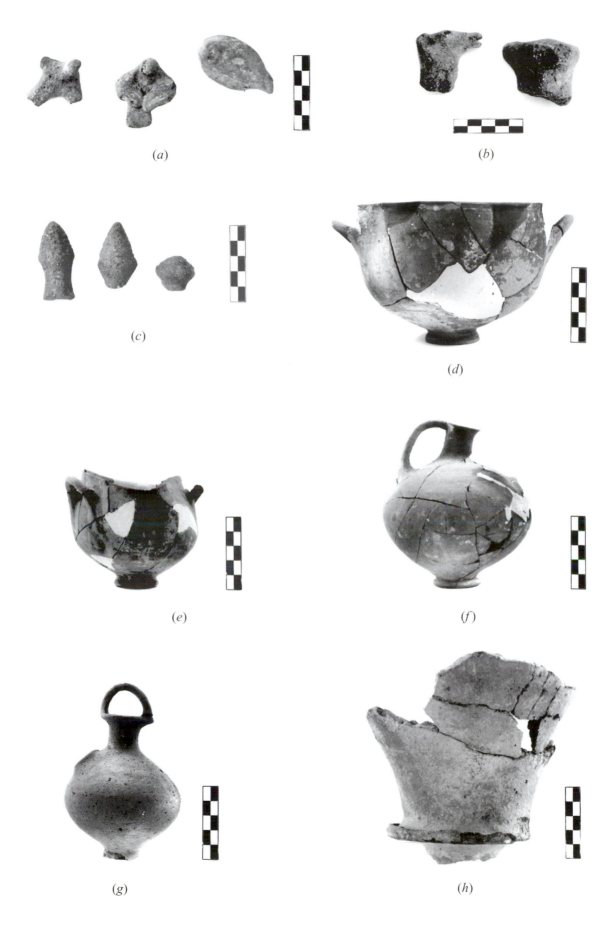

(a) K 1 bird attributes; (b) K 1 animal figurines; (c) K 1 goddess attributes; (d) deep bowl **K1.1**; (e) deep bowl **K1.2**; (f) thelastron **K1.4**; (g) thelastron **K1.7**; (h) chalice **K1.9**.

PLATE 8

*(a) Basin **K1.10**; (b) basin **K1.11**; (c) stirrup jar **K1.13**; (d) cooking dish **K1.16**; (e) cooking jug **K1.20**; (f) tripod **K1.21**; (g) juglet **K39.5**.*

PLATE 9

(a)

(b)

(c)

(d)

(e)

(f)

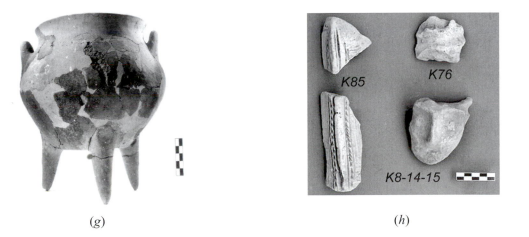

(g)

(h)

*(a) Jug **K11.4**; (b) jug **K11.5**; (c) thelastron **K11.6**; (d) pithos **K13.1**; (e–f) pyxis **K14.1**; (g) tripod **K14.2**; (h) goddess head K 8-18, stand or goddess crown K 76, rectangular stand K 85.*

PLATE 10

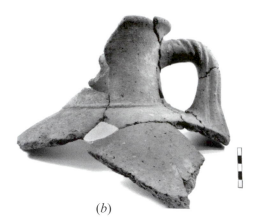

(a)

(b)

(c)

K100.2   K38.3   K21.1

K147.2   K61.6   K76.13

(d)

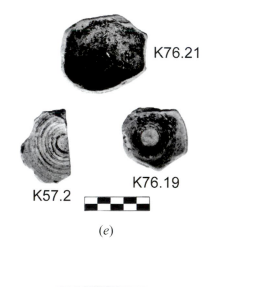

K76.21

K57.2   K76.19

(e)

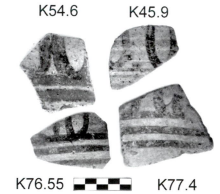

K54.6   K45.9

K76.55   K77.4

(f)

(g)

*(a) Hut urn **K16.1**; (b) amphora **K70.2**; (c) deep bowl **K76.1**; (d) deep bowl fragments; (e) deep bowl bases;
(f) stirrup jar fragments; (g) pyxis **K22.2**.*

PLATE 11

(a)

(b)

K.17

K23.8   K28.2

(d)

(c)

K23.9   K80.4

(e)

(f)

(g)   *(h)*

*(a) Pyxis **K22.3**; (b) pyxis **K22.6**; (c) lid **K22.9**; (d) tankard fragments; (e) tankard fragment **K23.9** and kylix fragment **K80.4**; (f) krater **K23.11**; (g) amphora **K23.17**; (h) thelastron **K23.18**.*

PLATE 12

K29.1   K66.1   K29.3

(c)

(d)

(a) Jug **K23.29**; (b) amphora **K23.73**; (c) deep bowl fragments; (d) larnax **K29.17**; (e) jug **K31.11**; (f) lid fragments; (g) hut urn **K33.2**.

PLATE 13

(a)

(b)

(c)

(d)

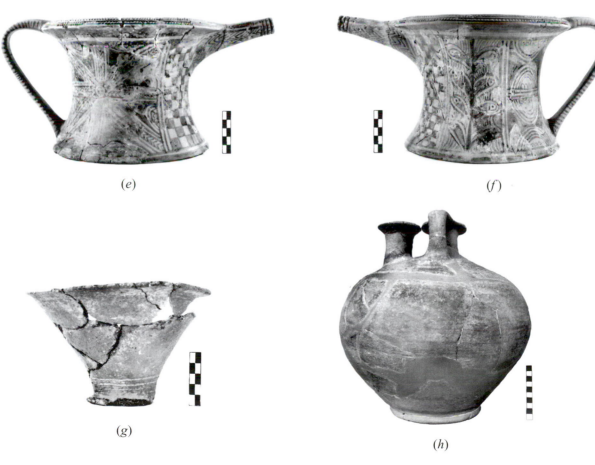

(e)

(f)

(g)

(h)

*(a) Stirrup jar **K33.4**; (b) deep bowl **K36.1**; (c) pithos **K36.2**; (d) pithos **K24.2**; (e–f) tankard **K26.4**; (g) kalathos **K26.7**; (h) stirrup jar **K26.10**.*

PLATE 14

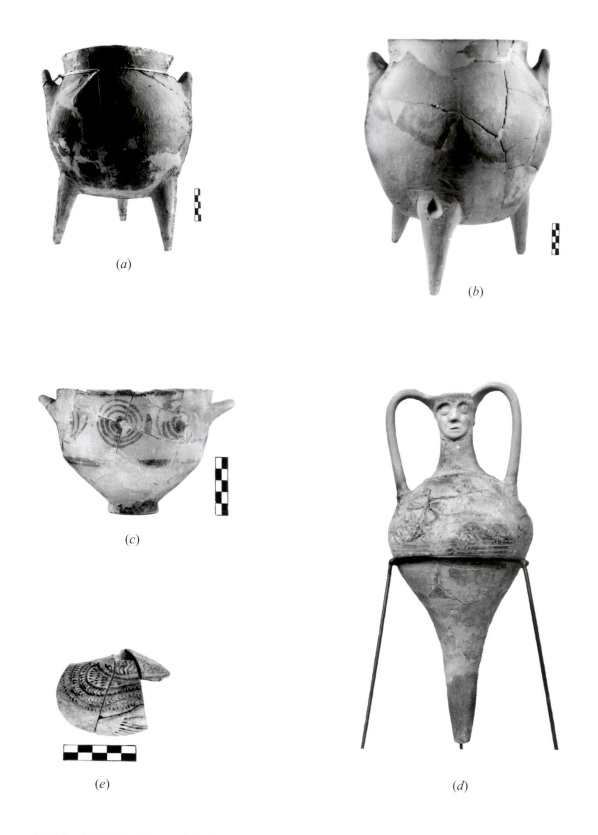

*(a) Tripod **K26.11**; (b) tripod **K26.12**; (c) deep bowl **K27.1**; (d) rhyton **K27.3**; (e) bird vase **K28.4**.*

PLATE 15

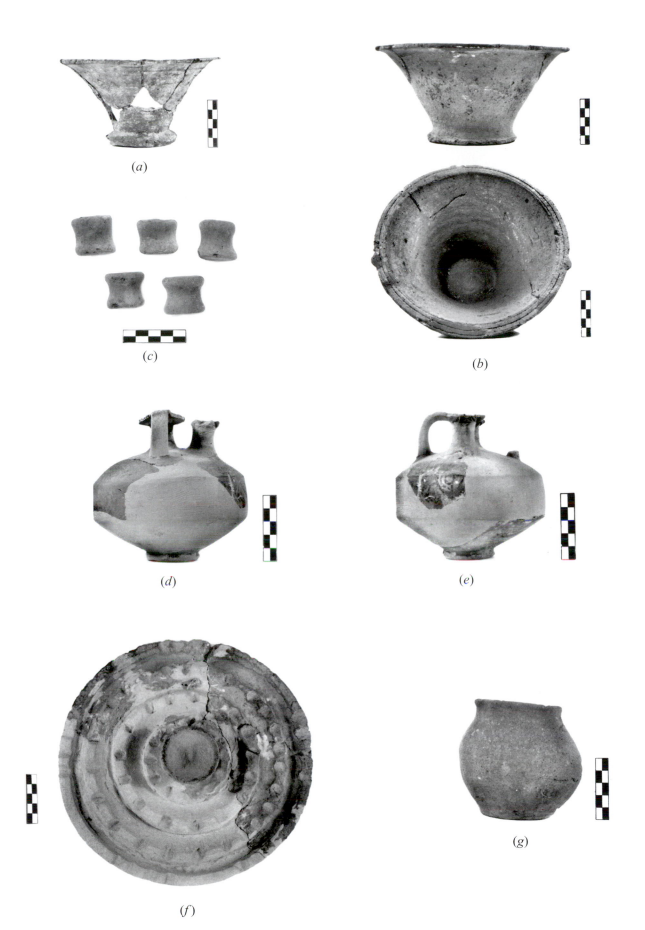

(a) Kalathos **K28.6**; *(b) kalathos* **K43.14**; *(c) K 44 spools; (d–e) stirrup jar* **K47.2**; *(f) lid* **K47.4**; *(g) cooking jug* **K47.5**.

PLATE 16

*(a) Deep bowl **K51.1**; (b) jug **K57.4**; (c) cup **K58.1**; (d) kalathos **K58.2**; (e) stand **K58.4**; (f) stand **K58.5**.*

PLATE 17

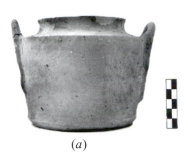

(a)

(b)

(c)

(d)

(e)

(f)

(g)

(h)

*(a) Pyxis **K61.12**; (b) tripod **K61.15**; (c) stirrup jar **K59.1**; (d) jug **K80.5**; (e–f) basket kalathos **K68.11**; (g) pyxis **K80.8**; (h) pyxis **K68.12**.*

PLATE 18

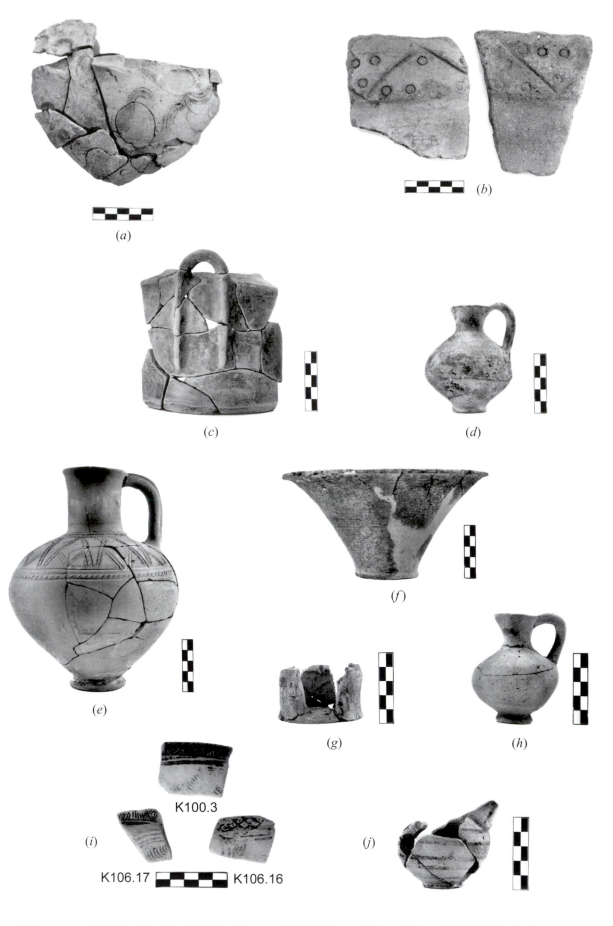

*(a) Stirrup jar **K83.2**; (b) pithos **K83.4**; (c) pyxis **K85.5**; (d) jug **K85.7**; (e) jug **K87.1**; (f) kalathos **K87.3**;*
*(g) hut urn **K69.2**; (h) juglet **K96.2**; (i) kylix fragments; (j) thelastron **K100.4**.*

PLATE 19

(a)

(b)

(c)

(d)

(e)

(f)

(a) Amphora **K90.3**; (b) krater **K79-89.18**; (c) pyxis **K116.1**; (d) stirrup jar **K116.4**; (e) deep bowl **K116.5**;
(f) jug **K116.6**.

PLATE 20

(a)

(b)

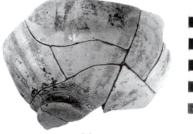

(c)

(d)

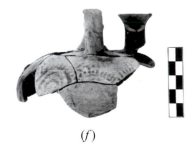

(e)

(f)

(g)

(h)

*(a) Jar **K116.7**; (b) pyxis **K75.9**; (c) deep bowl **K110.2**; (d) jug **K110.8**; (e) stirrup jar **K110.9**; (f) stirrup jar **K110.10**;
(g) kalathos **K110.15**; (h) lid **K110.19**.*

PLATE 21

*(a) Pyxis **K113.1**; (b) stirrup jar **K113.2**; (c) cooking slab **K113.5**; (d) cup **K114.2**; (e) pyxis **K114.3**; (f) pyxis **K114.4** and lid **K114.5**; (g) stirrup jar **K114.6**.*

PLATE 22

(a) Jug **K114.9**; (b) cooking jug **K114.10**; (c) deep bowl **K120N.1**; (d) bowl **K121.6**; (e) tankards **K77.1**, **K121.7**; (f) stirrup jar **K121.10**; (g) tripod **K121.13**; (h) deep bowl **K115.2**; (i) skyphos **K115.4**.

PLATE 23

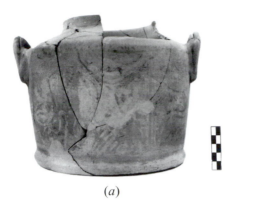

(a)

(b)

(c)

(d)

(e)

(f)

(g)

(h)

(i)

*(a) Pyxis **K115.7**; (b) hut urn **K115.8**; (c) stirrup jar **K115.9**; (d) scuttle **K115.13**; (e) jar **K115.16**; (f) plaque **K104.2**; (g) jug **K107.5**; (h) stand **K107.10**; (i) stirrup jar **K109.1**.*

PLATE 24

*(a) Krater **K122.3**; (b) hut urn **K122.4**; (c) rhyton **K123.1**; (d) deep bowl **K124.1**; (e) Byzantine sherd from K 127; (f) PG jug **V.1**; (g) bottle **M1.2**; (h) stirrup jar **M3.1**; (i) stirrup jar **M3.2**.*

PLATE 25

*(a) Stirrup jar **M4.4**; (b) stirrup jar **M4.5**; (c) mug **M4.7**; (d) skyphos **M8.1**; (e) krater **M8.2**; (f) stirrup jar **M8.3**;*
*(g) thelastron **M8.12**; (h) fenestrated stand **M8.4**.*

PLATE 26

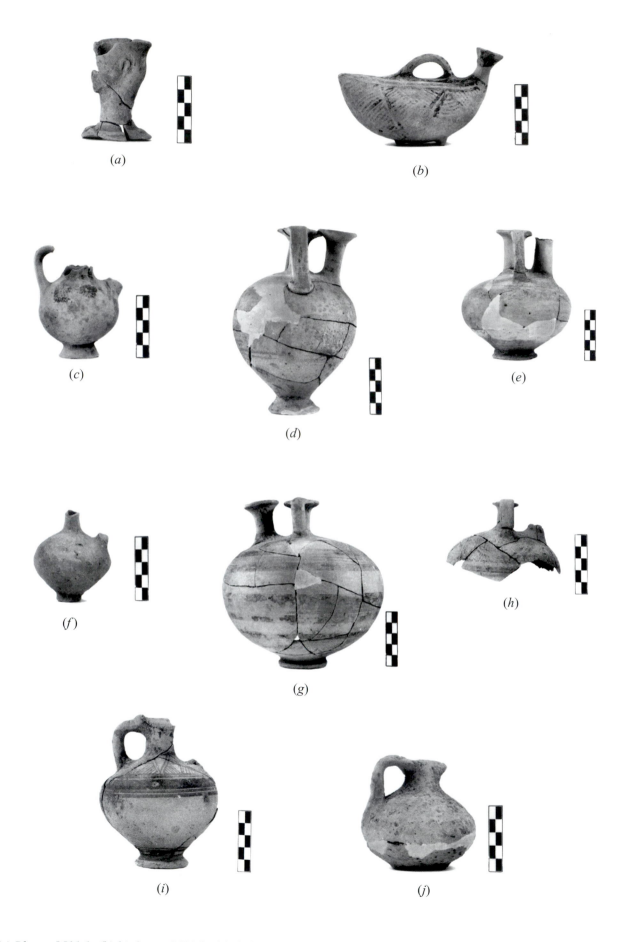

*(a) Rhyton **M11.1**; (b) bird vase **M11.2**; (c) thelastron **M11.3**; (d) stirrup jar **M11.4**; (e) stirrup jar **M11.6**; (f) juglet* ***M14.3**; (g) stirrup jar **M14.5**; (h) stirrup jar **M14.6**; (i) flask **M16.2**; (j) oinochoe **M16.5**.*

PLATE 27

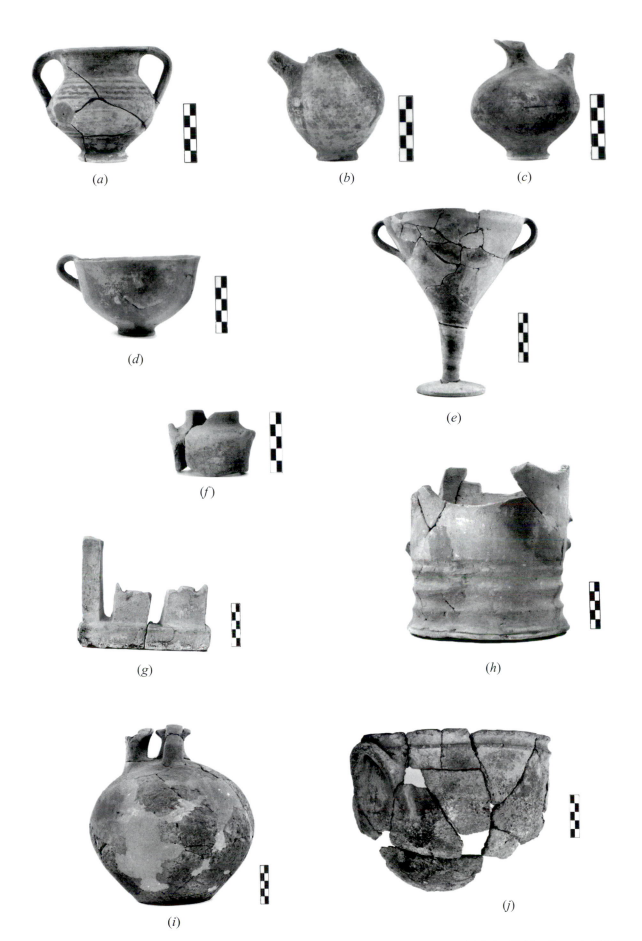

(a) Krateriskos **M17.1**; (b) thelastron **M17.5**; (c) thelastron **M17.6**; (d) cup **A3.1**; (e) kylix **K.15**; (f) pyxis **K.24**;
(g) fenestrated stand **K.32**; (h) snake tube **K.33**; (i) stirrup jar **K.36**; (j) coarse krater **K.40**.

PLATE 28

(a)

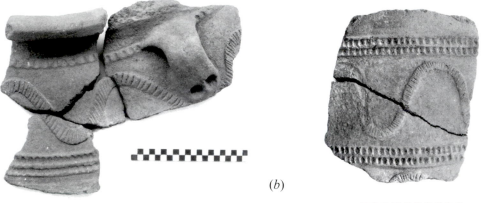

(b)

(c)

*(a) Stirrup jar **K.46**; (b) pithos **K.53**; (c) plaque, no good context.*

PLATE 29

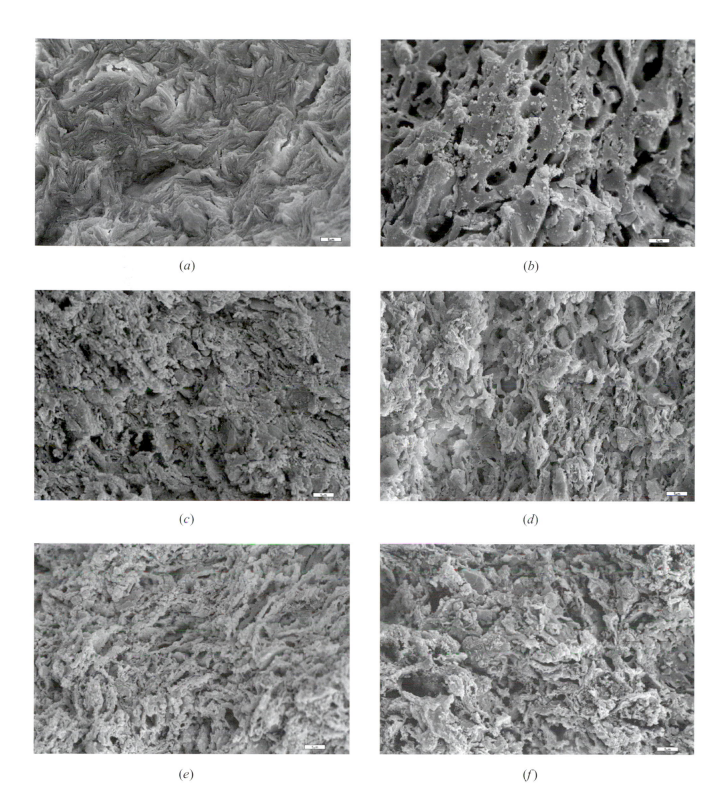

(a) Low calcareous group, body fragment, no vitrification (NV); (b) moderately calcareous group, sample KAR 06/ 32, advanced vitrification (V); (c) moderately calcareous group, sample KAR 06/ 78, no vitrification (NV); (d) highly calcareous group, sample KAR 06/ 10, extensive vitrification (Vc+); (e) highly calcareous group, sample KAR 06/ 27, initial vitrification (IV); (f) highly calcareous group, sample KAR 06/ 31, initial vitrification (IV).

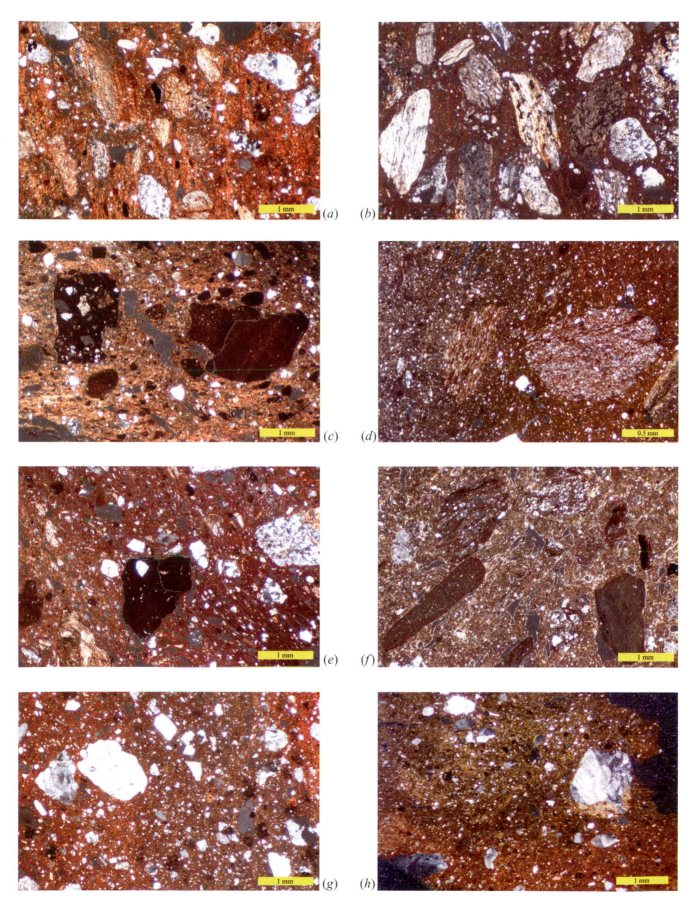

(a) Fabric 1, subgroup (a) (×25); (b) Fabric 1, subgroup (a) (×25); (c) Fabric 1, subgroup (b) (×25); (d) Fabric 2 (×25); (e) sample KAR 06/ 38 (×50); (f) sample KAR 06/ 18 (×25); (g) sample KAR 06/ 21 (×25); (h) sample KAR 06/ 2 (×25).

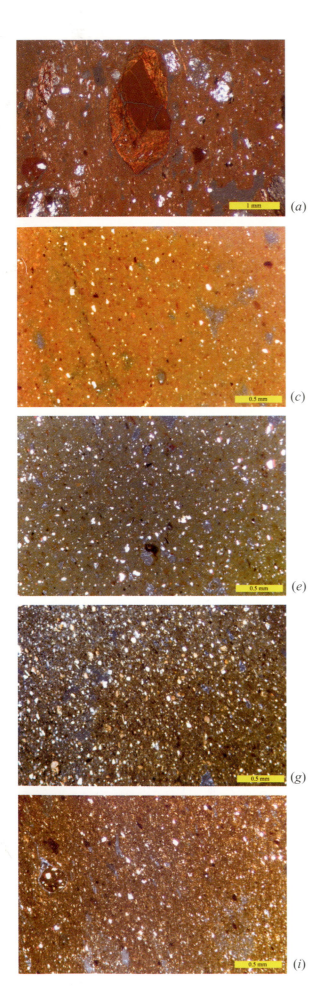

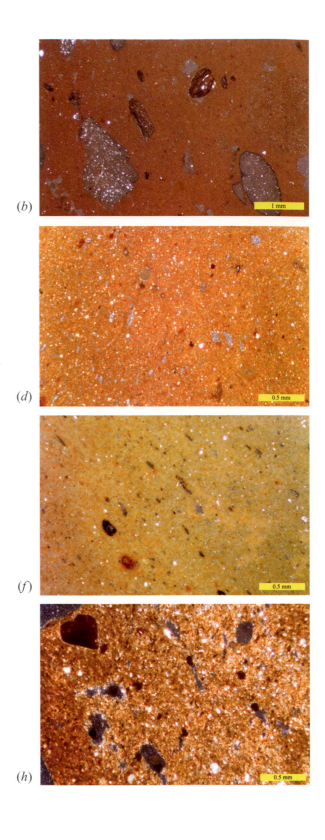

(a) Fabric 3 (×25); (b) Fabric 4 (×25); (c) Fabric 5 (×50); (d) sample from the Pediada Survey (×50); (e) sample KAR 06/ 15 (×50); (f) sample KAR 06/ 23 (×50); (g) sample KAR 06/ 37 (×50); (h) sample KAR 06/ 40 (×50); (i) sample KAR 06/ 41 (×50).